The Arizona Guide

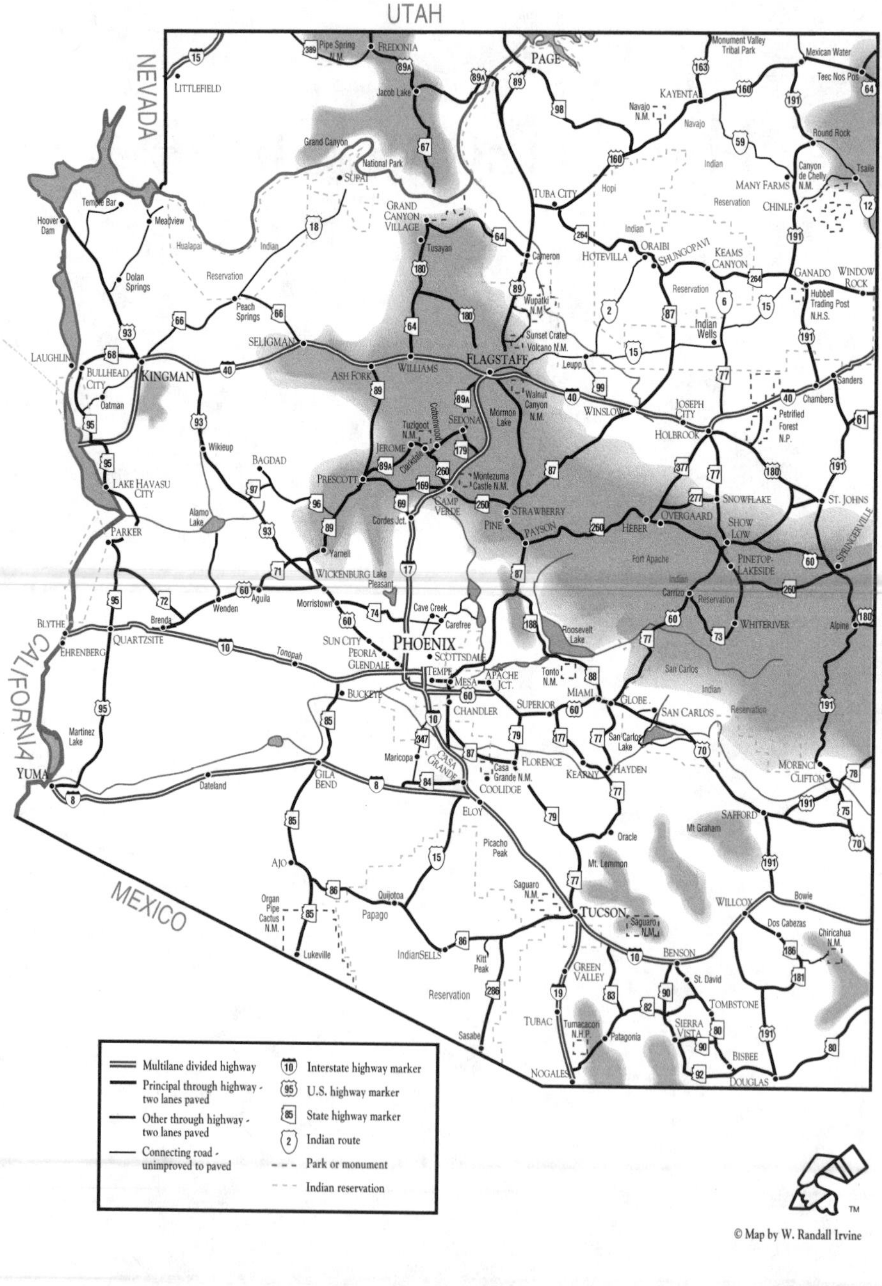

Arizona State Map

UTAH

NEVADA

CALIFORNIA

NEW MEXICO

MEXICO

Legend	
Multilane divided highway	Interstate highway marker
Principal through highway - two lanes paved	U.S. highway marker
Other through highway - two lanes paved	State highway marker
Connecting road - unimproved to paved	Indian route
	Park or monument
	Indian reservation

The Arizona Guide

Judy Wade

Photographs by Bill Baker

Fulcrum Publishing
Golden, Colorado

This book is dedicated to my sister Karen, the principal.
Although she gave me only an "A-" on the manuscript, she did say that she thinks
I "have great potential as a writer." Thank you, Karen. Next time I'll try harder.

—Judy Wade

Book design by Deborah Rich

The information in *The Arizona Guide* is accurate as of July 1998. However, prices, hours of operation, phone numbers and other items change rapidly. If something in the book is incorrect or if you have ideas for the next edition, please write to the author at Fulcrum Publishing, 350 Indiana Street, Suite 350, Golden, Colorado 80401-5093.

Library of Congress Cataloging-in-Publication Data

Wade, Judy.
The Arizona guide / Judy Wade.
p. cm.
Includes index.
ISBN 1-55591-374-1 (pbk.)
1. Arizona—Guidebooks. I. Title.
F809.3.W33 1998
917.9104'53—dc21 98-33649
CIP

Printed in the United States of America
0 9 8 7 6 5 4 3 2

Fulcrum Publishing
350 Indiana Street, Suite 350
Golden, Colorado 80401-5093
(800) 992-2908 • (303) 277-1623
website: www.fulcrum-books.com
e-mail: fulcrum@fulcrum-books.com

Contents

Phoenix and Environs 156

Tucson 200

Southeast and South Central—Old West Country 230

Arizona's West Coast 292

Author's Note

The "we" approach: This book is written in the first person plural because both of us, Judy Wade and Bill Baker, contributed to it. We traveled the state together, discovered more corners of Arizona than we knew existed and frequently engaged in heated discussions about where to turn and which direction to follow. We provided a balance for each other when one of us loved a place and the other hated it. When one lagged, the other pushed. One took photos while the other took notes. Hence, "we" wrote the book.

Introduction

Background Information

Multifaceted Arizona has been credited with having more personalities than almost any state in the union. From the cactus-dotted sands of the low desert to peaks in excess of 12,000 feet, covered with snow even in summer, Arizona's diversity is celebrated in all aspects of nature.

Dry sandy washes, placid lakes, shimmering rivers and dramatic canyons provide backdrops for appreciating the land in its natural state as well as for enjoying the improvements made by man. The red rocks of Sedona, Canyon de Chelly's well-preserved Indian ruins, the eerie beauty of Monument Valley, Window Rock's sacred history and the developing wine country of Sonoita/Patagonia all are part of Arizona's outdoor treasures.

Almost 30 million visitors come to the state each year, most of them arriving during winter months to take advantage of superb sunshine in Phoenix; others are drawn by the Grand Canyon, one of the seven natural wonders of the world, which by itself hosts more than 5 million visitors each year.

History

Admitted to the Union on February 14, 1912, as the nation's 48th state, Arizona is a U.S. youngster. To many it seems in a hurry to create the history it doesn't yet have. Others point to the ancient ones whose residence in what is now Arizona dates to prehistory as validation of a valuable past.

Three tribal groups—the Anasazi in the northern plateau regions, the Mogollon people who inhabited the northeastern and eastern mountain ranges and the Hohokam who were an agrarian culture living primarily on desert plains near rivers—lived honestly and well for centuries. The state's diversity of creatures, climate and resources furnished them with an affluence of life's necessities. Understanding the survival techniques of desert plants helps to comprehend the lives of these early Native Americans, who have left traces of their cultures in Montezuma Castle, Tuzigoot, Pueblo Grande and other ruins.

The peaceful desert began to change in the 1500s when the Spanish Conquistadors arrived. The introduction of horses and guns had a huge impact on the lives of the Native Americans, as did new crops and growing techniques. Settlers from the East began to discover the state's mining riches, farming possibilities and animal resources. Beavers in the Gila River Valley soon were hunted to extinction. Native Americans who had lived in the state for centuries became a nuisance as they resisted encroachment on their hunting and farming lands, and the military was called in. The bloody Indian wars of the 1800s permanently subdued them. Today, Native Americans in the state number more than 100,000, many living on 23 reservations that are home to 21 distinct tribes.

President Abraham Lincoln created the Arizona Territory in 1862. It has produced celebrities at least as exciting as those from any longer-lived state. Baseball great Reggie Jackson attended Arizona State University on a football scholarship, then went on to fame with the New York Yankees. Ghoulish rocker Alice Cooper played with a Phoenix band in his early days. Arizona has had a woman governor (Rose Mofford in 1988), an impeached governor (Evan Mecham in 1988) and a governor found guilty of bank fraud (Fife Symington in 1997). Presently it has another woman governor, Jane Dee Hull.

State Symbols

In a state whose history is filled with the symbolism of Native American cultures, it's not surprising that symbols still are an important part of Arizona's identity. In 1985 the state's school children were asked to vote on their choices for state mammal, fish, reptile and amphibian, choosing from a group preselected by the Arizona Department of Game and Fish. The Arizona legislature already had chosen the state bird, flower and tree. So in 1986 the following plants and animals became official emblems of the State of Arizona.

State Flower: Saguaro Cactus Blossom

This famous plant was a slam dunk in the flower category, mainly because it is the most recognizable cactus on earth. With its many arms and lovely waxy white flowers, it grows naturally only in Arizona and in a small portion of California, along the Colorado River where the two states share a border. Saguaro bloom in May with each blossom opening for just a few hours. You have to catch them in early morning because usually by noon they're closed, never to reopen. If the bats, bees and moths have done their pollinating job, fruit will appear in about a month. It is considered a great delicacy by finches, sparrows, cactus wrens and other desert birds, and within hours of turning pink will be pecked full of holes.

State Bird: Cactus Wren

You might hear the scratchy, strident call of this pretty desert bird long before you spot it. The largest member of the wren family, it is not colorful but is attractively patterned with shades of brown and white and interesting to watch for its flitty behavior. Cactus wrens are so-called because they depend on cactuses as a nest-building site, for protection and as a food source. Besides cactus fruit, they also eat the bugs and insects that live on the spiney plants.

State Tree: Palo Verde

This green-trunked tree is a classic example of how plants survive in the desert. Tiny leaves conserve water that is lost by broader-leafed plants. The green bark encourages photosynthesis as do leaves in other plants. In April and May it is covered with tiny yellow flowers that create a dramatic explosion of color.

State Mammal: Ringtail

A relative of the raccoon and about the size of a gray squirrel, the ringtail has a long, bushy tail that, at about 15 inches, is the same length as its body. It prefers rocky cliffs, caves, crevices and hollow trees and is nocturnal, so chances of spotting one are pretty slim. But you'll know if one has been in the area because of the vile, skunklike smell it emits when threatened or frightened.

State Reptile: Arizona Ridge-Nosed Rattlesnake

The beautiful white stripes on its brown face are said to be the inspiration for war paint worn by the Chiricahua Apaches. This small 24-inch snake is one of 11 rattler species that live in Arizona. Found at 5,000- to 8,000-foot altitudes in mountain ranges in south-central Arizona, it has a row of scales on its nose that give it its name. As with all rattlers, it's wise to give these a wide berth. They are protected, and it is illegal to kill or possess one.

State Fish: Arizona Apache Trout

Presently listed as threatened under the Endangered Species Act, this colorful fish readily breeds with other trout species such as rainbow, which have been introduced to Apache trout's natural streams. It lives in high mountain streams in central and eastern Arizona and is gaining ground again as a pure species as non-native trout are removed. The Apache trout is yellowish with dark spots and has an orange slash on its lower jaw.

State Amphibian: Tree Frog

The only time you'll probably ever be aware of this little hopper is during summer rains when it is very vocally looking for a mate. It rarely gets more than 2 inches long and lives above 5,000 feet in pine, oak and fir forests, using circular pads at the end of its toes to crawl into treetops and out along branches.

State Gem: Turquoise

This warm blue-green stone, used for centuries in Indian jewelry, now is a popular semi-precious stone often combined with silver.

State Flag

The state's copper industry and continued growth (which seems assured) are symbolized by a copper star rising from a blue field of honor in the face of the setting sun.

State Seal

The state motto, "Ditat Deus," which in Latin means "God enriches," is interwoven with the state's original major enterprises—reclamation, farming, cattle raising and mining, along with the date 1912, when Arizona was admitted to the Union.

State Name

Two Native American words, "Aleh-zon," meaning "Little Spring," are the derivative for the state name.

Geology and Geography

The nation's sixth largest state, Arizona covers 113,417 square miles that encompass three distinct geographical zones. The northern plateaus that we refer to as Canyon Country and Indian Country in this book bear signs of the volcanic activity that formed their peaks and valleys. The central mountains, where the Mogollon Rim marks the abrupt end of the plateaus, are covered with fragrant pine forests.

Cacti and wildflowers at Tonto National Monument.

High mountain lakes, winter resorts and hiking trails have made the rim the state's playground. We cover this in sections called Above and Below the Rim, and Central Arizona. The southern deserts, where Phoenix and Tucson have grown up, create the image that most out-of-towners have of the state. This is where saguaro cactuses grow in abundance, and where reliable sunshine and extensive irrigation systems sustain the bulk of the state's population. The Old West and the West Coast chapters deal with the southern deserts.

Arizona is the only state in which all four North American deserts are found. Within this abundance of aridity there is great diversity of plant and animal life. The **Sonoran Desert,** located in the southwestern part of the state, extends into California and is sometimes subdivided as the **Colorado Desert** and the **Arizona Desert.** It has more birds, plants and animals than any other desert, making up a species list that includes graceful fan palms, green-trunked palo verde and brushy mesquite. From magnificent bighorn sheep to little kangaroo rats, the range of species is enormous.

The **Chihuahuan Desert** gets more rain and has more limestone in its pale soil than the Sonoran Desert and is characterized by generally small, stubby growth except near riparian areas. It reaches north into Arizona from Mexico and is dotted with yucca and agave.

The **Mojave Desert,** the most arid of the deserts, stark and sparsely vegetated, touches the state's western edge where it adjoins California, extending into Nevada. Higher elevations make it the coldest of the deserts.

For decades Arizona has been known for its Five Cs—copper, citrus, climate, cotton and cactus. Despite the fact that developers are gobbling up fields at a great rate, irrigation sustains cotton as the state's number one cash crop. Fewer acres are planted, but technology allows higher yields per acre, so bottom-line production remains stable. You still can see cotton in the Phoenix area near Litchfield Park, along rural roads south of Chandler and in great quantity flanking US 70 west of Thatcher and Safford. October, a harvest month, is a good time to see the fluffy white bolls ready for picking. Yuma, on the Colorado River bordering California, and areas around Willcox in the state's southern part, produce vast fruit and vegetable crops.

Flora and Fauna

One of the state's biggest wildlife claims to fame is bird-watching, particularly for hummingbirds in Ramsey Canyon south of Sierra Vista. But other wildlife viewing opportunities, including fleet-footed pronghorns, desert bighorn sheep, white-tail deer, coatimundi, javelinas and more exist almost everywhere. See individual chapters (Outdoor Activities) for places to go and resources for more information. An excellent starting point to see what the state has to offer is the **Arizona-Sonora Desert Museum** in Tucson (see Tucson Museums).

Suggested Reading

Arizona Wildlife Viewing Guide (Falcon Press, 1995) by John N. Carr not only tells you where to go to see neat animals, but gives directions on how to get there.

70 Common Cacti of the Southwest, 100 Desert Wildflowers of the Southwest and *100 Roadside Wildflowers* (Southwest Parks and Monuments Association, Tucson) are part of a series of small books with excellent color photographs that help you identify the state's plants.

Climate and Weather

In Arizona it is quite possible to ski in the morning and play golf in the afternoon. In the Tucson area, for example, an early winter morning glide down the slopes of Mt. Lemmon easily can be followed by a quick 18 holes on a local course. In the Phoenix area, there's no question that summers are hot, and getting hotter. Weather bureau records show that as more and more people move into the Valley of the Sun, as more air conditioners and more cars blow off increasing quantities of hot air, and more desert is paved over to create highways and urban areas, temperatures go higher and higher, and stay there. Summer nights, which used to bring cooling relief to even the hottest August mornings, are not cooling off as much as they used to. *The Arizona Republic* labels it a phenomenon called "urban heat island," a problem that exists not only in Phoenix but in most large cities. So far the power is available to keep those air conditioners humming, and although pricey, there's no shortage of gasoline to fuel cars and their air conditioners. You can come to Phoenix assured of a cool experience, no matter what time of year.

The Heat Index

If you're from a part of the country where winter is hard, you're familiar with windchill factor. The Arizona equivalent is the heat index. You'll hear it in weather reports, and it often is referred to in newspaper weather columns. Basically it is an indicator of humidity. As moisture increases, the air temperature is perceived to be even hotter than it really is. For example, a 90-degree day with 60 percent humidity (which sometimes happens during the July and August monsoons) feels like the temperature really is 120 degrees. But a normal 100-degree summer day in Phoenix, with only 10 percent humidity, is felt at just what it is … about 100 degrees.

Statewide, temperatures have a huge variance. A January day in Flagstaff or the Grand Canyon will average about 41 degrees, while in Phoenix it will be shirtsleeve weather with a temperature averaging about 65, easily slipping into the midafternoon 80s. Flagstaff and the Grand Canyon regularly experience below-freezing temps from November through April, while Phoenix and Tucson may only occasionally dip below the 32-degree mark. Flagstaff has the summer advantage, with averages in the 70s and 80s, while Phoenix averages triple digits for much of June through September.

For state weather information visit **"The Weather Channel" on-line: www.weather.com/weather/us/cities/AZ**.

Visitor Information

General Information

Individual chambers of commerce and visitor centers are your best source of information for the specific areas you want to see. They're included in the Services section of each chapter. Overall state information and a comprehensive Travel Planner will be sent if, at least four weeks in advance, you contact the **Arizona Office of Tourism, 2702 N. 3rd St., Ste. 4015, Phoenix, 85004; (800) 842-8257 or (602) 230-7733, fax (602) 255-4601.**

The State of Arizona website, **arizonaguide.com**, links you to hundreds of sites within the state. Try this first when trying to locate something.

Other Websites

City of Tucson website: **mtcvb@azstarnet.com**
City of Phoenix website: **arizonaguide.com/phxcvb**

Native American Information

Native American Tourist Center
4130 N. Goldwater Blvd., #114
Scottsdale, AZ 85251
(602) 945-0771

The center will send pamphlets, brochures and information on Native American sites, casinos and other areas of interest in the state. There are 21 Native American tribes represented in Arizona, with 16 active casinos. There probably will be more, as many tribes have several authorized sites but have not yet opened casinos on all of them.

Native American Casinos

Harrah's Ak-Chin Casino
Ak-Chin Indian Community
Maricopa (south of Phoenix)

Cocopah Casino
Cocopah Indian Tribe
Somerton (near Yuma)

Blue Water Casino
Colorado River Indian Tribes
Parker

Ft. McDowell Gaming
Ft. McDowell Mohave-Apache
Fountain Hills (east of Scottsdale)

Spirit Mountain Casino
Fort Mohave Indian Tribe
Needles, CA (on Arizona border north of Lake Havasu City)

Gila River—Lone Butte
Gila River—Wild Horse Pass
Gila River Indian Community
Sacaton

Casino of the Sun
Pasqua-Yaqui Tribe of Arizona
Tucson

Paradise Casino
Quechan Indian Tribe
Yuma

Apache Gold Casino
San Carlos Apache Tribe
San Carlos

Desert Diamond Casino
Tohono O'Odham Nation
Sells

Mazatzal Casino
Tonto Apache Tribe
Payson

Hon-Dah Casino
White Mountain Apache Tribe
Whiteriver (3 miles from Pinetop)

Cliff Castle Casino
Yavapai Apache Nation
Camp Verde

Yavapai Gaming Center
Bucky's Casino
Yavapai-Prescott
Prescott

Tips for Visitors

Health

Not surprisingly, it's the sun that causes many of the health problems that visitors to the state encounter. *Sunburn* is typical, especially among winter visitors who want to return home with a trademark Arizona tan. Use a lotion with an SPF of at least 15 when going outdoors. *Dehydration* is common among hikers, cyclists and even golfers who, because of the dry climate in which perspiration evaporates quickly, lose fluids before they even realize they're perspiring. Symptoms can be dizziness, lightheadedness, intense thirst and a general feeling of weakness. If these occur, get into the shade as quickly as possible, and drink water. To prevent dehydration, always carry water with you, even if you're just going for a one-hour stroll. Drink before you get thirsty.

Telephone

Phoenix recently activated new area codes: 602 covers Phoenix and metro; 480 covers Scottsdale, Mesa, Tempe, Ahwatukee, Chandler, Gilbert, and other communities to the east and south; 623 covers areas mainly west of Central Avenue; and 520 covers regions outside the Phoenix area.

Mountain biking on the Old Stagecoach Road.

Getting There

See Phoenix (Getting There) for information on **Sky Harbor Airport** and **Greyhound Bus Lines.** From Sky Harbor, many airlines serve Tucson, and there are some that connect to even smaller cities such as Sierra Vista, Page, Lake Havasu, Flagstaff and Prescott.

Getting Around

Arizona is about as car-dependent as it gets. In Phoenix bus service is sketchy at best. There is no big, reliable mass transit system such as BART in San Francisco. All major rental car companies have offices at or near Sky Harbor. In addition, check the Yellow Pages once you're here for companies that may have good off-airport rates.

Information for Visitors with Disabilities

In many cases, this guide indicates when a trail or venue is wheelchair accessible, but in general, Arizona complies with the ADA, and there is no shortage of hotel rooms that can accommodate visitors with various disabilities, from wheelchair users to those who are sight or hearing impaired.

How the Book Is Organized

The Arizona Office of Tourism graciously agreed to share their sensible way of dividing the state. The only change we have made is to single out Tucson as an area all its own. There are eight geographic regions: (1) Northwest and Canyonlands; (2) Northeast and Indian Country; (3) East Central—Above and Below the Rim; (4) Central; (5) Phoenix and Environs; (6) Tucson; (7) Southeast and South Central—Old West Country; and (8) Arizona's West Coast. Each region is divided into cities or destinations and should be considered geographically, in the way one might cover it in a car. Especially in the Phoenix region, which is made up of more than 30 smaller towns and communities, text is organized in a logical geographical flow.

Festivals and Events

We have highlighted what we think are the most important events in each area, although there usually are many more. Contact local visitor centers and chambers of commerce for full calendars of events. A statewide calendar also is available from the **Arizona Office of Tourism** at **(800) 842-8257.**

Outdoor Activities

Bicycling

Mountain Biking

Some areas, like Sierra Vista, Sedona and Tucson are particularly off-road friendly. See Outdoor Activities in those areas for details. Many trails welcome mountain bikers, but riding in wilderness areas is prohibited.

Touring

In Tucson and Phoenix there are many bike lanes designated on city streets. In addition, you can ride just about anywhere that is safe. Sierra Vista has some interesting road rides, and there are good paved rides in Saguaro National Park in Tucson. Your best bet is to hook up with a local bike shop for information on friendly places to ride.

Fishing

The Thursday edition of *The Arizona Republic* (Phoenix's morning daily newspaper, sold all over the state) carries a rating of how the fish (and what kinds) are biting at local lakes. Ratings include good, fair and poor destinations with comments on which baits are successful, which fish are biting best, where in the lake they're hitting and what time of day to try for best results. Local lakes that are covered include Alamo, Pleasant, Horseshoe, Bartlett, Saguaro, Canyon, Apache, Roosevelt and San Carlos Lakes and the Colorado River. It also lists the mountain lakes where anglers can expect to have good luck.

Four-Wheel-Drive and Motorcycle Trips

Not usually called out as separate trips, we indicate when a four-wheel-drive vehicle is necessary to travel a particular route.

Arizona is a great state for motorcycling, which many riders consider about as close to seeing it from horseback as you can get. In Phoenix, **Western States Motorcycle Tours** rents Harley-Davidson, BMW and Suzuki motorcycles, stores your extra luggage, and sends you on your way. **9401 N. 7th Ave., Phoenix, 85021; (602) 943-9030, fax (602) 943-4212. Website: members.aol.com/AzMcRent/** (this is a really helpful home page that answers your questions quickly and with humor). **E-mail: AzMcRent@aol.com.** Company owner Frank Del Monte has written a helpful 144-page guide called *Motorcycle Arizona!* that lists tours of one day to one week throughout the state. Accompanied by easy-to-read maps and very specific directions, this guide is essential if you're biking the state for the first time. It's available for $9.95 in book stores, by calling **(602) 943-9030** or on-line at **members.aol.com/AzMcRent.**

Golf

Golfing is a huge sport in Arizona. We have listed favorite courses in just about every area, but many more are not mentioned, or there would be no room in this book to mention anything else. For a listing of hundreds of Arizona courses, by area and difficulty, check out Arizona Central on-line at **www.azcentra.com/depts/golf/azgolf/html.** Some have photos, course diagrams, and reviews.

Hiking and Backpacking

Because so much of Arizona is wide open space, it is prime territory for hiking. See individual areas for hikes of varying difficulties, including a spectacular Lost Dutchman Moonlight Hike listed under Apache Junction in the Phoenix chapter.

Although they are used for many types of recreation, state and national parks are listed because most (not the historic ones) offer hiking and backpacking. If you plan to use the

Organ Pipe Cactus National Monument near Ajo. Guide Will Nelson shows an organ pipe to a visitor.

parks a lot, check out the **Golden Eagle Passport** that admits the holder and passengers in a private vehicle for $50 a year. The **Golden Age Passport**, available to those 62 and older, is a lifetime entrance pass to most national parks. Both may be purchased at any federal area where an entrance fee is charged. The best way to get information quickly is to go to the official website of the National Park Service, **www.nps.gov.** Once you reach it, you may search by name for the park you're interested in, listed below.

National Park Service Units in Arizona

National Monuments

Canyon de Chelly
Casa Grande
Hohokam Pima
Montezuma Castle
Navajo
Organ Pipe Cactus
Pipe Spring
Sunset Crater
Tonto
Tumacacori
Tuzigoot
Walnut Canyon
Wupatki

National Parks

Grand Canyon
Petrified Forest
Saguaro

National Historic Sites

Fort Bowie
Hubbell Trading Post
Chiricahua
Coronado

National Recreation Area

Glen Canyon

State Parks

Arizona has some of the loveliest, best-kept state parks in the country, mainly because the Lotto system generates adequate funding. Most Arizona state parks charge an entry fee, usually nominal, but if you're traveling as a family fees can add up. You may purchase a $40 family pass that's valid for a year at the first park you visit, or from the **Arizona State Parks Dept., 1300 W. Washington, Phoenix, 85007; (602) 542-4174. Website: www.pr.state.az.us.** The State Park Service says that it is very important you call and verify camping availabilities and open hours before setting out, because sites fill up and hours change.

Alamo Lake State Park (near Lake Havasu)
P.O. Box 38
Wenden, AZ 85357
Phone and fax (520) 669-2088

Boyce Thompson Southwest Arboretum
(east of Phoenix)
37615 E. Hwy. 60
Superior, AZ 85273
(520) 689-2723, fax (520) 689-5858

Buckskin Mountain State Park
(near Lake Havasu)
54751 Hwy. 95
Parker, AZ 85344
(520) 667-3231
River Island phone (520) 667-3387,
fax (520) 667-3387

Catalina State Park
P.O. Box 36986
Tucson, AZ 85740
(520) 628-5798, fax (520) 628-5797

Cattail Cove State Park
P.O. Box 1990
Lake Havasu City, AZ 86405
(520) 855-1223, fax (520) 855-1730

Dead Horse Ranch State Park
675 Dead Horse Ranch Rd.
Cottonwood, AZ 86326
(520) 634-5283

Fool Hollow Lake Recreation Area
P.O. Box 2588
Show Low, AZ 85901
(520) 537-3680, fax (520) 537 4349

Fort Verde State Historic Park
Box 397
Camp Verde, AZ 86322
(520) 567-3275, fax (520) 567-4036

Homolovi Ruins State Park
HC63 Box 5 (87 N)
Winslow, AZ 86047
(520) 289-4106, fax (520) 289-2021
E-mail: homolovi@pr.state.az.us

Jerome State Historic Park
P.O. Box D
Jerome, AZ 83331
(520) 634-5381, fax (520) 639-3132

Kartchner Caverns State Park
Benson, AZ 85602
(520) 586-4110

Lake Havasu State Park
1801 Hwy. 95
Lake Havasu City, AZ 86406
Office phone (520) 855-7851 Windsor Beach phone (520) 855-2784
fax (520) 855-7423

Lost Dutchman State Park
6109 N. Apache Trail
Apache Junction, AZ 85219
Phone and fax (602) 982-4485

Lyman Lake State Park
P.O. Box 1428
St. Johns, AZ 85936
(520) 337-4441, fax (520) 337-4649

McFarland State Historic Park
P.O. Box 109
Florence, AZ 85232
Phone and fax (520) 868-5216

Patagonia Lake State Park
P.O. Box 274
Patagonia, AZ 85624
(520) 287-6965, fax (520) 287-5618

Picacho Peak State Park
P.O. Box 275
Picacho, AZ 85241
Phone and fax (520) 466-3183

Red Rock State Park
HC-02, Box 886
Sedona, AZ 86336
(520) 282-6907, fax (520) 282-5972

Riordan State Historic Park
1300 Riordan Ranch St.
Flagstaff, AZ 86001
Phone and fax (520) 779-4395

Roper Lake State Park
Rt. 2 Box 712
Safford, AZ 85546
Phone and fax (520) 428-6760

Slide Rock State Park
P.O. Box 10358
Sedona, AZ 86339
(520) 282-3034, fax (520) 282-0245

Tombstone Courthouse State Historic Park
P.O. Box 216
Tombstone, AZ 85638
(520) 457-3311, fax (520) 457-2565

Tonto Natural Bridge State Park
P.O. Box 1245
Payson, AZ 85638
(520) 476-4202, fax (520) 476-2264

Tubac Presidio State Historic Park
P.O. Box 1296
Tubac, AZ 85646
Phone and fax (520) 398-2252

Yuma Crossing State Historic Park
201 N. 4th Ave.
Yuma, AZ 85364
(520) 329-0471

Yuma Territorial Prison State Historic Park
Box 10792
Yuma, AZ 85366
(520) 783-4771, fax (520) 783-7442

Detailed maps of national forests and wilderness areas can be purchased from the Forest Service's Southwestern Regional Office. For a listing of available maps, including scale and cost, contact **USDA Forest Service, Public Affairs Office, 517 Gold Ave. SW, Albuquerque, NM 87102; (505) 842-3292.**

National Forest Service Offices in the White Mountains Area for the Apache-Sitgreaves National Forests

Forest Supervisor
Apache-Sitgreaves National Forests
P.O. Box 640
Springerville, AZ 85938
(520) 333-4301; TTY (520) 333-6292

Alpine Ranger District
P.O. Box 4619
Alpine, AZ 85920
(520) 339-4384; TTY (520) 339-4566

Clifton Ranger District
HC 1, Box 733
Duncan, AZ 85534
Voice and TTY (520) 687-1301

Chevelon Ranger District
HC 62, Box 600
Winslow, AZ 86047
Voice and TTY (520) 289-2471

Heber Ranger District
P.O. Box 968
Overgaard, AZ 85933
(520) 535-4481

Springerville Ranger District
P.O. Box 760
Springerville, AZ 85938
(520) 333-4372; TTY (520) 333-6335

Lakeside Ranger District
RR 3, Box B-50
Pinetop-Lakeside, AZ 85929
Voice and TTY (520) 368-5111

Horseback Riding

Because this is the Old West, of course there are many opportunities to ride. See individual areas as well as dude ranches listed under Where to Stay.

River Floating/Rafting

Arizona has some great white-water rafting and equally good float trips. Snow runoff flows from the White Mountains into the Salt River in the early spring, creating great conditions, and the Colorado River is legendary. See Outdoor Activities in the Phoenix and Environs region and Grand Canyon for rafting opportunities.

Skiing

Arizona's main ski areas—the SnowBowl near Flagstaff in the Coconino National Forest, Sunrise on the White Mountain Apache Reservation and Mount Lemmon near Tucson—generally get enough snow to have successful seasons. See individual areas for specifics on downhill and cross-country.

Seeing and Doing

Museums and Galleries

These range from small-town one-room affairs that may be interesting for their local perspective, to huge nationally acclaimed institutions that take a day to explore. Both have merit. We have listed the reasons we like each one and have tried to include enough information for you to make a decision. Galleries are a different matter. A few are listed, but art is so subjective that we hesitate to make any specific recommendations.

Scenic Drives

As with art, "scenic" is somewhat subjective, so we've pretty much stuck with pointing out drives that others have designated as scenic. Some are AAA-designated, and others are posted with the attractive little signs that the state of Arizona uses to tell you that what you're seeing is scenic—whether you think so or not. We love the desert, so naturally think almost everything here is scenic.

Where to Stay

Although most of the accommodations in Arizona are very special, some are included simply because they're the only ones in a particular town. In some cases, we refer to the fact that chain accommodations are available, occasionally highlighting one if it provides particularly good services, is an unusual value or is the best of a limited number of accommodations in a given area.

Hotels, Motels & Inns

Our favorites are the historic hotels, and they seem to be all over Arizona. From the elegant old Copper Queen in Bisbee, to Flagstaff's Weatherford, to the venerable Arizona Biltmore in Phoenix, they run the gamut from a bit dowdy to unsurpassed luxury. There are few youth hostels, and we have listed those we know about. The following scale approximates what a night's lodgings will cost based on double occupancy:

$	Less than $25
$$	$25 to $50
$$$	$50 to $100
$$$$	$100 on up (in tony areas it can really go up)

National Hotel/Motel Chain Toll Free Numbers

Best Western—(800) 528-1234
Comfort Inn—(800) 221-2222
Choice Hotels—(800) 221-2222
Clarion—(800) 221-2222
Days Inn—(800) 325-2525
Econo-Lodge—(800) 553-2666
Holiday Inn—(800) 465-4329
Motel 6—(800) 466-8356
Quality Inn—(800) 221-2222
Sleep Inn—(800) 221-2222
Super 8—(800) 800-8000

Camping

Campgrounds and RV parks are all over the place. Camping is popular because of the state's mild weather. In most parts you can camp year-round in relative comfort. Many RV parks specialize in accommodating the snowbirds that flock here to escape tough winters elsewhere. Local author James Tallon's book, *Arizona's 144 Best Campgrounds* (An Arizona Highways Book), has good details on what sites look like and what else there is to do in the area. State parks often have great facilities and many take reservations.

There are many Elderhostel programs in Arizona. Check them out by contacting **Elderhostel, 80 Boylston St., Boston, MA 02116; (877) 426-8056.**

There are 12 national forests in the Southwest, seven of which are in Arizona. The Apache-Sitgreaves, Coconino, Kaibab, Coronado, Prescott and Tonto National Forests all lie within state boundaries. For all national forests in Arizona except Kaibab, you can reserve a camp unit that usually has a parking space for a vehicle, table and fire pit or fireplace. Spaces may be reserved up to 240 days in advance, but you must call at least five days ahead of the time you want to be there. With this number you can reserve a campsite in 24 national forest campgrounds in Arizona. **(800) 280-2267, fax (301) 722-9802.**

Where to Eat

We have sampled the food at most of the restaurants listed in the book and admit that there seems to be a preponderance of pricey establishments. That's partially because fast-food chains, which make up the bulk of low-priced eateries in the state, are not listed. We tried to go into detail with those locally owned places we were particularly fond of. Meal costs are indicated based on the following categories:

$	Under $5
$$	$5 to $10
$$$	$10 to $20
$$$$	$20 and up

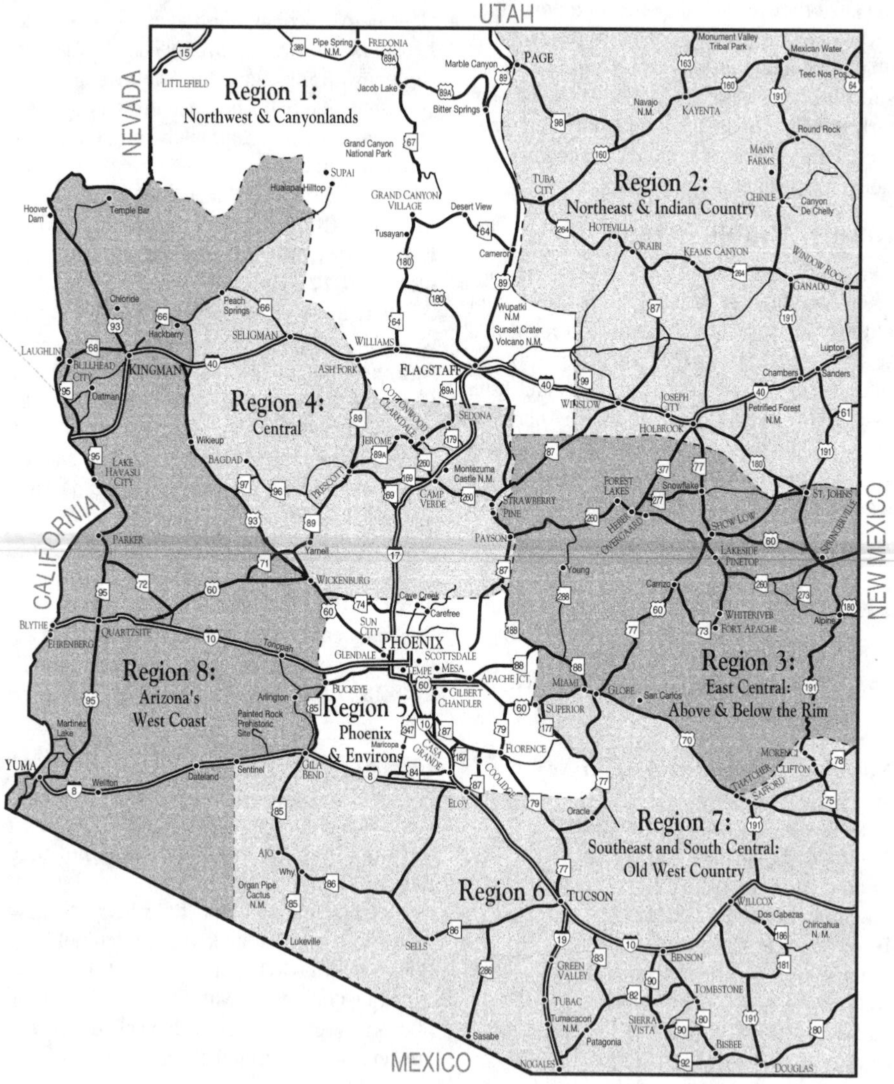

Region 1:
Northwest & Canyonlands

Region 2:
Northeast & Indian Country

Region 3:
East Central:
Above & Below the Rim

Region 4:
Central

Region 5
Phoenix
& Environs

Region 6

Region 7:
Southeast and South Central:
Old West Country

Region 8:
Arizona's
West Coast

Arizona Regional Map

The Arizona Guide

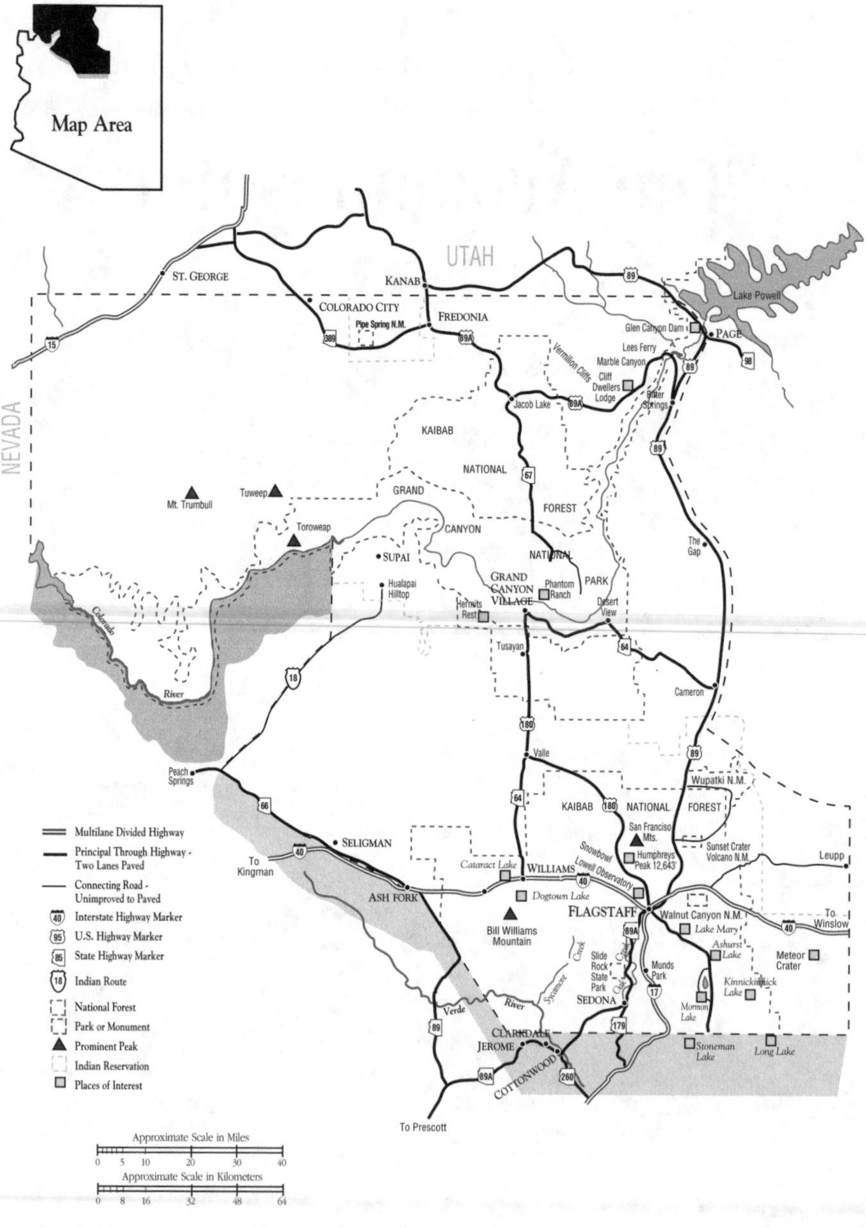

Map Area

UTAH
NEVADA
ST. GEORGE
KANAB
COLORADO CITY
FREDONIA
Pipe Spring N.M.
Lake Powell
Glen Canyon Dam
PAGE
Lees Ferry
Marble Canyon
Vermilion Cliffs
Cliff Dwellers Lodge
Bitter Springs
Jacob Lake
KAIBAB
NATIONAL
FOREST
GRAND
CANYON
NATIONAL
PARK
Mt. Trumbull
Tuweep
Toroweap
SUPAI
Hualapai Hilltop
Hermits Rest
GRAND CANYON VILLAGE
Phantom Ranch
Desert View
The Gap
Tusayan
Cameron
Colorado
River
Valle
Peach Springs
Wupatki N.M.
KAIBAB NATIONAL FOREST
San Francisco Mts.
Humphreys Peak 12,643'
Sunset Crater Volcano N.M.
Leupp
SELIGMAN
To Kingman
Cataract Lake
WILLIAMS
Snowbowl
Lowell Observatory
ASH FORK
Dogtown Lake
FLAGSTAFF
Walnut Canyon N.M.
To Winslow
Lake Mary
Ashurst Lake
Meteor Crater
Bill Williams Mountain
Slide Rock State Park
Sycamore Creek
Oak Creek
Munds Park
Kinnickinnick Lake
Mormon Lake
SEDONA
Verde
River
CLARKDALE
JEROME
COTTONWOOD
Stoneman Lake
Long Lake
To Prescott

Multilane Divided Highway
Principal Through Highway - Two Lanes Paved
Connecting Road - Unimproved to Paved
Interstate Highway Marker
U.S. Highway Marker
State Highway Marker
Indian Route
National Forest
Park or Monument
Prominent Peak
Indian Reservation
Places of Interest

Approximate Scale in Miles
0 5 10 20 30 40
Approximate Scale in Kilometers
0 8 16 32 48 64

Northwest and Canyonlands

Northwest and Canyonlands

The Arizona Strip

The 3.2 million acres of undeveloped land south of the Utah state line and north of the Grand Canyon is considered the Arizona Strip. This remote, wild and lovely area in the state's northwest corner is little known and lesser explored, not because of a lack of riches, but because access is difficult. It was one of the last places in Arizona to be inhabited by modern-day people. To get to other parts of the state from the strip, you have to drive around either end of the canyon. It contains eight wilderness areas: Beaver Dam Mountains, Cottonwood Point, Grand Wash Cliffs, Kanab Creek, Mt. Trumbull, Mt. Logan, Paiute and Paria Canyon-Vermilion Cliffs. One of the advantages of being so remote is that the Vermilion Cliffs area provides habitat for the California condor (see sidebar, page 6). The Bureau of Land Management (BLM), the largest owner in terms of acres, strictly limits development to keep the strip a pristine wilderness. The strip also includes jurisdictions of the National Park Service, National Forest Service and some Kaibab Indian Reservation land.

Although there are 5,000 miles of open roads, only I-15 and US 89A are paved. Some of the dirt routes seem to meander to nowhere, disappearing into washes, cliffs and canyons. Driving, however, is the chief means of exploring the Arizona Strip, but you must come prepared as it is a long time between gas stations and eateries. The BLM cautions that the winding, rough and rocky roads are not appropriate for motorhomes and travel trailers. If you're going off the paved roads at all, you should have a four-wheel-drive vehicle. The brown road signs belong to the BLM; the yellow, oval ones are county road signs.

For those uninitiated to the strip, the BLM has created Recreation Management Zones ranging from Zone 1, "Scenic and Historic Highways," which directs you to paved highways, to Zone 4, "Primitive Passages," which requires a four-wheel-drive or all-terrain vehicle, with a likelihood of getting help if stranded rated as "very low." Rangers say that being current on road and weather conditions is a must for safety.

Major Attractions

Lee's Ferry

About 15 miles below Glen Canyon Dam, this historic town is the jumping-off point for river rafting trips through the Grand Canyon and for backpackers hiking the Paria Canyon Primitive Area. A dozen or so companies offer white water trips on the Colorado River through the canyon. The May through September season is heavily booked for these three- to eight-day motorized and oar trips. Check the Grand Canyon National Park website at **www.the-canyon.com/nps/.**

Dominguez-Escalante

About 21 miles east of the town of Jacob Lake off US 89A, near Paria Canyon and the Vermilion Cliffs Wilderness, there is a roadside turnoff with interpretive signs. They explain the grueling journey undertaken in 1776 by Spanish priests Francisco Dominguez and Silvestre Escalante as they slogged on foot from Santa Fe, through Colorado to Utah, then back through northern Arizona to Santa Fe. There are a picnic area and trailheads for a number of hiking and equestrian trails, but no services or water.

Nampaweap Petroglyph Site

You have to walk about one-half mile from the parking area, but it's worth it to see hundreds of boulders covered with thousands of rock art images along a half-mile basalt cliff. There are no services, but hiking is not terribly difficult. The petroglyphs are located about 55 miles southeast of St. George, off a gravel road (BLM Road 1069 or County Road 5) that goes through Wolf Hole to the Mt. Trumbull area. Roads from Pipe Springs and Colorado City also lead to the site, but a good map is essential. A second interesting petroglyph site just across the Arizona state line in Utah has more than 500 individual rock art designs at the base of a 500-foot mesa. Take BLM Road 1069 over the border, 10 miles southeast of St. George.

Black Rock Mountain

In a gorgeous Ponderosa forest on a plateau, you can sit at a shady picnic table and look into Utah to the north, past the Virgin Mountains, and to the south for a sweeping perspective of Arizona. Take BLM Road 1069 south from St. George to Wolf Hole Valley, then go west on BLM Road 1004. At the edge of the wilderness area the road splits. Take BLM Road 1009 to the site.

Scenic Drives

The **Fredonia-Vermilion Cliffs Scenic Road** is generally considered the entrance to the Arizona Strip. It follows US 89A from the Navajo community of Bitter Springs south of Lee's Ferry, to the Mormon pioneer community of Fredonia, 85 miles to the west near the Utah state line. Approximately 3 miles south of Lee's Ferry, you cross the historic Navajo Bridge at Marble Canyon. It has been converted to a pedestrian bridge, with cars now using the newly completed larger and stronger bridge. The Navajo Bridge is famous for the views it provides of the Colorado River almost 500 feet below. The route passes through the Vermilion Cliffs area where condors recently have been released (see page 6) and on to House Rock Valley, a wide grassland where elk, antelope and bison frequently are spotted. At Jacob Lake, US 89A connects to AZ 67, which leads to the Grand Canyon's North Rim. From this point the road begins to climb with a series of sometimes unnerving switchbacks to the heavily forested Kaibab Plateau.

Where to Stay

Camping

Backcountry camping in undeveloped areas without a permit is allowed for a total of 14 days. The only full-service campground, with 75 developed sites, is in the **Virgin River Canyon Recreation Area,** about 20 miles southwest of St. George in the state's far northwest corner. Located between the Paiute and Beaver Dam Mountains Wilderness Area, set deep down in the gorge's multicolored walls, there are rest rooms, a picnic area, drinking water, showers, a dump station, electrical hookups, hiking trails, canoeing and fishing in the Virgin River. You might have to wade across the river to get to some of the trails. There is a fee for overnight camping. The campground is just off US 15 where it cuts briefly across Arizona between St. George, Utah, and Mesquite, Nevada, before you reach the town of Littlefield.

If you're thinking about spending any time at all in this area, it's essential to have the

Arizona Strip Visitor Map, a detailed chart of tiny roads and obscure places. It's printed on weatherproof stock, so it really will take a beating without falling apart at the folds. It is available for moderate cost at the field office in Utah, or in Phoenix at the BLM office (see Services).

Visitor Lodging

Hotels and motels with varying degrees of comfort are located in Mesquite, Nevada, at Jacob Lake and Fredonia and in St. George, Utah.

Services

BLM Arizona Strip Field Office

The office is located in St. George, Utah, about 5 miles north of the Arizona border. There is no Strip office in Arizona because there is no town to house employees and provide support services for the office. Open Mon.–Fri., 8 A.M.–5 P.M.; Sat., 9 A.M.–4 P.M. **345 E. Riverside Dr., St. George, UT 84790; (801) 688-3200.**

Bureau of Land Management Office

Open Mon.–Fri., 7:30 A.M.–4:30 P.M.; the public room is open 9 A.M.–4 P.M. **222 N. Central Ave., Phoenix, 85004-2203; (602) 417-9200, fax (602) 417-9399.**

Condors

On the brink of extinction, these magnificent birds are getting a new lease on life in the Vermilion Cliffs area of the Arizona Strip. The gigantic grayish-brown creatures are the largest land birds in North America, with a wingspan of more than 9 feet and body weight of 17 to 24 pounds.

The birds do not generally fit the romantic notion of endangered species, like the enormous gray whale, elegant peregrine falcon or diminutive spotted owl. The huge red-headed vulture is ugly, it feasts on carrion, and so far efforts to re-introduce it to the wilds have consumed more than $20 million in federal, state and local funding. Animal lovers maintain, however, that there is much romanticism in the great bird's soaring, graceful flight and its inquisitive, gregarious nature. Its feathers and bones have been a part of legend and ceremony within Indian mythology for generations. And scientists point out there is still so much we don't know about the world's creatures that it is foolish to think that any of them are disposable.

Those who remember seeing condors in the wild attest to the fact that they rely on soaring, rather than flapping flight. A condor roosts in a spot where it can launch itself easily with just a few wing-beats, using uplifting winds along mountain ridges to stay aloft. Graceful spiraling means that the bird is using a warm thermal updraft to gain altitude, after which it can glide for long distances before seeking another uplifting thermal.

Condors raise only one young every other year from a single pale aqua-colored egg placed in a remote cave, sheltered outcrop or crevice on a cliff. No nesting material is added. Baby condors develop slowly, not perfecting flying skills until they're almost a year old. Parents may continue to feed a chick for more than a year. Condors do not breed until age five or six.

In 1987 the last free-flying condors were captured in an attempt to save the species. There were just 27 birds remaining. Programs rebuilt the population so that in 1997, 15 condors were released in the Vermilion Cliffs area. As of this writing, 15 are still flying high, not all of them part of the original group. Each bird wears a tiny transmitter so that biologists can track them, not just for research but for the birds' safety. Their social nature encourages them to readily accept human handouts, an event that may encourage them not to return to the wilds. The closer condors are to civilization, the greater the danger of encounters with power lines and other hazards. The Vermilion Cliffs provide young condors with the good thermals critical for their flight development. Also, the cliffs are pockmarked with caves and ledges for roosting and nesting. Although condors were last sighted in the Arizona wilds in 1924, condor bones that date back 11,000 years have been found near the Vermilion Cliffs. It seems a natural site for releasing condors today.

Visitors can drive dirt roads and hike the area, high-powered binoculars poised for possible sightings. Often the condors may be seen from the pull-out parking places along US 89A between Lee's Ferry and House Rock Valley Road. Rangers say that travel off the highway is unnecessary and ill-advised.

To find likely spots for seeing condors, check out the project's homepage at **www.peregrinefund.org/vermil.html.** A chatty narrative tells how the birds are doing and where they've recently been sighted. The release of the condors is a joint project of The Peregrine Fund, the U.S. Fish and Wildlife Service, the Bureau of Land Management and the Arizona Game and Fish Department. For more information contact **The Peregrine Fund, 566 W. Flying Hawk Ln., Boise, ID 83709; (208) 362-3716, fax (208) 362-2376. E-mail: tpf@peregrinefund.org.**

Page and Lake Powell

It was 1956, Dwight D. Eisenhower was president, and Page, Arizona, had yet to make its appearance on any map. Today Page and Lake Powell are a dot and a spidery patch of blue that hang across Arizona's border with Utah. When in 1956 the U.S. Congress authorized the Bureau of Reclamation to build a dam on the Colorado River to supply water to the lower basin states of California, Arizona and Nevada, a construction camp was established to house workers. By the time the Glen Canyon Dam was completed in 1965, the camp, now known as Page, was an established city and the gateway to a new aquatic playground.

Page is named for John C. Page, a past Commissioner of the Bureau of Reclamation who oversaw the construction of Hoover Dam. Today Page has a population of about 8,200, a figure that swells considerably during pleasant summer months when visitors come to enjoy water activities.

Page is a Main Street town with a tidy, new look. A grassy city park, just behind the Chamber of Commerce office, provides a pleasant picnic place, alive with glossy black ravens that eye your lunch hopefully but keep a respectful distance.

Lake Powell tour boat gives visitors an overall view. Photo courtesy Arizona Office of Tourism/ Alan Benoit.

On Lake Powell Boulevard, "Church Row" is a ribbon of 11 places of worship, created when each congregation was offered a free plot of ground if it would build a church. From an elevation of 4,300 feet on Manson Mesa, Page overlooks Glen Canyon Dam and Lake Powell. While some consider its landscape bleak, others find majestic beauty in its sweeping vistas and low vegetation. During June, July and August high temperatures hover in the 90s, retreating to the chilly 40s and 50s in January and February. Summer is high season here, but many visitors prefer the serene and sunny days of May and October, free of the frenzy of kids out of school.

Glen Canyon Bridge, 700 feet above the Colorado River, offers a good view of the Glen Canyon Dam. When it opened in 1959, the bridge cut the driving distance from one side of the canyon to the other by 197 miles. With 250 square miles of blue water, Lake Powell, the reservoir created by the dam, is a maze of backwater canyons, quiet bays and tiny inlets. It is 186 miles long, has 1,986 miles of shoreline and 96 water-filled side canyons. It took until 1980 to fill the lake to its capacity, which puts its glossy surface 3,700 feet above sea level. Maximum depth at the dam is 560 feet. Lake Powell's easy-to-take, 75-degree summer water temp dips as low as 42 degrees in winter, its sheer mass keeping it warm enough to prevent freeze-over. The lake is named for Major John Wesley Powell, a Civil War veteran who explored the Colorado River in the late 1800s.

From the vantage point of a boat, great cliffs rise as much as 400 feet from the water's surface. Gray waterlines on canyon walls mark the lake's ever-changing level. High and low watermarks can have a 90-foot spread. What look like ancient hieroglyphics really are the marks of erosion. At one point, man-made cutouts in the rock, called Prospector's Steps or Miner's Stairs, rise from the water's edge, remnants of days when the canyon was mined. Two flights are visible. Locals say there are an additional four flights underwater that reach down to what was the canyon floor before the lake was filled. "Navajo tapestry" is the term given to the intricate stains on the canyon walls. Porous sandstone absorbs the colors created by minerals such as iron (red), manganese (black) and calcium (white) to create the rich patterns.

Major Attractions

Glen Canyon National Recreation Area

Everything that happens out of doors near Page happens in this enormous park. Established in 1972 as part of the national park system, it covers more than one million acres. National recreation areas are defined by the lakes and reservoirs they encompass, most of which were created by dams. Lake Mead, on the Arizona-California border, was the first.

Glen Canyon is the center point of the Grand Circle, an ecological aggregate of seven national parks, seven national monuments, as well as state parks and historic sites that encompass Indian ruins and geologic formations. National Park Service rangers are at most marinas, ready to answer questions. Vegetation in the recreation area is brushy, consisting of junipers and piñon pines at higher elevations, with yucca and prickly pear cactus further down. Seeps or springs from overhanging cliffs sometimes support gardens of maidenhair fern, monkey flower and (watch out!) poison ivy. Red-tailed hawks, ravens and peregrine falcons catch thermals near cliffs. Seldom seen, but in the area, are bighorn sheep and bobcats. You're more likely to catch a glimpse of a coyote or deer as you hike the area.

The canyon dates back 310 million years, a history that can be traced visually through the layers of sandstone that make up its walls. During the Cretaceous period, which began 135 million years ago, the sandstone cliffs on the canyon's north edge were formed, as were layers of tropic shale that bear fossil oysters, snails, sharks and other sea life. They confirm that Lake Powell is not the first body of water to fill the canyon.

The canyon's earliest residents were prehistoric Indians who hunted the plentiful bison

and mammoth that lived here 11,000 years ago. By 200 B.C., as the climate became drier, the Anasazi moved in and began to cultivate corn. These resourceful people left evidence of their culture in baskets, pottery and ruins that include Defiance House, located in the lake's Forgotten Canyon in Utah.

Glen Canyon Dam

This massively impressive 710-foot wall of concrete, crossing a deep sandstone gorge, holds back the mighty Colorado River. It is the last of eight dams built on the river. The site was chosen because the reservoir basin could safely hold an enormous amount of water, the canyon walls and bedrock foundation were strong and stable, and nearby Wahweap Creek supplied good rock and sand for making concrete aggregate. Power produced at the dam is sold to hundreds of cities in a six-state area. Much of it goes south for the summer to run air conditioners and to pump water for irrigation. In winter months the power goes north to help supply heating loads. Free self-guided tours of the dam and power plant take about 30 to 45 minutes, depending on how quickly you want to stride along. Pick up a tour booklet at the **Carl Hayden Visitor Center.** Scheduled guided tours descend 53 stories into the dam and are offered during the summer.

John Wesley Powell Memorial Museum

At this museum in downtown Page, you can not only check out history, but make reservations for lake, river, air and ground tours and get general visitor information. The area's past is illustrated in a sequence of black and white archival photos from the days when the river was first explored. The museum includes John Wesley Powell's family history, his adventures exploring the Colorado, along with Indian artifacts and an explanation of the canyon's geologic structure. If you don't think your camera adequately captured the grandeur of Antelope Canyon, professional photographs are available here along with a good selection of books on the area. Free admission. Open May to Sept., 8 A.M.–6 P.M., Mon.–Sat., and 10 A.M.–6 P.M. on Sun.; mid-Feb., Mar., Nov. to mid-Dec., 9–5 P.M., Mon.–Fri. Closed mid-Dec. to mid-Feb. Call, write, fax or e-mail for more information. Located at the corner of **Lake Powell Blvd. and N. Navajo, P.O. Box 547, Page 86040; (520) 645-9496, fax (520) 645-3412. E-mail: jwpmm@aol.com.**

Festivals and Events

Page Attacks Trash/Earth Day
mid-April

More than 4,000 residents and visitors spread out over Page and clean up the town, then come back to the central park to collect their T-shirt reward. Anti-trashers feast on barbeque provided by Salt River Project, the local utilities company, and cooked by the Elks Club. It's such an event that President George Bush declared it one of his Points of Light.

Lake Powell Air Affaire
early October

Billed as "The Best Little Air Show" in the Southwest, past celebrations have featured the Canadian Snowbirds, the Canadian Air Force's nine-plane precision jet team, as well as the U.S. Navy Leap Frog parachute team. Wing walkers, hot air balloons, radio-controlled models and more are part of this two-day event. Spectators sprawl in bleachers and rental chairs, slathered with sun screen and protected with brimmed hats. Room reservations, **(800) 654-5834;** air show tickets, **(520) 645-9373.**

Outdoor Activities

Biking

Rides range from mellow road cycling to tricky off-road treks. An easy four-mile route called The Chains takes you from Page to Lake Powell, where you'll be ready for a swim if you ride during summer months. Take US 89 toward the dam. A quarter mile before the dam, turn right on an unmarked gravel road and follow it to the end. Walk down to the lake. To check out Page, try the six-mile loop that follows Navajo Drive, Sage Avenue, Grand View Street and Rim View Drive.

Within the National Park, bicycles are permitted on established trails and roads only. An excellent park map and guide is available at the visitor center, where helpful rangers will point you in the right direction to find the best trails for riding. For more information, contact the **Carl Hayden Visitor Center, P. O. Box 1507, Page 86040; (520) 608-6404.** The Center is located at Glen Canyon Dam.

Getting There

Page is about 280 miles north of Phoenix and 125 miles north of Flagstaff on US 89. Most visitors make the easy drive by private car. By air, Great Lakes Air serves Page from Phoenix. During summer months, Scenic Airlines operates a daily flight from Las Vegas to Page. Other airlines offer service seasonally.

Boating

Houseboating

Houseboating and Lake Powell were made for each other, and in fact there are more than 500 of the floating condos available for rent. The lake's placid waters sometimes are upset by testy weather, so boaters have to be alert for the occasional storm that brings high winds and ocean-force waves. A good navigational map is essential for quick access to the closest arm as a protective retreat. These secluded inlets also make it possible for boaters to stay fairly remote even in the middle of summer. Much of the fun is simply anchoring for an on-deck barbeque, then watching stars appear in a smog-free sky.

Usually several couples or families get together to rent a houseboat, not only for the camaraderie but in order to have more than one boat driver. Houseboats can be as long as 59 feet with bunks for 12. Full briefings are held before anyone is allowed out on the lake. Piloting, navigating, docking, anchoring, refueling and pumping out are essential skills that must be learned.

Houseboats may be rented for as few as two days during the off-season from October through mid-May, but three-day minimums are usual the rest of the year. Most houseboaters rent a tag-along power boat for waterskiing or exploring places too small to accommodate the houseboat. If you're thinking about renting a houseboat during summer months, book as far ahead as possible. Some categories of boats are reserved during peak seasons up to a year in advance. For reservations call **Lake Powell Resorts & Marinas, P.O. Box 56909, Phoenix, 85079; (520) 645-2433.**

Marinas

Although most of the Glen Canyon Recreation Area is in Utah, one of its most important jumping-off points is **Wahweap Marina,** the largest of the lake's five marinas, 6 miles north of Page. Here you can rent houseboats and powerboats, fuel up, find fishing and water sports gear, groceries and general merchandise. Wahweap Lodge is a top notch place to overnight (see Where to Stay section) and the center of marina activities.

Bullfrog Resort & Marina (801-684-3000, Halls Crossing Marina (801-684-7000) and Hite Marina (801-684-2278) are in Utah. You may find yourself stopping at any of them if you're cruising the lake.

Dangling Rope Marina (520-645-2969) has an Arizona area code because it is in the middle of Lake Powell and gets its calls by cellular phone, but it is in Utah, about 40 miles up the lake from Wahweap. Accessible only by boat, it offers a year-round gas dock and pump-out station.

Boat Trips

Rainbow Natural Bridge

The best way to see this amazing sandstone formation is by water, either on the five-hour tour or in your private boat. It was featured in a 1909 *National Geographic* and by the following year it was declared a national monument. About 8 land miles north of the Arizona-Utah border and approximately 50 lake miles north of Wahweap Marina, it is the world's tallest known natural bridge. It remained relatively obscure until Lake Powell was filled in 1963, but today is one of the lake's most popular sites. Its 275-foot span arches to 290 feet, created over the centuries by a swift-flowing stream, forcing its way to the Colorado from Navajo Mountain. You disembark on a sturdy floating dock, and from there it is an easy quarter-mile walk to the bridge. The inspiring spectacle has deep spiritual meaning to Native Americans. Please be respectful, and do not walk under the bridge or beyond the viewing area.

Along the way, as your tour boat traverses the lake, you'll see natural rock sculptures that include Sleeping Indian and Eighteen Wheeler. On Antelope Island there are no antelope even though the National Park Service wanted to introduce them. They discovered that vegetation on the island is insufficient to support a herd.

Other Lake Tours

The *Canyon King,* a 95-foot paddle wheeler, does one-hour rides to Castle Rock and nearby sights. Some cruises include dinner. Other half- and all-day boat trips explore remote and beautiful canyons at a leisurely pace. Tours leave from Wahweap Marina. For information and reservations call **Wahweap Boat Tours** at **(520) 645-2741 or (520) 645-2433.**

Fishing

The lake attracts anglers after largemouth, smallmouth, and striped bass, as well as walleye, pike and scrappy little bluegill and crappie. There always seems to be a local tournament in progress, which is not surprising considering the great fishing on the lake and on the river below the dam. You must have an Arizona fishing license, as well as a Utah license if you plan to fish farther north. Purchase them at marina stores.

Bubba's Guide Service offers a nine-hour fishing day to pursue largemouth, smallmouth or striped bass and includes a guide, bass boat and gas, bait and tackle, lunch and soft drinks. **P.O. Box 3778, Page, 86040; (520) 645-5785.**

Four-Wheel-Drive Trips

Antelope Canyon

One of the most photographed (and most difficult to photograph) spots in the area, Antelope Canyon, also called Slot and Corkscrew Canyon, is a cavelike passage of petrified sand that winds for half a mile. Formed when rushing water swirled and curled through the soft pink sandstone to pour onto the canyon floor, it is a shadowy, ethereal place where the temperature stays about 70 degrees even during the heat of summer. Water-sculpted rock, impregnated with quartz crystal, reflect shafts of sunlight, creating ever-shifting rainbows and deep blue shadows. Clearly outlined against the sky 150 feet above the canyon floor, the formations called Weeping Eye and Eagles Head need no explanation.

Although the corkscrew portion covers barely a quarter mile, the canyon itself extends more than 25 miles from Lake Powell. Bring a flashlight for the darkest parts. May through July are the best times to photograph because the sun is high enough to shine down inside the canyon. The jeep trip leaves from downtown Page and heads past six steaming strobe-lighted stacks on the horizon, belonging to the 2,250-megawatt Navajo Generating Station. So much coal is produced on the Navajo and Hopi Reservations that much of it is transported 275 miles to Laughlin, Nevada, through a unique coal and water slurry pipeline. Where the jeep leaves paved Hwy. 98 for the canyon turn-off, members of the Navajo tribe staff the gate into the canyon. You must be with a licensed guide to go into the canyon. No private hikers or autos are allowed. At the end of 3.5 miles of shifty, sandy road, jeep tracks end at the canyon's mouth and you'll begin your stroll. This spot was in the news in August 1997 when 11 hikers were killed by a flash flood that swept through it. If there is rain anywhere in the area, postpone your trip. Companies with permits to tour the canyon include **Grand Circle Adventures, 52 6th Ave., Page, 86040; (520) 645-4010 or Lake Powell Jeep Tours, 104 S. Lake Powell Blvd., P.O. Box 1144, Page, 86040; (520) 645-5501.** For more information on tours contact **www.canyon-country.com.**

Golf

Glen Canyon Golf and Country Club

This older 9-hole course has been around for more than 30 years, but the new adjacent

18-hole course, Lake Powell National Golf Club, completed in 1995, brings total available holes to 27. The new course is a masterpiece of planning, incorporating the best of natural surroundings. It is set picturesquely on rolling dunes overlooking Lake Powell with views so spectacular it's hard to keep an eye on the ball and off the vistas. Some golfers come here just to play what's billed as the "longest and steepest hole in the Southwest." Four tees on each hole cater to a variety of skill levels. It has a pro shop, restaurant and grill. The courses are playable and open to the public all year, seven days a week. Greens fees take a drop from October to March. Tee times, recommended, are given seven days in advance. Located **next to the Marriott, 400 Clubhouse Dr., Page, 86040; (520) 645-2023.**

Hiking and Walking

Glen Canyon provides many areas for brief strolls, challenging day hikes and multiday backpack forays. It can be tough going, however, because it is a slickrock area with few marked trails. But orienteering is made somewhat easier because the lake often is in view. Nonetheless, hikers should be proficient with a compass and should have a good updated map, available from the **National Park Service (520-608-6404)** or at the **Carl Hayden Visitor Center** (see Services). Best hiking months are March through June, and September and October. In summer, water may be scarce so carry your own. If you drink found water, boil or treat it first as it may contain Giardia. Gnats and flies can be a problem in spring, so bring repellent.

The Horseshoe Bend View

This 0.75-mile moderate day hike starts at Milepost 545 on US 89 and winds to a spectacular view of the Colorado River as it makes a looping curve around a sandstone escarpment.

Wiregrass Canyon

A mellow 3-mile hike (gets hot in summer so do it early in the morning), it traces an easy-to-follow wash, passing a little natural bridge, balanced rocks and small arches. Side canyons offer good exploring. If there's a storm brewing, rethink your hike, because flash floods have been known to gush through the canyon. The trailhead is 10 minutes north of the dam. Follow US 89 in Big Water (in Utah), turn right onto UT 277, then right onto UT 12 and go 4.5 miles south on Warm Creek Road. Park where you see the sign "Wiregrass Canyon Backcountry."

Kayaking

Lake Powell is a great place for this shore-hugging sport because it has close to 2,000 miles of shoreline. Best time to paddle is September to May when boat traffic is at a minimum yet the weather is reliably sunny. Many places have kayak rentals, including **Red Rock Cyclery** (see Biking) and **Twin Finn Dive Center** (see Scuba Diving).

River Floating/Rafting

There's no white water on this last undammed section of the Colorado that winds south from Glen Canyon Dam. Usually a leisurely 15-mile float, it meanders past ancient Anasazi petroglyphs, affording great views of the Colorado's handiwork as it carved the canyon out of high desert plateaus. Sandstone cliffs hunker 2,400 feet above river level. Half-day and all-day (with lunch) tours are available. A number of companies do full motor and oar trips that range from four to 12 days. Rather than contact individual outfitters, you can save a lot of time by getting in touch with a company that books trips with more than a dozen outfitters. Once they know the sort of trip you're looking for, information will be sent. Contact **Rivers & Oceans, P.O. Box 40321, Flagstaff, 86004; (800) 473-4576 or (520) 526-4575.**

Scuba Diving

Those accustomed to Caribbean diving may find Lake Powell's dive sites a tad underwhelming, while others really get into the austere beauty of underwater pinnacles and sheer vertical walls. It is definitely worth at least a one-time dive, just for comparison's sake. These are altitude dives, so take that into consideration when calculating depth and time tolerances. Even beginning divers can wade into the water from a gently sloped shoreline to look at rock formations, walls, cracks, crevices, cliffs and an amazing array of articles dropped from boats (see Tracking the Trash, page 16). Sagebrush, blown into the water, replaces the coral reefs of the Caribbean. Local fish that reliably swim into view include smallmouth bass, bluegill, crappie, walleye, catfish and striped bass. Shad, the small inch-long feeder fish that provide meals for larger species, are especially spectacular on a night dive when they come close to shore in huge schools. For boat dives, **Navajo Canyon** has good year-round visibility. **Antelope Island** has easy access. Visibility can be as little as 7 feet in warmer water near the surface, with 60 to 80 feet of visibility usual at cooler depths during late fall and early spring when water temps are around 55 to 60 degrees. Wet or dry suits are a definite requirement. For truly hardy souls, drift diving in the Colorado River below the Glen Canyon Dam is available year-round. For information and gear rental contact **Twin Finn Dive Center, P.O. Box 4780, 811 Vista Ave., Page, 86040; (520) 645-3114. E-mail: twinfinn@page-lakepowell.com.**

Swimming

The lake is considered swimmable from June through October, and terrific in August when the average water temperature is close to 80 degrees. Be careful when swimming or diving as the water level frequently fluctuates. When it is particularly low, submerged salt cedar trees and cactuses become formidable deadheads.

Waterskiing

The lake's placid surface is ideal for waterskiing. It is prohibited in marked channels with heavy boat traffic and in narrow side canyons. Boats and equipment can be rented at many local shops.

Seeing and Doing

Nightlife

Ken's Old West Dining and Dancing, the local hangout, is so crowded most nights that you can't even get in. The rustic, wood-front place usually has a country western band. Line dancing is big here. Locals recommend the steaks and prime rib. **718 Vista; (520) 645-5160.**

Windy Mesa Bar has some of the best entertainment, varying from country to reggae to pop. Sunday is jam night. Pool tables and pinball machines keep an eclectic clientele entertained. **800 N. Navajo Dr.; (520) 645-2186.**

Gunsmoke Saloon offers dining, dancing and cocktails. During prime tourist months, May to October, a country and western music show is presented nightly. At 9 P.M. the saloon turns into a nightclub. It is adjacent to **The Dam Bar and Grille,** which offers good steaks and seafood in a setting that's a sort of shrine to Glen Canyon Dam. An etched glass dam and a 60 by 5-foot replica of the dam graces one wall. **644 N. Navajo; (520) 645-2161 (dinner reservations) or (520) 645-1888 (show reservations).**

Where to Stay

Hotels, Motels & Inns

With the exception of **Wahweap Lodge,** all of Page's motels are in about a 3-mile radius. During summer months reservations are a must. In the winter, if they stay open, most motels cut their rates by about half.

Courtyard by Marriott—$$$$

This attractive place definitely is a number of notches above the basic small-town motel. The territorial adobe-look hostelry offers lovely canyon, golf course or lake views from the balcony of each of its 153 rooms. The

Southwest-style lobby has a huge fireplace and massive mission furnishings that invite settling in to watch the flames. A workout room and heated outdoor pool and whirlpool are welcome amenities. A well-stocked gift shop carries sundries and reading material. In-room coffee means you don't have to traipse to the restaurant for your morning caffeine jolt. Rates June to September are highest, going down to the $$$ range during low season from November to June. **600 Clubhouse Drive, P.O. Box 4128, Page, 86040; (800) 851-3855 or (520) 645-5000.**

Wahweap Lodge—$$$$

This is Arizona's only resort on the shores of Lake Powell, offering great lake views from many of its 350 rooms. The fine-dining Rainbow Room and Itza Pizza, open summer months only (see Where to Eat) make it possible for you never to have to leave the resort and marina for your entire stay. Higher rates prevail April through October, falling to the $$$ range November to March. **100 Lake Shore Dr., Page, 86040; (520) 645-2433 or (800) 528-6154 (reservations).**

Lake Powell International Hostel—$–$$

As its name implies, you'll rub elbows with an interesting international clientele in this friendly place. Accommodations, in three different buildings, can handle up to about one hundred guests at a time. On warm summer evenings, everyone's out playing volleyball and badminton, and making plans for the next day's hikes. There are bunks in dorms, private rooms and a few private suites, all with linens furnished. Coffee and tea are always available, and guests can use a number of complete kitchens and an outdoor cooking area. **141 8th Ave., P.O. Box 1077, Page, 86040; (520) 645-3898.**

Bed & Breakfasts

A Room with A View—$$$

By city ordinance, bed and breakfasts in Page can have just two rooms for rent. Because it's a young city, these are not the Victorian 1920s or even World War II–era converted mansions awash with froufrou and potpourri, but sleek, newer homes with a couple of rooms outfitted for guests. The industry developed in Page as an outlet for the overflow from hotels. Most are open summer months only. A Room with A View has spacious rooms with private baths, one with a 6-foot marble tub. Cooked-to-order breakfasts. **P.O. Box 2155, Page, 86040; (520) 645-5763.**

Camping

Lake Powell Resorts and Marinas Wahweap RV Park

Full utility hookups are available all year, along with water, groceries, restrooms, showers, coin-operated laundry and LP gas. No reservations needed in winter, but they are essential during the summer. **(800) 528-6154.**

Lone Rock Beach

Free camping, with no facilities, is available here. Camp just across the border in Utah, or anywhere north of the dam and west of US 89 on BLM land. You can camp almost anywhere in Glen Canyon except within one mile of the marinas and Lee's Ferry, or at Rainbow Bridge National Monument.

Wahweap Campground

On the shores of Lake Powell, great vistas and proximity to water-based activities attract swarms of folks during summer months who quickly fill the 180 spaces. Open mid-March to the end of October for dry camping with no hookups. **P.O. Box 1597, Page, 86040; (520) 645-1004.**

Where to Eat

If you're putting together a picnic, try Safeway or Basha's, the two major grocery stores, for good deli items. (*Note:* That small refrigerator near the door as you leave Basha's isn't full of dark spaghetti. Those are live fishing worms, chilled so they stay calm and last longer.)

Rainbow Room—$$$$

At **Wahweap Lodge,** this elegant glass-walled restaurant has reliably good food as well as sweeping views of the marina and its goings on, Wahweap Bay and Castle Rock beyond. The adjacent **Driftwood Lounge** is quiet and low key. **(520) 645-2433.**

Peppers—$$$–$$$$

Inside the **Courtyard by Marriott,** predinner complimentary hors d'oeuvres in the pleasant upscale bar are substantial (full-size enchiladas some nights) and delicious. The dinner menu has a definite Southwest style to it, with spicy dishes a feature. During summer months ask to dine on the attractive patio. **Lake Powell Blvd. and US 89; (520) 645-5000.**

Navajo Room—$$$

Also at **Wahweap Lodge,** from June through the end of September, an expansive dinner buffet precedes colorful Native American dance entertainment. Buffet is at 6 P.M., entertainment begins at 8 P.M. **(520) 645-2433.**

Strombolli's—$$

The outdoor deck is the place to be for people-watching and to be in the thick of what's happening in Page. Hand-tossed pizza and microbrew draft beers are among its most popular fare, but baked calzones are the favorite of many. Don't be in a hurry. Relaxed service is just part of the ambiance. **711 N. Navajo Dr.; (520) 645-2605.**

Services

Carl Hayden Visitor Center

Serving the Glen Canyon National Recreation Area, the center is located at the Glen Canyon Dam in a building used jointly by the Bureau of Reclamation and the Park Service. Hiking and trails, camping, weather and other area information is available. The National Park Service provides an information center here to help with outdoor activities in the Glen Canyon Recreation Area. Open daily, 7 A.M.–7 P.M. in summer; 8 A.M.–5 P.M. other months. **Box 1507, Page, 86040; (520) 608-6404.** The Natural History Association operates a bookstore in the center, filled with good reference material including topographical maps, hiking books and sources for the history of the area. **P.O. Box 581, Page, 86040; (520) 645-3532.**

Page-Lake Powell Chamber of Commerce Visitor and Convention Bureau

This is your one-stop shopping place for information on area activities and events, and also for booking tours. Open daily, mid-May to mid-Oct., 7 A.M.–7 P.M.; open Mon.–Sat., 8 A.M.–5:30 P.M. the rest of the year. Located in Page Plaza, facing the road, near Safeway. **P.O. Box 72, Page, 86040: (888) 261-PAGE (7243) or (520) 645-2741, fax (520) 645-3181. E-mail: redrock@dcaccess.com. Website: www.page-lakepowell.com.**

Tracking the Trash

Anytime there's an aggregate of humanity at a special site, it's to be expected that a certain percentage will be insensitive to the garbage, refuse, trash, waste and debris that they leave behind. At Lake Powell, sudden gusts of wind can carry unsecured hats and towels into the lake, and items accidently dropped from boats will find their way to sandy shores. They end up as unsightly, unwelcome intrusions on an area that should be scenic and unspoiled.

Enter the Trash Tracker. This well-equipped houseboat scours the lake on 26 weekly trips each year, manned by volunteers who devote their days to corralling the visitor-generated junk that mars the lake's lovely beaches. Golf balls, swim suits, towels, shotgun shells, cans and bottles, motor parts, even barbecue grills, baby pacifiers and coins are among the "treasures" that the volunteers stuff into huge biodegradable garbage bags. Each volunteer has a "quota" of five bags per day. They often fill more.

The Tracker leaves from Wahweap Marina, towing the *Eliminator* (a bargelike craft in which retrieved detritus is stored) and a small runabout for forays away from the "mother ship." Volunteers, usually four per trip, plus a captain who doubles as a guide, sleep in bunks and share a head (bathroom). Each volunteer brings some groceries aboard and assumes cooking duties for one night.

The privately funded program is a huge asset to the underfunded National Park Service, which otherwise is charged with lake cleanup. Lake Powell Resorts & Marinas provides the houseboat, pilot and trash barge, with other donators picking up the tab for trash bags and motors. Volunteers work hard and should come prepared with hats, gloves, sun screen, hiking boots and long pants. Days are spent on the pick-up brigade, but evenings allow plenty of time for comparing the day's finds, relaxing, and enjoying the lake.

The Trash Tracker makes 26 runs from April to November each year. The program is enormously popular and takes just four volunteers per trip. Each must be 18 (many are seniors) in good enough shape to bend, lift and walk in summer temps that can top 100 degrees. Volunteer applications are considered on July 15 for the following year. Don't be surprised if there is a waiting list of a year or more, although last-minute cancellations do happen. You're welcome to join if you can do so at a moment's notice. For more information, and to apply, contact **Trash Tracker Coordinator, Glen Canyon National Recreation Area, P.O. Box 1507, Page, 86040; (520) 608-6404.**

Flagstaff

This remarkably lovely, clean, entertaining and altogether appealing town once was nothing more than a pit stop on Route 66. It was the place for an overnight in a neon-signed motor court on your way to the Grand Canyon or Las Vegas. And then visitors began to linger to enjoy crisp pine-scented air and explore the surrounding forests. Phoenix residents realized that Flagstaff's 7,000-foot elevation made for much more pleasant temperatures during July and August when the Valley of the Sun sweltered in triple-digit temps for weeks without relief. Flagstaff has a distinct four-season climate, with the first snow usually appearing in November and lasting into April. Because 20 inches of the white fluffy stuff generally fall in March, spring skiing is reliably good.

Today Flagstaff remains the seat of Coconino County, the country's second largest county, with an area of more than 11 million acres. This city of about 53,000 is surrounded by the **Coconino National Forest,** 1.8 million acres of pine trees, lakes and picturesque gorges that afford outstanding opportunities for recreation. The area boasts the highest point in the state, 12,643-foot Humphreys Peak, one of the San Francisco Peaks, which have become Flagstaff landmarks.

History

Settled in 1876, Flagstaff gets its name from a tall pine tree that was a trail marker for early travelers on their way to California. By 1882 the Atlantic & Pacific Railroad reached the town and a depot was built. The adjacent street became known as Railroad Avenue (it's now Route 66 or Santa Fe Avenue) and businesses flourished along its busy length. Saloons and houses of ill repute flourished as well, supplying entertainment for mill workers and construction crews from the Atlantic & Pacific Railroad. By 1891 Flagstaff was named county seat of newly created Coconino County.

Flagstaff narrowly missed being the motion picture capital of the world. Although accounts differ, the general story says that Cecil B. DeMille and producer Jesse D. Lasky came through Flagstaff on the train from New York in 1912, looking for locations to make "The Squaw Man," as well as a venue suitable for a permanent studio. They loved the scenery, the fresh air, the tall pines and the climate. But while they were there it started to snow. Coming from the East Coast with the express goal of finding a place with weather that would let them film in every season, the flurry rendered the town unsuitable. They proceeded to a small West Coast real estate development called Hollywoodland, and the rest, as they say, is history. Nonetheless, many movies and television programs have been shot in the Flagstaff area, which continues to attract film makers for the same reasons that DeMille and Lasky found it appealing.

Major Attractions

Lowell Observatory

Forever niched in the annals of astronomy as the site from which the planet Pluto was discovered by Clyde W. Tombaugh in 1930, this is an active research observatory that also shares its facilities with an interested public. The 1.5-hour tour starts with a half-hour slide show narrated by energetic students who lay the groundwork for the observatory's history and for understanding the studies and discoveries that have made it famous. Visitors usually are amazed to learn of the observatory's genesis as a place for Percival Lowell to pursue verification for what he thought were canals on the surface of Mars. He believed they were built by intelligent life to harvest water from polar ice caps. Only when V. M. Silpher used a spectrograph in conjunction with the enormous Clark telescope to document the theory of an expanding universe was the canal theory proved false. Each tour visits the site's library, a quiet and comfortable room built in 1916 that houses Lowell's collection of books, memorabilia from his life, and the original spectrograph used in the expanding cosmos study. Take a look at the "Saturn" chandelier, a precursor of the Art Deco style.

While on tour, guests are introduced to the huge Clark refractor telescope and are able to walk past Lowell's grave on a pine-covered hill. If viewing conditions are right on the nighttime tours, visitors can peer through a telescope at the fascinating celestial bodies in the night sky. The 103-year-old observatory was heavily involved in the Apollo program, hosting Buzz Aldrin and Neil Armstrong as students. Armstrong's signature is displayed in the library guest book. A gallery with interactive displays and a gift shop well stocked with trinkets as well as useful research books is in the main visitor center. To set myths to rest concerning the planet Pluto being named after Disney's daffy dog, guides explain that it was an English schoolgirl who suggested Pluto in honor of the Greek god of the underworld. Since it fit with the progressive sequence of Jupiter and Neptune, it was adopted. It also appeased those who thought the new discovery should bear the name of Percival Lowell, as the planet's astronomical symbol became P with a sub-L, which are Lowell's initials.

There are many programs and events throughout the year that affect the observatory's open hours, but generally it is open daily, 8:30 A.M.–5:30 P.M. Call first to hear a recording of scheduled events and night viewings. There is a small fee. Lowell Observatory is located on Mars Hill. From City Hall, where all main roads entering Flagstaff converge, drive west on Aspen Street four blocks to Thorpe Park. Turn left at the park, proceed one block, then turn right and follow the road up the hill. **(520) 774-2096.**

Walnut Canyon National Monument

Just east of Flagstaff, one of the loveliest canyons in the state is open for hiking and exploring. The Sinagua, canyon dwellers from 1120 to 1250, left a well-documented history in more than 300 cliff dwellings, two dozen of

which may be viewed from groomed trails. Artifacts found in the canyon verify that its residents were skilled traders. Bones of birds from Mexico, seashells and distinctive jewelry were no doubt traded for Sinagua pottery and obsidian. The canyon provided a comfortable living for its early residents, with fresh water for drinking and to nourish fertile garden plots flowing along its floor. Limestone cliffs, eroded by centuries of creek action, wind and rain, are layered with ledges that provided building sites for Sinagua cliff dwellings. Niched safely above the canyon bottom, families could keep a watchful eye for enemies as they caught cooling breezes.

Allow at least a couple of hours to see the museum and do a hike. The **Island Trail**, the monument's most challenging, descends 185 feet into the canyon for a one-mile round trip. Although most hikers dread the uphill return (you're at an elevation of 6,690 feet here), if your legs are not in great shape you may find that going down 240 steps is just as difficult as coming back up. However, the trail is paved and unless it is snowing it should not be difficult to navigate. The 25-plus cliff dwellings that it winds past are an ample reward. Another option is the **Rim Trail**, a mostly level 0.75-mile hike along the edge of the canyon that meanders through a special community of plants and animals. There is an elevation gain of only 20 to 30 feet, and the surface is smooth enough so that the trail can be negotiated in a wheelchair, along with someone to help brake and back up. You'll see flashes of blue Steller's jays among the pines, through which breezes truly do whisper. The Rim and Island trails are the only two that are self-guided.

A ranger-led **Ledge Hike** leaves Wednesday and Sunday at 10 A.M. for a 1.5-hour hike that covers 0.75-mile off-trail, going to a number of cliff dwellings that are not usually open to the public. For somewhat of a challenge, show up Saturday at 10 A.M. for the two-hour, 2-mile Ranger Cabin hike. Slopes are steep and you have to deal with loose footing and brush, so wear long pants. The reward is seeing the historic cabin first used by the National Park Service as ranger housing, then later as the original visitors center until 1939. You hike down a side canyon formed by one of the tributaries of Walnut Creek, then come back along a ledge past 30 cliff ruins that are closed to the public without a ranger escort. Reservations are a must for this hike.

Riordan Mansion State Historic Park in Flagstaff includes a unique two-family home built in 1904.

From the visitor center there is a spectacular view of the San Francisco Peaks. From left to right they are Mt. Eden, 9,280 feet; Mt. Agassiz, 12,300 feet; Mt. Fremont, 11,900 feet; Mt. Humphreys, 12,643 feet; and Mt. Doyle, 11,460 feet. The center has a good selection of books, and exhibits on the canyon's former residents. If you don't want to hike and prefer to simply sit and bird-watch, there are pleasant shady benches just for that purpose. There is no food sold here, but you can bring a picnic to enjoy at convenient tables. Weather can be very changeable. It is not unusual in the spring for a sunny day to turn into sleeting snow. The park is open daily, 7 A.M.–6 P.M. during the summer, 8 A.M.–5 P.M. during winter months. Trails close an hour before the park closes. Walnut Canyon is 7 miles east of Flagstaff off I-40. Take Exit 204 south 3 miles on a paved road to the visitor center. Small fee per vehicle. **(520) 526-3367, fax (520) 527-0246.**

Riordan Mansion State Historic Park

This unusual mansion will seem like a real step back in time to youngsters, but older visitors will no doubt remember many of the furnishings, especially in the kitchen, that were very much in use when they were kids. The whole story behind this quirky home seems like a set of mirror images, with brothers Timothy and Michael Riordan, prominent Flagstaff logging scions, marrying sisters Caroline and Elizabeth Metz. They built a sort of mansion-duplex, with private living quarters in separate wings for each family and a large central living room with fireplace and billiards table where the families gathered together.

Built in 1904, it was designed in the American Craftsman style by Charles Whittlesey, who also designed El Tovar Lodge at the Grand

Canyon. The rustic 13,000-square-foot log-slab building, with volcanic stone arches and wood shingles, was ahead of its time in many ways. It had a refrigerator, not an ice box, long before refrigerators were common. Interior "wells," open to the roof, provided natural air conditioning. Much of the original furniture remains, including a high-sided "jail chair" in which naughty children were made to sit quietly as they contemplated the error of their ways. Within an oval dining room, an elliptical table with no head or foot democratically assured that guests had clear views of each other and no one was seated in any particular place of honor. A wicker swing moves freely in the living room where Mary Riordan, in an oil portrait, has the unusual ability to follow visitors with her eyes wherever they move in the room. Mary, daughter of Timothy and Caroline, is the namesake of upper and lower Lake Mary, 10 miles southeast of Flagstaff. A Steinway piano is ready to be played, and Tiffany stained glass windows accent a number of rooms. Bedrooms look as though the occupants had left just moments ago, with clothing draped casually over chairs, and personal photos and the accouterments of private lives displayed on dresser tops. Only Timothy's half of the house currently is open to the public, as a family member lived in the other half until recently. It is being refurbished and is expected to become part of the tour by the year 2000.

You can pick up a pamphlet for a self-guided tour of the estate grounds where there are tables for picnicking, but you are permitted in the home only on a guided tour. When the guide instructs you to stay on the red carpet, pay attention. If so much as an errant toe slides off, you will be admonished in front of the group. The home is lavishly decorated for the holiday season. Open May to Sept., 8 A.M.–5 P.M. Guided tours leave on the hour from 9 A.M. to 4 P.M. Open Oct. to Apr., 11 A.M.–5 P.M., with guided tours on the hour from 12 noon to 4 P.M. Reservations are recommended. Small admission fee. **1300 Riordan Ranch St., Flagstaff, 86001; (520) 779-4395. Website: http://www.pr.state.az.us.**

Getting There

Flagstaff is situated at the junction of I-17 and I-40. It is 146 miles or about 2.5 hours north of Phoenix on I-17. **Amtrak (800-872-7245)** arrives and departs daily, eastbound morning, westbound evening. **America West Express (800-235-9292)** has scheduled service to Phoenix Sky Harbor International Airport from the new Pulliam Airport four miles south of Flagstaff.

Northern Arizona University

This respected university contributes a great deal to Flagstaff's sense of being a "young" town. Besides nearby outdoor recreational opportunities, students are drawn here for the university's excellent reputation and strong emphasis on teacher preparation. It began in 1899 as Northern Arizona Normal School, a teacher prep institution. In 1925 it became Northern Arizona State Teachers College, and in 1966 was accorded university status. Old Main was built even before that, in 1894, as a reform school. Seven university buildings are on the National Register of Historic Places. Today the campus covers 666 acres plus more than 4,000 acres that the School of Forestry uses as a lab forest. For information on visiting the campus call **Student Union Information (520-523-4636)** or the general switchboard **(520-523-9011),** from where you can be transferred to other departments.

Sunset Crater Volcano National Monument

About 15 miles north of Flagstaff, this extinct (at least it has been since A.D. 1065) volcano is part of the vast volcanic field that covers much of the terrain north of Flagstaff. It took 200 years from the last eruption for the field to calm down, and when it did it left this thousand-foot classic cinder cone. The lava has had a great influence on plant and animal life, which have had to adapt to a harsh environment. Some have evolved to become distinct species. Endemic to the area is a type of white or blue scorpion weed with a blossom that curves like a scorpion's tail. It blooms during the late summer rainy season as does the pink penstemon, also endemic, removed from the endangered species list in 1986. A single moderate fee will give you admission to both Sunset Crater and Wupatki. It is open daily, 8 A.M.–5 P.M. during the winter, 8 A.M.–6 P.M. in summer. Winter hours may be shortened to 9 A.M. so check before setting out. **(520) 526-0502.**

Wupatki National Monument

The fields and meadows that make up this monument immediately say that the people who once lived here were agrarian. Located on the southern Colorado Plateau in the rain shadow of the San Francisco Peaks, the area is studded with the remains of pueblos and small structures that once held stores and grains. The Anasazi and Sinaguan people settled here in about 1110, but within 200 years were gone. Legends and artifacts point to a migration to the Verde Valley and possibly to the Hopi mesas. Today the area is rich in archaeological sites. Pick up a guide in the visitor center. Although the ruins are widespread, all are within walking distance of parking areas along short trails. Located just behind the visitor center, **Wupatki Ruin** is the largest, with about 85 rooms that probably housed 200 residents when fully occupied. If the winds are right, you'll feel air rushing in or out of an interesting blowhole that is connected through a network of underground crevices to other blowholes.

Forest Service Road 545, a paved 35-mile scenic loop, connects Sunset Crater with Wupatki. If you start at Sunset Crater you're at about 8,000 feet, and you'll descend to about 4,500 feet at the one-time agricultural fields of Wupatki. From the crater's rough and rugged lava landscape you'll pass through Ponderosa forests and serene grasslands. You also can continue on US 89 for a straight and much shorter route.

Get in your car and drive less than five minutes to a smaller pueblo called **Wukoki Ruin** that may have accommodated just a few families. Follow the park road to well-preserved **Lomaki Ruin,** which once had two stories and six to eight rooms. From the **Citadel Ruin** on top of a volcanically formed rise, there is a good view of other ruins in the area. It gives a sense of how this once well-populated place must have functioned. The visitor center has a museum with artifacts from the site and a book store. It is open daily, 8 A.M.–5 P.M. during the winter, 8 A.M.–6 P.M. in summer. Winter hours may be shortened to 9 A.M. At this time there is no off-trail hiking, but plans for permit hiking are on the drawing board. Wupatki is located about 35 miles north of Flagstaff. Follow US 89 north to the signs, or follow the Scenic Loop described in the above paragraph. **(520) 679-2365.**

Festivals and Events

Pine Country Pro Rodeo

Third weekend in June

If you've never been to a rodeo, this is about as pleasant a setting as you'll find to view this favorite Southwestern festivity in which top national rodeo contenders gather to compete in classic rodeo events. June in Flagstaff is reliably sunny and warm without being hot. Held at the Coconino County Fairgrounds.

Flagstaff Festival of the Arts

July–August

This one-month music festival consists of a series of concerts featuring the classics, pops and ethnic music. National and international artists get together for afternoon and evening concerts held at Ardrey Auditorium on the Northern Arizona University campus.

Flagstaff Winterfest

February

When the temps are in the 70s in Phoenix and the Valley of the Sun, Flagstaff is reveling in the snow that makes this annual event possible. As one of Arizona's truly wintery sites, the city takes its position seriously, putting on nearly one hundred snow-related events that include dogsled races, nordic and alpine skiing competitions, snowmobile drag racing, snowboard and snowshoe events. Sleigh rides, historic walking tours and family snow games are part of the festivities.

A Celebration of Native American Art

May through September

The Special Exhibits Gallery at the Museum of Northern Arizona hosts this annual sale and show honoring the creativity of Native American artists, focusing on native arts of the Colorado Plateau. Artists in residence and exceptionally high quality Hopi, Navajo and Zuni art attract buyers from all over the country. It is fascinating for the serious collector as well as the casual browser. **(520) 774-5213.**

Outdoor Activities

Biking

Flagstaff's Urban Trail System (FUTS) for nonmotorized transportation is a great way to get around town and the area. The network of trails offers ready access to the campus of Northern Arizona University, forested areas, canyons, national monuments, cultural centers and historic downtown. FUTS interconnects with the Arizona State Trail, the Coconino National Forest trail system and the Flagstaff Bikeways System. You'll see recreational users, as well as the occasional business-clad cyclist, obviously on his way to work. The basic 18-mile trail, of bladed aggregate, is soft enough for runners and sturdy enough for mountain bikers. Cross-country skiers use it in winter.

Many of the trails used by skiers become hiking and cycling trails once the weather warms. **The Nordic Center,** 16 miles north of

In the Cococino National Forest near Flagstaff, a cyclist gets directions from a pasing logger.

Flagstaff on US 180, doubles as a mountain bike park May through October. Use fee for trails is waived during the summer and bike rentals are available on site. For information call **(520) 779-1951.**

Maps of forest service roads, many of which are great ways to explore back country on a mountain bike, are available from **Peaks Ranger District, Coconino National Forest, 5075 N. Arizona 89, Flagstaff, 86004; (520) 527-3600.**

Fishing and Lakes

Mormon Lake

Although it's the largest lake in Coconino county, it has a tendency to go dry, which is probably why the Mormon colony that tried to settle here in the late 1800s finally gave up. In good years, there are reports of large bullheads being pulled from its waters, but in bad years it can be a bog. There are trails for hiking around the lake, and camping at National Forest Service campgrounds at Dairy Spring and Double Springs. Water, rest rooms, showers and dump stations are available, but no hookups. At this 7,000-foot elevation, camping is comfortable only from May to September. The lake is located 25 miles southeast of Flagstaff on Lake Mary Road.

Stoneman Lake

You might find yourself completely alone in this ancient water-filled crater, which is reason enough to seek out the secluded little lake. Duck hunters frequented the place up until the early 1970s, and now anglers come to bag large northern pike and yellow perch. It is named for Gen. George Stoneman, who was part of the Mormon Battalion that crossed the state in 1846. Bring your own boat or canoe as there are no services. The lake is south of Mormon Lake on Forest Route 213, which also may be reached from I-17 by taking the Stoneman Lake exit (306) about 35 miles south of Flagstaff.

Golf

Elden Hills Golf Course

The area's only full-length public course, its pine-flanked fairways are breezy and pleasant, a cool alternative to courses in the Valley during the summer. Here golf season generally extends from March through November. Located in the old Fairfield Continental area in east Flagstaff, the par 72, 6,100-yard layout is a challenge for anyone who has a tendency to stray into the rough. **2380 N. Oakmont Dr.; (520) 527-7997; tee times (520) 527-7999.**

Hiking

The relatively flat cross-country ski trails of Nordic Center become agreeable hiking trails when it gets warm.

At the **Snowbowl,** the chair lift transports hikers through the Coconino National Forest to 11,500 feet at the top of Agassiz Peak for fabulous views that on clear days extend to the Grand Canyon, 80 miles away. Riders can hike back down the mountain or take the lift. To get to the Arizona Snowbowl Scenic Skyride, follow US 80 for about 7.5 miles to Snowbowl Road on the right. Follow Snowbowl Road for 7 miles to the top parking lot and look for the ski lift. It is open daily, mid-June to Labor Day, and on weekends after Labor Day. Tickets are moderately priced, with discounts for seniors. Children 5 and under riding with an adult are free. For Skyride information call **(520) 779-1951.**

Humphreys Peak Trail

The most popular trail within the Kachina Peaks Wilderness, this is a super area because there are no roads and no motorized vehicles. Even mountain bikes are not permitted. A number of trails are accessible from Flagstaff, with the most popular, the 5-mile Humphreys Trail, starting at the base of the ski area at the Snowbowl. This is Arizona's Mt. Everest. The trail starts at 9,500 feet and hits 12,643 feet at the summit, the state's highest point. Air is fresh and cool, but thin, so don't even think about this hike unless you're in good cardiovascular shape. The 4.5-mile hike begins in forested territory, becoming a field of volcanic rock that authenticates the peak's origins by fire. Signs caution you not to stray from the trail lest you damage delicate plant species that grow in the alpine tundra. It takes three to four hours to reach the summit, depending on how often you stop to rest. Most say the spectacular views are worth the effort. It's not difficult to understand why the Hopis and Navajos consider these peaks sacred. You can document your ascent by leaving a written comment in the metal ammo box that rests against a pile of rocks at the top.

The trail is accessible from late spring to early fall, but expect to find snow almost all the time except perhaps for September. Also starting from the Snowbowl parking lot, the **Kachina Trail** is a wonderful hike among shadowy tall timber that includes Douglas fir and Ponderosa pine. The whole hike is at about 9,000 feet so don't be surprised if you have to take things more slowly than you normally do. The trail is 5 miles one way, and makes a good day hike up to Schultz Tank and back. It connects with the Humphreys Trail and Weatherford Trail that will give you a tougher and longer way back if you want more of a challenge. **Inner Basin Trail** is an easy 4-mile round-trip hike with a 1,000-foot elevation gain. **Weatherford Trail** is a good 12-mile day hike to the saddle between Fremont and

Doyle peaks with about a 2,000-foot elevation gain. The **Bear Jaw** and **Aubineau** trails also are favored for day hikes. For more information contact the **Coconino National Forest, Supervisor's Office, 2323 E. Greenlaw Ln., Flagstaff, 86004; (520) 527-3600, or the Peaks Ranger Station, (520) 526-0866.**

Skiing and Snowplay

There are no overnight accommodations in any of Flagstaff's ski areas, but many hotels and motels in town offer ski packages that combine accommodations and more with lift tickets. If you simply want to play in the snow and build a snowman, there are a variety of locations close to Flagstaff where you can bury yourself in the chilly white stuff. For more information call the **Coconino National Forest Supervisor** at **(520) 527-3600.**

Arizona Snowbowl

This popular area among the San Francisco Peaks 14 miles north of Flagstaff has two mountain day-lodges with restaurants and lounges, four chairlifts, a 2,300-foot vertical drop, 32 trails, a rental shop and ski instruction for adults and kids. There are 50 miles of beginner terrain and a special area for snowboarders. Two new expert runs, Volcano and Lava, recently were added, giving the Snowbowl more advanced runs than any other state ski area. The season is generally mid-December to early March. During summer months the area offers scenic chairlift rides and mountain biking. Call the **Flagstaff Visitors Bureau (800-842-7293)** for a list of hotels in town. Take I-17 north to US 180 and exit on Snowbowl Road 8 miles north of Flagstaff. Lift tickets are moderately priced. Kids 7 and under and seniors over 70 ski free. **P.O. Box 40, Flagstaff, 86002; (520) 779-1951.** For a snow report call **(520) 735-7600.**

Along US 180

Toboggans and saucers are ideal for the small slopes that line US 180, between Flagstaff and Valle at the foot of the San Francisco Peaks. Wing Mountain, at Milepost 226, is a good one, as is Crowley, at Milepost 223. Parking lots usually are plowed at these two spots, but if the snow is really fresh, the plows may not have gotten there yet. Just be sure you park well off the road to be safe.

Flagstaff Nordic Center

For cross-country skiers, there are 25 miles of groomed trails for all skill levels. Sixteen miles north of Flagstaff on US 180, the center has a ski school, equipment rentals, guided tours and races. **(520) 779-1951.**

Seeing and Doing

Museums and Galleries

Museum of Northern Arizona

One of the outstanding museums in the state, be sure to allow at least two hours, more if possible, to truly appreciate everything here. Even before entering, take a moment outdoors

Exhibits at the Museum of Northern Arizona include a life-sized model skeleton of a dinosaur, which once roamed the piney woods that surround the museum.

Items at the Museum of Northern Arizona in Flagstaff include authentic Native American pottery, rugs, fetishes and silver jewelry made with turquoise.

to stand at the Rio de Flag Canyon overlook to enjoy the crisp air scented with Ponderosa pine that flourishes at this lofty altitude. In front of the museum, a little nature trail starts at the flagpole and follows the canyon rim to the east, then descends to the canyon floor via easy-to-negotiate steps, where it follows a creek. An additional loop ascends the canyon's far wall and eventually meets up with the original trail for a total distance of only about one-half mile. Placards dispense nature tidbits, such as how to recognize a Ponderosa (needles cluster in threes). Heed the markers for poison ivy and poison hemlock. If you touch the former or ingest the latter, you'll either end up with a horrible case of the itches, or dead, like poor Socrates.

When you walk into the museum, immediately turn around and take a look at the lovely Navajo rug draped over a pine balcony above you. Then proceed to the large window in front of you that overlooks a courtyard, with at least a dozen wild bird species flocking to the feeders. Broad-tailed hummingbirds, glossy black ravens, red-headed house finches, dramatic blue-crested Steller's jays and colorful hairy woodpeckers are among regular diners. A book at the window helps identify unfamiliar species.

Founded in 1928, the museum focuses on the Colorado Plateau and its biology, geology, anthropology and fine arts. Always a crowd-pleaser, the life-sized model skeleton of Dilophosarus, a flesh-eating dinosaur that once roamed these woods, greets visitors in the Geology Gallery. For a rest, curl up in front of the fireplace in the living room-like Babbitt Gallery to contemplate historic paintings donated by the pioneer Babbitt family of northern Arizona.

Here you'll find one of the best museum gift shops anywhere. Besides an extensive collection of books on museum-related subjects, there are excellent pieces of Native American art including Navajo rugs, Hopi pottery, fetishes and an outstanding selection of well-priced turquoise and silver jewelry. Besides being assured of authenticity (kachina dolls are made of genuine cottonwood roots, for example), there is no sales tax on items purchased here. Open daily, 9 A.M.–5 P.M. Closed Thanksgiving, Christmas and New Year's Day. Moderate admission. **3101 N. Fort Valley Rd., Flagstaff, 86001; (520) 774-5213, fax (520) 779-1527.**

Pioneer Museum

One of four branches of the Arizona Historical Society (Tempe, Yuma and Tucson are the other three), the museum is in the building that served as the county hospital from 1908 to 1938. Known then as the "poor farm" for the number of elderly men without families who ended up there, it has been a museum since 1963. A horse barn, root cellar and settler's cabin also are on the property. The collection, which gives a sense of the explorers, lumber magnates and railroad developers in Flagstaff's history, includes vehicles, farm machinery and other pioneer memorabilia. A 1929 Baldwin articulated locomotive and a Santa Fe caboose are favorites with children. During winter months the exhibit called "Playthings of the Past" draws together toys, games, dolls and children's books from years past. Another exhibit features medical instruments and equipment used by early Flagstaff physicians. Open Mon.–Sat., 9 A.M.–5 P.M.

Closed Sun., Christmas, New Year's Day, Easter and Thanksgiving. No fee, but donations are appreciated. Located on Fort Valley Road next to Sechrist School. **2340 N. Fort Valley Rd., Flagstaff, 86001; (520) 774-6272.**

Nature Preserves

Since 1994 the **Nature Conservancy Hart Prairie Preserve** has managed 245 beautifully undisturbed acres that contain a globally rare community of Bebb's willow trees. Herds of up to one hundred elk often pass through the preserve. At an elevation of 8,600 feet, golden aspens create spectacular fall color. In winter, the area is blanketed with snow. At present this is a closed preserve, which means you can't simply wander onto it at will. However, free guided hikes are offered Wednesdays at 10 A.M. and Sundays at 2 P.M. from about May 15 through Oct. 15. Winter cross-country ski weekends and summer hiking weekends are regularly scheduled. From the preserve office on US 180, you carpool for one-half hour on Forest Service roads to the preserve itself. The easy hike lasts about 1.5 hours, so plan on 2.5 hours total. An 1877 lodge called the Homestead can accommodate groups of up to 20 and may be reserved. The preserve is about 12 miles from Flagstaff. **2601 N. Fort Valley Rd. (same as US 180), Flagstaff, 86001; (520) 774-8892.**

Nightlife

The Museum Club

"The Zoo," as it is affectionately known, is a Flagstaff landmark and not to be missed. It's a bar, dance club, roadhouse and unquestionably a museum with so much history that it has been listed on the National Register of Historic Places. Noisy, rowdy and fun, it is constructed of native Ponderosa pine logs around five Ponderosa tree trunks, complete with branches, that have become part of the interior decor. When it was built in 1931 it was the largest log cabin in the state. It sits on a stretch of Old Route 66 now called Santa Fe Avenue.

You enter under the inverted fork trunk of a Ponderosa, past the watchful eyes of a door person who makes sure you're not under age, you're suitably dressed (shirt and shoes) and you won't cause problems. The reason it's called The Zoo is immediately obvious. Stuffed bear, bobcat, owls and peacock perch in tree branches above the dance floor, and a javelina snarls down at imbibers at the bar. The place once belonged to Dean Eldredge, who built it to house his collection of taxidermied animals, Indian artifacts and rifles. He apparently stuffed anything that moved, from fish to fowl. Only a few of his original mounts remain today, but others have taken over, assuring that the zoolike ambiance endures.

During the 1960s and 1970s big names that include Willie Nelson, Waylon Jennings and Wanda Jackson appeared at the club as they worked their way to stardom. Others, like Barbara Mandrell, would simply show up, grab a guitar and entertain. Today it continues to host up-and-coming country-western performers.

It's almost impossible not to have a good time here. Everyone's friendly, and if you don't know the dances being done on the floor, a resident dance instructor will gladly introduce you to the intricacies of the two-step. More than ten years ago the club's owner instituted Operation Safe Ride, providing free round-trip transportation to those who need it. There is a well-stocked shop with Route 66 souvenirs, and of course Museum Club T-shirts, some with big red Corvettes zooming across the front. **3404 E. Rte. 66; (520) 526-9434, fax (520) 526-5244. Website: www.flagguide.-com/museum club.**

Orpheum Theater

You probably don't go on vacation to go to the movies, but this 1916 theater is more than a place to view the flicks. It began by showing the silents, and still has two projection windows that date to the days when dual projectors were needed to show a full-length uninterrupted film. But the best part is that it has 900 seats, a balcony and a giant screen just like in the olden days. Now it shows all first-run features, complete with an updated sound system designed to knock your socks off. **15 W. Aspen; (520) 774-7823.**

Scenic Drives

Flagstaff to Valle

Along US 180 between Flagstaff and its junction with AZ 64 leading to the Grand Canyon, a section designated as a scenic road passes through tall pines and alpine meadows. Depending on season and rainfall, the roadside could be carpeted with brown-eyed goldeneye, yellow rabbitbrush and scarlet penstemon mixed in with piñon pines. During the winter the road often is banked with snow, pushed to the sides by diligent plows. The San Francisco Peaks in the distance look like someone should put a cherry on top. About 20 miles from Flagstaff the Kendrick Picnic Area has tables among the trees. Follow US 180 northwest from Flagstaff to the town of Valle.

Peaks Loop Drive

Great in fall because of the aspen, but also good almost any summer day when you're looking for a place to cool off, the 60-mile trip loops around the impressive San Francisco Peaks. From Flagstaff head north on US 89 and turn left onto Forest Road 418 just past the Sunset Crater turnoff. You'll start climbing, and it's hard to keep your eyes on the road and off the scenery. It's best just to pull off at a safe point and savor the Ponderosas and canyons from afoot. You can follow the road until it rejoins US 180.

Hart Prairie Road

This is really a side trip from the Peaks Loop Drive and is very popular in the fall. Besides great views of the San Francisco Peaks, aspen groves turn a brilliant golden yellow all along the roadside. There are plenty of places to pull off for a picnic or short hike. If you're already on Forest Road 418 simply turn left at Forest Road 15 for a tour south. If you're starting from Flagstaff, just go to Hart Prairie Road, take US 180 north to Milepost 235. Turn right onto Hart Prairie Road, which is Forest Road 15. Follow it until it returns to US 180, turn left and you'll be headed back to Flagstaff.

Where to Stay

Flagstaff has many types of accommodations in all price ranges, from budget chains to historic inns to cabins and bed and breakfasts. Rates change seasonally at most places, with summer rates the highest.

Hotels, Motels & Inns

Embassy Suites—$$$$

The accommodations here are pretty straightforward but worth mentioning because you have the advantage of a very comfortable bedroom and living room, both with TVs. The living room has a pull-out sofa bed that will sleep a couple of kids (or close friends). A refrigerator and coffee maker with regular and decaf keep you from searching for coffee in the morning. And when you do decide to integrate with the day, the room rate includes a full, cooked-to-order breakfast. In the evening, a free happy hour includes drinks and popcorn. Room rate is on a par with other area motels, and when you consider breakfast for two plus cocktails in the bargain, it looks even better. Off-season (winter) rates can be as much as $50 less than summer. **706 S. Milton Rd., Flagstaff, 86001; (520) 774-4333 or (800) 362-2779, fax (520) 774-0216.**

Arizona Mountain Inn—$$$

On 13 Ponderosa pine-blanketed acres surround by National Forest, this inn is ideal for families or a group of friends. Accommodations range from bed and breakfast rooms in a main lodge to separate cottages with one to five bedrooms, appropriate for up to 16 people. Rustic cottages with fireplaces are furnished with kitchen utensils and a barbecue. Pricing is according to the number of guests in the unit, with a four-night minimum during the summer. Go about five minutes southeast of Flagstaff, exit I-17 at Lake Mary Road and follow it one mile. The inn is on the left. **685 Lake Mary Rd., Flagstaff, 86001; (520) 774-8959.**

Montezuma Lodge at Mormon Lake—$$$

If you grew up "going to the cabin" during summer months, you'll love this quintessential lodge, with 18 rustic cottages scattered among 16 acres of densely wooded pine forest overlooking Mormon Lake. Squirrels pitter-patter across the cabin roof, jays and nuthatches chatter noisily just above your porch, and there isn't a civilized sound to be heard, except perhaps the slam of a car door. The Audubon Society recently identified 286 bird species in the area. Mismatched dishes and crisp little curtains that possibly were once flour sacks, braided rugs and knotty pine walls darkened by the years are part of what makes this lodge such a delight. Resident skunks, although not de-scented, will approach for a handout and refrain from turning their backs unless offended. The trailhead for three area hikes is just below the lodge. If you're there in the late summer and fall, you're almost certain to hear elk bugling in the distance. Monday through Thursday rates are slightly lower than weekends. Open May 1 to Dec. 1. Located about 25 miles southeast of Flagstaff, about a 35-minute drive. Take Lake Mary Road 20 miles south to Milepost 324. One-half mile past the marker, turn right onto Mormon Lake Road. Follow the road about 4 miles until you see the sign for Montezuma Lodge. Turn right at the sign and proceed one-half mile to the main lodge. **H.C. 31, Box 342, Mormon Lake, 86038; (520) 354-2220, fax (520) 354-2555.**

Mormon Lake Lodge—$$–$$$

Another great in-the-woods kinda place, this one has genuine log cabins, horseback riding through the pines and mountain bike rentals among its reasons to stay. The Lodge has one of the few open-pit steak houses still in operation. Besides the best beef available, the menu also features game and fish choices. On Friday and Saturday nights there's live country music in the 1880 Saloon, and the Cowboy Dinner Theater is really good, corny fun. There's cross-country skiing and snowmobile rentals during the winter. All cabins have full baths, and some have kitchenettes and fireplaces. Family cabins, with one and two bedrooms, are great for kids or for two couples. There is a considerable price difference between weeknights and weekends. Located about 30 minutes south of Flagstaff. From I-17 take Lake Mary turnoff, then head 21 miles to Mormon Lake turnoff. **P.O. Box 38012, Mormon Lake, 86038; (520) 354-2227, fax (520) 354-2356. Website: www.foreverresorts.com/mormonlake.htm.**

Weatherford Hotel once had Bill Boyd, "Hopalong Cassidy," as a desk clerk.

Hotel Weatherford—$–$$

This hostelry is a combination of a hotel and a historic landmark, with seven private rooms with baths and one room with facilities down the hall. One of the first brick structures in Flagstaff, the hotel was built by Texas cattleman John W. Weatherford in 1898 and enlarged the following year. Once the crown jewel of Flagstaff's hostelries, the three-story structure had a conservatory, dance pavilion, roof garden and sun parlor. It hosted William Randolph Hearst, Zane Grey and artist Thomas Moran. Carley Burch and Glenn Kilbourne, characters that Grey created for the novel *The Call of the Canyon,* came alive as the author toiled away in one of the hotel's upstairs rooms. William Boyd, better known as Hopalong Cassidy, worked here as a desk clerk.

In 1929 fire destroyed the Weatherford's ornate wood balconies, and during the next 40 years it went through a number of structural and ownership changes. In 1979 it was purchased and saved from destruction, and today is still in a renovation process. Layers of stucco have been removed to reveal a lovely old fireplace, and the second-floor ballroom has been carefully restored. The mirrored

Brunswick bar is an antique from Tombstone, wood floors gleam with their original luster, and stained glass windows have been added. If you call in advance, whether you stay there or not, the management will arrange a free tour. Also in the building is **Charly's Pub and Grill** (see Where to Eat). **23 N. Leroux St., Flagstaff, 86001; (520) 774-2731.**

Bed & Breakfasts

More and more of these small places, especially popular during summer, are popping up in Flagstaff.

Comfi Cottages of Flagstaff—$$$

Six individual cottages built in the 1920s and 1930s (one is from the 1950s) are scattered along quiet streets in an older residential neighborhood. One-, two- or three-bedroom places are completely equipped with the comforts of daily living including cable TV, phone, bicycles, even a picnic basket. When you check in you'll find the fixings for breakfast in your refrigerator. A favorite is the cottage at 710 Birch, one block from the city park and forest. The bathroom has a clawfoot tub and there's a fireplace in the living room. **1612 N. Aztec, Flagstaff, 86001; (888) 774-0731 or (520) 774-0731. Website: www.virtualflagstaff.com/comfi.**

Birch Tree Inn—$$$

Just around the corner from Comfi Cottages, this 1917 country Victorian home once was a fraternity house. Two energetic couples took it over, refurbished the whole place, and kept it low-key with no TVs or phones in the rooms. A pool table, reading material and TV are in the main floor parlor. In the summertime, arriving guests are offered iced tea and hors d'oeuvres on the veranda. There are five comfortable, homey second-floor guest rooms, all with queen beds except the Southwest room, which has a king. Two rooms have a shared bath. **824 W. Birch Ave., Flagstaff, 86001; (888) 774-1042 or (520) 774-1042. E-mail: birch@flagstaff.az.us.**

The Inn at 410—$$$$

Elegant by most B&B standards, the nine rooms in this 110-year-old brick California Craftsman home are filled with antiques and personal treasures that make you think the real occupants could reappear at any moment. Everything here is well thought out for the comfort of guests, including a garden room with a private entrance that is completely wheelchair-accessible. You'll wonder how the tree-trunk bed frame ever was placed in the Dakota Suite, since doors and windows are way too small. The room is paneled in weathered barn siding and has a wood burning fireplace. Besides a full, truly fabulous breakfast, cookies fresh from the oven are set out each afternoon. **410 N. Leroux St., Flagstaff, 86001; (800) 774-2008 or (520) 774-0088, fax (520) 774-6354. Website: www.bbonline.com/az/@410.**

Hostels

Grand Canyon International Hostel—$

This clean, cheerful place has dorms and private rooms in a historic building in old Flagstaff just south of the Amtrak station downtown. It's hard to miss. Just look for the 142-foot Downtowner neon sign. Linens and breakfast are included, and there are phones in every room. It has two big kitchens, a barbeque, laundry room and free tea and coffee. No lockout during the day, no curfew at night and no chores. Guests seem to gather in the cable TV room in the evening to chat over the day's experiences. They'll accept **1-800-COLLECT** calls for reservations. **19 S. San Francisco, Flagstaff, 86001; (520) 779-9421.**

Camping and RV Parks

J & H RV Park

Open April 1 to November 1, this popular park is tidy, well-kept and up to date. It has 55 full hookups, a general store, laundry, showers, recreation and TV rooms and 24-hour security. The park is located one mile past Townsend-Wynona Road on US 89. **7901 N. Hwy. 89, Flagstaff, 86004; (520) 526-1829.**

Bonito Campground

This unusual campground is about 18 miles northeast of Flagstaff just off US 89, in the middle of a grove of gorgeous Ponderosa pine. You actually camp on cinders that a thousand years ago catapulted out of a volcano that later became Sunset Crater Volcano National Monument (see page 21). At an elevation of almost 7,000 feet, it is a cool summer haven. It is run by the Forest Service and has 44 developed sites, drinking water and rest rooms, but no hookups. Its charm is in its remote primitiveness. For information call the **Coconino National Forest** at **(520) 526-0866.**

Where to Eat

Flagstaff has brilliantly avoided the fast-food chain mentality and instead has a wealth of eateries with truly outstanding food. That's not to say you can't find a Denny's, Domino's or Jack in the Box. They're there, but they seem to be secondary to the great grills, delicatessens and bakeries that dominate the dining out scene.

Beaver Street Brewery—$$

Wood-fired pizza and boutique beers are the drawing card to this lively brew pub. Set in a building that dates to 1938, painted wall signs are remnants of its days as a market. Opened in 1994, the Brewery has become a local favorite, especially for its rich, full-bodied Railhead Red Ale. Nut Brown and Indian Ale also are popular. Almost everyone opts for an appetizer fondue. The vegetable version, fragrant with sharp cheddar, caramelized onion and ale is served with bread cubes and chunks of squash, carrot and whatever's fresh. A classic Swiss fondue made with Gruyère, white wine and a splash of kirsch is served with bread cubes and fresh fruit. Their Caesar salad is garlicky and tasty, and the chili is not shy. You come here as much to try the great beer as you do to eat, but both experiences are reliably good fun. **11 S. Beaver St.; (520) 779-0079, fax (520) 779-0029.**

Charly's Pub & Grill—$$-$$$

In the historic Weatherford Hotel (See Where to Stay), this lively pub is likely to be crowded with students and young people from all over the world. Three different eating venues, all serving the same menu, have very different atmospheres. The pub part, with pool tables and a bar, is by far the most active. If you're looking to settle in for a nice, leisurely dinner, you'll probably want to go through the French doors into the quieter dining room with a fireplace. Or move to the next room, the Exchange Pub, which once housed Flagstaff's telephone exchange. A blackened-chicken Caesar salad has just enough garlic, and the sun-dried tomato, spinach and cheese appetizer is outstanding. The posole, a stew of pork, hominy and green chile served in a flour tortilla shell, is certainly worth a try, especially since it's likely to be awhile before you'll see it on another menu. The hotel is in historic downtown Flagstaff. **23 N. Leroux St.; (520) 779-1919.**

Pasto—$$-$$$

"Fun Italian Dining" is the way this place bills itself, but it's a lot more. Creative, imaginative food comes in portions so huge, you'd do well to consider splitting any order. Or, be prepared to ask for a doggie bag, assuming your dog eats things like Southwestern black-bean ravioli, tortelloni florentine, chicken vesuvio or artichoke orzo—just a few of the menu items that keep local patrons coming back (always a good sign) and hook newcomers for good. In downtown Flagstaff. **19 E. Aspen; (520) 779-1937.**

Historic Flagstaff Visitor Center is housed in the historic Amtrak station, which still welcomes passengers twice a day on eastbound and westbound trips.

Services

Flagstaff Visitor Center
1 E. Rte. 66
Flagstaff 86001
(800) 842-7293 or (520) 774-9554
fax (520) 556-1308
Websites: www.arizonaguide.com or wwwflagstaff.az.us.

This is worth a stop not only to pick up lots of good information, but to see the historic train station in which it is housed. Amtrak passengers arrive daily at the Tudor revival–style station built in 1926. **1 E. Rte. 66, Flagstaff, 86011; (800) 842-7293 or (520) 774-9541.**

I-10 Rest Area

On I-10, 16 miles south of Flagstaff there is a well-equipped rest area among the tall pines.

Fall Color

The annual burst of color produced by broad-leafed deciduous trees has been immortalized in songs like "Autumn Leaves" and idolized by dazzled spectators. Arizona's arid climate would seem unencouraging to trees that autumn can oxidize into the spectacular rusts and golds that prevail in the East and Midwest. In much of the state there are no distinguishable four seasons. But when fall comes to the Arizona mountains, there is a change in the way the air smells and in how sunlight filters through the trees, creating elongated shadows even at mid-day. Colors are at their best from the end of September through October.

In Northern Arizona, cottonwoods in **Canyon de Chelly National Monument** near Chinle take on a golden hue that changes to a vivid orange. Yellow quaking aspen shimmer in golden stands near **Flagstaff** at the Snowbowl. You can view them from aloft by riding the chair lift that operates Friday through Sunday. The riparian area along **Oak Creek Canyon** is thick with aspen, oak and sycamore. The reds are created by Rocky Mountain maple and big-tooth maple. Follow AZ 89A north of Sedona. During October, ranger-led walks are offered at **Slide Rock State Park** in Sedona. The **Payson** area is networked with hiking trails that include Horton Creek and Pine Creek Trails, where sycamores, maples and box elders flourish. Near **Pinetop-Lakeside** the Woodland Lake Loop is an easy and colorful hike. Central Arizona's **Verde Valley** glows with fall color from about mid-October on. A good vantage point is the Verde Canyon Railroad (see page 130). In southern Arizona in the **Chiricahua Mountains** near Willcox, oak, aspen, ash and burgundy big-tooth maples put on reliably colorful displays. In this same area, San Pedro and Southwestern Railroad trips leave from Benson (see page 282) Thursday through Sunday and follow along the **San Pedro River**, where cottonwoods acquire a classic autumn gold. The Nature Conservancy's **Ramsey Canyon** near Sierra Vista is brilliant with the reds of big-tooth maples. Even if it's quite late in October, you probably haven't missed the color show at **Boyce Thompson Arboretum** (see page 101). During November and even early December cottonwoods, willows and sycamores brighten the landscape.

The **Arizona Office of Tourism** has information on the best places to see autumn at work. Call **(888) 520-3444** and ask for the week's fall foliage report.

Williams

Named for legendary mountain man Bill Williams, whose statue greets travelers coming from the west, the town began along the Beale Wagon Road and the Overland Road, early exploration routes. The landscape is dotted with small piñon pines and distant dark cinder cones. Williams received the boost it needed to put it on the map when the railroad reached there in 1882, making it possible to ship lumber, cattle and sheep from the formerly remote area.

It didn't take long for residents to realize that Williams' proximity to the Grand Canyon, just 60 miles north, gave it a unique position in the tourism industry. By 1901 a spur line reached the scenic wonder, with a paved road following in 1929. When the Fray Marcos, one of the famous Harvey Houses, was built by the Santa Fe Railroad, Williams was securely niched as "The Gateway to the Grand Canyon."

By the time Route 66 went through in the 1930s, Williams' Wild West image had been shed, and tourists found a warm welcome in the dozens of family restaurants and neon signs of Motel Row. Williams became a "tourism town." But as a traveling public began to rely more heavily on automobiles than trains, rail service to the Canyon ended in 1968. In 1984 Williams was the last town along the old route to be bypassed by the new interstate highway system. Even as a special ceremony was being held to mark the historic event, a wave of nostalgia was beginning. Although many of the gas stations and other businesses suffered terribly, and even closed, others began capitalizing on a trend that had begun with the very first Route 66 bypass.

Today the business loop through Williams follows old Route 66, which was split into two one-way streets in the 1950s by highway engineers attempting to alleviate traffic congestion. The entire downtown area is on the National Register of Historic Places. A number of original 1940s neon signs still light up old Motel Row in East Williams.

Festivals and Events

Rendezvous Days

Memorial Day Weekend

Formerly called Bill Williams Days, the old-time mountain man encampment is re-enacted with black powder shooting contests and a parade featuring the famous Bill Williams Mountain Men. It commemorates the days when these rowdy guys were Indian scouts, trappers and guides for the military. A parade, covered wagon ride, arts and crafts booths, street dance on Sunday night with live music and a Saturday steak fry and dance are part of the festivities.

Mountain Village Holiday
Mid-November through New Year's

The whole town literally glows during the holidays as more than one-half million architectural lights outline buildings, businesses and structures in the park. Do your Christmas shopping in galleries, antique shops, specialty stores and historic buildings decked out in holiday finery. The celebration includes a night parade with decorated RVs, trucks, military vehicles and private cars. On weekends local merchants sponsor free hayrides and Santa welcomes children in the Youth Center next to the Visitor Center.

Outdoor Activities

Golf

Elephant Rock Golf Course

Recently rated the state's top nine-hole course by *The Arizona Republic,* this mature par 35 layout is named for a nearby rock formation. It was created in the 1930s on the town's north side by railroad workers and provides a pleasant challenge. A back nine holes is under construction. **2200 Country Club Dr., Williams; (520) 635-4935.**

Mountain Biking

There are two short but challenging mountain bike rides on abandoned sections of old Route 66, at the top and bottom of Ash Fork Hill. Ash Fork is north of I-40 at an elevation of 5,500 feet; Devil Dog is south of I-40 at 6,500 feet. You can easily do both trails in the same day. It can be hot during summer so take plenty of water and sun screen as there are no services. In the winter, mud and snow may make the routes impassable, so check with the Forest Service before starting out. The Forest Service also has an excellent trail map. **Williams Ranger District, USDA Forest Service, Rte. 1, Box 142, Williams, 86046; (520) 635-2633.**

Ash Fork Hill Trail loops along a 1922 section of Route 66 for 6 miles. A rough downhill is followed by a smooth but steep uphill. Rewards are great views of Picacho Peak and Bill Williams Mountain. You can add 2 miles to your ride by following Forest Road 6 through piñon and juniper woodland, where you may see red-tailed hawks and golden eagles soaring overhead, as well as deer and antelope moving slowly through the forest shadows. This hour-long ride will be longer if you take the time to enjoy your surroundings. To access the trail, take Exit 151 off I-40, 12 miles west of Williams. Take Forest Road 106 north to the parking area.

Devil Dog Trail begins on Forest Road 108 and loops for 5 miles at the top of Ash Fork Hill through cool pines. Where it becomes Forest Road 45, you're on a section of Route 66 built in 1922. You have the option of charging up Bixler Mountain for a side trip (only the hardy should try it), following Forest Road 45 at the point where it leaves the 1922 road. The old road then loops back to the starting point along a 1932 portion of Route 66 that at one time was paved. The whole ride can take as little as 30 minutes if you don't do Bixler Mountain. To access the trail, take Exit 157 off I-40, 6 miles west of Williams. Bear right under the underpass and turn left to the parking area on Forest Road 108.

Skiing

The slopes at **Williams Ski Area** won't thrill you if you're into extreme skiing, but they are wonderful family slopes with a T-bar and a rope tow. They're also safe and secure for beginners who might be intimidated by larger areas. In addition to five usually uncrowded runs, there are marked cross-country ski trails. Equipment rental is near the snack bar and warming lounge. When there's snow, it's open Thu.–Sun. Go south from Williams on I-40 to the ski area. **(520) 635-933.**

Seeing and Doing

Museums

Williams Depot

The 1908 depot is the jumping-off point for the Grand Canyon Railway. Built of solid-poured concrete, the building is the largest such structure in Arizona, part of which once was the original eight-room Fray Marcos Hotel. Its sturdy construction saved it from demolition. Most such buildings, made of wood, are razed to avoid paying taxes on them when they've outlived their usefulness. Since it would have cost more to demolish the building than to pay taxes, it was spared. The Railway Museum, located in what used to be the hotel dining room, is crammed with artifacts and photos that trace the line's history. Try your hand at sending Morse code over the wires. The museum is open from 7:30 A.M. to 5:30 P.M, with no admission charge. Outdoors, Locomotive Number 20, built in 1910, its tender and a restored 1923 Harriman coach car testify to the elegance of turn-of-the-century rail travel. The gift shop has an above-average selection of actually useful railroad souvenirs including model train equipment and guide books. If you missed breakfast, you can grab a quick continental version in the Santa Fe room before boarding. The sound of gunfire will draw you outdoors to the Old West Village and theme show, presented on scheduled train days. Watch out, because cranky cowboys cheat at poker and lure unsuspecting visitors into their scurrilous game.

Getting There

From Phoenix, take I-10 to I-17. Go north 146 miles to Flagstaff, to the junction with I-40. Follow I-40 west for 32 miles to Williams.

Tours

Grand Canyon Railway

The classic way to see the Grand Canyon is to start in Williams and ride this historic train through forest and high desert plains to the South Rim. Its history dates to 1901 when the Santa Fe built a spur from Williams to the Canyon, thereby opening passenger service. It was pioneer Arizona journalist and politician William O. (Bucky) O'Neill who promoted the railroad as a means to develop mining interests. The steam train chugged along the route for 67 years, opening to the world a wonder that previously had been visited mainly by miners. But with the popularization of the automobile and construction of reliable roads, the traveling public opted to drive the 64 miles north from Williams in their own transportation. The train made its last run on July 30, 1968, with just three passengers aboard.

But in 1989, in a serendipitous mix of environmental awareness and a desire to avoid what had become serious traffic congestion at the canyon, steam train service once again was deemed viable. Forward-thinking investors realized the potential of harnessing America's nostalgic love of trains and began renovating locomotives and coach cars. Today, refurbished steam engines with original gauges and whistles pull restored vintage rail cars that a responsive public keeps full. Three of the venerable locomotives were built in 1910. Turn-of-the-century steam engines are in service Memorial Day weekend through September. Diesel locomotives, a part of canyon

The Grand Canyon Railway leaves from Williams, with cranky cowboys aboard to provide entertainment.

The Grand Canyon Railway dome car affords excellent views as well as space for singing cowboys to perform.

railway history for the passengers and freight they pulled from the 1940s to 1960s, are used from October to Memorial Day weekend. The Harriman coach cars were built by Pullman in 1923, and the Coconino dome coach was built in 1954 for the Chicago, Burlington and Quincy, and Northern Pacific railways. A number of classes of service include coach cars with conventional train seating, a club car with mahogany bar and a domed observation car. The Chief has overstuffed club chairs and divans, an open platform and oversized windows. In this first-class car a continental breakfast is served on the way up, with hors d'oeuvres and champagne on the return trip. Singing cowboys provide on-board entertainment, and there is an almost guaranteed "holdup," complete with masked bandits, on every journey.

The morning train leaves Williams Depot at 9:30 A.M. and arrives at the South Rim at 11:45 A.M. The return trip leaves the Grand Canyon Depot at 3:15 P.M., arriving in Williams at 5:30 P.M. If you think that 3.5 hours at the canyon are enough for you, this can be a great day trip. Otherwise, book into a hotel (see Grand Canyon, Where to Stay), take your time exploring, and return the next day. Trains run every day except Dec. 24 and 25. There are many train and lodging packages that offer good value. For information call **(800) THE-TRAIN.**

Where to Stay

Hotels, Motels & Inns

Fray Marcos Hotel—$$$

This impressive hostelry, built in 1995, re-creates the style of the historic Williams Depot next door. It follows the same architectural theme as the original 1908 Fray Marcos built by the Santa Fe Railroad. It is named for Fray Marcos de Niza, a Franciscan monk traveling with Spanish explorer Coronado, who is said to be the first white man to visit what is now Arizona. The hotel's large high-ceilinged lobby has a massive Arizona flagstone fireplace flanked by enormous paintings of the Grand Canyon by southwestern artist Kenneth McKenna. The dark wood balcony and wrought iron chandelier help give it an "old-time" look. Don't miss the three lovely Remington bronzes in lobby niches. The one called *Rattlesnake*, with horse and rider both in the air, is remarkable. Rates are seasonal, with the lowest offered Nov. to Feb. High season is Apr. to Labor Day. **235 N. Grand Canyon Blvd., Williams, 86046; (520) 635-4010 or (800) 843-8724.**

Red Garter Bed & Bakery—$$$

This delightfully restored 1897 one-time bordello and saloon offers four rooms with private baths in a two-story Victorian Romanesque-style brick structure. The breakfast that's included is worth the stay. Don't miss the oat scones and sticky buns, served with coffee, juice and fresh fruit. They also offer homemade soups and fresh baked bread, and will pack a picnic lunch for the rest of your journey. Bakery is closed Mon. **137 W. Railroad Ave. (P.O. Box 95), Williams, 86046; (800) 328-1484 or (520) 635-1484. Website: www.-redgarter.com.**

Camping

Grand Canyon Red Lake Hostel & Campground

This is the closest hostel to the Grand Canyon, so it's always busy. Reservations are a must between May 1 and October 15. There are eight rooms that sleep four, but may be reserved privately for an extra charge. It has 14 RV hookups and ten tent sites. A gas station and country store with a good selection of Indian crafts and jewelry are next door. On AZ 64, 8 miles north of the junction with I-40. **(520) 635-9122** or **(800) 581-4753.**

Where to Eat

For superb breakfast, baked goods and more, stop at the Red Garter, listed above.

Miss Kitty's Steak House and Saloon—$$-$$$

You can ride your horse up to the hitching post at this large, noisy, friendly place where wagon wheel lamps light up a busy dining room and dance floor. Balconies draped with patriotic bunting enclose a second tier of diners. There usually is live entertainment, and playful "cowboys" may just steal you away for an impromptu "wedding" if you're not careful. But it's all part of the fun at this casual, welcoming place. In summer a great breakfast buffet is available from 7 to 10 A.M. Lunch and dinner entrees include lots of steak and prime rib, as well as chicken, ribs and salmon. If you're yearning to try jalapeño chili beer, with a real chili pepper inside the bottle, this is the place. Located next to the Ramada Inn. **642 E. Rte. 66; (520) 635-9161.**

Spenser's—$-$$

Inside the Fray Marcos Hotel, Spenser's is worth a stop just to see its amazing solid oak bar. It was crafted in 1887 in Shepherd's Bush, a small English village, for a pub called the Lion's Den. The pub proprietor paid cabinet maker George O. Spenser 200 pounds to make the bar, with the promise that he'd never have to pay for another drink. Spenser fared well, as he lived to age 84 and never missed a day at the Lion's Den. The light menu includes salads, soup, sandwiches and pizza. **(520) 635-4010.**

Services

Williams-Grand Canyon Chamber of Commerce, 200 W. Railroad Ave., Williams, 86046-2556; (520) 635-1418, fax (520) 635-1417. Website: www.amdest.com.

Grand Canyon

History and Geology

On its 1,450-mile journey from Colorado's Rocky Mountains to the Sea of Cortez in Mexico, the Colorado River has left a legacy of sublime beauty. Nowhere is that more evident than in the Grand Canyon. Since prehistory, when paleo-hunters drifted across the Southwest in search of game, the Grand Canyon has been home to someone. The Desert Archaic culture lived there ten centuries before the birth of Christ, and the Anasazi tended corn and bean fields as recently as 800 years ago. Spanish explorers, U.S. Army surveyors and Catholic missionaries also passed through the canyon.

More recently, the Navajo raised crops along the friendly Colorado River on the canyon floor. And today the Havasupai tend cattle and produce highly collectible basketry and beadwork on a reservation that is picturesquely niched in the western Grand Canyon.

The canyon's history is layered in its geology. Light-colored Kaibab limestone, filled with ancient fossils, caps the rim. A dozen layers down, black schist is striped with pink granite formed by fire more than two billion years ago. Over millions of years the Colorado River cut the canyon's depth, while erosion created its width, a vista-making 18 miles at the South Rim. Each year more than 5 million visitors are drawn by the canyon's incomparable panoramas and unique history.

North Rim

The Department of Transportation closes the Grand Canyon North Rim Parkway (AZ 67) around October 15, to reopen May 15, which coincides with the closing of National Park facilities. Most people visit during summer months, when facilities can really be overstressed. Portable facilities usually are available but are not always clean, so plan your rest stops. Yet the serene loveliness of the North Rim, in sharp contrast to the South Rim's hubbub, draws many hardy souls, most often in RVs or with tenting equipment. At the rim, near the Grand Canyon Lodge, there are a campground, camper store, service station and self-service laundry.

Grand Canyon Lodge—$$$

Also open mid-May through mid-October, this resort is a National Historic Landmark with cabins and motel rooms. The homey lodge has a western-style dining room with canyon views, as well as a sun room, snack shop, saloon and gift shop. You can book mule rides and bus tours at the hotel. Its 200 rooms fill up quickly, and no waiting list is kept, but sometimes there are last-minute cancellations, so it's always worth a call. **(303) 297-2757. Website: www.amfac.com.**

Kaibab Lodge—$$$

Located 18 miles from the North Rim and 5 miles from the park boundary, this truly rustic lodge is open mid-May through mid-October, coinciding with park openings. It has a series of cabin-style rooms with private baths and showers. There are no private cabins. There also are eight rooms in the Longhouse. Owners stress that this is basic lodging with nothing larger than a double bed, no phones or TVs. The lodge has a dining room where a large continental breakfast is served along with a dinner menu that changes nightly. **P.O. Box 2997, Flagstaff, 86003;** during summer, when the lodge is open, **(520) 638-2389;** during winter, when the lodge is closed, **(520) 526-0924;** outside Arizona, **(800) 525-0924.** The website, **www.canyoneers.com,** connects with **Canyoneers,** a river-rafting operation that does white-water pontoon boat and hiking trips. It links to Kaibab Lodge and **Kaibab Camper Village** near Jacob Lake, which is the only full-hookup camper and RV park on the North Rim.

South Rim

A master plan has been approved by the National Park Service that will change forever the character of visits to this landmark. For at least two decades it has been apparent that the huge number of visitors, topping 5 million in recent years, is taking its toll on the experience. Where once the biggest traffic problem was a "deer jam," waits of several hours just to enter the park have become commonplace. Among the plan's components is to remove 80 percent of private vehicles that now enter the park. A year-around shuttle system will be put in place to bring guests from remote parking lots, and a nonpolluting, in-park shuttle will quietly and efficiently take visitors from place to place once they're in the park. The 20 percent of private vehicles still allowed inside the park will belong to employees and hotel guests.

A proposed Heritage Educational Center will replace a parking lot and utility building, and an Orientation Center at Mather Point is expected to be operational by the year 2000. Two recently constructed lodges, Kachina and Thunderbird, are scheduled for demolition by about 2002 so that the area at the canyon's rim can become a true historic district, with major buildings all dating to the canyon's early days. The pace at which this plan proceeds is largely dependent on funding, which is expected to require $350 billion. But, say project creators, it ultimately will enhance the experience at the Grand Canyon and will encourage visitors to stay for a number of days rather than a number of hours as many now do.

In its effort to save all national parks, the National Park Service has increased fees at many of them. The Grand Canyon entrance fee for vehicles doubled in 1997, and a new back country permit of $20 plus a $4-per-person charge each night is now levied. The new auto entrance fee hasn't slowed visitors a bit. Eighty percent of the fees stay at the canyon, with the rest going to help bail out less affluent parks.

Fall is undisputably a lovely time to visit either the North or South Rim. But winter's another story. The North Rim, oftentimes completely snowed in, closes from the end of October through mid-May. Backcountry skiers and snowshoe trekkers may find it an accessible challenge, but should not proceed without first checking with the National Park Service regarding weather.

The South Rim, while open during winter months, often has below-freezing temps and blustery winds. On the other hand, a brilliantly crisp day that's cold but sunny, with a fraction of the touristy crowds that accumulate during the summer, has a lot of appeal. Most services such as bus trips and hikes with a ranger continue during the winter. Campgrounds remain open as do lodges and hotels.

The signature musical interpretation of the Grand Canyon, Ferde Grofe's *Grand Canyon Suite,* makes interesting listening as you hike or simply sit and view the spectacular chasm. It is divided into movements called "Sunrise," "Painted Desert," "On the Trail" (most familiar as the orchestra imitates the bray of a burro

Visitors come from all over the world to see the spectacular scenery of the Grand Canyon.

and the clip-clopping of hooves) and "Sunset and Cloudburst." This pleasant work of man is an apt accompaniment to a remarkable work of nature.

Festivals and Events

Grand Canyon Music Festival
September, first three weeks

Since 1984 this concert series has been held in the park, usually featuring chamber music, often including jazz and blues. Recently concerts have been presented at the Shrine of the Ages auditorium, an enchanting, intimate setting that accommodates just 310 patrons. The auditorium has a wall of glass that looks out onto the forest, while the music presents a perfect complement to the setting. The event typically attracts the nation's best chamber musicians. **P.O. Box 1332, Grand Canyon, 86023; (520) 638-9215.**

Outdoor Activities

Hiking

Bright Angel Trail

The park's most popular trail, it was constructed in 1891 so that miners could get to their claims. It involves a series of switchbacks that make the ascent longer but less strenuous than the Kaibab Trail. It is a 19-mile hike round trip, so a stay at the bottom is just about mandatory unless you're doing it by mule. On the canyon floor at Indian Garden, a grove of cottonwoods tells you there is water here. At this point water from the North Rim's Roaring Springs is pumped up to the South Rim and is its only water supply. There are stop-off stations at various points along the trail, and during summer months rangers patrol regularly, hoping to head off heat-related incidents.

South Kaibab Trail

Great views are the attraction on this ridgeline trail. But it's a challenge, dropping almost 5,000 feet in just over 6 miles. You can do a portion of the trail as a day hike, starting from the trailhead at Yaki Point and turning around at Cedar Ridge, which is tough as even here there is an elevation drop of almost 1,500 feet.

Canyon Mule Trips

For more than a hundred years the classic way to descend into the canyon has been astride a sure-footed, unflappable mule, a cross between a female horse and a male donkey. The four-legged taxis are used because they are more sure-footed than horses. More than one hundred mules are trained for canyon trekking, each with a 10- to 12-year work-life expectancy. When they retire, they are sold to petting zoos where they become "canyon celebrities." The animals are educated at special mule schools in Tennessee, where each one undergoes three years of training. Canyon officials boast that there has never been a mule with rider lost over the edge. Single-day and overnight trips are extremely popular, so it is essential to book early. Sometimes it is possible to snag a last-minute reservation because of a cancellation, so don't hesitate to put your name on a waiting list. To see the mules, go to the Bright Angel Trailhead where they're corralled.

Seeing and Doing

Museums and Galleries

Hopi House

At the South Rim, this historic gift shop recently underwent a ten-year restoration. Constructed in 1904, it was designated a National Historic Landmark in 1987. It was the first building designed by Mary Elizabeth Jane Colter, the renowned architect who is responsible for the look of many of the original Fred Harvey-owned buildings in the West. The structure was designed to present Hopi tribal arts and crafts in roomlike settings, and is built of native stone and wood. Stone from the original quarry, weathered by exposure to the elements, was a perfect match for the stone it replaced in reconstruction. It is located across from the main entrance to El Tovar.

Kolb Studio

Built on the very lip of the canyon in 1904 and enlarged in 1926, Ellsworth and Emery Kolb's photography studio was one of the canyon's earliest entrepreneurial endeavors. The industrious brothers would photograph mule riders as they began their descent into the canyon. But because the water supply at the rim was so restricted, they had to run the 4.5 miles to the bottom of the canyon to Indian Garden where there was sufficient water to process the film. Then, they'd charge back up, developed prints in hand, to sell them to mule riders as they returned to the rim. In 1911 the brothers made a daring river trip down the Colorado, which they filmed. Copies of the film are still being shown today.

Nightlife

The club scene is not exactly why you come to the canyon, and you won't find it here. But there are a number of pleasant places to go for a nightcap and conviviality. The **Bright Angel Lounge,** open daily from 11 to 12:30 A.M., has a full-service bar and live entertainment in the evenings Wednesday through Saturday. **Maswik Sports Lounge** in the Maswik Lodge has a big screen TV aglow with whatever sporting event is of the moment. Seven additional sets are scattered throughout the room. Open daily, 11–12:30 A.M.

El Tovar Lounge overlooks the canyon and when it's warm, drinks are served on the veranda. Settle in here while you're waiting for your dinner reservations. Open 11–12:30 A.M.

Getting There

To get to the South Rim from Phoenix, take I-17 north 146 miles to Flagstaff, to the junction with I-40. Follow I-40 west for 32 miles to Williams. Take Arizona 64 from Williams 63 miles to the South Rim. Or take the Grand Canyon Railway (page 35) from Williams.

Tours

Helicopter Tours

Strict regulations as to when and where aircraft can fly over the canyon have decreased noise impact to that of a bus operating within the park area. The only helicopters that you as a visitor will see (unless you take a helicopter tour) are those operated by the National Park Service on rescue flights, or flights to bring

The Grand Canyon Railway leaves daily from Williams and deposits passengers at the South Rim of the Grand Canyon to return the same day, or later in the week.

The El Tovar Hotel at the Grand Canyon, built in 1905, retains past elegance and charm.

supplies to the bottom of the canyon. Among the half-dozen companies that fly, **AirStar Helicopters** does a particularly good job of showing off the canyon. Non-English–speaking guests are given taped simultaneous translation of the English narration that they may patch into their camcorders to precisely accompany the video they are shooting. Tours of 25–30 minutes cover the Dragon Corridor and Central Canyon, 40–45 minute tours also take in the Colorado River at the point where it merges with the Little Colorado and 50–60 minute flights add even more pinnacles, buttes and spires. Flights leave from the Grand Canyon Airport near Tusayan. Call **(800) 962-3869 or (520) 638-2622.**

Where to Stay

Hotels, Motels & Inns

All of the Grand Canyon National Park Lodges are operated by Amfac Parks and Resorts, the official National Park Service concessionaire on the South Rim. Of the eight properties, four are located on the canyon's rim, three are within the park and one is just outside the park's south entrance. All rooms have phones and TVs, but there are no housekeeping units. Some accommodations close during winter months. Room rates do not change seasonally, but usually packages are available during winter months. Individuals can book as many as 23 months in advance. For reservations at all Grand Canyon properties call **(303) 29-PARKS.** If you're staying at any park hotel or lodge, just dial the operator to be connected to any other park service.

El Tovar Hotel—$$$$

Built by the Fred Harvey Company in 1905 and now a National Historic Landmark, it is the only lodging at the canyon that's considered a true hotel because it has room service and a concierge. All 77 rooms have just undergone renovation to restore the decor to its original soft pastels. Right on the rim and fashioned after hunting lodges in Europe, it is constructed of native stone and Oregon pine. Lovely and dignified, it is the most upscale of all accommodations at the Grand Canyon. It has a gift shop, elegant restaurant and lounge. Breakfast or lunch here, looking out over the canyon, is a must.

Kachina and Thunderbird Lodges—$$$$

These twin 104-room buildings have rooms facing the canyon or the park, and are right in the middle of everything that's going on at the South Rim. They may not exist much longer as they do not fit the historic ambiance of this part of the rim, but for the next few years, they offer modern motel-type accommodations. If you really don't want to be quite so much in the middle of things try Yavapai Lodge for peace and quiet.

Maswik Lodge—$$$

Located at the southwest end of Grand Canyon Village, it was named for a Hopi Kachina who is said to guard the canyon. It has 278 rooms, and sometimes is the last to fill up. So try here if all else fails. Rustic cabins also are available during summer months. It has a gift shop, restaurant and lounge.

Yavapai Lodge—$$$

With 385 rooms, this is the park's largest lodge. Actually it's a series of lodge buildings in a piñon and juniper forest about a mile from the canyon rim, adjacent to the visitor center and the village business area. It is not unusual to see mule deer grazing outside your window, jays and nuthatches in the trees and squirrels and chipmunks being adorable in hopes of a snack. Don't feed them. It's against park regulations.

Bright Angel Lodge and Cabins—$$–$$$

Almost everyone who stays overnight at the canyon wants to book here because the name, Bright Angel, is so well known. But with just 37 rooms and 49 cabins you should reserve early. It overlooks the Canyon's rim and provides dramatic views from many rooms. Designed in 1935 and built of log and native stone, it is the point from which mule rides depart for descents into the canyon. In the lobby, a carved wood thunderbird was named the "bright angel of the sky" by architects. It has a restaurant and lounge.

Phantom Ranch—$

At the bottom of the canyon, accessible only by mule, foot or river raft, there are dormitory-type accommodations, segregated for male or female hikers. Hikers also can reserve meals at the Phantom Ranch Dining Hall. If you're even thinking of doing this, reserve well ahead as accommodations fill up more than a year in advance. You also can book overnight mule trips that include three meals and cabin accommodations.

Where to Eat

There are several good choices for mealtimes, ranging from fine dining to basic fast fare. Although there are no dress codes you probably won't be comfortable showing up for dinner at El Tovar or Arizona Steakhouse in shorts and a T-shirt. For dinner reservations, from any of the hotels or lodges inside the park, use a house phone and dial 6431.

Arizona Steak House—$$$–$$$$

Located on the rim at the Bright Angel Lodge with huge windows affording a canyon view, the specialty here is steak. A fresh catch of the day is also reliably good. Open seasonally for dinner from 5 to 10 P.M. Reservations are not accepted, so during busy summer months show up before 5 or you could have a wait of up to an hour.

El Tovar—$$$–$$$$

The elegant dining room in this famous hotel is lined with murals depicting the Hopi, Apache, Mojave and Navajo cultures. Service is still as impeccable as it was when crisply clad Harvey Girls served fresh oysters and imported Roquefort to well-heeled diners. Truly a fine dining experience with canyon views from many tables, dinner reservations are in high demand. Reservations are not accepted for breakfast (try the asparagus and boursin omelette) or lunch. For dinner reservations call **(520) 638-2631, ext. 6431** from outside the park.

Bright Angel Coffee Shop—$$–$$$

At the Bright Angel Lodge, this is a good family restaurant, open for three meals a day. Though always busy, it doesn't have the long waits that build up at the Steak House. Well-prepared fare includes Southwestern entrees, sandwiches, pasta, omelets and vegetarian dishes. Opens at 6:30 A.M. for breakfast, closes at 10 P.M. Reservations are not accepted.

Bright Angel Fountain—$$

Also at Bright Angel Lodge, it has take-out service for hot dogs, sandwiches, muffins and more. Hours are seasonal, but during summer months it's always open to dispense hefty servings of ice cream.

Maswik Cafeteria—$–$$

It opens at 6 A.M. to accommodate guests taking the many tours and rafting trips, with early departures from the Maswik Lodge tour desk. This food court offers lunch and dinner with daily specials that feature pasta, Mexican food and sandwiches to go. Beer and wine are available.

Yavapai Cafeteria—$–$$

The spacious, bright dining room has greenhouse window seating. You feel like you're eating under a waterfall when it rains. Lines move quickly and efficiently, serving up fare that ranges from pancakes and pizza to burgers and fried chicken. Open seasonally, 6 A.M.–11 P.M. Beer and wine are available.

Babbitt's—$
This market and deli has groceries and will make sandwiches to go. Open 7 A.M.–7 P.M. Located across the parking lot from Yavapai Lodge. There are also Babbitt's in Tusayan and Desert View.

Outside the South Rim

Tusayan

This little town, just beyond the park's southern boundaries in the Kaibab National Forest, exists primarily to supply visitor support. It has a number of lodging options including **Moqui Lodge ($$$; 520-638-2424).** With 136 rooms, it is sometimes a good bet if lodging right at the canyon is full. It is the headquarters for the Apache Stables horseback riding facilities. The lodge restaurant is open daily for breakfast and dinner. Specialties are Mexican dishes and American favorites. The atmosphere is casual, catering to families. The lounge is low key and subtle, good for sipping a great margarita while regrouping for the next day's hiking. Open April through November. Tusayan has a McDonald's, Taco Bell and Burger King, as well as a barbecue place and a steakhouse. The Imax Theatre presents a 34-minute film, *The Grand Canyon—The Hidden Secrets,* from 8:30 A.M.–8:30 P.M. every hour on the half hour. At 9:30 P.M. a second feature on the eruption of Mount St. Helens is shown. The 70-foot screen is truly a remarkable way to view aerial footage and river-running scenes. There is a post office at the Babbitt's store, which also carries groceries, general supplies, books, magazines and takeout deli food.

Valle

This small town 25 miles south of the canyon has a Days Inn, restaurant, gas station and small market. Bedrock City, that oh-so-blue-walled area to the west of AZ 64, is a Flintstones-themed "prehistoric park" where kids can ride a train through an "active volcano." The Flintstone and Rubble houses are there, as is a gift shop with more Flintstones stuff than ever you imagined. Fred's Diner is open for three meals, serving Bronto Burgers, Dino Dogs, Gravelberry Pie and other themed fare. The AAA-approved campground has pull-through sites with full hookups, and also has tent camping with showers and rest rooms. Once closed during winter months, it now is open all year. Valle is located at the intersections of US 180 and AZ 64, south of the Grand Canyon. **(520) 635-2600.**

Planes of Fame Air Museum

Open since 1995 and growing every year, this museum is part of the much larger Planes of Fame Museum in Chino, California. Many of the vintage aircraft are flyable, with others in the restoration process. In the collection is a Lockheed C-121A Constellation, the old "Connie" that was the VIP transport for General Douglas MacArthur during the Korean War. You can tour its interior. Morbid but interesting is the Japanese-piloted World War II suicide rocket called the Yokosuka Ohka, whose name means Cherry Blossom. The one at the museum was captured on the island of Okinawa. A Hawker Hunter, the first genuinely transonic British service aircraft had its initial flight in 1951. The airport itself sometimes accommodates overflow traffic from the Grand Canyon Airport, and often gets traffic that has been diverted because of weather conditions. Open daily, 9 A.M.–5 P.M. in winter, and until 6 P.M. in summer. Closed Thanksgiving and Christmas. Small admission. **HCR 34 Box B, Valle, Williams, 86046; (520) 635-1000.**

West Rim

Peach Springs

Situated on the Hualapai (say Wall-a-pie) Indian Reservation where Grand Canyon National Park reaches its most southern point, for years the only reason to go here was to get permits for backcountry trips. When I-40 bypassed Peach Springs in the early 1970s, everything pretty much closed except a deli and a service station. But for the last ten years this area has been re-emerging as the jumping-off point for exploring the canyon's West Rim, which is uniquely different from the tourist-jammed South Rim more than 100 miles to the northeast. There is little traffic, few buildings and almost no commercial enterprises or other signs of man's intrusion. Here, the Hualapai have stewardship over almost one million acres of land, 108 miles of which is Grand Canyon frontage.

Grand Canyon West

Located 92 miles northwest of Peach Springs via some paved and some unimproved county roads and about 3 miles from the rim, it is the starting point for a 4.5-mile bus tour. Don't expect luxury or air-conditioning—these are 1975 vintage Bluebird school buses. It proceeds to Eagle Point for a look at rock formations, then to Guano Point to see remains of tram towers used in the 1950s as part of a system to harvest bat guano from a mine on the canyon's north face. The location, on a sharp bend in the Colorado, creates a spectacular view, much wider than on most rim sites. At Guano Point a lunch of chicken or beef barbeque, tortillas, beans and corn is served as part of the tour. There are picnic tables, or if it's windy, you can eat inside the little tram-works house. There are no walls or guard rails, so Hualapai guides warn you to stand back from the canyon's edge, especially if the wind is blowing.

Hualapai River Runners

This Native American-owned and operated company does one- and two-day raft trips on the lower Colorado. Trips include navigating

A Native American Guide from the Hualapai Reservation takes guests in a yellow bus to the West Rim of the Grand Canyon.

nine rapids in motorized pontoon boats, hiking to Travertine Falls and lunch at Separation Canyon. The trip leaves from Hualapai Lodge and travels through the Lower Granite Gorge from Diamond Creek to Pierce Ferry. Hualapai guides share legends about their culture and point out sights in nature. It is offered from April to October. For reservations call **(800) 622-4409 or (520) 769-2219.**

Hualapai Lodge—$$$

Opened in 1997 in Peach Springs, it is located between Kingman and Seligman on the longest remaining stretch of Route 66. Sixty large, comfortable rooms, a restaurant open for three meals and a gift shop occupy a two-story building. For reservations call **(888) 216-0076 or (520) 769-2230.**

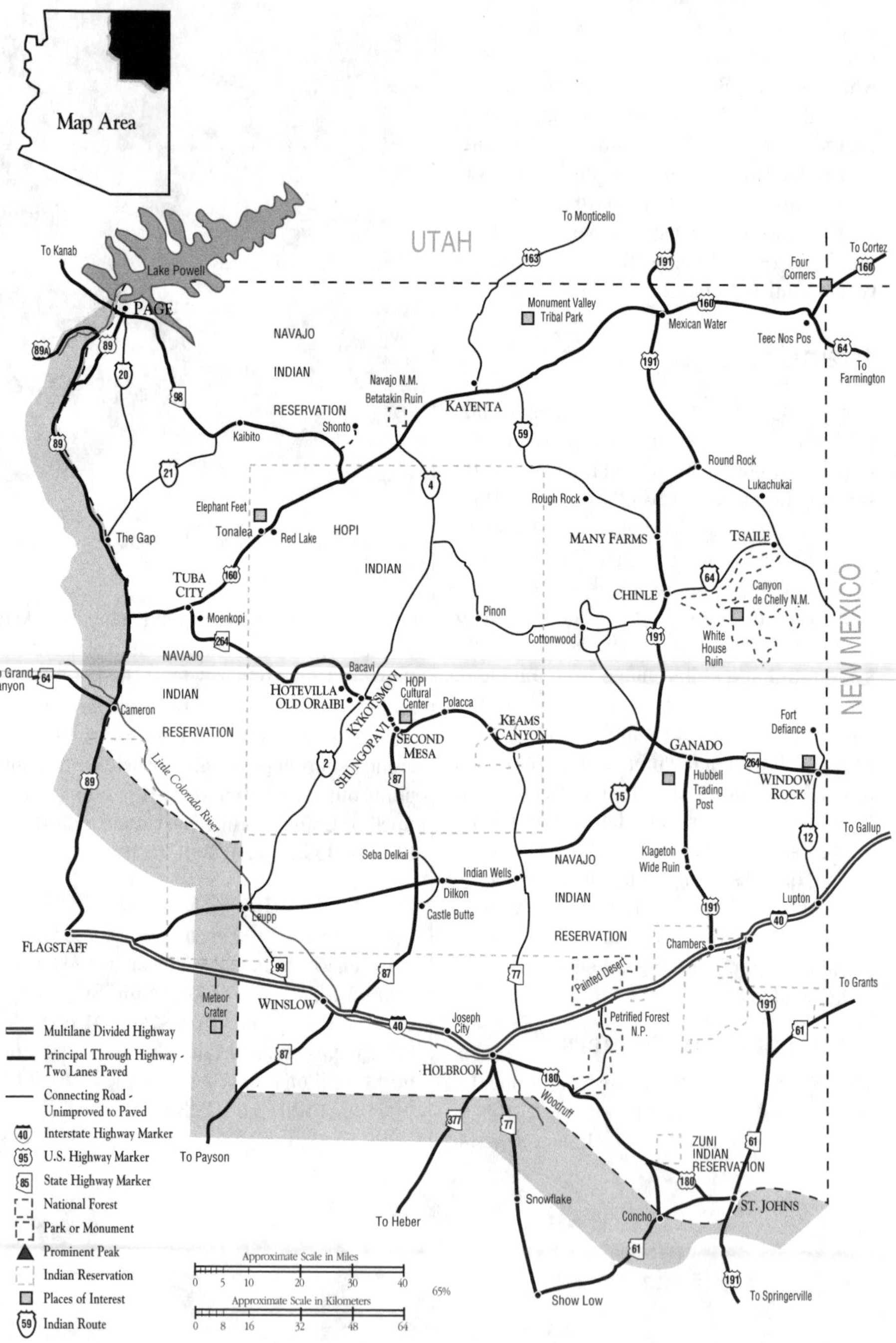

Map Area

UTAH
NEW MEXICO
To Kanab
Lake Powell
PAGE
To Monticello
To Cortez
Four Corners
Monument Valley Tribal Park
Mexican Water
Teec Nos Pos
To Farmington
NAVAJO INDIAN RESERVATION
Navajo N.M. Betatakin Ruin
KAYENTA
Shonto
Kaibito
Round Rock
Lukachukai
Rough Rock
Elephant Feet
Tonalea
Red Lake
HOPI INDIAN
MANY FARMS
TSAILE
The Gap
TUBA CITY
Moenkopi
Pinon
CHINLE
Canyon de Chelly N.M.
White House Ruin
Cottonwood
To Grand Canyon
NAVAJO INDIAN RESERVATION
Bacavi
HOTEVILLA
OLD ORAIBI
KYKOTSMOVI
HOPI Cultural Center
Polacca
KEAMS CANYON
SHUNGOPAVI
SECOND MESA
Cameron
Fort Defiance
GANADO
Hubbell Trading Post
WINDOW ROCK
Little Colorado River
To Gallup
Seba Delkai
Klagetoh Wide Ruin
Indian Wells
Dilkon
Castle Butte
NAVAJO INDIAN RESERVATION
Lupton
Leupp
FLAGSTAFF
Chambers
Painted Desert
To Grants
Meteor Crater
WINSLOW
Joseph City
Petrified Forest N.P.
HOLBROOK
Woodruff
To Payson
ZUNI INDIAN RESERVATION
Snowflake
Concho
ST. JOHNS
To Heber
Show Low
To Springerville

Multilane Divided Highway
Principal Through Highway - Two Lanes Paved
Connecting Road - Unimproved to Paved
40 Interstate Highway Marker
95 U.S. Highway Marker
85 State Highway Marker
National Forest
Park or Monument
Prominent Peak
Indian Reservation
Places of Interest
59 Indian Route

Approximate Scale in Miles
0 5 10 20 30 40
Approximate Scale in Kilometers
0 8 16 32 48 64

65%

Northeast and Indian Country

Northeast and Indian Country

Navajo Reservation and Environs

On a map, Arizona's far northeastern corner appears bare and featureless. In its center the vast 27,543-square-mile Navajo Reservation wraps around the Hopi Reservation in a giant cartographic hug. The reservation is located primarily in Arizona, but extends into Utah and New Mexico. The entire expanse is crossed by few main roads, their wiggly courses dotted with isolated Indian-named towns. Yet this is an area that reflects Mother Nature's smile. She took her time as she molded, sculpted, and composed. Some believe that she purposefully situated this stunningly beautiful area in a place that the elements treat harshly. When given to the Navajos, the land was thought to be practically valueless. But discovery of oil and other mineral resources, and development of tourism in recent years, have proven the land's richness.

This is an enigmatic part of the state, filled with hidden places waiting to be discovered. The Navajo people, called Dine', say that there are dozens of things there that no white man has ever seen. Exploring even those that are known is truly a journey to foreign lands.

About 200,000 Navajo live on the 16-million-acre reservation, which is larger than the entire state of West Virginia. The reservation is a unique blend of traditional and modern ways. You will hear Navajo spoken as often as English, sometimes mingling in a single conversation. The language is so complicated that during World War II, Navajo men were employed as Code Talkers to communicate in their native language to baffle the enemy. The "code" was never broken. Although differences between Navajo and European-American cultures rapidly are being erased, some old customs prevail. Generations ago photographing or sketching a Navajo would have been offensive, and the person would have edged away. Some still will, so the courteous thing to do is to request permission before photographing. Don't be surprised if you are asked for a small fee. Eye contact may be considered rude, and touching usually is reserved for close friends and family. Open friendliness may not be forthcoming. Don't be put off. Just remember that you are on their land; they were here first, and their culture deserves respect.

The Navajo Reservation observes daylight savings time, while the rest of Arizona doesn't. The reservation is on Mountain Daylight Time, which means that from May through October it is on New Mexico, not Arizona time. If you're on the reservation in the summer, remember that the time in Phoenix, the Grand Canyon and elsewhere will be an hour earlier. Alcoholic beverages are prohibited on the reservation. Most of the land is open range, so watch for cattle when driving. The accommodations mentioned here are not necessarily favorites, but we list them because there are so few places to camp and to stay in this area.

Four Corners Monument Navajo Tribal Park

In the northeast corner of the reservation is the only place in the country where it's possible to stand in four states at the same time. A concrete monument marks the point where Utah, Colorado, New Mexico and Arizona meet. Incorporating the seals of all four states and bearing the inscription "Four States Here Meet in Freedom Under God," it rests on a corner of each state, all of which are on Indian land. At the visitor center, open year around, Navajo craftspeople sell jewelry and traditional Navajo food. There are picnic tables and rest rooms, but no water. The monument is located one-quarter mile west of US 160, 6 miles north of Teec Nos Pos and 40 miles southwest of Cortez, Colorado. The park is open May to Aug., 7 A.M.–8 P.M., and late Aug. to Apr., 8 A.M.–5 P.M. There is a small fee. **Navajo Parks and Recreation Dept., P.O. Box 9000, Window Rock, 86515; (520) 871-6647.**

Kayenta

This small, weathered town in the northeastern part of Navajo County is 20 miles south of the Utah border. It is generally considered the jumping-off point for visiting the Navajo National Monument, 20 miles to the west, and Monument Valley to the north. Peabody Coal Company owns and operates two mines in the area, which fuel electric power plants. There is a **Holiday Inn** (see Where to Stay) that is not particularly memorable, but during busy summer months it can be a good fallback place to stay when lodgings closer to Monument Valley are full. Its restaurant is open for three meals a day. The **Best Western Wetherill Inn (520) 697-3231** has clean rooms for slightly less. You can get groceries at two markets and stop at the **Navajo Nation Visitor Center** to buy jewelry and other crafts. The center is open on weekdays with varying hours, closed on weekends.

Navajo National Monument

About an hour and a half east of Page off US 160, west of Kayenta, the Navajo National Monument protects cliff ruins hidden in deep canyons, built and occupied 700 years ago by the Anasazi. If you visit in winter, be prepared for strong winds and snow at this 7,300-foot elevation. Summers are warm and pleasant. The elaborate cliff dwellings at Keet Seel and Betatakin ruins are both remarkably well preserved. A third, Inscription House, is closed to the public.

Betatakin Ruin

Most visitors simply hike the 1-mile round-trip paved Sandal Trail that goes to an overlook facing the Betatakin Ruin. Bring your binoculars because you won't get very close. It is open year-round during daylight hours. The walk takes about 45 minutes with frequent stops to catch your breath if you're not in shape. For more hiking and a lovely view of the piñon and juniper forest, veer off onto the Aspen Forest Trail that descends partway into Betatakin Canyon. For a close-up look at the Betatakin Ruins you must take a 5-mile round-trip, ranger-guided tour that's fairly strenuous, and descends 700 feet into the canyon (remember, that's 700 feet that you also have to come back up). First-come tours are limited to 25 and begin in early May at 10 A.M. daily. From Memo-

Monument Valley, on the Navajo Reservation, has spectacular scenery often seen in motion pictures, TV shows and commercials.

rial Day through Labor Day two hikes are offered at 9 A.M. and 12 noon. After Labor Day, tours go back to one a day at 11 A.M., and are discontinued in October. This is a very popular hike, so show up early to claim a ticket.

Keet Seel Ruin

The only way to get to this dramatic cliff dwelling, located 8.5 miles from the visitor center, is by hiking or on horseback. Those who have done it say it is well worth the effort. A National Park Service backcountry permit is necessary. A local Navajo family provides horses for the day trip to the ruin for a fee, but hiking permits are free. The visitor center at Navajo National Monument has lovely Native American jewelry of excellent quality, including pieces of snowflake obsidian. The museum has a walk-in replica of a Betatakin family home, an example of a living unit within a pueblo. The center is open 8 A.M.–4:30 P.M., mid-Dec. to March; 8 A.M.–6 P.M. May to early Sept.; and 8 A.M.–5 P.M., mid-Dec. and March to May. Take US 160, 18 miles south of Kayenta and turn right (northwest) on AZ 564 to the park. **HC-71, Box 3, Tonalea, 86044; (520) 672-2366.**

Scenic Drive

Recently designated a scenic highway by the Arizona Department of Transportation, the 23-mile stretch of US 163 that extends from Kayenta through the magnificent rock formations of Monument Valley and on to the Utah state line is an hour well spent. The paved, two-lane highway passes 7,101-foot-high Agathla Peak on the east and wanders through small Navajo communities, where in summer the residents often sell arts and crafts along the roadside.

Monument Valley Navajo Tribal Park

On Arizona's border and extending north into Utah, this magnificent expanse of red sandstone is a 30,000-acre Navajo Tribal Park within the 16-million-acre reservation. Its spires, buttes and mesas have been shaped over 50 million years as wind, rain and temperature chafed away at layers of crumbling rock. Today, imaginations create stone creatures in the mind's eye—Bear and Rabbit, the King on his Throne, Three Sisters, Elephant Butte—all are clearly discernible on a monolith-studded landscape beneath a crisp, dazzling sky.

A 17-mile dirt road winds through Monument Valley and is open to private vehicles, which do quite well by avoiding patches of loose sand that can envelop a tire and devour it whole. A plus for traveling by car is that you can roll up windows and turn on air-conditioners in defense against the fine red, blowing dust that scratches eyes and penetrates cameras. An alternate plan is to take one of the open-air trams that leave from the visitor center. Driven by local Navajo guides, they stop at all the usual scenic sites and have the advantage of being allowed into shadowy canyons and remote spots that prohibit private cars.

The cliff-dwelling Anasazi lived in Monument Valley more than 1,500 years ago, mysteriously abandoning their homes in the 1300s. Today close to 300 Navajos are settled here, some in traditional dome-shaped hogans, spinning wool by hand to create treasured Navajo rugs and tending herds of cattle and sheep. Other families choose present-day manufactured homes, some with electricity and running water.

A classic stop for all visitors is John Ford Point, named for the famous director of 1930s and 1940s westerns. Beginning with *Stagecoach,* released in 1939, many of these early flicks featured the scenic spit of land as a backdrop. *How the West Was Won,* released in 1962, and the 1988 film *Back to the Future III* all were filmed here. Another landmark, Right Mitten, has had luxury automobiles helicoptered to its flat top to create dramatic footage for a television commercial. Rain God Mesa was the altar at which medicine men prayed for life-sustaining moisture and which shelters a sacred burial ground.

Sometimes it is possible to stop at a traditional hogan made of sticks and mud where Navajos offer rugs and jewelry for sale. The atmosphere is low-key and respectful, with no pressure put on the visitor to make a purchase. Along the windy road, it is common to see herds of wild horses, untamed for generations. They race beside towering cliffs, impossible to catch, savoring the sheer pleasure of running free. They belong to no one, but somehow belong to everyone who appreciates the captivating loveliness of Monument Valley. The Valley is about 320 miles from Phoenix. There is a small entrance fee. Navajo-escorted tours may be booked at the Visitor Center and range from 3 hours to all day. **Monument Valley Navajo Tribal Park, P.O. Box 360289, Monument Valley, UT 84536; (801) 727-3353.**

Where to Stay

Goulding's Lodge—$$$$ (summer); $$$ (after mid-October)

About 4 miles west of the monument entrance, just inches over the Utah state line, it's the only hotel in Monument Valley. Balcony rooms have majestic views. It has a small indoor pool, restaurant, gas station and general store. The land once belonged to Harry Goulding, who started a trading post there in the 1920s. His home and store, adjacent to the current motel, now are a small museum. **Goulding's Lodge, Box 360001, Monument Valley, UT 84536; (800) 874-0902 or (801) 727-3231.**

On the Navajo Reservation in the Monument Valley, traditional earthen hogans provide snug homes.

Holiday Inn—$$$$ (summer); $$$ (winter)

If Goulding's is full, this is a good fallback choice. It's in Kayenta, about 25 miles to the south, at the junction of US 160 and 163. Rates are high for basic accommodations, but places to stay are few and far between up here, and summer months are busy. **Holiday Inn, Box 307, Kayenta, 86033; (800) 465-4329 or (520) 697-3221.**

Camping

Mitten View Campground has tent and RV sites with showers and 64 hookups. It is at the entrance to the 17-mile trail that loops through Monument Valley. Spaces are on a first-come, first-served basis. Call the **Monument Valley Tribal Park** at **(801) 727-3353** for camping information. Another camping and RV option, **Goulding's Campground** is near the lodge and has 60 RV hookups, showers and a children's playground. Facilities, including the laundry and pool, are closed during winter months, but visitors are still welcome to park there. For information call **(801) 727-3231.**

Tsaile

The best reason to stop at this reservation town is to visit the **Navajo Community College,** used as much to educate Navajo youth as it is to preserve the culture, says director Edsel Brown. Two-year courses prepare students for college life off the reservation. The four-story, hogan-shaped building is constructed around a traditional eight-sided hogan, the college's center. Students come to this peaceful room to study and to reflect. By taking the time to spend a few quiet moments here, it is easy to feel the influence of an ancient culture and religion. The third and fourth floors house a terrific museum with works by Navajo artists that include silver-work, rugs, wool, baskets and pottery. The bookstore is a treasure trove of information on the Navajo culture. The college grounds have the traditional hogan layout, with each side having a use, like a room. The dining hall (corresponding to a hogan cooking area) is in the center, for example, and sleeping quarters (dorms) are on the west. The door faces the sunrise so occupants can welcome the new day. The traditional way to enter a hogan is to walk around to the left. Students and personnel are proud of their college and glad to take the time to explain it, so don't hesitate to ask. The museum and gallery are open weekdays 8:30 A.M.–4:30 P.M., and you usually may walk around the rest of the campus any time. For information call **Navajo Community College, Tsaile, 86556; (520) 724-6600.**

Coyote Pass Hospitality

This hogan-style bed and breakfast, for lack of a better way to categorize it, is designed to let visitors sample the Navajo culture by actually living it. Their literature cautions that it is not for everyone, and it surely isn't. In a hogan with a single room, mattresses lie on a dirt floor, water comes from a pail and dipper, there may be rudimentary electricity and bathrooms are out back. The upside is that the personal request of each guest is thoughtfully considered. Recently a pair of British sisters who wanted to learn Navajo weaving techniques were introduced to a pair of Navajo sisters who taught them. You may be faxed an advance book list so you can prepare for your visit. This isn't just an overnight stop. You plan a stay which is then styled around your particular method of learning about the Navajo culture and of experiencing life as a Native American. **P.O. Box 91-B, Tsaile, 86558; (520) 724-3383 or (520) 724-3258.**

In Canyon de Chelly, these Anasazi Ruins, called White House, were occupied about 1080–1275 A.D.

Canyon de Chelly

Take a look at a map and you'll see that Canyon de Chelly (pronounced Shay) National Monument spreads like the talons of an eagle, with the two fingers of Canyon de Chelly on the south and Canyon del Muerto (Canyon of the Dead) on the north. For 50 million years streams from the nearby Chuska Mountains have followed their courses, creating sheer, sculpted red sandstone passages that trace history in their many layers. Other elements—probing tree roots, seeping water that freezes, soil acids and wind—continue the process of change. Glossy ravens and red-tailed hawks joyride on updrafts along terra-cotta cliffs. The spirits of the Anasazi linger in petroglyphs and dwellings niched among ridges and protected ledges. For them the canyon was a welcoming place, sheltering a peaceful people whose frequent ceremonies gave thanks for the rich, moist soil that produced reliable crops of corn.

The best way to see Canyon de Chelly is to first view it from the north and south rims by car, to get a sense of its enormity. Then, the safest means of exploring its depths is on a tour in a tram or jeep equipped with large tires, specifically adapted to foil the canyon's shifting, sandy bottom. Brief, late afternoon rains are common in summer, and can turn the canyon floor into quicksand.

The most widely photographed ruin is Junction House, which lies at the point where the canyons converge. Its 15 rooms are easy to see from below as well as from across the canyon at Junction Overlook. Hand and toeholds are clearly visible, carved into the cliff by the Anasazi so they could reach this lofty dwelling. Further into de Chelly the **White House Ruin,** so called because some walls still bear traces of the original white plaster, once consisted of approximately 60 rooms and four kivas. The ruin overlooks a shady spot alongside a cottonwood-lined creek, a favored rest stop for jeep tours where Navajos often spread blankets to display jewelry and crafts. **Standing Cow Ruin,** named for the white cow pictograph on the canyon wall beside a Navajo stone hogan, befuddles archaeologists because it is situated on the site of an Anasazi ruin. Usually the Navajo shun places of the "ancient ones" as they call the Anasazi. The cow probably is of Navajo origin.

A few Navajo families live in the canyon, but most are here just during summer months, making a living by selling crafts and jewelry to visitors. Most come into the canyon during the day, returning to homes in the nearby town of Chinle at night.

The extensive pictographs (painted pictures) and petroglyphs (carved or incised symbols) found in Monument Valley and Canyon de Chelly were left by both Anasazi and Navajo cultures. Believed to have intricate meanings, they in fact express a language of their own. Those with horses date to the 16th century and later, when the Spanish introduced ponies to the Anasazi. Others clearly date to the Spanish era, such as the pictograph near Standing Cow Ruin in Canyon del Muerto that shows a rider with a cross on his cape, and riders with what appear to be rifles. Whatever these enigmatic markings say, they are just part of the spectacle of towering cliffs and memorable dwellings that honor nature and an ancient way of life. Some speculate their messages are best left uncovered, permitting them to keep shadowy secrets that perhaps were never meant to be revealed. Canyon de Chelly is 96 miles and about a 90-minute drive southeast of Monument Valley. Hiking and horseback riding (with a guide), and four- and six-wheel-drive vehicle tours may be booked at historic **Thunderbird Lodge (800-679-2437 or 520-674-5841),** one-half mile from the visitor center. Private individual cars are not permitted. **Justin's Stables** provides spirited horses that, along with a guide, will take you into the canyon. Located at the mouth of the canyon. **P.O. Box 881, Chinle, 86503; (520) 674-5678.** For general information contact the **Visitor Center, Box 588, Chinle, 86503; (520) 674-5500.**

Where to Stay

Thunderbird Lodge ($$$), a historic property within one-half mile of Canyon de Chelly, was originally a trading post built around 1902. It simply grew, with successive owners, to accommodate the increasing flow of visitors to the spectacular canyon. The surrounding massive cottonwood trees are reminders of that era. It has a restaurant and gift shop with a separate "rug room" filled with beautiful Navajo rugs. The cafeteria is open daily, 6:30 A.M.–9:30 P.M. **P.O. Box 548, Chinle, 86503; (800) 679-BIRD or (520) 674-5841, fax (520) 674-5844.**

The **Holiday Inn** ($$$) at the mouth of Canyon de Chelly has a pool, cable TV and restaurant. **Holiday Inn, P.O. Box 1889, BIA Rte. 7, Chinle, 86503; (800) 465-4329 for reservations; (520) 674-5000, fax (520) 674-8264.** The **Canyon de Chelly Motel** is located in downtown Chinle one block east of US 191, 3 miles from the visitor center. It has a full service restaurant and indoor swimming pool. **(800) 327-0354 or (520) 674-6875, fax (520) 674-3715.**

The **Navajo Nation Inn** ($$$) is unremarkable except that it is the only game in town. It is about 60 miles west of Canyon de Chelly in the town of Window Rock. It has a restaurant and plainly furnished standard, double and king rooms. **48 W. Hwy. 264, Window Rock, 86515; (800) 662-6189 or (520) 871-4108, fax (520) 871-5466.**

Window Rock, a giant sandstone formation, is 47 feet high. Water once flowed through it.

Spider Rock RV and Camping Too (520-674-8261) is located 10 miles east of the visitor center on the South Rim Drive. It has 50 RV sites and 20 regular campsites on natural land with no hookups as of this writing. It is nothing special, but is one of the few campgrounds in the area.

Window Rock

The geological formation that gives this place its name once had water flowing through it. Centuries of wind and blowing sand also have helped to sculpt this 47-foot opening. Navajo legend says it was made by the Giant Snake, who once crawled along the expanse of sandstone, eventually creating a passage through it. You can't climb up to the hole, but you can hike around it. The rubble at the foot of the window are remnants of a prehistoric pueblo.

The small town of Window Rock is the capital of the Navajo Nation, which is governed by an elected tribal council headed by a tribal chairman. The council is made up of representatives of various election districts. This is in keeping with the Navajo heritage, which never has had hereditary chiefs. When in session, delegates call each other by traditional clan names, and proceedings are mannerly and polite. The 88-member council, which includes a number of women, has 110 chapters and meets four times a year.

Navajo Tribal Council Chambers

The hogan-shaped chamber is made of sandstone quarried from the same type of rocks that surround it. Window Rock presides over all. Ponderosa pine beams came from higher elevations, and wall-sized murals by Navajo artist Gerald Nailor were completed in 1935. They depict the history and progress of the Navajo Nation, portraying significant events including the introduction of the Navajo and Spaniards, the signing of the Treaty of 1868 permitting Navajos to return to their homeland, the discovery of oil and other events. The Santa Fe Railroad donated the bell at the entrance, used to call members to session. It commemorates the service of the thousands of Navajos who worked to build and maintain the Santa Fe line. Although tours aren't scheduled regularly, if the chamber's front door is open, come in and take a look. If it is locked, come around to the back and perhaps a worker will give you a brief peek. For information on tours of the council chambers contact **Navajo Council Chambers, P.O. Box 1400, Window Rock, 86515; (520) 871-6417.** The building is located in **Window Rock Tribal Park,** which has trails, water, rest rooms and picnic tables. For information on the park contact **Navajo Parks and Recreation Dept., P.O. Box 9000, Window Rock, 86515; (520) 871-6647.**

Navajo Arts & Crafts Enterprise

This large retail store promotes and nurtures Navajo art. Rugs, silver, jewelry, paintings, kachinas, baskets, sand paintings and more, all authentic and of top quality, are for sale. The Enterprise brings materials at wholesale prices to artists in communities all over the reservation, which it buys back in the form of finished goods. Craftspeople are encouraged to develop marketable ideas so you're pretty well assured of finding something new each time you visit. Designs here tend to be traditional as most customers are Navajo, but more experimental designs are creeping in. The Enterprise also purchases from other Nations, including Zuni, Hopi and Santo Domingo. Anything you purchase here has its authenticity guaranteed. There also are shops in Kayenta and Chinle, and there is an especially large and well-stocked store in Cameron, near the junction of US 89 and AZ 64 southeast of the Grand Canyon. Open 8 A.M.–5 P.M., Mon.–Fri.; closed Sat. and Sun. Located near the junction of AZ 264 and Route 12; **(520) 871-4090.**

Navajo Nation Museum, Library and Visitor Center

Recently relocated into new, expanded quarters, the museum is a repository of bits of Navajo history that include the development of the designs and symbols used in silver and weaving techniques. Historical displays explain the evolution of the Navajo culture. Open 9 A.M.–6 P.M., Mon.–Fri.; 9 A.M.–5 P.M., Sat. year-round, although winter hours sometimes are shorter. Located a block east of the Navajo Nation Inn at AZ 264 and Loop Road. **P.O. Box 49509, Window Rock, 86515; (520) 871-6673.**

Navajo Nation Zoo and Botanical Park

Known locally as The Zoo, this small place differs decidedly from what you might expect. Don't look for manicured lawns and high-tech exhibits. Rather, in this area of just 12 inches of rainfall a year and a frost-free season of only one hundred or so days, it's apparent that nature is harsh. Sturdy junipers, Indian rice grass, lupine, Navajo and other high desert plants do well, however. Animals include those that figure in Navajo history and culture, as well as native and domestic creatures that exist in the area today. Bears, cougars, Mexican wolves, coyotes, deer, elk, bobcats, raccoons, prairie dogs and a pronghorn live there. Goats, Navajo churro sheep and rabbits represent domestic stock. Birds of prey, a roadrunner, a sandhill crane, wild turkeys, snakes, lizards and turtles are at home here. Exhibits and examples of traditional Navajo dwellings, along with the animals, educate school children. It is located on the north side of AZ 264, one-quarter mile east of its intersection with Indian Route 12 North. Follow the pink bears from the turnoff to the entrance. You can accomplish a worthwhile visit in about an hour. Open daily, 8 A.M.–5 P.M., except Christmas and New Year's Day. Free admission. **P.O. Box 9000, Window Rock, 86515; (520) 871-6573.**

Fort Defiance

Six miles north of Window Rock at the junction of Navajo Routes 12 and 7, this small town is the site where Colonel Edwin Sumner built the state's first military outpost in 1851. He built it on Bonito Creek and named it Fort Defiance because it flew in the face of the Navajo desire for it not to be there. The Navajo did their best to discourage it, but the Army prevailed. The fort served as the headquarters for Colonel Kit Carson's Navajo Campaign in the summer of 1863, during which the Native Americans were removed from the area. Although nothing of the old fort remains, an Indian school and Bureau of Indian Affairs Administrative Office are located there.

Ganado Hubbell Trading Post

Trading posts date to early days when wool, hides, meat, woven materials, whatever the Navajos had to convert to money, were exchanged by traders for cash.

The Hubbell Trading Post is everything a genuine trading post should be, with many bonuses tossed in. It is the oldest continuously operated trading post on the Navajo Reservation. As were other posts, most long gone, it was the contact point at which the Navajo culture and newcomers became acquainted with each other. It became a social center and journey's end for the Native Americans who traveled on horseback to exchange their wares for supplies and trade tokens. John Lorenzo Hubbell bought the post when he was just 23, and soon gained a reputation of being fair and honest with all comers. He was born in 1853 in Pajarito, New Mexico, and quickly assimilated the Navajo lifestyle and language, which put him in demand as a Navajo interpreter. His insistence on superior craftsmanship influenced the high quality of rugs and silver jewelry for which his post became famous. He helped develop the Ganado-style rug, today a classic Navajo design. At one time he and his sons owned 24 trading posts in Arizona and New Mexico. In historical context, this was a difficult time for Native Americans, who were being herded onto reservations and struggling to adjust to a new way of life. Hubbell helped ease the way by acting as a spokesman and go-between with a world that to the Navajo was completely foreign. In 1912, when Arizona was admitted to the Union, he was elected one of the state's first senators.

The post hasn't changed much over the past half century. Declared a National Historic Site in 1967, its shelves are stocked with canned goods, flour, sugar and coffee, with hardware hanging from the ceiling. Counters are built higher than those in a conventional store, to prevent a customer from reaching across and grabbing, and to allow the trader to duck down behind in case bullets started flying. In the rug room, intricately woven products of Navajo looms are casually stacked, each tagged with a weaver's name and a price. A single mound may hold tens of thousands of dollars' worth of rugs (see sidebar, page 57). As you enter the main store, you're walking into a room dubbed the "bull pen," where trading and socializing had equal importance. The process often lasted several days, with overnight guests staying in hogans built especially for that purpose. Although John Hubbell has been gone since 1930, buried on Hubbell Hill overlooking the trading post, things still operate much as they did in the old days. Navajo weavers bring their wares and leave with needed supplies. The post has some of the state's best prices on rugs and jewelry.

Next door to the store is the Hubbell home, an adobe built in 1902, where Hubbell lived with his wife and four children. Tours are conducted during summer months when there is enough visitor demand. The home, with a massive-beamed ceiling, baskets tacked between the beams and amazingly beautiful rugs everywhere, is a showplace of fine books and paintings that are unexpected in this remote place.

The visitor center usually has rug weavers and silversmiths demonstrating their craft who will graciously pose for photos. Picnic tables are just outside the center, but there is no overnight camping. Hubbell Trading Post is on the Navajo Reservation 1 mile west of Ganado and 55 miles northwest of Gallup, New Mexico. The main east-west road is AZ 264 (Navajo Route 3). Coming from the south, take I-40 to US 191 and head north. The post is open daily, 8 A.M.–5 P.M. (6 P.M. in summer), except Thanksgiving, Christmas and New Year's Day. For more information contact the **National Park Service, P.O. Box 150, Ganado, 86505. Website: www.wmonline.com/attract/pforest/hubbell.htm.**

Navajo Rugs

Navajo rugs are one of the most beautiful Native American traditions. Each is a unique work, a product of the weaver's talent, patience and imagination. Although modern dyes and yarns influence the finished products, many weavers still use wool from their own and neighbors' sheep, carding and spinning it themselves.

Quality of each rug will differ. A crisp, flat, tightly woven design will bring more money than one made of nubby, poorly carded wool with loosely woven spots. However, traders will tell you that it is important to choose a rug that you love, one whose appeal will endure. If you are attracted to a nubby, textured surface, you can see beauty in the fact that the rug was made by older hands that may have lost some of their strength, and guided by aging eyes that may not see designs as sharply as they once did.

Among the easiest-to-recognize Navajo rug designs is **Ganado,** which always has a red background. Geometric crosses and zigzags, often with emblems that look like Greek keys, a central design and a solid border are characteristic. It is named for the town of Ganado, home of the Hubbell Trading Post.

Similar to a Ganado is a **Klagetoh,** which usually has a gray background with black, red and white in an uncomplicated main design. **Chief** is the oldest recognized design, characterized by simple bands of red and black. It usually is square so that when the rug is folded the design looks the same as when the rug is fully open.

Two Grey Hills and **Burntwater** are very different from the Ganados because they contain no red, are much subtler, and generally have a more intricate design. Two Grey Hills are among the most expensive because the wool is natural and undyed. The shadings of brown, white and black are created by using wool from different sheep, which requires a time-consuming carding process. Lovely Burntwater rugs are particularly in vogue now because of trends in decorating to pastels and natural tones. Subdued geometric

To weave navajo rugs, some women even shear the sheep, card the wool and dye it, then spin the yarn to create the beautiful intricate patterns and colors in the rugs.

patterns are interwoven in murky yellow, brown, terra cotta, even rose, lilac and pastel blue.

Yei and **Yeibichai** designs contain human figures. The Yei are intermediaries between the gods and the Navajos, and Yeibichai are human dancers that represent Yei. Both patterns are particularly appealing because they are among the few Navajo designs that feature recognizable human figures, although greatly stylized. **Pictorial** rugs also may have human figures but the design will be present-day, similar to the *naive* or *naif* designs of other cultures. It is not unusual for Pictorial rugs to show pickup trucks and trains, along with trees, flowers, sky and other natural elements.

Hopi Reservation

Completely surrounded by the Navajo Reservation, the Hopis on this 1.6-million-acre reservation represent one of the oldest cultures in North America, predating the Navajos, Apaches and certainly the white man. Oral tradition says that they came originally from South America. At one time their lands extended from the Grand Canyon to the New Mexico Border and south to the Mogollon Rim. They had a highly developed agricultural society, an amazing feat considering the harsh desert climate. Although contact was limited, the Hopis acquired horses, burros, sheep and cattle from the Spanish during the 1500s and 1600s. Smallpox was an unwelcome Spanish acquisition, devastating the Hopi population and reducing it from about 10,000 in 1634 to fewer than 3,000 several years later. Navajo marauding, unchecked by ruling Mexico in the early 19th century, also decimated their numbers and further reduced Hopi lands. In 1962, as a result of a lawsuit brought by the Hopi, they were given exclusive use of a specific area and joint use, with the Navajo, of a larger area, to which the Navajo previously had prevented Hopi access. To this day the conflict is ongoing, say many Hopis. Today there are close to 10,000 tribal Hopi members, about 7,000 of whom live on the reservation. About 70 percent rely on the sale of arts and crafts for part of their living, constantly striving to weed out bogus products.

Twelve Hopi villages are poised on, or located at the bottom of, a series of three mesas that project out from Black Mesa to the north. Loosely strung along AZ 264, most Hopis live in or near these villages. Proper behavior when visiting any village means no photography, recording or sketching of villages or ceremonies. Please heed the restrictions, as in the past actions of thoughtless tourists have resulted in the closure of various areas, some of which have just recently been reopened to visitors. The Hopi Reservation is highly sacred to those who live there. There are no areas set aside for visitors to hike, bike or walk. So please do not attempt to explore on your own, and leave an area immediately if asked to do so. **Keams Canyon** is the first town as you head west into Hopi territory, but it isn't one of the villages. It's a government town with the Bureau of Indian Affairs Hopi Administrative Agency headquarters at its center. The canyon, lined with cottonwoods, can be a cool place to picnic. **McGee's Indian Art Gallery** has a good selection of Indian handwork, and you can stay at the 20-room **Keams Canyon Motel (520-738-2297)** where rooms are in the $$ range.

First Mesa

Fifteen miles west of the town of Keams Canyon, the first three Hopi villages are poised on top of First Mesa, with **Polacca,** at its foot, as an access point. A steep, winding road snakes up the side of the mesa to the villages. The feathered sticks you may see along the roadside are Hopi prayer sticks, called *pahoes*. The most spectacular and the most restricted of the First Mesa villages is **Walpi,** which dates to A.D. 1100. On a narrow promontory that drops off steeply on three sides, ancient stone buildings sit next to structures of concrete block in an amazing juxtaposition of centuries. Stones in the ancient buildings, brought by hand to this remote place, are smaller than those in the two more recent villages, which were brought by cart. The 360-degree views are breathtaking. The peace-loving residents planned it that way, so that anyone approaching from any direction was visible when still miles away. As you walk you'll see patterned pottery shards, remnants of the work of artists of centuries ago who plied a craft that the Hopis of First Mesa are famous for today. Kachina dolls and weavings also are among their art forms. If you pick up a pottery shard, be sure you replace it once you've examined it. It is strictly forbidden to take anything from the mesa. You also may find a tiny shell or a bit of a feather that has fallen from a ceremonial costume during a lively dance. A handful of families still live in Walpi, mostly older Hopis who were born in the low-ceilinged houses. A few sell arts and crafts to visitors, but with neither electricity nor water, life is primitive. A half-hour walking tour of Walpi is conducted on request (you're not allowed in without a guide), led by a Hopi guide who knows the history and nuances of this ancient place. You can drive to **Hano/Tewa** and then to **Sichomovi,** the first two villages on First Mesa, and leave your car at Ponsi Hall where you arrange for a guided walking tour. For information contact **First Mesa Consolidated Villages, c/o Tourist Office, P.O. Box 260, Polacca, 86042; (520) 737-2262.**

Second Mesa

Ten miles west of First Mesa, at the junction of AZ 87 and AZ 264, is **Secakuku Trading Post,** which also has a restaurant and grocery store. The **Honani Gallery** has a good selection of well-crafted jewelry. The villages here are **Shungopavi, Sipaulovi** and **Mishongnovi.** Hopis living here are known for their coiled baskets, kachina dolls and silver overlay jewelry. The **Hopi Cultural Center** is on this mesa, with a restaurant and motel connected to the museum and gift shop. The restaurant has good basic fare as well as Hopi tacos, and tostadas served on fry bread. The museum has a good representation of Hopi ceremonial objects and dress, and the baskets and pottery for which Hopis are famous. Open Mon.–Fri., 8 A.M.–5 P.M.; Sat.–Sun., 9 A.M.–3 P.M. Closed weekends, mid-Oct. to mid-Apr. **(520) 734-6650.** The **Hopi Cultural Center Motel** has 33 rooms in the $$$ category, a price that goes down during winter. It's the only motel in the area, so reservations usually are needed. **P.O. Box 67, Second Mesa, 86043; (520) 734-2401.**

Third Mesa

Another ten miles west, Third Mesa has villages scattered throughout the western part of the Hopi reservation. Here craftspeople excel at making wicker baskets, kachina dolls, fine weavings and silver overlay jewelry. **Oraibi** dates to A.D. 1100 and is generally considered the oldest continually inhabited settlement in the country. **Hotevilla** is the most recently established village. Following an altercation between two chiefs in Old Oraibi in 1906, the group supporting the loser, You-ke-oma, broke off and set up its own village. Today village men plant vegetables along the slopes of the mesa. **Bacavi**, located just across from Hotevilla, was established by clans from Hotevilla as a result of yet another clash. Near the bottom of Third Mesa, **Kykotsmovi,** one of the youngest villages, branched from Oraibi in the 1800s. The **Hopi Tribal Offices** are located here. Although there is no formal visitor center, information usually is available at the public relations office within the tribal offices. Call **(520) 734-2441, ext. 106** to reach the Public Relations Dept. In town you can get groceries and some supplies at **Kykotsmovi Village Store.**

Tuba City

Located on the Navajo Reservation, yet named for a Hopi chief, Tuba City is actually about 47 miles northwest of Hotevilla, which is on First Mesa on the Hopi Reservation. The 80-room **Tuba City Quality Inn** with rates in the $$$ category can be a good base for exploring the area. Call **(520) 283-4545** for reservations, which are necessary in summer. A few fast food places also are strung along US 160. The town of **Moenkopi** on the Hopi Reservation is just two miles southeast of Tuba City. This Hopi village was once a Mormon settlement.

St. Johns

St. Johns is located in the southern part of Indian Country near the junction of AZ 61 and US 191/180. If you approach this little town from the south, you'll drive through rolling grasslands that supplied early ranchers with unlimited grazing land. You can see for more than 50 miles in any direction. About 27 miles north of Springerville on the banks of the Little Colorado River, St. Johns originally was called El Vadito, which means Little Crossing. In 1879 Mormon pioneers changed it to San Juan, which was almost immediately anglicized to its present form. At an altitude of 5,725 feet, it is the site of a 16,000-pound woolly mammoth discovery, and dinosaur bones found in the area attest to its ancient dwellers. More recently, in 1540, Coronado crossed the river here. Generations later descendants of the conquistadors returned to settle. As the seat of Apache County, its history is preserved in the **Apache County Historical Society Museum.** Open Mon.–Fri., 9 A.M.–5 P.M. Donations accepted. Its displays include mammoth tusks, miniature dioramas that depict Navajo life, lovely old handmade quilts and other trappings of daily life in early St. Johns. **180 W. Cleveland (P.O. Box 146), St. Johns, 85936; (520) 337-4737.** The **Equestrian Center of White Mountains** is a renowned mecca for horse shows, dressage and hunter-jumper competitions as well as ongoing clinics and camps. On Memorial Day weekend the annual High Country Stampede is held here.

Concho Valley Country Club

Surprisingly popular considering its relatively remote location, this little club is about 15 miles southwest of St. Johns. The 18-hole, 6,656-yard course (from the championship tees) plays to a par 72 and has a number of tricky water hazards created by a spring-fed stream that wanders among greens and juniper-framed fairways. The year-round course and adjacent lounge attract out-of-the-area players with golf packages that include overnight accommodations. Located about 20 miles northeast of Show Low on AZ 61 near the town of Concho. **(800) 658-8071.**

St. Johns Chamber of Commerce, in the same building as the museum, is open 9 A.M.–5 P.M., Mon.–Fri. **P.O. Box 178, St. Johns, 85936; (520) 337-2000.**

Lyman Lake State Park

Boaters love this 1,200-acre park because the 1,500-acre lake is so large that there is no restriction on boat size. There is, however, a no-wake (5 mph) restriction at the lake's west end to accommodate fishermen who regularly pull limits of walleye, largemouth bass and channel cat from the clear waters. So far as aesthetics go, some people are unsettled by the otherworldly landscape, perceiving it as desolate. Others appreciate the pristine contours and sparse vegetation, interrupted only by scattered stands of cottonwoods. The park is in the far south reaches of the Painted Desert (see page 64) and in the ancient past was a vast lake. Today's lake, named for Mormon Bishop Francis M. Lyman, was formed in 1915 when the Little Colorado was dammed to create an irrigation reservoir. Snowmelt from Mount Baldy and the Escudillo Mountains keeps it filled. There are paved boat ramps, rest rooms and showers. The campground has 38 hookups with shelters, 40 developed campsites as well as beach camping with few facilities. There is a pleasant picnic area with tables and shelters. Best seasons to visit are spring through fall. At this 6,000-foot elevation winters can be brutal. On Saturday and Sunday, from Memorial Day weekend through Labor Day weekend, the park pontoon boat will take a maximum of 14 visitors across the lake for a **Petroglyph Hike.** The 10 A.M. tour covers a moderately difficult petroglyph trail that leads to a number of rock art sites. The 2 P.M. tour, reached via the park van, goes to Rattlesnake Point Pueblo Ruin, a 14th-century excavated site consisting of several rooms. Yes, those are genuine buffalo at the entrance, correctly called American bison, a herd of seven at this writing. They were introduced by the St. Johns Chamber of Commerce in the 1960s simply to add a bit of local interest. The stock is rotated regularly to keep the herd viable. Located 10 miles south of St. Johns on AZ 81/US 180/191. **P.O. Box 1428, St. Johns, 85936; (520) 337-4441, fax (520) 337-4649.**

Raven Site Ruin

Part of an active archaeological dig, this 800-room pueblo was a major pottery production and trade site during its occupied days from around A.D. 1000 to 1450. It is named Raven Site for the images of the glossy birds found on excavated pottery, proving that the ancestors of today's noisy creatures lived in the area centuries ago. Prehistoric cultures often had bird names for their clans. One of the site's most interesting programs involves inviting the public to participate in hands-on archaeology projects to learn the processes of restoration, reconstruction and preservation that help ancient people tell their tale. You may participate in one-day or week-long digs, which include bunkhouse lodging and meals. Special two-hour and half-day hikes into the fossil beds and petroglyph areas may be arranged. Reservations are required.

At the museum site, two ancient trucks that long since saw their last flat tire are now display stands for petrified wood, which may be purchased. The museum has a truly fascinating display of pottery, ladles, arrowheads, deer and antelope bones fashioned into awls and weaving tools and other artifacts obtained from the site. If you can stand the overwhelming smell of mothballs, pop into the door marked "Insect Room" to see a display of the creepy crawlies, including tarantulas and scorpions, that are part of the state's insect population. They're all safely skewered behind glass. The knotty pine-paneled gift shop has good handcrafts, carvings, baskets, jewelry, and on the second floor, a fine selection of kachinas and Navajo rugs. The site is open May to mid-October with self-guided tours daily at 10 A.M. and 5 P.M. and guided tours at 11 A.M. and 2 P.M. daily. Guided petroglyph hikes are held at 9 A.M. and 1:30 P.M. daily. Small fee. The museum and gift shop are open daily, 10 A.M.–5 P.M. There is space available for tenters and self-contained RVs. Raven Site and the White Mountain Archaeological Center are located 16 miles south of St. Johns, 5 miles south of Lyman Lake and 12 miles north of Springerville on US 180/191. **HC 30, St. Johns, 85936; (888) 333-5859 or (520) 333-5857.**

Holbrook

This little town at a 5,000-foot high desert elevation along Historic Route 66 has a rich western history, and also serves as a jumping-off point for the Petrified National Forest and the Hopi, Navajo and Apache Reservations to the northeast. When the railroad reached this point in 1881, it brought savvy money men who recognized the land's potential to nourish livestock. It became part of the Aztec Land & Cattle Company, which owned more than 2 million acres of prime grazing land. Nicknamed the Hashknife Outfit because its curved-T cattle brand looked like the chopping utensil used by the ranch cook, its cowboys were the roughest, toughest hombres ever to invade the West, so goes the legend. Holbrook remains a ranching center today, although on a smaller scale.

Festivals and Events

Old West Days

first Saturday in June

A quilt auction, arts and crafts sales, roping demonstrations, a Bucket of Blood 21-mile bike race, 10K run and more make this one-day festival a favorite annual event.

Indian Dances

June through August

Monday through Friday during early evening hours, young people of Navajo and Hopi ancestry perform culturally related dances on the historic courthouse lawn. Accompanied by drum music and dressed in native costumes, they present colorful powwow-type performances.

Major Attractions

Petrified Forest National Park

Millions of years ago, the forces of nature replaced the woody pulp of ancient trees with bright jasper and quartz crystals, as well as iron and manganese, creating a rainbow forest of petrified logs and fossils. The dusky reds, pinks and coppery yellows echo the shades used by present-day Southwestern Indian artisans. This 146-square-mile park is one of breathtaking scenery and is a respected center for scientific discovery and archaeological research. Established as a national monument by Teddy Roosevelt in 1906 and elevated to national park status in 1962, its protection put an end to decades of destruction by visitors who saw the unusual logs as decorative accents for yards and gardens.

The 100,000-acre park's ecosystem dates back 230 million years to the Triassic period of the Mesozoic era, when bizarre, early life-forms worked their way toward becoming dinosaurs. The park's Chinle Formation is recognized as one of the world's most complete examples of the Triassic period. The visitor center at the park's north end is a good place to get an overview of what you're going to see, and to learn about recent dinosaur discoveries. The Rainbow Museum, just inside the park's southern border, is filled with Triassic skeletons. Highlights are the Puerco Indian Ruins, where foundations of rooms and a kiva are remnants of a large agrarian culture that lived along the Puerco River. Agate House, dating to A.D. 1150, is an easy one-half mile walk from the main road parking lot along a path studded with huge logs. Built about 900 years ago of chunks of petrified wood, it is partially reconstructed.

Once viewed as simply a lovely curiosity, the Petrified Forest continues to reveal fossil beds, petroglyphs and other elements that help scientists understand the history of the earth. You can take the 27-mile drive through the park in 45 minutes if you don't stop. But the best tactic is to allow a full day, pausing at places that interest you. Spend an extra day and you can hike into one of two wilderness areas. Be prepared for rarified air at the park's 5,400-foot elevation, and be sure to take water, especially during summer months when temperatures can be an arid 100-plus.

There are no campgrounds or lodging in the park, but you usually can find a place to stay in Holbrook or Winslow. Although it is forbidden by law to remove any pieces of petrified wood from the park (rangers estimate they lose a ton of petrified wood a month to visitor thievery, some of which comes back when the takers realize it brings bad luck), you can purchase them for a very small amount at several Holbrook shops. Since only 10 percent of the forest is protected, there is plenty on private land. The park is open daily, 8 A.M.–5 P.M., with extended hours during summer months, when budget and staffing permit. Small entry fee. The museum is at the southern entrance, at Rainbow Forest, 20 miles southeast of Holbrook on US 180. **(520) 524-6822.**

The Painted Desert

The northern reaches of Petrified Forest National Park have become known as the Painted Desert for its multicolored formations pigmented by minerals that reflect light. Although all part of the same geologic formation, the Painted Desert portion has spectacular overlooks and particularly vivid colorations. Try to be here in the early morning or late afternoon when the less direct rays of the sun bring out exceptional richness of color. Painted Desert Visitor Center at the north end is smaller than the center and museum at Rainbow Forest on the south, but has a good video that introduces you to the park. Usually open the same hours as Rainbow Forest Museum, but that can change, so call first. This entrance is located off I-40, 25 miles northeast of Holbrook. **P.O. Box 2217, Petrified Forest, 86028; (520) 524-6228.**

Seeing and Doing

Holbrook Visitor Center and Museum

The 1898 Navajo County Courthouse, now a well-planned visitor center, was the oracle from which justice was dispensed for 78 years. In 1976 all county offices were moved to a location south of Holbrook (named for Henry Randolph Holbrook, who was the chief engineer for the Santa Fe Railroad when it reached the town). For five years the stolid building was vacant. Then it was rescued by the Navajo County Historical Society, which encouraged local residents to donate furniture, keepsakes and photos to chronicle area history. More than a dozen exhibits depict early Holbrook life, including a drugstore and soda fountain complete with prescriptions, wire-back chairs and soda glasses. It looks as if the guests have just finished slurping up a sweet concoction. Upstairs the original courtroom, judges' chambers and law library remain much as they were when in use. Don't miss the jail cell near the entrance. It was shipped to Holbrook from St. Louis and used until the building closed. Prisoners' graffiti still decorates the walls, verifying that this grim, dark place afforded little in the way of entertainment. No one ever escaped. Open daily, 8 A.M.–5 P.M. Donations accepted.

E. Arizona St. and Navajo Blvd; (520) 524-6558.

Rock Art Canyon Ranch

About 13 miles from Winslow and 19 miles from Holbrook is a remote area with some of the finest Anasazi petroglyphs in the Southwest. Cowboys take you on a tramlike vehicle to Chevelon Canyon, which at one time supported a large pre-Columbian population. On the walls of this spectacularly lovely gorge, with the river a gentle flow at its bottom, are hundreds of well-preserved petroglyphs. The Baird family, owners and stewards of this natural treasure, are multigeneration residents of the area and delightful hosts. You can do a whole-day excursion, adding hiking and a wagon ride to your petroglyph excursion. Or you can go for just half a day, tailoring the time to your desires. For groups, a barbecue dinner may be served in a building filled with artifacts. The ranch has the last remaining bunkhouse of the Hashknife Outfit, now restored. The important thing to the Bairds is that you have an interesting, relaxing time, and come away with an appreciation of an area and a lifestyle that exists in very few places. The ranch is open May 1 to Oct. 30 for meals and is open year-round for tours. Closed Sunday. You'll definitely need directions on how to reach the remote ranch, so be sure to call or write first. **Brantley Baird, P.O. Box 224, Joseph City, 86032-9999; (520) 288-3260.**

Jack Rabbit Trading Post

This is one of those "Hey dad, we wanna stop" places, hyped by an endless succession of signs with the silhouette of a huge black and yellow jackrabbit poised for a giant leap. It's filled with the expected souvenirs and jackrabbit-shaped gew-gaws, but also has a good selection of turquoise jewelry, various rocks, geodes and crystal and books about Route 66. Its claim to fame is cherry cider. Between Holbrook and Winslow on Route 66 near Joseph City. **P.O. Box 38, Joseph City, 86302; (520) 288-3230.**

Where to Stay

Hotels, Motels & Inns

Off-season (winter) rates are a bargain in this area, if you aren't afraid of cold and snow.

Wigwam Hotel—$$

This is another of those "Hey Dad, we wanna stay in a teepee, can we please, please, please?" places. There's no question that this village of conical overnight accommodations appeals to the spirit of adventure in every child's heart, and the kitsch buried in many adults. It's Holbrook's most photographed site. Never mind that it was only the Plains Indians that used teepees, and this sort of structure historically was found only in the Midwest. The concrete and wood wigwams were opened in 1950 along what was then Route 66 by Chester Lewis and still are in the family. They mimic other similar wigwam villages that appeared across the country in the 1940s and 1950s, as a postwar public responded to no more gasoline rationing and took to the road. Recently revovated, the wigwams have one or two double beds, a private bath and simple furnishings. During summer months advance reservations are essential. **811 W. Hopi Dr., Holbrook, 86025; (520) 524-3048.**

In the Winslow-Holbrook area, this kitschy trading post celebrates its position on Historic Route 66.

Campgrounds

Cholla Lake Park

The largest body of water in northeastern Arizona, the 360-acre lake is leased to Navajo County by Arizona Public Service, a state power company. Swimming, boating and fishing are among the activities, but most people come to use the campground because it is close to the Petrified Forest. There are full hookups, dump station and rest rooms. Showers are available from mid-Mar. until Nov. 1. A ranger is on site. The park is located 8 miles west of Holbrook, one mile off I-40 at Exit 277. For reservations call **(520) 288-3717.**

Holbrook Petrified Forest KOA

Open all year, this is the closest campground to the Petrified Forest and Painted Desert, which are 17–22 miles away. The 132-site park has long, level pull-through spaces and a pleasant grassy tent area. It is open year-round, but the pool is swimmable only from May 1 until Oct. 15. From I-40/AZ 77 take Exit 289 and go south 1.4 miles to Hermosa Drive, turn left (east) and go 200 yards to the entrance. **102 Hermosa Dr., Holbrook, 86025; (800) 562-3389.**

Services

Holbrook Chamber of Commerce is located in the same building as the Navajo County Museum, **100 E. Arizona St., Holbrook, 86025; (520) 524-6558 or (800) 524-2459, fax (510) 524-1719.**

Winslow

Between Holbrook and Winslow, I-40 parallels old Route 66 for most of the way, but the historic road's personality has been submerged by the new highway. Winslow came into being in 1881 when the Atlantic and Pacific Railway sited a terminal here and named it after General Edward Francis Winslow, railroad president. Before that, a number of Native American tribes crossed the Little Colorado River at what is now Winslow as they ventured south and west to trade.

In old photos, Winslow's streets are lined with motor courts and diners that catered to a postwar motoring public. But in 1979 Winslow was bypassed by I-40, and the town languished. Reminders of these days exist side by side with authentic cowboys who attest to the town's enduring ranching importance.

Today Winslow is reinventing itself as a mecca of nostalgia, depending on tourism for much of its income. When the Eagles sang about the town in the 1970s on their "Take It Easy" album, the "Standin' on the corner in Winslow, Arizona" lyrics gave the town an additional bit of cachet. Reminder Advertising, an office supply company with a good selection of books, now occupies the building on the song's corner at Second Street and Kinsley. A large sign identifies the famous spot, making it perhaps the most photographed site in Winslow. The original sign was stolen several years ago, but within days an anonymous benefactor installed the one that's now there, thus assuring the corner's immortality.

Festivals and Events

West's Best Rodeo

mid-September

In addition to sanctioned rodeo events, a new component called Standin' on a Corner-Winslow Heritage Days has been introduced to this two-day festival. Events, held in City Park four blocks north of historic Route 66, include an International Gallery of Taste featuring ethnic dishes with local origins and a display and sale of quilting, carving, silversmithing and more by local artists and crafters. Local groups including gospel singers, Native American dancers, Mexican folk dancers and others usually perform.

Christmas Parade

Saturday before Thanksgiving

For more than half a century Winslow has been home to the state's largest Christmas parade. It draws more than one hundred entries while the town in general is packed with bands and equestrian groups. Shriners from all over the state don classic makeup and costumes to become clowns. If you long for the style in which a small town celebrates, this is the place to be.

Seeing and Doing

Old Trails Museum

This eclectic place holds one of the best collections of Route 66 memorabilia around. It's easy to spend a couple of hours here. You'll find a little bit of everything, including an original Route 66 sign studded with "reflector marbles," precursors of today's reflective paint. Just inside the door is a copy of the famous Eagles album on which Winslow is mentioned. Train buffs will appreciate the tableware, timetables and posters from the Santa Fe Railroad and the days when passengers stopped at luxurious La Posada Harvey House. Museum hours vary, so it's best to check first. **212 N. Kinsley, Winslow, 86047; (520) 289-5861.**

Homolovi Ruins State Park

More than 300 archaeological sites include four major 14th-century pueblos of the Homolovis, called Anasazi by archaeologists. These people were ancestors of the Hopis. As with many such sites, much has been lost to collectors and antiquities dealers, but enough crumbling walls and pottery shards remain to paint a vivid picture of the civilization as it once was. Hopis consider this a sacred site. It is illegal to remove anything. The visitor center has good background information on the park and conducts a number of programs and activities, mainly during summer months. You can hike among pueblo ruins, and bring a picnic to the campground and day use area where there are grills and tables. Fifty-two spaces with hookups, plus rest rooms and showers are not heavily used. The park is 3 miles northeast of Winslow. Take I-40 to Exit 257 and continue 1.3 miles on Hwy. 87. **HC63-Box 5, Winslow, 86047; (520) 289-4106. E-mail: homolovi@pr.state.az.us.**

Brigham City

Restoration is in progress to bring this slice of history back to the point where it can adequately convey what life once was in this Mormon community. In 1876 a group of families arrived at the northeast edge of what is now Winslow, along the Little Colorado River, to build a settlement that would attract additional pioneers. But within two years, it was clear they'd built on a flood plain. After a number of washouts and an ongoing struggle with alkaline water, the community was abandoned. Very little is left of the 7-foot-high fort walls, sawmill, crockery plant and homes. Check at the Old Trails Museum to find out how the project is progressing.

Meteor Crater

This gigantic, privately owned hole in the ground was created 49,000 years ago when a massive meteor impacted with earth at nearly 45,000 miles per hour. You'll be awed by the enormous chasm, which you can view from observation decks that overhang the rim. If you think the topography looks like a moonscape, so did NASA, who used the site to train Apollo astronauts. **The Museum of Astrogeology** at the crater has excellent information on the crater's formation and the role it plays in earth and space sciences. You can touch a 1,406-pound meteorite, the largest piece of the main rock that has been found. Snacks may be purchased to enjoy in Astronaut Park where tables and facilities invite relaxing (you aren't allowed to bring in your own food). Meteor Crater is 20 miles west of Winslow. Exit I-40 at the Meteor Crater exit (239) and travel 6 miles south. Open May to Sept., 6 A.M.–6 P.M.; Sept. 16 to May 14, 8 A.M.–5 P.M. Moderate fee. **P.O. Box 181, Flagstaff, 86002-0070; offices (520) 289-5898; crater (520) 289-2362.**

Where to Stay

Hotels, Motels & Inns

La Posada—$$$

Although still a work in progress as of this writing, close to three dozen rooms are ready for guests. Built in 1930 as the last of the chain of luxury resorts along the route of the Santa Fe excursion trains, this former Harvey House is getting a second chance at life and has become a catalyst for the town as a whole to revitalize. It closed in 1957 when the popularity of railroads succumbed to burgeoning automobile travel, and the railroad made it their office headquarters. It was designed by Mary Colter, an innovative architect now considered ahead of her time for her environmentally sensitive structures. She also created most of the other Harvey Houses, including Bright Angel Lodge at the Grand Canyon. The rambling Spanish tile-roofed building, made of steel, brick and concrete, is structurally perfect, say its new owners. Fluorescent lights and dropped ceilings added in the 1950s have been removed to reveal graceful arches, murals and lovely structural details. Rooms are being renovated in their former colors and style. Many have original fixtures and floors. La Posada recently was placed on the National Register of Historic Places. Although a fraction of the original number of trains now tootle past, the charming inn appeals to a new generation of travelers fascinated by how the West used to be. **303 E. Second St., Winslow, 86047; (520) 289-4366. E-mail: laposada@igc.org.**

Camping

Meteor Crater RV Park

As you get off I-40 heading toward the crater, this newer park offers desert landscaped pull-through spaces and full hookups. Facilities including showers, rec room, playground, laundry, country store and gas station are new and clean. Spaces usually are available, but in prime summer months reservations are recommended. Tent spaces available. Call **(520) 289-4002 or (800) 478-4002.**

Where to Eat

Falcon, The Family Restaurant—$–$$

When Pete Kretsedemos traveled through Arizona by train as he returned from the service, he fell in love with the state and vowed to come back. He opened this homey eatery in 1955, selling thick hamburgers for 45 cents. Travelers along Route 66 gobbled them up, and now the children of these travelers return to the Falcon along with the locals, who have eaten here for generations. A complete lunch, for under $5 including soup and dessert, can consist of meat loaf, chicken and noodles, liver and onions or other home-style fare. Homemade soups and pies are a specialty. On tables, "IQ Testers," those wood triangles studded with golf tees, challenge diners to leave just one tee standing. The adjacent cocktail lounge has a complete liquor-bottle chess set on display. **1113 E. Third St.; (520) 289-2342.**

Services

Winslow Chamber of Commerce

There is a small room with displays of area Indian cultures here, as well as a good selection of printed material on regional places of interest. **300 W. North Rd. (P.O. Box 460), Winslow, 86047; (520) 289-2434.**

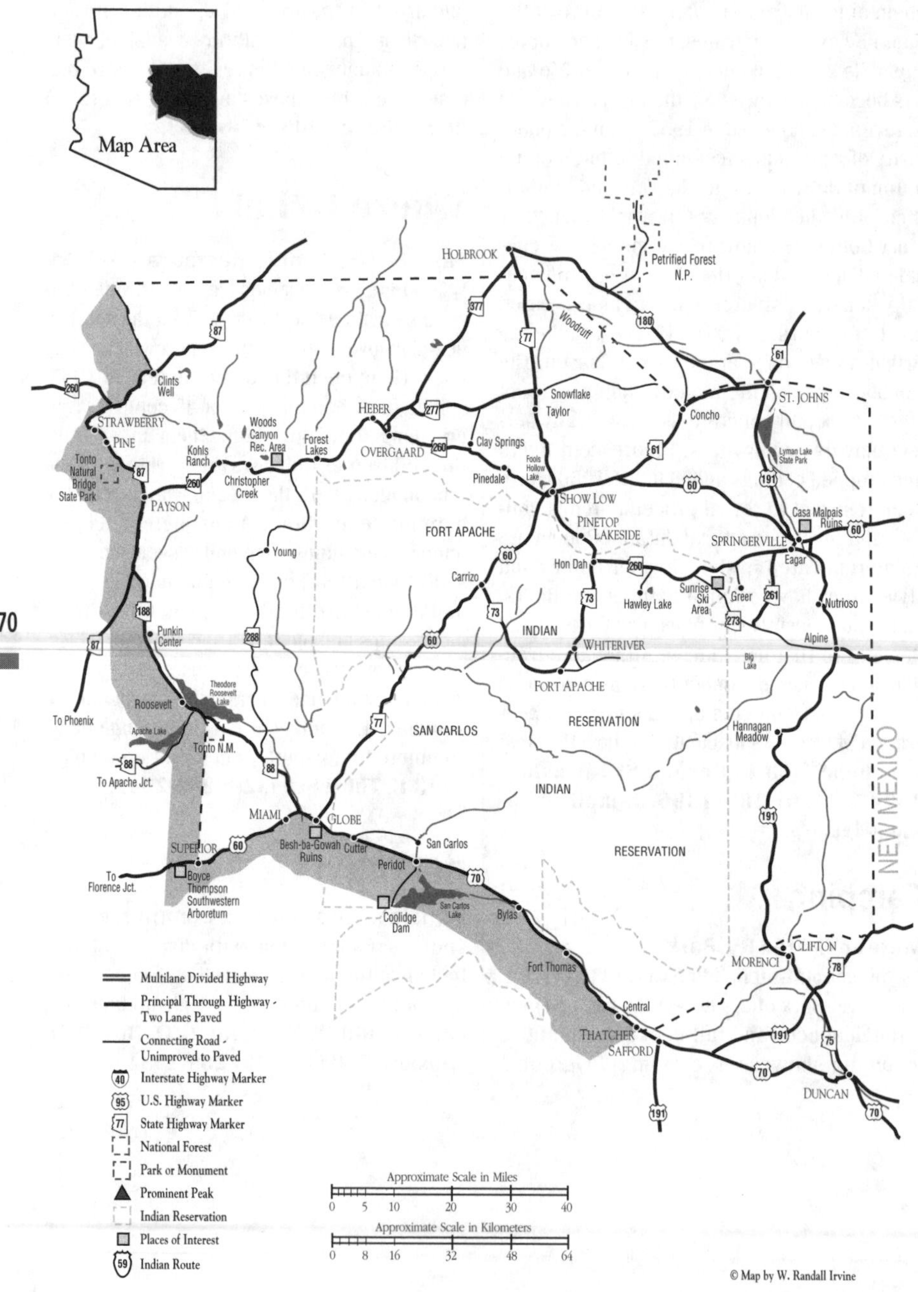

East Central—Above and Below the Rim

East Central—Above and Below the Rim

Springerville and Eagar

These small sister cities located in Round Valley, a high mountain bowl just outside the northern boundary of the Apache Sitgreaves National Forest, make a good starting point for recreation opportunities in the entire area. From its beginnings as a trading post in the late 1800s, run by Henry Springer for whom the town is named, Springerville has become a headquarters for lumbering and cattle ranching. An 18-foot statue on Main Street across from the post office, *The Madonna of the Trail*, is one of twelve such monuments built across the country in the 1930s as a tribute to the contributions made by pioneer women. Eagar is named for three Mormon pioneer brothers. The first, John T. Eagar, settled 4 miles south of Springerville in 1871. Keep your eyes open for pronghorns while in this area. They look like small deer with a fluffy white rump and often sprint across meadows near highways. Two significant seasonal events are the **Christmas Electric Light Parade**, held in early December, followed by the **Christmas Eve Festival of Lights**, and the **4th of July Annual Round Valley Western Celebration and Rodeo.**

Major Attractions

Casa Malpais Archaeological Park

Ancestors of the Zuni and Hopi, known as the Mogollon people, originally occupied this prehistoric site whose name means "house of the badlands," believed to have been built between 1250 and 1380. The 1.5-hour guided tour winds past an astronomical observatory, a ceremonial plaza and a Great Kiva, probably once roofed. The site can be windy, and at one point you scramble down a rope ladder and climb up a rocky tunnel, but the view on top is terrific. If you're at all interested in ruins, it is well worth the time. A short interpretive trail has two dozen stopping points with informational signs. Tours originate from the museum in downtown Springerville, where excavated artifacts are on display. The site is 2 miles north of Springerville on AZ 60. The museum also serves as the chamber of commerce office and is open daily, 9 A.M.–4 P.M. Tours leave at 11 A.M. and 2:30 P.M. Small fee for tours. Mailing address is **P.O. Box 31, Springerville, 85938.** The museum is located at **318 E. Main St., Springerville; (520) 333-5375.**

Renee Cushman Art Museum

Housed in a special wing of the meeting house for the Springerville and Eagar Third Wards of the Mormon Church, this small but important collection was a gift to the Church from Renee Scharf Cushman. It includes an engraving attributed to Rembrandt, three Tiepolo pen drawings, and dozens of other works of European art and furniture that date from the Renaissance to the early 20th century. Open by appointment only, which may be arranged through the Round Valley Chamber of Commerce, **(520) 333-2123.**

Little House Museum

Put together and maintained through the efforts of a local historian, this museum presents life as it was in log cabins during the days of outlaws and ranching. Niched among the crevices of the Little Colorado River canyon, it traces local history with photos, mementos and lifestyle memorabilia. It is noted for its exceptionally good collection of antique nickelodeons, player pianos and music boxes that still work. The museum is on X Diamond Ranch property. Open May 15 to Labor Day. Tours (the only way to see the museum because much of the contents are quite fragile) are offered Thu. through Sun. at 11 A.M. and 1:30 P.M., and Mon. at 1:30 P.M. The museum is closed Tue. and Wed. Located 7 miles west of Eagar on South Fork Road, 3.2 miles south of AZ 260. **(520) 333-2286.**

Where to Eat

Los Dos Molinos—$$$

The food here is so hot, they sell T-shirts and temporary tattoos attesting to the fact that diners ate here and survived. But you have only to ask for less fiery fare, and it will be served to your liking. Located on **E. Main St.; (520) 333-4846.**

Mike's Place—$$$

On the east edge of Springerville, this eatery is noted for its steaks cooked over an open fire. They're huge. **65 N. D St. and Hwy. 60; (520) 333-4022.**

Where to Stay

Hotels, Motels & Inns

Among the no-surprises accommodations are the **Springerville Inn** with 55 rooms and a restaurant **(520-333-4365)** and the 49-room **Reed's Motor Lodge (800-814-6451 or 520-333-4323),** both in the $$ category and located right in Springerville.

Hannagan Meadow Lodge—$$$–$$$$

On the Coronado Trail about 53 miles south of Springerville, this is where you go when you really want to leave the madding crowds behind. At 9,100 feet, the historic lodge is the highest year-round occupied facility in Arizona and is about as remote as you can get and still have running water. Yet there are a very good dining room, country store and gas station on site. The lodge was built in 1926 and completely renovated in 1996, bringing rooms and cabins well into the comfort range that most travelers expect. Lodge suites with private baths are located on the second and third floor of the main lodge. Rustic, authentic log cabins are set back from the main road, up a small hill

among pine and aspen. During winter months the lodge rents skis and snowmobiles as well as ice skates to try on the lodge's outdoor rink. Dogsled races are a favorite participation event. During summer months guests usually come for hiking, fishing, mountain biking and horseback riding. **HC 61, P.O. Box 335, Alpine, 85920; (800) 547-1416 or (520) 339-4370.**

Services

The **Round Valley Chamber of Commerce** serves Springerville, Eagar, Alpine and Greer. It is in the same building as Casa Malpais Museum at **318 E. Main St., Springerville, 85938; (520) 333-2123.**

Alpine

Coronado Trail Scenic Byway

Between Springerville and Morenci, US 191 wiggles along high mountain roads through the Apache-Sitgreaves National Forest and some of the state's most scenic countryside. It is said to be the route taken by Francisco Vasques de Coronado more than 400 years ago as he searched for the fabled Seven Cities of Cibola. Exceptional views are the main focus of this spectacular drive that winds for 121 miles through craggy mountains and fragrant pines. From Alpine, going south to Morenci, it's pretty desolate so be sure your gas tank is full and you have emergency road equipment. The good news is that the road is paved and in good condition, unless you cross it in early spring just after winter has taken its toll. The drive is particularly popular from the middle of September through October when fall oxidizes the oak, maple, mountain ash and aspen into brilliant colors. It is not a good idea to attempt the entire trail during winter months as it may be impassable in spots because of heavy snowfall. However, the sections at either end are reliably open. Beginning from Springerville, the road descends almost 5,000 feet, passing through life zones similar to those between Canada and Mexico. Along the way, you'll come to **Nelson Reservoir,** which is stocked with trout and has rest room and parking facilities as well as boat launch ramps.

The town of Alpine looks like an Austrian village with its pine-covered slopes and views. It is at the intersection of US 191 and US 180, which enters from New Mexico. The chamber of commerce hosts a January dogsled race, and the Alpine Ranger District hosts a Winter Fest that includes a snow sculpture competition, ski events, sled races and a toe-warming bonfire. During summer months hiking is a popular sport. There are several restaurants in town and during the winter you can rent cross-country ski equipment. For information contact the **Alpine Chamber of Commerce, Box 410, Alpine, 85920; (520) 339-4330.** Call well in advance as they'll return only local calls, but will send information on request.

About 22 miles south of Alpine on Forest Road 29B there is a small campground at **Hannagan Meadow.** A 4,000-foot drop at **Blue Vista Overlook** creates dramatic views of the Blue Range Mountains and the valleys below. A short nature trail begins at the parking lot. The old mining towns of Morenci and Clifton mark the trail's end (see page 291 for more on Morenci and Clifton). The drive takes about four hours if you keep moving. For more information contact the **Alpine Ranger District** at **(520) 339-4384.**

Big Lake and Crescent Lake

The season at these scenic little lakes lasts from about the end of April to sometime in November, depending on weather. At 9,229 feet, it cools off to jacket weather even at summer's peak. The attraction is trout fishing, including rainbow, brook and cutthroat, and good bank fishing from the dam. It's said that more trout are taken from Big Lake than any other Arizona water, which stands to reason since it is stocked each spring and fall with more than 300,000 fish. But many campers come just to enjoy the cool pine air and peace and quiet. There are a store and boat rental, but no accommodations.

The largest campground, Rainbow, has 157 full hookups, clean rest rooms, showers and spaces that allow for privacy. **Brookchar** and **Cutthroat Campgrounds** are for tent camping only. **Rainbow** and **Grayling** are for RVs and tent camping. A store and marina are close by. From AZ 260 about 3 miles west of Eagar, turn south onto AZ 261 and follow it to AZ 273, a total of about 24 paved miles, to Big

Lake. **Winn Campground,** 2 miles from AZ 273, has amenities. You may reserve any of these campgrounds by calling **(800) 280-CAMP.** About 10 miles south of Big Lake, **Buffalo Crossing Campground** is at the east fork of the Black River. There are a number of remote first-come, first-served campgrounds in this area. The Forest Service has an office near Crescent Lake, which is your best bet for getting maps and information on camping in the area.

Greer

A wonderfully remote small town 5 miles south of AZ 260 at an elevation of 8,525 feet, Greer sits in a valley that is most people's idea of what a high alpine valley should be. It has fewer than a hundred permanent residents, most of whom run the charming lodges that accommodate winter snow-seekers and summertime guests looking for a heat escape. It is named for Mrs. Ellen Greer, whose cattle-raising family established the town in the late 1800s. Entering town, you'll pass a cross-country ski area with 37 miles of groomed trails. Sunrise Ski Area is about 16 miles away. North of town three small lakes are stocked with trout as are the headwaters of the Little Colorado River nearby. Take AZ 373 south from AZ 260 about 16 miles west of Eagar and proceed 5 miles to Greer. The paved road ends there. For more information call the **Round Valley Chamber of Commerce, 318 E. Main St., Springerville, 85938; (520) 333-2123.**

The **Butterfly Lodge Museum,** a log cabin built in Greer in 1914, is named for the area's proliferation of the fluttery creatures. It was the home of author James Willard Schultz and later his artist son, Hart Merriam Schultz, also named Lone Wolf to honor his mother's Blackfoot Indian heritage. The cabin is listed on the National Register of Historic Places. Open Memorial Day to Labor Day, Fri.–Sun., 10 A.M.–5 P.M. A small donation is requested. Located on AZ 373 just north of Greer.

Outdoor Activities

Fishing

The Greer Lakes, which include Bunch, River and Tunnel Reservoirs, are well stocked with large rainbow and brown trout. Those who know say that at River the shallow areas on the south side of the lake are best. The lake has rest rooms and a boat launch. Fly fishing is the method of choice at Tunnel, which also has a boat launch.

Hiking

Butler Canyon Nature Trail provides a soothing stroll along a path lined with interpretive signs that identify trees and plants, and explain geological features. Look for the marked trailhead just before you enter Greer. On the other side of town, a marked forest hiking trail winds along the creek and leads to Sheep's Crossing.

Trail Rides

With so many great places to hop on a horse and explore, horseback riding is big in this area. **Lee Valley Outfitters** does one- and two-hour, half- and all-day rides as well as hayrides. On AZ 373, one-quarter mile from the AZ 260 turnoff. Look for the Spade Ranch sign. Call **(520) 735-7454.**

Where to Eat

Greer as a whole is so tiny that you can simply drive along the town's one road and pretty much see it all. A number of resorts including **Big Ten, Greer Lodge** and **Greer Mountain Resort** have restaurants, but they may be open seasonally. **La Ventana at the Peaks Resort** has the area's most upscale menu with more sophisticated fare. The restaurant opens for dinner Friday and Saturday evenings, except during winter months, and also has Sunday brunch during the summer. **Cattle Kate's Boarding House** is open the year-round and serves three meals a day. **Molly Butler Lodge** is open for dinner throughout the year. **Snowy Mountain Inn** is open daily for dinner during summer months, closed Mon.; open weekends and holidays for dinner the rest of the year.

Where to Stay

Camping

Fairly new and set among towering Ponderosas, **Rolfe C. Hoyer Campground** is about a mile north of Greer on AZ 373. Hookups, showers, toilets and its proximity to town make for easy, civilized camping without sacrificing an in-the-woods feeling. Call **(520) 735-7313.** Overflow camping is available 2 miles north at **Benny Creek Campground,** close to the Greer Lakes that have reliably good trout fishing.

Lodges and Cabins

Wonderful guest accommodations that range from basic housekeeping cabins to elegant lodges line the narrow road that meanders through the pines. Most have minimum stays on weekends and holidays.

Red Setter Inn—$$$$

This bed and breakfast is a hand-hewn log lodge with guest rooms on three levels. Some rooms have whirlpool tubs, fireplaces and private balconies overlooking the river. **P.O. Box 133, Greer, 85927; (520) 735-7441, fax (520) 735-7425.**

Big Ten Ski Resort—$$$–$$$$

Open all year, there are nine rustic yet modern cabins set among the pines and completely furnished for housekeeping. The Big Ten pizza and chicken restaurant is on site and has carry-out. **P.O. Box 124, Greer, 85927; (520) 735-7578, fax (520) 735-7390. E-mail: bigten@cybertrails.com. Website: www.wmonlilne.com/bigten.**

The White Mountain Lodge—$$$

Built in 1892 as a family home, the lodge's rooms include a full breakfast. Housekeeping cabins have fireplaces. Open all year. **P.O. Box 143, Greer, 85927; (888) 493-7568 or (520) 735-7568, fax (520) 735-7498.**

Greer Lodge—$$$–$$$$

Overlooking the Little Colorado River, the Greer Lodge has spacious, airy rooms that open onto a main living room from two floors. Housekeeping cabins are scattered around the property. The lodge is open all year; the riverview dining room and lounge are open during the summer and on a limited winter schedule. **P.O. Box 244, Greer, 85927; (520) 735-7216.**

Molly Butler Lodge—$$–$$$

Built in 1910, this lodge has rustic, homey rooms. Open all year. **P.O. Box 134, Greer, 85927; (520) 735-7226.**

Greer Mountain Resort—$$$

Located just north of town, this resort has an RV park with eight full hookups, as well as rooms, cabins and an on-site restaurant. **P.O. Box 145, Greer, 85927; (520) 735-7560.**

Snowy Mountain Inn—$$$

Situated on 100 quiet, off-the-road acres, this inn has main lodge rooms and log cabins. A private pond for guests only is stocked with catch-and-release rainbow trout. **P.O. Box 337, Greer, 85927; (520) 735-7576.**

Services

The Round Valley Chamber of Commerce serves Greer and is located in Springerville at **318 E. Main St., Springerville, 85938; (520) 333-2123.**

Show Low

The town is "named after a turn of a card" say its brochures. If you believe a pair of partners homesteaded 100,000 acres, then had a falling-out and agreed to settle their differences in a poker game, then the town's name makes sense. Marion Clark and Croyden E. Cooley played a game called Seven Up that went into the wee, small hours. Cooley needed a single point to win. According to accounts, Clark then said "you show low, and you win." When Cooley cut the deck he turned up an unbeatable card, the two of clubs. The main street, Deuce of Clubs Blvd. (same as US 60) is named for that card. With the Mogollon Rim just to the south and the White Mountains to the southeast, Show Low has become a big outdoor recreation hub. It is 175 miles northeast of Phoenix and 195 miles north of Tucson. The **Freedom Fest,** held the 4th of July, is a fun, typically small-town celebration with a parade, softball tournament, a huge fireworks display and arts and crafts show at the Main Street Market Place. **Theatre Mountain,** which operates April to October, is an acclaimed community group of thespians that presents a series of comedies, musicals and melodramas at 7:30 on Friday and Saturday nights. Special Thanksgiving and Christmas presentations also are part of the schedule. Check with the Chamber of Commerce (see Services) for a schedule.

Major Attractions

Show Low Historical Museum

In an unimposing store front in what used to be the police department (a jail cell still exists), this collection of local memorabilia includes prehistoric Indian artifacts, a Silver Creek Railroaders display, an old time kitchen and photos of Show Low as it once was. The museum is open May 1 to Oct. 25, Tues.–Sat., 1–5 P.M. **542 E. Deuce of Clubs Blvd., Show Low; (520) 532-7115.**

Outdoor Activities

Fishing

Fool Hollow Lake Recreation Area

This 149-acre lake is surrounded by 800 acres of recreation area on Forest Service land. Fishermen can launch boats at two separate ramps to pursue bluegill, bass, channel catfish, walleye, crappie and rainbow trout. Motors up to 8 hp are allowed. There are 92 RV hookups and 31 developed tent sites, each with picnic tables, water and fire rings. The center has five shower buildings with rest rooms, a dump station and fish-cleaning station. This great site appears to be underused on winter weekdays, but overflows during July and August. Spaces are wooded and well planned so that each has maximum privacy. Developed campsites for tent camping in Bald Eagle Loop have wonderful views of the lake through fairly heavy woods. During summer months, a campground host is in residence in a marked space. Located on Show Low's northwest edge. Take AZ 260 west 2 miles to Old Linden Road. Turn right and proceed another 2 miles. Signs will direct you to Fool Hollow. An on-site manager may be reached at **(520) 537-3680.**

Show Low Lake County Park

Also called Navajo County Park, early spring trout fishing is the attraction here. So say anglers who seem to have equally good luck from the shore or from a boat. It's not surprising since the 100-acre lake is stocked weekly with 1,800 of the feisty fish during summer months. With an average depth of about 20 feet, the lake also has catfish, bluegill, walleye and largemouth bass. It holds the state record for yielding a 12-pound walleye. No live bait is permitted. Tent and RV sites with picnic tables are set among pines. Facilities include a small store, showers and bathrooms, boat rental and launch and dump station. The park is leased from Phelps Dodge Corporation, which built the dam here to provide water for its mining and metallurgical operations at Morenci under a water exchange agreement with the Salt River Project. The park is located 6 miles south of Show Low on Show Low Lake Road, one mile off State Route 260. **(520) 537-4126.**

Nature Preserve

Pintail Lake Wild Game Observation Area

This preservation area was built in the late 1970s by a young biologist named Allen Severson, and within a single season had attracted capacity numbers of birds. Migratory geese, ducks and other water birds rest here among unique grasses and reeds. You can get close-up looks at various species (depending on the time of year) from observation platforms and an enclosed blind. The lake's slender, white-breasted namesake likes the preserve so well it has become a permanent resident. Informative signs along the entrance trail, leading to the blind, point out local vegetation. The fences are there to keep free range cattle out, not to confine creatures in the preserve. Try to get there in the early morning or at dusk for best sightings. Take AZ 77 about 3.5 miles north of Show Low, turn east on Pintail Lakes Road and proceed one-half mile. A one-quarter mile paved trail, wheelchair accessible, leads to the lake.

Golf

Silver Creek Golf Club

This public 18-hole, par 71 championship course in the White Mountains has lots of undulation in and around the bunkered bentgrass greens, creating challenging play. There are four sets of tees, the longest at 6,813 yards, playing to a par 71. Although about 35 snow days a year make the course unplayable, it is considered a four-season course. Located 7 miles north of Show Low and 5 miles east of AZ 77 on White Mountain Lake Road. Call for tee times. **(520) 537-2744.**

Show Low Country Club

With grass fairways and bentgrass greens, this par 70 course has distinctively different front and back nines. One meanders through the pines, the other through the meadows. Both are scenic and playable the year-round. On the western side of Show Low at the intersection of AZ 260 and Old Linden Road. Call for tee times. **(520) 537-4564.**

Where to Stay

Hotels, Motels & Inns

For more of a selection of resorts (although there are some in Show Low) head south to Pinetop and Lakeside. Here there are plenty of choices for uncomplicated overnights in basic motels, most along Deuce of Clubs Blvd. in the $$–$$$ range.

Mogollon Rim

This unique geologic feature is named for Don Juan Ignacio Flores Mogollon, from 1712 to 1715 the Governor of the Province of New Mexico, which was a portion of New Spain at that time. It forms a natural division between the Colorado Plateau and the Gila-Salt River watersheds, extending from northwestern Arizona into New Mexico and marking a fault line that runs through the state. Massive uplifting during the Paleozoic Era created the sheer walls of horizontally layered sedimentary rock at a time when the area was populated with fishes, sea life and primitive forms of emerging mammals. Simply put, it is a 200-mile-long escarpment from the edge of the Colorado plateau that is sheer and steep in some places, more gentle in others, that was created 600 million years ago. The best-known section, and the most spectacular in terms of scenery, is the portion that begins just beyond Payson below the rim and extends to Pinetop/Lakeside, on top of the rim. If you do the Mogollon (pronounced Muggy-own) Rim Interpretive Trail (see page 84) the vistas provided by scenic overviews will help you understand how these cliffs were created. You also can see how the storm patterns coming in from the Pacific and Gulf of Mexico are affected by the massive rim. One reason that the area is so lush is that clouds, in their effort to float over the rim, release the heavy rain that they're carrying. Moisture falling on top of the rim flows into the Little Colorado River. Below the rim, rainfall trickles to the Gila, Salt and Verde Rivers.

The Pines Resort—$$$–$$$$

This totally civilized, cozy and comfortable place offers 46 luxury one-, two- and three-bedroom condominiums with fireplaces and full kitchens. **2700 S. White Mountain Rd., Show Low, 85901; (800) 537-4632 or (520) 537-1888.**

The 200-mile escarpment called the Mogollon Rim is sheer and steep in some places, and is heavily wooded, providing wonderful hiking and camping opportunities.

High Country Bed and Breakfast—$$$–$$$$

We didn't stay here, but friends recommend any of the four quiet and charming rooms here in the tall pines. **1291 B. E. Woolford, Show Low, 85901; (520) 532-0567.**

Camping and RV Sites

Though the campground at Fool Hollow Lake serves mainly RVs, there is a picturesque area for tenters. See Fool Hollow Recreation Area.

Pine Shadows Mobile Home & RV Park. The upscale adult park is open May 1 to Nov. 1 and has 129 spaces with hookups, telephone lines and cable TV. **4951 S. White Mountain Rd., Show Low, 85901; (520) 537-2895.**

Where to Eat

All you have to do is cruise Deuce of Clubs Blvd. and take your pick. Most restaurants are in the

$$ price range. **Guayo's (520-537-9503)** in town, and **La Casita (520-537-5179)**, 4 miles south on AZ 260, are part of the group of 11 top-notch Mexican restaurants operated by the Esparza family. They've been local favorites for almost 20 years. **Branding Iron Steak House (520-537-5151)** serves up great steaks for lunch or dinner. Others along the boulevard are **Pat's Place (520-537-2337),** open for breakfast, lunch and dinner with pizza, burgers, sandwiches and spaghetti; and **JB's Restaurant (520-537-1156),** with great baked goods and a buffet. Upstairs is **One Eyed Jacks Bar & Grill (520-537-7460),** the place to go to watch sports on big screen TV.

Services

Show Low Chamber of Commerce, 951 W. Deuce of Clubs Blvd.; (mailing address) P.O. Box 1083, Show Low, 85901; (888) SHOW-LOW; (520) 537-2326 (phone and fax). E-mail: slcofc@whitemtns.com.

Pinetop and Lakeside

This lovely little resort community lures residents from other, hotter parts of the state to its cool altitudes with the slogan, "If you're hot, we're not!" It's almost impossible to tell where Pinetop starts and Lakeside leaves off, but if you have to have a defining feature, Lakeside is further to the northwest and closer to Show Low. Together they make up the hub of the White Mountains resort area. During summer months the traffic on AZ 260, the main street for both towns, can be so heavy that you wonder if anyone is left in any other part of the state. But somehow it all works out, and by early evening most folks have settled into their cabins. Summer mornings can be in the brisk 60s, but days heat up to almost 80 degrees, so if you're hiking be sure to have sunscreen and water. What Phoenicians call monsoons (see page 172) manifest themselves in the White Mountains as cooling showers, briefly sprinkling most afternoons. When the sun sets it can be downright chilly, especially if you're camping.

As long as a thousand years ago, Native Americans lived in the White Mountains. Coronado, in his quest for gold, marched through the area in 1540. By the late 1800s Mormon settlers arrived. As were many towns in the area, Pinetop was founded by Mormons. Pinetop was first called Penrod after William L. Penrod, one of the early pioneers whose family built a sawmill here before the turn of the century. Lakeside, another Mormon settlement, was called Fairview and Woodland until Show Low Creek was impounded to form a lake in the 1890s. It became known as Rainbow Lake, and along with other area lakes now reminds many visitors of northern Minnesota. From early in its history the area has been recognized as a prime vacation spot. Records from the 1920s show that there already were Boy and Girl Scout camps here more than 70 years ago.

Festivals and Events

Arts and Music Festival
mid-June

On a three-day weekend vendors gather at the Woodland Road festival site to sell unique arts and crafts, including ceramics, pottery, jewelry and woodworking items. Food and beer booths, carnival rides for kids and a variety of musical performances are included. The outdoor stage is in-the-round, so there isn't a bad seat in the house.

White Mountain Native American Art Festival
end of July

This popular event, more than a decade old, honors Native Americans through recognition of their cultures. Close to one hundred artisans display and sell their creations and demonstrate how their particular crafts are perfected. Carving, weaving, flint knapping, pottery making and painting are among the skills taught. Native American dancers and storytellers are always popular performers, and visitors can sample fry bread, Navajo tacos, acorn stew, Apache burritos and other ethnic dishes. Events are held at the festival grounds on Woodland Road.

White Mountain Bluegrass Festival
mid-August

Mountain music, cloggers, gospel music, nightly jam sessions as well as craft and food booths are part of this annual festival held in the cool pine woods. If you've longed to make this sort of music on your own, workshops are part of the celebration. There is an entrance fee and some camping available at the site. All events and activities take place at the festival site off Woodland Road about 1 mile south of the traffic light at White Mountain Blvd. (Hwy. 260). Parking is free. For more information contact the **Pinetop-Lakeside Chamber of Commerce** at **(520) 367-4290.**

Fall Festival
late September

If you don't believe that Arizona has a glorious display of fall colors, just head to the White Mountains anytime between the end of September and mid-October (see page 32). Yellow and gold aspen, red bigtooth maples, scarlet sumac and more proudly display their colors. Pinetop/Lakeside celebrates the event with a local talent show, a chili cook-off and a carnival. One of the most popular events is the Run to the Pines Car Show that draws more than 500 pre-1973 vehicles to compete for awards in the categories of Best Paint, Best Engine, Best Interior, Longest Distance and more. Games and music from the 1950s and 1960s also are part of the festivities.

Outdoor Activities

White Mountains TrailSystem

This 180-mile network of pathways and tracks extends across the Lakeside Ranger District of the Apache-Sitgreaves National Forest in a series of multiuse loops and trails. Eventually all loops will connect with each other and with neighboring Forest Service districts, providing opportunities for a number of skill levels. The trails are designed for hiking, mountain biking and horseback riding and range from easy to difficult, with many of the moderate trails suitable for an enthusiastic beginner. Well marked with blue diamond-shaped signs, they range from 4 to 16 miles in length, with trails appropriate for short brisk walks, day hikes and overnight backpacking. An excellent TrailSystem guide is available from the sources below.

It lists difficulty level for each mode of transportation, highlights, distance and trailhead access. The final two trails, 6.5-mile Los Burros, whose trailhead is near McNary on the White Mountain Apache Reservation, and the more difficult 16-mile Ghost of the Coyote that begins west of Show Low on Burton Road, were officially opened in June 1997. **Lakeside Ranger Station, RR3, Box B-50, Lakeside, 85929; (520) 368-5111.** Or, **Apache-Sitgreaves National Forest, Supervisor's Office, Box 640, Springerville, 85938; (520) 333-4301 or TTY (520) 333-6292. Website: www.wmonline.com/attract/trails/hiketip.htm.**

Biking

Many of the trails in this area, part of the White Mountains TrailSystem, remain underused by mountain bikers. A popular trail heavily used by hikers, equestrians and mountain bikers, the **Springs Trail,** a quick 3.8-mile loop, involves smooth and technical riding. It parallels Thompson Creek, crossing it at one point. Connectors to the **Blue Ridge Loop** and **Country Club Loop** (clearly marked) can give you a longer, more challenging ride. To access the Springs Trail take AZ 260 south to Buckprings Road and go 0.6 mile to Forest Road 182. Turn left onto Forest Road 182 (road to Sky Hi Retreat) and go 1.1 miles to the trailhead on the left. For a complete book of mountain bike trails that are part of the TrailSystem, see page 83.

Hiking

Ice Cave Trail

Listed in the TrailSystem guide, this 3.5-mile route is moderate for hikers and equestrians, but difficult for mountain bikers because it has a steep, rocky descent. It probably is named for the cave it passes, from which a flow of cool air continually rushes. You can't enter the cave because it is protected by a fence, but the trail is scenic, winding along Porter Creek and Scott Reservoir. Elevation goes from 6,700 to 7,200 feet, so if you're not accustomed to high altitudes, take it easy. This trail connects to **Blue Ridge Trail,** an 8.7-mile loop, but to do just the 7-mile round-trip Ice Cave Trail, simply turn around and retrace your steps when you hit Blue Ridge. To reach the trailhead, from the Lakeside Ranger Station, travel south on AZ 260 to Porter Mountain Road (FR 45) and turn left. Proceed one mile. The trailhead is on the right.

Mogollon Rim Interpretive Trail

Easy and fairly level, the trail is extremely popular because it follows the very edge of the Mogollon Rim, providing absolutely amazing views. The one-mile loop takes a leisurely hour. The first one-half mile is paved and wheelchair accessible. Shaggy Ponderosa pine, Douglas fir, piñon pine and many types of gnarled, wind-twisted juniper and oak grow along with manzanita and mountain mahogany. Interpretive signs explain that in A.D. 1300 there probably were more people living along the rim than there are now. The early residents used the Ponderosa for fire wood, its gum for healing cuts and scratches, and its needles, when steeped in hot water, created a broth that could cure a cough or cold. You're likely to see Abert squirrels, the ones with light-colored tails, basic gray and ground squirrels, bright blue Steller's jays and probably huge ravens. To access the trail from Pinetop-Lakeside, follow AZ 260, 3 miles west, then north of the Lakeside Ranger Station. Just past Camp Tatiyee, watch for the Mogollon Rim Trail sign. From Show Low go 7 miles south on AZ 260 and watch for the trail sign between Mileposts 347 and 348. Proceed through the V-shaped walk-through and follow the signs.

Woodland Lake Park

This delightful city park is the hub of the White Mountains TrailSystem and has several trailheads including those for Walnut Creek, Pinecrest and Meadowview, although its main function is as a day-use area. It has ramadas with picnic tables, some of which are quite isolated in the woods, a large kids' playground, tennis courts, softball fields, boat dock and fishing. Llama hikes sometimes are offered during summer months. The Woodland Lake Loop is a 1-mile, level, easy walk around the lake. The park is open daily, 6 A.M.–10 P.M. From Highway 260 turn west at Frontier State Bank onto Woodland Lake Road (watch for the green Woodland Lake Park sign) and follow it 0.2 mile to the park.

Fishing

Lakes and streams in the White Mountains are stocked regularly with native Apache trout as well as rainbow, brook, brown and cutthroat. Other species include walleye, bluegill, large and small-mouth bass, catfish, northern pike and arctic grayling. Because many lakes and streams are located near campgrounds, an outing can be a family affair with hiking and mountain biking trails, boating opportunities and birdwatching available for nonanglers.

Near Springerville and Eagar, **Becker Lake** regularly produces large rainbows. **Big**

Bonito Creek, on the White Mountain Apache Reservation, is not only a beautifully wooded area with bear and javelina, but also a good place to snag brown and rainbow trout. Large trout are the attraction at Big Lake near Alpine (see page 74 for detailed information).

At **Fool Hollow Lake** just north of Show Low (see page 78) more than half a dozen species are easy to catch. **Lyman Lake State Park** (see page 61) between St. Johns and Springerville is stocked around Memorial Day by Arizona Game and Fish with 30,000 rainbow trout and channel catfish, thus assuring good summertime catches. It's weedy, small and not particularly picturesque, but if you want to strap on waders or launch a small boat, **Mexican Hay Lake,** 15 miles southwest of Springerville, has been known to yield some real lunkers. **Show Low Lake** (see page 78) near Show Low is a good family fishing site and reliably holds at least six hungry species. Dry fly fishermen say that **Trout Creek** south of Hon-Dah is good for rainbow, brook and brown trout.

On the Apache Reservation, **White River North Fork** is heavily fished because during spring and summer months the tribe stocks it twice weekly. Reports are that Apache trout and brown trout are abundant in the upper areas, while small-mouth bass are best catches in the part below White River and Fort Apache. It's easy fishin' with all the comforts of a well-appointed park at **Woodland Lake** (see page 84) in Pinetop-Lakeside. Go for trout, crappie, bass and bluegill. **Hawley Lake** on the Reservation is one of the few lakes open during the winter, when ice fishing is offered. You also can ice fish at **Luna Lake,** one-half hour south of Springerville. To obtain a permit to fish on the streams and lakes in the White Mountain Apache Reservation, write or call **Fort Apache Game and Fish, P.O. Box 220, Whiteriver, 85941; (520) 338-4385.**

Troutback Flyfishing Guide Service creates customized lake or stream fishing packages for individuals or groups. Because it holds a special use permit with the White Mountain Apache tribe, it has access to areas not open to the general public. The company offers full and half-day trips as well as lessons to introduce novices to the sport. **P.O. Box 864, Show Low, 85902; (520) 532-3474.**

For specific seasons, license requirements, boating restrictions, campground facilities, exact locations, and to find out what's biting where, you can contact any of the following White Mountains chambers of commerce: **Pinetop-Lakeside (520) 367-4290; Round Valley (Eagar, Greer, Springerville) (520) 333-2123; Show Low (520) 537-2326.**

Getting There

The Pinetop-Lakeside area is 190 miles north of Phoenix, about a 4-hour drive, and 90 miles east of Payson, about a 1.5-hour drive. From the Phoenix area there are two routes: From the East and Southeast Valley, take US 60 (Superstition Freeway) through Globe and the Salt River Canyon to Show Low, and proceed south on AZ 260. From the Northeast Valley, Scottsdale, Paradise Valley and Fountain Hills, take AZ 87 north, and AZ 260 east to the area.

Horseback Riding

As for hiking and mountain biking, the White Mountains TrailSystem is your best bet for riding. **Porter Mountain Stable** offers organized one-hour to full-day rides into the Sitgreaves National Forest, including lunch, as well as evening rides with sunset suppers. The stable is located 1.5 miles north of AZ 260 on Porter Mountain Road in Lakeside. Turn east at Milepost 350. **(520) 368-5306.**

Skiing

Sunrise Park Resort

About 200 miles from Phoenix or Tucson and 30 miles east of Pinetop-Lakeside on the White Mountain Apache reservation, this is the Southwest's largest ski area. Its 800 acres are mostly intermediate and beginner runs, with 20 percent of the runs in the expert range.

There are 65 trails on three mountains with five mountain day-lodges. The snow-making machine usually assures at least some skiing, no matter what the weather conditions, although an ample supply hasn't been a problem in recent years. All runs are open to snowboarders. Ten lifts serve all three mountains. Also offered are ski lessons, cross-country skiing and snowmobiling. For a state usually considered a desert, the skiing here is remarkably good, with three 11,000-foot peaks creating terrain that is not so much difficult as it is interesting. There also are groomed cross-country ski trails and a ski rental facility. In summer the area draws hikers and trout fishermen to Sunrise Lake, within walking distance of the hotel. Scenic chairlift rides, hiking and mountain biking also are popular in the area. The 100-room **Sunrise Park Resort** is on-site with prices in the $$$ range. Call **(800) 55-HOTEL.** From Pinetop-Lakeside take AZ 260 east to AZ 273 and the access road with the resort sign. For a snow report call **(800) 772-SNOW.**

Seeing and Doing

White Mountain Apache Reservation

Bordering the Pinetop/Lakeside area to the east, this enormous piece of land covers 1,644,874 acres and is home to some of the area's biggest attractions, including Fort Apache, Hon-Dah Casino and Sunrise Ski Area. The Salt River Canyon (see page 100) is located in the reservation's southern section.

Fort Apache

In 1870 the U.S. Army established an outpost at Camp Mogollon, now called Fort Apache, that was the headquarters for the 1st Cavalry and 21st Infantry. Its purpose was to protect trade routes, to assure the safety of early settlers and to train Indian scouts, among whom was Chief Alchesay. Army scout Croydon E. Cooley, one of the participants in the famous card game that gave Show Low its name, did his job well, and through his efforts this region was spared the violent wars that plagued southeastern Arizona around the same time. Fort Apache includes what is left of General Crook's headquarters, now a small museum. Officers' quarters and horse barns look like they're about to collapse but until recently were used as a school, opened when the fort was abandoned in 1922. Take a short walk along a dirt road up the little hill to the right for a look at the rock-walled cemetery where the men from opposing sides now are buried side by side. The Apache Cultural Center traces the fort's history with photos and old military gear. It also sells some Apache crafts. Fort Apache is located 4 miles southwest of Whiteriver off AZ 73. The Fort is open Mon.–Fri., 7:30 A.M.–4:30 P.M. in summer, one-half hour later in winter. For more information call **(520) 338-4625.**

Hon-Dah Casino

This large, low, natural wood building with a bright turquoise roof is hard to miss. It is the biggest thing in Hon-Dah. To the Apaches its name means "welcome." If you're a slots aficionado, you're practically guaranteed to feel comfortable in a place that has the greatest number of nickel slots in the state. Unlimited progressive jackpots, video gaming that includes poker, keno and blackjack, and live gaming in the poker room are all big attractions. On the 1.6-million-acre White Mountain Apache Reservation, it's one of the few Native American casinos in the state that has live, Vegas-style entertainment in the adjacent Timbers Lounge & Showroom. The Indian Pine Restaurant offers truly fine dining with an excellent selection of fish and beef dishes as well as pasta and pizza. The wine list features a lovely Australian chardonnay. Located 3 miles south of Pinetop. **(520) 369-0299.**

Scenic Drives

General Crook Trail

This trail through the Sitgreaves and Coconino National Forests, also called Forest Road 300, in many places is a faithful parallel of the trail that U.S. Army General George C.

Crook established to move his troops and equipment from Fort Whipple in Prescott to Fort Apache in the White Mountains. It follows the lip of the Mogollon Rim, providing remarkable views. You can hike most any part of the route, or drive along FR 300, which has a fairly decent gravel surface in some areas and is simply graded and drained in others. The road is accessible from a number of points along AZ 260 including Woods Canyon Lake. It can be bumpy and rough, but the scenery and vistas are well worth it. There are about a dozen campgrounds, and you can camp wherever it isn't posted. An excellent hiking map of the Mogollon Rim, produced by *Arizona Highways* magazine in cooperation with the U.S. Forest Service, shows the trail in good detail. It also defines 20 additional hiking trails that branch off from or are near the Rim Trail. It may be ordered from *Arizona Highways* for about $4 by calling **(800) 543-5432.** In the Phoenix area call **258-1000.** Or fax orders to **(602) 254-4505.**

Shopping

The big draws in this area are antiques, collectibles and high-class junque, purveyed from more than a dozen shops strung along White Mountain Boulevard (AZ 260). Just get in your car and hop from place to place. Most shops also are in the business of buying, so if you're looking to cash in on family heirlooms, bring them along.

Where to Stay

You'll find a wide range of accommodations that include rustic little housekeeping cabins tucked away in the woods, luxurious lodges, modern condominiums and basic motels in the Pinetop-Lakeside area. Even some of the budget chains have fireplaces and whirlpool tubs. If you're looking for a resort or cabin, try to plan ahead so that you can get brochures from a number of places to compare what they have to offer. A few of our favorites are listed here, and the very helpful **Pinetop-Lakeside Chamber of Commerce (520-367-4290)** will be happy to provide you with a complete list.

Cabins and Resorts

Northwoods Resort—$$$–$$$$

These charming, white-with-blue, wood-frame places could have jumped off the pages of an Austrian Alps brochure. One- and two-bedroom housekeeping cottages, exceptionally well furnished, are scattered over quiet, wooded grounds. For ultimate privacy, request Honeymoon Cottage #15. It faces the woods, has a spa tub, fireplace, and a wraparound wood deck. Located off AZ 260 at Milepost 352. **P.O. Box 397N, Pinetop, 85935; (800) 813-2966 or (520) 367-2966, fax (520) 367-2969. Website: wwwwmonline.com/northwds/northwds.htm.**

Lake of the Woods—$$$

Here you'll find log cabins in the trees and on the shores of a beautiful little pine-fringed private lake. One- and two-bedroom housekeeping cabins and two larger chalets have two-night minimums. You can rent fishing boats (people-power only, no motors). Fishing is free (no license) for guests. Open the year-round. Located off AZ 260, 7 miles south of Show Low in Lakeside. **P.O. Box 777, Lakeside, 85929; (520) 368-5353.**

In the $$–$$$ Range—

Cozy Pine Cabins (520-367-4558) in Pinetop has six housekeeping cabins; **Hidden Rest Resort (800-260-REST or 520-368-6336)** in Lakeside has 11 housekeeping cabins, some with fireplaces, some with in-room two-person spas; **Meadow View Lodge (520-367-4642)** in Pinetop has ten housekeeping cabins; **Mountain Haven Inn (520-367-2101)** in Pinetop has ten housekeeping cabins; **Rainbow Lake Lodge & Resort (520-368-6364)** in Lakeside has 17 housekeeping cabins; and **Whispering Pines Resort (520-840-3867)** in Pinetop has 28 housekeeping cabins.

RV Parks

Ponderosa RV Resort

Exclusively for those 55 and better, this is a long-term place where guests often stay for up to a year, although overnighters are welcome when spaces are available. Full hookups with paved streets, shade trees, laundry and bathrooms. From Highway 260 in Lakeside, turn south on Woodland Road, and continue one-half mile to the resort. **Rte. 1, Box 570, Lakeside, 85929; (520) 368-6989 (phone and fax).**

Hon-Dah RV Park

Across the street from the casino on the White Mountain Apache Reservation, more than 120 full-hookup sites have satellite TV and phone connections. There are showers, laundry facilities and a recreation room. **(520) 369-7400.**

Camping

Some of the most enjoyable camping in the state is in this area. The 1.6 million acres of the White Mountain Apache Reservation have some of the best-maintained, most remote and picturesque sites. It's best to start by contacting the **Whiteriver and Outdoor Recreation Division, P.O. Box 220, Whiteriver, 85941; (520) 338-4385 or (520) 338-4386, fax (520) 338-1712.** Camping permits are required for each family unit, and camping is restricted to designated areas. Sites may have picnic tables, fire rings, trash barrels, toilet facilities and water outlets, but not all sites have all amenities. There are 36 campgrounds in the Apache-Sitgreaves National Forest, with amenities that range from full RV hookups to primitive camping with cleared areas only. During busy summer months you can make reservations at least five days in advance by calling **(800) 280-CAMP.** Forest Service offices in the area that you'll be visiting also will have camping information.

Where to Eat

There are dozens of places along White Mountain Blvd. Just take your pick.

Charlie Clark's—$$$–$$$$

This log-sided steakhouse has been around since 1938 and features mesquite-broiled chicken and steak as well as huge prime rib and baby-back ribs. Casual and friendly, it's about as close to nightlife as you'll get around here, with live country western music on specified nights. Open for lunch and dinner. Bar opens at 11 A.M. On AZ 260 in the east end of Pinetop, at Main and Penrod. **(520) 367-4900.**

The Christmas Tree—$$$–$$$$

Named for the lighted pine that stands at its entrance, this upscale eatery is famous for its chicken and dumplings. Chicken livers, honey duck and a good selection of fresh fish are menu staples. Open at 5 P.M., Wed.–Sun. **Woodland Rd. and Hwy. 260, Lakeside; (520) 367-3107.**

Chalet Restaurant & Lounge—$$$

A good traditional menu at this family-friendly place includes liver and onions, country fried steak, beef stroganoff, pasta primavera as well as steaks and chicken. Open at 5 P.M., Mon.–Sat. For reservations call **(520) 367-1514** after 3 P.M. **348 W. White Mountain Blvd., Lakeside.**

Chuck Wagon Steak House and 1890 Saloon—$$$

Those who've eaten here say you'd better have a big appetite or count on asking for a doggie bag. Steaks, burgers, chicken and pork are grilled western-style over mesquite, then served with cowboy beans, steak fries, sautéed mushrooms, onions and homemade bread. The saloon has a full bar. Open daily at 4 P.M. in summer, Wed.–Sat. in the winter. **On Porter Mountain Rd. off AZ 60; (520) 368-5800.**

Pinetop Cafe—$$

Great breakfast cafe with a huge menu; it's also open for lunch and dinner. You can chow down on biscuits and gravy, hot cakes and all the stuff you don't eat at home. They have a full bar. Hours vary with the seasons. **436 E. White Mountain Blvd., Pinetop; (520) 367-2517.**

Services

Pinetop-Lakeside Chamber of Commerce, 592 W. White Mountain Blvd., Lakeside, 85929; (520) 367-4290.

Town of Pinetop-Lakeside, 1360 N. Neils Hansen Ln., Lakeside, 85929; (520) 368-6700.

U.S. Forest Service, Lakeside District, RR3, Box B-50, Lakeside, 85929; (520) 368-5111.

Snowflake and Taylor

The neatly tended fields and farms of this gently rolling countryside look much like those of Minnesota and Wisconsin. The towns are named for Erastus Snow and William J. Flake, Mormon pioneers who arrived in 1878 in hopes of colonizing the area for the church. Taylor is named for John Taylor, a president of the Church of Jesus Christ of Latter-Day Saints who was on the same mission. Together they purchased the 5,640-foot-high town site, then known as Stinson's Ranch, for 500 head of cattle. Snow, Flake and Taylor still are prominent family names in the area. This pair of small towns, 16 miles north of Show Low in the valley formed by Silver Creek, has more than one hundred historical homes. Half a dozen are listed on the National Register of Historic Buildings. Among them are good examples of Victorian, Georgian, Greek Revival, Gothic, Colonial and Neoclassical architecture, all part of Brigham Young's master plan for a utopian community. Today the towns still serve as a center for Mormon experience in the Southwest.

A **Historic Walking Tour** map, available from the chamber of commerce, directs visitors to 26 buildings that include the 1889 Greek Revival home of Charles L. Flake, the 1893 Gothic Revival home of John A. Freeman, and the impressive Victorian mansion of James M. Flake, built in 1895. Part of the historic homes tour, the Stinson House is now the **Stinson Pioneer Museum,** built in 1873. It contains memorabilia donated by local residents, including an Edison phonograph, a replica of an early kitchen, and a photograph of William Jordan Flake in prison stripes, jailed for polygamy. A display traces the long, cruel 1846 route of the Mormon Battalion in which 400 ill-equipped and underfed men walked more than 2,000 miles at the behest of President James K. Polk, who hoped to rid the Midwest of Mormonism. The museum is open 9 A.M.–3 P.M., Mon.–Fri.; and 9 A.M.–3 P.M., Sat. Closed Dec. to May. Donations accepted. **102 N. First East, Snowflake, 85937; (520) 536-4331.** The **Pioneer Days Celebration,** held in July, honors the community's builders with a rodeo, ball games, dances, crafts demonstrations, a parade and more.

Where to Stay

Putter's Paradise RV Park

With 90 full hookups and generous spaces, this may be one of the area's best kept secrets, so far as RVers are concerned. But the real lure is the Snowflake Golf Course next door. The RV park is almost entirely populated with golfers who come for the package deal that allows two to play 18 holes a day for a week, for $45. The course is lush and green, and playable the year-round—even in winter when the rye and bluegrass fairways and bentgrass greens are dormant. You can get some great long drives on frozen ground, jokes the pro. Packages may be arranged through the RV park or the course. The course and park are adjacent to each other on AZ 77 about 3 miles west of Snowflake. Summer reservations are essential. **P.O. Box 336, Snowflake, 85937.** Or, **Snowflake Golf Course, Heber Road & Country Club Dr.; (520) 536-7233.**

Where to Eat

Katy's Kountry Kitchen—$-$$

Located on the main drag, this very low-key restaurant has earned a local reputation for its BBQ ribs and homemade baked beans. Breakfast omelettes are more than hearty, filling a 12-inch oval platter, and lunch burgers with fries are huge. The rough-cut knotty pine walls, open beam ceiling and western relics hung on the walls set the tone of the place. Open for breakfast, lunch and dinner seven days a week. **201 N. Main St.; (520) 536-5450.**

Services

The **Snowflake Chamber of Commerce** in the same building as the Stinson Pioneer Museum is open 9 A.M.–3 P.M., Mon.–Fri.; and 9 A.M.–3 P.M., Sat., May to Dec. There are public rest rooms at the Chamber. **P.O. Box 776, Snowflake, 85937; (520) 536-4331.**

Heber and Overgaard

These twin towns, located about 54 miles east of Payson on AZ 260, don't have a lot to tempt you to tarry. You generally just pass through on your way between the Pinetop-Lakeside area and Payson. Heber was a Mormon settlement established in about 1880 and named for Heber C. Kimball, a chief justice of the State of Deseret, 1883.

Navajo County Tall Timbers Park, a pleasant day-use site, is located just outside of Overgaard coming from the east. Most of its traffic comes from groups who live in the surrounding area and reserve the pavilion, then use the racquetball, softball, basketball, volleyball, horseshoes and shuffle board courts. But if you're just passing through, it is a good place to relax with a picnic or get out and stretch your legs. From this point a 12-mile dirt road accesses Forest Road 300, the Rim Trail Road. Snow covers the park and closes it during the winter. During summer months a ranger is on site. For park information call **(520) 535-3404.**

Between Heber and Payson, sufficient snow keeps the cross-country ski facility, at **Forest Lakes Touring Center and Cabins,** active from about January 1 until mid-March. There are 27 miles of groomed double-set trails, with additional ungroomed trails on the other side of AZ 260. They rent skis, poles and boots, and sell trail day-passes. Snowshoeing here is fun, and instructors say it is a good way for parents to move alongside a very young child just learning to ski. Open 8 A.M.–5 P.M. during ski season.

In summer, guests come for day trips to nearby Black Canyon Lake and Willow Springs Lake. The touring center has six rental cabins with kitchenettes open year-round in the $$–$$$ range. The center is located just past Milepost 288 on the south side of road, 14 miles west of Heber. For information call **(520) 535-4047.**

Between Heber and Show Low, **Webwood Acres RV Park and Campground** is a well-kept, off-the-beaten-track area in the tall pines on the edge of the national forest. There are 21 large RV sites with sewer, water and electric hookups, and a separate tent and group-camping area. There are flush toilets, exceptionally clean showers and a laundry room with curtains in the windows. Kids and teens can hike and toss horseshoes, but some have discovered they can take their computers to the laundry room and plug them in to play games. The room also has a large table with puzzles, board games and paperback books. Open mid-Apr. to mid-Oct. From AZ 260 between Mileposts 320 and 321, take Forest Road 139 north about 3 miles to the Webwood Acres sign and turn right. **P.O. Box 914, Clay Springs, 85923; (602) 396-2868.**

Roosevelt Lake and Dam

This impressive construction feat, 76 miles northeast of Phoenix, corralled the Salt River and Tonto Creek, which are fed by snow runoff from the White Mountains. The result created central Arizona's largest lake. Construction of the Theodore Roosevelt Dam began in 1903. When it was dedicated in 1911, the year before Arizona became a state, it was the largest masonry dam in the world. It was part of President Roosevelt's plan to grow the West by constructing a system of irrigation works that would store, divert and develop available water sources. In 1996 modifications were completed using steel reinforced concrete that heightened the dam by 77 feet. The lake's surface area was expanded by 1,862 acres, immediately increasing recreational opportunities. The **Roosevelt Lake Visitor Center,** located 1.5 miles east of the dam, has exhibits, videos and an interactive computer system to let you test your knowledge of how water affects this arid environment. For a true Kodak moment, step out to the back patio. Open daily, 7:45 A.M.–4:30 P.M. For information call **(520) 467-3200.**

Tonto National Monument

Four miles east of Roosevelt Dam and one mile off AZ 88, this Salado cliff dwelling was relatively undiscovered until construction began on the dam. In 1907 it was declared a National Monument. The Salado people lived here for about 300 years, abandoning what must have been a comfortable living site between 1400 and 1450. Archaeologists have found decorated earthenware, probably made by the Salado, as well as sea shells from the Gulf of California, and Mexican macaw feathers that affirm an established system of trade. This was a primarily agrarian culture that built canals to irrigate corn, beans, cotton and pumpkins, supplemented by the deer, quail, rabbit and other game that flourishes in the area. Native plants such as the saguaro cactus that grow here today supplied moist, tender fruit. The Lower Ruin, a small village, consists of 16 ground floor rooms plus a 12-room annex. Interesting features are saguaro cactus ribs covered with clay and used as beams to create a roof. A mano and metate (grinding stone and basin) remain in a room that probably was used for communal food preparation. The larger Upper Ruin had 32 rooms on a first floor, with eight additional rooms forming a second story. A self-guided tour winds upwards 350 feet to the Lower Ruin for a close-up look. It also affords sweeping views of the Tonto Basin, which helps place the site in context as a desirable dwelling place. The path is paved and easy to negotiate, but the rapid elevation gain may dictate frequent stops to catch your breath. The Upper Ruin is accessible only with a park guide, with tours scheduled as interest warrants. Be sure to take water, especially in summer.

As in many parts of the desert, March and April are wild flower months when clouds of yellow brittlebush, little Mexican gold poppies, blue lupine and an occasional firecracker penstemon line the hiking path. The visitor center, which is wheelchair accessible, has a good video that explains the park's history and geology. Displays on the culture and crafts of the Salado further detail their lives at this site. There is no camping here, but a picnic area about one-half mile from the ruins has tables and shade. Open daily, 8 A.M.–5 P.M., except Christmas Day. From Globe, take AZ 88 west, or AZ 188 south from Jake's Corner and Punkin Center. From Phoenix and Apache Junction, for an interesting but slower and rougher route take the Apache Trail, AZ 88 (see page 187). For more information call **(520) 467-2241.**

Where to Stay

Roosevelt Lake RV Park & Motel—$$

On AZ 88 as you approach Roosevelt Lake, there is a cluster of services that include Spring Creek Store and a Texaco station. The RV park here has pull-through spaces and full hookups including cable TV. The motel has standard rooms and kitchenettes with all cooking and eating utensils. Although the site itself is not particularly picturesque, its obvious attraction is that it is within minutes of the lake.

Camping

Facilities for camping at Roosevelt Lake are widely considered the best of any desert lake in the state. Visitors come to fish, launching small car-top boats as well as large trailered craft. Three great campgrounds, developed by Tonto National Forest, offer a variety of choices. Cholla and Windy Hill are available for individuals; Grapevine is reserved for groups of 15 and more. Volunteer camp hosts usually are on site. Sites have shelters, drinking water, fire pits, picnic tables, showers, flush toilets and fish cleaning stations. In addition to the following two campgrounds, there is primitive shoreline camping at **Bermuda Flat, Cholla Bay** and **Bachelor Cove.**

Cholla Campground

The nation's largest all solar-powered campground, Cholla is covered with thick brush for privacy, yet has refreshing lake views. A number of short walking trails branch off, leading through brush and along the lake. It has about 200 sites on six loops, one of which is reserved for tent camping. Loops are named for various types of cholla cactus and include Teddy Bear and Jumping. There are four shower buildings and ten rest room facilities. It is wheelchair accessible. Cholla is 5 miles northwest of Roosevelt Dam. From Phoenix, take AZ 87 north 60 miles to the junction of AZ 87 and 188. Turn right and follow AZ 188 for 28 miles to Cholla. Or from the Miami-Globe area, take AZ 88 northwest 32 miles to its junction with 188. Take 188, 5 miles to Cholla. For information call **(520) 467-3200 or fax (520) 467-3239.**

Windy Hill Recreation Site

This larger 347-site campground is on the opposite end of the lake from Cholla, on a peninsula jutting out into the lake. The nine loops (one just for tents) are named for local creatures like Jack Rabbit and Coyote. It has two high-water and two low-water boat ramps. Vegetation is sparse here, but the campground is fairly new, and with enough rain it will grow. There are several barrier-free, wheelchair-accessible camp units. From Phoenix take AZ 87 north about 60 miles to the junction with AZ 188. Turn right and follow 188 for 33 miles to the junction with AZ 88. Continue on AZ 88 east for 4 miles to Forest Road (FR) 82A. Turn left and proceed 2 miles to the site. Coming from the Globe-Miami area, take AZ 88 north 25 miles to the junction with FR 82A. Turn right and proceed 2 miles to the site. For information call **(520) 467-3200 or fax (520) 467-3239.**

Grapevine Campground

For groups only. Call the above number for information.

Superior, Globe and Miami

These interesting small towns are about an hour's drive from Roosevelt Lake along AZ 88, or you can come from the Phoenix area along US 60. Coming from Phoenix you travel through beautiful saguaro-studded landscape. As you gain elevation the mountains at varying distances appear in shades of gray, as in an uncomplicated watercolor painting. The road follows the bases of massive rock formations. Out of Superior it climbs to picturesque Mountain Pass, through a tunnel where Queen Creek has carved a steep canyon in the craggy Pinal Mountains. From the bridge you get a good look at uplifted layers that provide a framework for understanding area geology. The vegetation changes dramatically over the 2,000-foot elevation gain.

As did most of the towns in this area, **Superior** grew up around a mine, the Silver King, opened in 1875. The rubble piles along the road north of town are mine tailings from the Magma Copper Mine, earlier called the Silver Queen, and the abandoned smelter is another remnant. Exit US 60 to see what remains of this town. Along Main street the Magma Hotel is boarded up, and the only businesses that seem to be functioning are the bars.

Between Superior and Globe-Miami, US 60 is designated as the **Gila Pinal Scenic Road.** Although it is two lane, there are frequent pullouts for passing. Everywhere there is evidence, in tailings and scars on the landscape, of the industry that gave Arizona one of its nicknames, the Copper State. **Globe** and **Miami,** just 5 miles apart, are linked by their mining history as well as US 60. They first flourished during gold and silver days. The discovery of high grade copper ore in the surrounding mountains forever established their identity as mining towns. The Old Dominion Copper Company, one of Globe's first, is among the most famous mining names in the world. During the area's salad days, mining created an affluent upper class of mine managers and executives, as well as a solid middle class made prosperous by the mines. Cattle ranching flourished as well, nourished by grasslands kept green by a stable water supply. But by 1931 the Old Dominion closed down. Copper ore was playing out and the Great Depression was taking its toll. Miami continued to function as a center for ore processing, but on a diminishing basis. In 1982 a final blow was dealt to the area when copper prices tumbled from more than a dollar a pound to less than 60 cents. Businesses foundered and workers moved to other areas.

In the last few years copper prices have rebounded and the Carlota Copper Company has reopened a mine in Globe. Boards have been removed from businesses along Broad Street and new restaurants welcome eager customers. Globe's history is a major draw. Many buildings, solidly constructed in the first place, have endured for decades with enough vitality to give them second lives. Old hillside homes are being bought up and restored. Mining is still the biggest industry, but tourism is fast gaining a toehold in the local economy. Globe is picturesque in a quirky sort of way, with skeletons of mining equipment creating sculptures against a skyline of old open-pit mine tailings. You'll feel especially welcome here because locals have learned the importance of promoting tourism and the pitfalls of an economy that is dependent on copper mining alone.

Festivals and Events

Boomtown Spree

mid-April

True mine aficionados come to Miami for this three-day event, which features the Arizona State Mining Championships. The strenuous day-long competition of individual events includes hand mucking, spike driving, individual and team machine drilling and hand drilling. These skills, essential to the miner's trade, have become much admired, competitive talents. The event, held off and on since 1939, includes a parade, barbecue and fun run.

Copper Dust Stampede Pro-Rodeo

mid-April

This celebration in Globe has everything a rodeo should have—an Old West dress-up competition, three rodeo performances with all the classic rodeo events including PRCA sanctioned bull-riding and calf-roping and a parade with rodeo queens. Team riders through historic downtown Globe, a little buckaroo rodeo for kids ages 3 to 8, and a traditional country western dance cap it off. The rodeo is held at the Gila County Fairgrounds over a Friday and Saturday.

Historic Home & Building Tour

weekend in late February

Globe's Golden Age is the basis for this celebration highlighting the historic homes and buildings that date to the turn of the century and before. Local antiques dealers get together for a show, and quilters participate in a display and sale of their handiwork at the Cobre Valley Center for the Arts.

Annual Apache Jii Day

late October

Jii, the Apache word for "day," an Indian celebration held in downtown Globe, features talented dancers, singers and storytellers from around the Southwest. It's definitely worth going, if only to see the beautiful ceremonial costumes. The Hoop, Jingle and Eagle Dances usually are part of the schedule. The famed Apache Crown Dancers are among the day's highlights. This is an excellent opportunity to see and purchase Native American arts and crafts, worked on all year for this event. Traditional food is available. This one-day event is a good day trip from Phoenix as accommodations in Globe often are booked months in advance.

For information on any of these events contact the **Globe-Miami Chamber of Commerce, 1360 N. Broad St., P.O. Box 2539, Globe, 85502; (800) 804-5623 or (602) 425-4495, fax (520) 425-3410.**

Outdoor Activities

Hiking

The **Pinal Mountain Recreation Area** is within the Globe Ranger District of the Tonto National Forest, about 25 miles from Phoenix and due south of Globe. Summer hiking is popular at these higher elevations because of cool temperatures, but winter with its snow and cold is only for the most intrepid souls. Picnic sites are scattered throughout the area.

Your best bet is to stop at the **Globe Ranger District Office of the National Forest Service in Six Shooter Canyon, Rte. 1, Box 33, Globe, 88501; (520) 425-7189.** From US 60, go left on Oak Street, continue two blocks to Broad Street and bear right at the Y. Follow signs to the office. You can pick up trail guides and get reliable directions. Once there, you're within less than 1 mile of many of the trailheads.

Pioneer Pass Toll Road Trail

This flat, gentle trail for hikers and equestrians was built originally as a toll road to the Pioneer Mine. There are scenic views of Upper Pinal Creek and thick stands of pine. About 3.2 miles one way, the trailhead is at the junction of Icehouse Canyon Road and Six-shooter Canyon Road, near the ranger station.

Sierra Ancha Wilderness

This difficult-to-access wilderness area is rough, rugged, primeval and one of the most scenic areas of the state. The effort, however, is worth it. Filled with high vertical cliffs protecting prehistoric Indian ruins, elevations vary from 4,000 to 7,400 feet. The wilderness is south of the town of Young, but most often accessed from Claypool, between Miami and Globe. By taking AZ 88 north to AZ 288 and continuing north, you are within striking distance of a number of trailheads, beyond which a four-wheel-drive vehicle usually is required. Trails are open for hiking and horseback riding. For the most up-to-date and reliable information, before heading into this area contact the **Pleasant Valley Ranger District, P.O. Box 450, Young, 85554; (520) 462-3311,** or the main office of **Tonto National Forest, 2324 E. McDowell, Phoenix, 85006; (602) 225-5200.** A booklet will be mailed to you on request.

"Rollin' on the River" becomes the song of choice as rafters challenge the quirky Salt River.

River Rafting

Despite the ongoing controversies about water, or lack of it, rafting and floating are popular sports in Arizona. Rafting a river gives you a look at scenery you may see no other way, and if done properly, has low impact on the environment. The state of Arizona requires that rafting guides have first-aid training. Many have Advanced Wilderness First Aid and Wilderness First Responder training as well.

Spring Rafting: March Through May

Salt River rafting depends on snow melt from the White Mountains, which most years provides enough runoff to guarantee a brisk-running river. It's the basis for a good time that ranges from mellow to real high-class abuse. Everything that happens on the Upper Salt River is regulated by the White Mountain Apache Tribe, which owns the land. Private rafting companies pay fees to obtain permits to operate on the Salt. You are not permitted to launch your own raft, and many areas are closed even to hiking. This wild river, whose chilly water requires wet suits, is located above the dam systems so melted snow for white water makes it the earliest spring-running river in the country. The unregulated flow creates some spectacular rapids. You may glimpse an American bald eagle soaring on thermals.

Many trips put in at the US 60 bridge, where guests get suited up and receive paddling instructions, then load into rafts. Rapids are rated on a scale of difficulty from one to six as established by the American Whitewater

Affiliation, with a Class 1 defined as "easy, with riffles and small waves, few obstructions," and a Class 3 as "Intermediate, with moderate, irregular waves which may be difficult to avoid ..." Among the rapids on this stretch is a Class 2 called Kiss and Tell, named for the way the water rushes at a solid rock wall. If inept paddlers allow the raft to bump the rock sideways (the kiss), the raft will tip, bouncing passengers into the chilly flow. On sunny weekends when the river is awash with paddlers, dozens of other rafters can watch smugly (the tell), hoping they aren't next into the drink.

The challenging swirl of Maytag Rapids leaves no doubt about the origins of its name. Mescale, which has been as tough as a Class 4, catapults even an occasional guide into the rushing water. At this time of year, most rapids are ones and twos, but if conditions are right, you'll hit an occasional more challenging rapid. Lunch is set up at a convenient stop, after which rafts continue on to cover a total of about 15 miles of quirky river, arriving at the takeout point at Salt Banks.

Returning to the put-in point requires a conveyance vehicle that's able to negotiate a primitive, single-lane, gravel road, roughly carved from the sheer canyon wall. The transport of choice usually is a bright orange school bus that drivers understatedly dub "a durable vehicle." Rafters may rate the toughest rapids a three but we feel the bus ride back is a definite five.

Far Flung Adventures offers one-, three- and five-day trips in self-bailing rafts with all necessary equipment and comfortable campsites. Camping trips cover a 50- to 60-mile scenic stretch, and one-day trips go from Horseshoe Bend to Salt Banks. **Box 2804, Globe, 85502; (800) 359-2627 or (520) 425-7272.**

Blue Sky Whitewater does one- and two-day trips that include gear, wetsuits, booties, paddle, jackets, food and beverages. Two-day trips include waterproof bags as well. The one-day trip covers 10 miles and 12 rapids. Add another 18 miles downstream for the two-day trip. **143 N. High St., Globe, 85501; (800) 425-5253.**

Sun Country Rafting has one-day tours that cover 10 river miles; two-day tours that cover 20 miles; and 32-mile, 3-day tours. **(800) 272-3353.**

The portion of the Salt River within the Tonto National Forest may be rafted non-commercially by applying for a permit. Request an application packet from **River Permit Coordinator, Tonto National Forest, 2324 E. McDowell, Phoenix, 85006; (602) 225-5200.**

Summer Rafting: June Through August

You can float an 8-mile stretch of the mellow Gila River in comfortable six-person, self-bailing rafts piloted by expert guides. Inflatable kayaks also are an option. You'll see graceful great blue herons, flycatchers, circling vultures and possibly deer. On BLM land, the Gila flows from San Carlos Lake at Coolidge Dam. The lake belongs to farmers who use it for downstream irrigation. The rafting season basically coincides with the growing season. Water is shut off around the first week of September because growing season is over, effectively terminating summer rafting within a week. With never more than a couple of small rapids, there are opportunities to swim in the cool, clean water. The day includes a picnic lunch on sandy shores. Wear your swimsuit but bring a coverup and plenty of SPF 15. Tubing is not recommended because of the large number of submerged logs and clogs of brush. The trip meets at Winkelman City Park in Winkelman, about 90 minutes from Phoenix. Take US 60 east to Superior, then go south from Superior on AZ 177. For information and reservations call **Blue Sky Whitewater** at **(800) 425-5253.**

Seeing and Doing

San Carlos Apache Reservation

This 1.8-million-acre reservation straddles Graham, Gila, and Pinal Counties and includes

Apache Tears

A beautiful Apache legend, centuries old, centers on Picket Post Mountain near the city of Superior. A group of warriors were once cornered by Spaniards. If captured, the braves would become lifelong slaves in Spanish gold mines. But to flee meant tumbling over a precipitous cliff and certain death. Since slavery was an impossible concept for them, the braves chose death.

Later, as the women of the tribe prepared the bodies for burial, they heard a whisper on the wind: "Thy bitter tears shall be turned into beautiful stones, for I should not have made those cliffs so high." The Apaches say the breeze still carries the message of the women's broken hearts. As you walk near Picket Post Mountain, don't be surprised to hear the whispers, then look down to see glossy black Apache tears scattered among the rocks and vegetation. The satiny stones are nodules of obsidian, a glass formed by rapidly cooling lava. The stones are common around Picket Post Mountain, which has volcanic origins.

Native Americans discovered that because obsidian is brittle and heat-sensitive, it fractures sharply, making it ideal for arrowheads, knives and other pointed tools and weapons. Such tools are relatively rare, and each source of obsidian has slightly different characteristics, so archaeologists use them to trace ancient trade routes. Occasionally nodules are red or brown if iron oxide dust is present. Sometimes they are naturally faceted. A type known as snowflake obsidian is dotted with flecks of translucent quartz crystals called cristobalite. Another type, rainbow obsidian, gleams with multicolored iridescence. The semiprecious gemstones are used in jewelry but most often they are simply carried as a token of good luck to encourage the watchful eye of the spirits.

At one time it was possible to prowl a site on the eastern slopes of Picket Post to search for Apache tears, but it is now closed for safety reasons. The stones are inexpensive and widely available at souvenir and mineral shops throughout Arizona. The world's largest Apache tear, a baseball-sized, gem-quality piece of obsidian, is on display at the **World's Smallest Museum** in Superior at Buckboard City, located on US 60 on the west side of Superior. Smaller Apache tears also are for sale. For information call **(520) 689-5800.**

mountains, waterways and Sonoran desert. It was created in 1871 to convert the Apaches to farmers, an enterprise doomed to failure by the very nature of its residents. Over the years the reservation was reduced five times to accommodate the mining industry. In the fall, well into November, miles of golden cottonwoods and salt cedar, also called tamarisk, enrich the Gila River banks in bright contrast to shadowy hills and blue skies. Bird-watchers come to view wintering bald eagles as well as migratory waterfowl on San Carlos Lake, on Talkalai Lake (named for a turn-of-the-century San Carlos Apache policeman) and on many stock ponds. Mountain biking devotees can cruise around San Carlos Lake, down the 700 Road (maps are available at the Recreation & Wildlife Dept., see below) or up the 900 Road. Indian Route 8, 50 miles of paved road, leads to the beautifully wooded Point of Pines area. Be sure to bring water as there is none available on this route.

On the reservation about 20 miles east of Globe, the San Carlos Apache Recreation and Wildlife Office issues hunting, fishing and camping permits for the reservation and can provide trail maps and recreation advice. It is worth the stop for its display of taxidermy-preserved creatures that inhabit the area. Black bear, desert bighorn sheep, puma, deer, fox, birds and fish all have the office as their final resting place after being bagged as trophies from past hunts. The office is open daily, 8 A.M.– 4:30 P.M.; Sun., 8 A.M.–12 noon. On US 70, 20 miles east of Globe, just past Milepost 272 as you head east. **P.O. Box 97, San Carlos, 85550; (888) 275-2653, (888) 475-2344 or (520) 475-2343/2653.**

San Carlos Lake

Created by Coolidge Dam in 1930, this lake became a watery cemetery as it covered an Apache graveyard dating to the 1800s. The U.S. government offered to move the graves before the lake was filled, but Apache leaders felt that disturbing their sleeping brothers would be a desecration, so they accepted the offer to cover the graves with a cement slab. Also at the bottom of the lake are the remains of Camp San Carlos, the original Indian agency station abandoned in 1900. The 19,900-acre lake has excellent bluegill, black crappie, flathead catfish and largemouth bass fishing. You can drive around its perimeter by taking Reservation Road 3 from US 70 at Peridot, about 15 miles east of Globe. The road crosses Coolidge Dam and continues around the lake, rejoining US 70 near Calva. The drive has pretty views of flat-topped mesas and rock formations. In spring elegant, torchlike yuccas dot the desert. San Carlos Lake Marina, a fairly new facility about 7 miles off US 70 on Reservation Road 3, has picnic ramadas, rest rooms and a large boat ramp. Groceries, beer, wine, fishing licenses, bait and camping permits are available at the marina store, behind which is a small RV park with hookups. The setting is quite pretty, with red cliffs and vistas looking east across the lake. For information and RV spaces call the store at **(520) 475-2756.** There are small campgrounds at other points around the lake, including Soda Canyon Point.

On the San Carlos Apache Reservation, the Cultural Caenter offers a good selection of Native American crafts.

San Carlos Apache Cultural Center

This small museum and crafts center on the San Carlos Apache Reservation merits a look-see for the way it details the tribe's history in well-designed tableaus and old photographs. One display shows the Changing Woman ceremony that celebrates the transformation of a girl into adulthood. Old photos show the reservation land being ravaged by an 1874 order of President U.S. Grant to allow copper mining and grazing. In an 1886 photo, the Army recruits Apaches as scouts. Paintings by Native American artists depict tribal scenes, spirits and Apache daily life. The center also is an excellent place to purchase Apache burden baskets, conical receptacles woven of willow and other fibers, often accented with buckskin fringe and metal cones. You're likely to hear Apache spoken here, even though English is the first language on the reservation. Manager Herb Stevens will happily show you (and sell you) jewelry made by local artists from peridot, a light green semiprecious stone that is mined on a nearby mesa, one of only three places in the world that the gem is found. Darker colored stones are of higher quality.

The center is located in the village of Peridot on AZ 70 approximately 20 miles east of Globe. As you go east it's just at the top of a little rise at Milepost 272. You have to watch carefully or you'll miss it. If you come to the Recreation and Wildlife Office, turn around, you've gone too far. Open Tue.–Sat., 9 A.M.–5 P.M. Tribal members free, small charge for others. **P.O. Box 760, San Carlos 85550; (520) 475-2894 (phone and fax).**

Apache Gold Casino & Resort

One of the many low-key casinos that flourish on Arizona's Indian Reservations, this one is filled with a sea of quarter slots. It also has bingo, video and progressive poker as well as live poker, keno and a well-priced buffet. The impressive sculpture that greets visitors, the Apache Games Warrior, holding a hoop and stick, represents traditional games of chance played by the Apaches. The casino is appropriately named for a legend that says the Apache Indians buried a cache of gold deep in a mountainside, which was eventually unearthed by the Mexican Peralta clan. They disappeared, and with them the gold, which occasionally surfaces in myths and legends. There are a Best Western (ask about well-priced Stay and Play packages), convenience store and 60-space RV park with full hookups on the site. An 18-hole golf course is set for competition early in 1999. Located on US 70, 5 miles east of Globe, just inside the boundary of the San Carlos Apache Reservation. Call **(520) 425-7800 or (800) APACHE3.**

Scenic Drives

Highway Mine Tour

This drive may be somewhat questionable as scenic, but if you're interested in the mines that made Miami and Globe famous, and if you see beauty in piles of slag, tailings and oddly shaped equipment, this is for you. The chamber of commerce (see Services) has a brochure with map that directs you to six mines, or their former sites, along AZ 60. The drive begins 6 miles west of Miami between Mileposts 238 and 239, at the Pinto Valley Mine, and proceeds toward Miami-Globe. Other stops are at Milepost 242 at the Blue Bird Mine, at Miami Town Park, at the Cyprus Miami Mining Corp. across from the Copper Hills Inn (look for the FLOSBEs, see page 105), at the Sleeping Beauty Mine that now produces turquoise, and at what is left of the Old Dominion Mine.

Salt River Canyon

This wild and beautiful gorge, a rafter's favorite, exists because the melting snow in the White Mountains flows into the Black and White Rivers, which in turn converge to create the Salt River. Over millions of years it has carved out Salt River Canyon, sort of a Grand Canyon that you can drive into. The Pima Indians named the river for the water's brackish taste that comes from several large salt springs near the western edge of the White Mountain Apache Reservation. It is a natural border between the San Carlos Apache Reservation on the south and the White Mountain Apache Reservation on the north. As you leave Globe heading northeast on US 60/AZ 77, you'll notice that there are no more saguaros at this 5,000-foot altitude. They've been replaced by scrub oak, piñon pine and manzanita spread over gently rolling hillsides, as well as a stand of cottonwoods along Seven Mile Wash. About 40 miles north of Globe at Seneca, which is not much more than a boarded up store, you begin a 6 percent grade down to the bottom of the canyon and the bridge, built in 1934, that crosses the Salt River. The scenery is spectacular, but stay alert. The 2,000-foot descent is 9 miles of wide, well-paved switchbacks that create white knuckles in some but that others find exhilarating.

About a third of the way into the canyon you can pull out at an overlook called Hieroglyphic Point where there are excellent views and petroglyphs carved into black boulders lining the slope below the road. If you're an intrepid hiker, you can scramble up the rocky trail that leads to an even higher vantage point. Back on the highway heading north, just before crossing the bridge there is a small slump-block building with ornamental grating that looks like an office, but it's actually a rest room with composting toilets.

Outside, interpretive signs explain how the bridge was built and tell you that the canyon is inhabited by black bear, javelina, raccoons, mule deer and other mammals. Bald and golden eagles and osprey are frequently seen. Smallmouth bass, bluegill, channel catfish and squawfish live in the river. If you need to gather your nerve before proceeding up the other side of the canyon, break out a picnic and enjoy the views, stroll across the walking bridge for a great photo opportunity, and follow paved paths to the river's edge. A gas station and small market are just north of the bridge.

Those with a high-clearance four-wheel-drive vehicle in the mood to explore can take the turnoff just north of the bridge and follow the dirt road that parallels the river as it heads west. The left fork doubles back under the bridge and heads toward Apache Falls. The right fork takes you past a few primitive campsites along the river to Cibecue Creek, the end of the road for passenger vehicles.

On the way out of the canyon, Beckers Butte Overlook is a worthwhile vantage point for a stop and a few photos looking back at the colorful bridge. The overlook faces its namesake on the canyon's far side.

Because this is Indian-owned land, you must have a permit to get off Highway 77 at any point. They are available for $5 at the Salt River Canyon Inn at the bridge and at a number of outdoors shops in Phoenix.

Parks, Gardens & Preserves

Boyce Thompson Southwestern Arboretum

Plan to spend several hours in this remarkably lovely place near Superior. The 350-acre haven for desert plants, surrounded by the Tonto National Forest, was endowed by William Boyce Thompson in the 1920s. He wanted to establish a place where plants from the world's arid and semiarid regions could be studied, a goal admirably fulfilled in this living laboratory. Many of the drought-resistant plants developed here have become part of Arizona's general landscaping designs. The arboretum, in the shadow of Picketpost Mountain and straddling Queen Creek Canyon, creates a number of life zones in which low-desert, high-desert, and even higher-altitude plants flourish. More than 3,000 water-efficient species from all continents grow here. The arboretum is a project of the University of Arizona, Arizona State Parks and a private operating foundation that supplies volunteers and generates funding through memberships, contributions and endowments. Sales held early in April and in the fall offer Arizona-appropriate plants to visitors. Each September the Arboretum holds a fun event called Bye Bye Buzzards, at which lovers of the unlovely creatures gather to say "arrivederci, vultures," (the correct avian term for buzzards) and send the birds on their migratory way. Lest anyone question why a bird that considers roadkill a gourmet meal is worthy of honor, arboretum officials point out that the birds are true custodians of the desert. They eat nothing live, they take only waste and leave only bones. A bird walk and a program by an animal rescue and rehab organization that

Boyce Thompson Southwest Arboretum is filled with great examples of desert vegetation and exotic plants.

brings creatures in the getting-better process to exhibit to guests follow the vulture send-off.

Trails

Pick up a Main Loop Trail guide at the visitor center and set out for a 1.5-mile, two-hour walk. You'll pass plants typical of the Arizona desert as well as cactuses that represent different geographic areas of the United States. Farther along grows an oddity called a boojum tree, named for the mythical creature in Lewis Carroll's poem "The Hunting of the Snark." Ayer Lake, from which the Arboretum draws its water, shelters two endangered fish species—the Gila topminnow and the desert pupfish. Don't miss the fragrant herb garden or the demonstration garden that explains how to use water-efficient plants in residential landscaping. On other self-guided trails tour an area with landscape trees suitable for south-central Arizona and an extensive cactus garden. Interpretive ramadas along the way afford opportunities for "seeing and smelling."

The strange-looking boojum tree is named for a mythical character in a Lewis Carroll story.

Birds and Animals

Because any stream or water hole in the desert draws animals, more than 300 species live at the arboretum. Snakes, tortoises and toads are dawn and dusk creatures, while lizards enjoy mid-day sun. The presence of night-roaming javelina, deer, coyote, raccoons and ringtails is verified by their droppings, often found near trails. Chipmunks and squirrels are frequently spotted during the day. Pack rats have become so abundant that the resident tortoise shell cat, Miss Kitty, has "ratting" as her primary job description.

Birders make the arboretum a favorite rendezvous because of its 200-plus resident, wintering and migratory avian species. The riparian communities along Queen Creek and Silver King Wash are particularly rich in bird life, especially during winter months when migrants move in from colder climes. Expect to see pine siskins, a number of goldfinches, evening grosbeaks, flickers, phoebes, shrikes and vireos. Stop at the platform at Ayer Lake to see mallards, redheads, ring-necked ducks, buffleheads, mergansers and other water birds. Bald eagles and northern harriers pass through, and several hawk species are seen less frequently.

The gift shop carries an excellent selection of nature books, the expected T-shirts and trinkets, and an unexpected collection of lovely baskets, made by the Tarahumara Indians of Mexico's Copper Canyon. Water fountains are available throughout the property. Rest rooms are at the visitor center and the Smith Interpretive Center. The shady picnic area, beside Silver King Wash, has water, tables and barbecue pits. Pets are welcome but must be kept leashed. The arboretum is located 3 miles west of Superior and 60 miles east of Phoenix on US 60. Open daily, 8 A.M.–5 P.M., except Christmas Day. **37615 E. Hwy. 60, Superior, 85273; (520) 689-2632, fax (520) 689-5858. Website: www.ag.az.edu/bta.**

Museums

Bacon's Boots and Saddles

This fascinating store might seem to belong more appropriately in a Shopping category, but it also could go in Museums or in History. Edwin Bacon, 70, has been making saddles for more than 50 years. His son Earl, 48, works with him. In the Keegan Building, built from adobe in 1895 and partially rebuilt with brick, the pair turn out exquisite handmade saddles that begin at about $1,700 and can go as high as $4,000. But they last forever, says Ed. On the day we visited, Ed was repairing a saddle he made in 1979. The cowboy-owner had given it so much use that his rope had burned the leather off the horn, and Ed was replacing it. Besides the workmanship that involves hand sewing with flaxen linen threads, the aesthetics of each saddle make it a work of art. Elaborately drawn-in floral designs are hand-tooled to create intricate tapestries in leather. The father and son make about 20 saddles a year, putting more than 80 hours of work into a plain saddle, and upwards of 100 into the fancy models. There is a wait of almost a year from the time orders are placed, which pour in from all over the world. If you don't have time to wait for a saddle, drop in this friendly place anyway and pick out a new set of Western duds. The store stocks great boots, hats, jeans, shirts, pants and all the accouterments to make you look like you belong in a saddle whether you do or not. Open Mon.–Sat., 8:30 A.M.–5:30 P.M. Closed Sun. **290 N. Broad St., Globe, 85501; (520) 425-2681.**

Gila County Courthouse

In downtown Globe, the 1906 Gila County Courthouse has been recycled into the Cobre Valley Center for the Arts. In use for 70 years, it was placed on the National Register of Historic places in 1975 and vacated in 1976. Although its bright, airy rooms are now filled with contemporary art, many traces of the old building's grandeur remain. Banisters along the staircase to the third floor are covered with copper from the Old Dominion Mine. The courtroom has become a theater. Excellent local art in stained glass, ceramics, painting, sculpture, photography, jewelry, prints and more is on display and for sale. Plan to spend at least an hour browsing. Open daily, Mon.–Sat., 9 A.M.–5 P.M.; Sun., 12–4 P.M. **101 N. Broad St., Globe, 85502; (520) 425-0884.**

The Cobre Valley Center for the Arts occupies the old Gila County Courthouse building, built in 1906 in Globe.

Gila County Historical Society Museum

This 1914 building used to be the Old Dominion Mine Rescue Station and now houses relics and artifacts from mining days. Mining equipment sits outside, while inside rooms have been re-created to include a mine superintendent's office, a lady's boudoir and other scenarios typical of the era. Open Mon.–Fri., 10 A.M.–4 P.M. Next to the Chamber of Commerce office on Hwy. 60. **1330 N. Broad St., Globe 85502; (520) 425-7385.**

Archaeological Sites

Besh-Ba-Gowah Archaeological Park

There's no hands-off attitude at this 700-year-old pre-Columbian pueblo, whose name comes from the Apache language and means "place of metal" or "metal camp." It has been restored so that visitors can walk into rooms, climb

Besh-Ba-Gowah, a Salado Indian village in Globe, is partially reconstructed to its A.D. 1450 state.

ladders and see the pottery, utensils and furnishings that belonged to this ancient culture. It is thought that the Hohokam were the earliest residents here, leaving around A.D. 1100 to be replaced a century later by the Salado, who constructed the pueblo that stands today. They, too, abandoned the site sometime after 1400, and it became home to the Apaches in the 1600s. It's easy to spend an hour exploring the ceremonial chamber and household rooms where all that's missing are cooking smells and snoozing dogs. The visitor center has the world's largest single collection of Salado pottery, which includes basic utilitarian vessels as well as intricately decorated pots and jars. A small ethnobotanical garden demonstrates the relationships between people and their environment, and illustrates how native plants were used by the Salado. The site can be hot and dusty, so bring water. At the bottom of the hill as you approach the park are several sheltered picnic tables. Open daily, 9 A.M.–5 P.M., except Christmas Day, New Year's Day and Thanksgiving. Most portions of the pueblo are wheelchair accessible. Located on the outskirts of Globe, off Jess Hayes Street. **150 N. Pine St., Globe, 85501 (mailing address only); (520) 425-0320.**

Where to Stay

Hotels, Motels & Inns

Noftsger Hill Inn—$$-$$$

If you had a crush on perky Miss Blanders in third grade, here's your chance to relive school days on your terms. This stately inn, built in 1907 as the North Globe Schoolhouse and later renamed the Noftsger Hill School, sits atop a hill overlooking Globe. Front rooms offer a view of the rugged Pinal Mountains, while those in the rear face the Old Dominion Mine. Arizona luminaries including former governor Rose Mofford were educated here. So much of the school's personality remains that it even has the warm, furniture-polish smell of a schoolhouse. As you stand in the main hallway, it's not difficult to imagine the sound of running feet on the hardwood floors and the cheerful chatter of kids released from their studies. Classrooms, now guest rooms, have high ceilings and original blackboards on which visitors have recorded their comments. One-time coat closets contain clawfoot tubs and pedestal sinks. Owners Frank and Pam Hulme have furnished the inn with mining-era antiques and art, complemented by Mission-style furniture. Rooms with private baths have king or queen beds. A full breakfast is included. **425 North St., Globe, 85501; (520) 425-2260.**

El Rey Motel—$-$$

You'd almost expect to see a little 1930s Chevrolet coupe parked outside this vintage motor court. It looks much like it did in the 1930s and 1940s. However, the Southwestern ranch style, so popular at a time when motoring was the means of choice to explore the country, has been updated with modern comforts. **1201 E. Ash St., Globe, 85501; (520) 425-4427, fax (520) 402-9147.**

Apache Gold Casino Best Western—$$$

This is a good bet if you plan to spend time at the casino. A covered walkway joins the motel with gaming areas as well as the Wickiup Buffet and Apache Grill that serve reliably good, well-priced meals. Rooms are spacious, comfortable and quiet. Located on Hwy. 70, 5 miles east of Globe. **P.O. Box 1210, San Carlos, 85550; (800) APACHE-8 or (520) 492-5600.**

Best Western Copper Hills Inn—$$$

We list this comfortable, reliable chain motel here because it is conveniently located at the junction of US 60 and 70, and it has refrigerators and coffee makers in the rooms. Even though it is on a fairly busy highway, rooms are well insulated and noise doesn't seem to be a problem. The restaurant is open for three meals a day. **Rte. 1, Box 506, Miami, 85539; (800) 825-7151 or (520) 425-7151.**

Camping

There are a number of campgrounds in the Pinal Mountain Recreation Area (see Hiking for how to get to ranger station). At Pioneer Pass along the banks of Upper Pinal Creek, at 6,100 feet, there are about two dozen tent sites, rest rooms and fire grills. Water is available May through October. At Pinal Recreation Site, among tall stands of Ponderosa pine and white fir there is tent space for 22 families, picnic tables, rest rooms, fire grills and water in summer. With just six tent sites at Upper Pinal Recreation Site on the north side of Pinal Peak, it remains quiet and lovely. It has picnic tables, rest rooms, fire grills, two wind shelters and water in summer. For more information on these sites contact the **Globe Ranger Station** at **(520) 425-7189.**

FLOSBEs (pronounced FLOSBIES)

Miami takes an interesting, creative approach to reclaiming the hills of dusty mine tailings that have existed for decades. *Four Legged Organic Soil Building Engineers* (FLOSBEs), known as cattle to most people, rise to the task. Usually thought of as eaters and destroyers of grass, an expert in range management, Terry Wheeler, has devised a way to employ the beasts to restore the grasslands. He began thinking of the chemically depleted, pulverized rock mine tailing as soil, rendered sterile and potentially unproductive by mining operations. He noticed that deer and cattle left manure on the fringes of some of the tailing deposits, and in these places, things were growing. So he tried spreading hay over the dead hills, then penning cattle in selected areas. The small herd slowly stomped the hay into the tailings and ate their way across the hills, doing what cattle do best, making manure. This accomplished the first step in making the mounds fertile and productive. Now cattle droppings fertilize the vegetation, which in turn flourishes so the FLOSBEs have more food.

Where to Eat

For its size, Globe has an unusually large number of excellent Mexican restaurants, almost all of them family-run. A number of small, individually owned eateries, without a trace of chain-food mentality, also offer food truthfully labeled genuine home cooking. Along US 60 on the city outskirts there's no shortage of pizza and burger chains.

Guayo's—$$

Run by the third generation of the Esparza family with a fourth on the way up, the food here is flawless Mexican at its best. The place opened in January 1970. Owner Eddie Esparza jokes that in those early days customers were asked if they'd like their food "with or without [mine] tailings," so fierce were the winds that blew dust from the nearby mines against the little prefab building. Over the years Guayo's was enlarged and improved to today's casually comfortable dining room. Eddie's grandfather, also an Eddie, was nicknamed Guayo, and the name stuck to the restaurant he founded. The family says their grandparents figured that if they owned a restaurant, they'd never starve. It's one of 11 Esparza-owned restaurants in the state. Specialties like green-chili enchiladas and superb beef tamales are served on cheerful Fiesta ware, to top with an unusual, slightly sweet salsa, or a variation with a bit more authority, but still not killer. The restaurant uses fresh, not powdered chili, and the pre-meal bowl of mixed corn and flour tortilla chips is decidedly not prepackaged. **On AZ 88 about 1 mile north of the junction with AZ 60, at the east end of the Apache Trail, between Miami and Globe; (520) 425-9969.**

Globe Brewery & Barbecue Company—$$-$$$

In Globe's historic downtown district, this new (scheduled to open late in 1998) eatery occupies multi-levels of a hand-hewn stone building built in 1905. The 1915 Otis four-level rope-and-drum elevator is still in operating condition. The 20-foot Brunswick-Balke-Collander back bar on the main floor was made in 1888. A copper brewhouse, a glassed-in Cigar Room on the mezzanine, Old West vaudeville-style entertainment and a sports lounge with competition darts make the brewpub a multifaceted place to eat and be amused. Despite its historic personality, food is very contemporary, with nary a fried morsel on the menu. Rather, the chef concentrates on dishes that appeal to today's health-conscious consumers without neglecting favorites like thick steaks and juicy prime rib. Signature breads and desserts are made in the brewpub's bakery, with brewed-on-site beers changing frequently. **190 N. Broad St., Globe, 85501; (520) 425-8227. E-mail: globebrewery@gila.net.**

One man's trash is another man's treasure at the antiques and collectibles shops in Globe.

Guayo's El Rey—$$

This Guayo's El Rey is run by Greg Esparza, brother of Eddie Esparza (who owns the other Guayo's, page 105). The smoke-free atmosphere alone attracts many diners to this low-key place in the town of Miami. Everything is fresh daily and made from scratch. You won't find enchilada sauce from a can here! Specialties are beef and chicken tacos and outstanding chili rellenos. The real draw is the homemade salsa, a family tradition since 1938, when Greg's grandparents had the place. Can you get the recipe? "Sorry, my grandpa would hate me if I gave it out," says Greg. On Sunday, when they're open for breakfast, they'll sell as many as 60 gallons of menudo, the classic hangover remedy. Also on the Sunday menu are chorizo and eggs, huevos rancheros, and the traditional American ham or steak and eggs. The decor is authentic Mexican, with wrought iron and cheerful colors, and comfortable booths and tables, Open for lunch and dinner except Wednesdays. It is located one block from U.S. 60 in downtown Miami. **716 Sullivan St., Miami 85532; (520) 473-9960.**

La Luz del Dia Bakery—$

Rib-sticking breakfasts are served all day at this little Mexican cafe, where a steaming pot of menudo is always ready, and huevos rancheros come with warm, fresh tortillas just right to wrap around the accompanying pinto beans. Sit at the yellow formica counter, the three booths, or genuine 1950s-style tube-leg table and chairs and try to decide between the short stack of pancakes or chorizo and eggs (hot Mexican sausage with eggs any style). Look up to see the painted tin ceiling where a second floor once existed. The aroma of fresh empanadas, Mexican baked bread and cookies wafts through the cafe from the bakery in the back, where bread and hamburger buns are baked daily. The specialty of the house is a fried tortilla with green chile and beans, lettuce, tomato and cheese. Everything here is good and gets even better when you realize it's almost impossible to order anything over $4. Owners Ernie and Carmen Vasquez are almost always there. Open Mon–Fri., 7 A.M.–4:30 P.M.; Sat., 7 A.M.–3 P.M. **304 N. Broad St., Globe, 85501; (520) 425-8400.**

Copper Hills Inn, Dining Room and Coffee Shop—$$-$$$

In the coffee shop, where coffee is free if you're a motel guest, chatty waitresses fill you in on local happenings and tell tales of foreign tourists who expect tomahawk-wielding Indians and tobacco-chewing cowboys to pop out from behind every saguaro. Food is basic, good and comes in large portions. The cocktail lounge, adjacent to a larger dining room, is friendly and casual as are most eateries in Globe. Yes, that is an original DeGrazia mural on the wall behind the bar. There is live entertainment on Tue. and Thu. evenings. **On US 60-70 between Miami and Globe; (520) 425-7151.**

Services

Globe-Miami Chamber of Commerce, 1360 N. Broad St., P.O. Box 2539, Globe, 85502; (800) 804-5623 or (520) 425-4495; fax (520) 425-3410.

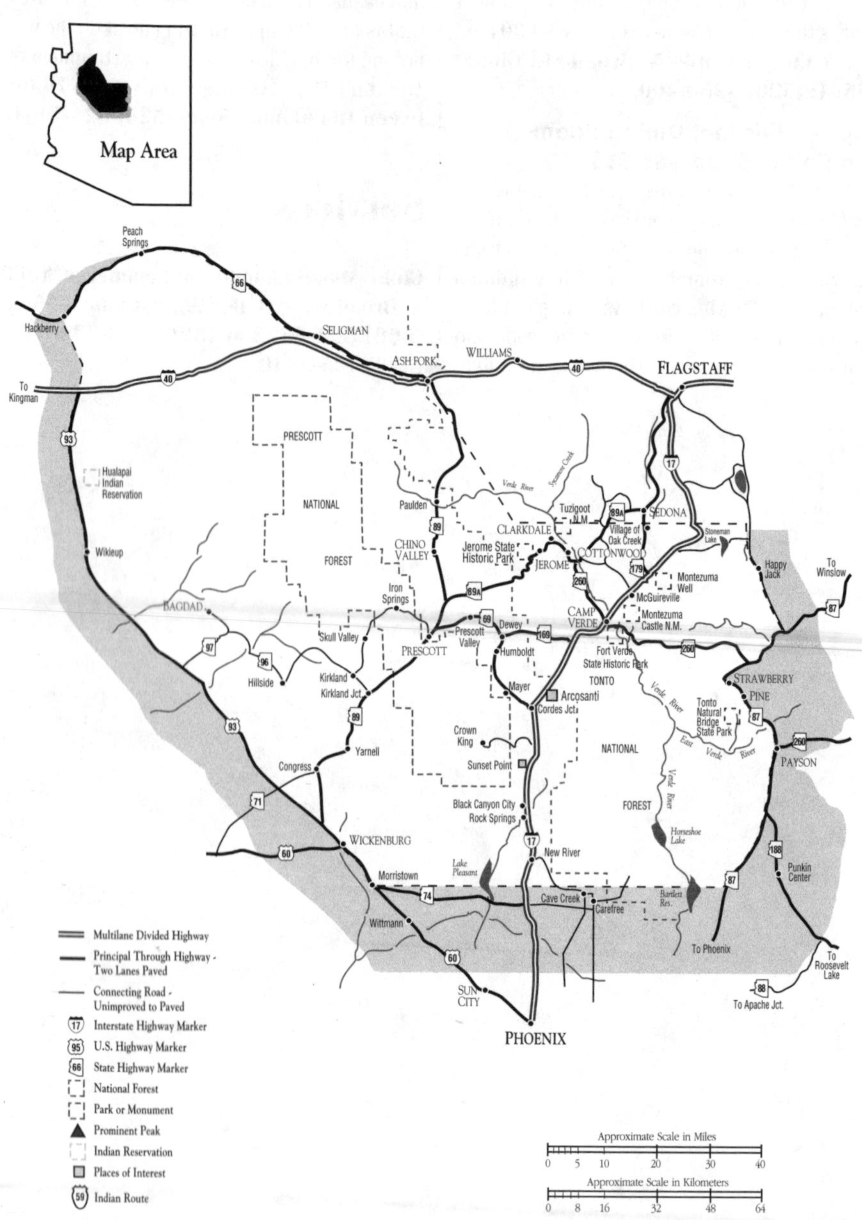

Map Area
Peach Springs
Hackberry
SELIGMAN
ASH FORK
WILLIAMS
FLAGSTAFF
To Kingman
PRESCOTT
NATIONAL
FOREST
Hualapai Indian Reservation
Wikieup
Paulden
CHINO VALLEY
Verde River
Sycamore Creek
Tuzigoot N.M.
SEDONA
CLARKDALE
Jerome State Historic Park
JEROME
COTTONWOOD
Village of Oak Creek
Stoneman Lake
Happy Jack
To Winslow
Montezuma Well
McGuireville
Montezuma Castle N.M.
CAMP VERDE
Iron Springs
BAGDAD
Skull Valley
Prescott Valley
Dewey
Humboldt
PRESCOTT
Fort Verde State Historic Park
TONTO
STRAWBERRY
PINE
Hillside
Kirkland
Kirkland Jct.
Mayer
Arcosanti
Cordes Jct.
Tonto Natural Bridge State Park
East Verde River
PAYSON
Crown King
Sunset Point
NATIONAL
Yarnell
Congress
Black Canyon City
Rock Springs
FOREST
Horseshoe Lake
WICKENBURG
New River
Lake Pleasant
Punkin Center
Morristown
Cave Creek
Carefree
Bartlett Res.
Wittmann
To Phoenix
To Roosevelt Lake
SUN CITY
To Apache Jct.
PHOENIX
Multilane Divided Highway
Principal Through Highway - Two Lanes Paved
Connecting Road - Unimproved to Paved
Interstate Highway Marker
U.S. Highway Marker
State Highway Marker
National Forest
Park or Monument
Prominent Peak
Indian Reservation
Places of Interest
Indian Route
Approximate Scale in Miles
0 5 10 20 30 40
Approximate Scale in Kilometers
0 8 16 32 48 64

Central Region

Ash Fork and Seligman

Three forks of Ash Creek converge here, one of which was followed by the railroad that brought copper ore from the now-ghost-town of Jerome. At one time the town jewel was the elegant Escalante, one of the West's Harvey Houses. Today its claim to fame is its flagstone quarries that ship the Arizona building stone to all parts of the globe. You can visit an old west Settler's Cemetery with cross-marked graves and etched sandstone tombstones. The town sits comfortably on Route 66, just barely bypassed by I-40, near the junction with AZ 89 that leads south to Prescott. It has markets, motels, service stations, a KOA and several restaurants. **Ash Fork Chamber of Commerce & Tourism Center** (located under the big Santa Fe Railroad water tower), **P.O. Box 494, Ash Fork, 86320-0494; (520) 637-2531.**

By the time you reach Seligman from Williams, you've made a gradual 40-mile, 2,000-foot descent, leaving Ponderosa pines behind as you enter juniper territory. Seligman is a must for Route 66 fans (see sidebar, page 111). This friendly little town midway between Flagstaff and Kingman was founded in 1886 at an Atchison, Topeka and Santa Fe main junction that had repair facilities, so train traffic was heavy. Seligman takes its name from a pair of East Coast investment banker brothers who helped finance the railroad's southern route. Between Kingman and Williams, the vast open country that surrounds Seligman provides ideal habitat for the pronghorn, so numerous they were chosen as the mascot for Seligman High School athletics. As you drive along, watch for these light buff-colored creatures streaking across the landscape at speeds up to 75 mph.

During the heyday of Route 66, the town flourished with motor courts and cafes. Today it is a pleasant, touristy place of about 900. Angel Delgadillo, a native and semiretired town barber, keeps his memento-filled shop, really more of a museum, open to tourists. Look for the "Route 66 Memorabilia" sign on the left as you enter town from the east. Angel won't take regular appointments, but if you catch him at the shop and can convince him you're a true Route 66 aficionado, he'll snip away as he answers your questions. Pick up a walking tour guide at the visitor center for detailed information on what to see on foot.

Where to Stay

There are seven motels in the budget category. The KOA, on the west side of town right on Route 66, has a pool, volleyball court and two playgrounds as well as showers, bathrooms, grocery store and laundry room. Tent sites are available. **Seligman KOA, P.O. Box 156, Seligman, 86337; (520) 422-3358 or (800) 562-4017.**

Where to Eat

The Snow Cap—$

Angel Delgadillo's brother, Juan, runs this unforgettable walk-up stand a few doors down from the barber shop. "Do you want yesterday's coffee or tomorrow's?" he'll query with a grin as he "squirts" you with a string of plastic mustard. "Eat here and get gas," says the Snow Cap's business card. Despite the humor, burgers are juicy and shakes are thick and rich. Located in Seligman's center on Route 66. **(520) 422-3291.**

The Copper Cart—$-$$

For more than 40 years this family-owned eatery has served, it says, "the best coffee on

Route 66." The building remains little changed from its construction in the early 1950s, next to the main Atchison, Topeka and Santa Fe rail line. Railroaders have always frequented the place, as have Grand Canyon visitors and the intrepid rafters who challenge the Colorado River. The specialty is a half-pound of grilled ground beef with gravy, salad and all the trimmings. On Route 66 on the west side of Seligman. **(520) 422-3241.**

Services

Seligman Chamber of Commerce
P.O. Box 65
Seligman, 86337
(520) 422-3939

Seligman Route 66 Visitors Center
217 E. Rte. 66
P.O. Box 426
Seligman, 86337-0426
(520) 422-3352, fax (520) 422-3642

Route 66: Niched Forever in Northern Arizona History

Why has a simple ribbon of tarmac created such a surge of nostalgia? It existed just 47 years, from 1937, when the final piece was paved between Chicago and Santa Monica, to 1984, when its last active section was bypassed by the new four-lane I-40 at Williams. Martin Milner, who starred as Tod Stiles along with George Maharis as Buzz Murdock in the *Route 66* television series of the 1960s, has no explanation for its resurgence of popularity. But he looks back on the show with a great deal of fondness. "We made 116 episodes, and no more than half a dozen actually were filmed on the real Route 66. But that didn't seem to matter. It was the sense of adventure and escape that kept viewers coming back," he says.

Called America's Mother Road, the route was the pathway West during the dust-bowl days of the 1930s for Depression-era workers looking for a better way of life. In the post-war 1950s, it was traveled by vacationing American families enjoying the new prosperity. Today its nostalgia value is what attracts travelers. Angel Delgadillo, president of the Arizona Chapter of the Historic Route 66 Association, says that people want to go back to a slower era. "We're such a young nation. We've destroyed so much of ourselves. We've plowed it under. People want to return to the America of yesteryear before it is completely gone."

Route 66 enters Arizona on the east, at Lupton on the New Mexico border,

Old Route 66 Visitor Center in Hackberry is filled with memorabilia and souvenirs of the Old Road in use for 47 years.

and roughly parallels I-40 to Holbrook. Mostly, the historic route now is the main drag through small towns left isolated by the superhighway bypass. A few notable stretches of Route 66 remain. A piece swoops north from Seligman through Peach Springs, where Mormons planted the flowery fruit trees many decades ago, and continues through Truxton to Hackberry, where an old general store has been converted to a particularly wonderful Route 66 visitor center by folks who obviously love the old road, before it finally wanders on to Kingman.

The most spectacular, however, is the stretch from Kingman to Oatman, where switchbacks and narrow pavement press a driver to choose between watching the road and enjoying the see-for-days vistas. The old route continues along a particularly desolate stretch to Topock on the California border.

An excellent little reference for anyone thinking about traveling Route 66 is the book written by Tom Snyder, founder and director of the US Route 66 Association. Called *Route 66 Traveler's Guide and Roadside Companion,* it has maps showing driveable portions of the old highway with recommendations for stops along the way. It is published by St. Martin's Press and is available in most bookstores.

The Historic Route 66 Association, with chapters in all eight of the states that the road crosses, is dedicated to preserving the old route and the memorabilia that surrounds it. Each year the organization sponsors an Annual Fun Run, a three-day event held the last weekend of April in which cars travel the entire continuous 160 miles of Route 66 from Seligman to Topock. You can "Run What Ya Brung" as flyers say, or show up in a historic vehicle, which is what most participants do. Classic Thunderbirds, Ford Fairlanes, Chevys, Pontiacs, Buicks and others from past decades are spiffed and shined to brand-new elegance. Women don pink poodle skirts, put their hair in pony tails, and slide into saddle shoes, while men Bryl Cream their hair and roll packs of cigarettes into T-shirt sleeves. Towns along the route come alive as the caravan leaves Seligman for Kingman, where bed races, slow drags and a barbecue in the park are main events. The next day the cars arrive in Oatman, practically overwhelming this funky little mountain town with their shiny magnificence. Topock hosts an awards ceremony and closing reception. For more information on the Fun Run, contact the **Historic Route 66 Association of Arizona, P.O. Box 66, Kingman, 86402; (520) 753-5001.** A glossy *Route 66* magazine, published quarterly for $3.95 per issue, is available at **326 W. Rte. 66, Williams, 86046; (520) 635-4322, fax (520) 635-4470. E-mail: hwyrvreworldnet.att.net.**

Prescott

Pine-scented air and Arizona history characterize this mile-high city. At 5,374 feet above sea level, it sits comfortable in the largest stand of Ponderosa pine in the world, on the craggy slopes and in the gentle foothills of the Bradshaw Mountains. Thumb Butte, the town landmark, stands sentrylike in the background. Surrounded by more than a million acres of national forest and the 1,400-acre Yavapai Indian Reservation, Prescott is a cool retreat from Arizona's low desert heat. During summer months, it fills with folks from Phoenix in an escape mode. Prescott adopted the slogan "Everybody's Hometown," and it definitely has that sort of feeling. Transplanted Midwesterners, many of whom have arrived in Prescott via California, especially identify with the town square and Victorian homes. More relics of earlier times are found in the antiques and collectibles shops, most of which are located on Cortez between Gurley Street and Sheldon. Prescott is in a growth pattern, partially because of an influx of retirees over the last decade, but three institutions of higher learning—Yavapai College, Prescott College and Embry Riddle Aeronautical University—attract young people as well.

The country's attention was turned to Prescott when gold was discovered in 1838, followed by another big strike in 1861. Then-president Abraham Lincoln saw it as a source of funding for the North during the Civil War, and in 1864 created the Arizona Territory. Prescott is named for historian William Hickling Prescott. Believing the area's Indian ruins were of Aztec origin, the founding fathers named the city streets—Montezuma, Cortez, Alarcon—after figures chronicled in Prescott's book on Mexico. It was the state capital until November 1, 1867, when that honor shifted to Tucson. The capital moved briefly back to Prescott before Phoenix permanently garnered the title in January 1899. At one time Prescott was named Granite for the large deposits of this attractive building stone just north of the city. In 1900 much of Prescott, mainly wood frame buildings, went up in smoke when an inebriated miner knocked over a kerosene lamp in a lodging house. So what you see now are mostly post-turn-of-the-century buildings.

Festivals and Events

Frontier Days

Fourth of July weekend

As many as 100,000 people attend this annual event, so if you're even thinking of going, get campground or hotel reservations early. If you can't find a place, call the Prescott Chamber of Commerce (see Services) for a list of available options. Home of the oldest continuous rodeo in the United States, going strong since July 4,

1888, and now held at the Yavapai County Fairgrounds, Prescott pulls out all the stops for this celebration, beginning with a parade that attracts entries from around the state. Another big draw is the arts and crafts show, along with food booths, in Courthouse Plaza. There's also a carnival with typical rides and a truly fine fireworks display on the fourth.

Arizona Cowboy Poets Gathering

mid-August

Cowboys have a tradition of writing, reciting and singing about the lives they lead. Held annually for more than a decade, the event promotes that tradition and gets bigger every year as more and more poets come together to share their music, stories and love of the West. If you've ever wanted to pen an ode, you can attend free workshops that help you get in the spirit of writing while you pick up tips from established, acclaimed poets. In the evening, top-name Western entertainers perform. Events are held at **Sharlot Hall Museum, 415 W. Gurley St., Prescott, 86301; (520) 445-3122.**

Faire on the Square

Labor Day weekend

Close to 200 of the best handcrafters in the Southwest show up for this event. It is Prescott's premier arts and crafts show, and is juried so you know that the best of the best will be represented. Many people come up from Phoenix for the day, not only to enjoy cooler weather but also to buy Christmas gifts. Held in Courthouse Plaza. For information call **(800) 266-7534.**

Outdoor Activities

Prescott National Forest is the area's biggest recreational draw. Lakes, hiking trails, campsites and an equestrian facility are all within minutes of Prescott. The forest covers more than 1.25 million acres, most of which is accessible to varying degrees year-round.

Hiking and Backpacking

Fall and spring are the recommended seasons for hiking because they tend to be cool and dry. You need to keep in mind that you're in the mountains, and on any given hike the elevation change can make a huge difference in temperatures. Some trails have elevational changes of more than 3,000 feet, which can mean the difference between temperatures in the mid-50s and those below freezing, with a foot of snow, all in the same day. For all trails listed, except the Ackerman, contact the **Bradshaw Ranger District** at **(520) 445-7253** for maps and more information.

Ackerman Memorial Park Trail

This easy loop trail takes about an hour and passes through rolling hillside with a few great views. To reach the trailhead, take Virginia Street east off Gurley about .4 mile. The road dead-ends at the trailhead, where there is limited parking. When you start out you'll have the choice of going to the picnic area to your right, from where you can follow a rough, rocky creek bed. Or take the main trail on the left that winds up Old Water Tank Hill, elevation 5,605, for a good view. When you return to your car, if you're into old cemeteries, drive down the dirt road another 0.3 mile, and you'll end up at the International Order of Odd Fellows cemetery, where graves date to the late 1800s.

Thumb Butte Trail

This heavily used hikers-only trail is just 10 minutes or 2.5 miles from downtown Prescott and is a good way to get acquainted with hiking in the area. Interpretive signs identify plant life, and directional signs keep you on the right path. Rated moderate for the steep climb to a ridge below Thumb Butte, it is 1.4 miles long and will take you about 45 minutes one way. The trailhead is at the Thumb Butte recreation site. Take Gurley Street west for 2.5 miles to Thumb Butte Road and continue for 1.5 miles to the site. Toilets and picnic tables are just across the road from the trailhead.

Little Granite Mountain Trail

There is a good network of trails in and around the Granite Mountain Wilderness. This one follows the southwestern border, with views of Skull Valley. It is open to biking, hiking and equestrian use. Trails are clearly defined but can be confusing without a map because they crisscross each other at a number of points. Hiking time is about 1.5 hours for the trail's 3.3-mile length, rated moderate.

Aspen Creek Trail

Rated easy and offering scenic Prescott-area views, this 2.2-mile trail begins about 30 minutes out of Prescott and takes about 1.5 hours one way. It overlooks Spruce Mountain, Mount Union and the Wilhoit area. Climbing sharply from Copper Basin Road, it is used most frequently by hikers, but is open to mountain bike and equestrian use as well. If you hike it in summer, expect extreme heat and come prepared with adequate water. Take Montezuma Street (AZ 89) south from Prescott 1.1 miles to Copper Basin Road. Turn right on Copper Basin Road and continue for approximately 4.7 miles to the trailhead on the left. Other intermediate trails around Prescott include the West Spruce Trail and Clark Spring Trail.

Golf

Even though Prescott gets a light dusting of snow most winters, courses usually are playable all year.

Antelope Hills

It has two 18-hole municipal golf courses, one ranked fifth in the state among public courses. The 6,778-yard North Course has challenged golfers since 1956 with its unforgiving par 72 fairways that wind through stands of cottonwoods, elms, spruce and poplars. The South Course, 7,014 yards playing to a par 72, is a putter's trial, giving anyone's short game a real workout. There is a full-service restaurant and bar, driving range and complete pro shop. **1 Perkins Dr.; (800) 972-6818 or (520) 776-7888.**

Horseback Riding

Groom Creek Loop Trail

This 9-mile loop is a good day ride, passing through one of the most impressive stands of Ponderosa pine in the forest. A horse camp, exclusively for mounted campers, is located just south of Groom Creek, where most riders access the trail. The trail follows forested areas almost entirely, climbing to the top of Spruce Mountain, then returning via a 4-mile downhill back to the Groom Creek area and the camp. It is approximately 6.5 miles south of Prescott on Senator Highway, which becomes Forest Road 52.

Woodchute Trail

In the Chino Valley Ranger District, bulldozers making way for cattle watering tanks on Woodchute Mountain built this trail, open to hikers and equestrians only. In the late 1800s miners from the town of Jerome got their shoring timbers for the mines from Woodchute Mountain, cutting all the Ponderosa pine, so that the trees you see growing here now all are second growth. The trail, not recommended for winter use because it often is clogged with snow, climbs 2.75 miles from the south trailhead to the top of Woodchute Mountain and continues an additional 3.5 miles down on

Getting There

Prescott is located in central Arizona, 96 miles northwest of Phoenix and 90 miles southwest of Flagstaff. From Phoenix, take I-17 north to AZ 69 and continue west on 69 through Humboldt to Prescott. In town, AZ 69 changes names to Gurley Street, which is the main drag. Or from I-17 take AZ 169 through Dewey to Prescott. On I-17 north out of Phoenix there is a rest area at Milepost 252. From Flagstaff take I-17 south to AZ 169, and follow 169 into Prescott. An alternate, slower, but more scenic route from Flagstaff follows AZ 89A, which winds through Oak Creek Canyon and Sedona. **Prescott Transit Authority (520-778-7978)** provides transportation to Sky Harbor International Airport in Phoenix, 102 miles south. From **Prescott Municipal Airport** there is scheduled passenger service to Phoenix on America West Express.

the north side. It can be accessed from the Potato Patch Campground just east of the Summit on AZ 89A.

Four-Wheel-Drive Trips

Bradshaw Backcountry Tours

If time is limited and you want to see some of the Prescott National Forest and surrounding territory, a four-wheel-drive tour can be the best way to do it. Bradshaw has jaunts from two hours to all day, taking in pine forests, great views and history. Guides are well versed in local lore. **(520) 445-3032.**

Seeing and Doing

Arcosanti

This unusual "city" is located at Cordes Junction, about 23 miles east of Prescott. "An Urban Laboratory," says the large brown sign at the property entrance. Off to the right, over rolling prairie, a group of unimpressive buildings snugs into the desert landscape. But appearances are deceiving, and it soon becomes apparent that this futuristic site, as planned by Italian architect Paolo Soleri, is truly a combination of architecture and ecology. "Arcology," as he calls it, purposes to create new urban habitats. It was begun in 1970 and so far is less than 5 percent complete. When finished, this prototype will house 6,000 residents in compact structures on 25 acres of a 4,000-acre preserve. You approach Arcosanti from the back, so it is only when you take the one-hour tour (the only way you're allowed to walk around the grounds) that you get a sense of Soleri's direction. Many of the multifunction buildings are apses, quarter-circles, allowing them to be warmed by the sun in winter but shielded in summer. Tours begin at the visitor center, which presents artwork and an explanation of Arcosanti. The lower tier houses a cafeteria and bakery. The tour takes visitors past a ceramics studio and a foundry where Soleri windbells are forged to help fund the project. At any given time about a hundred students and workshop participants are in residence. A limited number of rather spartan rooms and one apartment may be rented for overnight stays. They're popular with guests who come for the musical events scheduled from May through October. Among the most popular, the light and sound show is projected onto a natural mesa that faces Arcosanti.

Arcosanti, Paolo Soleri's "urban laboratory" in Cordes Junction, is designed to someday be a city of 6,000.

To get to the complex, take I-17 north from Phoenix to the Cordes Junction Exit 252. Skip the McDonald's and the Subway at this exit in favor of the bakery and cafeteria at Arcosanti, which have more interesting fare. Following the Arcosanti signs, you'll reach a 2.5-mile stretch of dirt road that will take you 15 minutes to cover because of its washboard conditions. Proceed slowly and you'll be okay. Tours are held daily on the hour, 10 A.M.–4 P.M. The cafeteria is open noon–3 P.M. and the bakery is open 9 A.M.–4 P.M. You can browse the gift shop at no charge, but there is a charge for tours. **HC 74, Box 4136, Mayer, 86333 (mailing address); (520) 632-7135, fax (520) 632-6229.** From the Phoenix area call **(520) 254-5309. Website: www.arcosanti.org/.**

Bucky's Casino

On the Yavapai Indian Reservation within the Prescott Resort, this unintimidating casino offers 5-cent, 25-cent and $1 slots as well as video poker machines. For even more slots (175 to be precise), head across AZ 59 to the Yavapai Gaming Center and its 150-seat Bingo Hall. The casino is open 24 hours. **Corner of AZ 69 and Heather Heights; (800) SLOTS-44.**

Farms and Orchards

Young's Farm

In Dewey just east of Prescott, this working farm has something going on all year. The produce barn opens the first weekend in July. Just-picked sweet corn is available through September. You choose your own ears from large wagons, loaded in the fields and brought to the barn. Melons start in early July and by late that month, green beans are in. Home canners come here to stock up. In the fall the farm is a pumpkin center, and around the holidays fresh turkey and ham are the attraction. Produce prices are not much less than at supermarkets, but you always are assured of absolute freshness. A general store stocks kitchen gadgets, canned jams and jellies, hand-crafted items and more. Kids like the petting zoo with its gentle cows, goats and other farm animals. The craft barn and critter corral are open daily, 9 A.M.–4 P.M. The farm restaurant is open daily, 6 A.M.–4 P.M., serving up basic fare in generous portions. It's definitely good for an hour or two of browsing around. Located at the intersection of AZ 69 and AZ 169 east of Prescott. From Phoenix, take I-17 north to Cordes Junction, then take AZ 69 west to the junction with AZ 169. Watch for the Young's Farm sign on the right. **P.O. Box 147, Dewey, 86327; (520) 632-7272, fax (520) 632-5953.**

Poppy Hill Farm

Vine-ripened tomatoes the year around, cabbage, kohlrabi, beets, Swiss chard, peas, cucumbers, broccoli, winter and summer squash, peppers, peaches, pears and apples are available seasonally. It's all chemical-free, organically grown. Don't be dismayed if no one seems to be around. Just honk and someone will appear from the fields or greenhouses to help you. Oftentimes there isn't a great selection of ready-picked vegetables on display at this small farm. Rather, tell them what you want and if it's ripe and pickable, you'll get it fresh from the garden. Open Mon.–Sat., 8 A.M.–4 P.M. Five miles from AZ 69 on the north side of AZ 169 near Dewey. **(520) 632-8598.** For more information on seasonal availability of fresh produce in this area contact the **Yavapai County Cooperative Extension, 500 S. Marina, P.O. Box 388, Prescott, 86302; (520) 445-6590.**

Museums and Galleries

Sharlot Hall

At this skillfully recreated living history museum, docents relate tales of early Prescott as they point out artifacts from settler days. The museum is actually a group of historic buildings clustered together in a gardenlike setting. Spread across three acres, exhibits explore the Arizona Territory in the 1860s. The 1877 William C. Bashford House, which serves as the gift shop, is one link in the chain that helps connect the dots of Prescott's history. An 1864 governor's mansion, built of Ponderosa pine logs, and the 1875 John C. Fremont House show how the fifth territorial governor lived. Central to the grounds is an unusual windmill, built in the 1870s in Springfield, Ohio, and freighted via train to Prescott.

The grounds are planted with old-time flowers that include hollyhocks, columbine and daisies. The Territorial Women's Memorial Rose Garden is filled with a fragrant collection of "antique" as well as newly developed rose varieties. It is dedicated to women born before 1900, who lived in Arizona before 1912, and who were part of the state's development. Near Fort Misery, the oldest log building associated with the territory of Arizona, a kitchen garden flourishes with beans, tomatoes, beets and other vegetables that were summer staples more than a hundred years ago. The museum is named for its founder, Sharlot Mabridth Hall, a poet and historian with a passion for preserving Arizona history. Her efforts to save the territorial Governor's Mansion grew into

The Phippen Museum in Prescott features art of the American West. It is picturesquely sited overlooking the dramatic rock Granite Dells.

the movement created in the museum campus that exists today. Open Apr. to Oct., 10 A.M.–5 P.M., Mon.–Sat.; 1–5 P.M., Sun.; Nov. to Mar., 10 A.M.–4 P.M., Tue.-Sat.; 1–5 P.M., Sun. The archives are open 10 A.M.–5 P.M., Tue.–Fri.; 10 A.M.–2 P.M., Sat. Closed Thanksgiving, Christmas and New Year's Day. Small donation requested. **415 Gurley St., Prescott, 86301; (520) 445-3122.**

Phippen Museum

A bonus to visiting this picturesquely sited museum is driving through landscape that is rough with massive boulders that make up the Granite Dells. Six miles from downtown Prescott, this rambling, rustic ranchhouse-like gallery features art of the American West. Historic Western paintings as well as those by contemporary artists are featured. The permanent collection features the bronzes and paintings of George Phippen, who founded the Cowboy Artists of America. Changing exhibits touch on historical themes, as did a recent show on early transportation in Arizona, and on specific artists and their work. It also houses historic artifacts. Open daily, except Tue., 10 A.M.–4 P.M.; Sun., 1–4 P.M. Small admission fee. **4701 Hwy. 89 North, Prescott, 86301; (520) 778-1385.**

Smoki Museum

This worthwhile museum looks like an Indian pueblo. Since its opening in 1935 it has preserved collections of pre-Columbian and contemporary pottery, as well as jewelry of shell, stone and turquoise. Its most unusual feature, its construction of native stone and wood, includes pine logs used for columns, vigas and latillas and for door and window enclosures. On your right as you enter is a display showing how a piece of pottery, found in shards, is reconstructed to remain authentic. A Hopi-style kiva is the museum's centerpiece. Even the reception desk is sandstone, built in place after the museum opened. Don't bother trying to identify the Smoki tribe. The word has been conjured up, created in the 1930s by a group of non-Native American professionals who set out to preserve Native American culture, dances and artifacts. They considered themselves much like the Moose, Elks or any other philanthropic group. Open in the summer, Mon., Tue., Thu., Fri., Sat., 10 A.M.–4 P.M.; Sun., 1–4 P.M.; closed Wed. The museum is closed Oct. 1 to Apr. 30. **147 N. Arizona St., Prescott, 86304; P.O. Box 10224, Prescott, 86304 (mailing address); (520) 445-1230.**

Courthouse Plaza

Prescott's white granite courthouse, surrounded by shady elm trees, statues and thoughtfully placed benches, is the centerpiece of a true town square, reflecting the Midwestern and New England heritage of many of Prescott's first residents. At one entrance a statue of local hero Rough Rider Buckey O'Neill greets visitors. O'Neill served as sheriff of Yavapai County, then mayor of Prescott, a position he resigned to join the Spanish-American War effort. On July 2, 1898, he was fatally wounded on San Juan Hill. A statue called "Cowboy at Rest" reminds guests of the area's Western heritage. A plaque tells of Prescott's founding in 1864 on Granite Creek, a source of placer gold. The original courthouse was erected in the Plaza during Prescott's days as the state's territorial capital. When it burned in the early 1900s, the present white-columned capitol was built to serve as the seat of government for Yavapai County.

Whiskey Row

During the late 1800s the block facing Courthouse Square on the west included 20 saloons and restaurants where hard-driving miners and cowboys came to enjoy booze, food and ladies of the evening. If you stand near the courthouse and look across Montezuma Street to face this once-notorious block, you can easily see the remnants of those days. The Palace Hotel at 120 S. Montezuma was destroyed except for its ornate back bar, which had come to San Francisco by ship and was then laboriously transported overland by wagon. When fire broke out, reverent patrons picked up the bar and carried it across the street to Courthouse Plaza. The St. Michael Hotel, built in the Second Renaissance Revival style, replaced a smaller hotel built in 1890. The chamber of commerce has an excellent brochure for $1 that outlines a walking tour of historic downtown buildings. It has detailed pen and ink sketches of many, and paragraphs about their architectural style and history.

Mount Vernon Street

Along this elegant street, locust trees shade carefully restored Victorian homes that tell of a time when bright entrepreneurs saw money to be made in farming and sheep herding. Many homes were built as badges of their success. They are part of Prescott's Last Territorial Period, which began in 1900 immediately after the fire of 1900 destroyed 11 blocks in the center of the city. The last homes of this period were built about 1912. Many now are charming bed and breakfast inns. You can see a number of them along Mount Vernon Street as well as South Pleasant.

Bashford Court

This three-level atrium mall, across Gurley Street from the courthouse, is filled with interesting shops and boutiques. A favorite, on the first floor, The Raven purveys Poe memorabilia and writing paraphernalia, including cards, pens, stationery and other fun stuff. If you collect Christmas tree ornaments, don't miss the Mountain Christmas shop, just across from the Prescott Brewing Company.

Bead Museum

Even if you think you don't care beans about beads, you'll find this unusual museum interesting. Its purpose is to collect and preserve, identify, document, and display beads and ornaments used by people from ancient times to the present. Exhibits, especially those from other parts of the world, change regularly. The sheer number of beads is pretty amazing. Enter through the shop next door. Open Mon.–Sat., 9:30 A.M.–4:30 P.M. No admission charge. **140 S. Montezuma, Prescott, 86303; (520) 445-2431 (phone and fax).**

Prescott Arts Gallery

Dozens of accomplished local artists show at this large, pleasant gallery on Whiskey Row. Jewelry, glass, woodwork, weaving, pottery, photography and other media are well priced and definitely worth a look. Here you can pick up unusual gifts to augment the T-shirts that you'll inevitably be taking home. Open daily, 10 A.M.–6 P.M. **134 S. Montezuma, Prescott, 86303; (520) 776-7717.**

Scenic Drives

Crown King to Prescott

As you travel north along I-17 out of Phoenix to Prescott, you're following one of the earlier major highways in Arizona, still called the Black Canyon Freeway by many. It is the main north-south thoroughfare for the central part of the state. Leaving populated areas, the scenery changes to include flat-topped mesas and low, craggy mountains, all of which were mined in one way or another. At the Bumble Bee exit you can leave I-17 (if you have a high-clearance vehicle) and head into the mountains, following county roads on a windy route that starts out paved and quickly becomes graded dirt. You go through the ghost town of

> ### "Naked Kachinas"
>
> No one's quite sure whether it's a demonstration of whimsey or an effort to make elaborate electrical transmission line towers a palatable piece of the horizon. In the eyes of some, the symmetrical, angular "arms" and geometric shapes of these wire-strung towers resemble what might be skeletons of the famed Hopi kachinas. You'll notice a concentration of them along I-17 just past Milepost 252, as well as in dozens of other places in the state.

Bumble Bee to Crown King, where there are a small cafe, general store and gas station. You might want to stop for a rest before tackling the next 40 miles to Prescott, which wind around tight mountain curves. It's difficult to believe that this primitive road, carved out among the piñon and Ponderosa, once was a main stagecoach route. About 22 miles from Crown King is Palace Station, a log cabin stage stop, now on the National Register of Historic Places. You should be able to get a historical brochure here when you get out to stretch your legs. You'll then pass the ruins of the old Senator Mine on the north side of Mt. Union, one of the richest sources of gold ore in the 1860s. Campgrounds and an equestrian camp tell you you're getting closer to a more civilized area, and within about 7 miles of Prescott, you're back on pavement. This is Senator Highway, which changes names to Mount Vernon and passes through a neighborhood of gracious, beautifully restored Victorian homes.

Where to Stay

Because Prescott is such a popular vacation destination, you'll find ample lodging in all price ranges.

Hotels & Resorts

Forest Villas—$$$

This lovely hotel looks far more expensive than it is. The elegant lobby has a grand staircase that's truly worthy of the name, yet somehow you don't feel out of place shouldering your backpack and treading up to the second floor in your Reboks (there is an elevator). Rooms are large and comfortable with small balconies just big enough to enjoy the morning coffee you brewed with your in-room coffee maker. Most rooms have gorgeous mountain views. The expansive continental breakfast includes Danish, bagels, muffins, toast, cereal, fruit, coffee and juice and more. The lobby champagne bar offers favorite vintages, top notch bubbly as well as mixed drinks. From the heated pool you look up at the mountains. One of the hotel's most convenient features is an underground parking garage from which an elevator takes you to your floor. Located 4 miles east of Courthouse Square on Highway 69 at the Lee Boulevard Stoplight, convenient if you're coming in from Phoenix. Look up to your right when you're at the light at Lee Circle and you'll see the hotel. The entrance is another 200 yards ahead on your right. **3645 Lee Cir., Prescott, 86301; (800) 223-3449 or (520) 717-1200, fax (520) 717-1400.**

Prescott Resort—$$$–$$$$

On a bluff overlooking forests and granite mountains, the resort contains Bucky's Casino where slots and poker machines are permitted because the resort is on the Yavapai Indian reservation. Paintings and sculptures by nationally recognized local artists give a gallery feel to the resort's public areas. It has a pool and workout facilities. Rooms have refrigerators and coffee makers, and some have balconies with great views. The 180-degree vistas looking out over the city from the hotel restaurant, the Thumb Butte Room, make it a favorite local dining spot. **1500 Hwy. 69, Prescott, 86304; (800) 967-4637 or (520) 776-1666.**

Historic Hotels

Hotel St. Michael—$$–$$$

Built in 1900 on old Whiskey Row and now on the National Register of Historic Places, it is said that the gargoyles decorating this turn-of-the-century hotel are purposely ugly. Each was named after one of the county commissioners at the time, who refused to allow the hotel's builder to erect a hotel higher than three stories, the height restriction imposed by building codes then in effect. Although never quite achieving the luxury that its builder aspired to, a number of restorations make it comfortable and up to date. Located directly across from Courthouse Square, museums, shops and restaurants are within walking distance. The hotel lobby opens onto a series of shops themed to the 1900s. To be sure your room looks out at the square and not at a brick wall, request a courthouse view when booking. A continental breakfast is included with room rate. **205 W. Gurley; (800) 678-3757 or (520) 776-1999, fax (520) 776-7318.**

Hassayampa Inn—$$$–$$$$

The state's hot weather gave this inn its beginnings. In the preair-conditioned 1920s, as Phoenix developed into a metropolis, its most affluent citizens sought relief at the Hassayampa from the soaring summer temperatures in the Valley of the Sun. Mile-high Prescott, an easy day's drive north, was the destination for many. City fathers soon saw the need for a luxury hotel to accommodate these visitors, and in 1927 the Hassayampa Inn became a reality. Named for the nearby Hassayampa River, the new four-story building immediately lived up to its purpose, delighting guests with its elegant lobby and porte cochere. But by the mid-1950s the hotel had become run down as it found itself competing with newer inns with more modern amenities. In 1986 the Hassayampa underwent a complete renovation, adding air conditioning and new furnishings. Today 68 refurbished rooms and a restored lobby return it to its status as Prescott's Grand Dame of hotels. The lobby is decorated in the original Art Deco style, and an old fashioned elevator takes guests to upper floors. For a possible taste of the supernatural, ask for balcony suite number 428. Past guests and housekeepers swear they've seen the ghost of Faith, a young woman who was spending her honeymoon at the hotel the first year it opened. Her new groom dashed out to get a pack of cigarettes and never returned. The distraught Faith hanged herself, and some say her spirit lingers there today. **122 E. Gurley; (800) 322-1927 or (520) 778-9434.**

Hotel Vendome—$$$–$$$$

Small and elegant, its two stories hold 17 rooms and four suites. Built in 1917 and renovated in 1994, the hotel retains its yesteryear charm with a wide white-railed front porch and tales of a resident ghost. Rooms all have cable TV and private baths, some with clawfoot tubs. Guests can order wine and beer at the hand-carved cherry-wood bar, where a large continental breakfast also is served. **320 S. Cortez, Prescott, 86303; (520) 776-0900.**

Bed & Breakfast Inns

Rocamadour—$$$–$$$$

In the scenic Granite Dells four miles north of Prescott, this B&B has some of the elements of Chenonceau as well as a decidedly Southwest ambiance. Rocamadour, meaning "rock lover" in French, reflects the background of owners Mike and Twila Coffey who operated the Chateau de Trucy in Burgundy. Rocamadour is decorated with gorgeous antiques and offers four guest rooms for adults looking for privacy in gorgeous surroundings. One room has an onyx whirlpool tub, a cottage has a hot tub and deck, and a suite has a fireplace, full kitchen and patio. Full breakfasts are served in a dining room with a French country style. A favorite guest activity is a challenging 15-minute hike up the rock trail that faces the inn. The reward at the top is an expansive view of Willow Lake. The Coffeys say they do not typically accept kids or pets, but you could ask. This is a place best savored as a twosome. **3386 N. Hwy. 89, Prescott, 86301; (888) 771-1933, (520) 771-1933.**

Pleasant Street Inn—$$$–$$$$

Built in 1906, this sleek blue Victorian was moved to its present site in 1990, just a swing ahead of the wrecking ball that would have demolished it to make room for a new police station. It has four rooms, two of which are suites that can accommodate up to four guests. A full or continental breakfast is included and served in the dining room or on the covered porch. **142 S. Pleasant St., Prescott, 86303; (520) 445-4774.**

Prescott Pines Inn—$$$–$$$$

Out a ways from most of the other B&Bs, this inn includes a 1902 two-story main house and five guest houses for a total of 12 rooms in all, some with gas fireplaces. Some rooms have small refrigerators and microwaves, some have complete kitchens. This is not a true B&B since breakfast is not included (for a small charge a huge breakfast is available by reservation) but coffee, tea, juice and an endless jar of chocolate chip cookies always are at hand. Kitchen rooms open onto a flagstone patio with a barbeque grill, shade trees and an abundance of song birds. A large chalet also is available. Located 1.3 miles south of Courthouse Square on AZ 89S, on the east side of town at the edge of the Prescott National Forest. **901 White Spar Rd. (Hwy. 89S), Prescott, 86303; (520) 445-7270.**

RV Parks

Rafter Eleven

One of you must be 55 or older to stay in this attractive mobile home and RV park, named for a former cattle brand. It has ample spaces with picnic tables shaded by cottonwood trees. It's okay if you have your grandkids with you, but not permanently. It attracts a lot of full-timers, with longer stays the norm, but during the off season it often is possible to get in for just a night or two. Located in Dewey, 12 miles east of Prescott, 78 miles north of Phoenix on AZ 69. **11250 E. Hwy. 69, Dewey; (520) 772-8266.**

Willow Lake RV & Camping Park

This scenic park is located in the Granite Dells in the Heritage Park area north of Prescott. Willow Lake, dry for years, received a recent infusion of snowmelt that has filled it to its banks. Two hundred tree-shaded spaces are available with full hookups. Separate areas are set aside for tent camping and for guests with kids. A laundry room, showers, pool and convenience store are on-site. From the junction of Hwy. 69 and US 89, go 3.5 miles north on US 89, turn left onto Willow Lake Road and proceed 2.25 miles to Willow Creek Road. Turn right and proceed 1.25 miles to Heritage Park Road, turn right and the park is one-half mile down the road. **1617 Heritage Park Rd., Prescott, 86301-6010; (520) 445-6311 (phone and fax) or (800) 940-2845.**

Point of Rocks RV Park

Spaces with full hookups for 96 RVs dot the pleasant grounds in the Granite Dells, shaded by cottonwoods and piñon pines. Located about a block from Watson Lake, the park has a laundry room and showers. The lake itself is much different from the steep-walled canyon lakes and intrigues with its softly eroded rocks and explorable inlets. Located about 4 miles north of Prescott, just off AZ 89 about one-quarter mile north of Willow Lake Road. **3025 N. Hwy. 89, Prescott, 86301; (520) 445-9018.**

Campgrounds

There is camping at Lynx Lake from Apr. 1 to Nov. 15 and at White Spar the year-round, although there is no water in winter. For reservations, call the **National Forest Reservation Center** at **(800) 280-2267** at least ten days in advance. Granite Basin Campground sits on the edge of a very small lake that usually has plenty of crappies and sunfish. The setting, amid a forest of boulders, makes it seem private and protected. Take Iron Springs Road about 4 miles north of Prescott, and turn north on Forest Road 374. At Indian Creek, open May 15 to Sept. 30, and Granite Basin, open all year, camping is first-come, first-served.

Where to Eat

Kendall's Famous Burgers and Ice Cream—$

This 1950s-style diner makes a convenient stop for light fare while you're exploring Prescott's downtown area. Order your burger (quarter pounders are good) at the back counter, then hit the ice-cream bar where your malt or shake will be mixed fresh while you wait. Across from Courthouse Plaza. Open Mon.–Sat., 11 A.M.–8 P.M.; Sun., 11 A.M.–6 P.M. **113 S. Cortez St.; (520) 778-3658.**

Prescott Brewing Company—$$
In Bashford Court, this award-winning microbrewery turns out beers that have garnered honors at the Great American Beer Festival for a number of years. The staff will let you "journey down the path of production" they say, if time allows and they're not in a brewing cycle, so you can see just how these acclaimed brews are created. Before you get into the menu, decide on the beer you'll stick with for your meal by ordering a selection of 4 oz. samples for under a buck each. At any given time they'll have their Lodgepole Light, Liquid Amber (our favorite), Prescott Pale Ale and Petrified Porter, as well as a number of specialty beers. Kids love old-fashioned cream soda by the pitcher. The menu features exceptionally hearty burgers, sandwiches, pizzas and inventive appetizers like stuffed mushrooms and artichoke hearts with beer mustard. The beer bread's a decided do-not-miss. Parking on the street may be hard to find, but there's a large parking lot behind the building off Montezuma Street. Open Sun.–Thu., 11 A.M.–12 midnight (menu served until 10 P.M.); Fri. and Sat., 11 A.M.–1:00 A.M. (menu served until 11 P.M.). **130 W. Gurley St.; (520) 771-2795.**

Zuma's Woodfire Cafe—$$
As soon as you walk into this terra-cotta colored Mediterranean style building, you smell the fragrance of the pecan logs firing the ovens. If you sit in the lower dining room you can watch the chefs shoveling pizzas in and out of the ovens, preparing salads and cooking pasta. The copper-walled display kitchen is as much a part of Zuma's as is their well-prepared food. Pizza, salad and pasta make up their menu and might sound a bit humble. But clever items like Thai peanut and chicken pasta, penne vodka pasta, Peking duck pizza and grilled albacore salad (ask for the albacore rare—it's delicious) take dishes well beyond the ordinary. Their wine list has a good variety and is well-priced. You can dine al fresco on either of two patios, which are warmed by fire pits on chilly evenings. Open Sun.–Thu., 11 A.M.–10:30 P.M.; Fri. and Sat., 11 A.M.–11 P.M. **124 N. Montezuma St.; (520) 541-1400.**

At the historic Palace, a smiling bartender serves at a back bar that was saved from the 1900 fire.

The Palace—$$–$$$
On Whiskey Row, this historic bar and one-time hotel specializes in steaks and seafood in very large quantities. The original establishment burned in the 1900 fire, but the ornately carved 1880s Brunswick bar survived and is used today in the Palace, rebuilt in 1901. Recently extensively remodeled, it traces history in framed photos and clippings that line the walls. Fare ranges from grilled roast beef and cheddar sandwiches for lunch, to barbequed ribs, T-bones, salmon and trout for dinner. It's worth a stop here just for a beer, to chat with friendly bartenders and take a leisurely look at the back bar that so narrowly escaped destruction. Open for lunch and dinner. **120 S. Montezuma St.; (520) 541-1996.**

Peacock Room (Hassayampa Inn)—$$$–$$$$
Three-diamond cuisine in this lovely old hotel dining room is always a special occasion. Rich mahogany and flowered upholstery are

restorations of its Art Deco beginnings in 1927. As you enter, just before the maitre d' station on the right, there's an old photo of how the dining room originally looked, with a lunch counter and solid wall where etched glass panels now create an artistic focal point. The menu, a changing melange of continental and American-style, consistently wins awards. Open for breakfast Mon.–Sat., 7–11:30 A.M.; 7 A.M.–1 P.M., Sun.; lunch, 11:30 A.M.–2 P.M., Mon.–Sat.; dinner, nightly from 5 P.M. **122 E. Gurley St.; (520) 778-9434.**

Services

The helpful volunteers at the **Prescott Chamber of Commerce** can supply you with everything from hiking trail maps to pamphlets on the town's history. **117 W. Goodwin St., Prescott, 86302; P.O. Box 1147, Prescott, 86302 (mailing address); (800) 266-7534 or (520) 445-2000. Website: www.prescott.org. E-mail: Chamber@prescott.org.**

Verde Valley

Arizona's midsection is a cummerbund of green forests and flowing streams, Indian ruins and historic sites, preserved (one hopes) forever as part of the state park system. A string of small towns follows along the central part of the Verde River. This mellow waterway begins in the Chino Valley near the town of Seligman, flows through the Verde Valley, briefly becomes part of Horseshoe Lake, and finally ends up joining the Salt River above Granite Reef Dam. The part most commonly called the Verde Valley extends from the Clarkdale area in the north to past Camp Verde in the south. The town of **Camp Verde** marks the Valley's southern entrance and originally was populated by miners who poured into the area to seek their fortune. These new residents severely hindered the hunting and gathering economy of the Native Americans, so the Tonto Apaches and Yavapais raided Verde Valley fields for corn. In 1865 the military secured the area to protect settlers, who farmed the rich river valley, from Apache raids.

Northwest of Camp Verde, off AZ 89A, the ghost town of **Jerome** clings to the side of Cleopatra Hill. Part of Mingus Mountain, which once yielded copper in great abundance, the little town has expansive views of the Verde Valley. If you think you're feeling an earthquake, you probably aren't. The hill on which Jerome is built is honeycombed with old mine tunnels that shift constantly, creating earth movements that frequently cause small but definite tremors on the surface. Eugene Jerome, an early financier and a well-known New York City attorney, agreed to underwrite a speculative mining venture on the condition that the town carry his name. In 1882, Territorial Governor Frederick Tritle connected with Jerome while casting about for financing for a mining operation in the Black Hills that form one side of the Verde Valley. During the 1920s, this hillside town's salad days, 15,000 people had homes on the mountainside. About half of today's population of 403 are full-time working artists, their wares available in a number of shops along Hull Avenue and Main Street. Not all mining memories are visual. A shrill noon whistle still blows as it did during mining days. You can walk just about anywhere you want to go in Jerome, so park in one of the small city lots, if you can find a place, and set out on foot to explore.

Five miles from Jerome, at the upper end of the Verde Valley, a one-time smelter town called **Clarkdale** dates to 1912. Ore from Jerome was processed here, then cast and shipped as ingots to alleviate the expense of transporting ore across the country. The last smelter smokestack in Clarkdale came down in 1966. Small, tidy frame houses that date to 1913 still line the historic district. Today's Main Street is clearly recognizable in photos from the 1920s. The original town, next to Clarkdale, was first named Verde, then later Clemenceau, for the French Premier Georges Clemenceau. The school-cum-museum still bears his name.

Cottonwood, named for the cottonwood trees that flourish in this rich riparian area, lies 8 miles southeast of Clarkdale. Cottonwood began as a trading center, purveying supplies and the necessities of life to those attracted by the mines. As late as the 1930s Apaches lived along the Verde River in wickiups made of willows lashed together with bear grass. Today Cottonwood is something of a retirement destination, favored for its reasonable cost of living and slower pace. While not age-restricted, retirees make up more than half the residents of a new Del Webb community called Cottonwood Ranch.

Festivals and Events

Sizzling Salsa Sunday

first Sunday of May

The Verde Valley's Mexican heritage is remembered on Cinco de Mayo with a salsa contest among Verde Valley restaurants. Mariachis, a street dance, food and craft booths and piñatas for kids to swing at are part of the celebration. Various cities in the valley host different events, but you can be sure that Cinco de Mayo will be celebrated in some way in all of them.

Jerome Home Tour

mid-May

The buildings on this tour once served as apartments or room and boarding houses for miners, grand Victorian homes for mine executives or sturdy frame dwellings for mine middle management. Today they are part of an annual home tour that also may include shops, businesses and restaurants essential to a thriving community. Among the buildings usually open to visitors, Surgeon's House is poised on a lofty knoll with a commanding view of the hillside (see Where to Stay).

Fort Verde Days

second weekend in October

For more than 25 years, Camp Verde has celebrated its history with precision cavalry displays, a small rodeo and an art show that attracts craftspeople from around the state. People dress up in period costume and really get in the spirit of the event.

Outdoor Activities

Hiking

Northeast of Camp Verde, West Clear Creek surges across more than 40 miles of wilderness. Twenty of these follow the Mogollon Rim and make up the West Clear Creek Wilderness. A rewarding hiking venue, trails are generally challenging, scenery is spectacular and nature is at its best. Soaring red-tailed hawks, icy pools, stands of cottonwoods and willows seem more like a rainforest than an area surrounded by desert.

Easiest of the hikes include the Bull Pen, at the creek's western end, and the Calloway and Maxwell trails, near the creek's upper end. Summer hiking is best because the creek is flowing yet not unmanageable. However, it's also the time annoying gnats and poison ivy flourish. For more information contact **Beaver Creek Ranger Station, H.C. 64, Box 24, Rimrock, 86335; (520) 567-4501.**

Horseback Riding

Horseback Adventures

Look for these stables at Cowboys and Outlaws Wild West Town. Owner Bill Jones says that he offers "horses matched to your skills and adventures matched to your imagination." The company's trail rides cover some of the best the Verde Valley has to offer. One parallels Beaver Creek near Montezuma Castle, and another follows the General Crook Trail in Copper Canyon. An all-day ride covers piñon-covered Pine Mountain. Overnight rides also are available. Located at I-17 and Middle

Verde Road off Exit 289. **P.O. Box 593, Camp Verde, 86322; (520) 567-5502.**

Seeing and Doing

Historic and Archaeologic Sites

Fort Verde State Historic Park

The 1870s are preserved here with four fort buildings that demonstrate just how tough life could be a hundred years ago. On most weekends, "reenactors" in period costume play the roles of soldiers, wives, doctors and cavalry officers. In summer it's so hot that "the only shade's a swarm of flies" says one "soldier," authentically (and not too happily) clad in a wool uniform over wool underwear. The fort "doctor" will tell you he got the job for being able to "take off a leg in one minute or less without killing the patient through blood loss or shock." The park is open daily, 8 A.M.–4:30 P.M., except Christmas Day. There is a very small fee. Located one block East of Main Street (AZ 260) in downtown Camp Verde. **125 E. Hollamon; (520) 567-3275.**

Montezuma Castle National Monument

Three miles north of Camp Verde, Montezuma Castle is one of the best-preserved examples of cliff dwellings in the country, even though Montezuma was never there and it is definitely not a castle. Settlers named it, believing it was built by Aztec refugees fleeing from the Spanish conquistadors in Central Mexico. More than 800 years ago, it housed Sinagua Indians (the name means "without water" in Spanish), who found a cool shady home beneath overhanging cliffs and a ready water supply in Beaver Creek. The five-story dwelling was constructed around 1150. By the 1300s the civilization here was at its peak with as many as 50 people making their home in 20 different rooms. But a century later the site was abandoned for reasons unknown, and the Sinagua left the Verde Valley completely. Because of their sheltered position, the ruins are well preserved, but visitors have not been allowed to climb up to them since 1951.

Remnants of another larger pueblo that stood six stories high and had about 45 rooms remain in low rock walls that outline portions of the bottom floor. It is believed that wood ladders connected various levels. Its unprotected position allowed the elements to erode it to what you see today. The level, hard-surface walking trail is accessible to wheelchairs. Bring a picnic lunch to eat at tables beneath sycamores along the creek. Even in midsummer the shade and (usually) a breeze keep temperatures tolerable. Benches and drinking fountains are scattered along the walkway. The

Getting There

The Verde Valley is crossed by I-17 about 1.5 hours north of Phoenix. You can exit I-17 and follow AZ 260 in either direction and be in the Verde Valley.

A costumed reenactor at Fort Verde State Historic Park in Camp Verde helps bring history to life.

Even though they belonged to the Sinagua Indians, Montezuma's castle is named for someone else.

visitor center has excellent displays that explain area history and contain artifacts from the castle. The castle is about 90 miles north of Phoenix and 50 miles south of Flagstaff, off I-17 at Exit 289. Open daily, 8 A.M.–5 P.M. during winter months, and 8 A.M. to 7 P.M. (or sundown) from Memorial Day to Labor Day. Small admission. **(520) 567-3322, fax (520) 567-3597.**

Montezuma Well

Near Montezuma Castle and part of the monument, this limestone sink was formed by the collapse of a huge underground cavern that was then filled by continuously flowing springs. At the same time that 50 Sinagua lived at Montezuma Castle, more than one hundred lived here, building irrigation channels from the well to feed their crops. Remains of their ditches are here, as well as a Hohokam pit house built about 1100.

Tuzigoot National Monument

Another Sinagua village of the same era as Montezuma Castle, this restored site once sheltered more than 450 people. First settled around 700, Tuzigoot (the name means "crooked water" to the Apache) grew over a 400-year period. The Verde Valley was a living grocery store, with antelope, deer and small game. The meadow above the river produced grains and beans. The river itself was filled with fish and turtles, and attracted migratory Canada geese, white wing doves and a variety of ducks. These life-sustaining features made it a natural settling place. Pick up a booklet at the visitor center for a self-guided tour along the one-quarter mile trail through the ruins. The original two-story pueblo, rising 120 feet above the valley, had 77 ground floor rooms with ladders leading to the upper floor. A second-story viewpoint, with the same panoramas that attracted the Sinaguans, looks out over Mingus Mountain. Long after the Sinagua left, around 1400, miners discovered that the area produced some of the richest copper deposits in the world. The mining city of Jerome is visible on the mountain's upper slopes. The adjacent visitor center is particularly interesting for its display of pottery, turquoise and shell jewelry, and stone axes and tools that were discovered while excavating the site in 1933 to 1934. Tuzigoot became a national monument in 1939. Open daily, 8 A.M.–7 P.M., Memorial Day to mid-Sept.; 8 A.M.–5 P.M., the rest of the year. Small fee. Tuzigoot is between Clarkdale and Cottonwood off AZ 279 at Broadway Road. **(520) 634-5564.**

Jerome State Historic Park

As you enter Jerome, turn off at Milepost 345 for great views of the Verde Valley and a look at the adobe Douglas Mansion. Never meant to be a family home, it was built by the owner of the Little Daisy Mine as a place to wine, dine and lodge mining officials and investors. The 8,700-square-foot mansion, constructed in 1916 for $150,000, now houses artifacts and exhibits that tell of the town's heyday and the mining industry that supported it. Guides will point out the central vacuum cleaning system, an innovation for its day. A picnic area has tables, and rest rooms are in the museum. Open daily, 8 A.M.–5 P.M., except Christmas Day. Small fee. **P.O. Box D, Jerome, 83331; (520) 634-5381, fax (520) 639-3132.**

Parks

Dead Horse Ranch State Park

This pretty 325-acre park (one of our personal favorites) is filled with great wildlife. Easy hikes of just a few hours wind along the Verde River riparian area and near a large fishing lagoon. Hiking trails begin at picnic areas and follow the banks of the river. At an elevation of 3,300 feet it's far enough above the Phoenix area to attract campers escaping summer heat. But its best months are spring and fall, when days are cool and nights are crisp. More than 150 bird species have been identified here. Around the river and lagoon we have seen great blue herons, bitterns, mallards, cinnamon teal, gadwall and other water birds. The small footprints in the wet sand are likely those of beavers and raccoons, and the larger canine ones belong to coyotes, distinguishable from domestic dog prints because coyotes walk in a straight line, their slow, loping gait leaving sets of four aligned prints. Dogs leave side-by-side tracks like humans. A number of types of hawks, bald eagles and turkey vultures soar overhead, and at least three hummingbird species frequent the park.

Each October the four-acre lagoon is stocked with catfish for Verde River Days. Enough bass from previous stockings survive that at least one grew to ten pounds before recently succumbing to a fisherman's lure. In winter catfish and trout are stocked as well. We have visited this lovely riparian area on a weekday morning and found ourselves blissfully alone on some of the longer trails. Two first-come first-served campgrounds have pull-through and back-in sites with rest rooms and showers, and several day use sites have rest rooms. The park is wheelchair accessible. Open daily, 8 A.M.–8 P.M., for day use, open for camping 24 hours. The ranger station is manned various hours depending on season and day of the week. The park is located in Cottonwood just off 10th Street. **675 Dead Horse Ranch Rd., Cottonwood, 86326; (520) 634-5283.**

Old Town Cottonwood

The area around the Sundial Inn in Cottonwood is considered Old Town. At one time the big cottonwood trees in the wash just north of what is now the visitor center provided a protected site for wagons that belonged to ranchers and cattlemen. They stopped overnight, sitting around their campfires, swapping stories and sharing camaraderie that happened all too infrequently among those who lived on far-apart ranches. Most of the buildings in Old Town were built before 1925 and are clearly recognizable as belonging to that era. They now house shops, art galleries and antiques stores, a vintage clothing boutique, cafes and delis. Movies are shown nightly at the Old Town Palace Theater. **Mount Hope Foods (520-634-2546)** just across the street and around the curve from the Sundial Inn at **1123 N. Main St.** has been the area's natural foods center for 30 years. It stocks a good supply of organically grown fruits and vegetables, dried nuts and fruits as well as teas and homeopathic remedies. We stop to buy local pine nuts, usually at reasonable prices. The **Old Town Association Visitor Center (1101 N. Main St.; 520-634-9468)** was once the old town jail. The original cells are there and a 1950s mural by local artist Randolph Pyne recently was uncovered and restored. It shows red rocks and the San Francisco peaks as well as residents and workers of the area.

Dead Horse Ranch State Park in the Verde Valley has a pleasant lake that is regularly stocked.

The Verde Canyon Railroad takes passengers through the Sycamore Wilderness area on a vintage train.

Museums

Clemenceau Heritage Museum

It began life in 1926 in Cottonwood as Clemenceau Public School, providing kindergarten through ninth grade education mostly for the children of mine workers. The smelter closed in 1937, but the school remained open until the last classes were taught in 1986. Shortly thereafter local volunteers requested a portion of the building to use as a small museum, then filled it with artifacts and photographs of the Verde Valley from years gone by. There is an operational model railroad of the 1895 to 1953 era, with little well-crafted ore cars and a steam locomotive, and a replica classroom. Other parts of the building still are used as district administrative offices. Open Wed., 9 A.M.–noon; Fri.–Sun., 11 A.M.–3 P.M. **11 N. Willard, Cottonwood, 86326; (520) 634-2868.**

Train Tour

Verde Canyon Railroad

The Sycamore Wilderness Area and North Verde River Canyon, known as the "other" Grand Canyon, are among the state's most beautiful untouched places. The only way to see this carefully protected region is on the Verde Canyon Railroad, an excursion train that does a 3-hour, 40-mile round trip into otherwise inaccessible wilderness. March through June the high desert canyon is a'bloom with Indian paintbrush, daisies, ocotillo and other cactuses and wild flowers. Cottonwood and aspen create a blaze of color in the fall. The railroad dates to 1911 when it hauled copper along the river. Today it transports passengers on the Clarkdale-Perkinsville round trip in Pullman Standard coach cars built in 1946–1947. Cowboy balladeers entertain as guests look out at giant cottonwoods, hovering eagles, 700-foot sandstone walls and great blue herons. The old depot and water tower still stand along the tracks. Vintage FP7 engines pull the train along at a sedate, rattly 12 miles per hour, allowing occasional sightings of mountain lions, wild turkeys and javelinas. The engines (it takes two to pull the train with its maximum of 340 passengers) were built in 1953 for the Alaskan Railroad by the Electro-Motive Division of General Motors. The impressive eagle paintings on the engines were done by wildlife artist Doug Allen. Each passenger has an inside seat, but open gondola cars are ideal for snapping photos.

The train leaves from the new depot in Clarkdale, which has a gift shop, reservation offices, minimuseum and snack bar with patio dining. Take a few minutes to browse the historic photographic display. There is a snack bar on each coach. Special inn and train tour packages are available through the Southwest Inn at Sedona and Sedona Super 8 Motel. Trains leave daily at 1 P.M., except Tuesdays when the engines are down for maintenance and Mondays during the summer. Moonlight excursions are sometimes are available. Advance reservations are required. **300 N. Broadway, Clarkdale, 86324; (800) 293-7245 or (520) 639-0010, fax (520) 639-1653. E-mail: verdecanyonrr@verdenet.com.**

Walking Tour

Local historian and author Nancy Rayne Smith

will take individuals and groups on walking tours of Jerome, covering the town's history, building by building. If you have a particular interest, such as architecture, a tour can be tailored to your needs. Tours are by reservation only, primarily during summer months because it's pretty cold to walk around Jerome in winter. **(520) 634-8654. E-mail: nrsmith@verdenet.com.**

Four-Wheel-Drive Tours

Tours from one hour to half a day are available along mountain trails, led by Copper Canyon Tours owner Clay Miller, who's been leading them for years. The Iron Horse Expedition goes to 6,000 feet, following the narrow gauge railroad bed built for what was billed as the "crookedest railroad in the world" because of the mountain switchbacks it had to maneuver. The railroad was built in 1895 for the train that hauled ore from Jerome's mines as well as the occasional passenger. Other tours cover area geology, Native American heritage and myths and legends. **P.O. Box 591, Jerome, 86331; (520) 634-3497.**

Nightlife

Blazin' M Ranch Chuckwagon Suppers and Western Stage Show—$$–$$$

This family-oriented place is a combination theme park, dinner venue and cowboy show. Times and days vary with the season, so call ahead to see when dinner and the show are scheduled. Then arrive at least an hour earlier to browse through the Old West town and shops. The Blazin' M has always been a dairy farm and cattle ranch, its roots evident in the yard full of friendly farm animals and small ponies ready to give young wranglers a thrill. For dinner you sit at family-style picnic tables, drinking sarsparilla, then watch a show that includes a medley of cowboy songs and comedy routines filled with good times and simple humor. As an example of what to expect, servers will tell you they put your cowboy beans on your plate upside-down "so they'll give you only the hiccups." One of the cowboy entertainers talks about his girl named Bureau—"A big wide thing with drawers." You get the idea. In Cottonwood, adjacent to Dead Horse Ranch State Park. **P.O. Box 160, Cottonwood, 86326; (800) WEST643 or (520) 634-0334.**

Where to Stay

Hotels, Motels & Inns

Sundial Motel—$$

This unpretentious little place, built in 1921 in a sort of Indian-Spanish style in Cottonwood's Old Town, is a budget gem. The outside is faced with natural river rock, and an interior courtyard welcomes with tables and umbrellas. Rooms have TV, a microwave and a small refrigerator, so you can tuck in for several days or a week (rates are less by the week) to explore the area. Some rooms have kitchenettes. Don't expect the Ritz, but you'll be comfortable, and the price definitely is right. **1034 N. Main St., Cottonwood, 86326; (520) 634-8031.**

Little Daisy Motel—$$–$$$

The motel is named for the Little Daisy Mine, properly known as the United Verde Extension Mine, and for the original Little Daisy Hotel, built in 1918 and still standing but not open in Jerome. This tidy, light blue frame motel has kitchenettes and rooms that will accommodate a family. Kitchen utensils are available on request. It's an affordable alternative to Sedona's pricey digs just 16 miles north. **34 S. Main St., Cottonwood, 86326; (520) 634-7865, fax (520) 639-3447. E-mail: littledaisy@sedona.com.**

The Surgeon's House—$$$–$$$$

Built in 1917 for the man charged with keeping mine workers healthy, this lovely home is poised above the main town of Jerome and has what can be described only as breathtaking views of the Verde Valley that reach all the way to the Red Rocks of Sedona. Andrea Prince furnished the home, which is on the National Register of Historic Places, with charming personal antiques and mementos. A cool, shady garden adjacent to the dining room is a quiet place to relax. The master suite has a private balcony. Rates include a full breakfast, homemade snacks and complimentary beverages. Take the cobblestone driveway off Clark Street past the Episcopal Church that is now the Jerome Historical Society. **P.O. Box 998, Jerome, 86331; (800) 639-1452 or (520) 639-1452. E-mail: surghouse1@juno.com. Website: www.virtualcities.com.**

Jerome Grand Hotel—$$$–$$$$

Opened in July 1996, this super hotel is an example of recycling at its best, and now is a national historic landmark. Built in 1926 as the United Verde Hospital, it was one of the most modern hospitals of its day. It closed in 1950 but its owner, Phelps Dodge Mining Company, kept it in medical readiness until the 1970s in case it was needed. After being purchased in 1994 and undergoing three years of renovation, guests no longer feel like they should strip for surgery. The original Otis elevator is in service, and the Kewanee boiler system that heated the hospital still warms guest rooms. At 5,260 feet (just up the road from the Surgeon's House) it has 180-degree valley views, extending to the San Francisco Peaks. Relax in a 1920s style lounge or dine in the Grand View Restaurant, open for three meals a day. Don't let the narrow cobblestone street put you off. Go slowly and follow it to the top. It's worth it. The hotel is walking distance (mostly uphill) from downtown Jerome. **200 Hill St., Jerome, 86331 or P.O. Drawer H, Jerome, 86331 (mailing address); (520) 634-8200, fax (520) 639-0299.**

Cliff Castle Lodge—$$$

This Best Western is also notable as a gaming place, with the Yavapai Apache Cliff Castle Casino part of its complex. Rooms with balconies have king or queen beds. There are a large pool and a restaurant. Surprisingly, when you stay at the hotel you won't hear noise from the casino. Because it has so many rooms you often can get a room here at the last minute when all else is full. Located at I-17 and Middle Verde Road, 3 miles north of Camp Verde on Montezuma Castle Road. **P.O. Box 3430, Camp Verde, 86322; (800) 622-7853.**

Camping & RV Parks

See Parks for camping in Dead Horse Ranch State Park. The two mentioned here are notable for being cool and pleasant in the summer, but they also fill up very fast.

Rio Verde RV Park

Located on AZ 89A just north of Cottonwood, right on the Verde River, this RV park has large, shady spaces with full hookups. It's next door to the White Horse Inn. **(520) 634-5990.**

Turquoise Triangle RV Park

On the Verde River, this RV park has 60 full hookups. Spaces lined with huge cottonwood trees keep it cool, even in summer. Located on AZ 89A just south of the river. **(520) 634-5294.**

Where to Eat

At the I-10 exit for the Verde Valley there are a Denny's, Dairy Queen, Burger King and McDonald's. You'll have to get a mile or so further from the freeway to Camp Verde for other eateries, or head in the other direction to Clarkdale, Cottonwood or Jerome.

Custard's Last Stand—$$–$$$

In downtown Camp Verde, you can't miss the big fake horse in front of this low western-style building. Open daily, 10 A.M.–8 P.M. for breakfast, lunch and dinner. Huge burgers are its stock-in-trade. **On Main Street; (520) 567-9900.**

The Ranch House—$$$

The setting, on Beaver Creek Golf Course at Lake Montezuma, makes this a good place to relax and enjoy a well-prepared meal. Mesquite barbecued items are a specialty. Open Sun.–Thu., 6 A.M.–8 P.M.; Fri.–Sat., until 9 P.M. Take Lake Montezuma Road about 5 miles off I-17 to Lake Montezuma. **(520) 567-4492.**

Jerome Palace—$–$$

Voted by Jerome businesses as the town's best restaurant, it's also known as the Haunted Hamburger for its half-pound creation of the same name that's smothered with a ton of toppings. Located at one of Jerome's highest points, across from the Surgeon's House and down the street from the Jerome Grand Hotel, the building was built in 1908 as a boarding house. The small outdoor balcony has views to rival the burgers. Open daily for lunch and dinner, 11 A.M.–9 P.M. **410 Clark St., Jerome; (520) 634-0554.**

The White Horse Inn—$$–$$$

Locals say they go here for the best burgers in Cottonwood. With specials like pork chops and mashed potatoes, you know this is not the place to come if you're counting calories. Food is almost overwhelmingly hearty and you'd better eat up because waitresses, often jeans-clad grandmothers, really care whether or not you finish your cowboy beans. Open for lunch and dinner, and it has a full cocktail lounge. On AZ 89A just north of the Verde River bridge in Cottonwood. **(520) 634-2271.**

Clarkdale Antique Emporium & Soda Fountain—$–$$

Browse through remnants of yesteryear, then hop on a stool at the old-fashioned fountain for a further taste of the past. Sodas, sundaes and pies with a giant scoop of ice cream are among the present-day crowd pleasers. **907 Main St., Clarkdale; (520) 634-2828.**

Services

Cottonwood-Verde Valley Chamber of Commerce is located at the junction of AZ 89A and AZ 260. A separate room with tables and chairs is lined with brochures, so you can take the time to figure out what you want to do and ask questions before you leave. Open daily, 9 A.M.–5 P.M. **1010 S. Main St., Cottonwood, 86326; (520) 634-7593, fax (520) 634-7594.**

Camp Verde Chamber of Commerce occupies an old painted adobe school built in 1911. The original red oak floor creaks in friendly fashion as you come in. Located downtown near First and Main Streets across the parking lot from the town hall, where there are public rest rooms. Open Mon.–Fri., 9 A.M.–5 P.M. **P.O. Box 1665, Camp Verde, 86322; (520) 567-9294.**

In the same building as the Chamber of Commerce, the **Camp Verde Historical Society (520-567-4707)** is a good source of information to help put the Verde Valley in historical perspective.

Sunset Point Rest Area, on I-10, 53 miles north of Phoenix, is a large, busy rest area with covered ramadas, bathrooms and drinking water. Good interpretive signs explain the valley you're overlooking.

Payson

Completely encircled by the 2.9-million-acre Tonto National Forest, this woodland mountain town is one of Arizona's oldest communities. At an elevation of 5,000 feet and located in the state's geographic center, Payson is "The Heart of Arizona" to the locals. Never a rich town, its pine-covered slopes have come into their own in terms of real estate value in recent years. The craggy, tree-studded hills, favored sites for upscale vacation homes, attract residents of the steamy-in-summer Valley of the Sun in droves.

The area takes its animals seriously. Coming down off the Rim from the Heber area, countless roadside signs caution drivers to watch for elk. One of the cleverest, a four-parter, says: *YOU SPEED ... YOU CHOOSE ... HIT AN ELK ... YOU BOTH LOSE.* All that's missing are the words BurmaShave at the end.

Payson got its name from an Illinois senator who never even saw the place. It was christened in Senator Payson's honor because, in 1884, he was instrumental in getting a post office for the town, then called Union City. Early residents, mostly miners, were lured by tales of mineral wealth in the surrounding mountains. When the stories didn't pan out, they stayed anyway, enticed by the mild four-season climate and the fact that all of them were basically in the same boat. Zane Grey was drawn to Arizona in general and the Mogollon Rim area near Payson in particular by the wild and untamed mountains. He penned many novels in a small two-bedroom cabin at 6,500 feet just beneath the Rim. A 1990 forest fire destroyed the cabin, but plans to reconstruct a replica are in the works.

Festivals and Events

World's Oldest Continuous Rodeo

mid-August

Celebrated for more than one hundred years, this PRCA-sanctioned event draws entrants and spectators from all over the country. It's a fun, colorful competition, held among the tall pines in a place that's cool when temperatures in the most heavily populated portions of the state are in triple digits. Events include barrel racing, bull riding, team roping, bareback riding, calf roping, saddle bronco riding and steer wrestling, with participation by both cowboys and cowgirls. The four-day event, held at the Payson Rodeo Grounds, also includes an elaborate parade, dances, and queen and junior queen coronation. On Sunday morning there's even a cowboy church service at the arena.

Old Time Fiddlers Contest

late September

During this thoroughly enjoyable weekend, Arizona fiddlers and musicians gather to compete for state championship titles. They play a very specific type of music that has its roots in mountain and rural areas and is preserved by a dedicated group. Fiddlers range from youngsters just learning to old-timers who have mastered the art of "fiddlin'," which has little to do with playing the violin. There also are storytellers, a fiddle-making demonstration, folk dancers and arts and crafts booths. The event usually begins with a "21-fiddle salute."

Major Attractions

Tonto Natural Bridge State Park

Fourteen miles north of Payson on the west side of Highway 87, this unusual state park is home to a wonder that has taken thousands of years to create. Hidden in a pine-studded valley, the world's largest natural travertine bridge spans a 400-foot tunnel 183 feet above little Pine Creek. It was so well concealed, it took a prospector being chased by Apaches in 1877 to stumble on it. Over the centuries water seeping from the creek undermined a portion of travertine to create a tube that eventually became a natural bridge.

First, view the bridge from above, then clomp down Gowan Loop Trail, a narrow half-mile path to a series of boardwalks, where you can stand in a shadowy fern-draped grotto practically underneath the bridge. The springs that created the bridge are still at work today. If you opt for the short way back to the top, you'll hand-over-hand your way up cables on either side of an extremely steep trail. Be sure you're in good shape, or return the way you came. The Pine Creek Trail extends for one-half mile to the Pine Creek natural area. A quaint old lodge, once used by Zane Grey and Al Capone, is settled comfortably in an orchard of apple, pear, plum and apricot trees in a pretty meadow above the bridge. Built in 1927 by Beryl Goodfellow and Andy Ogilvie, it accommodated travelers who came to see the unusual natural bridge. Purchased by the state of Arizona in 1991, you can tour the three-story lodge, furnished with antiques and original fixtures. A Victrola scratches out tunes in the foyer, and the Goodfellow Room has its original porcelain tub and wicker bed. Lodge tours are offered Friday and Saturday if a volunteer is available. A small herd of javelina has migrated into the area, there is a resident deer population and bird-watching is excellent. Just move quietly and nature will come out to greet you. Open daily, Apr. to Oct., 8 A.M.–6 P.M.; Nov. to Mar., 9 A.M.–5 P.M. Closed Christmas Day. No pets. Small fee per vehicle for use of the park. The park office is one-half mile off AZ 87, 14 miles north of Payson. **(520) 476-4202.**

Christopher Creek and Kohl's Ranch

About 18 to 22 miles east of Payson, these two little communities have become summer getaway destinations for heat-suffocated Phoenicians. See Where to Stay for more information.

Outdoor Activities

Hiking

Fossil Springs Wilderness

This 12,000-acre protected area has a wonderful hike from near the town of Strawberry to

Fossil Springs. This reliable water source produces a pleasant 72-degree gush that creates a little environmental oasis populated with lush trees and plants, and more than one hundred bird species. In canyon walls near the spring, you can see small fossilized shells, remnants of a vast sea that covered this area 350 million years ago. You can swim in the pools that have formed along the creek, but the water is not reliably safe for drinking. The wood flume directs water to the turbines of the Irving and Childs Power Plants that depend on it for power generation. From AZ 87 in Strawberry (Strawberry Lodge is on the corner) turn west on Fossil Creek Road (Forest Service Road 708) and go past the school house 4 miles on the dirt road. Turn right to the marked trailhead parking lot. The Upper Trail is a dusty, 2.5-mile trek that descends about 1,300 feet from the trailhead to the springs. The Flume Trail also leads to the springs, covers about 4 miles, and is accessed about 5 miles farther along Fossil Creek Road. It is longer, about 4 miles total, but easier because the grade is gentler. To do both trails, leave one car at the Upper Trail head and another at the beginning of the Flume Trail, where you'll end your hike. Motorized and mechanical equipment, including mountain bikes, is not allowed on the trail. For information contact the **Pine-Strawberry Chamber of Commerce** at **(520) 476-3547.**

Horseback Riding

Kohl's Stables

The stables are located at Kohl's Ranch 17 miles northeast of Payson on AZ 260. You can pop in and do a one-hour, two-hour or half-day ride along easy trails, with a guide who knows the area and its history, and is more than willing to talk about it. This isn't the Wild West experience, where you charge off into parts unknown, clinging to the back of a barely broken steed. Rather, these are enjoyable family rides taken only with a guide. If you've seen the area as a hiker, this can add another dimension to your appreciation. Rides are moderately priced, and horses are in good shape. Call **(520) 478-4211** and ask for the stables.

Five miles north of Payson, Shoofly village was home to a prehistoric culture between A.D. 1000 and 1250.

Parks, Gardens and Lakes

Woods Canyon Lake

Between Heber and Payson, this pretty little 52-acre lake is stocked with trout and large-mouth bass. To get there, follow Forest Road 300 from AZ 260 for about 5 miles. This is probably one of the most scenic stretches in the state. Every few hundred yards there is a vista point with a parking lot from which you can get unparalleled views of the Mogollon Rim. From this area, you may pick up several trailheads including the Willow Creek Trail and Crook Trail. There are two campgrounds and a well-stocked store at the lake. From Memorial Day to Labor Day you can join in Friday nature walks, Saturday hikes to a nearby sinkhole and assorted organized Sunday hikes. Make reservations by calling **(800) 280-CAMP** and ask for Aspen or Spillway Campgrounds. A day-use picnic area has tables and fire pits. From AZ 260 take the Forest Road 300 exit, marked with a green sign that says Woods Canyon Lake.

Seeing and Doing

Shoofly Village

You really have to use your imagination to picture what this one-time village must have been like when occupied. All that's left are the outlines of more than 80 rooms and courtyards, with remnants of a perimeter wall that encloses about four acres. A ring of trees identifies the location of the wall. At an elevation of 5,240 feet, on top of Houston Mesa just under the Mogollon Rim, the area is covered with low scrub and junipers and was active between

A.D. 1000 and 1250. The people who lived here had close ties to the Hohokam and Salado prehistoric cultures. A small reconstruction shows how dwelling walls were built of wood, adobe and stone. A one-quarter mile interpretive trail, some of it paved and wheelchair accessible, has excellent signs that help visualize how the site once looked. There are rest rooms and picnic ramadas. Located 5 miles north of Payson. Take AZ 87 north from Payson to the Houston Mesa Road and turn east. At the fork in the road, with the sign for Mesa del Caballo subdivision, take the right fork. The parking lot is just beyond the fork.

Museum of the Forest

Three green, wood frame buildings on the shore of a small lake in Green Valley Park house artifacts and photos that show the history and lifestyle of Payson pioneers, including the cavalry that came to secure the area under General Crook. Displays trace local Arizona culture and ecology. The statue in front of the museum, a firefighter in full gear, honors the forest firefighters who died protecting lives and trees. A tour starts in the original 1930s forest ranger's residence, now the museum store. You can pick up good reference material here on Payson's history. The center building is a re-creation of the Herron, Payson's finest hotel at the turn of the century, which burned to the ground in 1918. Behind the hotel the tower with the little house on top is the original Forest Ranger's Station. In the last building you can see how the first forest ranger, Fletcher Beard, conducted business from his office from 1908 to 1913. Staffed by volunteers, the museum's open hours are short, but it's well worth your while to plan around them. Open Wed.–Sun., 12–4 P.M. From the Beeline Highway take Main Street west about 1 mile to Green Valley Parkway (just before the lake) and turn right. **700 Green Valley Pkwy., Payson, 85544; (520) 474-3483.**

Strawberry Schoolhouse

The little town of Strawberry, about 20 miles north of Payson (3 miles north of Pine) lies in the shadow of the Mogollon Rim. Strawberry has become something of a retirement destination as well as a favorite place for summer visitors. Named for the wild strawberries that once grew here, it is at a cool 6,000-foot elevation. Its claim to fame is Arizona's oldest school. Built in 1885, the interior of this one-room log building has been restored to its pre-1900 status. It has interior wainscoting as

In Payson the Museum of the Forest honors those who fought forest fires, and houses artifacts and photos that help trace the area's history.

Getting There

Payson is about 75 miles northeast of Phoenix via AZ 87, known as the Beeline Highway. As of this writing, the highway is four-lane in some spots and two-lane in others. Additional lanes are under construction, scheduled for completion sometime in 2001.

Payson Municipal Airport offers charter service and is open to private aircraft. There is a fly-in campground adjacent to the runway. **Payson Express** provides shuttle service to and from Payson and the Greater Phoenix area, with door-to-door service, or daily service from Phoenix Sky Harbor Mon.–Sat. **P.O. Box 2601, Payson, 85547; in Payson (520) 474-5254; in Phoenix (602) 256-6464, fax (520) 474-1368.**

well as wallpaper, and was considered quite elegant in its day, especially for a student population that totaled just 22 pupils during the 1889–1890 school year. From AZ 87 in Strawberry, take Fossil Creek Road about 2 miles to the schoolhouse. Open summer weekends and by appointment. Call the **Pine-Strawberry Historical Society** at **(520) 476-4324.**

Walking Tour of Pine

A number of early rock and log cabins remain in present-day Pine as reminders of its establishment by Mormon pioneers in 1879. Most have been updated to become cafes and gift shops, but enough structure remains to capture the original character. Stop in at the chamber of commerce to pick up a self-guided walking tour map. There is a very small charge.

Mazatzal Casino

Run by the Tonto Apache Tribe and named for the Mazatzal (pronounced Ma-ta-zal) Wilderness, it's typical of Indian gaming sites in the state. It offers a "Hot Time in the Cool Pines," it says, with 318 player-friendly slot machines, $25,000 keno, high stakes bingo and a card room. The Cedar Ridge Restaurant serves above-average casino food, and you can take a break in the Apache Spirits Sports Bar. Open 24 hours a day, 7 days a week. Located on Payson's south edge on the Beeline Highway (AZ 87) at Milepost 251, the first light as you enter from the south. Turn right into the casino. **(800) 777-PLAY.**

Where to Stay

Hotels, Motels & Inns

Inn of Payson—$$$

This newish motel is pleasant and quiet, with patio rooms facing the pool or a grassy garden area. Large, comfortable rooms have coffee makers and mini-refrigerators. A full-service restaurant, Michael's at the Inn serves continental breakfast, lunch and dinner. **801 N. Beeline Hwy., Payson, 85541; (800) 247-9477 or (520) 474-3241.**

Pueblo Inn—$$$

You can't miss this adobe-style building on the south side of AZ 260 as you come into town from the east. It looks just like its name. Rooms are well furnished and exceptionally comfortable. For a real treat book yourself into one of the luxury rooms that has a two-person spa, coffee maker, refrigerator, fireplace and wet bar. Winter prices are slightly less than summer. **809 E. Hwy. 260, Payson, 85541; (800) 888-9828.**

Majestic Mountain Inn—$$$

This brand new inn has deluxe rooms with fireplaces and in-room, two-person spas. All rooms have coffee makers, wet bars and refrigerators, and most look out over an uninterrupted expanse of pine forest. It can be a quiet, romantic getaway as well as a comfortable home base for exploring the area. **602 E. Hwy. 260, Payson, 85541; (800) 408-2442 or (520) 474-0185.**

Lodges & Cabins

Strawberry Lodge—$$–$$$

This is one of those delightful little gems that you can't help but love. The Turner family bought it more than 35 years ago when it was a hunting lodge, and now Jean Turner, born in 1918, runs it with cheerful hospitality. The dining room is famous for its well-priced family specials that include fried chicken, meatloaf, prime rib, ribs and more. Don't miss their fabulous fruit pies and outstanding buttermilk pie. Jean says that locals, once named the Spit 'n' Whittle Club, meet about 6:30 A.M. to discuss the problems of the world. "Then they come back around 3 to see if anything has changed," she laughs. Small, comfortable rooms, some with fireplaces, have no phones or TVs. Summers are busy, with winter snow days also popular, so call for reservations. Located on AZ 87 in downtown Strawberry. **HCR 1 Box 331, Strawberry, 85544; (520) 476-3333.**

Kohl's Ranch Lodge—$$$–$$$$

People have been coming to this cool creekside location 17 miles northeast of Payson for more than 75 years. Before that, Native Americans lived here along the banks of Tonto Creek. In 1927 the Kohl family bought grazing land here, and the ranch became a community center for parties and get-togethers. The present lodge, built in the 1940s, has 41 comfortable rooms decorated in a Western theme. When booking, be sure to ask for a room on the creek side. You won't be directly on the creek (that's where the cabins are) but you will be on the side away from the road. Some of the rooms have fireplaces, refrigerators and coffee makers. There also are eight one- and two-bedroom cabins on the creek that have individual decks, outdoor spas and fireplaces. These can get a bit pricey, but if two couples split the tariff, it ends up about the same as a lodge room for each. Since this is Zane Grey country, movies made from the famous author's books are shown in the lodge loft on Friday, Saturday and Sunday, and on request. There is a small market with gifts, supplies and books about the area, including Zane Grey novels and Tony Hillerman's current favorites revolving around the ambitious antics of Sgt. Jim Chee of the Navajo Tribal Police. See Where to Eat for Zane Grey Dining Room. Open year-round. **E. Hwy. 60, Payson, 85541; (800) 331-5645 or (520) 478-4211.**

Christopher Creek Lodge—$$–$$$

You really can be right on the creek in these rustic log and stone cottages. Although they look as if they were built years ago, they have modern facilities. Most have fireplaces and can accommodate a family or two couples. There also are motel-type rooms, not nearly as charming as the cottages, but if you're just looking for a place to headquarter while you tour the area, they can be a good home base. Firewood provided. Located 21 miles east of Payson on AZ 260 in Christopher Creek. **Star Route, Box 119, Payson, 85541; (520) 478-4300.**

Happy Jack Lodge & RV Park—$$$

This remote, quiet resort on top of the Mogollon Rim is a haven for the goshawk and spotted owl in an area of fragrant Ponderosa that has survived the logging industry. The one-time logging camp has been renovated to accommodate today's guests and has a lodge, RV park with full hookups (may be open summer months only so check first) and kitchenette cabins. There are five major fishing lakes and streams within a 25-mile radius and a network of old logging roads to explore on foot or with a mountain bike. Located 39 miles north of Payson. Stay on AZ 87 north from Payson to Forest Road 3 (if you're coming south from Flagstaff, it's also called Lake Mary Road), and continue north 2 miles to the lodge. **P.O. Box 19569, Happy Jack, 86024; (520) 477-2805, fax (520) 477-2806.**

Camping & RV Parks

Campgrounds in the area are located north and east of Payson, mostly along the rim. Call the Payson Chamber of Commerce (see Services) for an up-to-date list before you set out. One of the closest and most beautiful, **Ponderosa Campground,** is about 15 miles east of Payson in a huge stand of its namesake pines that truly "whisper" in the wind. There are 60 spaces with water, a dump station and rest rooms. Open May to Sept. It is located along State Route 260 about 15 miles east of Payson. Others in the area, like **Christopher Creek Campground,** fill up so quickly that it's almost pure luck if you manage to snag a space there.

Where to Eat

Fast food chains are strung along the major highways that intersect in Payson.

Zane Grey Dining Room (Kohl's Ranch)—$$$

People staying in Payson often make a late afternoon drive out to Kohl's Ranch to look around, have a drink at the Cowboy Bar, and stay for dinner in the Zane Grey Dining Room. Low-key and casual, it has comfortable booths and good, hearty food. Thursdays are all-you-can-eat barbecue beef rib nights, and prime rib is always available. Open daily for breakfast, lunch and dinner. Located 17 miles northeast of Payson on AZ 260. **(800) 331-5645.**

Creekside Steakhouse & Tavern—$$-$$$

About 22 miles northeast of Payson on AZ 260, this rustic tavern has been a stopping-off point for 25 years for people driving down off the Rim. Portions are huge, so the kitchen will fix many sandwiches by the half. On the menu for years, the Mad Jack with chilies, cheese and bacon was one of our favorites. Half a dozen steak selections range from petite to enormous. Stop in the bar to see generations of initials carved in its rugged top. Service is friendly and "down home," and there's live bar entertainment on weekends. Open daily, 6 A.M.–10 P.M. In Christopher Creek. **(520) 478-4557 or (520) 478-4389.**

Mario's—$$-$$$

Besides being a great place to watch sports, Mario's has outstanding hand-tossed (we took their word for it) pizza, subs, a good selection of pastas and some truly tasty vegetarian specialties that include spinach ravioli and vegetarian pizza. It's worth a stop just for their homemade bread. Happy hour, Mon.–Fri., 5–7 P.M., really gets happy. They'll package up food for takeout, too. Open daily, Sun.–Thu., 10:30 A.M.–9 P.M.; Fri. and Sat., 10:30 A.M.–10 P.M. Located at the east end of a shopping center across from Safeway. **600 E. Hwy. 260, Payson; (520) 474-5429.**

The Oaks—$$$

One of the area's fine-dining restaurants, it occupies a classic frame building set back from the road, and has a reputation for attentive but unpretentious service. The dinner menu changes every month, and a nightly special is offered. Prime rib always is on the menu, as is an excellent, generous Caesar salad. It's a popular place among the locals for its expansive Sunday brunch. Reservations are recommended. Open Wed.–Sun., 11 A.M.–2 P.M. for lunch; Wed., Thu., and Sun., 5–8 P.M., Fri.–Sat., 5–9 P.M. for dinner. **302 W. Main St., Payson; (520) 474-1929.**

Services

As you approach Payson on AZ 87 from Phoenix, the new Mazatzal rest area is open at the Hwy. 188 junction, the turnoff to Roosevelt Lake. The location is scenic as well as practical, so it's a good place to stretch your legs.

Payson Chamber of Commerce is located in a small building at the corner of West Main and the Beeline Highway (AZ 87/260). There is a large parking lot behind the building. Open Mon.–Fri., 8 A.M.–5 P.M.; Sat.–Sun., 10 A.M.–2 P.M. **100 W. Main, P.O. Box 1380, Payson, 85547; (800) 6-PAYSON or (520) 474-4515, fax (520) 474-8812. E-mail: pcoc@netzone.com. Website: www.rimcountry.com.**

Pine-Strawberry Chamber of Commerce is located on the west side of AZ 87 in Pine, on the corner of Old County Road. Staffed by volunteers, it may be open just a few hours a day. **P.O. Box 196, Pine, 85544; (520) 476-3547.**

Sedona and Oak Creek Canyon

Considered by many one of the state's loveliest areas, Sedona also is known as a place of healing and emotional rejuvenation. In the mid-1970s a group of spiritualists declared that Sedona has four electromagnetic energy sources called vortexes. Consequently there are a number of practitioners of alternative healing who regularly schedule seminars and events here. You can pick up a vortex map at the chamber of commerce. Sedona also is an arts center with more than 40 galleries. Everyone comes to Sedona during the summer, when its elevation makes it cooler than the Valley of the Sun. December, January and February are considered low season and preferred by many visitors for the crisp, cool weather, occasional snow and dearth of tourists.

Sedona's namesake, Sedona Schnebly, moved here with her husband Carl from Missouri in the early 1900s. Because they owned the only home large enough to accommodate paying guests, the pair soon became known for their hospitality to travelers making the exhausting journey between Flagstaff and Jerome. When Carl applied for the area's first post office, his first choices of names were Oak Creek Crossing and Schnebly Station. The Postmaster General rejected them because the cancellation stamp didn't have room for so many letters. So Carl named the town for his wife, Sedona, who's six-letter name not only fit the stamp but had a melodious ring that appealed to everyone. In prehistory, the Anasazi fished Oak Creek, and farmed and hunted in the area, which at one time was a major trade route crossroads.

Festivals and Events

Jazz on the Rocks
mid-September

This is one of the most celebrated jazz and blues festivals anywhere, partially because of its scenic setting in red rock country, but also because it attracts top performers. Louis Bellson, Count Basie's Orchestra, Gerry Mulligan and other jazz notables have appeared in the past. Local groups perform in area restaurants during the festival, giving everyone a chance to join in the fun. **(520) 282-1985.**

Sedona Sculpture Walk

first weekend in October

Held at Los Abrigados Resort & Spa, the 3-day event attracts more than one hundred artists and sculptors from across the country. Artistic themes range from Native American to Western, contemporary and abstract. For information call the **Sedona Arts Center** at **(520) 282-3809.**

Red Rock Fantasy

late November to mid-January

More than one hundred thousand people come annually to this spectacular holiday light display that gets its glow from more than a million lights. Fifty families from around Arizona are chosen to create unique light displays that they set up on the 22 acres of Los Abrigados Resort, competing for the votes of visitors who choose the best display. An ongoing crowd-pleaser called Dancing Lights, located creekside in the Sycamore Grove, involves tiny twinklers performing a synchronized dance to holiday and classical music. Tickets are available at the admission booth at Los Abrigados. **160 Portal Ln., Sedona, 86336; (520) 282-1777. Website: www.sedona.net/fun/fantasy.**

Outdoor Activities

Biking

There are lots of outstanding trails in the area and bike shops with rentals to help you get out on them. **Sedona Red Rock Pathways** project aims to connect most of the area with a series of bicycling trails. At present a good, fairly easy one-way route begins on AZ 89A, along **Lower Red Rock Loop,** and winds through **Red Rock State Park,** ending up on Verde Valley School Road. Don't try to continue to the Upper Loop Road as it is narrow with no room for bikes. Hard-core cyclists bike the steep **Schnebly Hill Road,** which can be rocky and dusty. Try it, if a great view is enough reward for you. Forest Service roads offer good riding, but remember that in the Coconino National Forest designated Wilderness Areas are not open to cyclists. **Dry Creek Road** is not too difficult and connects with **Boynton Pass Road,** also marked. Pick up Dry Creek Road in west Sedona off AZ 89A. Riders also use AZ 89A, where it is four-lane, but many cyclists are not comfortable with the amount of traffic, especially during summer. It's well worth $4.95 to pick up the Experience Sedona Recreation and Activity map at the Sedona Chamber of Commerce. It details hiking and biking trails all over the area.

Mountain Bike Heaven has double suspension bike rentals and will get you on your way with maps and suggested rides. Open daily, Mon.–Fri., 9 A.M.–6 P.M.,; Sat.–Sun., 9 A.M.–5 P.M. **1695 Hwy. 89A, Sedona, 86336; (520) 282-1323. Website: www.mountain-bikeheaven.com.**

Desert Jeep & Bike Rentals has bikes, technical assistance and dual full-suspension bikes. Located at the Desert Quail Inn on AZ 179 near Jack's Canyon Road. **6626 Hwy. 179, Sedona, 86351; (888) GO-4-JEEP or (520) 284-1099. E-mail: gjeep@sedona.net. Website: www.desertquailinn.com/jeep.-html.**

Sedona Bike & Bean Shop dispenses cappuccino and espresso along with its bike rentals. They'll show you a 3-D topographic map that helps you plan your ride. If you're looking for a riding companion, ask about the group rides that run daily. Located off AZ 89A in uptown Sedona. **376 Jordan Road; (520) 282-3515. Website: www.bike-bean.com.**

Four-Wheel-Drive Tours

A number of area operators go out to the red rocks, with varying focuses for their tours. Your best bet is to study the brochures, find out exactly how many guests go at one time and where the tour stops for photo opportunities. Most companies will pick you up and return you to your hotel. Some will rent you a jeep, but unless you know the area well, you may miss the best parts. Also, licensed companies have permits to go where private vehicles aren't allowed. Most can get you to a point where you can see the history of the area layered in the rocks.

Pink Jeep Tours

For years this company has taken guests right up rock walls and out onto trails that bear no resemblance to roads. Choices include winding among spires and pinnacles, which guides point out are different from mountains, looking at rock art and ancient ruins, checking out canyon lands and ancient geologic formations and viewing areas that are sacred to Native Americans. Guides are among the most knowledgeable in the area. **240 N. Hwy. 89A, Sedona, 86339; P.O. Box 1447, Sedona, 86339 (mailing address); (800) 999-2137 or (520) 282-2137. Website: www.pinkjeep.com.**

Sedona Red Rock Jeep Tours

Their specialized Vortex Tour visits at least three of the vortexes for which the area is famous. Whether or not you believe in vortex power, it can't hurt to learn where one comes from and why many people believe it can be used in healing. The company also offers archaeological, sacred earth, dawn and sunset tours. Located in Uptown Sedona at **270 N. Hwy. 89A, Sedona, 86339; P.O. Box 10305, Sedona, 86339 (mailing address); (800) 848-7728 or (520) 282-6826, fax (520) 282-0254.**

Golf

Oakcreek Country Club

This 6,800-yard, par 72 championship course, designed by Robert Trent Jones, is a challenge to golfers for its tree-lined layout. Thirty years old, it's been around long enough to be well-settled, and is open year-round. The signature 187-yard, par 3, 4th hole is tucked cleverly into a red rock formation. **690 Bell Rock Blvd., Sedona, 86351; (520) 284-1660.**

Sedona Golf Resort

They call it Golf on the Rocks, which pretty well describes this 18-hole championship course designed by Gary Panks. The 6,640-yard layout plays to a par 71, and winds through the red rocks that have made Sedona famous. Its famous par 3 11th hole begins at the course's highest point and shoots 200 yards to a right-sloping green. It may be one of the few courses in the country with bunkers of red sand. A dining room opens for breakfast and lunch. Located on AZ 179, 7 miles from I-17. **7260 Hwy. 179, Sedona, 86351; (520) 284-9355.**

Getting There

Sedona is a 2-hour drive north of Phoenix. From I-17 take Exit 298 onto AZ 179 and proceed 15 miles to Sedona.

Hiking

Red Rock and Slide Rock State Parks (see Seeing and Doing) have many great trails, including the easy, almost-level Pendley Home-

Famous red rock formations of Sedona.

stead Trail at Slide Rock that meanders through the apple orchard. Another beautiful hike follows a narrow side canyon off Oak Creek called **West Fork.** It is particularly lovely in fall when the giant cottonwoods along the canyon floor burst into color. The fairly level trail crosses the creek at several points and is cool and shady. Pick up the trailhead 3.2 miles north of Slide Rock State Park on AZ 89A. As you head north, on your left is a parking area with a path leading down to the creek. Just on the other side of the creek are the ruins of an old cabin and trail markers. Everyone seems to hike **Red Rock Crossing** because it is easy, do-able even by fairly young children and the definitely unfit. From the parking lot a cement walkway ends at Oak Creek, continuing on as a dirt trail to Cathedral Rock. The trailhead is off Upper Red Rock Loop Road. Once you're on it, just follow the signs. **Long Canyon Trail,** an easy 4.5 miles, leads to some lovely petroglyphs. From Dry Creek Road follow signs to Boynton and Long Canyon, turn right at Long Canyon Road, and the trailhead is one-half mile ahead.

In Sedona, the shopping area of Tlaquepaque is named for its Mexico counterpart. Arranged like a small village, small shops and boutiques open onto shady courtyards.

Hot Air Balloon Flights

Northern Light Balloon Expeditions

Seeing the red rocks from above may be even more spectacular than from ground level. Colors take on a different dimension, and formations have new shapes and forms. Best of all the ride is quiet, the stillness interrupted only by the occasional blast of the propane burner. Hotel pickup and return. **P.O. Box 1695, Sedona, 86339; (800) 230-6222. E-mail: balloon@sedona.net.**

Seeing and Doing

Tlaquepaque

Pronounced "T-laca-pocky," it looks like a cool, charming Spanish colonial village, and it is indeed named for the town in Guadalajara. But this town is an upscale arts and crafts center near Oak Creek, with boutiques, galleries and restaurants. Although you'll find a few, there is no T-shirt-and-ashtray mentality here. It's been planned so no shop competes with another, so you won't see endless rows of the same merchandise. The series of small pathways and graceful arches, with individual courtyards shaded by huge sycamores, creates a village feeling. Most shops are open daily, 10 A.M.–5 P.M. Located adjacent to Los Abrigados Resort just south of the "Y" on AZ 179 in Sedona. **P.O. Box 1868, Sedona, 86339; (520) 282-4838.**

Parks

Red Rock State Park

This extensive park and center for environmental education preserves one of the loveliest parts of Oak Creek. It is crosshatched with easy hiking trails of one to two miles. Allow at least an hour in the nature center to learn about what you'll see out in the park. The wheelchair access ramp leading to the center is imprinted with tracks of bear, bobcat, great blue heron, raccoon and other creatures of the area. The park, at one time slated to become a housing development, was part of the Smoke Trail Ranch, originally purchased by TWA owner Jack Frye who bought it in 1941 as a vacation retreat. Migrating birds, in April and November, share the forest with resident ravens, jays, Gila woodpeckers and Say's phoebes. Alders, cottonwoods and sycamores create fall color. The park's 286 acres once sheltered the Sinagua and Yavapai Indians, drawn to the Oak Creek area by its life-sustaining natural resources. Solar-powered toilets with circulating fans are placed along trails. A nature walk is held daily at 10 A.M. to acquaint visitors with the park's ecology. A spectacular overlook called Eagles Nest is the destination of a guided hike held Sat. at 8 A.M. May to Sept., and at 9 A.M. Oct. to Apr. There is a small per-vehicle entrance fee. Open 8 A.M.–6 P.M. during the summer, 8 A.M.–5 P.M. in the winter. It is located on Red Rock Loop Road off AZ 89A about 5 miles south of Sedona. **4050 Red Rock Loop Rd., Sedona, 86336; (520) 282-6907, fax (520) 282-5972.**

Slide Rock State Park

Nature has worn a 30-foot water slide between steep, extremely slippery red rock walls along Oak Creek in this 43-acre natural recreation area. For the summertime activity of water sliding, wear old heavy-duty denim shorts and tennis shoes, but be forewarned, the water temperature is a chilly 65 degrees, or less. From the parking lot to the slide it's an easy stroll through an apple orchard, in full fragrant bloom by mid-April, that dates to 1912. Thirteen apple varieties including red delicious, Arkansas black and Jonathan are grown here and sold at the refreshment center as cider, caramel apples and just plain apples for eating out of hand. Harvesting takes place in September and October. On Saturday, you can join a ranger-narrated history program at 1 P.M. in spring and fall, and 9 A.M. in summer, that focuses on the Pendley homestead, owned by the family that planted the original apple trees. Sunday bird walks leave at 8 A.M. April through

Slide Rock State Park is named for the rock and gushing water that have ruined countless pairs of jeans.

November. There are picnic tables, grills, a snack bar, hiking trails and rest rooms at the site. Small per-vehicle entry fee. Located 7 miles north of Sedona on AZ 89A. Open 8 A.M.–7 P.M. during the summer, 8 A.M.–5 P.M. during the winter and 8 A.M.–6 P.M. during the fall and spring. **P.O. Box 10358, Sedona, 86339; (520) 282-3034, fax (520) 282-0245.** For current water quality conditions, call **(602) 542-0202.**

Scenic Drives

This whole area is so scenic it's difficult to drive anywhere without coming upon a view. But here are a few of our favorites.

Loop Trail

Loop Trail is less than a half hour's drive, so go slowly and savor the scenery. From AZ 89A at the edge of Sedona heading for Cottonwood, turn left onto Upper Red Rock Loop Road. After a few miles the pavement ends, but the dirt road is graded and fine for regular automobiles. You pass distant red rocks, rolling farmland and in the fall, trees in full color. The pavement resumes at just about the point where you pass the entrance to Red Rock State Park. Continue on 3 miles to AZ 89A. You're now off the Loop Trail, but since you're in the area, you might as well continue on for another short segment. Turn right (back toward Sedona) and continue about a mile to Dry Creek Road (FR 152) and turn left (north). Follow it another mile to FR 152C and turn right. You can park and hike to Devil's Bridge, a spectacular natural arch in the red rocks.

Red Rock Scenic Road

This is the classic route taken by many visitors to Sedona, and offers much of the scenery that everyone looks for. From I-17 turn left onto AZ 179 and follow it about 14 miles into Sedona. It passes some of the area's famous rock formations including Cathedral Rock on the left and Bell Rock on the right, easy to recognize from their descriptively named outlines. Don't miss the Chapel of the Holy Cross 1 mile off AZ 179 on Chapel Road. Your view of it from the highway is the best, but once you reach the red cliffs among which it is set, you'll be treated to even better views of the spectacular red rocks. Open daily, 9 A.M.–6 P.M.

Where to Stay

Hotels, Motels & inns

Sedona Inn—$$$

This Best Western is out of the ordinary for its decks that provide 360-degree views of the red rocks. Complimentary continental breakfast, heated pool and whirlpool, in-room refrigerators and coffee makers make it a singularly pleasant place to stay, without the resort tariff. Located 1.5 miles west of the center of town, off AZ 89A and Soldiers Pass Road. **(800) 292-6344 or (520) 282-3072.**

Southwest Inn—$$$$

The Santa Fe-style inn offers a picturesque red rock setting and all the civilized accouterments you'd expect—fireplaces, phones, modem jacks, refrigerators, coffee makers, hair dryers, decks and patios. There are a pool and continental breakfast. The inn partners with the Verde Canyon Railway on accommodations and train packages. **3250 W. Hwy. 89A, Sedona, 86336; (800) 483-7422; (520) 282-3344, fax (520) 282-0267. E-mail: info@swinn.com. Website: www.swinn.com.**

Los Abrigados Resort & Spa—$$$$

Part of the charm of this timeshare, which also welcomes overnight guests, is that everything is right here—spa facilities, fine restaurants (see Where to Eat), comfortable rooms with microwaves, small refrigerators and coffee makers, and shopping next door at Tlaquepaque. Some rooms have patio spa tubs for bubbling under the stars. If it has a fault, it's that a few rooms are a bit claustrophobic because the patio looks out onto an enclosed area. When booking, ask about the view. Located just south of the "Y" on AZ 179 in Sedona. **160 Portal Ln., Sedona, 86336; (520) 282-1777.**

Enchantment—$$$$

Absolutely a Big Splurge, Enchantment is truly worth it if you want to be totally pampered. This resort with spa, hidden in Boynton Canyon, includes guest rooms and two- and three-bedroom casitas. You come here to unwind, play tennis, hike among the red rocks, to be massaged and have facials. Three-day packages bring the cost down considerably, so ask when booking. **525 Boynton Canyon Rd., Sedona, 86336; (800) 826-4180 or (520) 282-2900, fax (520) 282-9249.**

Hostels

Hostel Sedona—$

Just behind Los Abrigados Resort, you'll find Hostel Sedona. A newer place still getting situated, the hostel offers 12 bunks, two private rooms, communal kitchen, chore list and storage for gear. The hostel is conveniently located less than a mile from downtown Sedona and is wheelchair accessible. From AZ 179 south of the "Y" take Ranger Road to Brewer Road, go left, then take another immediate left into the hostel. Or from AZ 89A west of uptown Sedona, take Brewer Road south past Ranger Road. Take the next left into the hostel. **5 Soldiers Wash Dr., Sedona, 86336; (520) 282-2772.**

RV Parks & Camping

Sedona RV Resort
There are almost 200 RV hookups and tent sites at this upscale park, picturesquely sited among the red rocks. It has paved roads lined with shade trees, picnic tables and barbecues, even hair dryers in the shower room. Tent sites have electric hookups. Located 2 miles southwest of Sedona on AZ 89A toward Cottonwood. **6701 W. Hwy. 89A; (800) 547-8727 or (520) 282-6640.**

Rancho Sedona RV Park
Along Oak Creek, this luxury 10-acre park has full hookups, large shade trees, access to the creek, rest rooms, showers and laundry facilities. The park is close enough to downtown Sedona and Tlaquepaque that you can walk, and a free shuttle runs from 8 A.M.–10 P.M. For a premium price you can have a large executive site on the creek. Exit AZ 179 at Schnebly Hill Road and turn left onto Rancho Sedona. **135 Bear Wallow Ln.; (520) 282-7255.**

Lo Lo Mai Springs Outdoor Resort
This pleasant 26-acre park hugs Oak Creek for almost a mile, with shaded RV sites that have patios and full hookups. Tenters can set up camp in secluded sites at the edge of the creek. There are rest rooms, swimming pool and spa, showers and laundry, a convenience store and clubhouse. Hiking trails radiate out from the park in a number of directions. Located 9 miles southwest of Sedona. Take AZ 89A southwest from Sedona toward Cottonwood. Approximately 8 miles from Sedona go left on the Page Springs-McGuireville turnoff (AZ 50). Continue approximately 1 mile to the entrance of Lo Lo Mai Springs. **11505 Lo Lo Mai Rd., Page Springs, 86325; (520) 634-4700.**

Where to Eat

Joey Bistro—$$$
You might not immediately catch on to the significance of this friendly Italian place's name until you realize that the huge photos on the walls are all famous Joeys—Joe DiMaggio, Joe Bonano, Josef Stalin—they're represented, larger than life, looking down at your plate of pasta. The menu is definitely a notch or two above your average Italian fare, with interesting pastas combined with vegetables, fish and meat in pleasing blends. The wines-by-the-glass menu is extensive enough to offer good choices, so you don't have to commit to a whole bottle until you've tried what's inside. Wines are mainly Italian with some Californias. Call ahead to ask about the specials, such as pasta night, when menu prices on selected items can be less than half the normal tariff. Cover your eyes when the dessert tray comes, unless you want to expend beaucoup d'calories. Open for dinner from 5 P.M. Located at Los Abrigados Resort. **160 Portal Ln., Sedona; (520) 204-JOEY.**

Knotty Pine Cafe—$$$
Casual, family eatery with genuine knotty pine walls, ceilings and floors. Located at Junipine Resort on Oak Creek, it is a pleasant .75-mile drive north of Slide Rock State Park, 8.5 miles from Sedona. Almond-crusted Oak Creek trout and barbecued pork ribs draw diners from as far away as Phoenix. Open daily for breakfast, lunch and dinner Mar. through Oct.; open Thur.–Sun. Nov. through Feb. **8351 N. Hwy. 89A, Oak Creek; (520) 282-3375.**

Hot Rocks Pizza—$$–$$$
If you've decided to eat in, have Hot Rocks deliver a Posse Grounds (a Sedona landmark) pizza overflowing with chicken, olives, jalapenos, cheddar, tomatoes and onions. The vegetarian White Buffalo is fragrant with olive oil, garlic, onions and artichokes. Or, ad lib your own when you call. Delivery available from 10:30 A.M.–9 P.M. **(520) 282-7753.**

The Sage—$$
This vegetarian restaurant actually attracts more nonvegetarians than dedicated vegans for its superfresh, delicious cuisine. There really isn't a set menu. Rather, check the blackboard for daily specials that can include pasta with mushroom sauce, eggplant/lima bean stew, peppers and pasta. There's a daily lunch buffet with dishes like hummus and chips, pasta tossed with vegetables and olive oil,

potato salad, coleslaw, and always fresh rolls and breads. Tira misu is a dessert specialty. During summer, meals are served in the creamy-pastel-decor dining room or on an outdoor patio. Open daily for lunch and dinner. Except Tues., open for lunch only. **2611 W. Hwy. 89A, Sedona; (520) 204-2079.**

WenDeli's Delicatessen—$$

They'll pack a picnic to take to the red rocks. Specialties are fruit salad and generous sub sandwiches with all the trimmings. Located in the uptown area next door to TCBY. Open daily 8 A.M.–4 P.M. **276 N. Hwy. 89A, Ste. B., Sedona; (520) 282-7313.**

Services

Sedona-Oak Creek Canyon Chamber of Commerce, P.O. Box 478, Sedona, 86639; (800) 288-7336 or (520) 282-7722, fax (520) 204-1064. Website: www.arizona-guide.com/sedona.

Yarnell and Wickenburg

YARNELL

About 25 miles southwest of Prescott lies Peeples Valley, a lush pastureland named for prospector A. H. Peeples, who led other adventurers into the area in 1863. Looking down into the valley from the east side of Weavers Mountain is Yarnell, a pleasant little town north of Wickenburg that shares a common history with many of Arizona's small towns. Peeples' venture unearthed gold on a mesa near present-day Yarnell that turned out to be the richest placer gold discovery ever made in the state. Small claims were staked and the area slowly grew, until 1889 when prospector Harrison Yarnell struck gold near Antelope Peak, east of what now is Yarnell, and gave the town its name. When it was no longer profitable to extract gold from underground, sometime in the early 1940s, the mines were abandoned.

Never a boom town, Yarnell was content to stay small, serving the ranchers and miners that called it home. At 4,800 feet its mild climate attracted permanent residents, including retirees, artists and those involved in local service industries. Each May, Yarnell Daze celebrates the town's history with a parade, an antique automobile show and street vendors. Today it has several antiques shops and galleries. Many residents work at nearby ranches or in Prescott and Wickenburg. There are a gas station and a bank. But the town's character may be about to change. A Canadian mining company is proposing an open pit mine on Yarnell Hill south of town. Speculators say that over a six-year period the mine would gradually erode the top of the hill until it would no longer exist. Although opponents are vocal, proponents point to the town's history and say what the heck, it always was a mining town and always will be. Yarnell is 28 miles north of Wickenburg on AZ 89. Information is available at Hill Top Realty on AZ 89 at 163 Broadway. Or contact the **Yarnell-Peeples Valley Chamber of Commerce, P.O. Box 275, Yarnell, 85362.**

WICKENBURG

It's hard not to like a town that erects a "No Fishing From Bridge" sign over a river that's perpetually dry, flowing 20 feet below the surface at this point and for most of its 100-mile course through the desert. From the late 1800s when Wickenburg was a boom town celebrating its glory holes and copper mines, it has had a sense of humor about itself. Tales of its wealth were so exaggerated that any raconteur of overstated stories became known as a "Hassayamper" in honor of the dry Hassayampa River. To local Native Americans, its name means "river that flows upside down." Legend says that if you drank from it, you'd be unable to tell the truth. Today, the small Sonoran desert town 60 miles northwest of Phoenix doesn't have to try all that hard to retain its Old West ambiance. Surrounding ranches, dude and working, lend credibility to the cowboy you see at the local sandwich saloon decked out in spurs and chaps. Three Western apparel and tack shops reinforce the image that helps sustain the charm that makes tourism Wickenburg's most important economic staple. Its population of around 5,000 more than doubles during winter months.

The Yavapai Indians were the sole inhabitants of the Wickenburg area until the late 1500s, when the first Spaniard, Antonio de Espejo, took a look at the area. He claimed to have discovered gold, but it wasn't until 1863, when German immigrant Henry Wickenburg began working the famous Vulture gold mine on the river's banks, that its reputation as a mining center was validated. But the Vulture had checkered success, sometimes yielding its riches with barely a whimper, other times bankrupting the company that owned it. It's one of the reasons that the mine changed hands so many times. Wickenburg sold it after just two years and turned to farming. No one is sure if the mine is named for the birds that circle in this desert environment or the manner in which so many hopefuls fell prey to the allure of gold, only to find the Vulture Mine too stubborn to release its riches. Fortunately the Hassayampa River channel supported agriculture.

As more and more people moved into the area, confrontations over water became frequent until six passengers were killed in a stagecoach ambush just outside of town. Blame was placed on Mexican bandits, Yavapai and even Americans masquerading as Native Americans. But the truth of the 1871 Wickenburg Massacre was never fully revealed. In 1891 the railroad came to town, linking Wickenburg to Phoenix, and by the 1920s a tourism trade was well established. Cattle ranches became dude ranches and well-heeled tourists became repeat visitors.

Festivals and Events

Apple and Peach Picking at Date Creek Ranch

weekends in July

Beginning July 4, you pick your own peaches and apples at this rustic ranch. You'll be given a bag (or you can bring your own), and wire mesh pickers are also available to reach those high-up prizes. You can also buy grass-fed beef. Located in the foothills of the Date Creek Mountains north of Wickenburg. Take US 93 past Wickenburg to Milepost 177 and turn right. Follow the signs to the ranch. **(520) 776-8877.**

Fiesta Septiembre

early September

This salute to the area's Hispanic heritage has been held for more than a decade. It draws a goodly crowd from Phoenix, which helps support the respected groups that entertain. They often include Ballet Folklorico troops from a number of Mexican communities, mariachi bands and an arts and crafts mercado. Foodies can watch a tortilla-making demonstration and sample traditional foods. Events are held in the downtown area around the Desert Caballeros Western Museum.

Bluegrass Festival & Fiddle Championship

mid-November

This spirited event, going on for almost 20 years, features at least three prominent bands plus fiddle competition in more than a dozen categories. Competitors vie for some serious prize money here. There are an arts and crafts fair, food and kids' activities. Held at Constellation Park.

Outdoor Activities

Four-Wheel-Drive Tours

Wickenburg Jeep Tours

For some basic desert four-wheeling, they'll take you to the old San Domingo Mines, to the Box Canyon riparian area, past petroglyphs and through desert brush and scrub. A little humor and history are mixed with educational information about desert plants and animals. Tours are 2.5 to 3 hours long. Open Oct. 1 to May 31. **295 E. Wickenburg Way, Wickenburg, 85385; (800) 596-JEEP or (520) 684-0438.**

Getting There

Wickenburg is 60 miles northwest of Phoenix. Take I-17 north to AZ 74 (Carefree Highway), and follow it west to US 60. Follow US 60 north to Wickenburg. Or, you can take US 60 all the way from Phoenix. This diagonal road faithfully follows the Atchison, Topeka and Santa Fe Railroad line that was Wickenburg's original link to Phoenix. However, it is absolutely ablaze with traffic lights and can move at a month a mile during morning and evening rush hours.

Seeing and Doing

Nature Conservancy Hassayampa River Preserve

The Hassayampa River, which rarely makes an appearance in its sandy bed south of town, bubbles to the surface 3 miles to the southeast where it supports one of Arizona's finest Sonoran Desert streamside habitats. The Nature Conservancy manages a 5-mile stretch that flows the year-round. Its grassy banks, lined with cottonwoods and willows, form a ribbon of green, a favorite spot for picnickers and hikers. It preserves a cottonwood-willow forest (especially lovely in the fall), inhabited by Harris and zone-tailed hawks, vermilion flycatchers, Abert's towhees and more than 200 other bird species that are drawn to this area by reliable water and food supplies. Guests come to spot mule deer, mountain lion, bobcat, javelina and ringtailed cats that come to the river's edge to drink, their presence verified more by their tracks than actual sightings. Although with enough patience, anything is possible. The visitor center is an 1860s adobe built by Frederick Brill, an early rancher. An easy hike through the preserve follows a trail from the visitor center along the river. A loop around Palm Lake leads to an area alive with ducks, other waterfowl and shorebirds. The preserve is open Wed.–Sun., Sept. 16 to May 14, 8 A.M.–5 P.M. Summer hours are 6 A.M.–12 noon. The preserve is located about 8 miles south of Wickenburg on the west side of US 60 near Milepost 114. **Box 3290, Wickenburg, 85385; (520) 684-2772.**

Desert Caballeros Western Museum

This truly nifty museum, on two levels, details Wickenburg's history from prehistoric times through its mining days, using miniature dioramas and a full-size reproduction of a turn-of-the-century town. The country store is so well stocked you'll want to shop. It also has an outstanding collection of Western art including works by Russell, Remington, Catlin Phippen and others. The poignant life-sized bronze statue in front, of a cowboy kneeling in gratitude beside his tired horse, is called "Thanks for the Rain," created by famed cowboy artist Joe Beeler. Open Mon.–Sat, 10 A.M.–4 P.M.; Sun., 1–4 P.M. Small admission. **121 N. Frontier St.; (520) 684-2272; gift shop (520) 684-7075. E-mail: dcwm@-primenet.com.**

Vulture Mine

Looming on the horizon like a roughed-up thumb, Vulture Peak, at the east end of the Vulture Mountains, defines an area once rich in ore. A great self-guided tour directs you among tumbledown structures, once an assay office, bunkhouse, store and more. You can easily spend a couple of hours here, reading the interpretive signs and trekking up to the Glory Hole. For a more in-depth study of the mine, the on-site caretakers offer guided tours for ten or more. Tours are offered daily, Oct. to Mar., 8 A.M.–4 P.M., and on a reduced schedule the rest of the year. Small fee. The mine is located west of town on Wickenburg Way. Turn south on Vulture Mine Road to the mine entrance. For information call **(602) 859-2743.** This is a cellular phone number, so you must dial the 602 area code even if you're calling from the 602 area.

Robson's Arizona Mining World

This re-creation of a rough-and-tumble mining town brings together machinery, artifacts and antiques from the days when gold was king.

At Merv Griffin's Wickenburg Inn, a resident wrangler guides a guest party on a trail ride.

Located in the Harcuvar Mountains at the site of the once-flourishing Nella-Meda gold mine about 26 miles west of Wickenburg, 14 original buildings date to the mine's active days. A barber shop doubling as a surgery, a mercantile, print shop, saloon and more invite exploration. Open Oct. 1 to May 31, weekdays 10 A.M.–4 P.M., weekends 8 A.M.–6 P.M. Small fee. Take US 60 west from Wickenburg, then turn right (north) on AZ 71. Watch for the signs. For information call **(520) 685-2609.**

Scenic Drives

North of Wickenburg just as you cross the line from Maricopa into Yavapai county, the stretch of US 93 called the Joshua Forest Parkway is either stunningly beautiful or depressingly desolate, depending on your point of view. Those voting for beautiful find the Joshua trees (see sidebar, page 153) fascinating and the rolling, rocky countryside a treasure to explore. The two-lane road has occasional passing areas, and there is a roadside table with a ramada about 8 miles into the drive. Just before the Burro Creek Bridge going north, which spans an impressive chasm that surpasses its "creek" denomination, there is a pullout with good views of the Juniper Mountains to the west. By the time you cross the attractive trickle called the Big Sandy River and reach the wide spot in the road known as Wickieup, the scenery becomes pretty ordinary. But you might want to stop at the Subway for a snack, or for gas, or to look at the Indian jewelry there. The historical marker just north of Wickieup tells you that you're looking at the Big Sandy Valley, first explored by the Spanish in 1582. It became an important agricultural, mining, milling and smelting area in its early days.

Where to Stay

Guest Ranches

Good information is available on-line from Dude Ranchers' Association at **www.duderanch.org** and at **www.arizonaguide.com/azduderanch.**

Merv Griffin's Wickenburg Inn—$$$$

This inn has been around since 1974 and recently was purchased by entrepreneur and entertainer Merv Griffin. One of its many charms is that it sort of snuggles into the desert at the end of a winding dirt road. Buildings are gently tucked into hillsides and sheltered by a rolling landscape, becoming a true part of the desert in the midst of a 4,700-acre preserve. Because it was planned as a time-share, the casita accommodations have small stoves, refrigerators and coffee makers. Some casitas have private rooftop decks with fireplaces. It has tennis courts, a new swimming pool and spa including a children's pool with sandy "beach," an arts and crafts room and nature trails. Remarkably pristine acreage is crossed by trails for accompanied, open trail and sunset rides. A real guest-pleaser, during the cattle drive steers are driven into the open range for guests to help round up and herd back to the arena. The object is not to lose any along the way. Located 8 miles north of Wickenburg on AZ 89, about a 90-minute drive from Phoenix. **34801 S. Hwy. 89, Wickenburg, 85358; P.O. Box P, Wickenburg, 85358 (mailing address); (800) 942-5362 or (520) 684-7811.**

Rancho de los Caballeros—$$$$

This resort-style ranch was named for the grand tradition of the Spanish caballeros, the "gentlemen on horseback," who explored and settled the Southwest. At the ranch your attention is about equally divided between dude activities and the 18-hole private golf course that winds among upscale homes. Various rides accommodate equestrians of all abilities. There's even a pony named Shorty who's good with children. There are four tennis courts, trap and skeet shooting, hayrides, cookouts and a swimming pool. Tile-floor guest rooms and suites have handcrafted furnishings brought from Mexico and Santa Fe, so the overall look is rustic but the comfort level is high. Some rooms have kitchenettes and wet bars. Open Oct. to May. Take US 60 for 3.5 miles west of Wickenburg and turn south on Vulture Mine Road. **1551 S. Vulture Mine Rd., Wickenburg, 85390; (520) 684-5484.**

Motels

None of these are standouts, but if you're not staying at one of the dude ranches, they are your only choice for good, basic accommodations. One of the newest, **Las Viajeros (800-915-9795),** on US 93 on the north edge of town, has a pool and continental breakfast included in the room rates. The **Best Western Rancho Grande Motel (800-528-1234)** in downtown Wickenburg has some kitchenette units. The 29-room **Americinn,** on US 60 just south of town, is the closest motel to the Hassayampa Preserve, and it has a pool and spa. It is adjacent to The Willows restaurant, open for three meals a day, closed Mon. **850 E. Wickenburg Way; (800) 634-3444 or (520) 684-5461.**

Where to Eat

The expected chains like McDonald's, Denny's and Taco Bell are part of Wickenburg's dining out scene, as are two pizza parlors, a couple of steak houses and a deli. But the real gems are little places like those listed here.

Anita's Cocina—$-$$

The giant taco salad and super duper tostada (order it only if you're starving) are delicious, and remarkably well priced. This unpretentious two-room place isn't fancy, but service is friendly and the food's great. Located just a block off Wickenburg Way, the main drag. **57 N. Valentine; (520) 684-5777.**

Custer Cowboy Cafe—$-$$

"We pride ourselves on the size of our portions. If for any reason you feel you did not get enuf food for the money you paid, you just let us know and we will give you more, guaranteed," signed Jim Bob and Tina Custer. This little sign on the tables pretty much expresses the character of this genuine-cowboy-owned cafe. Walls are covered with framed belt buckles won in rodeo events and photos of bronc and bull-riding contests. Come here for a breakfast steak that'll keep you busy for awhile and home fries, boiled, diced and crispy-browned without being greasy. It's not unusual to see a grizzled cowboy pause when his meal is served, remove his hat and bow his head for a brief grace before diggin' in. Open daily, 6 A.M.–8 P.M. Located on US 93 just north of town. **666 N. Tegner St., (520) 684-2807.**

Services

Wickenburg Chamber of Commerce, P.O. Drawer CC, Wickenburg, 85358; (800) 942-5242 or (520) 684-5479.

Trees Shaped Like Joshua

Joshua trees.

The Joshua Tree is one of many plants and animals with a Biblical connection. It was named by Mormon pioneers following the call of Brigham Young to journey to Salt Lake City. They thought the tree branches resembled the arms of Joshua motioning them even further westward in their quest for the Promised Land. When silhouetted against a red desert sunset, a fertile imagination and inventive eye can surely discern "arms," wispy "hair" and perhaps a scraggly beard. This is truly a living thing whose beauty is unquestionably subjective. Its contorted configurations are considered grotesque by some and eerily beautiful by others. Some see the tree as a fascinating example of nature's sense of humor. Once viewing a Joshua tree, it is impossible to remain neutral about its attractiveness, or lack of same.

Found in the desert from California to Utah and in parts of Arizona and Nevada at elevations between 2,000 and 6,000 feet, the Joshua tree bristles with dagger-shaped, spine-tipped leaves and greenish-white flowers in long clusters, which bloom from February to late April, generally at their best in March. Blossoms open quite unspectacularly for just one night, then close to remain on the tree for two to three weeks. The tree can reach a height of 40 feet, but most specimens here range from 20 to 30 feet.

Without a tiny creature called the yucca moth to pollinate the blossoms, the Joshua tree wouldn't be able to flower. One cannot exist without the other. The female moth collects the tree's pollen in a ball and carefully spreads it within the flower, fertilizing the seeds. She's not an altruistic conservationist. She's just assuring her offspring a food source when they hatch from her eggs. The hungry larvae eat only a few seeds, however, leaving more than enough to be scattered across the desert by the wind. Although the tree may propagate via its root system, it must have the seeds it produces in pollinated flowers to establish itself in new areas.

The Joshua tree's shallow root system and top-heavy growth pattern cause it to cling tenaciously to sandy desert soil. It may not bloom every year, choosing to display its blossoms based on nature's distribution of rainfall and warm weather. It grows slowly, taking its time to develop new branches and blooms, adding just one-third to one-half inch each year. Because it doesn't have rings like a conventional tree, it is difficult to determine the age of a Joshua tree. But if the harsh desert environment allows, the many-armed elders can survive for several hundred years.

Besides its interesting architectural appearance, the Joshua tree provides a focal point for a complex wildlife community. Oftentimes a graceful red-tailed hawk or canny sparrow hawk uses the tree's topmost reaches as a lookout point for its next meal. Noisy cactus wrens flit and chatter among its branches as they nibble away at insects. Woodpeckers sometimes work their rapid-fire techniques on the fibrous trunk in a search for bugs.

Creamy, waxy podlike Joshua tree flowers supply food for more than two dozen bird species. The fleshy fruits, and later the dry seeds, are an important food source for ground squirrels.

The shaggy trunks provide fibers that augment the nest-building materials of desert birds. Fallen trees provide a safe haven for the seldom-seen desert night lizard. Termites find protection from heat and cold in the decaying fiber and convert plant energy to animal energy. Stink bugs munch on the tree's fibrous trunk, helping transform its nutrients into another living form. So even as it dies the Joshua gives life.

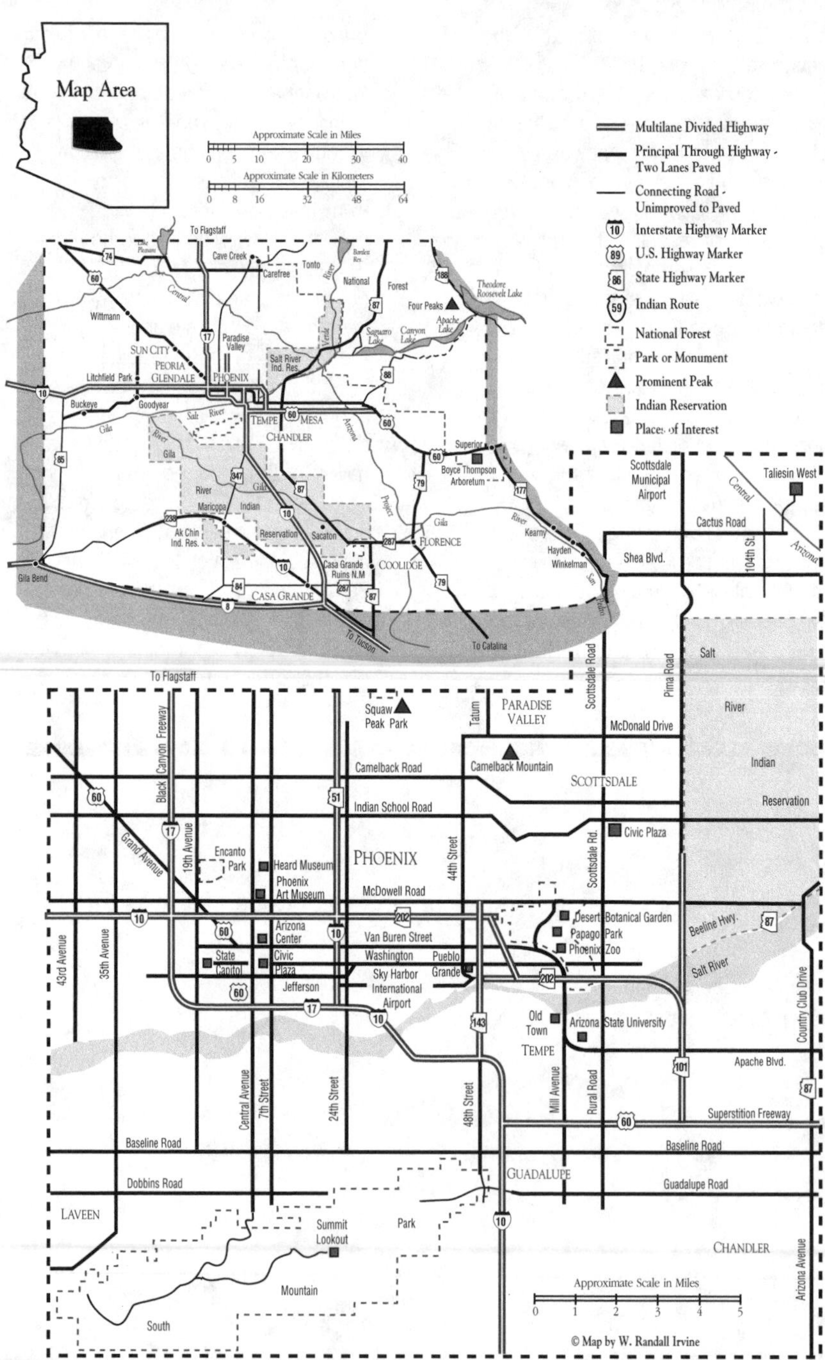

Phoenix and Environs

Phoenix and Environs

The Valley of the Sun

Although they strive to maintain separate images, Phoenix, Scottsdale, Mesa and Tempe blend into one geographically indistinguishable urban area in a smooth segue of suburbanism, with differences marked by little green signs telling you you're entering one or the other. Rapid growth has created panoramas of red tile roofs as subdivisions eat up the desert at what some clock as an acre an hour. An astonishing 22 incorporated cities cover more than 9,000 square miles in Maricopa County. Economically the distinctions are clear. Scottsdale's upmarket persona is a decided contrast to the lower-key lifestyle of Mesa. Yet all are part of the Valley of the Sun, an apt appellation considering that it averages 300 sun-filled days each year. It helps keep the 150-plus golf courses green and grassy, no doubt part of what attracts the 12 million people that visit the Valley each year. Old sol is around for 86 percent of daylight hours, creating a pleasant average yearly temperature of 72 degrees with almost no humidity. And despite its desert location, there are six lakes within a 75-minute drive of Phoenix. They create an eclectic mix that makes this one of the fastest-growing areas of the country. It doesn't seem destined to stop anytime soon. The flip side of all this sunny news is that during the Valley's hottest months, June, July and August, records put the average high at 102 to 105. Days that top 110 degrees are common, and recorded 120-degree days have been verified. The 72-degree average mentioned above kicks in from November through April, when days are absolutely lovely and temperatures rarely rise above 82 degrees.

Phoenix

In 1997 Phoenix became the nation's sixth largest city, nudging out San Diego for what many residents consider a dubious honor. Projected population for the year 2000 is 1,298,121, with 2.7 million people currently calling Maricopa County home. The median resident age is 31.1 years, more than 25 percent of whom are under the age of 18. Despite its reputation as a retirement city, Phoenix has a decidedly youthful orientation. Less than 10 percent of the population is over the age of 65.

Geographically larger than Los Angeles, Phoenix spreads over more than 100 square miles, yet has no efficient public transportation system. This means that people depend on their cars, often creating serious air pollution problems. Traffic on I-10 entering Phoenix from the south or coming in from the west on any given business day can be bumper to bumper. Yet new residents continue to arrive. Cost of living remains just a hair above the national average, due in part to reasonable housing costs. Many homes are in tightly packed subdivisions where only a wall assures any privacy. But it's one of the few cities where, in 1998, you could buy a home with a pool, albeit small, in some areas for under $100,000.

Never taking itself too seriously, the city's sense of humor emerges in brochure copy that places it "along the banks of the Salt River." The Salt is mostly banks and very little river, with a thin, crystal trickle sometimes crawling along its sandy bottom. It hasn't seen a steady flow of water in a century. Unless of course it's been raining, in which case the Salt occasionally overflows its banks with great enthusiasm, spilling onto the adjacent landscape, providing much-needed moisture for desert plants and animals. It's all part of the charm of the desert that entices 27 million visitors to the 48th state each year.

First-time visitors sometimes are intrigued by desert landscaping rather than lawns in front of homes. Others are amazed that in the middle of a desert there are so many lush, green golf courses. Ever since the web of canals called the Central Arizona Project guaranteed a continuing water supply from the Colorado River, Phoenix has figured its water needs were taken care of. Yet water is at the center of a never-ending controversy, some saying there is enough for decades to come, while others assert that with nonstop development, quirky weather and greater-than-anticipated water use, nothing but a cough of dust will emerge from city faucets within just a few years. As of 1997, water in the Valley of the Sun was distributed in these proportions: about 50 percent to crop irrigation; about 30 percent to home use; about 6 percent to Native American water rights, and the remainder to industry and miscellaneous.

History

Most of the world's great cities have grown up along the banks of rivers. Phoenix falls right in line. A visit to the ruins at Pueblo Grande, just east of Downtown Phoenix, clearly shows how the Hohokam depended on the Salt River. One of the city's present-day canals follows the route of a canal constructed prior to 1400 to irrigate crops.

Not much was happening in the Phoenix area once the Hohokam mysteriously left around 1450. Coronado, Cardenas, Alarcon and Diaz explored some of the state in the name of Spain, and Spanish padres established the Mission San Xavier del Bac south of Tucson in 1797. In 1821 Arizona became a Spanish province. In 1850 the Arizona-New Mexico territory was created, by 1860 a small settlement was thriving on the banks of the Salt River, and in 1870 a group of local residents formally laid out a town site. Suggested names were Stonewall, after Stonewall Jackson, and Salina. But one of those first entrepreneurs saw the new city as rising from the ashes of a previous civilization, evidenced by the canals, and the name Phoenix was approved. Settlers followed the Pima and Maricopa Indian tradition of growing cotton and other crops, and in 1879 the first factory was built for producing artificial ice. In 1887 with the tracks for the railroad completed, the first train roared into the depot. In 1889 the city received recognition when Prescott reluctantly relinquished the title of territorial capital to Phoenix. By the time Arizona became the 48th state, on February 14, 1912, Phoenix was a true city, with regal Victorian homes not far from what became a busy railroad-centered downtown.

Yet in the eyes of the world, Phoenix is a young city. In 1940 its population was just 65,000. By the early 1960s it was still under one-half million. And then the widespread availability of air conditioning, in addition to evaporative cooling, made the desert a much more attractive place to live.

Festivals and Events

Fiesta Bowl
December 31

It's billed as Arizona's Biggest Party. Considering that festivities begin in September for this end-of-year event, it may be true. The Tostitos Fiesta Bowl Football Classic, played at Sun Devil Stadium, includes golf and tennis tournaments, soccer and running events, parties, a formal ball and tours scheduled over the months preceding the game. On New Year's Eve, from 4 P.M. to midnight the night before the game, the Fiesta Bowl Block Party is held in downtown Tempe. In the western version of the midnight Times Square Ball Drop, a 225-pound tortilla chip plummets into a 15-foot jar of salsa. With big-name bands, fireworks, carnival rides plus souvenir and food booths, it's easy to understand why more than 150,000 guests attend annually. For ticket information call **(602) 967-4877.**

Fiesta Bowl Parade
December 30

A highlight of the overall Fiesta Bowl celebration, the parade generally features two dozen bands, more than a dozen elaborate floats, and equestrian, honorary and specialty groups that can include folkloric dancers and jump rope teams. Usually starting at 11 A.M., the parade begins at Bethany Home Road and proceeds south on Central Avenue to Thomas Road. You can rent bleacher and chair seats along north Central, but most parade-goers simply line the avenue on foot.

Spring Training
month of March

Major league baseball's spring training has been a tradition in Arizona and Florida since 1909 when the Chicago White Sox started playing their first exhibition games in Yuma and Tucson. By 1947 the New York Giants and the Cleveland Indians had become part of the athletic migration. The Arizona Diamondbacks, the state's own new major league team, play at Bank One Ballpark. Altogether ten ball clubs comprise the Arizona Cactus League, whose teams train in the state each spring.

More than 125 games begin in late February or early March and continue for approximately a month. Ticket prices depend on venue, but generally cost under $5 for lawn seating where offered, to $12–$19 for preferred seating. Most games begin at 1 P.M. Tickets are available at game time, but the surefire way to nab choice seats is to order tickets by mail. A number of area hostelries have Spring Training Hotel Packages that guarantee premium Cubs box seats with a hotel room. For information on schedules, times and advance ticketing, contact the **Mesa Convention & Visitors Bureau, 120 N. Center St., Mesa, 85201; (800) 283-6372 or (602) 827-4700.**

Team	Home Stadium Site
Anaheim Angels	Tempe
Arizona Diamondbacks	Tucson (spring training only)
Chicago Cubs	Mesa
Chicago White Sox	Tucson
Colorado Rockies	Tucson
Milwaukee Brewers	Phoenix
Oakland A's	Phoenix
San Diego Padres	Peoria
San Francisco Giants	Scottsdale
Seattle Mariners	Peoria

Arizona State Fair

late October through early November

The 13-day event runs the gamut from nontraditional, space-themed attractions including a UFO encounter to more fairlike barnyard animals, fast rides and artery-clogging foods. One year may feature rhythm and blues performers, with mainstream music the next. Grandstand events usually include an all-Indian rodeo, horse shows, boxing, monster trucks, a demolition derby and more. Presently events are held at the Arizona State Fairground at 19th Avenue and McDowell, but call **(602) 252-6771** to check before setting out as the venue may change.

Way out West Oktoberfest

first weekend of October

Held in Tempe, this beer-and-bratwurst fest began in 1973 as a salute to Tempe's sister city, Regensburg, in Bavaria. It is now the main fund raiser for the Tempe Sister City organization and includes a polka band from Germany, burritos along with bratwurst, mimes, magicians, organ-grinders, 200 storybook characters in costume and 25 different beers. The West meets the wurst in Hayden Square in downtown Tempe.

ArtWalk

year-round

Scottsdale's art district hosts walks to its famed galleries on Thursday evenings from 7 to 9 P.M. Oftentimes walks are themed, such as the Fall Cowboy Artists of America event that coincides with the sale and show at the Phoenix Art Museum. Visiting artists usually are on hand to chat about their works. At any given time at least 40 galleries will participate.

Thunderbird Balloon Classic

early November

A spectacularly colorful event, going on for more than 20 years, it gets bigger every year. In the past, special-shape hot-air balloons have included the Korbel "Champagne Bottle," "Magic Carrots" sponsored by Home & Garden, the Burger King "Whopper," Planter's "Mr. Peanut," Sea World-Busch Gardens' "Air Shamu" and Famous Footwear's "Big Foot." In all, more than one hundred of the hot air classics lift off and fill the skies over the McDowell Mountains and the Sonoran Desert. In addition to balloon races and evening balloon glows, events include exhibits, arts and crafts displays, interactive games, food, rides and entertainment at the Polo Field at WestWorld in Scottsdale. **(602) 978-7790. Website: www.t-bird.edu/press/balloon23.htm.**

Tempe Fall Festival of the Arts
early December

As a refreshing alternative to mushing through the malls, many area shoppers wait for this event to stock up on holiday gifts. Artists are at work, musical groups are playing and caroling, and usually the days are sunny and warm. Arts and crafts, pottery, hand-blown glass, clothing, jewelry and other gift items are generally part of the mix. Everything is handmade, nothing is premanufactured, and a "jury" decides which craftspeople will be allowed to sell, so quality of merchandise is consistently high. The third-largest arts festival in the country, it is held Friday through Sunday, 10 A.M.–6 P.M., in a five-block area in downtown Tempe. Plentiful parking is scattered throughout surrounding lots, so be prepared for a bit of a walk.

Getting There

Phoenix Sky Harbor International Airport is served by 18 major carriers—Aeromexico, Air Canada, Alaska, America West, American, American Trans Air, British Airways, Continental, Delta, Frontier, Mesa, Northwest/KLM, Scenic, Southwest, TWA, US Airways and United. The airport is 15 minutes from downtown, and within 15 to 30 minutes of major area hotels and resorts. British Airways has daily nonstop service from Gatwick Airport and Air Canada offers daily nonstops to Toronto. This number of airlines coming into a single city helps create a competitive atmosphere that tends to keep fares down, even during prime winter months.

Greyhound provides bus service. The main terminal is located at **2115 E. Buckeye Rd.** in Phoenix, with suburban stations in Apache Junction, Chandler, Mesa and Tempe. For fare and schedule information call **(800) 231-2222.**
Amtrak discontinued train service to Phoenix in 1996.

Outdoor Activities

(See South Mountain Park under Seeing and Doing for urban hiking, mountain biking and scenic drives, as well as individual Valley of the Sun cities.)

Golf

With 150-plus golf courses dotting the Phoenix area, you're never more than a chip shot away from the links. Here there are more courses per capita than in any state west of the Mississippi, creating available tee times even during the practically ideal golf months of January through April when average high temperatures range from 65 to 83 degrees. The Arizona Central website has a Course Surfer that lets you find courses by location, by course name, by city name and by your preference of price and difficulty. Go to **azcentral.com** and, at the bottom of the page, click on "Guide to more than 200 Arizona courses."

Talking Stick Golf Club

Just opened at the end of 1997 on the Salt River Pima-Maricopa Indian Community, this truly spectacular 36-hole facility was designed by two-time U.S. Masters Champion Ben Crenshaw and partner Bill Coore. The North course is a low-profile desert grasslands setting, while the South course is elevated, with scalloped bunkers and more treed areas. Talking Stick is the Southwest headquarters for the Golf Digest Instructional Schools. Located on the corner of Alma School and Indian Bend Roads. **(602) 860-2221.**

Troon North Golf Club

In Scottsdale, the club is designed around mature cactus and rock outcroppings that dramatically enhance its two courses. Each, over 7,000 yards, plays to a par 72. Recently both were ranked the #1 and #2 public access courses in the state by *Golf Digest.* Although pricey, its reputation assures that it is always busy. **(602) 585-5300.**

Grayhawk Golf Club

The new Raptor course, considered one of Scottsdale's most picturesque, is backdropped by the McDowell Mountains. Famed golf architect Tom Fazio designed the 7,000-yard, par 71 layout. A second course, par 72 Talon, recently was selected as one of *Golf* magazine's "Top 10 You Can Play." **(480) 502-1800.**

Raven Golf Club

Near South Mountain in central Phoenix, this club has large greens and forgiving fairways. Formerly agricultural land, the course is flanked by mature pine trees, framing mountain views. **(602) 243-3636.**

Ocotillo Golf Club

Located south of Phoenix in Chandler, this golf club has three 9-hole courses with the Gold-Blue course combination playing to a par 72. Rolling farmlands with 7 miles of shoreline create water on almost every hole, with hazards diminished by ample fairways. **(602) 220-9000.**

Hiking

(See also South Mountain Park under Seeing and Doing.)

Camelback Mountain

This Scottsdale landmark is widely used for recreation, particularly the Echo Canyon area with a steep and challenging 1-mile hike to the top of the camel's head. If the evening news reports a helicopter rescue of a hiker from Camelback, you can bet it's from this area. Stay on the trail, bring plenty of water and enjoy the city view from the top. Access is from Echo Canyon Parkway on McDonald Drive in Paradise Valley. To be assured of a parking place, arrive very early in the morning.

Papago Park

If you like the kind of hike that has a destination, the Hole-in-the-Rock trek can fill the bill. There really is a hole, at the top of a marked trail that is advanced beginner or low moderate in difficulty. Once at the top you can see most of the park including the Phoenix Zoo.

River Floating

Salt River Recreation supplies tubes and shuttles for what has become a revered summer pastime in the Phoenix area. From May through September the Salt River (usually) provides cool mountain-stream waters for a mellow float that gets you away from the heat of the Valley of the Sun. Rent a tube where you put in. Rent an extra for your ice chest so your drinks and food can float right along with you. Everyone gets on the river at a central point, then at designated points, leaves the river to catch a shuttle bus back to their cars. The usual technique is to gather tubes in a circle and link them together with a center tube to hold the cooler. On a hot summer weekend the river is almost choked with boom boxes, rafts, tubes and the ubiquitous Styrofoam cooler. Trips of 1.5 to 4 hours, 5 hours on weekends, are offered. Rest rooms, soft drinks, popcorn, ice cream, hats and visors, T-shirts, ice chests and more are available at tubing headquarters. Caution: Arizona's summer sun can be devastating to unprepared skin. Be sure to wear a hat, slather yourself with at least SPF 15, and even though you'll be wearing a swimsuit, cover up with a long-sleeve shirt. Tube rentals are about $9. Children should be age 8 or older. From I-60 in Mesa take Power Road northeast for 15 miles to the well-marked Salt River Recreation Headquarters. **P.O. Box 6568, Mesa, 85216; (480) 984-3305, fax (480) 984-0875.**

Hot Air Ballooning

There may be no better place to enjoy this sport than the Sonoran desert at dawn. Tethered to a multistriped orb of ripstop nylon, skimming the tops of saguaros and palo verdes, few sounds mar the silence. Drifting upward the feeling is of incredible freedom. Below, brown and white cattle and an occasional jackrabbit, startled by the balloon's shadow, scurry for cover. A covey of round, top-knotted Gambel's quail hides under a mesquite bush. A velvety golf course is dotted with bright-shirted players. As the balloon gains altitude, multiarmed saguaro cactuses grow small, and the sun turns the mountains warm shades of yellow and red. Settling back to earth can be a tricky maneuver because air is layered, affecting the top of the balloon differently from the basket. But bumps usually are mild, and with a ground crew to steady the gondola, landings are uneventful. The traditional bottle of champagne is at the ready, along with orange juice in concession to the early hour. Among the Phoenix-area companies that soar are: **Unicorn Balloon Company of Arizona, Inc., (800) 468-2478 or (602) 468-2478; Hot Air Expeditions, (800) 831-7610 or (602) 788-5555; Rainbow Balloon Flights, (602) 258-2812 or (800) 378-0470.**

Seeing and Doing

Downtown Phoenix and Central Avenue

A decade ago downtown streets were practically deserted after about 6 P.M. on weekdays. Office workers scurried to the suburbs and home. But now, a re-energized downtown entices people to linger for evening events, and to return to downtown for dinner and entertainment.

Arizona Center

This $515-million complex consists of eight blocks of restaurants, shops and night clubs. Its boutiques and vendor carts, spaced among palm trees and fountains, draw visitors in search of take-home gifts and items distinctively Arizona. A new 24-screen movie complex has just opened. It's the place to come for dinner before the theater, a sporting event or a presentation at symphony hall, and is always a good bet for a meal on a cool patio at an interesting restaurant. **Lombardi's** at the Arizona Center, **Mi Amigo's Mexican Restaurant** and **Sam's Cafe** (Southwestern food) all are good choices.

Orpheum Theater

Built in 1929 at a cost of $750,000 in the Spanish Baroque Revival style so popular at that time, this beautifully restored theater was considered the most luxurious playhouse west of the Mississippi. It hosted the best of vaudeville, including W. C. Fields and Mae West. In 1984 the City of Phoenix purchased the theater and placed it on the National Register of Historic Places. Intricately carved sandstone gargoyles leer from lofty perches. Located at the corner of Third Avenue and Adams Street. Free tours by appointment. **(602) 252-9678.**

Herberger Theater Center

This lovely live theater venue has two small stages for intimate productions that include children's theater, ballet, performances by the Arizona Theatre Company and others. Check to see what's playing. Located in the heart of downtown across from Civic Plaza. **222 E. Monroe St.; (602) 254-7399.**

Arizona Science Center

This is one of our very favorite places to bring out-of-town guests, especially those with children. From the time you get a look at its sweeping exterior curves and angles you have a pretty good idea that what's inside will be terrific. The $47-million center, opened in 1997, is filled with more than 350 interactive exhibits geared for everyone from toddlers to grandparents. Don't miss the giant nose, with

The Arizona Science Center, in downtown Phoenix, delights kids and adults with hands-on exhibits.

The Heard Museum is one of the world's foremost repositories of Native American art and artifacts.

"cilia" that can be irritated by "dust particles." Kids throw nerf balls up a pair of giant nostrils, and when the nose has had enough, it erupts in a startling sneeze. Another display features a field of shaggy little creatures that shake and shudder in an electromagnetic field in time to music that you select. Upstairs you can "fly" a Cessna in a wind tunnel. There is an Iwerks theater, a 203-seat planetarium that hosts laser light shows and simulated heavenly events. Open daily, 10 A.M.–5 P.M., except Thanksgiving and Christmas. Admission varies, beginning with a base price for exhibits only, with the Iwerks and planetarium additional. You can park in a garage at Monroe and Second Streets. Call for a schedule of special exhibits, planetarium shows and events. **600 E. Washington St.; (602) 716-2000, fax (602) 716-2099. www.azscience.org.**

Sports Venues

Phoenix's major league baseball team, the Arizona Diamondbacks, got their own stadium in 1998. Changing forever the downtown Phoenix skyline, the dramatic 48,500-seat **Bank One Ballpark,** nicknamed BOB, is designed with a retractable roof and natural grass playing surface. Six private party suites, full-service restaurants, a food court, swimming pool and picnic area make the park a multiuse venue. (See Spring Training, page 159).

Next door is the 19,000-seat **America West Arena,** home of the National Basketball Association's Phoenix Suns and the Phoenix Coyotes of the National Hockey League. The Arizona Cardinals NFL football team plays a full season at **Sun Devil Stadium,** part of Arizona State University in Tempe.

Heard Museum

This unforgettable museum was founded in 1929 by Dwight B. and Maie Bartlett Heard to house their personal collection of primarily Native American art. It is internationally acclaimed for its artifacts documenting the history of native cultures, as well as the ongoing special events that include Native American hoop dancers and artists demonstrating ancient crafts. It promotes appreciation and respect for native people and the products of their cultural heritage, which include pottery, baskets, jewelry, weavings and an extensive kachina doll collection donated by former Arizona senator Barry Goldwater. A recent $16.2 million expansion added galleries and a studio for artists in residence. Saturdays usually feature Native American music and dance performances or artists' demonstrations. Be sure to allow time to browse the Museum Shop and Book Store for top quality authentic Native American baskets, pottery, textiles, jewelry and other crafts. The museum's premier event, the Heard Museum Guild Indian Fair and Market, held in early March, draws visitors from all over the country. Open Mon.–Sat., 9:30 A.M.–5 P.M.; Sun., noon–5 P.M.; closed major holidays. Moderate admission. The museum is located one block east of Central Avenue and three blocks north of McDowell Road. **22 E. Monte Vista Rd., Phoenix; (602) 252-8848.**

Phoenix Art Museum

A recent $25-million renovation and expansion more than doubled the size of this respected museum. Unique architectural details give it an unusual quality of liveliness not often seen in museums. Those details include imaginatively placed openings in walls and windows that create visual cues to help visitors orient themselves. Permanent collections cover three areas of emphasis: Art of Asia, Art of the

Americas and Europe to 1900, and Art of Our Times: 1900 to the Present. A child-friendly gallery called ArtWorks offers youngsters a creative way to look at art. The Throne collection of miniature rooms appeals to children and adults. Fans of Phoenix artist Philip Curtis will appreciate the newly opened gallery that features his distinctive work. Half-hour gallery talks, called "ArtBreaks," are offered at 12 noon Tuesday through Sunday. Family programs and performances are offered on the third Sunday of each month, free with general admission. Don't miss the Gallery Store, where the merchandise reflects the collections and exhibits currently in progress. Located at the corner of Central Avenue and McDowell Road. **1625 N. Central Ave.; (602) 257-1222.**

Heritage Square

It may not seem particularly exciting to visitors from the East and Midwest, where vintage homes are fairly common, but to Phoenicians, whose city is comparatively young, this collection of historic buildings dating to the late 1800s is an essential link to the past. They were part of the city's original development and have been restored and decorated to reflect a period in history when elegance was an anomaly in the Old West. The Eastlake Victorian Rosson House, built in 1895, is a classic example of the architecture of the time. The Carriage House, once a mule barn, is now a sandwich and gift shop. Lunch, tea and pastries are offered at the Teeter House Victorian Tea Room, and the Arizona Doll & Toy Museum is in the Stevens bungalow. Heritage Square is located between 6th and 7th Streets, between Monroe and Adams, near the Science Center. Homes are open varying hours for tours, some with a small admission charge. You can get a self-guiding brochure by stopping at Heritage Square offices in **The Duplex. 115 N. Sixth St., Phoenix; (602) 262-5029.**

Coronado Historic District

We often take visitors on a drive through this area to prove to them that Phoenix really does have a quite interesting recent history. The area bounded by Virginia Avenue, McDowell Road, 7th Street and 16th Street at one time marked the northernmost edge of Phoenix' prime residential area. When a trolley line was established along Brill Street in 1910, the area became more accessible. Homes here were generally built between 1910 and 1940, and represent the diversity of the city's population at that time. There are some magnificent mansions, many restored to a comfort level that satisfies present-day owners. Other, humbler dwellings were built in the Craftsman style so popular in California at that time. Also represented are mission style, charming English cottages and basic bungalows. While some have been subjected to anachronistic additions and expansion, many others have been beautifully restored, so you get a definite feeling for the streets of decades past.

Phoenix Park 'n Swap

The area's biggest flea market, swap mart, whatever you want to call it, is the place to come for tools, stereo stuff, clothes, antiques and assorted garage sale cleanouts. Held in the parking lot near Greyhound Park, it's been going on for decades, and is a regular weekend stop for many bargain hunters. Haggling is part of the fun. Get real, we've got the deal, they say. And they usually do. Open Wed. evenings, Fri., Sat. and Sun. from 6 A.M. Nominal admission. **3801 E. Washington St.; (602) 273-1250.**

Other Valley of the Sun Areas

Horse Racing

For decades Turf Paradise has occupied the corner of 19th Avenue and Bell Road. Racing is exciting, but the place itself is understated. You can sit and watch from the grandstand, clubhouse or Turf Club, or just hang out at the rail where you can actually get dirt in your face. The club features parimutuel wagering with a minimum bet of $2. Post time is 12:30 P.M. and the season generally runs from the end of September to the beginning of May. **(602) 942-1101.**

Museums and Galleries

Hall of Flame

Trucks, horse-drawn and mechanized, and hand-to-hand implements used between 1725 and 1955 are part of the world's largest collection of fire fighting equipment. Children may explore a tyke-friendly area with a small replica fire truck and a large, real 1951 vehicle. They can try on turnout gear, helmets and coats worn by firefighters. A Safety House helps them pick out fire hazards, then use a bedroom window as an escape route. Special kids' story hours and workshops are scheduled regularly. Contact the museum for times and dates. Located in Papago Park. Open Mon.–Sat., 9 A.M.–5 P.M.; Sun., noon–4 P.M. Small fee. **6101 E. Van Buren; (602) 275-3473.**

Historical Sites and Ruins

Pueblo Grande Museum and Cultural Park

Located close to downtown Phoenix, this prehistoric Hohokam village site along the Salt River was home for more than 1,400 years to people who engineered hundreds of miles of canals, cultivated corn, beans and squash, and constructed towns of adobe. They grew cotton to weave fine-textured fabrics for their clothing. They disappeared sometime during the fifteenth century. The crumbling walls and outlines of buildings that now remain are not spectacular as ruins go. But as you stand on the platform mound ruin, possibly the homesites of Hohokam elite, the roar of jets shakes your thoughts—Sky Harbor Airport is just a few miles away. In three out of four directions, your line of sight encounters traffic-clogged freeways. The centuries superimposed give many observers cause to reflect.

Most visitors start with the brief orientation video explaining why the Hohokam chose the site. A hands-on room, geared for youngsters but interesting to adults as well, invites visitors to assemble puzzles, create a rubbing and learn about the Hohokam culture through interactive exhibits. The main gallery, the repository for all items of interest unearthed during excavation anywhere in Phoenix, has "dug" bottles as well as ancient artifacts discovered during archaeological exploration. Changing exhibits may include local art and photographs as well as displays dedicated to Native American culture.

The one-third-mile-long ruin trail, accessible to wheelchairs, wanders up and over a 30-foot mound about the size of a football field. In the middle foreground an active canal, lined with palo verde trees, follows the route of an original Hohokam canal. Many Phoenix canals are so sited, testifying to the wisdom of ancient peoples as they used the water from the then-mighty Salt River to create a green and fertile valley. The gift shop stocks a good selection of native crafts and reference materials. The park is the only National Historic Landmark in Phoenix. Call ahead for a schedule of events and workshops. Small admission fee. No admission charge on Sun. Open Mon.–Sat., 9 A.M.–4:45 P.M.; Sun., 1–4:45 P.M. **4619 E. Washington St., Phoenix, 85034-1909; (602) 495-0901, fax (602) 495-5645.**

Parks and Gardens

Desert Botanical Garden

The nationally acclaimed 150-acre Desert Botanical Garden provides an excellent starting place to become acquainted with the desert. It exhibits, conserves and studies the world's arid-land plants, with special emphasis on the ones native to the Southwestern United States. Nature trails run through the garden, with interpretive signs and helpful docents to introduce guests to the mysteries of the many-armed saguaro cactus and the secrets of the colorful Gila woodpecker. At the gift shop, look for treasures with a Southwest flavor to take home, as well as books about the desert and its inhabitants, lovely pottery and T-shirts with creative designs that take them out of the "souvenir" category. During February, March and April Mother Nature schedules her own very special event. The wildflower season bursts into bloom in the desert in general, and in a concentrated way at the garden. It's possible to see a range of flowers and cactuses in bloom that would take weeks to track down in the open desert. For desert plants to take home, including those not widely available elsewhere, check the March and October dates for Landscape Plant Sales. Helpful attendants will advise you on which ones will flourish in other parts of the country. One purchaser is successfully growing prickly pear cactus in Wisconsin. Open daily, except Christmas Day, Oct. to Apr., 8 A.M.–8 P.M.; May to Sept., 7 A.M.–8 P.M. Located in Papago Park at 64th St. and McDowell Road. **1201 N. Galvin Pkwy., Phoenix; (602)754-8190; events hotline, (602) 754-8134; TDD (602) 481-8143. E-mail: desertgdn@aol.com.events.**

Chinese Cultural Center

The Walk with the Emperor garden at this colorful restaurant and office complex has handcrafted pagodas and koi ponds that are landmark replicas of five ancient Chinese cities. Just a few of the eight planned Far Eastern restaurants are open as of this writing, with a museum and galleries scheduled for completion around 2001. Come for lunch and stroll the serene gardens. **668 N. 44th St., Phoenix, 85016; (602) 955-7229.**

Phoenix Zoo

If you compare it with the famed San Diego Zoo, this smaller facility pales. But it certainly is worthy of a stop. It is the nation's largest privately owned, self-supporting zoo. You can meander on four separate trails that represent Arizona, Africa and the tropics, plus a children's trail. The zoo is home to 1,300 animals that live in environmental settings, including 200 endangered species from around the world. Open 9 A.M.–5 P.M. Summer hours, 7 A.M.–4 P.M., are in effect May 1 to Labor Day. **455 N. Galvin Pkwy., Phoenix; (602) 585-8233.**

South Mountain Park

The mound of mountains that borders the city's southern edge makes up the largest municipal park in the world, truly a treasure that so far has managed to stave off encroaching development. Within almost 17,000 acres there are picnic areas, five lookout points, and trails that range from mellow mile-long strolls to challenging hikes of a dozen miles and more, well-preserved petroglyph sites, and on weekends, lots of people. Because the park is a preserve, everything within its boundaries is protected by law. It provides a home for coyotes, javelinas, cactus wrens, gilded flickers, Gila woodpeckers, Gambel's quail, tiny yellow-headed verdin and dozens of other species. It is a favorite of mountain bikers and equestrians as well. At its 2,692-foot summit, a series of radio towers, capped with flashing red beacons, both orient and warn away planes headed for nearby Sky Harbor International Airport.

Remnants of civilizations that have used the park date to prehistoric times, with the ephemeral Hohokams among the more recent residents. They lived all over the Valley of the Sun (see Pueblo Grande), leaving their mark in hundreds of petroglyphs. Although many sites are remote and difficult to reach, some are easily accessible on nonchallenging trails. From the 48th Street parking lot take the Desert Classic Trail just five minutes around the base of the mountain to the west, and you'll be standing in front of a group of vivid petroglyphs, centuries old.

Hiking

One of our favorite, easy strolls begins at the East Gate off 48th Street and simply follows the dirt road in Pima Canyon. It parallels a wash on one side where we often spot coyote tracks, and on the other are cliffs where we've watched a pair of red-tailed hawks build a nest and produce a pair of chicks. For a longer hike, still just over 2 miles, take the Pima West Loop north from the North Ramada and circle around to connect with the Pima East Loop. The Mormon Loop Trail branches off from the National Trail, gains a bit of elevation and presents more of a challenge. A large sign at the 48th Street entrance details all the trails, so you can pick and choose before you set out.

Mountain Biking

You see mountain bikes on trails throughout the park, but the favorite, and biggest challenge is the 14.3-mile National Trail that runs along the park's middle. You have to allow the better part of a day to bike it. You'll probably spend 4 to 5 hours on the trail and several more recuperating. If the elevation gain of more than 1,000 feet doesn't get you, carrying your bike over rock outcroppings and picking yourself up from sliding through loose gravel probably will take their toll. The reward is great views and seeing Indian petroglyphs. You'll want to do this in winter months, as there aren't enough cool morning hours in summer (even if you start at dawn) to keep you comfortable for the whole ride. You can access the trail from the park's 48th Street entrance. Leave your car in the lot and follow a busy (on weekends there are lots of hikers, walkers, families with kids) dirt road (nonmotorized use only) about one-quarter mile to a sign that says National Trail. A 17-mile round-trip ride begins with an almost-flat trail, the Desert Classic, that starts from the East ramada in Pima Canyon and follows the southern base of the mountains to Telegraph Pass Trail, where you start to gain elevation. Turn right onto National Trail, then to the dirt road, and return. It's a good trail for beginners to hone skills and also is easy enough to get your heart rate up.

Horseback Riding

At the Pointe Hilton Resort near South Mountain, Trailhorse Adventures offers scheduled rides at varying times and days of the week, depending on the season. Rides leave from the stables on Pointe Parkway, winding first through suburbia, but quickly get into the park's Pima Canyon area. Most are geared for dudes, but if you happen to hit a group of more advanced riders, the leaders are happy to speed things up a bit. A historical trail ride and an Indian ruin ride include box lunches. For information call **(800) 723-3538; www.trailhorseadventures.com.**

Scenic Drive

The best vantage point from which to put Phoenix in perspective is Dobbins Lookout. The 180-degree view of the Valley of the Sun encompasses the misty Superstition Mountains to the east, unmistakable Camelback Mountain, a cluster of high rises marking Downtown Phoenix, and the Bradshaw and Estrella Mountains to the west. On a clear day you can see Phoenix, Mesa, Tempe, Scottsdale and half a dozen other Valley towns. The memorable panorama reveals the area's multifaceted personality, as well as the brown cloud that has earned the city a number of wrist slaps from the EPA in recent years. From the Central Avenue entrance follow paved Summit Road to the north-facing lookout.

All trails in the park are clearly marked. Be sure to carry water. Cell phones do work in the park. There is a manned office at the main entrance at the south end of Central Avenue. For more information on South Mountain Park, and for trail maps, contact the **Phoenix Department of Parks and Recreation, 10919 S. Central Ave., Phoenix, 85040-8302; (602) 495-0222, fax (602) 495-0212.**

North Mountain Park

Part of the Phoenix Mountain Preserve, the same system that protects South Mountain but in a different geographical area, this 10,000-acre preserve has one central 7,000-acre section and several other chunks of parks. All are webbed with hiking trails with easy access to trail heads from many points in the residential area that surrounds it. The 10-mile-plus Charles Christiansen Trail is the most popular with hikers, equestrians and mountain bikers. It basically traverses the whole preserve.

Squaw Peak Park

When you see helicopters hovering over the peak, also in the Phoenix Mountain Preserve, it's a pretty safe bet they're extricating someone who's gotten in trouble on the Squaw Peak Summit Trail. This 1.2-mile route has an elevation gain of more than 1,200 feet and is favored by true exercise enthusiasts. For a much easier and safer trail, take the Squaw Peak Nature Trail, a complacent stroll that gets you away from the city in minutes. Wildlife is similar to that found at South Mountain. We take out-of-town guests here to get a feel for the Sonoran desert without a lot of strenuous hiking. The 1.5-mile loop will take well under an hour, even moving at a snail's pace. For information call **(602) 262-7901.**

Where to Stay

Because it is such a popular winter travel destination, places to stay in the Valley of the Sun range from the most basic digs to off-the-charts luxury and elegance.

Bed & Breakfast Inns

La Estancia—$$$$

Maybe because it's such a big city with hundreds of hotels and motels, Phoenix has very few small inns and bed and breakfasts. Just down the street from the elegant Royal Palms, La Estancia is one of the few remaining private homes that were scattered through a fragrant orange grove at the base of Camelback Mountain. Wealthy owners from the east came to spend winters in the reliable Phoenix sunshine, shuttering their homes during hot summer months in the days before air conditioning. The Monterey Revival style mansion, completed in 1929 for hardware entrepreneur Charles Pratt, has five rooms with private whirlpools, a pool, courtyard and deck. A full breakfast is included. From July to Sept. rates are lower. **4979 E. Camelback Rd., Phoenix, 85018; (602) 808-9924 or (800) 410-7655.**

Maricopa Manor—$$$$

Another delightful B&B, it once sat on the far north edge of Phoenix. When city growth encompassed the small, Spanish-style bungalow by the 1970s, it was purchased and expanded to become a family home. Today there are six rooms and suites with private baths. Decades-old citrus trees shade a walled courtyard. Breakfast in bed is assured, because muffins, fruit and juice are delivered to your room in a wicker basket. Each room has a refrigerator and microwave, and some have fireplaces. **15 W. Pasadena Ave., Phoenix, 85013; (602) 274-6302 or (800) 292-6403; www.maricopamanor.com**

Historic Properties

Royal Palms—$$$$

This absolutely wonderful place, once great, turned tacky and then re-emerged to outdo even its former self. In 1928 the Royal Palms was the winter home of Cunard Steamship executive and entrepreneur Delos Cooke, who died in 1931. By 1948 investors opened it for guests, naming it for the palms that line its driveway. Longtime Phoenicians remember it as one of several inns—Jokake, which was torn down to make room for the Phoenician, Smoketree and Hermosa—that became functionally obsolete. During its first incarnation, the inn featured entertainment by Carmen Cavallero, Hildegard, Frank Sinatra, Tony Martin and other idols of the era. Today, luxury casitas, and villas with private patios and outdoor showers are each individually decorated. No question it's pricey, but for a big splurge it's definitely the place to go, especially during July and August when rates on casitas are less than half of the winter high-season tariff. The rate includes two full breakfasts at T. Cook's (see Where to Eat) and a minibar stocked with soft drinks and fresh fruit. **5200 E. Camelback Rd., Phoenix, 85018; (602) 840-3610. (800) 672-6001; www.destinationtravel.com.**

Wigwam Resort—$$$$

In Litchfield Park west of Phoenix, this venerable resort owes its existence to the motor car. When Goodyear Tire & Rubber discovered that cotton extended the life of automobile tires, the company required a dependable local supply of the high quality fiber. World War I had closed off Egypt as a source, and boll weevils had ravaged Georgia's cotton. So Arizona became the site. A 13-room guest lodge was built to house visiting Goodyear executives. By 1929 the "wigwam" as it was affectionately dubbed had become so popular that it opened to the public as a resort. A year later a nine-hole golf course was added, and today it is the only Valley resort with three championship courses. It includes 300 guest casitas, four fine restaurants, two pools and nine lighted tennis courts. The original 1919 main lodge, now the Fireplace Room, displays photographs of guests in cool white 1920s resort wear and ranch dress of the 1940s and 1950s. It has gained a national reputation for its exceptional selection of wines and spirits. **Litchfield Park, 85340; (623) 935-3811.**

Arizona Biltmore—$$$$

Opened on February 23, 1929, 8 miles northeast of Phoenix, the hotel blends with the saguaros and chaparral as though it's been there for ages. Today luxury homes and golf links surround it. The Biltmore was the dream of architect-builder Albert Chase McArthur and his two brothers, who set out to create a grand and lovely resort hotel to present the

Inspired by the architecture of Frank Lloyd Wright, the Biltmore has welcomed guests since 1929.

desert and romantic West to the rest of the country's social elite.

McArthur, once an apprentice draftsman to Frank Lloyd Wright, employed Wright's principles of using indigenous materials in harmony with surrounding landscape. A copper roof, a tribute to the state's flourishing mining industry, is still a distinctive feature. Concrete blocks were designed by a prominent Southwestern sculptor and cast in a small factory on site. Imprinted with a geometric palm-tree pattern, they have come to be known as "Biltmore Block" and provide a striking element in the hotel's exterior appearance. Rooms have gone through many updates to include minibars and voice mail, but the Wright direction prevails in mission-style furnishings and western-design lamps à la the 1930s. The two-story lobby remains almost unchanged and the original pool is still lined with famed Catalina tile, manufactured on Wrigley-owned Catalina Island and brought by the family to the Biltmore. Ask for a room in the main building to stay in the hotel's oldest part. **24th St. and Missouri, Phoenix, 85016; (800) 950-2575 or (602)955-6600.**

Luxury Resorts

The Pointe Hilton on South Mountain—$$$$

South of the hubbub of Phoenix but close to all that's happening, you could settle in here for a stretch without ever getting into your car. The adjacent par-70 golf course is a highly acclaimed desert-target/links layout, and the fitness club is state of the art. Ten tennis courts and stables just across the street make this a complete vacation destination. All accommodations are suites. Check summer rates for real bargains. **7777 S. Pointe Pkwy., Phoenix, 85044; (800) 747-7111.**

The Pointe Hilton at Tapatio Cliffs—$$$$

This hotel offers the same high quality and level of luxury as the South Mountain Hilton, with The Falls, a three-acre oasis of pools, terraces and outdoor dining as a focal point. All rooms are suites, and the Tocaloma Spa and Salon has a great loofah treatment that really rubs you the right way. **11111 N. 7th St., Phoenix, 85020; (602) 866-7500 or (800) 572-7222, fax (602) 993-0276.**

The Pointe Hilton at Squaw Peak—$$$$

On the slopes of North Mountain, this Spanish-Mediterranean resort sits next to the mountain preserve, so hiking and mountain bike trails are just outside your door. There are seven pools, four lighted tennis courts and an extensive spa and salon. The "River Ranch" has a lagoon pool, 130-foot slippery rock slide and sports pool for water volleyball and basketball. All rooms are suites. **7677 N. 16th St., Phoenix, 85020; (800) 876-4683 or (602) 997-2626.**

Hostels

The Metcalf House Hostel—$

This is the only hostel in Phoenix that we know of, and it's a good one. It has 35 beds and a large common room, all part of a great old home built in a sort of Craftsman-cottage style. Call the hostel for the phone number of the local taxi, which charges a small fixed rate to transport you from the airport or bus station. Located on 9th Street between Portland and Roosevelt, 2 blocks east of 7th Street. **1026 N. 9th St., Phoenix, 85006; (602) 254-9803.**

Where to Eat

Planet Hollywood, Hooters, Hard Rock Cafe, Houston's, most of the successful upscale chains you'd expect to find in a big city are here. A few are worth special mention.

LON's at the Hermosa—$$$$

This very popular place (reservations essential) combines historic Arizona ambiance with award-winning regional cuisine. The 1930s hacienda-style adobe is filled with Southwestern furnishings and cowboy artwork, which creates a comfortable, casual atmosphere for food that is absolutely delicious without being pretentious. The chef plans portions that are not overwhelming so you can order an appetizer, salad, entree and dessert without feeling like you've overindulged. Knowledgeable jeans-clad waiters are happy to advise and explain any dish. One of the best entrees is the sesame seared ahi tuna with mango relish. Our favorite entree is mahi mahi on roasted peppers with snow pea salad. The vanilla bean brulee comes perfectly caramelized, with a light mango sauce. Open for lunch and dinner. **5532 N. Palo Cristi Rd., Paradise Valley; (602) 955-8614 or (602) 955-7878 restaurant.**

T. Cook's at the Royal Palms—$$$$

The best strategy here is to go for breakfast so you can experience the ambiance and skills of the chef withour paying dinner prices. Most truly fine restaurants open only for lunch and dinner, but because this one serves Inn guests, it opens early. You certainly may order your basic muffin and tea, but the reason you're here is to try things like the grilled potato pancake with smoked salmon, or maple french toast with homemade sausages. It will cost you the same as a really good lunch, so go late in the morning and call it lunch. "Rustic Mediterranean" best describes its atmosphere, where the lingering aroma of spit-roasted specialties attests to a truly creative menu. Food is beautifully prepared without undue froufrou, and portions are large. The dining room has a tree growing in its center, a reflection pool on one side and a grassy courtyard on the other. **5200 E. Camelback Rd.; (602) 808-0766.**

Durant's—$$$$

A Phoenix legend for decades, you can't go wrong with a huge steak or fresh seafood. Take some time to study the truly extensive wine list. **2611 N. Central Ave.; (602) 264-5967.**

Lombardi's—$$$-$$$$

In the Arizona Center in downtown Phoenix, it serves upscale Northern Italian food that's not an overgross in the calorie department. Outstanding focaccia bread comes warm and fragrant from wood-burning ovens. Ask about nightly seafood specials, always fresh, sometimes served with an inventive pasta. With an early 5:30 dinner reservation you still have time to make opening curtain at the Herberger Theater, or slip into your seat at a sporting event. Afterward, stop in for a creme brulee, Tuscan bread pudding or icy gelato. Open for lunch and dinner. **455 N. 3rd St.; (602) 257-8323.**

Stockyards Restaurant and 1889 Bar—$$$-$$$$

Until the 1960s, when the breeze wafted less-than-lovely aromas from East Washington Street near the railroad tracks, Phoenicians shut their windows. The Livestock Exchange, overlooking the world's largest feedlot with 200 acres of pens accommodated up to 40 thousand head of cattle. A small coffee shop served cattlemen. When it burned in 1954 it was replaced by today's building. The decor is 1890s, with old photographs chronicling the restaurant's history. The smelly stockyards are long gone, but the tradition of serving great beef lives on. Open for lunch and dinner. **5001 E. Washington St.; (602) 273-7378.**

Vincent's on Camelback—$$$$

For years the quintessential place to see and be seen, the award- winning American Southwestern cuisine is the same high quality as ever, served in a charming country French setting. Duck tamales and checkerboard cake are classics. Open for lunch and dinner. **3930 E. Camelback Rd.; (602) 224-0225.**

Sam's Cafe—$$$

At Biltmore Fashion Park, 24th Street and Camelback in a super trendy area, it's the place to lunch after a tough morning's shopping. The outstanding Southwestern menu has great fish tacos and black bean soup. Their signature is a white chocolate tamale, a skinny shaft of sweetness wrapped in a corn husk and presented frozen at the end of your meal. Open daily at 11:00 A.M. for lunch and dinner. **2566 E. Camelback Rd.; (602) 954-7100.**

Rustler's Rooste—$$$

A civilized cowboy experience that includes live country western music and dancing along with outstanding steaks and prime rib is guaranteed at this lively eatery. On the northeast nose of South Mountain, it advertises "Beef 'n Brew With a View" and it delivers on all three counts. During winter months, if you come for early dinner and watch the sun set you don't have to become part of the high-steppin' crowd that shows up later. **7777 S. Pointe Parkway; (602) 431-6474**.

Pica Poco—$$

It's OK to try your high school Spanish in this small, bright and cheery cafe that looks like it belongs South of the Border, because almost everyone also speaks English. Colorful Mexican art decorates walls, reflecting the heritage of its owner, who uses his home-cooked memories as the basis for soft tacos, ceviche, tostadas and more. Margaritas and Mexican beer, too. Open daily 11 A.M.–9 P.M. **3945 E. Camelback Rd.; (602) 912-0048.**

Services

The Arizona Republic and the *Arizona Business Gazette* have a wonderfully helpful website that hosts other websites for various organizations. The site also offers ever-changing news topics from the *Republic*. In the fine print you'll find a guide to more than 200 Arizona golf courses, Arizona sports information, a travel and lodging guide and more. **Website: www.azcentral.com.**

Arizona Office of Tourism, 2702 N. 3rd St., Ste. 4015, Phoenix, 85004; (800) 842-8257. Call the 800 number to receive a large packet of information on visiting the state.

Phoenix & Valley of the Sun Convention & Visitors Bureau, One Arizona Center, 400 E. Van Buren St., Phoenix, 85004-2290; (602) 252-5588.

Many companies offer personalized van tours from Phoenix to other parts of the state. One that we like is **Open Road Tours, (800) 766-7117** or **(602) 997-6474.**

Monsoons

For many, the word monsoon creates images of turban-wrapped, white-skirted servants in an aged, grainy black and white film set in a jungle, scurrying to batten shutters against an onslaught of wind, rain and other nasty surprises from the elements. In Arizona, monsoon means the season between sometime in early July and the middle of September when the southern part of the state gets most of its rain. The word monsoon refers to a wind pattern that affects a large climatic region and reverses direction seasonally, but in common usage it covers the entire process. Moisture from the Gulf of Mexico and the Gulf of California flows into the state when hot summer desert air rises and moist air replaces it. It doesn't have to rain to be a "monsoon day." As defined by meteorologists, it is officially any day when the dew point, an indicator of the amount of moisture in the air, reaches 55 degrees or higher. The monsoon season begins officially when the dew point, as recorded at Sky Harbor Airport, hits 55 for three consecutive days.

Arizonans have a sort of love-hate relationship with the monsoons. Combined with the most intense solar heat of the year, they create undesertlike humidity that makes evaporative coolers ineffective and requires air conditioners to work even harder. Thunderstorms build quickly, creating flash floods, dust storms and winds that have been known to uproot manufactured homes, take roofs off buildings and strew branches and debris across city streets. On the other hand, for the brief time it actually rains, the desert can be blessedly cool. And these rains, which account for 40 to 50 percent of Arizona's annual precipitation, bring the spectacular desert bloom that occurs in April.

Recently it has been debated whether the cement and asphalt city center, referred to in local news accounts as an "urban heat island," chases away the monsoons. Because the city holds heat and remains up to 15 degrees warmer than the surrounding desert, which cools naturally at night, some theorize that storms are deterred from passing over Phoenix. So far no statistics bear out that theory, but unquestionably downtown Phoenix, and ever-expanding areas in Scottsdale, Tempe, Mesa and other surrounding cities, are heat capsules.

If you're caught in an Arizona monsoon, stay in your car and wait the storm out. If it becomes so dusty or rainy that you can't see to drive, pull as far off the road as possible, turn off your lights and keep your foot off the brake pedal so other cars won't think you're moving in traffic and possibly rear-end you. If you can continue driving, remember, the road will be slick. There isn't enough rain in Arizona to keep the roads washed clean. Don't cross flooded washes. If you stall and the rain continues, you easily could be swept away. If you're on foot, don't stand under a tree, especially a palm tree, which acts as a lightning rod. Get out of a canyon or wash immediately.

Scottsdale

This pleasant resort town had its beginnings in the 1880s when the Rev. Winfield Scott, a Civil War veteran, retired to a little farm on a plot of land east of Phoenix. Others arrived to farm and to run cattle and sheep. As recently as the 1940s, sheep herding along Scottsdale Road was a spectator sport. In 1951 the entire town budget was operated from a cigar box at the fire station. Almost 50 years later such big-city badges as a Nieman-Marcus, countless luxury resorts and a population of about 180,000 take Scottsdale well out of the small-town category. The distance between the northern and southernmost points is 31 miles. Landmark Camelback Mountain parallels the road that bears its name, defining some of Scottsdale's most upscale areas, and on its north side, Paradise Valley. "The West's Most Western Town" as it proudly bills itself, retains some of its once-rowdy image in Old Town Scottsdale, but it is well balanced by upscale restaurants, trendy boutiques, a thriving arts scene and galleries galore.

Adjacent to Scottsdale but very much its own city, **Paradise Valley** could be considered the area's Beverly Hills. Single-family homes are the only structures allowed, except for historic properties like the Hermosa Inn (see Where to Stay) and golf courses. Most homes are set on very large plots, some also protected by walls. A drive through its quiet streets reveals glimpses of how the likes of the Goldwater family, Dan Quayle and Alice Cooper live.

Frank Lloyd Wright's famous school of architecture, Taliesin West, is open for tours of the architect's home and classroom.

Seeing and Doing

Taliesin West

If you've seen Taliesin East, you'll be absolutely stunned at how different it is from this Frank Lloyd Wright enclave. The curiosity is not so much in the structures themselves, but in how the same principles of design can successfully apply in two such diverse areas. The architect built his studio, home and architectural campus here in 1937, and occupied it until his death in 1959. Recognized as an architectural masterpiece and declared a National Historic Landmark, it began when Wright sought a winter home for himself and for his architectural school located in Wisconsin. He found the desert climate appealing, and its rocks, boulders and subtle colorations irresistible. He linked the elements of his school with walkways and terraces, adding fountains as a contrast to the surrounding Sonoran desert. Taliesin West remains much as it was in Wright's day, with revered portions such as the Garden Room practically untouched. Visitors enter through a low-ceilinged stone-walled vestibule, typical of his compression of space technique, that bursts into a large, well-lighted area covered with a translucent roof that makes it seem even more expansive. Wright-designed furniture and the famous Music Room are much in use today. You can walk around most of the exterior, but the only way to see interiors is by guided tour as Taliesin West is still a working educational facility. A variety of tours are offered seasonally, ranging from one to three hours. Taliesin is located at the intersection of Cactus Road and Frank Lloyd Wright Boulevard (about 114th Street) in North Scottsdale. Call **(480) 860-2700.**

Art Galleries

The city of Scottsdale helps create a market for the work of local artists because, by city ordinance, 1 percent of all capital improvement funds is allocated to public art. Scottsdale Civic Center is enhanced by 23 outdoor sculptures that are part of the collection. More than one hundred galleries make Scottsdale an internationally recognized art market. They are primarily located along Main Street, on Marshall Way, on Fifth Avenue and in Old Town near the Civic Center. (See Phoenix, Festivals and Events, for Thursday night ArtWalks.)

McCormick-Stillman Railroad Park

This park, an absolute must for younger kids, features a 5/12-scale steam locomotive that chugs a 1.25-mile route around the park and lake. It leaves from Stillman Station, a 5,200-square-foot replica of a historic depot in Clifton, named for Guy Stillman who donated the train. The park opened in 1975 on land donated by Anne and Fowler McCormick, on the edge of the one-time McCormick Ranch. Extensively renovated, the park includes a 1940s aluminum carousel, rest rooms, a snack bar and an area for birthday parties and other celebrations. At holiday time the station, train and whole back loop are covered with lights. The park is located on the southeastern corner of Scottsdale and Indian Bend Roads. In the winter, open 10 A.M.–5:30 P.M. Summer hours vary. **7301 E. Indian Bend Rd.; (480) 994-2312.**

Rawhide

Come to this fun, rowdy 1880s Western town for a full day of family fun. The largest Western-themed attraction in Arizona, it has two dozen shops to keep adults happy while young ones hang out in Kids' Territory. Visit the petting ranch, museum and interesting Native American village. The obligatory cowboy gunfights are staged regularly. Special events include the Haunted Express, safe trick or treating, and in the fall, a sundown

cookout and western show. If you've never tried rattlesnake, you'll have your chance at the Rawhide Steakhouse and Saloon, which also serves great ribs and huge steaks. Open daily for dinner, seasonally for lunch. **23023 N. Scottsdale Rd.; (480) 502-1880.**

Salt River Indian Reservation

Home of the Salt River Pima-Maricopa Indian Community, this is the most urbanized of any Arizona reservation. On the south it shares a border with the city of Mesa, and parallels Scottsdale on the west. Despite its location, tribal members cultivate about 12,000 of the reservation's 52,600 acres, producing cotton, melons, potatoes, onions and carrots. For general information about the reservation call the Community Relations Office at **(480) 874-8056.** On the reservation, the **Hoo-hoogam-Ki Museum** displays baskets, pottery and artifacts typical of the Maricopa and Pima tribes. Open

Mon.–Fri., 10 A.M.–4:30 P.M. From Oct. to May it also is open Sat., 10 A.M.–2 P.M. Token fee. Follow Longmore Road north from McDowell Road. The museum is at the southeast corner of Longmore and Osborn. **10000 E. Osborn Rd.; (480) 874-8190.** For games of chance, visit **Casino Arizona (480) 850-7777.**

Fountain Hills

This mostly residential bedroom community's claim to fame is the 560-foot fountain that spurts higher than the Washington Monument, every 15 minutes, from 10 A.M. to 9 P.M. daily. **Fort McDowell Casino (480-843-3678)** is operated by the Yavapai here. **Fountain Hills Chamber of Commerce, (480) 837-1654.**

Where to Stay

Scottsdale has everything from over-the-top luxurious to basic and simple accommodations. We've listed some of our favorites, but your best bet is to get the "Destination Guide" from the Scottsdale Chamber of Commerce and Visitors Bureau (see Services).

Luxury Resorts

Scottsdale Princess—$$$$

Many guests settle into a room or casita at this sprawling hotel and never leave. Nine tennis courts and two championship 18-hole golf courses, three swimming pools plus walking trails and a spa can keep most people occupied. Located about 20 minutes north of downtown Scottsdale. **7575 E. Princess Dr., Scottsdale, 85255; (480) 585-4848.**

The Phoenician—$$$$

For sheer opulence, this palacelike resort has it all. To many it symbolizes luxury. Even if you aren't staying here, you can stroll through the Italian marble lobby (guest rooms have marble baths and berber carpet), have lunch at Windows on the Green, take a look at the cabana-flanked pools and waterfalls and have a drink at the bar. **6000 E. Camelback Rd., Scottsdale; (480) 941-8200. Website: www.thephoenician.com.**

Spas

The Spa at Camelback Inn

This uniquely Southwestern spa features an adobe clay purification treatment inspired by the ancient healing rituals of Native American cultures. Classes, yoga, wraps, treatments and massages, too. **5402 E. Lincoln Dr., Scottsdale; (480) 948-1700.**

The Centre for Well-Being at the Phoenician

One of the best in the area, it offers extensive treatments and programs including personal training and nutrition for couples, as well as a meditation atrium and aerobics studio that overlooks the golf course. The Choices Bar in the spa offers sixteen still and sparkling waters from around the world. Southwestern body treatments use desert plants and minerals such as aloe vera, jojoba and sage that are native to the area. **6000 E. Camelback Rd., Scottsdale; (480) 941-8200 or (480) 423-2452 spa direct.**

Where to Eat

El Chorro Lodge—$$$$

Even though it's been around for six decades, El Chorro does not rest on its laurels. If you ate here 20 years ago, you would still find many of the same things on the menu today like breaded chicken livers sauteed with bacon, eggs benedict, chicken-fried steak with mashed potatoes and gravy, shad roe on toast. Additions like mesquite-broiled chicken and blackened swordfish are a concession to a new generation of heart-healthy diners. Take the time to appreciate the John W. Hampton cowboy sculpture at the entrance, and the photos of countless celebs who have enjoyed El Chorro over the years. Open daily for lunch and dinner. **5550 E Lincoln Dr., Scottsdale; (480) 948-5170.**

Marquesa—$$$$

At the Scottsdale Princess, this Five Diamond restaurant creates Catalan cuisine that uniquely blends Italian, French and Spanish influences. Tapas and dinner are served seven nights a week. This is where you come to celebrate a special occasion, or to create a real impression. We love to bring guests to the Spanish market-style Sunday brunch. With dozens of food stations including outdoor grills on which fresh fish, chops and vegetables are freshly cooked, it is truly spectacular. **7575 E. Princess Dr., Scottsdale; (480) 585-4848.**

Los Olivos Mexican Patio—$$$

Since 1948 this casual place has served handmade tortillas along with some of the best enchiladas anywhere. Owned by the Corral family since it opened, it has a staunchly loyal local following. The adobe-walled building dates to 1928 when it was a chapel. Reasonably priced and low key, this is our favorite place to go for Mexican food. Open for lunch and dinner. **7328 E. Second St., Scottsdale; (480) 946-2256.**

Pinnacle Peak Patio—$$$

A long-time local favorite since it opened in 1957, Pinnacle Peak Patio, a 15-minute drive north of Scottsdale's center, delivers the cowboy experience with gusto. At one time practically isolated on a tiny dirt road, housing developments now surround it. In the 1960s, driving "all the way to Pinnacle Peak" for dinner was a real journey. Although homes have crept near and the dirt road is now paved, its character remains. It still serves platter-sized steaks and mesquite-grilled chicken along with cowboy beans and crispy salads. If you wear a necktie, be prepared to have it snipped off to become a ceiling decoration. And if you order your steak well done, you can count on finding an old leather boot, neatly garnished, on your plate. A country-western band plays nightly. Open for lunch and dinner. **10426 E. Jomax Rd., Scottsdale; (480) 585-1559.**

Roaring Fork—$$$

Formerly called Brio, this open, airy cafe's recent renovations include acquiring a new chef-owner who specializes in (what else with a name like Roaring Fork?) American western cuisine. Far from pretentious, the uncomplicated menu features good beef items a tad more substantial than Southwest fare. The misted patio is a good alternative to indoor dining except during July and August monsoons. Open for lunch, Mon.–Fri., 11:30 A.M.–2 P.M.; for dinner, Sun.–Thu., 5–10 P.M., and Fri.–Sat., 5–11 P.M. **7243 E. Camelback Rd., Scottsdale; (480) 947-0795.**

Terra Cotta—$$$

The aroma of fare from the wood grill wafts through this casual place, named for the predominant color on floors, walls and tablecloths, accented with soft Southwest greens and blues. The patio puts you outdoors, but there's not much charm in overlooking a parking lot. You're better off indoors where the attraction is great contemporary Southwestern cuisine. In the Borgata of Scottsdale. Opens at 11 A.M. **6166 N. Scottsdale Rd., Scottsdale; (480) 948-8100.**

Safari Hotel Coffee Shop—$$

Old-timers remember the Safari as *the* resort hotel along Scottsdale Road. Now its claim to fame is its all-night coffee shop, a longtime favorite stop for that final coffee nightcap after closing the Scottsdale bars. Waitresses are straight out of Alice's Restaurant, with many claiming upward of 20 years' tenure serving the mixed crowd that wanders in here. The blue cheese dressing is still as great as it was in the 1960s. **4611 N. Scottsdale Rd., Scottsdale; (480) 945-0771.**

Sugar Bowl Ice Cream Parlor—$$

When you want to toss caution and calories to the winds, plan a stop here for a frozen extravaganza. A Scottsdale landmark, it's been around since the 1950s when real cowboys tied their horses to hitching rails when they came into town. Don't miss the Camelback soda. They also have a good sandwich and salad menu. Open daily at 11 A.M. **4005 N. Scottsdale Rd., Scottsdale; (480) 946-0051.**

Services

Scottsdale Convention and Visitors Bureau, 7343 Scottsdale Mall, Scottsdale, 85251; (800) 877-1117 or (480) 945-8481, fax (480) 947-4523; events line (888) 936-7786.

Tempe

With a population of 157,000 in about 40 square miles, Tempe is Arizona's fifth largest city. More transplanted Midwesterners live here than any other region of the United States. Historic Mill Avenue, around which the city grew up, is alive with shops, hotels, restaurants and art festivals. Tempe's founder in 1871, Charles Trumbull Hayden, ran Hayden's Ferry across the Salt River, which flowed vigorously at that time. He also built a flour mill, still in operation today. The name Hayden figured prominently in Arizona history, as Charles Trumbull Hayden's son, Carl, was a U.S. congressman from 1912, the year Arizona became a state, until 1937, when he became a U.S. senator, an office he held until 1969. Tempe, originally called Hayden's Ferry, was renamed Tempe by an English tourist who thought it looked like Greece's Vale of Tempe.

A diverse group of farmers, Hispanic homesteaders, gold prospectors and hopeful entrepreneurs made up Tempe's early population. By the turn of the century, Victorian homes, Hayden's mill and a lumber yard verified that Tempe was a real city. When the price of cotton bottomed out in the early 1920s the city, by this time surrounded with huge cotton fields, went into an economic slump that didn't get any better with the countrywide Depression of the 1930s. But things were looking up by the 1940s, when Tempe Normal School became a four-year liberal arts college, welcoming returning service men from World War II. For years the city prospered. Then, as shopping malls drew consumers away from the city's center in the 1970s, Mill Avenue became a sort of hippy-dippy hangout for the bearded and long-haired. Today it is revitalized, with coffee houses, boutiques, restaurants and shops housed in newly constructed buildings designed à la the past.

At first you may think you'll never find a parking space in downtown Tempe. Look for green parking signs directing you to parking lots off the main drag. FLASH, the free city bus shuttle, serves downtown Tempe and Arizona State University (ASU). You can simply hop on and off.

Seeing and Doing

Arizona State University

Tempe is obviously a college town. Just walk along Mill Avenue to see throngs of students on bikes, toting books and just hanging out. The 650-acre campus, landscaped with citrus trees, palms and assorted cactuses, is just south of downtown Tempe. It opened in a single one-story building as the Territorial Normal School in 1885, became Tempe State Teachers College in 1925, and in 1958 attained university status. The three-story red brick building built in 1898 when it was called the Arizona Normal School is now Old Main, the oldest building on campus. The 43,000-student institution is one of Arizona's three state universities, along with University of Arizona in Tucson and Northern Arizona University in Flagstaff. Gammage Auditorium, the last public building to be designed by Frank Lloyd Wright and a community center for the performing arts, regularly hosts symphony concerts and Broadway shows. Both the Sun Devils and the NFL's Arizona Cardinals play their games at ASU's Sun Devil Stadium.

Campus Walking Tour

Seeing the campus on foot provides an overview and allows you to stop at some of the highlights. **Nelson Fine Arts Center** houses the ASU Art Museum's five galleries and outdoor sculpture courtyards. The collection includes paintings, sculpture and crafts of the 19th and 20th centuries as well as an interesting selection of Latin American art. During the school year, you can linger at the Galvin Playhouse in the complex for breakfast or lunch, served from 7 A.M. to 1:30 P.M. The **Moeur Building,** a WPA project built during the Depression, stands out as the only adobe building on campus. It houses the Mars Global Surveyor Space Flight Facility, which supports the Thermal Emission Spectrometer (TES) experiment. The

Mars Global Surveyor spacecraft, launched in 1996 with TES aboard, will send back data from Mars into the year 2000. NASA TV is part of the viewing area, open to the public Mon.–Fri., 8 A.M.–5 P.M. The **Law Library** is designed to look like an open book. Noble trees, some of them more than 80 years old and over 90 feet tall, line **Palm Walk.** At the **Bateman Physical Sciences Center,** there are regularly scheduled planetarium shows. Call **(480) 727-6234** for show information. At the **Meteorite Center** specimens of what look like pretty dull rocks are actively used for space research. Open Mon.–Fri., 8:30 A.M.–4 P.M. The small **Geology Museum** houses gemstones, fossils, minerals and more, but the show-stopper, the six-story Foucault Pendulum, shows the rotation of the earth. Open Mon.–Fri., 9 A.M.–12:30 P.M. The **State Arboretum** weaves among campus buildings with color-coded plant markers that help identify the ten vegetation categories represented. **ASU Visitor Information Center** has brochures for the self-guided tour. Open Mon.–Fri., 8:15 A.M.–4:45 P.M. **826 E. Apache Blvd., Tempe; (480) 965-0100.**

Tempe Historical Museum

This hands-on museum lets you play rain god and divert water from the Salt River into agricultural fields. It's one of the exhibits that helps detail Tempe's past through an understanding of what goes on today. An "archaeological dig" replicates the way artifacts are unearthed. On the walls, old photos establish a time line of Tempe's development. Serious historians can spend time in the library where files, microfilm and tapes preserve Tempe's history. Microfilm copies of newspapers from the 1890s to 1950s provide one of the most accurate accountings of what life was like as the city developed. Changing exhibits recently have included Victorian Secrets, a lingerie retrospective, and a history of the Cactus League. A staffed satellite tourism office in the museum foyer stocks brochures and maps. There is a small fee for the museum. Open Mon.–Thu. and Sat., 10 A.M.–5 P.M.; Sun., 1–5 P.M. Closed

Fri. and major holidays. Located on the corner of Rural Road and Southern Avenue. **809 E. Southern Ave., Tempe 85282; (480) 350-5100.**

Petersen House Museum

About a mile west of the Historical Museum, this Queen Anne Victorian, built in 1892 by pioneer farmer Niels Petersen, once was one of the most elegant homes in the Salt River Valley. Its furnishings reflect Arizona's territorial days as well as the 1920s. Interior detailing includes hand-stenciled wallpaper, ornate moldings and intricate curlicues so typical of the era. The tour is self-guided. Small donation. Open Tue., Thu. and Sat., 10 A.M.–2 P.M. **1414 W. Southern Ave., Tempe, 85282; (480) 350-5151 or (480) 350-0900.**

Arizona Mills

Opened with much fanfare in November 1997, this 1,480,000-square-foot outlet-style mall's racetrack layout allows you to enter at one point, hit all the stores and end up back where you started. Its art gives it more charm than most such malls. "Red Rock Towers," a stone and ceramic collage, sits at the main entrance, "Copper Mine Two," a series of asymmetrical panels framed in turquoise, and a stylized cactus called "Saguaro Totem" decorate other entrances. Inside six "neighborhoods" divide the mall and are identified by specially themed works of art. You'll see a mural of the ruins at Montezuma's Castle, petroglyphs, indigenous trees and more incorporated into the overall design. You easily can spend the day here. American Wilderness, J.C. Penney Outlet, Marshall's, Ross, Burlington Coat Factory, an IMAX theater and a 24-plex theater are part of the retail mix. In the parking lot there are two recharging stations for electric vehicles. Located off US 60 and I-10. **(602) 491-9700.**

Rio Salado

A retail complex, residential area and meandering urban park along the dry Salt River is a work in progress at this writing, with a 2-mile lake expected to open mid-1999. Plans call for an inflatable dam to corral waters to form a lake that will be home to water birds and riparian vegetation as well as paddle boats. If plans go as expected, Arizona's largest hotel, the Peabody Tempe (complete with famous Peabody ducks), will be completed on the lake's shore by the end of the year 2000. A golf course, equestrian center, walking trails, playing fields and more will be part of the finished complex.

Where to Eat

Monti's La Casa Vieja—$$–$$$

A favorite family eatery since 1956, Leonard Monti Sr. opened his restaurant on the home site of Tempe's founder, Charles Trumbull Hayden. The 1872 building marks the city's birthplace, and has welcomed generations of eager steak-eaters with its garlicky, juicy steaks and prime rib. Local athletes like it, they say, for the huge top sirloins. Open Sun.–Thu., 11 A.M.–10 P.M.; Fri. and Sat., 10 A.M.–midnight. **3 W. First St., Tempe; (602) 967-7594.**

Rainforest Cafe—$$–$$$

In Tempe in the new Arizona Mills megamall at the junction of I-10 and US 60, you come for the theme park atmosphere as much as for sustenance. Waiters are "safari guides," the hostess is a "tour guide," and lunch is a "rainforest adventure." It really does look and smell like someplace in the heart of Costa Rica, with mist rising from jungle plants, splashing waterfalls and "rain" dripping from greenery that covers walls and pillars. Every 20 minutes or so you can expect a "thunderstorm" complete with lightning and unsettled elephants trumpeting in the background. It's noisy, fun and totally visual, and the food's not bad either. Vegetable sandwiches, flatbread pizza and salads are reliably tasty. The full bar is smoke-free, as is the restaurant. To its credit, the cafe donates money tossed into the Atlas fountain to organizations that support environmental causes. Open Mon.–Sat., 10:30 A.M.–11 P.M.; Sun., 10:30 A.M.–9 P.M. **(602) 752-9100.**

Gordon Biersch Brewing Company—$$

Four flagship German-style lagers brewed on site make this casual micro-brewery and restaurant a new favorite. Pilsner, Blonde Bock, Marzen and Dunkles are complemented by seasonal beers all brewed with yeast and hops from Germany. An eclectic menu and friendly setting make it as popular with the college crowd as it is with the professor set. Open daily, 11 A.M.–1 A.M. **420 S. Mill Ave., Tempe; (602) 736-0033.**

Services

Tempe Convention and Visitors Bureau, 51 W. Third St., Ste 105, Tempe 85281; (602) 894-8158, fax (602) 968-8004.

Mesa

Mesa was established in February 1878 by 80 Mormon pioneers from Salt Lake who figured that the location, on a flat-topped tableland about 3 miles above the Salt River, was good for agriculture. The name Mesa means "table" in Spanish. With a population of 350,000 it is the second-largest city in the Valley of the Sun, with a projected population of 425,000 by the year 2000. It enthusiastically welcomes snowbirds to dozens of RV parks, and has hotel accommodations at the Mesa Pavilion Hilton, the Sheraton Mesa and the Holiday Inn. It hosts the Chicago Cubs for Spring Training (see Spring Training, page 159).

Seeing and Doing

Arizona Temple of the Church of Jesus Christ of Latter-Day Saints

Mesa's Mormon beginnings are abundantly evident in this impressive monument. The groundbreaking took place in 1922, and the temple was completed in 1927 at a cost of $800,000. Built of crushed rock from nearby Tempe butte quarry, its concrete frame is reinforced with 130 tons of steel that make it practically indestructible, said the builders at the time. The exterior finish, faced with a terra cotta glaze, repels dust so well that elders say it has never been cleaned. More than 72,000 square feet and 193 rooms are used for marriages and other ceremonies. Non–Mormons are not allowed inside the temple. Most interesting to visitors are the beautifully maintained gardens and rich architectural details. In December, more than 400,000 lights decorate the grounds and building, and the largest Easter pageant in the world dramatizes the resurrection of Christ. The visitor center, open daily, 9 A.M.–9 P.M. (10 A.M.–10 P.M. from the day after Thanksgiving until New Year's Eve), has replicas of rare religious art, and invites visitors to view a video explaining the basic doctrines of the Mormon Church. **525 E. Main, Mesa, 85211; (520) 964-7164.**

Champlin Fighter Aircraft Museum

Considered by some the Smithsonian of fighter aircraft, two hangars house the world's largest private collection of flyable vintage fighter planes. You can see fragile wood and fabric planes from World War I like the Fokker Triplane and Sopwith Camel, the heavy iron Goodyear F2G-1 Corsair and P-38 from World War II, and U.S. and Soviet-built jets that flew in Korea and Vietnam including the McDonnel-Douglas F4 Phantom. In May, on Barnstormers and Bi-Plane Day, you can actually catch a ride with a pilot in one of these open-cockpit beauties. The American Fighter Aces Association headquarters is at the museum. To be an "ace" a pilot must have five verified downings of enemy aircraft in aerial combat. Open daily, Apr. 15 to Sept. 15, 8:30 A.M.–3:30 P.M.; Sept. 16 to Apr. 14, 10 A.M.–5 P.M. Moderate admission. Located at Falcon Field off McKellips Road. **4636 Fighter Aces Dr., Mesa, 85215; (602) 830-4540.**

Mesa Southwest Museum

More of an experiential visit than a simple museum stop, it is filled with re-creations of Hohokam Indian dwellings and a real jail. The museum traces the area's development from prehistory to the present. Changing exhibits mean you'll see something new every time you go. Kids like the hands-on opportunities, like gold-panning, and the controlled terror created by the roar of animated full-scale dinosaurs. Small fee. Open 10 A.M.–5 P.M., Tue.–Sat.; 1–5 P.M., Sun. **53 N. MacDonald St., Mesa; (602) 644-2230.**

Golf

Mesa offers golf packages for those who come to play the 13 courses that participate. Golfers call one of 11 hotels to select the course or courses they prefer to play, and the hotel handles the rest. Tee times may be guaranteed up to 90 days prior to arrival. Similar packages are available for Chicago Cubs and Arizona Cardinals games.

Services

Mesa Convention and Visitors Bureau, 120 N. Center, Mesa, 85201; (800) 283-MESA or (602) 827-4700. Website: www.arizonaguide.com/mesa.

In and Around Phoenix

EAST OF PHOENIX

APACHE JUNCTION

Because it is so close to lakes and the Superstition Mountains, this little town, for years a sort of suburban trailer park to Phoenix, is on a definite economic upswing. It's a new town, incorporated in 1978 in Pinal County, in an area left untouched by early miners because it was the homestead of hostile Apaches. What put it on civilized maps was the discovery of gold at Goldfield in 1893. Building Roosevelt Dam gave the city a real boost because the Tonto Wagon Road (Apache Trail) was built to access the construction site, and telephone and telegraph lines were strung from Mesa, through Apache Junction, to the dam. The construction of both Mormon Flat Dam, which formed Canyon Lake in 1925, and Horse Mesa Dam, which created Apache Lake in 1927, helped further establish the town. By 1922, US 60 to Globe had been completed, creating a circle route that Americans, made newly mobile by the automobile, found fascinating.

Festivals and Events

Lost Dutchman Days
end of February

This fun, down-home event features a Senior Pro-Rodeo, marching band competition as part of one of the area's biggest parades, an art show, carnival and entertainment. Of course the Lost Dutchman and his burro play a prominent part in the festivities.

Outdoor Activities

Superstition Mountains

The Superstition Wilderness area east of Apache Junction appears in a number of places in this chapter. Its general background revolves almost entirely around gold. Early legends say that the Aztecs buried gold in the mountains after the 1519 Spanish invasion of the Mexican mainland. The conquistadors and later the Jesuits supposedly hid their treasures in the Superstitions. The Peralta family from Arispe, Sonora, owned (so goes the tale) a dozen extremely rich mines in the area. As the Mexican-American war wound down in 1848, the Spanish hurried to wrest whatever gold they could from the mountains before the Southwest came under the flag of the United States. Apaches protected "their" gold by sending anyone who came searching on a quick trip to the hereafter. And then German prospector Jacob Waltz showed up, evaded the

Apaches, and is said to have discovered the mines' whereabouts. When he died, a bag of extremely rich gold ore was discovered under his bed.

For decades these tales have fired the imagination of movie makers. Parts of *Lust for Gold,* produced in 1949 by Columbia Pictures starring Glenn Ford and Ida Lupino, were filmed in the Superstitions. The construction of Apacheland, an 1880s Western movie town, drew more production companies and became home base for *Arizona Raiders,* starring Audie Murphy; *Charro,* filmed in 1968 with Elvis Presley; Marty Robbins in the 1972 film *The Drifter; The Gambler,* starring Kenny Rogers; and the epic *How the West Was Won.* One of the classic landmarks of the Superstitions, Weaver's Needle, a volcanic spire, juts 4,535 feet into the sky. The spire was probably named for scout and guide Pauline Weaver (a man), one of Arizona's first white settlers.

Hiking

Many marvelous hiking trails cross the 160,000 acres that make up the Superstition Wilderness area of the Tonto National Forest. You'll see easy-to-access trailheads marked all along AZ 88. Motorized vehicles and mechanized equipment are prohibited unless specifically authorized.

Peralta Trail

Heavily used and readily accessible, this 6.2-mile trail is not recommended for horses because it can have uncertain footing. From the trailhead to Fremont Saddle the elevation gain is more than 1,000 feet, but scenery and desert vegetation are interesting. From US 60, 8.5 miles past Apache Junction, take the Peralta Road 77 turnoff. The trailhead is about 8 miles north on this road. You may also access the shorter, but steep and rocky, 3.4-mile Bluff Spring Trail at this point.

Dutchman's Trail

This long, 18.2-mile trail crosses a number of other trails in the Wilderness, some heavily used. Access it at First Water trailhead by driving east on US 60 toward Apache Junction. At Exit 196 take Idaho Road and proceed north 1 mile to AZ 88. Turn right and continue approximately 3.5 miles to Forest Road 78, near Mile Marker 200. Turn right and follow Forest Road 78 approximately 3 miles. For a shorter hike, you can access the 3.3-mile Second Water Trail at this point, which passes through Garden Valley.

For maps and trail guides for these trails contact the **Tonto Basin Ranger District, Hwy. 88, HCO 2 Box 4800, Roosevelt, 85545; (520) 467-3200, fax (520) 467-3239.**

Lost Dutchman Moonlight Hike

This is a very special hike, not to be missed if you can work it into your schedule. Once a month during the winter, on a Saturday night as close to the full moon as possible, rangers lead a 2.5-mile hike along the base of the Superstition Mountains in Lost Dutchman State Park. The two-hour hike is eerily lovely. You'll see saguaros silhouetted against the moon, hear coyotes yip in the distance and thrashers and night birds call as they flit among creosote and manzanita. At one point the ranger stops to tell the tale of Indian Canyons, inhabited by the Thunder Gods, now turned to stone and visible in the silvery light as stolid rock formations. As the ranger talks, Native American chants issue from a tape player. Before the hike the bearded Lost Dutchman himself puts in an appearance, telling his tale, and explaining why his gold will never be found—at least not so far. Some of the trail covers rocky and uneven ground so you should be in pretty good condition and have no problems with night vision. Bring a flashlight and meet at the Cholla group ramada after checking in at the ranger station. There is a small vehicle fee. These hikes have become so popular that, as of this writing, reservations were being considered. See Parks and Gardens below for directions to the park. For information call **(480) 982-4485.**

If you think you'll be the lucky one to find the Lost Dutchman mine, you can get outfitted for treasure hunting and prospecting at **Pro-Mack South** in Apache Junction. Mining supplies, metal detectors, even free panning lessons and training videos are available. **940 W.**

Apache Trail, Apache Junction, 85217; (800) 722-6463 or (480) 983-3484.

Horseback Riding

Many visitors to Arizona look for a real Old West experience, like riding off into the sunset.

Don Donnelly Stables takes would-be cowpokes on dude-friendly horses into the fabled Superstition Mountains on rides that last an hour or overnight. You also can arrange three to eight-day horseback vacations, from February through November, riding for 6 to 8 hours every day. But at the end of the day you have tents, hot showers and entertainment. The stables are open all year. **6010 S. Kings Ranch Rd., Gold Canyon, 85219; (800) 346-4403 or (520) 982-7822.**

Lakes

Saguaro Lake

It's difficult to place this lake in sensible reading order. If you look at a map, the lake is obviously the third and last in the chain of lakes that eventually return to the Salt River. But the lake can't be accessed from the Apache Trail, as can Canyon and Apache Lakes. The usual route is to take AZ 87 north from Phoenix, and exit at the marked sign. The **Desert Belle (480-984-5311),** a comfortable pontoon boat, offers 90-minute lake tours the year-round. It's a smooth glide in the open air or under cover in the boat's midsection. The tour goes to Stewart Mountain Dam, which creates the lake, accompanied by narration that fixes the lake's time in history and explains the vegetation on its sandy shores.

Canyon Lake

Located 14 miles northeast of Apache Junction on AZ 88, it is the middle of the three lakes (the other two are Saguaro and Apache) that form a chain below Roosevelt Lake along the Salt River. Held back by the Mormon Flat Dam built in 1925, it was known as Mormon Lake until the 1940s. A replica paddle wheel steamboat, the **Dolly (480-827-9144)**, does 90-minute narrated cruises, some of which include lunch or dinner. Passengers sit on

On Canyon Lake, east of Phoenix, the Dolly steamboat takes guests on brunch and dinner tours of the lake.

shaded upper and lower decks as the boat glides past steep canyon walls and spectacular scenery. You may glimpse desert bighorn sheep and bald eagles. Anglers say that depending on water level and stocking schedules, bass, crappie, bluegill and walleye are catchable. You can rent boats and get fishing supplies at the **Canyon Lake Marina.** There are 10 RV spaces with electric and water hookups and 17 spaces with no hookups, as well as tent camping right on the lakeshore at **Laguna Beach Campground (480-944-6504).** The campground has tables for day use and its own private beach with swimming area. The **Lakeside Restaurant and Cantina (480-380-1601)** is open daily for three meals (hours vary by day and season), served indoors or out, overlooking the lake. It is open for breakfast Saturday and Sunday the year-round. For a good day trip, rent a slow-moving pontoon boat, basically a floating porch, and watch the passing scenery. Pack a picnic and a cooler full of cold drinks, slather on the number 15 and you're set. There are a number of picnic grounds where you can tie up, and lots of canyons to explore. Call **Canyon Lake Marina (480-944-6594)** for rental information.

Apache Lake

The only way to reach this lake, midway between Roosevelt Dam and Tortilla Flat, is via the Apache Trail, one of the reasons why you often encounter boats being trailered along this twisty route. The 18-mile-long, skinny body of water has a marina with boat rentals, launch ramp, fishing and camping supplies and a grocery store. There is an RV campground with hookups and showers and an area for tents. For something even more civilized, the 58-unit **Apache Lake Motel (520-467-2511)** has kitchenettes, a restaurant and bar. Call for reservations, essential most weekends and almost always during the summer.

Golf

Gold Canyon Golf Resort

This foothills course recently took nine of its existing 18 holes, built an additional nine and created the spectacular new Mountain Course that plays to 6,008 yards from the blue tees. The remaining nine are now the Resort Course. In an area where most courses are relatively flat, the variances in topography and elevation changes in the Superstition Foothills make it not only interesting but also scenic. (See Where to Stay for directions.) For tee times call **(480) 982-9449.**

Four-Wheel-Drive and Ecological Tours

Apache Trail Tours

One of the best ways not to miss any of the great stuff (like big horn sheep, old mines, running streams and waterfalls) is to hook up with an experienced guide who has a vehicle that can take an off-road beating. Apache Trail Tours uses genuine Jeep® Scramblers to bounce along desert roads, or simply to follow the Apache Trail. Tours of four hours to all day can be arranged, some incorporating hiking, with a driver-guide who really knows the area. Before setting out, owner Jodi Akers carefully explains the "leaverite" concept to all clients. "If you find something that interests you, take a look, take photos, even pick it up. But then, you leaverite there," she says. The office is at Goldfield Ghost Town. **(480) 982-7661. Website: www.arizonaadventures.com/apachetrail.**

Walk Softly Tours

With levels of difficulty that range from "mind-boggling" to "heart-stopping," these ecologically sensitive tours are among the best for introducing newcomers to the Sonoran Desert flora and fauna, and to indigenous cultures. A tour called Mile in their Moccasins is a half-day odyssey to an Indian reservation led by a native guide. Another, A Walk on the Wild Side, is an all-day hike through back country into a desert canyon filled with unusual rock formations and desert oases. The company partners with the Arizona American Indian Tourism Association, the Forest Service and the BLM. **P.O. Box 5510, Scottsdale, 85261-5510; (480) 473-1148, fax (480) 473-1149. Website: www.walksoftlytours.com. E-mail: round_up@msn.com.**

Seeing and Doing

Parks and Gardens

Lost Dutchman State Park

At the base of the Superstitions, the park's proximity to Phoenix creates heavy use. Still one of the loveliest parks in the state system, its magnificent saguaro cactuses and ocotillo thrive in this part of the Sonoran Desert. For years the legend of the Lost Dutchman mine has lured adventurers to look for the golden treasure supposedly hidden there by miner Jacob Waltz. One theory, which supports the mine's obscurity, is that in the 1880s an earthquake rocked this area, shifting sight lines and moving landmarks that Waltz had used to pinpoint the mine's location. There are campsites here, but no hookups. Saturdays at 10 A.M., rangers lead a leisurely nature hike along park trails, which averages 2 to 3 miles and lasts about 1.5 to 3 hours. The park is located five miles northeast of Apache Junction on AZ 88, the famous Apache Trail. **6109 N. Apache Trail, Apache Junction, 85219; (480) 982-4485.**

Scenic Drives

Apache Trail

This rugged route follows AZ 88 over the historic Apache Trail, passing Tonto National Monument, Roosevelt Lake, Tortilla Flat and Lost Dutchman State Park, ending in Apache Junction or Globe, depending on which end you use as a starting point. When you drive it (you can do it in a passenger car), be aware of trail etiquette. The vehicle coming up hill has the right of way, and if you are a slower-moving vehicle, use pull-outs to let the traffic behind you pass.

The trail was built around the turn of the century as a construction road to get materials through the Superstition Mountains to the site of the new Roosevelt Dam. Once the dam was complete the road was forgotten, except by intrepid souls looking for adventure. But by the 1950s, it was rediscovered for its scenery, and also for the challenges it posed. On a map it looks like a pretty benign 48-mile stretch of some paved, some gravel road, giving no hint of the vast volcanic fields and buttes it crosses. It can take a couple of hours, or much longer, depending on your tolerance for jouncing around and how many times you stop. If you start from the Apache Junction end, the first place of note that you come to, 4.5 miles from Apache Junction, is **Goldfield** (at right). At 5.5 miles you come to **Lost Dutchman State Park** (see page 186). A sign lets you know that you're entering Tonto National Forest, unusual because the "trees" are cactus and scrub, but spectacularly beautiful and blissfully free of commercial signs or billboards. The terrain was created more than 29 million years ago during the Tertiary Period. The road follows the shores of **Canyon Lake,** which is about 15 miles into the trail (see Lakes, above). About two miles past Canyon Lake and 15 miles from Goldfield you come to the town of **Tortilla Flat** (see page 188).

Five miles beyond Tortilla Flat there is a new rest area with spectacular lookout points. Here the pavement ends, and so do most signs of civilization. But this is why you're on the trail in the first place. After an ascent, drivers have to be alert for the steep downhill along Fish Creek Hill, a real misnomer because the creek is almost always dry and certainly hasn't supported fish for decades. The downhill, however, really gets your attention as it descends sharply along a sheer cliff. As you leave Fish Creek Canyon, one of the trail's most famous landmarks, Geronimo Head, lies in front of you. Try to relax and enjoy the scenery until you come to the next civilized sign, the turnoff to **Apache Lake.** Stunning views overlook the massive cliffs of Goat Mountain and Four Peaks. If you scan the ridge lines you could spot a desert bighorn sheep. At this point you are about 14 miles from Roosevelt Dam (see page 92) where you again pick up the paved road, and from where you can continue on into Globe on AZ 88.

Goldfield

Once a booming mining town as a result of the 1892 gold strike in the Superstitions, today Goldfield has been rebuilt into more of a theme park than a town. In its first incarnation Goldfield existed for just five years, from 1893 to 1897. In today's version, you can explore the **Lost Dutchman Museum (480-983-4888),** which explains the geologic history of the mountains that yielded all that gold. You may join the countless visitors who have pored over the 23 maps, all purporting to lead to the Dutchman's gold. The **Superstition Scenic Narrow Gauge Railroad (480-983-0333)**

Goldfield Ghost Town in the Superstition Mountains has mine tours, gold panning, live rattlers and more.

At Tortilla Flat, dollar bills line restaurant walls, a custom that helped down-and-out travelers.

leaves from Goldfield on a tour through the Superstition foothills, past old mining claims in the Goldfield district. Other features include a live rattlesnake exhibit, a mine tour, an Indian jewelry shop and **Mammoth Steak House & Saloon (480-983-6402)**, a truly funky place with stuffed elk, mountain lion and other Arizona critters watching you eat. A hundred feet of hitching post out front accommodates cowboy guests. There's live entertainment along with char-broiled steaks. Goldfield is open daily, 10 A.M.–6 P.M. There is no charge to park and walk around. Located 3.5 miles north of Apache Junction on Hwy. 88. **(480) 983-0333.**

Tortilla Flat, population 6, lies 15 miles beyond Goldfield. It began in 1904 as a stage coach stop on the Apache Trail, the first of two stops between Phoenix and the Roosevelt Dam construction site. The second stop was at Fish Creek Hill. A 1987 fire pretty much leveled the town and destroyed many of the wood frame buildings that had been part of a restoration. The rebuilt version features an ice cream and candy store. Try the prickly pear ice cream to curb the fire of the chili served next door at the Superstition Saloon, where an estimated $15,000 in dollar bills hang on every available inch of wall space. Local lore says that early travelers left change at the tavern to help the next sojourner through this remote place. The wooden Indian who guards the saloon door, and bar stools worn smooth by countless derrieres, are examples of chain saw art. Saddles serve as other stools letting you ride into the sunset as you sip your beer. There are public rest rooms in the saloon. The town is generally alive from 10 A.M. to 5 P.M. daily. For information call **(480) 984-1776.**

Historic Drive

Beginning in Apache Junction and ending in Lordsburg, NM, the Old West Highway drifts for 203 miles, passing through pieces of history that span more than 600 years. An excellent booklet, written by Arizona journalist Sam Lowe, takes you mile by mile across this intriguing route. From Jacob Waltz, the Lost Dutchman and the Superstitions to the Tonto National Monument Cliff Dwellings, to the copper mines of Globe-Miami, through the Apache San Carlos Reservation and on to Safford, it follows US Hwys. 60 and 70, with plenty of side trips. The booklet is available for $4.95 from **The Old West Highway Committee, P.O. Box 2539, Globe, 85502; (800) 804-5623.**

Where to Stay

Gold Canyon Golf Resort—$$$$

This is a very special place, snugged into the Superstition Foothills, made up of large casitas with patios that have great desert views. Once called Gold Canyon Ranch, the name was changed to call attention to the 18-hole golf course (see Golf). New casitas have fireplaces, wet bars and some have a private spa. If you don't care about tee times and handicaps, there are tennis courts, a pool and riding stables. For one of the most enjoyable times in the desert, sit on your patio in the early morning while aggressive cactus wrens visit in search of a handout. During a full moon, the silhouettes of saguaros are spectacular. Located 35 miles east of Mesa off US 60. Signs on the highway point you in the right direction. **6100 S. Kings Ranch Rd., Gold Canyon, 85219; (800) 624-6445 or (480) 982-9090.**

Where to Eat

Mining Camp Restaurant—$$$

Open November to May, this good-fun place is built of Ponderosa logs and surrounded by buildings that replicate an old mining camp. Meals are served family style from big bowls and platters, with "all you can eat" a mandate rather than an option. The specialty is barbecued ribs accompanied by coleslaw, baked beans, homemade raisin bread and prospector cookies for dessert. If you're looking for continental cuisine, this is not the place. Open Mon.–Sat., 4–9 P.M.; Sun. and holidays, 12 noon–9 P.M. Located north of Apache Junction on AZ 88 about a mile south of Goldfield. For reservations call **(480) 982-3181.**

Services

Apache Junction Chamber of Commerce is open Mon.–Sat., 8 A.M.–5 P.M., except summer months when the office is closed on Sat. They have lots of good pamphlets, plus a knowledgeable staff. **1001 N. Idaho Rd., P.O. Box 1747, Apache Junction, 85217-1747; (800) 252-3141 or (480) 982-3141.**

NORTH OF PHOENIX

CAREFREE AND CAVE CREEK

Unique mineral outcroppings and boulders, flanked with majestic saguaro cactuses and a background of craggy little mountains, become focal points in a fascinating high desert landscape that backgrounds these two towns. Carefree lies in the lee of Black Mountain, an extinct volcano covered with huge boulders. Along with larger Continental Mountain, it creates a rugged natural skyline. Two adjacent but very different communities, Carefree is a planned enclave where multimillion-dollar homes are so well situated they seem part of the landscape. A good afternoon's trip from Phoenix can include a leisurely drive among magnificent homes, with a stop to eat at the Sundial Center. The exclusive, discreet, gorgeous and very expensive Boulders Resort is tucked into giant rock formations here. Cave Creek, a onetime mining town that dates to an 1874 gold strike, is typically high desert. Homes have views of Elephant Butte, so-named because its outline resembles that of a kneeling pachyderm. Drive north on Scottsdale Road, past Carefree Highway, and you're in Carefree.

LAKE PLEASANT REGIONAL PARK

Within a 25,000-acre park, Arizona's second largest lake was created when Waddell Dam stopped the flow of water along the Agua Fria River, which is fed by the Colorado River and runoff. It is part of the Maricopa Water District, intended to develop arid lands into agricultural opportunities. The 1926 dam was replaced by the current structure, completed in 1993 and named for Donald C. Waddell, who helped garner financing for the first dam. The earth-filled dam is 4,700 feet long and 300 feet high, holding back a lake that can fluctuate almost 200 feet. The lake is named for Carl Pleasant, an engineer involved in the 1926 construction. Its long sweep makes it good for sailing, and anglers say that largemouth bass fishing can be outstanding. You need an Arizona license, and there is a limit of six largemouth per day. Crappie, bluegill, carp and channel catfish also are plentiful. A nesting pair of bald eagles are part of the wildlife that surrounds the park, as are gray fox, javelina, mountain lions, bobcats and mule deer. Frequently spotted wild burros are descendants of those used in the late 1800s by miners trying their best to wrest, with minimal results, something valuable from the hills. The saguaro-studded shores and the general aridness can make things crushingly hot. But for those who are summer-starved by asphalt and concrete, this expanse of blue water is a true oasis.

A favorite sustenance stop on the way back to Phoenix is the Wild Horse, not known for its extensive menu (burgers, grilled ham, hotdogs and chips are about it) but it bases its widespread reputation on its sumptuous, well-priced cheeseburgers. On the Carefree Highway, 6 miles west of I-17. **8415 W. Carefree Highway; (602) 566-0740.**

Getting There

From Phoenix, take I-17 north to the Carefree Highway, also called AZ 74 (Exit 223), turn left and continue 7 miles to the park entrance. Facilities are clearly marked.

On the Water

Fishing boats, ski boats and power skis may be rented at **Lake Pleasant Regional Park (623) 780-9875**. Houseboats also are available. The **Desert Princess (623-780-9875)**, a comfortable launch-type boat, does sightseeing, lunch and dinner cruises. Call for schedule. A new general store and deli purveys necessities, including sandwiches, beer, anchors and lures for a fun day at the lake. **Pleasant Harbor Marina (623-566-3100)** has boats for rent and places for you to trailer your own craft. It is open from 7:30 A.M. to 5 P.M. daily. For information on the RV park and on camping at Lake Pleasant, call the port of entry to the RV park at **(623) 501-1035.**

Camping

Two newly opened campgrounds on the lake's west side, **Desert Tortoise** with 151 semi-improved sites with grills and shade, and **Road Runner** with 74 full hookups, are open the year-round. **Pleasant Harbor RV Resort** is spic and span and looks like it was built yesterday, but it's been here long enough for trees to create shade for its 200 sites. Most are claimed during winter months by snowbirds anchored here until the flakes back home melt away. But overnighters are welcome if space is available. It has large circular rosette spaces with tables, a heated pool with plenty of loungers, clubhouse with big screen TV, game room, shower facilities, laundry and small store. It's okay to bring your boat as a parking lot accommodates trailers. The park is close to the marina, overlooking the lake. **P.O. Box 1869, Sun City, 85372-1869; (800) 475-3272 or (623) 566-1035.**

Picnicking

About two dozen sites with tables and grills border the lake, and you also can use vacant RV sites at Desert Tortoise.

Visitor Center

The Overlook Building has interpretive displays and great lake views. **(623) 780-9857.**

Soaring

The friendly skies are particularly welcoming near Lake Pleasant at **Turf Soaring School,** where thermals off the desert give new meaning to the phrase "up-up-and-away." You take off in a tandem-seating glider, you in front and the pilot behind you, towed by a powered plane. Once airborne, cars on the ground become ants and fields turn into patchwork quilts. Then the pilot tells you to pull the red knob. This detaches your sailplane from the tow plane, and you soar and climb, catching thermals in exactly the same way that hawks and eagles do. If you've never tried this and want to experience the exhilaration of floating free, go for it. The company has eight sail planes and three tow planes, and flies every day that the weather permits. Take I-17 north to the Carefree Highway exit and continue west to 99th Avenue. The school is located at Carefree Highway and Lake Pleasant Road. **8700 W. Carefree Highway, Peoria, 85382; (602) 439-3621.**

WEST OF PHOENIX

GLENDALE

This town of about 200,000, the Valley's third largest city, was established in 1892 and capitalized on its past to turn itself into an antiques hub. A cotton and farming center early on, it is still surrounded by producing fields. Original hundred-year-old brick storefronts like the Old Towne shopping area line Glendale Avenue, downtown's main street. Restored Craftsman bungalows, a general store, soda fountain, teahouse and other remnants from a gentler era give the place an almost-Midwest feeling. **Sahuaro Ranch Park,** at 59th Avenue and Mountain View Road and listed on the National Register of Historic Places, preserves an early 20-acre homestead. A free trolley loops through Old Towne and Catlin Court, one of the main shopping districts. For more information, contact the **Glendale Marketing/ Communications Dept., Tourism Division, 5859 W. Glendale Ave., Glendale, 85301; (623) 930-2960. Website: www.arizonaguide.com/glendale.**

THE SUN CITIES

For a look at a first-class way to spend retirement years, drive through any of these master-planned active retirement communities that welcome residents age 55 and better. The original Sun City, with a population of 38,000, sold out years ago but now attracts a second generation of retirees, drawn to well-kept resale homes in tidy neighborhoods. The 7,000-seat outdoor amphitheater is the venue for a continuing stream of nationally known performing artists. **Sun City West,** opened in 1978, has more than 25,000 retirees enjoying an active lifestyle. There are a few new homes available, but most new construction is going on at **Sun City Grande,** opened in 1996. For information on any Del Webb community call **(888) 932-2639.**

SOUTH OF PHOENIX

GUADALUPE

Thirty years ago Guadalupe was way south of Phoenix, just a little village that you zipped by on I-10 on your way to Tucson. Now it is surrounded by the homes and businesses of Tempe on three sides, and the I-10 freeway that marks the Phoenix boundary on the west. As it was then, its population of about 6,000 is Yaqui Indian, with Mexicans the more recent arrivals. Until recently the Yaquis lived much as they have for decades. In the 1800s they cultivated sustenance crops along the Salt River, with enough left over to sell to early Phoenix residents. A 40-acre parcel, given to the Yaquis by President Woodrow Wilson in the early part of the century, was formally named Guadalupe in honor of Nuestra Señora de Guadalupe, the Mexican Virgin Mary. When the area called Ahwatukee began to develop in the late 1970s on the Tempe-Phoenix border and Tempe found itself in an accelerating growth spiral, Guadalupe felt the squeeze. Yet it managed to hang on despite the fact that its 450 acres are being eyed by developers.

Our Lady of Guadalupe Church, in the town center, is the site of elaborate Christmas and Easter celebrations, but most days it is a quiet, cool refuge for simply sitting and thinking. The **Guadalupe Farmer's Market** on the corner of Calle Guadalupe and Calle del Yaqui (Priest Road) is a fragrant repository of absolutely fresh, delicious vegetables, with hot roasted chiles always available. Depending on the season, locally grown tomatoes, squash, melons and more are in stock. The village's other big draw is a marvelous Mexican seafood restaurant called **San Diego Bay.** Formica-topped tables, plastic booths and fluorescent lights do not exactly make for great atmosphere, but that's not why you come here. All fish is absolutely fresh. The ceviche appetizer served on a crisp corn tortilla is flavorful and moderately spicy, and red snapper Veracruz, with mounds of fresh chopped vegetables, is unsurpassed. If you're there for dinner, see if they have a pot of clam soup brewing. This clear, fragrant broth with pieces of chewy clam is delightful. Wash it all down with a frosty Negro Modelo and you're in heaven. The unobtrusive little restaurant is located across from the Farmers Market in a big blue mercado. Open daily for breakfast, lunch and dinner. **9201 Avenida del Yaqui; (480) 839-2991.**

CHANDLER

This one-time agricultural town southeast of Phoenix wanted to be the Salt River Valley's answer to Pasadena, California. It was founded in 1912 by Canadian immigrant Dr. Alexander John Chandler, a veterinary surgeon, who purchased 80 acres of land from the federal government in 1891. He became a farmer and an expert in irrigation, a process essential to the success of farming in this arid land.

Settlers soon discovered that water was at a premium, and the newly formed Salt River Project limited each landowner to 160 acres that could be irrigated. This put a decided crimp in Chandler's ability to farm his land, which had by that time increased to 18,000 acres. So he became one of the first land developers, advertising plots to Easterners. Three hundred eager buyers were brought by train to a "town" that consisted of the subdivision office, a place to eat and a small grocery store. But it eventually grew to become a place of lovely homes, hotels and resorts.

The Chandler area, south of Phoenix, once a farming and ranching area, still retains a peaceful, rural feeling.

The town got a boost with the opening of the San Marcos Resort on November 22, 1913. The gala was attended by Governor W. P. Hunt and Vice President Thomas Marshall. It became the first Arizona hotel to offer guests the complete resort experience, with golf, tennis, horseback riding and polo among its attractions. Fred Astaire, Joan Crawford and Clark Gable were on its glittering guest list. The dining room, awash in crystal and silver, featured ostrich from local farms. By this time ostrich farming had become a thriving industry with the increasing demand for the big birds' plumes, which had become a trendy women's fashion accessory. Chandler incorporated in 1920, built a high school, jail and other trappings of an established community. It received a population boost in 1941 with the opening of Williams Air Force Base, and has continued to grow to its present population of about 150,000. Adjacent to Chandler in the community of **Sun Lakes,** almost 15,000 moderately affluent seniors enjoy the amenities of a resort retirement development.

The **Arizona Railway Museum (480-821-1108)** is a small non-profit museum dedicated to the preservation and restoration of Arizona's railroad history. The outdoor display features a number of railroad cars, including a tank, refrigerator, dome, and flat car as well as the staple boxcars and cabooses. Those who aren't captivated by cabooses will appreciate the collection of railroad china that includes the most common of all Southern Pacific china, "Prairie Mountain Wild Flower," first used in the 1930s. Open Saturdays and Sundays from Labor Day to Memorial Day, 12–4 P.M., or by calling and making arrangements. **399 N. Delaware St., Chandler 85224; (480) 821-1108; www.siege.net/~arm.**

Sheraton San Marcos Resort—$$$$

Calling itself Arizona's Original Golf Resort, this lovely old hotel, on the National Register of Historic Places, is a good example of how updating can be accomplished to accommodate a present-day desire for amenities without losing a sense of the past. Built in 1913 adjacent to the central square, it is the focal point of downtown Chandler. The town's founder, Dr. Alexander John Chandler, saw the hotel as an anchor in a master-planned community. It has had it ups and downs, closing its guest accommodations in 1979 and reopening seven years later after a complete renovation. Today its 295 rooms are lovely and welcoming. Even if you don't stay here, stop by for lunch to see the classic architecture. The 18-hole PGA championship golf course has challenged players for more than half a century. Many package deals bring somewhat pricey winter rates into a more affordable range. From mid-May to early September room prices are less than half of those from December through April. **One San Marcos Pl., Chandler, 85224; (800) 325-3535 or (480) 963-6655, fax (480) 899-5441; www.sheraton.com.**

Copper Canyon Brewing & Ale House—$$$

This microbrewery has at least six of its own brews available at any given time. The four permanent selections plus two that rotate always offer a good choice of lights and darks, ale, porter and usually something more experimental. This is not your smoky, crowded Saturday-night-get-blasted place. Rather it is sleek, techy and modern with ceiling pipes exposed, a look that seems to go down well with the largely professional crowd. Open for lunch and dinner. **5945 W. Ray Rd., Chandler; (480) 705-9700.**

Services

Chandler Chamber of Commerce, 218 N. Arizona Ave., Chandler, 85224; (480) 963-4571, fax (480) 963-0188.

AHWATUKEE FOOTHILLS

Really part of Phoenix, this burgeoning community of close to 100,000 represents a good share of Phoenix' growth. At one time Phoenix reached no further than South Mountain, but in the 1970s far-sighted developers saw the beauty in the mountain's southern slopes and began building. Today a dozen or more subdivisions are selling homes at a brisk pace. Proximity to the hiking and biking trails in South Mountain Park and five golf courses are among the area's draws. You can stay at the **South Mountain Quality Inn (480-893-3900)** or the **Grace Inn Best Western (480-893-3000),** both at the Elliott Road exit off I-10. **Matthews** restaurant in the Grace Inn has a good lunch buffet. The **Macaroni Grill (480-705-5661)** at I-10 and Ray Road is convenient for lunch or dinner. For information, call the **Ahwatukee Chamber of Commerce** at **(480) 961-2384.**

Between Phoenix and Tucson

FLORENCE

The county seat for Pinal County, this charming little town is often overlooked as a destination, which is too bad because it has interesting things to see. Positioned away from an interstate, it remains small-town, even though the name Florence and prisons have become synonymous in Arizona. Florence has five places of incarceration: two private prisons that contract to import prisoners from other states, one Immigration and Naturalization Service detention center, one county prison and the state prison, which moved here from Yuma in 1909 and is the largest of the five. The population of Florence, around 3,800, swells to 11,500 when you add the prison population—not all bad considering that state revenue sharing is based on the larger population. Among half a dozen good family-owned restaurants there is only one fast food outlet in town, which city officials dub "a mistake," although it is on the outskirts so it does not intrude on historic downtown. For fast food you can go 10 miles down the road to much newer Coolidge, founded in 1926.

The Florence after whom the town was named remains elusive. Some say it was named by Territorial Governor Richard McCormick for his sister, and other sources claim that Governor Anson Safford named it for his sister. Both could be true, as Florence was a popular name in 1866 when the town was established. In the late 1800s it became a stagecoach hub and the agricultural center of the upper Gila River. That it is a true Arizona territorial town is immediately evident in the architectural styles of the 139 structures that make up its nationally registered historic district. Current badges of memorabilia include a water tower bearing the town name, a TrueValue Hardware, and Rexall Drug complete with the old orange and blue sign. Florence is located at the junction of AZ 79 and AZ 87/287, about an hour's drive from either Phoenix or Tucson. From Phoenix take I-10 to Exit 185 and follow signs to the east. From Tucson take AZ 79 (Oracle Road) through Oracle Junction north to Florence.

Seeing and Doing

Pinal County Courthouse

This impressive brick and gingerbread building with mansard roof and dormers is Florence's best example of Victorian architecture. Built in 1891 at a cost of $29,000 and an additional $5,765 spent on jail cells, it is the oldest public building in daily use in the state. No one seems to know why the painted wood tower clock has shown 11:46 since the day it was built. Inside, tall narrow doors with transoms are anachronistically flanked by glowing soda machines. Years of paint clog the intricacies of a sweeping carved wood staircase, which historians say is made of redwood. But the beauty is still there in a building that has good bones, so take the time to admire its flamboyant exterior, then stroll the quiet hallways inside. Located at Pinal and 11th Street.

McFarland State Historic Park

Named for the U.S. senator, governor and supreme court justice who founded the Arizona State Parks system in 1957, this low wood ranch-style building was the first Pinal County Courthouse, built in 1878. You can see its adobe construction through a "window" carved in the plaster that now covers the exterior. The building's incarnation as the county hospital for almost 50 years is traced in exhibits of enameled basins and bedpans, a cruel-looking tonsil guillotine and gynecological instruments and a vacuum-pressure pump used by eye, ear, nose and throat doctors in the days before Dristan. The most compelling exhibit may be that of the World War II Prisoner of War Camp in Florence. From 1942 to 1946 it held 13,000 prisoners, mostly Italian and German soldiers captured in North Africa and Europe and shipped to the United States to relieve England's overcrowded prisons. Prisoner documents, records and photos verify that soldiers were much the same the world over. In back, the Ernest W. McFarland Library and Archives houses personal McFarland family memorabilia. Small fee. Open Thu.–Mon., 8 A.M.–5 P.M. Located at Main and Ruggles. **P.O. Box 109, Florence, 85232; (520) 868-5216 (phone and fax). Website: mcfarland_foundation-@azfamily.com.**

Pinal County Historical Museum

When we picked up a battered geography text here, among its pages we found a sheet of child-drawn doodles scratched on the back of a yellowed application form for a 1920s Ohio automobile registration. The youngster who learned from that book would be hard pressed to recognize the geographic world as it exists today. Morbidly fascinating are the hangman's nooses and wood gas chamber chairs that actually saw active duty. Displays of electrical insulators and barbed wire, farm and mining machinery, sun-colored amethyst and carnival glass, and huge tomes of prison records tell of Florence's early days. Just across the street, Main Street Park has picnic tables and ramadas. Donations welcome. Open Apr. to Nov., Wed.–Sun., 12 noon–4 P.M.; Dec. to Mar., Wed.–Sat., 11 A.M.–4 P.M.; Sun., 12 noon–4 P.M. Closed July 15 to Aug. 31. **715 S. Main St., Florence, 85232; (520) 868-4382.**

Walking Tour of Historic Florence

Pick up a map at the chamber of commerce, which is headquartered in an 1890 building,

once Brunenkant's Bakery. Other historic structures include the Church of the Assumption, its original part dating to 1870; the brick-on-adobe Cosgrove House on Baily Street, built in 1878; and the 1879 Elena Llescas House, constructed in the Sonoran style. The first Saturday in February a Tour of Historic Florence is held from 11 A.M. to 3 P.M., with trolleys taking visitors among the various sites.

Where to Eat

Murphy's—$–$$

This low-key soup and salad restaurant may look familiar to movie buffs. It doubled as the drugstore in the 1985 motion picture *Murphy's Romance* starring Sally Field and James Garner. Walls are lined with movie memorabilia, and the classic May/December romance flick runs on video as you eat. Food in this self-serve place is health-conscious and delicious.

The sandwiches on the menu are a concession to the men in town whom owner Sandy Tyus says "took awhile to learn that you really can fill up on soup and salad." Open for lunch Mon.–Fri., 11 A.M.–2 P.M. **310 N. Main St.; (520) 868-0027.**

Services

Greater Florence Chamber of Commerce

The visitor center here is extensive, and is staffed with helpful folks. **291 N. Bailey (P.O. Box 929), Florence, 85232; (800) 437-9433 or (520) 868-9433, fax (520) 868-5797. Website: www.florenceaz.org.**

GILA RIVER INDIAN RESERVATION

Bordering the south end of the East Valley, this 584-square mile reservation in Maricopa and Pinal Counties, with a population of 12,000, is much publicized for its Indian gambling casinos, convenient to Phoenix players.

Seeing and Doing

Gila River Arts & Crafts Center

The center offers more than just arts and crafts. You may browse through a museum and replicated villages of various Indian cultures. We spent more than an hour in the exhibit that uses the words of indigenous peoples to explain how their ancestors lived during the past 2,000 years. A 10,000- to 20,000-year-old mammoth tusk, discovered on the reservation in 1987, verifies the presence of ancient creatures. Photos are all that exist of extensive ruins called Snaketown. They were excavated, then covered up again to preserve what the Indians consider sacred ground. Other old photos tell the story of 110,000 Japanese who were forcibly evacuated and confined at the Gila River Internment Center on the reservation at FDR's 1942 decree. The shop area sells authentic silver and turquoise jewelry, baskets, pottery and more. Basketry from the Tarahumara Indians in Mexico's Copper Canyon, very different in material and design from the Pima baskets, also is sold here. Outdoors in Heritage Park, re-creations represent villages of the Papago, Pima, Maricopa, Hohokam and Apache Indians. The heat is killer at midday during the summer. But other times of the year it's a pleasant, level walk. You can get full meals and cool drinks in the restaurant. On Thanksgiving weekend, the Native American Dance Festival includes spectacularly costumed performers from eight different tribes, as well as arts and crafts demonstrations. The center is open daily, 9 A.M.–5 P.M. Located between Phoenix and Casa Grande off I-10 at Exit 175. **P.O. Box 457, Sacaton, 85247; (480) 963-3981.**

CASA GRANDE

Although it has had a post office since 1880, this town began as just a stop on the Southern Pacific Railroad. Its borders, marked by vast fields of green bushes with fluffy bolls as well as feed lots, confirm that two of Arizona's Five "Cs," cotton and cattle, are alive and well here. A number of RV parks with signs declaring they cater to "Over 55" show that the area has been discovered by snowbird retirees. Many see it as a lower priced alternative to Phoenix or Tucson, yet it is close enough to both to benefit from their shopping and cultural opportunities.

Seeing and Doing

Outlet Malls

Casa Grande's biggest current claim to fame may be its two outlet malls, located about halfway between Phoenix and Tucson. **Factory Stores of America (800-SHOP-USA or 520-421-0112),** on I-10 at Exit 194 (Florence

Boulvard), features about 30 stores including Farberware, VanHeuseun, Westport and Adidas. Just a few exits farther south, **Tanger Factory Outlet Center (520-836-0897 or 800-4TANGER)** has more than 50 stores including Barbizon Lingerie, Big Dog, Guess?, Koret, Levi's, Liz Claiborne, Springmaid-Wamsutta, Reebok and more. Take Exit 198.

Casa Grande Valley Historical Society

If you're into old stone buildings, stop at this museum just to see its remarkable architecture. Built in 1927 as the First Presbyterian Church of Casa Grande, the natural fieldstone structure now belongs to the historical society, which uses the former social hall for its Heritage Hall Museum. It traces the area's rural life with photos of early farming equipment and relics from the late 19th century mining boom. Open Tue.–Sun., 1–5 P.M., Sept. 15 to Memorial Day weekend. Minimal donation. Located two blocks east of the junction of Pinal Avenue and Florence Boulevard. **110 W. Florence Blvd., Casa Grande, 85222; (520) 836-2223.**

Where to Stay

Francisco Grande Resort and Golf Club—$$$

This 160-room luxury resort, one of the area's few multistory buildings, is visible on the flat desert for miles. Palms mark fairways along an 18-hole golf course, open to the public. It offers some real golf package bargains. **26000 Gila Bend Highway (AZ 84); (520) 836-6444 or (800) 237-4238.**

Services

Greater Casa Grande Chamber of Commerce has area information and public rest rooms. Open Mon.–Fri., 9 A.M.–5 P.M.; Sat., 10 A.M.–4 P.M.; Sun., noon–4 P.M. **575 N. Marshall St., Casa Grande, 85222; (800) 916-1515.**

GILA BEND

Traveling west from Casa Grande, at the point where AZ 85 converges with I-8 there is a rest area with a shaded table but little else. You might wonder why this super-four-lane exists out here in the desert, apparently linking nothing but little agricultural towns. Its *raison d'etre* is that it goes all the way from Texas to San Diego on the California coast.

The town of Gila Bend is located at the point where the Gila River changes its southerly flow and turns to the west. Father Eusebio Kino visited the spot, once a Hohokam village, in 1699. A popular site for many cultures, the river supplied water for irrigation, thus assuring a food supply. Today, farmers cultivate more than 90,000 acres in the area, with alfalfa, cotton, wheat, barley and a few experimental jojoba fields among the principal crops. If you're coming from the east on I-80, about 4 miles before you enter town, a sign points out the Butterfield Trail. When you get into town and stop at the museum, you'll find a replica of the early Butterfield Stage office in Gila Bend. In 1858 the town was established as a stage stop on the route between St. Louis and San Francisco. The 2,800-mile trip took 25 days at an average speed of 5 miles per hour and cost $200 per person plus meals.

Seeing and Doing

Painted Rocks Park

Located on the road to Painted Rock Dam, which creates the largest flood control reservoir in the state, this Bureau of Land Management park protects extensive petroglyphs along a winding trail through a huge rock mound. There are 30 tent or RV sites, vault toilets, picnic areas, fire grills but no showers. Take I-8, 12.5 miles west of Gila Bend to Exit 102 and continue north 10.7 miles to Painted Rocks Park. The petroglyphs are accessible from Painted Rock Road on a one-half mile graded dirt road. They once served as a landmark for travelers along the Butterfield Stage route. For information call the **BLM Field Office** at **(602) 580-5500** Mon.–Fri., 7:30 A.M.–4:15 P.M., or call the **Gila Bend Chamber of Commerce** at **(520) 683-2002.**

Gila Bend Museum and Tourist Office

Here, displays of Hohokam pottery and Papago baskets tell of the hunters and trappers in pursuit of the "hairy dollar bill"—the beaver—that once was abundant along the fast-flowing Gila River. Other exhibits trace the town's Native American history and its connection with the railroad. You can pick up a driving tour map that directs you to the Sanuc District of the Tohono O'odam Nation and the former site of the ancient village. The map also guides you to the ruins of the old adobe St. Michael's Catholic Church, an Indian ceremonial mound that dates to the 900s, and the Stout Hotel at Pima and Capitol, built in 1929 and visited by Tom Mix, John Wayne and Myrna Loy. The office is open daily, 8 A.M.–4 P.M. **644 W. Pima St., Gila Bend, 85337; (502) 683-2002, fax (502) 683-6430.**

Casa Grande Ruins National Monument protects mysterious ruins between Phoenix and Tucson that puzzle archaeologists.

ELOY

Jumping from an airplane may not be everyone's cup of tea, but at Skydive Arizona you can see what it's like and decide if you want to try it. The little town of Eloy is home to the largest skydive training facility in the world. Professional jumpers, those that compete internationally, come here to train. But so do average folks who just want to see what the sport is all about, and "get their knees in the breeze," as school instructors say. No one dives solo the first time. Students are harnessed to instructors. If that's all you want to do, you can stop there. But after a few tandem jumps and hours of training, you may choose to jump solo. The school is located midway between Phoenix and Tucson 4 miles off I-10 near the city of Eloy. **4900 N. Taylor Rd., Eloy, 85231; (800) 858-5867 or (520)466-4777, fax (520) 466-4720. E-mail: SkyAZ@aol.com. Website: www.skydive-az.com.**

Seeing and Doing

Scenic Drive

A pleasant alternative to I-10 between Phoenix and Tucson, the **Pinal Pioneer Parkway,** AZ 79, branches south from US 60 near Florence Junction. You may also access it from AZ 87/287 through Coolidge and Florence. The Parkway opens a window on the Sonoran Desert scenery before billboards and red-tile roofs. If you're not speeding, you'll glimpse, on small placards, the names of some of the cactuses you're seeing. Near the start of the drive you can turn west on AZ 87 for a visit to the Casa Grande Ruins National Monument.

Casa Grande Ruins National Monument

These impressive ruins, the remains of an ancient Hohokam farming village that surrounded a Great House, have puzzled observers since Father Eusebio Kino and his group of missionaries came upon the deserted village. Over the centuries the elements and looters took their toll, until Casa Grande was declared the country's first archaeological preserve. Today a shelter protects the ancient four-story building, which archaeologists believe dates to before 1350 and is the tallest, most massive of any Hohokam structure known to exist. The building's walls face the four compass points. Various openings align with heavenly bodies, perhaps to reveal the best times for planting and harvesting. On a gravel path, vegetation placards point out creosote, prickly pear, saguaro and other desert plants. Pick up a pamphlet for a self-guided tour through the ruins. Guided tours are sometimes scheduled, so call ahead. It's not a good idea to visit at high noon in the middle of summer, as the monument will be hot, and desert winds may make it truly uncomfortable. Early mornings are best during summer months. You can bring a lunch and picnic at shaded tables on the grounds. The monument is open daily, except Christmas, 8 A.M.–5 P.M. Small fee. From I-10 take the Coolidge exit (AZ 387) and follow the signs about 15 miles to the monument entrance off AZ 87. **1100 Ruins Dr., Coolidge, 85228; (520) 723-3172.**

Rattlesnakes

Although their danger is somewhat exaggerated, quite a few rattlesnakes live in the Valley of the Sun, as in most desert climates. You rarely find them in residential areas, but they sometimes linger in places with new construction. Baby rattlers are born in August and September—and arrive with fangs. They give no warning because their rattles have not yet developed. They're born with a little budlike tip on their tail and a second one develops in about a month. Well over half of the baby rattlers, at less than a foot in length, fall prey to hawks and other raptors. Survivors seek shelter under shady rocks and bushes, where you're most likely to encounter them. So be careful where you put your hands, don't lean against a rock or canyon wall if there is a ledge just above or next to you, and wear high-top shoes or boots with pants that flop over the tops. If you do hear a hiss or rattle, stand still until the snake moves away. For snakebite information in the Valley of the Sun, call the Samaritan Regional Poison Center at **(800) 362-0101.** In the unlikely event that you are bitten, call 911.

Picacho Peak State Park

That large, looming pinnacle to the west of I-10 about midway between Phoenix and Tucson has served as a travelers' landmark for centuries. The 3,382-foot eroded lava flow, distinctively shaped and formed by wind and weather, is the site of Arizona's largest Civil War battle. The Butterfield Overland Stage once used the pass it guards. More than 100 campsites with hook-ups are available (the higher ones have wonderful nighttime views of lights below) on a first-come, first-served basis, and picnic areas with shade ramadas are scattered throughout the park. In the spring, if winter rains have cooperated, wildflowers absolutely explode along the roads and on the slopes. In March more than one hundred "soldiers" stage a reenactment of the famous Civil War battle, blasting away on foot and horseback with black powder rifles.

Hiking

The Calloway Trail offers an easy 1.5-mile round-trip. Or you can tackle Hunter Trail where you hand-over-hand yourself upwards by gripping steel cables. You can stop halfway, admire the valley and Santa Cruz River, then go back. Or if you're feeling particularly robust, continue another mile to the peak. Sunset Vista Trail, another toughie, also takes you to the summit. This close to I-10, you'll find civilization within minutes in the form of restaurants and gas stations. Take the Picacho exit off I-10, about an hour south of Phoenix. **(520) 466-3138 (phone and fax).**

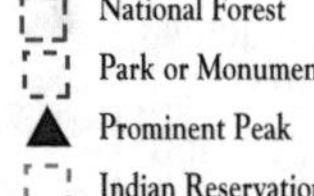
Map Area
Tucson
National Forest
Park or Monument
Prominent Peak
Indian Reservation
Places of Interest
Multilane Divided Highway
Principal Through Highway - Two Lanes Paved
Connecting Road - Unimproved to Paved
40 Interstate Highway Marker
95 U.S. Highway Marker
85 State Highway Marker
15 Indian Route
To Phoenix
Map is *not* to exact scale
SUMMERHAVEN
Mt. Lemmon Highway
Santa Catalina Mountains
Coronado National Forest
Oro Valley
10
Ina Rd.
Sabino Canyon
Hitchcock Highway
Skyline Dr.
De Grazia Studio
77
Sunrise Dr.
Fort Lowell Park Museum
Catalina Highway
Silverbell Road
Saguaro National Monument West
Oracle Rd.
Arizona Historical Society
Swan Rd.
Craycroft Rd.
Tanque Verde Road
Grant Rd.
Gates Pass Road
Speedway Blvd.
Arizona-Sonora Desert Museum
U of A
Broadway
Old Tucson Studios
Randolph Park
Old Spanish Trail
TUCSON
Kinney Road
Alvernon Way
Wilmot Rd.
Kolb Rd.
Saguaro National Monument East
Davis Monthan Air Force Base
Freeman Rd.
Ajo Way
Mission Road
Tucson International Airport
19
86
Pascua Yaqui Ind. Res.
10
Old Spanish Trail
Colossal Cave
BUS 19
San Xavier Ind. Res.
San Xavier del Bac Mission
Vail
To Nogales
Exit 279
To El Paso

Tucson

Tucson

In 1869 J. Ross Browne's book, *Adventures in the Apache Country: A Tour Through Arizona and Sonora,* described Tucson as "A city of mud boxes, dingy and dilapidated, cracked and baked into a composite of dust and filth littered about with broken corrals, carcasses of dead animals and broken pottery."

Today's Tucson is a sophisticated city of about 850,000, a pleasant blend of metropolis and small town that mixes the best of the West with trendy resorts, velvety golf courses, outstanding restaurants and an active arts scene. At an elevation of 2,389 feet, almost 1,300 feet higher than Phoenix, it stays a bit cooler than its neighbor to the north. More than 350 days each year are sunny and fair, according to the Tucson Bureau of the U.S. Weather Service. With a metropolitan area covering nearly 500 square miles, the city sprawls north, from a reemerging downtown, toward the picturesque Santa Catalina Mountains, one of five ranges that surround the city. It sits in the eastern portion of the high Sonoran desert, the only place in the world where saguaro cactuses grow naturally. Tucson is flanked by Saguaro National Park East and West where you can see the largest concentration of these "giants with arms" anywhere.

Tucson is a civilized city, one of just 14 in the country with a resident symphony, as well as opera, theater and ballet companies. An event called Downtown Saturday Night features gallery open houses (there are more than 35 in the downtown area), musical performances and street dancing. Thursday Night Artwalks have become a choice way to get acquainted with the Tucson arts scene. Led by docents, visitors move among galleries that welcome guests with coffee and cookies. Oftentimes displaying artists are on hand to talk about their work.

It's difficult to get lost in this well-laid-out city if you remember that the biggest mountain range, the Santa Catalinas, will always be to the Northeast. Main east-west streets will usually end up feeding into I-10 if you're trying to go north, and main north-south streets usually feed into I-10 as it skirts the south of the city or I-19, which is another north-south thoroughfare. You do have to watch street signs because they can be misleading. Street names frequently change and you can drive for miles before you realize you're on the wrong one. For example, where Kolb/Grant crosses Tanque Verde, the sign facing westbound says Kolb, but it says Grant for eastbound drivers. You have to look behind you to realize you've just missed your turn. Just stay alert and you'll be okay.

Tucson's website (see Services) suggests that you get your bearings by going up Sentinel Peak, the large hill with the white "A" emblazoned on it. You can see it from I-10 as you head south through Tucson. The annual whitewashing it receives from the University of Arizona freshman class keeps it sparkling clean. From here you'll see the ring of mountains that surrounds the city. It's easy to identify the 9,000-foot-high Santa Catalinas on the north and northeast, Rincon Mountains to the east, Santa Rita Mountains to the south and southeast, Tucson Mountains on the west, and the Tortolita Mountains on the northwest.

History

Tucson is the oldest continually inhabited settlement in the country. As early as A.D. 100 the Hohokam people raised crops along the soil-rich Santa Cruz River and charted their activities in petroglyphs, visible today in Saguaro National Park West at Signal Hill. The Spanish arrived in the late 1600s to find the peaceful Pima Indians living near what is now downtown. In 1775 Irishman Hugh O'Connor, in his explorations for Spain, founded the walled presidio of San Agustin del Tucson as protection against the Apaches. Almost a century before, the area had been called "chuk shon" by the Pima Indians. An interpretive translation is "spring at the foot of a black mountain" referring to the Santa Cruz River that follows an uneven above- and below-ground flow. The word became anglicized as "Tucson."

The city, briefly part of Mexico in 1821 when it became independent from Spain, returned to U.S. jurisdiction when it was sold as part of the Gadsden Purchase in 1854. The Butterfield Stage clattered through Cochise territory and on to Tucson in the 1860s. Remnants of Tucson's unruly frontier origins live on in lively country and western bars. Ethnic Indian, Mexican and Spanish roots are evident in the no-high-rise architecture and popular Southwest-style decor. And the Wild West thrives at places like Old Tucson Studios (see Major Attractions). Nicknamed "Old Pueblo" for its original walled presidio, Tucson once was the capital of the Arizona Territory, a title it lost to Phoenix even before Arizona became a state in 1912.

Festivals and Events

La Fiesta de Los Vaqueros

mid-February

Tucson's biggest rodeo and the largest outdoor midwinter rodeo in America, it has thrilled crowds for more than 70 years. The celebration features a parade around the rodeo grounds, the world's largest such nonmotorized event. Tickets are required. **(520) 741-2233.**

Tucson Gem & Mineral Show

February

The world's largest show of its kind, it attracts an international assemblage of buyers and dealers in gems, minerals, fossils, jewelry and other lapidary-related items. The wholesale and retail shows are held separately. Some participants come simply to exhibit fabulous finds and collections. The show offers special displays from museums and private collectors and seminars to help educate the novice as well as the seasoned lapidary enthusiast. Held at the Tucson Convention Center. For information contact the **Tucson Gem and Mineral Society** at **(520) 322-5773.**

Pima County Fair

middle of April

If you're accustomed to Midwest fairs, held in the fall of the year and filled with farm equipment, Arizona fairs will seem quite different. The emphasis is more on fun and games. This 10-day event always begins the second Thursday of the month and has competitions in home arts, fine arts and hobby categories. Four-H and Future Farmers of America (FFA) kids proudly display their projects, and you can stroll down a huge carnival midway. **11300 S. Houghton Rd.; (520) 762-9100.**

Located on the Tohono O'odham Indian Reservation, Kitt Peak is favored by astronomers for clear, clean air that is unaffected by city light pollution.

Major Attractions

Kitt Peak

Even if you're not a Trekkie and stars are something you prefer to see on the silver screen, Kitt Peak is worth an afternoon just for the sheer beauty of the stark white domes poised on various crests, blending with cumulus clouds against a sheer blue sky.

Approaching along the valley floor, you'll see the first white dome one-half hour before you reach your destination. As you drive through the saguaro studded Sonoran desert, an occasional roadrunner darts in front of you. A steep paved road kinked with switchbacks begins a 12-mile upwards spiral. Some find the sharp cliffs and drop-offs unsettling, but the pavement is wide, well maintained and perfectly safe. Sometimes during winter months a buildup of ice and snow may close the road.

One of seven national observatories, Kitt Peak was chosen as an observation point because of the dry atmosphere that guarantees an average of 260 clear days a year. Winter months are driest, and therefore most reliable. The observatory closes during August, when Arizona experiences what it calls its "monsoon" season. A second reason the location is so suitable is its relative isolation from light pollution, yet it is only 56 miles from Tucson's airport and city amenities.

Kitt Peak is located on the second largest Indian reservation in the United States. A 1958 lease for the lofty 6,875-foot high site, negotiated with the Tohono O'odham Tribal Council, is in effect "until the end of time," say its terms. The Tohono O'odham, also called Papago, have stipulated that the observatory cannot be used for military purposes, which means no Star Wars or spy satellites. The observatory shop in the visitor center helps perpetuate the Tohono O'odham's culture by offering beautifully designed woven baskets for sale, with all proceeds going to Native American artisans. Prices for these lovely works of art are kept lower than you'll find elsewhere because the shop charges no sales tax and the baskets are purchased directly from the artists. You'll also find interesting T-shirts, posters and astronomy-related books.

Here displays demystify the working of telescopes, and a huge cylinder of fused quartz, the core removed from the Mayall 4-meter telescope mirror, helps explain how light-gathering (rather than magnification) works. Another display reveals how the stars we see now may no longer exist because of the time it takes for the light from distant sources to reach earth. Exhibits demonstrate why no one ever "looks through a telescope" anymore. There is nothing to look through. Charge-coupled devices (CCDs) now convert light into digital form for computer storage so that astronomers work at video screens rather than eyepieces. LTOs, large telescope operators, adjust and position the telescopes to accomplish specific tasks. Astronomers almost never touch the telescopes.

The National Optical Astronomy Observatories, under contract with the National Science Foundation, oversees site operations on Kitt Peak. Responsible for the world's largest collection of telescopes, which includes 22 optical and two radio telescopes, the observatory provides major telescope facilities for the world's astronomers and has ongoing research programs in observational astronomy.

Telescopes are accessible to professionals as well as students through an application system. Once an application is accepted, the astronomer comes to the observatory on the specified dates and hopes that viewing conditions are optimal. If they aren't, he or she must reapply for new dates.

A guided tour, free because the observatory is funded with taxpayer dollars, begins with an overview of the observatory's operations. Sixty employees arrive by bus each day, and lunch at the full-service cafeteria. A sign asks guests to be quiet in deference to "day sleepers," astronomers in residence who work at night. Just outside the visitor center a glass case protects a large rock slab, found on the site during construction, that bears intricate Hohokam petroglyphs. Some of the figures may represent the ancestors of the mountain lions, bobcats, coatimundis, black bear, snakes, mountain goats, deer and javelina that live on the mountaintop today.

Of the 24 operational telescopes on Kitt Peak, visitors can visit three. The 2.1-meter telescope is closest to the visitor center, up a short hill then up four flights of stairs inside the dome. The dome turns noisily while a viewing slit accordians open to aim the scope heavenward. The telescope is tilted at the same angle as the earth's axis, which simplifies the job of accurately tracking the stars. It is used to view very distant stars and galaxies. Moons and planets are too close for this scope. The 2.1-meter telescope, considered old technology, depends on a large single-glass mirror. The "2.1" refers to the diameter of its primary mirror, constructed in 1963. A sample of the glass with its microscopically thin mirror coating is on display in the visitor center.

You also can look at the world's largest solar telescope, the McMath-Pierce, installed here in 1974. Its 500-foot length, 300 feet of which are underground, houses mirrors that produce a 30-inch image of the sun displayed on a TV monitor. The scope looks like a giant grasshopper poised for an angled leap. You may also visit the 4-meter Mayall telescope, the fourth largest optical telescope in the world.

Getting There

Tucson is about two hours south of Phoenix on Interstate 10. Because a number of other highways spoke out from it, the city is a convenient hub for exploring all of southern and eastern Arizona.

Tucson International Airport is served by Aerolitoral, Aeromexico, America West, American, Continental, Delta, Southwest and United Airlines. The airport is located about 20 minutes west of downtown. Call individual airlines or the **Tucson Airport Authority** at **(520) 573-8100,** or you can fly into Phoenix and use surface transportation for the remaining two hours to Tucson. A number of companies offer sedan service from Phoenix Sky Harbor Airport to many Tucson destinations. One of them is the **Arizona Shuttle (800-888-2749).**

Those seriously interested in astronomy can sign up for a 3-hour stargazing program that begins one-half hour before sunset. Through the observatory's new 16-inch telescope, on any clear night, you can see planets, star clusters, galaxies and nebulae. A box dinner is included in the cost. All-night programs with an astronomer may be arranged.

Kitt Peak is 56 miles southwest of Tucson via AZ 86. The observatory is open to the public daily, 9 A.M.–4 P.M., except Thanksgiving, Christmas Day and New Year's Day. Daily one-hour guided tours begin at the visitor center at 10 and 11:30 A.M. and 1 and 2:30 P.M. Most visitors take an additional hour to visit the telescopes not covered on the tour. You also can do a self-guided tour. Temperatures on Kitt Peak are as much as 20 degrees cooler than on the valley floor. Those with cardiac and respiratory concerns should remember the 6,000-foot-plus altitude and be aware that there are steps and steep hills to some of the telescopes. There are no food or gas facilities, but public rest rooms are adjacent to the parking lot. You can picnic near the parking lot, but there is a better picnic area with tables, a ramada, drinking water and rest rooms about a mile down the hill from the visitor center. **National Optical Astronomy Observatories, P.O. Box 26732, Tucson, 85726; Kitt Peak Visitor Center, (520) 318-8726 or (520) 318-8200 (recorded information). Website: www.noao.edu.**

Arizona-Sonora Desert Museum

One of Tucson's jewels and not to be missed, this ever-changing attraction will occupy most of a well-spent day. Set away from the city on almost one hundred acres of desert that is still truly wild (only 30 acres are under exhibit), it is part zoo, part museum and part botanical garden. More than 300 species of animals and 1,300 kinds of plants of the Sonoran Desert region exist happily in natural settings. The concept of featuring communities of plants and animals rather than individual species makes a visit similar to a journey through a succession of habitats. From a mountain canyon with pine trees you stroll into grasslands, for example, leaving behind black bears, wolves, Steller's jays and other woodland creatures. It's as if you were walking down a mountain slope into high desert grasslands where the vegetation becomes clumps of bear grass, yucca and ocotillo. This is where the prairie dog colony frolicks. If you come in the morning you'll see the clownish creatures sunbathing on mounds above their burrows. A cutaway exhibit shows the elaborate layout of tunnels that supports a colony. Other habitats are home to mountain lions, white-tailed deer, Mexican wolves and desert bighorn sheep. The hummingbird aviary is filled with dozens of the iridescent winged creatures that often will perch within feet of observers as if posing for the camera. The vegetation here represents the actual plants and flowers that hummers use for food in the wild.

A cactus garden displays more than 140 species of Sonoran Desert plants, a half dozen of which are endangered. A cool, dim, walk-through underground replica of a limestone cave has sleeping bats clinging to walls and ceilings. Other exhibits explore cave development, fossils and a packrat midden.

Two gift shops stock an outstanding selection of nature products and books including educational items, perfect to take home for the grandkids. There are two restaurants, a coffee bar and a picnic area just down the road from the museum entrance. While enjoying a quiet picnic lunch we were approached by a pair of shy, hopeful coyotes banking on a handout. The parking lot is wheelchair-accessible, as are most areas of the museum. During the summer, try to get there first thing in the morning, when animals are at their most active and temperatures haven't yet started to soar. When you call the museum, if you're put on hold, you won't get elevator music. You'll hear the sounds of desert birds, flowing water and gentle breezes. Open daily, Mar. to Sept., 7:30 A.M.–6 P.M.; Oct. to Feb., 8:30 A.M.–5 P.M. From Tucson take Gates Pass to Kinney Road, or simply follow Kinney Road to the entrance. **2021 N. Kinney Rd., Tucson, 85743; (520) 883-2702, fax (520) 883-2500. Website: www.desert.net/museum.**

University of Arizona

Tucson almost didn't get the University of Arizona, even though the 13th Territorial Legislature approved $25,000 for its founding, 27 years before Arizona was a state. Oddly enough the money was there but the land wasn't. Lawmakers assumed that Tucson could come up with a place to put the institute of higher learning, once funding was available. This miffed local citizens especially since the state capital site had gone to Phoenix, and neither the state prison nor the asylum for the insane were offered to Tucson. At the last minute, just before the Legislature reclaimed the funds, a saloon keeper and two gamblers donated 40 acres of land, deemed almost useless because they were "way out east of town." By 1891 classes were in session with 32 students and six teachers, and what was to become one of the top research universities in the nation had its beginnings.

You can easily take a day exploring the campus and spend very little because most museums charge no admission. The Flandrau Science Center has minimum charges for some events. Stop by the visitor center at the corner of Cherry Avenue and University for a fistful of brochures and a campus map. You'll find public parking directly behind the center (bring quarters to feed the meter). The visitor center is open Mon.–Sat., 7:30 A.M.–5 P.M.; Sat., 9 A.M.–1 P.M., during the school year. For summer hours and more information call **(520) 621-5130.**

Plant Walk

One of the brochures available at the visitor center directs you to a campus walking tour that identifies plants of the Sonoran Desert as well as "imports," brought by people from the East and Midwest as they migrated west. A grove of olive trees, west of Park Avenue in front of Gila, Maricopa and Yuma halls, dates to 1889 when they were planted to test their adaptation to Arizona's arid conditions. Today they're thriving.

Flandrau Science Center

If you've parked behind the visitor center and stuffed enough quarters in the meter, you'll have plenty of time to walk across the street to Flandrau Science Center. It's filled with hands-on exhibits designed to engage and educate people of all ages. If you arrive on a summer afternoon, don't be surprised to find the Planetarium Theater filled with five-year olds enthralled as they encourage "Hector Vector Star Projector" to make simulated heavenly bodies appear in a pseudo sky. The theater also features laser light shows set to music. A public observatory has a 16-inch professional telescope available to visitors on clear nights Wed.–Sat. throughout the year. Viewing is free. Call **(520) 621-4310** for current astronomy information. Pick up star charts, science kits and other educational toys at the science and astronomy store. Parking is free evenings and weekends. You can bring a picnic to enjoy on the mall, and visit other campus museums while you're here. The building is open Mon.–Fri., 9 A.M.–5 P.M., and Sat.–Sun., 1–5 P.M.

The Flandrau Science Center at the University of Arizona in Tucson offers great laser light shows.

Weather permitting, it also is open Wed.–Thu., 7–9 P.M., and Fri.–Sat., 7–12 P.M. For program information and telescope hours call **(520) 621-4515** during weekday business hours or **(520) 621-STAR** for recorded program information.

Mineral Museum

Located on the lower level of the Flandrau Science Center, this quiet, well-lighted place is filled with specimens that range from meteor fragments to precious gems. Special emphasis on Arizona's rich mineral history includes its status as the copper state. As you walk down the stairs to the museum, notice the murals. Painted walls mimic the geologic layers that you would pass through if you were descending into the Grand Canyon. Closed Fri. and Sat. evenings.

University of Arizona Museum of Art

With a permanent collection of more than 4,500 works, this museum needs a minimum of an hour's browse. A single large room holds the Retablo of Ciudad Rodrigo that dates to the late 15th century and consists of 26 separate panels, depicting scenes from the New Testament. Works by Rodin, Tintoretto, Picasso, Matisse, Kandinsky, Durer, Rembrandt van Rijn, Goya, Daumier, Manet, Whistler and others round out a truly impressive collection. Located on the corner of Speedway Boulevard and Park Avenue in the northwest corner of the campus. The museum is open Labor Day to mid-May, Mon.–Fri., 9 A.M.–5 P.M.; Sun., noon–4 P.M. From mid-May to Labor Day, Mon.–Fri., 10 A.M.–3:30 P.M.; Sun., noon–4 P.M. Closed Sat. For more information call **(520) 621-7567.**

Center for Creative Photography

Across from the Art Museum, the center, a combination museum and research institution, houses a collection of more than 70,000 fine prints. Photographers come to use the extensive archives and library, and everyone enjoys the changing exhibits in the main gallery. Look here for postcards to send home. Dozens of racks have interesting, off-beat, lovely and funny cards that you probably won't find elsewhere. You can park for the center, as well as the art museum, in the Visitor Section of the Park Avenue Garage on the northwest corner of Park and Speedway, then walk through a tunnel under Speedway to the center's front door. Free admission. The building is open Mon.–Fri., 8 A.M.–5 P.M.; library is open Mon.–Fri., 10 A.M.–5 P.M.; the gallery is open Mon.–Fri., 11 A.M.–5 P.M. Everything is closed Sat. and open Sun., 12 noon–5 P.M. **(520) 621-7968, fax (520) 621-9444. Website: www.ccp.arizona.edu/ccp.html.**

Arizona Historical Society Museum

Just a two-block walk south on Park from the photography center, you can explore a replicated underground mine tunnel and see how fashions have changed since the Spaniards came to the state in 1539. Authentically furnished period rooms and a transportation hall with wagons, buggies and buckboards give a realistic sense of the past. Recent changing displays have included an interactive exhibit that invited visitors into the lobby of a territorial hotel and a photographic exhibit of the restoration of Mission San Xavier south of Tucson. The Society's archives often are used by scholars researching Arizona history. Open Mon.–Sat., 10 A.M.–4 P.M.; Sun., 12 noon–4 P.M. Free admission. Located at the corner of Second Street and Park. **949 E. Second St.; (520) 628-5774, fax (520) 628-5695.**

History of Pharmacy Museum

This isn't just your basic one-room small museum. It's part of all four floors of the Pharmacy Building, and contains more than 60,000 bottles, books, drug containers, salesmen's sample kits and more. When you get off the elevator on the first floor you're in a territorial pharmacy, surrounded by polished mahogany and etched stained glass. It dates to the 1870s. Grab a self-guided tour brochure from racks in the lobby of most floors and take half an hour or so to enjoy looking at pre-Advil remedies that include a fertility drug called Syrup of Figs that cost $1 and guaranteed "A Baby in Every Bottle." A Materia Medica cabinet, with 300 numbered samples of herbs and remedies in hinged-lid metal boxes with glass windows, helped yesterday's pharmacy students learn their drugs. Open Mon.–Fri., 8 A.M.–5 P.M. Free admission. **1703 E. Mabel (corner of Mabel and Warren); (520) 626-1427.**

Outdoor Activities

Golf

Tucson truly is a golf oriented city, mainly because the weather allows for year-round play. Three new courses—Raven at Sabino Springs, Rancho Vistoso and Torres Blancas—each have 18 holes of challenging desert terrain as well as stunning views of the Sonoran desert. Some are very expensive, but greens fees drop as much as 70 percent during summer months. If playing in 100-degree-plus heat isn't appealing, do what the locals do; get the earliest possible tee time so you're off the course by midmorning. The day's most extreme heat doesn't hit until midafternoon.

Resort, Private and Semiprivate Courses

El Conquistador Country Club

The 18-hole Sunrise and Sunset courses flow along the desert's natural contours, with rabbits and roadrunners common visitors. For more variety in landscape, the Sunrise course has a greater number of elevated tees and greens. The slightly more challenging Sunset course follows shallow ravines that make it much easier to get into trouble. **10555 N. La Canada Dr.; (520) 544-1800.**

La Paloma Country Club

The 27 holes here, on three nine-hole courses, are uniquely designed to blend with rather than dominate the desert. Dotted with stately saguaros, the dramatic landscape makes it difficult to keep an eye on the ball. Jack Nicklaus designed these courses in the foothills along Sunrise Drive in an area once thought unsuitable for a golf course. **3660 E. Sunrise Dr.; (520) 299-1500.**

The Lodge at Ventana Canyon

The Canyon course and the Mountain course, both Tom Fazio-designed championship 18-hole PGA courses, wind through the natural rock features of the Catalina Mountain foothills. Guests at Loews Ventana Canyon Resort have playing privileges on the Canyon Course on odd numbered days and the Mountain Course on even numbered days. **6200 N. Clubhouse Ln.; (520) 577-4015 or (520) 577-4061.**

Tucson National Golf Resort

This semiprivate course hosts the Tucson Chrysler Classic each February, in which 156 top pros compete for a million-dollar-plus purse. The 3,470-yard orange course, 3,638-yard gold course and 3,222-yard green course make up 27 challenging holes. **2727 W. Club Dr.; (520) 297-2271.**

Public Course

Raven Golf Club at Sabino Springs

On this outstanding public course, desert creatures still come to drink at the lateral-hazard pond on number 12. The natural spring once provided water for the native Hohokam. Designed by Robert Trent Jones Jr., the course's construction seems to have done little violence to the rocky outcroppings and huge stands of cactuses that give it its personality. It follows the natural contours of the Santa Catalinas' lower slopes, and in doing so creates sweeping views of the city below. **9777 E. Sabino Greens Dr.; (520) 749-3636.**

Municipal Courses

The city has a good choice of municipal courses that can become crowded during winter months. Call individual courses for tee times.

Randolph North

This longish course has hosted PGA tournaments, and welcomes top female professional golfers in March for the Welch's/Circle K Championship LPGA. The mature eucalyptus and pines verify that the course, a traditional country club layout, has been around for awhile. **600 S. Alvernon Way; (520) 325-2811.**

Dell Urich

You might remember this as the old Randolph South course if you've been here before. Completely reconstructed, it reopened in spring of 1996. **600 S. Alvernon Way; (520) 325-2811.**

Fred Enke

If you've never played a real desert course, here's your opportunity. Prickly pear, saguaros, cholla and other cactuses are part of this limited-turf course where other courses might have lakes and sand traps. Greens (exceptionally large), tees and ball landing areas are planted with grass, but most of the rest is pretty much natural desert. Just navigating the hilly course can be a challenge. Unless you have lots of stamina, opt for a cart here. **8251 E. Irvington Rd.; (520) 296-8607.**

El Rio

For those whose long game isn't their strongest, this older course provides a good challenge. Measuring 6,013 yards from the regular tees, it is relatively flat with few trouble spots. It was the original site for the Tucson Open, and before the city of Tucson bought it, it was the city's first country club. **1400 W. Speedway; (520) 623-6783.**

Horseback Riding

Along with the variety of dude ranches in the Tucson area (see Where to Stay), many local stables offer trail rides that cover interesting terrain. They are not as active in summer as in winter and in fact some of the stables send their steeds north to cooler climes during hot months. Call first to find out where their rides go. Reservations usually are necessary.

Pusch Ridge Stables

They offer rides into the Catalinas with mounts for all levels from definite dudes to accomplished equestrians. You can do a one-hour ride or set up a two- or three-night pack trip into the mountains. Specialty, dawn and sunset rides are available. **13700 N. Oracle Rd.; (520) 825-1664.**

Pusch Ridge Equestrian Center at the Sheraton El Conquistador Resort

Their main barn is at the address above, but they have a beautiful equestrian center at the resort, as well as rides into the Catalinas. The center has riding rings and English and Western instruction. This is especially good for riders who haven't been on a horse for awhile and just need a few pointers in the ring, so they can go out on the trail with confidence. Kids and family rides are a specialty. **10000 N. Oracle Rd.; (520) 825-1664.**

Desert High Country Stables

Rides into the Tucson Mountains and other pretty areas with lots of saguaros furnish an experience much different from mountain riding. Choose this stable if you're a photographer or want great sightseeing along with the ride. **6501 W. Ina Rd.; (520) 744-3789.**

Walking Winds/ El Conquistador Stables

Located half a mile south of the entrance to Catalina State Park, they'll take you into the Catalina Mountains on well-mannered horses. The ride through the state park follows ancient Indian trails, while another goes into the Coronado National Forest wilderness area. "No riding past housing developments," they say. One-, 1.5- and 2-hour rides leave daily. Ask about cookout rides, often available during the winter. **10811 N. Oracle Rd.; (520) 742-4200.**

Van and Four-Wheel-Drive Tours

Old Pueblo Tours

If you'd like to get acquainted with Tucson and leave the driving to someone else, this small company takes you around in a 14-passenger minibus that has a comfortable wide center aisle and an ice chest full of drinks. Terri, the owner, has really boned up on the area. If she can't answer a question, chances are she'll be able to produce a book or reference that can. A day tour of about 6.5 hours stops at De Grazia's Gallery in the Sun, the Arizona Historical Society Museum, Old Town Artisans, "A" Mountain and Mission San Xavier del Bac. The van will pick you up at various points throughout the city. Tours are guaranteed to please, or your money back. **(520) 795-7448.**

Mountain View Adventures

A guide in western boots and a Stetson driving a jeep stocked with an ice chest and soft beverages will pick you up at your hotel (or other predetermined spot) and drive you into the Coronado National Forest. If you have a limited amount of time, this is a good way to get acquainted with the outdoors surrounding Tucson. Guides will help you identify funny things with spiky appendages, spot desert creatures that otherwise might blend in with their surroundings and entertain you with a repertoire of tales and legends that may or may not be rooted in fact. You decide. Two-, 3.5- and 4.5-hour tours have a two-person minimum. Children under 12 pay half price. **4245 N. Campbell Ave., Tucson, 85719; (800) 594-9644 or (520) 881-4488.**

Skiing

Tucson is one of the few areas where you can ski in the morning, then play golf in your shirtsleeves in the afternoon. **Mt. Lemmon Ski Valley** is the southernmost ski area in the country. At 9,100 feet in the Santa Catalina Mountains a one-hour, 35-mile drive northeast of Tucson, the area gets about 200 inches of snow that keeps slopes covered from about mid-December through April. It has 15 trails, a chair lift and two rope tows. There are a snack bar, cafe and rental shop on the mountain. Private cabin rentals usually are available in nearby Summerhaven. During summer months take the chair lift for a scenic "sky ride." Forest Service trails all over the mountain are especially popular in summer because the area is a reliable 30 degrees cooler than Tucson. For more information and a snow report call **(520) 576-1321.** For recorded information call **(520) 576-1400.**

Hiking and Mountain Biking

The Tucson area is filled with outstanding hiking opportunities throughout the front range of the Catalinas for all fitness levels. *Bicycling Magazine* recently rated Tucson one of the top three cities for two-wheel pursuits, for its myriad trails and great scenery. The Santa Catalina ranger district of the Coronado National Forest encompasses about 262,000 acres directly around Tucson, and the 300,000-plus Nogales Ranger District includes most of the Santa Rita Mountains south of the city. Both are loaded with miles of back country roads and trails, with opportunities for everybody including motorized users.

Tucson Mountain Park

Mountain bikers are the largest users of this county natural resource park. Its 26 miles of protected and preserved trails are open to all nonmotorized users including hikers, equestrians and mountain bikers. Located 14 miles west of Tucson. Take Speedway west through Gates Pass to the park.

Saguaro National Park West

Just next door to Tucson Mountain Park, this saguaro forest covers 25,000 acres, 13,700 of which are federally designated wilderness. More than 50 miles of trails are open to hikers and equestrians. One favorite, Sweetwater Trail (see below) offers tremendous views. At this time there is no mountain biking in the park except on dirt roads shared with cars, but some trails should be open to cyclists by the end of 1998. **(520) 733-5158.**

Saguaro National Park East

This 65,000-acre park near the Rincon Mountains has more than 75 miles of top recreational trails for hikers and equestrians. A 2.5-mile segment of single-track trail runs through the middle of Paved Loop Drive and is open to mountain bikes. It is the first single-track, shared-use trail to allow mountain bikes in the U.S. national parks. The Cactus Forest Trail, just 2.5 miles long but spectacularly beautiful, can be made into a longer ride by continuing on to Cactus Forest Drive, a paved road that loops through more gorgeous Sonoran desert. **(520) 733-5153.**

Aspen Draw Trail

This 1.5-mile trail on Mt. Lemmon is all uphill one way and all downhill the other if you make it a 3-mile round trip. It leaves from Ski Valley, the region's premier ski area, 30 miles northeast of Tucson.

Ventana Canyon Trail

This breathtakingly beautiful canyon has a trailhead just next door to the Ventana Canyon Resort. Craggy and rugged and decorated with a stand of mature saguaros, it is often used by hotel guests. Begin the clearly-marked access trail, owned by Pima County, at the trailhead at the back of the resort's employee parking lot, where there are spaces for about two dozen trail-user cars. Dogs are not allowed on the access trail. The route meanders in and out of a wash bed following the path cut in 1902 by a mining exploration party. About one-half mile in on your left, the cactus that looks like it has a gnarly growth at the top is actually a crested saguaro. Cardinals appear as bright flashes of red among cactus and scrub. Cactus wrens, quail, dove, Gila woodpeckers, thrashers and hummingbirds make up a rich bird population here. For a short hike, many visitors proceed the 2 miles to Maiden Pools, a point along the creek where water collects, then turn around. The ventana (means "window" in Spanish) for which the trail is named, is a picturesque hole in a rock about 6 miles up the trail. The grade is fairly level with one long moderately steep climb onto a plateau. Pick your way carefully and you'll be fine. If you start out on a short hike about 6 A.M., even on a hot July or August day, rugged granite cliffs and scrub will shade much of the trail. You should be cool until about 7:30 A.M.

Sweetwater Trail

In the west unit of Saguaro National Park, this 6.4-mile round trip starts at a Pima County trailhead at the end of El Camino del Serro at the far west side of the Park. It's the formal access into the west unit of the Park from the east side (Tucson metro) of the range. The trail provides great vistas of the Tucson basin and the saguaro forests. It connects to other trails in the system including a short spur that takes you up to Wasson Peak, at an elevation of 4,687 feet, the highest point in the Tucson mountains. (See Madera Canyon, page 238, for additional area hiking opportunities.)

The *Southern Arizona Trails Resource Guide* by John Dell and Steve Anderson is an excellent primer of basic information for anyone wanting to access the best trails in southern Arizona. It has the nitty gritty information that hikers, mountain bicyclists, equestrians and OHV enthusiasts really need. It tells where the trails are, what they're open for, and what special precautions to take when using Arizona trails. A special section covers current trail projects, programs and events. The book is available at outdoor stores and through the nonprofit **Pima Trails Association, P.O. Box 41358, Tucson, 85717.**

Seeing and Doing

Sabino Canyon

You don't have to hike or bicycle to enjoy this exquisitely lovely canyon that winds up the slopes of Mt. Lemmon in the Santa Catalina foothills, but they are the most popular options for exploring. The canyon was closed to private motor vehicles in 1981. You can birdwatch, picnic, even swim when the natural pools along Sabino Creek are full enough. You don't even have to leave the visitor center to see white wing doves, little ground doves, roadrunners, cardinals, round Gambel's quail and half a dozen other native birds. They're attracted to this lush riparian area because of an ample food and water supply.

Sabino Canyon is in Coronado National Forest, which covers Southern Arizona like a patchwork quilt with more than a dozen detached areas designated as national forest. Over the centuries it has been used by many cultures. The canyon was home to the Clovis people 12,000–15,000 years ago, who sustained themselves by hunting abundant bison and mammoths. More recent residents, the Hohokam farmers knew how to get the most from the desert with sophisticated irrigation systems. When Europeans arrived in the 1500s, the Pima and Papago Indians were hunting game in the canyon and depended on Sabino Creek for water.

By the 1940s the canyon had become such a popular recreation spot that the Civilian Conservation Corps, along with other government bodies, constructed bridges, picnic tables and retaining walls. Present-day users hike along trails established a hundred years ago by pack animals bearing supplies for summertime residents and Army personnel in temporary encampments.

Today's visitors find tranquility along Sabino Creek, which flows all but a month or two out of the year. Hiking and biking trails are so extensive it is possible to feel quite alone. The creek's whiskey color comes from tannin found in oak tree roots and pine needles. Its waters support crayfish and sunfish and are an essential source for rock squirrels and other small mammals that live in the canyon. If time is short, your best bet is to hop on the tram for the 50-minute, 3.8-mile round-trip ride to the end of the paved road and back. You can get off and on as often as you like, reboarding any passing tram at designated points to get to the next stop, or to return to the visitor center. Stops 1 and 6 have picnic tables, stops 1 and 2 have water, and there are rest rooms at all stops except 2 and 7. Some visitors ride the tram to stop 9 and do the easy downhill hike back. Others use the tram to get to trailheads that lead into other parts of the canyon. From stop 9, you can access more than 300 miles of hiking trails in the Catalinas. The round-trip fare is moderate, with no charge for toddlers. Trams leave from the visitor center every half hour June to Dec., 9 A.M.–4:30 P.M. Other months they leave every half hour on weekends and holidays, and hourly, on the hour, on weekdays, 9 A.M.–4 P.M.

The canyon is closed to cyclists (who are required to observe a 15 mph speed limit) on Wednesdays and Saturdays.

Hikers headed for the Bear Canyon Trail and Seven Falls, a particularly lovely destination in the Pusch Ridge Wilderness, can catch a shuttle seven days a week, every hour on the hour, 9 A.M.–4 P.M., to the Bear Canyon trailhead. The hike, rated moderate by the Forest Service, is about 4.5 miles round-trip and takes about 3 hours on a wilderness hiking trail along Bear Creek. The Bear Canyon shuttle charges a small fee.

April through June and September through December, evening moonlight rides take guests into the canyon at a slower pace than daytime rides, and without narration. The trip leaves at 9 P.M., takes about 75 minutes and stops at the top. Prepaid reservations only, which are nonrefundable. For information and reservations call **(520) 749-2327.**

The visitor center and canyon entrance is about 13 miles from downtown Tucson. From Tanque Verde Road go north on Sabino Canyon Road about 4.5 miles to the canyon entrance, which is clearly marked. The canyon is always open, and the visitor center is open daily, 8 A.M.–4:30 P.M. For the Santa Catalina Ranger District Office call **(520) 749-8700.** For recorded information call **(520) 749-2861.**

Mt. Lemmon

This is Tucson's premier playground. The cool, conifer forest at its 9,157-foot summit, fragrant with aspen, Douglas fir and Ponderosa pine, becomes a favored destination when the desert floor heats up to 100 degrees-plus during summer months. The mountain is named for botanist Sara Lemmon, who identified and named many new plant species on a horseback expedition with her husband in 1881.

The Mt. Lemmon Highway leading to Summerhaven and the summit was completed in 1951 and recently reconstructed with wider and more frequent turnouts, new overlooks and better parking areas. During construction, cuts were left uneven and craggy rather than sheer to blend with the cliffs sculpted by nature. As you climb the 25 miles to the summit, you leave the saguaros of the Lower Sonoran Life Zone, pass through riparian areas, an oak woodland community, the Upper Sonoran Life Zone, a transition zone with juniper and piñon pine, on through evergreen woodland vegetation to lush pine forest. There are 15 picnic and camping areas and more than 140 miles of hiking trails on Mt. Lemmon, all maintained by the Forest Service.

Mt. Lemmon Hiking, Picnic and Camping Areas

MILEPOST 0–2: Trailhead marker for Soldier Trail.

MILEPOST 2–5: Trailhead marker 706 for Babat Duag Trail.

MILEPOST 5–6: Entrance to the Molina Basic picnic and campground, open during winter months. It has solar compost toilets.

MILEPOST 10–12: Bear Canyon picnic area.

MILEPOST 12: Entrance to General Hitchcock Campground.

MILEPOST 12–14: Trailhead marker 21 for Green Mountain Trail.

MILEPOST 17.2: Rose Canyon Recreational Area Entrance. Picnicking, trout fishing and camping at Rose Canyon Lake. No boating or swimming. A fee is charged.

MILEPOST 18.6: Primitive camping and picnicking area with no facilities. The helicopter pad here is for emergency and Forest Service use.

MILEPOST 19.7: Turnoffs for half a dozen children's camps.

MILEPOST 19.8: Palisades Visitor Center has displays and a book store. Open daily, May to Oct.; Fri.–Sun., Oct. to May.

MILEPOST 21.6: Spencer Canyon Campground, open May 1 to Oct. 1. Fee area.

MILEPOST 21.8: Trailhead Marker 22 for Box Camp Trail.

MILEPOST 22.2: Trailhead Marker 16 for Butterfly Trail.

MILEPOST 23.4: Sykes Nob picnic area, one-quarter mile off the main road to the left.

MILEPOST 23.4–23.5: Inspiration Rock picnic area has three picnic sites.

MILEPOST 24: Loma Linda picnic area.

MILEPOST 24.6: Trailhead marker for Oracle Trail is one-quarter mile down the Old Mt. Lemmon Control Road.

MILEPOST 25: Summerhaven. This little village grew up around summer cabins that started appearing in 1916. There are restaurants, gift shops and a picnic area on the other side of Summerhaven. From here it is 1.5 miles to Mount Lemmon Ski Valley, the southernmost ski area in the country. There is no gas here, so fill up before you leave the valley floor.

Parks and Gardens

Catalina State Park

This beautiful 5,511-acre park is set at the foot of the west face of the Santa Catalina Mountains, which form a background for the entire city of Tucson. Within the Coronado National Forest, just 12 miles north of the city, the park feels wild and remote. The geological formations on the north side of Pusch Ridge are spectacular from the park. The Romero Ruin Interpretive Trail, a popular, easy hiking route, winds through typical desert vegetation to the site of an ancient Hohokam village. For a challenge, try the Romero Canyon Trail, a 14.4-mile round-trip that goes from 2,700 to 6,000 feet. Though not a true technical climb, several places become a scramble. The Sutherland Trail, a real killer, eventually ends up at the top of the Catalinas and Mount Lemmon. You can backpack in and spend the night before returning. The two trails roughly parallel each other, and are tied together by the Mount Lemmon Trail, so for some real high-class abuse, you can do them as a loop. The rewards are coming across cool ponds that support a variety of wildlife, and in some cases being entirely isolated. Don't hike alone, though. There are no rescue services along the way. The park rangers are very helpful, and will provide you with a trail map and latest trail information. There is an equestrian center in the park, and many trails are ideal for riding. Less strenuous pursuits include picnicking (there are tables and grills) and birdwatching. The Audubon Society holds a Friday morning bird walk that begins between 7 and 8:30 A.M., depending on time of year. Call the ranger station to verify. There are 48 campsites in the park with water, rest rooms, showers and a dump station, open all year. The park is on AZ 77 north of Tucson, about 6 miles north of Ina Road on the right. **P.O. Box 36986, Tucson, 85740; (520) 628-5798, fax (520) 628-5797.**

Tohono Chul Park

As you stroll the trails of this lovely park, you'll see much the same flora and fauna that you'd see in the desert, except here they're more concentrated and labeled with informative signs. If you time it right, you can catch a docent tour to fill you in on interesting facts that you might otherwise miss. You also can pick up a self-guiding booklet for 25 cents (they're in coin boxes and at the visitor center) that reveals just enough detail to help you understand the desert without boring you with an overdose of statistics.

Tohono Chul, which means "desert corner" to the Tohono O'odham Indians, is a nonprofit desert preserve that exists on contributions, voluntary admissions and memberships. The 48-acre park has been donated, over time, by several generous philanthropists. Although very close to a busy intersection, traffic sounds all but disappear once you begin your walk. You're likely to see little top-knotted Gambel's quail scurrying under low-hanging branches, and cardinals creating a splash of red against the green branches of paloverde trees. Hummingbirds are permanent residents. If you're lucky you'll spot a phainopepla that looks like a black cardinal. It's the bird responsible for the spread of desert mistletoe, winding among host tree branches throughout the Southwest. The birds consider the mistletoe berries a delicacy, and often nest in mistletoe-infested trees to be close to a food source. You also see cactus wrens, easily spotted if you follow the sounds of their strident *chirrups*. The wren's messy nest, usually composed of randomly placed sticks and twigs, can become exceptionally creative. On our last trip there we discovered a nest into which one enterprising cactus wren has woven a length of toilet tissue, its tail fluttering cheerfully in the breeze.

The Geology Wall represents the structure of the Catalina Mountains, the range that you see when you're standing at the wall and looking straight ahead. Eight illustrated panels explain two billion years of the mountains' geologic history, and give a sense of Tucson's place in time. The Children's Garden is planted with thorn-free, kid-friendly plants. Older children can follow a map to locate the vine-covered topiary coyote and the enchanted throne room. Youngsters are invited to dabble in flowing water and pools. Crops grown locally by indigenous peoples, as well as those introduced by the Spanish, flourish in the Ethnobotanical Garden. Area residents often visit the Demonstration Garden to get ideas on how to xeriscape their yards using water-conserving fountains and arid-adapted plants. The Exhibit House, a 1937 restored adobe, has changing art and cultural exhibits, and the park's two gift shops have an unusually interesting variety of items from local artists and craftsmen. Don't miss the pool of bright blue desert pupfish. This endangered species was named 50 years ago by ichthyologist Carl L. Hubbs, who thought their animated antics looked playful, like a bunch of puppies.

Free docent walks concentrate on birds, art and general desert plants. Walks are offered regularly, but less frequently during the hotter months of June through September. The park is open daily, 7 A.M.–sunset. The Gift Gallery is open daily, 9:30 A.M.–5 P.M. **7366 N. Paseo del Norte, Tucson, 85704; (520) 575-8468 (recorded information), fax (520) 797-1213; exhibit house gift shop, (520) 297-4999.**

Docent-led hikes are held regularly at Tohono Chul Park, which means "desert corner."

Saguaro National Park

This two-part park (half is to the east of Tucson, the other is to the west) was recently upgraded from a National Monument to a Park, much to the delight of desert lovers who welcome the additional protection for its fascinating 91,327 acres. In Saguaro Park East a paved 8-mile drive through a thick saguaro cactus forest introduces you to Sonoran Desert life in general. There are two picnic areas along Cactus Forest Drive. At the visitor center, a 15-minute slide presentation helps you identify what you'll see in the park. Displays include skeletons of desert creatures, a saguaro cross-section and books to help identify plants and animals. The visitor center is on Freeman Road south of Old Spanish Trail. **(520) 733-5153.** Saguaro Park West's popular Bajada Loop Drive winds through a saguaro forest along a dirt road. There are four picnic areas along park roads. The Red Hills Visitor Center is at the park entrance off Mile Wide Road. **(520) 733-5158.** (See page 211 for bicycling and hiking in the park.)

Mission San Xavier del Bac

It took 14 years of off-and-on labor, from 1783 to 1797, to build this lovely church on the Southwest side of Tucson. Even before that, in 1692, Father Eusebio Kino visited the site and named it San Xavier in honor of St. Francis Xavier, the illustrious Jesuit Apostle of the

At San Xavier del Bac Mission, called the White Dove of the Desert, Catholic Mass is said daily.

Indies. The mission was built for the Tohono O'odham Indian community, which it serves today. Called the White Dove of the Desert because of its striking appearance from afar, it is a beautifully balanced blend of Byzantine, Moorish and Mexican Renaissance architecture. An interior renovation completed by Italian craftsmen in mid-1997 revealed detailed frescoes and colorful murals that were cleaned and restored, giving it new status as the Sistine Chapel of North America. Carved wood figures and the ornate altar are treasured examples of Mexican baroque art. On the left as you enter is a reclining statue of St. Francis Xavier. As you face the mission, note that the tower on the right is missing. One legend says Apaches destroyed it in the late 19th century. But, records have shown, it simply was never completed because of lack of funds. A new legend says that if ever the tower is completed, the mission will be destroyed. During winter months, especially on weekends, visitors crowd the mission. But if you can go on a weekday, you may have the place to yourself, if just for a few moments. It is not difficult to imagine the murmur of prayerful voices responding in Spanish as an 18th century priest raises a golden chalice. A new museum opens onto a cool courtyard, creating much more of a feeling of what the mission must have been like at one time. The museum features old vestments and religious artifacts as well as books and crafts. Across from the mission small shops purvey jewelry, dream catchers and pottery friendship bowls with linked figures. This is a good place to find reasonable prices on lovely Tohono O'odham baskets. San Xavier is open daily, 8 A.M.–6 P.M. Mass is said daily at 8:30 A.M., and at 8, 9:30 and 11 A.M., and 12:30 P.M. on Sunday. Tours are self-guided and admission is free. You can see the mission as you drive south from Tucson about 8 miles on I-19. Exit at Mission Road. **Franciscan Friars, 1950 W. San Xavier Rd., Tucson, 85746; (520) 294-2624.**

Biosphere 2

In 1991 in a valley north of Tucson, eight researchers and more than 3,800 plant and animal species entered an experimental self-contained enclosure that was to be their home for two years. The event made headlines worldwide as television footage showed the researchers being air-locked into the domelike, giant glass greenhouse, sort of a human terrarium. With seven different ecological systems, Biosphere 2 is the largest totally enclosed, self-sustaining ecosystem ever constructed. Designed with more than 6,500 individual panes of glass, it cost more than $150 million to build. With its Bucky Fuller geodesic construction and weblike network of glass, it has an otherworldly, science fiction–fantasy aura that captures the imagination of the ecologically concerned and environmentally aware.

The three-acre glass and steel complex, covering an area larger than three football fields, contains a rainforest, savannah, marsh, ocean, desert, farm and microcity. All air, water, plants and animals in the system sustain one another. Close to 100 percent of the air, water and waste is recycled.

But the design and placement of Biosphere 2 did not provide adequate oxygen and other material needed to sustain life over a long period. The Biospherians emerged in 1993, with hard-core researchers skeptical about the contribution the experiment had made to the scientific community. Today no one lives in Biosphere 2 (our planet earth is Biosphere 1), but you can visit the complex and take a tour that reveals the conditions under which the Biospherians lived. Research currently being carried on will be used to predict the progress and effects of tropical deforestation, global warming and ozone depletion. The Visitor Center offers multimedia presentations and interactive science exhibits.

In 1996 Columbia University's prestigious Lamont-Doherty Earth Observatory took over management of the project and helped restore the facility's credibility as a serious research center. Detailed tours show living quarters, the communal dining room, library and kitchen. An "ocean," complete with simulated waves, and neatly tended gardens demonstrate how it was hoped the Biospherians would remain self-sustaining. Despite their best efforts, however, the orchard area produced enough beans for just two cups of coffee per person per month, and a glass of goat's milk once a week was a real treat.

You can make a day or a weekend trip to Biosphere 2, staying at the Biosphere 2 Hotel, a 36-suite property poised on a small hill overlooking the Biosphere itself. Large rooms have view terraces, well-stocked wet bars, and there is a pool, tennis court and exercise facilities. The Biosphere's Canyon Cafe is open for three meals a day. In typically cyberspace fashion, you can cruise the Internet while sipping a cup of coffee and crunching a biscotti. A docent will help steer you through data related to the planet earth and its environments.

Across from the cafe, a park and pond area is aflutter with wild birds, including the vivid red northern cardinal and industrious cactus wren. Bring a jacket for an evening stroll through the Sonoran foothills. Nights are almost guaranteed to be clear, cool and starry. Constellations appear with a desert clarity found only in places that are removed from city lights.

From the parking lot a shuttle will take you to the main entrance, where you'll be directed to the visitor center. Here, a half hour video fills in the Biosphere's background. A half hour tour then leaves for the greenhouses, which hooks up with a tour to the Biosphere, on the hour. The tour involves lots of walking, but everything is wheelchair accessible, including the Biosphere itself, which has a lift that goes to the living quarters.

Biosphere 2 is located 35 miles northeast of Tucson, just off Highway 77 and Biosphere Road near the town of Oracle. Guided tours are offered daily, 8 A.M.–5 P.M., and discounts are offered to Arizona residents. Cost-effective packages for two include an overnight in the Biosphere Hotel, admission to Biosphere 2, dinner and breakfast. **Columbia University/ Biosphere 2, P.O. Box 689, Oracle, 85623; (800) 828-2462 or (520) 896-6200, fax (520) 896-6471. Website: www.bio2.edu\\.**

Davis-Monthan Air Force Base

In 1927 Col. Charles Lindbergh dedicated Tucson's second landing field, readied for military operations, to two Tucson residents who had died in separate aerial accidents while serving the U.S. Army. Second Lt. Samuel H. Davis and Oscar Monthan became the new field's namesakes. Early on, the base was used to service transient aircraft bound for California. It wasn't until 1941 that the Army stationed units at the base, just in time to go on 24-hour alert after the Japanese attack on Pearl Harbor. Subsequently Davis-Monthan was used to train and prepare bomber crews for battle, and after the war became a separation center to process soldiers returning to civilian life. The Air Force inherited the installation in 1948, and personnel became involved in strategic missions with the Titan II missiles and U-2 reconnaissance forces. In 1964 an additional wing began training crews for the F-4 Phantom, and training continues as its main function today. In 1989–1990 D-M personnel helped secure and defend Panama's main airport, and later supported Operations Desert Shield and Storm. From Kolb Road as you pass the base, you'll see row upon row of mothballed aircraft, stored by Aircraft Maintenance and Regeneration Center. You can take a guided bus tour to the flight line for a look at aircraft currently on active duty, as well as the aircraft storage facility. Free 1.5-hour tours leave Mon., Wed. and Fri. at 9 and 10:30 A.M. Reservations are a must. For recorded information call **(520) 228-3358.**

El Presidio Historic District

This is quite literally Tucson's birthplace. Pit houses and pottery shards left by the Hohokam date the site to A.D. 800. In the 18th century the Spanish built the walled fort called San Agustin del Tucson, a presidio used as a safe haven from Indian attack. Today the neighborhood is on the National Register of Historic Places. Within its boundaries, roughly St. Mary's/6th Street on the north, Granada on the West, West Alameda on the south and Court on the east, are examples of architecture dating to the 1800s, when walls were made of adobe and mesquite wood was used to frame doors and windows. The arrival of the railroad in 1880 created an architectural revolution. Previously unavailable building materials now were priced within the budget of many residents who brought their own notions of design, reflected today in the interesting mix of architecture within the area. Among the most notable structures is the **Stork's Nest,** so-called because it was a lying-in home from 1922 to 1946. At 182 North Court Avenue, it now houses the office for Southwest Parks and Monuments Association. For an interesting blend of Mexican and Anglo, see the **McCleary House** at 241 West Franklin. Walls 22 inches thick attest to the home's Mexican heritage, with a wide porch that heralds the Victorian era decorating the front. For the Spanish Colonial Revival style, as interpreted by noted architect Henry Trost, explore the design of **The Owls Club** at 378 North Main Avenue. Built in 1902, it was occupied by the last of a group of wealthy bachelors, Leo Goldschmidt, who made it his home until 1944. Other interesting buildings in the community are in the California Mission Revival style, and there even are a few California and Craftsman bungalows to see. A self-guided walking tour brochure with detailed descriptions of 14 historic properties is available at Old Town Artisans (see below) and at the Tucson Museum of Art.

Old Town Artisans in Old Tucson is filled with interesting shops and has a great restaurant.

Old Town Artisans

This little gem of an area, within the El Presidio Historic District, hides in downtown Tucson among a forest of office buildings with few signs to point you in the right direction. It is a bit difficult to find, but ultimately worth it. Visit the block-long, restored, 1850s adobe marketplace, filled with the works of hundreds of artists and craftsmen, as well as imports from Latin American cultures. The building once protected the Mexican settlement of Tucson from Indian attacks.

Before you get involved in what's for sale, take time to appreciate the building's architecture and history. As with traditional Spanish structures, the walls are built right on the lot line, with all activity focused on a center courtyard. If you enter through the door on the corner of Telles and Meyer you'll be in SoWest Territories, Inc. Look up to your right where the wall joins the ceiling and you'll see traces of the original wallpaper. On the opposite wall, a saguaro skeleton has been used as a lintel. As you stroll through the Pot Shop you can see the original saguaro-skeleton beams supporting the ceiling. Next door, charcoal-stained staves from old whiskey barrels create a ceiling, while the original red oak floor creaks pleasantly underfoot. High on the wall, original wall paper is printed with swagged ropes, a remnant of more elegant days.

The building doesn't look like much from the outside, but its interior has witnessed a lively past. It once afforded office space to assayers who measured miners' gold and shelves for Yuen Lee to sell groceries to the miners for their return trips. Early records show a "ladies' nurse" tenant, an essential caregiver in an era when ladies of the evening were an accepted part of a community's nightlife. In 1888 Julius Goldbaum turned the building into a residence and distillery. The family sold the building in the mid-1920s. Over the decades incarnations continued until a developer purchased it in 1978 and began the restoration to create its present persona. Cocina Restaurant (See Where to Eat) is always open for lunch. It's a good idea to call for directions, depending on where you're coming from. Exit Interstate 10 at St. Mary's and proceed on St. Mary's past Main, until you pass the Tucson Electric Power building on the left. Turn right on Meyer Ave. and go three blocks to the Old Town Artisans Complex on the left. You can park in the lot straight ahead. The shops are open Mon.–Sat., 9:30 A.M.–5:30 P.M.; Sun., noon–5 P.M. Sun. hours are a bit iffy during the summer, so it's best to call first. **186 N. Meyer Ave., Tucson, 85701; (520) 623-6024 or (800) 782-8072.**

Old Tucson Studios

Destroyed by fire in 1995, this family-oriented, theme park-cum-studio was back in operation less than two years later. You can stroll the streets walked by John Wayne and other greats of western movie history, spending an entire day reliving how the West was once. At the Grand Palace, saloon girls draped in feathers and sequins show off their garters in a high-kicking revue, and a sultry chanteuse ends up on the lap of at least one gent in the audience. "Cecil Bee DeVille" demonstrates how movies are made, with clever bad guys outsmarting an inept deputy. Toddlers can visit the Petting Zoo where burros, sounding like squeaky doors, nudge pockets for handouts. Five different shows are presented at intervals throughout the day. You'll receive a schedule when you enter so you can plan your strategy. Always a crowd-pleaser, the live gunfight features high falls and lots of shooting. Old Tucson studios began in 1939 as a set for the motion picture epic *Arizona,* starring William Holden and Jean Arthur. Since then more than 300 productions have been filmed here, and it continues as a sought-after venue for motion picture and television productions. The studio remains open during shooting, so it's possible to get a behind-the-scenes look at how Hollywood really works if you're lucky enough to be there on a shooting day. For filming information call the main studio number and a menu selection will

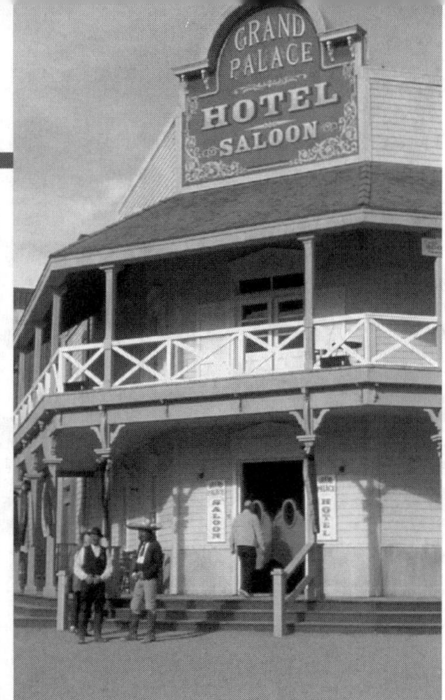

Old Tucson Movie Studio and Fun Park is peopled with characters out of the Old West.

Besides outstanding collections, the Museum Shop at the Tucson Museum of Art has interesting jewelry, handcrafts and art at reasonable prices.

give you a schedule. From late Dec. to mid-Apr. it is open daily; open 9 A.M.–7 P.M. and 10 A.M.–6 P.M. the rest of the year. Closed Thanksgiving and Christmas Day. Children 3 and under are admitted free. Located in Tucson Mountain Park 12 miles west of Tucson. From Tucson take Speedway or Ajo Way west and follow the signs. **201 S. Kinney Rd.; (520) 883-0100.**

Museums and Galleries

Tucson Museum of Art

Part of the city's Historic Block downtown, this respected establishment has been thoughtfully constructed with low-rise sensibilities to blend with its revered surroundings. Yet inside it is classically contemporary with linear sight lines creating spatial dividers. It neighbors with five distinctive homes built between 1850 and 1907 and a sculpture garden. The Plaza of the Pioneers is a pleasant, shady place for a rest. The museum's permanent 4,000-work-plus collection focuses on art of the Americas, including pre-Columbian, Spanish Colonial and Contemporary American. The Campbell Collection of Western Art, a group of paintings and sculptures that reflect the imaginative spirit of the Southwest in days past, is displayed in the renovated Edward Nye Fish House for ten months of the year. Called the Goodman Pavilion of Western Art, the historic home also displays other western collections. In the museum proper, exhibits rotate and include work in all media. Docent-led tours are held daily. Stop by the Museum Shop to see interesting jewelry, handcrafts and art. A scale model of the Historic Block (see below) gives you a sense of your location in the downtown milieu. Small charge for adults. Children 12 and under are admitted free. Admission is free on Tue. Open Mon.–Sat., 10 A.M.–4 P.M., Sun., noon–4 P.M. Closed Mon. during June, July and Aug. and on major holidays. **140 N. Main Ave.; (520) 624-2333.**

Historic Block

Actually part of the art museum that maintains and preserves these historic homes, this city block was once bounded on the south and north by the wall of the original presidio. Three feet thick and almost twelve feet high, it was built over a seven-year period by the Spanish military to enclose their enclave, and was completed in 1783. La Casa Cordova, thought to be the oldest remaining residence in Tucson, was built in 1848. Open to the public, it features two period rooms that show the lifestyle of the late 1800s. The Romero House, part of the Tucson Museum of Art School, is now a pottery studio. Next door is the 1855 adobe Stevens house. And the youngest of the historic properties, the J. Knox Corbett house, was used as a law office until 1970. Docents lead guided tours of the Historic Block Wed. and Thu. at 11 A.M., Oct. 1 to May 1 at no charge. Meet in front of the art museum on Main Street. For more information call **(520) 624-2333.**

Pima Air and Space Museum

This extensive indoor-outdoor museum features more aircraft of more different types than you'd ever figure to see in one place. Almost 200 vintage and present-day aircraft are displayed in hangers and tie-downs. Because many are outdoors, during hot summer months it's a good idea to plan your visit as early in the day as possible. You enter under a huge Sikorsky Skycrane helicopter used for transporting heavy loads and proceed into a cool gallery with planes parked and hanging everywhere. Straight ahead the exhibit "Women Aloft" has photos of early stewardesses, called flight attendants now. Directly outside of this first building is the last prop-driven Air Force One, used by John F. Kennedy as well as Lyndon Johnson. It went into service in 1961, and although jets were available then, this plane, a Douglas DC-6, was preferred for its ability to land at smaller airports. Pre-transistor equipment includes an old Hallicrafter radio with vacuum tubes. Three separate cabins—for the president and his aides, the press (with a wireless teletype), and the Secret Service (with pull-down berths)—lead to a complete kitchen. A separate seat was designated for an extra pilot, always carried when the president was aboard. Although this aircraft usually had a crew of three, it always held a crew of five on presidential flights. Volunteers take visitors on scheduled 15-minute guided tours of Air Force One.

The plane that everyone comes to see is the Lockheed SR-71 Blackbird, the strategic reconnaissance aircraft, operational from 1966 to 1990. It flies at Mach three–plus, three times the speed of sound. As a one-time Blackbird pilot put it, "It flies real high, at 80,000 feet, where you see black above you, blue below you, and the only identifiable thing is the curve of the earth." The sleek, black aircraft, poised like a pointy-nosed insect, once flew coast to coast in 68 minutes 17 seconds.

The museum includes four hangers plus a World War II barracks with additional aviation exhibits. A separate section is devoted to the famous 390th Bomb Group and 390th Strategic Missile Wing. Here you'll find the famous B-17 Flying Fortress. If you're a real flight aficionado you can spend all day here. For most, a couple of hours will do nicely. There are a snack bar and ramada with picnic tables. The gift shop has flight-related items including "flight suits" for youngsters. Open daily, 9 A.M.–5 P.M., except Christmas Day. Also closed Mon. and Tue., May to Oct. 1. No one is admitted after 4 P.M. From I-10 take the Valencia Road exit, and continue east 2 miles to the museum entrance. Moderate fee. **6000 E. Valencia, Tucson, 85706; (520) 574-9658.**

DeGrazia Gallery in the Sun

If you think this famous Southwest artist did little more than paint appealing, big-eyed children, you're in for a revealing treat. Considered foremost among American Impressionists, Ettore "Ted" DeGrazia produced an enormous body of work in his lifetime. The gallery itself, actually more a museum built to the artist's design, houses his most famous collections that focus on subjects of deep interest to DeGrazia. Permanent themed exhibits include Padre Kino, Papago Legends, Yaqui Easter, Bull Fight and Retrospective collections. The renowned Cabeza de Vaca collection illustrates the journey of the dauntless adventurer, the first non-Indian to travel in Arizona, New Mexico and Texas. The Retrospective collection includes paintings from 1925 to 1972, clearly tracing DeGrazia's artistic evolution, embodying the free, unrestrained style that characterizes his work. Because the number of works is too great to show all at one time, some galleries are designated for rotating exhibits so that all eventually will be available to the public. DeGrazia's ceramics, bronzes and enamels also are on display. Next door in the charming little Mission in the Sun, hand-built by DeGrazia and his Indian friends some years before the museum, interior walls are alive with whimsical angels, children, deities and other appealing figures.

DeGrazia was born in 1909 in Morenci, a Phelps Dodge mining town near the state's eastern border. He graduated from the University of Arizona in 1945, his work already beginning to be recognized. His subject matter, the Southwest and Mexico, was not widely known. So when the subtle desert colors and Indian way of life made their way into mainstream art circles, the artist drew national attention. The gallery is located in north Tucson. Take Swan Road north of Sunrise Road and turn right at the gallery sign. Open daily, 10 A.M.–4 P.M. Donations are appreciated. **6300 N.**

Swan Rd., Tucson, 85718; (800) 545-2185, (520) 299-9191 or (520) 299-9192.

The Yozeum

This hands-on museum, devoted solely to the yo-yo and its place in history, really has its ups and downs (somebody had to say it). Since first marketed by Donald Duncan in 1929, there's hardly a kid alive that hasn't tried Walkin' the Dog or Around the World. But it's not just kids that come here. Adults seem the most fascinated by the collection that includes a 14-karat gold yo-yo used as a party favor by the Vanderbilt family in the 1930s. There is a sterling silver version, as well as one marketed by Tiffany. Some yo-yos are smaller than a penny, one giant is six feet across. Among the most popular are the promotional yo-yos, marked with names of sports teams and events, companies and corporations, and even the White House that appears in gold on a yo-yo, presented as a gift at an official dinner. If you want to hone your yo-yo skills, visit the Yozeum the first Saturday of the month for a lesson. If you're lucky, a museum "yocent" will render an impromptu teaching session on other days as well. The museum is open Tue.–Fri., 9 A.M.–5 P.M.; Sat., 9 A.M.–1 P.M. Admission is free. **2900 N. Country Club Rd.; (520) 322-0100.**

Casinos

Both of these typical Indian casinos are open 24 hours a day, 7 days a week. **Casino of the Sun (7406 S. Camino de Oeste; 800-344-9435 or 520-883-1700),** on the Yaqui Reservation, has more than 500 slot machines plus keno, bingo and pull tabs. It has an inexpensive buffet and snack bar. Located five minutes west of I-19 off Valencia Road. A new card room with live poker recently opened at the **Desert Diamond Casino (7350 S. Nogales Highway; 520-294-7777),** located on the San Xavier Tohono O'odham Reservation. Otherwise you'll find the expected keno, slots and high stakes bingo beginning at 11 A.M. with the last late-night session starting at 9:45 P.M. Near the Tucson International Airport one mile south of Valencia Road.

Shopping

In Tucson, you can uniquely satisfy the urge to acquire with high quality Native American pieces that include jewelry, baskets, kachinas, fetishes and more. In Tucson's city center, more than 35 art galleries, antiques shops and crafts stores line Congress Street and the Downtown Arts District. For more artsy finds, search out one-of-a-kind items on 4th Avenue between downtown and the University of Arizona. The Old Town Artisans complex, near downtown's Museum of Art, brings together a fine group of purveyors of Southwestern wares (see page 218). For things truly Tucson, you can bring home locally bottled salsas and ristras (dried chili pepper strings). If you'd like a touch of the Sonoran Desert at your house, a number of local cactus farms and nurseries will ship your spiny souvenirs back home.

Where to Stay

Tucson is blessed with a goodly number of luxury resorts, historic hotels, middle-of-the-road chains and budget hostelries. Decide what it is you're after and which part of town you want, and you can narrow the choice considerably. We've listed a range of accommodations, with various prices and types of experiences. If you are simply passing through, by all means opt for one of the reliable chains off I-10 or I-19. Otherwise, read on. During summer months even the priciest digs lower tariffs to a very reasonable level. So don't just assume that a place is out of reach price-wise. Call the hotel directly (they'll usually give a better deal than the reservation center's 800 or 888 number) and ask for their lowest-price room, then ask if there are any discounts on top of that, such as AAA, corporate or senior discounts.

Luxury Resorts

Loews Ventana Canyon Resort—$$$$

In the Big Splurge category, but definitely worth every penny. You might not need the three phones in your room, but you'll love the spalike tub big enough for two. The resort, settled comfortably on 93 acres of plateau, provides impressive views of the city below. Behind the resort (take a look at the huge fish in the koi pond) a short nature path leads to an 80-foot waterfall that is fed by springs in the Catalinas, then flows into a small lake near the Flying V Restaurant. You don't have to leave your workout regimen at home, because at the Spa and Tennis Center there are eight lighted tennis courts, a weight and exercise room, a mirrored aerobics studio, water aerobics and outdoor lap pool, two championship golf courses (see Golf) and a par course. Leave time for a relaxing massage. Although winter months are pricey, room rates during summer are less than half of winter rates. See Where to Eat for the hotel's Flying V Bar and Grill. **7000 N. Resort Dr., Tucson, 85750; (800) 234-5117 or (520) 299-2020, fax (520) 299-6832.**

Sheraton El Conquistador—$$$$

You can relax for a week or more here and never miss the outside world. With 31 lighted tennis courts and two pro shops, it is the largest tennis resort in the West, as well as the largest golf facility, with one 9-hole and two 18-hole courses (see Golf). Its own equestrian center offers organized rides including breakfast rides and sunset champagne rides. **1000 N. Oracle Rd., Tucson, 85737; (520) 544-5000, fax (520) 544-1222, TDD (520) 544-1833.**

Westward Look Resort—$$$$ (but can be $$$ during the summer)

An all-time favorite because of its absolutely civilized approach to guests. The only Arizona resort to receive AAA's Four Diamond Award for 15 consecutive years, but it is far from the most expensive. Built as a private residence in 1912, guest rooms are discreetly scattered throughout shady grounds, home to rabbits and a variety of colorful birds including brilliant cardinals and soft gray doves. Exceptionally large rooms have a seating area with couch, refrigerator, coffee maker with coffee and a balcony or patio. It is a great tennis retreat, with eight courts and a USPTA instructor available. Three pools, basketball and sand volleyball courts and a nature/jogging trail encourage you to stay and enjoy the property. Be sure to book a massage or facial at the Wellness Center. You can tuck in here for days, just enjoying the property and its amenities. Golfers who stay here have special privileges at the Raven Golf Club at Sabino Springs. For a special occasion dinner, try the Gold Room with its fantastic sunset views, highly recommended. If you've never tried ostrich, it's on the menu here. **245 E. Ina Rd., Tucson, 85704; (800) 722-2500 or (520) 297-1151.**

Generations of guests have enjoyed the venerable Westward Look Resort, which also has a top spa.

The Miraval, Life in Balance Resort—$$$$

This classy, contemplative spa says it's the place to come to get your "life in balance." The picturesque location, in the shadow of 10,000-foot-high Mt. Lemmon, is in itself enough to render you boneless. Public rooms are exquisitely decorated with Navajo rugs, Saltillo tile floors and subtle Southwest colors. Man-made streams trickle among rooms grouped in "neighborhoods." The average stay here is three days (although you can do just an overnight or even a Day Spa program), tailored to your goals—weight loss, de-stressing, hiking and riding or just getting away from it all. One of the most unusual programs is Miraval's Equine Experience. Its proponents say you have to try it to understand it, sort of like hanging wallpaper or having a baby. Through working with horses (no riding is involved) you learn how you create your own personal stress, how body language contributes to and conveys that stress, and how you can unlearn the behavior by communicating at a most basic level. Unlike many spas, there is a full bar. Located in Catalina, north of Tucson. **(800) 232-3969 or (520) 825-4000.**

Inns & Historic Hotels

Arizona Inn—$$$–$$$$

This small, lovely 86-room Tucson resort has matured as gracefully as any well-bred 65-year-old. Within its brick and adobe walls, fourteen acres of low haciendas and lush gardens are quiet, serene and welcoming. The civilized custom of afternoon tea is carried out unhurriedly in the teak-floored library. Guests relax into high-backed chairs to be warmed, if the season is right, by a grand fireplace. The Inn's founder, Isabella Greenway, set out to create a homelike retreat in the 1930s, filling it with furnishings made by disabled doughboys from World War I, who came to Tucson for medical care at the Veterans' Hospital. She accented the rustic decor with 19th century Audubon prints and African art acquired on safari. It remains civil and understated, as if it belongs to a quieter era, because Mrs. Greenway's granddaughter looks after the Inn with the same practiced eye as her predecessor. Come here for a quiet sojourn, to enjoy the flower-scented grounds and a leisurely dinner in the Inn's superb restaurant (see Where to Eat). **2200 E. Elm St., Tucson, 85719; (520) 325-1541.**

The historic Arizona Inn in Tucson, built in the late 1930s, is famous for its abundant gardens and gourmet restaurant.

Hacienda del Sol—$$$–$$$$

Strolling the grounds of this one-time adobe girls' school, it's not hard to imagine primly frocked young ladies gathered in the shady courtyard to do their sums. Today's guests stay in updated courtyard rooms with a Southwest decor, in newly built suites, and in spacious casitas. In 1941 when it shifted gears to accommodate guests, it became a favorite hideaway for Spencer Tracy and Katherine Hepburn and served as home base for Joseph Cotten while he filmed the 1946 film *Duel in the Sun*. The resort maintains a strong sense of the past without sacrificing comfort. The overstuffed leather sofa in the pine-beamed living room clearly belongs to the 1940s, and the library includes early school yearbooks. Stables, a pool, tennis courts and hiking trails are scattered over 34 peaceful acres. Low season rates from July 1 to August 31 are a real bargain. **The Grill at Hacienda del Sol** (see Where to Eat) is a true dining experience. **5601 N. Hacienda Del Sol Rd., Tucson, 85718; (800) 728-6514 or (520) 299-1501.**

The Lodge on the Desert—$$$

Built in the 1930s, this lovely small hotel with just 40 rooms in the middle of a quiet residential district has been owned by the same family since it opened. The grounds, naturally desert landscaped, help create the feeling that you're miles away from civilization. Only the occasional intrusion of aircraft noise from nearby Davis-Monthan Air Force Base verifies that the real world is just around the corner. Rooms are large and inviting, some with fireplaces that are welcome during winter. **306 N. Alvernon Way, Tucson, 85711; (800) 456-5634 or (520) 325-3366, fax (520) 325-5834. E-mail: lodgeonthedesert.juno.com.Xavi.**

Hotel Congress—$$

This downtown Tucson landmark was built in 1919 to serve passengers of the Southern Pacific Railroad as they journeyed to and from what was then a little desert cow town. The classical brick and marble structure, once the height of elegance, had a guest register with the signature of the infamous John Dillinger. In the 1930s a fire devastated the third floor, which was never rebuilt. Although the hotel was refurbished, the Depression years precluded the Congress being as grand as it once was. Today, thanks to a 1985 purchase that led to its restoration, the hotel has piloted the development of the downtown Tucson Arts District, and is once again a charming place to stay. Its Old West personality is preserved in the deco-style Native American lobby designs painted by artist Larry Boyce, and in guest rooms furnished with the original mirrored vanities and metal bedsteads. Residents say it has the liveliest nightclub in town, and in fact the rooms directly over the Club Congress have a discount rate because "the nightclub and its patrons may generate a great deal of noise during peak hours" says hotel literature. Earplugs are available free at the front desk (no joke). Youth Hostel rooms also are available. Don't miss the great breakfast pancakes in the little coffee shop. **311 E. Congress, Tucson, 85701; (520) 622-8848, fax (520) 792-6366. Website: www.hotcong.com/congo/. E-mail: hotel@hotcong.com.**

Dude Ranches

These modern-day versions of the Old West provide rough and ready experiences tempered by well-behaved horses and 20th century amenities. A stay gives you access to the once-rowdy world of wranglers and rustlers while maintaining firm footing in the present. Horses called Diablo and Lightning may be misnomers. Most establishments, or "guest ranches," are family-friendly (some prefer children older than 11) and laid back, generating an unusually high percentage of repeat guests, some of whom return for generations. Many ranches have no TV, no phones in rooms and no newspapers. It's part of the experience of getting away from it all and establishing a closeness with nature and the outdoors. Some ranches close for the summer. See also Wickenburg Dude Ranches and Grapevine Canyon Ranch near Pearce. For centralized information about Arizona Dude Ranch Vacations call **(800) 444-DUDE. Website: www.gorp.com/oldwest.**

Tanque Verde Ranch—$$$$

This picturesque, century-old slice of real Arizona history considers itself one of the last luxurious outposts of the Old West, and apparently guests do too, as they return by the dozen year after year. The ranch has more than 120 well-trained ranch horses, some for walking rides with beginners and others for loping with more experienced riders. Located 35 minutes due east of downtown Tucson, in the foothills of the Rincon Mountains, Tanque Verde has been owned by the Cote family since 1957, a name Minnesotans will recognize because the family also owns Grand View Lodge near Brainerd. Rides often wind through the spectacular Saguaro National Park, bordering the ranch where saguaro cactus form a stately forest. In addition to trail rides, guests make use of indoor and outdoor pools, tennis courts and nature and exercise hiking trails. A series of evening programs includes line dance instruction, talks on astronomy and star gazing and wildlife lectures. Sixty-five lodge rooms and desert-view patio casitas, some with fireplaces, include three meals a day in the rate. **14301 E. Speedway, Tucson, 85748; (800) 234-DUDE.**

White Stallion Ranch—$$$$

This warm, friendly ranch, within ten minutes of Tucson shopping and city amenities, sits on the other side of the hills so there is a feeling of remoteness. The small (29 guest rooms) ranch has been run by the True family since 1965. It encompasses 5 square miles of desert, two of which are adjacent to Saguaro National Park. Wood-paneled rooms have comfortable, rustic pine furnishings. The Happy Hour Saloon stocks healthful fruit juices as well as stiffer stuff. Meals are set at long wood tables so getting to know fellow guests happens naturally. Those who would rather pet a horse than ride one can use the pool, play tennis, soak in the hot tub, hike in the desert or get involved in a volleyball game. **9251 W. Twin Peaks Rd., Tucson, 85743; (888) 977-2624 or (520) 297-0252.**

Home Stays

Mi Casa Su Casa/ Old Pueblo Home Stays

A service that's been offered in Europe for years is now available in Arizona. You typically are lodged in a private home where accommodations can range from modest to luxurious. The service matches guests with homes, based on information given by the guests. For example, in one home Greek and English are spoken. In another, pets are welcome. If you're coming from a two-story typically Midwest farm home, or a Manhattan high rise, staying in a low-profile ranch home that sprawls among cactuses and coyotes could be a real cross-cultural experience. The service has many listings in the Tucson area as well as more than 200 in other parts of the state. Prices vary widely, depending on type of accommodation and season. The service also lists bed and breakfast inns statewide. **(800) 456-0682 or (602) 990-0682, fax (602) 990-3390. E-mail: MICASA@PRIMENET.COM. Website: www.azres.com.**

Where to Eat

Tucson's dining scene includes the sophistication you'd expect to find in a well-bred city. On the other hand, roistrous cowboy steak houses, trendy cafes and bistros, basic coffee shops and fast food are readily available. The city has too many great Mexican restaurants to make an accurate count. Many of the best lie in the city's southern part, where its deep Hispanic-Latino roots began. Because Tucson was once part of Sonora across the border in Mexico, mainstays of that area such as burritos, tamales and enchiladas are a part of many menus. The Native American culture is apparent in blue corn tortillas and fry bread. Don't make the mistake of thinking that Mexican food is just hot stuff folded in tortillas. Some of its best is seafood, which includes shrimp, sea bass (sometimes on a menu as cabrillo) and other sea creatures that became part of the Mexican diet because they were readily available in surrounding waters. Just look around, read posted menus and you'll find you could easily eat your way through Tucson and never duplicate your order.

Basic, Middle-of-the-Road

City Grill—$$$

A display kitchen, two tiers of tables and booths and open beams make this a pleasant place to eat. The eclectic-trendy menu with pizza from a wood-fired oven and crispy salads made with a treasure hunt of greens includes something for just about everyone, from vegetarian to grilled meat aficionado. Fresh grilled seafood (yes, even in the desert seafood can be fresh) is another specialty. Its location, in the foothills area north of Speedway, is convenient as a jumping-off place for exploring Tucson. Open for lunch every day at 11 A.M., closes Fri. at 11 P.M., Sat. at 10 P.M. and Mon.–Thu. and Sun. at 9 P.M. **5350 E. Tanque Verde Rd., Tucson; (520) 733-1111.**

Cocina—$$$

We love this casual place after a day of sightseeing. In the courtyard at Old Town Artisans (see page 218), it is set in a shady patio, further cooled on warm days by micromisters. For the uninitiated, misters are cooling systems that periodically emit a blast of superfine water vapor that evaporates almost instantly in Arizona's dry air. The cooling effect, sometimes as much as 20 degrees below the ambient temperature, is instant and refreshing. Air conditioned indoor rooms are decorated with art objects from next-door shops. Display shelves show off cloudy, iridescent "dug" bottles that were unearthed when the courtyard was excavated. Morphine, opium, ladies leg ale bottles and other vessels attest to an era when fun was free-wheeling and unregulated. At Cocina's Court Street entrance, the base of old gasoline pumps and a front facade at a 45-degree angle to the street tell of the days when the restaurant was a corner gas station. The Southwest menu features black bean chili, gazpacho, a quesadilla made with mesquite roasted vegetables, and other items from the mesquite grill. They have a good selection of California wines. Open for lunch 7 days a week, open for dinner, Thu., Fri. and Sat., 5–10 P.M. **201 N. Court, Tucson, 85701; (520) 622-0351.**

Tea Room at Tohono Chul Park—$$

Combine brunch, lunch or a light supper at this pleasant courtyard tea room with a visit to Tohono Chul (see Parks and Gardens). That's what we did one June morning, and we loved their muffins and scones hot from the oven. Or try the grilled vegetables on foccacia or shrimp, jicama and avocado salad with orange chipotle dressing for lunch. Tea is served from 2:30–5 P.M., featuring finger sandwiches, scones, pastries and jam. Beer and wine are available. Open Oct. to mid-Apr., 8 A.M.–5 P.M.; mid-Apr. to Sept., 8 A.M.–8 P.M. **7366 N. Paseo de Norte; (520) 797-1711.**

Big Splurge Gourmet

Dining Room at the Arizona Inn—$$$$

This is one of our favorite romantic dinner places. In one of Tucson's loveliest historic hostelries (see Where to Stay), the dining room is noted for continental gourmet food served in a quiet, gracious atmosphere. At various times of year meals are served on patios, in the courtyard or on the terrace. This is a lovely place to linger over lunch. Be sure to stroll through the comfortable library and around the inn's flower-banked grounds for a look at elegance that dates back to the 1930s. Open for breakfast, lunch and dinner with a lovely Sunday brunch. **2200 E. Elm St., Tucson; (520) 325-1541, fax (520) 881-5830.**

Janos Restaurant—$$$$

After 15 years downtown this Four Star, Four Diamond restaurant has moved to the foothills on the grounds of the Westin La Paloma. The decor is a stunning blend of French and Southwestern custom and antique furnishings. Panoramic views, elegant service and a carefully chosen wine list, with several Arizona wines, are keeping newcomers and longtime fans happy. The name of owner-chef Janos Wilder has become synonymous with French-inspired Southwest cuisine. Come here for a big splurge and know it will be more than a meal—it will be an event. Open at 5:30 for dinner Mon.–Sat. **3770 E. Sunrise Dr.; (520) 615-6100. E-mail: janosrest@aol.com; website: janos.com/janos/.**

Ventana Room—$$$$

More marriage proposals have been made at table #21 of this fine dining restaurant than they can count, say the staff. One look and we knew why. The candlelit table is hidden behind a two-way fireplace, so that couples look over the flames to a panoramic city view beyond. A harp plays softly in the background. Service here is impeccable. The menu includes lightly seared fois gras as a starter, and fresh fish, usually grilled then embellished with an authoritative sauce. Open for dinner Sun.–Thu., 6–9 P.M.; Fri.–Sat., 6–10 P.M. Reservations suggested. Located in Loews Ventana Canyon Resort. **7000 N. Resort Dr., Tucson; (520) 299-2020.**

Daniel's—$$$–$$$$

This fashionably understated eatery is a study in deco. Fresh fish and pasta done in the Northern Italian style are always outstanding. It is famous for its desserts, so a good ploy is to go for lunch, order something light, then have dessert and skip dinner. Scotch connoisseurs will have something to chat over with the bartender, because the place offers a selection of close to one hundred single-malt scotches. Misters and heaters make it possible to eat on the outdoor patio the year-round. **4340 N. Campbell Ave., Tucson; (520) 742-3200, fax (520) 529-1907.**

Flying V Bar & Grill—$$$–$$$$

It's worth a stop here just to read the menu, but be sure not to miss the gorgeous view. Strong Latin and Southwest influences have helped shape offerings that include mesquite grilled ostrich fajitas, three-citrus chicken with black beans, and absolutely delicious grilled and chilled shrimp with jicama and avocado. A spa menu, with nutrition information available on request, includes swordfish fajitas with jicama and salmon burrito with cucumber salsa. If you're not acquainted with Southwest cuisine, stop here for a drink and tapas, served all day. These delicious little samplings include smoked salmon quesadilla, beer-batter jalapenos with chorizo, ten-bean turkey chili and oyster shooters with ancho-chile salsa. You can sample 30 kinds of tequila served as a shot with traditional sangrita chaser, or in a supersize margarita. At Loews Ventana Canyon Resort. **7000 N. Resort Dr., Tucson; (520) 299-2020.**

The Grill at Hacienda del Sol—$$$–$$$$

Furnishings custom-made in Mexico, wrought iron chandeliers, and a personality that feels old but is up to the minute in terms of cuisine characterize this fine restaurant. A seared ahi appetizer arrives warm and buttery, and the mesquite roasted pork loin represent the scope of the chef's expertise. An in-depth wine list includes a few local Arizona vintages. **5601 N. Hacienda del Sol Rd., Tucson; (520) 529-3500.**

Mexican

The greatest concentration of Mexican restaurants in the area is in the district along South 4th Avenue in south Tucson. El Dorado Bar & Restaurant, La Indita (Mexican-Indian) and others cluster there, although there are several out on Oracle Road as well.

Cafe Poca Cosa—$$$

This colorful, lively place has furnishings from Guatemala and works by local artists on the walls. Hip servers dressed in black present the daily menu on a chalkboard. Don't look for your typical cheese-smothered border food. The outstanding menu features a selection of cuisines that represent various regions in Mexico. Mole sauces and traditional dishes with new twists are specialties. **88 E. Broadway; (520) 622-6400.**

El Charro Mexican Cafe, Gift Shop & Bar—$$–$$$

Run by the Flores family since 1922, this downtown favorite is said to be the oldest Mexican restaurant in the country. Its food will tell you why it has endured. They bill their fare as "Tucson-style Mexican food," which means it has grown up pleasing the palates of the locals, who swear by it. The restaurant is on the walking tour of the historic El Presidio neighborhood, and was built by Jules le Vlein, a French master stoneworker. Go early, or linger afterwards to spend time in the gift shop, which is open late. **311 N. Court Ave., Tucson; (520) 622-1922.** Other locations at El Mercado on Broadway and at Tucson International Airport.

Guillermo's Double L Restaurant—$$–$$$

This place gets consistently high ratings when inspected by the health department, always a good sign for any restaurant. It's been in the same family since 1948, remaining popular because of an extensive menu of Sonoran-style Mexican food. Be sure to order at least one margarita. They're hand-mixed, not mangled into slush by a blender. Corner of South 4th Avenue and 29th Street. **1830 S. Fourth Ave., Tucson; (520) 792-1585, fax (520) 622-1660.**

Cowboy Steakhouse

Li'l Abner's—$$$

This is where you come for the urban cowboy experience, to have your tie snipped off if you're wearing one and to tear into a steak that weighs upwards of a pound. In an old Butterfield Stage stop, the atmosphere is rustic and down to earth. Steaks are broiled over open mesquite fires, with ribs, chicken and seafood also on the menu. If you've never tried the two-step, come on a Friday or Saturday night when a western band encourages diners to give it a try. Open at 5 P.M. for dinner only. **8500 N. Silverbell Rd.; (520) 744-2800.**

In a Class by Itself

Eegee's—$

Something of a Tucson tradition, Eegee's are slushy, slurpy desserts sold at take-out stands throughout the city. You eat them with a spoon from Styrofoam cups until they start to melt, then finish with a straw. Standard flavors are lemon, strawberry and piña colada plus a flavor of the month. They also have Teegees, which are basically iced tea with lemon. Seventeen Tucson locations.

Services

Metropolitan Tucson Convention & Visitors Bureau

130 S. Scott Ave., Tucson, 85701; (888) 638-8350 or (800) 638-8350. These numbers operate 24 hours and connect you to a visitor information specialist, or give you an automated choice to order brochures. **(520) 770-2143, fax (520) 884-7804.** Their entertaining website provides instant information on attractions, accommodations and activities. **Website: www.arizonaguide.com/visit-tucson. E-mail: mtcvb@azstarnet.com.** Requests for information can be e-mailed at any time.

Old Pueblo Trolley, Inc.

Historic electric streetcars follow a track between the University of Arizona and the Fourth Avenue business district. Call for fares, days and hours of operation. **360 E. Eighth St., Tucson, 85705; (520) 792-1802.**

Sun Tran

Tucson has public service citywide for just 75 cents a ride. It may take a bit of planning to get from place to place if you rely on this service alone, but it can be done. Call for help in trip planning. **Tucson Transit Management, P.O. Box 26765, Tucson, 85726; (520) 792-9222, fax (520) 791-2285.**

Map Area

- Multilane Divided Highway
- Principal Through Highway - Two Lanes Paved
- Connecting Road - Unimproved to Paved
- (40) Interstate Highway Marker
- (95) U.S. Highway Marker
- (85) State Highway Marker
- (15) Indian Route
- National Forest
- Park or Monument
- Prominent Peak
- Indian Reservation
- Places of Interest

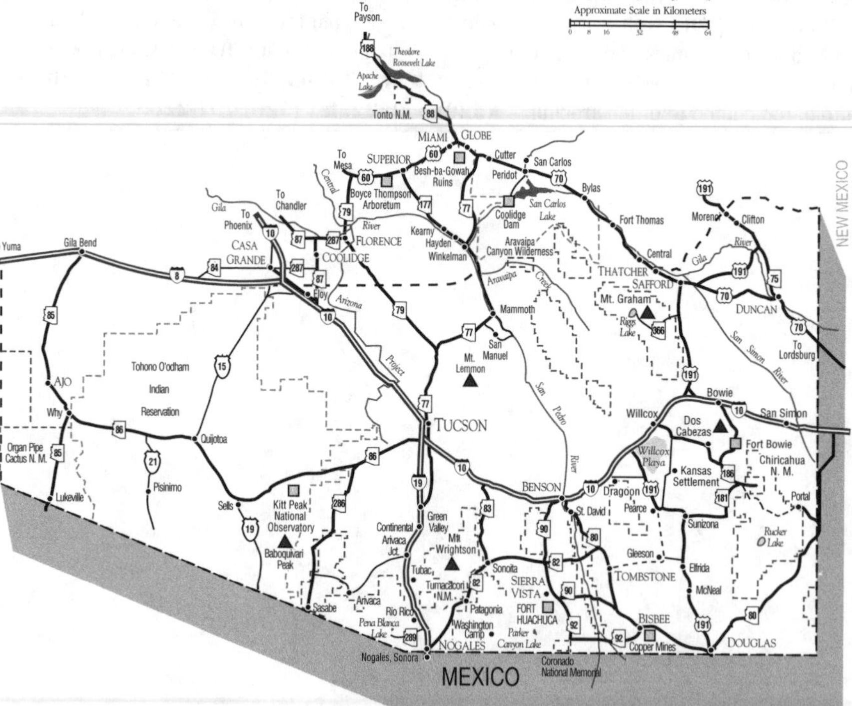

Southeast and South Central—Old West Country

Southeast and South Central—Old West Country

Most of this part of the state is in the Chihuahuan Desert, except for Tucson, which clings peninsula-like to the Sonoran Desert. The area embraces everything from lofty, snow-crowned mountain peaks to saguaros to Douglas fir and is enriched by a history colored with Indian lore that tells of tribes coming to an uneasy peace with encroaching white settlers. The Butterfield Stage rattled along dusty, rocky routes and Cochise holed up here in his legendary stronghold. It is dotted with separate parcels of the Coronado National Forest, appearing as scattered patches of green on area maps. It also has an enormous diversity of wildlife, including the greatest concentration of hummingbirds in the country in Ramsey Canyon.

Ajo

Just because it's located in the middle of nowhere, this amiable little town gets short shrift in the visitor department. But it is well worth the time to linger. It is within easy striking distance of both Organ Pipe National Monument and Cabeza Prieta National Wildlife Refuge. Once thought of as just a place to pass through on the way to Rocky Point in Mexico, it now is becoming a destination of its own. Winter visitors swell its population from about 2,000 in summer to upwards of 6,000 in winter. There's no doubt that this was a copper mining town. Just look at the mounds of tailings, 2,400 acres of them, creating light vertical ridges that define Ajo's eastern border. Mining began here in 1911 with the discovery of a new leaching process that required a well, which still sparkles at the bottom of the mine.

When the mine and smelter closed in 1985, Phelps Dodge, which owned just about the whole town, sold off its executives homes and the population plummeted. But as did many Arizona mining towns, Ajo pulled itself together and prospered. Retirees came, attracted by affordable housing, a low cost of living and great sunny weather. Today the town centers around a tidy plaza with palm trees and benches. Everyone comes here to stretch out on the grass since most homes have desert yards with few green lawns. A Catholic and a Protestant church overlook arched arcades that shelter shops and restaurants. Built in 1917, the plaza's red-tile-roof architecture is reminiscent of Spanish Colonial towns in Mexico. This look garnered it the role of a Mexican town in the 1972 motion picture *Pocket Money* with Lee Marvin and Paul Newman. The large, impressive building just off the plaza is Curleys School, once operated by Phelps Dodge and now closed. Its new owners have scheduled it for a second life as apartments. On the hill above the town is the hospital, closed since the mine shut down, and four small pastel homes that once housed mine managers, nicknamed Four Little Angels for their lofty perch. Although the word "ajo" means garlic in Spanish, it is more likely that the town is named for the Tohono O'odham word that means "place of colored clay."

Major Attractions

New Cornelia Mine

Standing at the chain-fenced overlook into the gaping mine pit gives a profound sense of how completely man can revise a landscape. At one time railroad tracks spiraled up the sides of the pit so that ore could be removed. Closed since 1985 because of falling copper prices, it is set to spring back to life. The Phelps Dodge company expects it to be operational sometime before 2003 to provide more than 400 jobs. The smoke-belching smelter will not be reopened, much to the relief of residents. Rather, ore probably will be moved by train to a large smelter in Morenci in eastern Arizona. The pit as it exists is 1.5 miles wide and 1,100 feet deep. The vivid green lake at the bottom is 35 feet deep, providing firm evidence of a ready water supply. During its lifetime the mine employed about 1,500 men, yielded about 3 million tons of low-grade copper ore that produced about $8.4 billion in copper, as well as bits of gold, silver and molybdenum. In the process it devoured three hills. Its mellifluous name is that of the wife of an early copper promoter. Today there is a small museum and satellite chamber of commerce at the mine overlook staffed by volunteers, some with good stories to tell since they once were part of the mine workforce. Open Tue.–Sat., 10 A.M.–4 P.M. Closed Memorial Day to Labor Day **(520) 387-7746.**

Ajo Historical Museum

This little building is down the hill to your right as you stand at the mine overlook. Once St. Catherine's Indian Mission, it now houses a re-created blacksmith shop, dentist office and print shop as well as artifacts and photos from Ajo's mining days. Open daily, 12 noon–4 P.M. May be closed during some summer months, and winter hours are iffy because it is staffed by volunteers, so call first. Located just beyond the mine overlook. **(520) 387-7105.**

Will Nelson's Ajo Stage Line

An excellent way to explore the area comfortably and to cross into Mexico for a brief South of the Border experience is to hook up with Will. He guides day trips as far south as Puerto Penasco, a fishing village on the Gulf of California, and to El Pinacate, the ring of ancient volcanoes known to past Native Americans as the Stone People. He also does overnight camp-outs, hiking treks and fishing trips. A four-day/three-night trip covers the 17th century Spanish missions established by Padre Kino. Call for availability and information. **1041 Solano, Ajo, 85321; (800) 942-1981 or (520) 387-6467, fax (520) 387-5419.**

Seeing and Doing

Cabeza Prieta National Wildlife Refuge

Managed by the U.S. Fish and Wildlife Service, this huge 860,000-acre refuge is a panorama of rugged mountains, lava flows, wide valleys and sand dunes that shift and change with the sweep of winds across its broad expanse. It shares a 56-mile border with Mexico. The name means Black Head in Spanish, in reference to a prominent lava-blackened granite peak within its boundaries. Established in 1939, it protects desert bighorn sheep, Sonoran pronghorns and lesser long-nosed bats. You'll probably see lots of reptiles as lizards, rattlesnakes and sidewinders (a type of rattlesnake) are comfortable in this hot, dry climate. The entire area is noted for inhospitable terrain, requiring careful planning and proper equipment to penetrate innermost areas.

Note: *Take caution.* Part of the refuge is within the Barry M. Goldwater Air Force Range and has been used for gunnery and bombing practice since World War II. Stuff that can hurt you may be lying around, or partially buried. If it looks dangerous, don't touch it. Make a note of where it is and let the refuge staff know. When "the range is hot," meaning there is air-

to-air gunnery practice in airspace above parts of the refuge, you won't be allowed in. These schedules are known in advance so call first.

El Camino Del Diablo (Highway of the Devil)

About 120 miles of this historic, dusty and difficult route that links Mexico with California passes through the refuge. The two-track trail requires a sturdy four-wheel-drive vehicle with high ground clearance. For safety and ecological reasons no off-roading is permitted. There is a small visitor center located on the north edge of Ajo on AZ 85 where you must stop for permits. **1611 N. Second Ave., Ajo, 85321; (520) 387-6483.**

Organ Pipe Cactus National Monument

This may be the most under-appreciated national monument in the state, which is too bad because it encompasses an outstanding variety of Sonoran Desert plants and animals, preserving a major ecosystem in almost unspoiled condition. The largest national monument in the lower 48 states, it is named for the stately cactus with arms that stem from a central ground-level base (unlike the saguaro with arms that branch from a single large trunk) similar to pipes that serve a giant organ. The monument, and about an 80-mile additional radius, is U.S. habitat for the organ pipe, although the cactus is also common in the state of Sonora, Mexico. The park's south-facing slopes are liberally scattered with these great plants. In May, June and July they produce delicate lavender-pink blossoms that open for a single night, then close forever. If pollinated by bats or moths, they produce a juicy fruit called pithaya, a favorite of cactus wrens. Other vegetation includes fuzzy-looking cholla, feathery mesquite, ironwood, prickly pear, palo verde, unmistakably scented creosote, spidery ocotillo and countless wildflowers along washes and roadsides.

Ajo Mountain Drive

This 21-mile, one-way loop through the monument follows graded dirt and paved roads and is passable in a passenger car if you're careful. Don't cross washes if water is running through them. Pick up a road guide (50 cents) at the visitor center, fill your water bottles and set out. The guide numbers correspond to clearly marked trail placards, pointing out types of plants, scenic views and geologic formations. Don't miss the window rock at about 9.5 miles at Milepost 13, formed by wind erosion and the expansion and contraction of freezing and thawing water. At Milepost 15, Estes Canyon, there are picnic tables and solar toilets, but no water.

Camping at Organ Pipe

About 1.5 miles from the visitor center, well-planned spaces with natural foliage have water, rest rooms, grills, tables and dump station, but no hookups. Expect to be visited by quail, roadrunners, cardinals, cottontails and jackrabbits. Spaces are first-come, first-served. Back country permits for primitive camping are available at the visitor center. Easy hiking trails near the visitor center are most enjoyable October through April when it isn't so hot. The one-mile Campground Perimeter Trail is a good introduction to desert vegetation. The Desert View Nature Trail, a 1.2-mile loop, has great views and interpretive signs. The 2.6-mile, round-trip Palo Verde Trail goes from the visitor center to the campground. For a workout, try tackling the Bull Pasture Trail, a tough 4 miles with considerable elevation gain. The payoff is a sweeping view of the valley below. Easier but equally rewarding is the Victoria Mine Trail, a 4.5-mile round-trip that leads to the mine for which it's named. From the trails you can look south into Mexico. The visitor center, located near the monument's entrance, is the best place to get information on hiking conditions and scheduled programs. It has good "touch" exhibits that include small animal skeletons and portions of desert plants. Located 22 miles south of Why on AZ 85. **Rte. 1, Box 100 Ajo, 85321 (mailing address); (520) 387-6849.**

Where to Stay

Inns & Bed & Breakfasts

Voted one of the top 50 inns in America by *Inn Times*, the **Mine Manager's House Bed and Breakfast** ($$$) is poised on a hill that affords a 30-mile view. Built in 1919 for the manager of the New Cornelia Company and his family, it has five rooms with private baths. Rates include a full, cooked breakfast. **601 Greenway Dr., Ajo, 85321; (520) 387-6505, fax (520) 387-6508.**

The Guest House Inn ($$$) was built in 1925 by Phelps Dodge for visiting company officials, and still reflects the desire to create a lasting impression with luxury furnishings and accommodations. There are four rooms with private baths. Full, cooked breakfast included. **700 Guest House Road, Ajo, 85321; (520) 387-6133.**

RV Parks

There are half a dozen places along AZ 85 to park your RV for one night or for an entire winter season, as many snowbirds do. **Ajo Heights RV Park (2000 N. Hwy. 85, Ajo, 85321; 520-387-6796)** has 32 large sites with full hookups, cable TV, phones; many sites with great views. **Belly Acres (2030 N. Hwy. 85, Ajo, 85321; 520-387-6962)** has shade trees and spaces with patios, tables and barbecue facilities. **La Siesta Motel and RV Resort (2561 N. Hwy. 85, Ajo, 85321; 520-387-6569)** offers modest rooms in the $$ category as well as spaces with full hookups, telephones, cable TV, pool and tennis court. **Shadow Ridge RV Resort (431 N. 2nd Ave. [Hwy. 85], Ajo, 85321; 520-387-5055)** gets top ratings from RV publications for its classy clubhouse, laundry room and fitness center. It has 78 full hookup spaces plus overflow areas with electricity and TV.

Where to Eat

Among good places to refuel in Ajo is **Plaza Ice Cream & Deli,** a traditional rest stop for travelers on their way to Rocky Point. In front of a one-time movie theater, umbrella tables sit under a shady arcade. Specialties are New York–style deli sandwiches (they're huge) and hand-dipped ice-cream treats, all at very modest prices. Owner Rose Sophy creates most of them herself. Open daily, 9 A.M.–5 P.M. **28 Plaza Street; (520) 387-DELI.** There's good Mexican food at **Don Juan's,** kitty corner across Taladro St. from the chamber of commerce.

Tohono O'odham Reservation

The town of Sells sits in the southernmost corner of the Tohono O'odham Reservations, which include the Gila Bend and San Xavier Reservations. The reservation extends from Ajo on the west, sweeps south into Mexico, is bordered by the Baboquivari Mountains on the east, and ranges north to within a few miles of the city of Casa Grande. Big landmarks on reservation land are Kitt Peak Observatory and San Xavier del Bac Mission. The town of Sells, on AZ 86 between Ajo and Tucson, is the tribal capital. On the reservation's eastern edge, distinctive Baboquivari Peak is revered as the home of I'itoi, creator of the Papagos.

Lukeville

This little town adjacent to the Mexican border exists as a border crossing point and Immigration and Naturalization Service office. Recently a new duty-free store has been opened, and there is a campground with hookups and adjacent motel.

Services

Ajo Chamber of Commerce, 321 Taladro, Ajo, 85321; (520) 387-7742.

Green Valley and Tubac

This part of the Santa Cruz River Valley south of Tucson is an especially lovely riparian area (once you get off the freeway) in the spots where the Santa Cruz River chooses to flow above ground. Green Valley and Tubac, each with a distinct personality, cluster along the ribbon of I-19.

The 5,000-acre community of **Green Valley,** located 25 miles south of Tucson, was once part of the original San Ignacio de las Canoa land grant conveyed to the Spanish monarchy more than 400 years ago. In essence a retirement community with a few family subdivisions mixed in, it has an appealing desert beauty. The pretty Santa Rita Mountains provide views to the east, and the huge open-pit copper mine, known historically as the Duval Copper Mine and run by Cypress Amax Minerals Company of Colorado, is to the west. From the freeway you'll see it as a distant large berm, kept watered and covered to hold down dust and minimize eyesore potential. The big attraction in Green Valley is golf. Two of the town's seven courses are private, with the remaining five open to public play (see Outdoor Activities).

Just 23 miles south of Green Valley off I-19, **Tubac** has become a hub of artistic activity reminiscent of Santa Fe, with more than 120 galleries and studios, shops and restaurants gathered in a four-block area. It flourishes with exhibitions and performing arts presentations September through May, and tends to slumber during the heat of summer. It bills itself as the place "where art and history meet" and it does have plenty of both. The entire little town is quite literally an arts and crafts center, now so trendy that decorators and designers from Phoenix and Tucson regularly trek south in search of accent pieces and accouterments to please clients. You easily can spend half a day poking into interesting shops, studios and galleries, many with truly wonderful locally produced art. Styles and influences include western, Arizona, Mexican Impressionist and contemporary. There are plenty of small interesting restaurants, many accessed by little alleyways that open onto sunny patios. Pick up a visitor's guide at any of the shops when you arrive, open it to the large center map, and you can choose your route.

Festivals and Events

Annual Tubac Festival of the Arts

February

The premier arts festival of Southern Arizona, it usually begins the first weekend of February and runs for nine days. It consists of more than a hundred crafts and merchandise booths, a juried fine arts show and tons of food. Merchants and artists who have permanent shops in Tubac are joined by area craftspeople who set up outdoor booths and stands. For information call the **Tubac Center of the Arts** at **(520) 398-2371.**

Anza Days

third weekend in October

In Tubac, this cultural celebration commemorates the trek of Spanish explorer Juan Bautista de Anza from Sonora to California with reenactments by costumed volunteers. Riders in Spanish military garb brandishing shields and lances make a colorful appearance, and foot and mounted soldiers perform precision drills. Native American music and dances from the Apache, Tohono O'odham and Mexican cultures are presented. Much of the fun of this festival is getting into the spirit of the old days, imagining how things must have been. Tubac's shops and galleries are open for browsing when you tire of historical pursuits. For information call **(520) 398-2252.**

Outdoor Activities

Golf

As courses in Phoenix and the Valley of the Sun become ever more crowded and expensive, the great unsung links between Tucson and the border are just now starting to get the play they deserve, say dyed-in-the-wool golfers.

Haven Golf Course

This par 72, 6,829-yard public course is the oldest in Green Valley. Pretty fairways are wide enough so that even real duffers can stay out of trouble. Mature trees and attractive ponds backgrounded by the Santa Rita Mountains make it scenic, with a cool feeling even when temperatures soar. It has a pro shop, practice range, lounge and food service. **110 N. Abrego Dr., Green Valley; (520) 625-4281.**

San Ignacio Golf Club

This championship desert course, designed by Arthur Hills, meanders through groves of mesquite and around water. Because it is at 3,000 feet, it tends to stay cool. Bentgrass greens are well kept. It has a pro shop, practice range, restaurant and lounge. Well-priced golf packages that include accommodations in nearby condos can make this a pleasant vacation for families and nongolfing spouses. John Jacobs Golf Schools are offered throughout the year. **4201 S. Camino del Sol, Green Valley; (520) 648-3468.**

Torres Blancas Golf Club at Santa Rita Springs

Green Valley's newest 18-hole championship course opened in winter 1995 and is doing its best to be one of the most attractive. Roughs hydro-seeded with brilliant red Mexican hats, golden marigolds and other wild flowers form a colorful contrast to Bermuda fairways and greens. A National Archaeological Society Hohokam Indian burial ground is on the first fairway. It recently was given Audubon Society sanctioning as a course that provides habitat for migrating birds. Four sets of tees per hole are reportedly user friendly from the forward tees and a definite challenge from the rear tees. A new clubhouse was completed in 1997. **3233 S. Abrego Drive, Green Valley; (520) 625-5200.**

Tubac Golf Resort

At an elevation of 3,400 feet, this well-designed 18-hole course 40 minutes south of Tucson is considerably cooler than city courses. Traditionally designed with bentgrass greens and wide Bermuda grass fairways flanked by cottonwood trees, it is kept green by the nearby Santa Cruz river. The course's 16th hole was featured in the movie *Tin Cup*. The Spanish-style resort offers comfortable rooms (see Where to Stay) that can be a good home base for exploring the area. At La Montura restaurant, inventive cuisine is served in an 1800s building, once the stables for the Otero Ranch that became Tubac. Located 40 miles south of Tucson at Exit 40 off I-19. **One Otero Rd., Tubac; (520) 398-2211.**

Rio Rico Resort & Country Club

Also part of a resort complex (the resort is on the other side of the freeway) at 4,000 feet, Rio Rico is ruggedly beautiful and can be quite a challenge. It hosts the Arizona PGA Tour and Senior PGA Tour qualifying tournaments each year. Designed by Robert Trent Jones Sr., it has bentgrass greens and Bermuda grass on tees and fairways, overseeded with rye in winter. The front nine follows the base of a small mesa, with the back nine leveling out along the Santa Cruz riverbed. The demanding, close-to-nature 18 holes total 7,119 yards. Deluxe room and golf packages are available. East side of I-19 at Exit 17. **1069 Camino Caralampi, Rio Rico; (800) 288-4746 or (520) 281-8567.**

Hiking

Madera Canyon

East of Green Valley in the north and middle of the Santa Rita mountains in the Coronado National Forest, Madera Canyon is a very special place for outdoor lovers. North-flowing Madera Creek trickles along its bottom, eventually joining the Santa Cruz River to create the riparian habitat that supports more than 220 bird species. Serious birders are attracted by the great number of rare species including the elegant trogon and magnificent hummingbird, as well as elf and whiskered screech owls. Although March is considered the beginning of birding season because hummers and owls arrive then, migrating species make the canyon a rich birding area all year long. July through early September are prime hummingbird months. The area has many trails for hiking and mountain biking, including one that's wheelchair-accessible. Major trails off the canyon range from 2.5 miles to 8.1 miles and longer. Some are easy and well graded (Bog Springs and Nature Trail are easy, short hikes if time is limited), while others can be steep and difficult, but all offer the kind of mountain scenery and fresh, clean air that clears your mind. Shady picnic areas with tables and barbecues are scattered throughout the canyon. Stop at the Santa Rita Lodge (see Where to Stay) about a mile from the end of Madera Canyon Road for books, trail guides and information about the canyon. The lodge has a register to sign before you hike that lets others know where you're planning to go and when you expect to return. The Super Trail is a favorite of many hikers. This exceptionally scenic trail meanders 4.5 miles to Josephine Saddle, but you can go all the way to Mt. Wrightson for a 16.4 mile round-trip. Drive to the upper end of Madera Canyon, where a sign indicates parking for trails. The trailhead is in the north corner of the parking lot. (See also Tucson, Hiking and Mountain Biking, for more outdoor opportunities.) From I-19 take Exit 63, which winds about 15 miles to the canyon. Or, from AZ 83 via Greaterville Road there is a lovely scenic drive over about 23 miles of dirt road.

De Anza Trail

Extending 4.5 miles along the Santa Cruz River from Tubac to Tumacacori, it is part of the National Historic Trail that follows the 1775 route between Nogales, Ariz. and San Francisco. Juan Bautista de Anza, the commander of the Tubac Presidio, Fray Francisco Garces and 240 immigrants who had dreams of finding an overland route to California used this trail. Plans are underway to include the 600 miles of the route that lie in Mexico, beginning in Culiacan, Sinaloa, which would make it the first International Historic Trail. The portion between Tubac and Tumacacori is open to hikers and equestrians, with plans in the works for a bike route along back roads between Nogales and Tubac. The Tubac trailhead is at the south side of the picnic grounds, south of the State Historic Park Museum. The trail crosses the Santa Cruz River several times, following a pleasant riparian area lined with cottonwoods. The river may be dangerous if it's been raining and the water level is high. It's best to hike early in the morning and carry lots of water, as the trail gets hot during the day. Do not drink the river water. For more information call **(520) 398-2252.**

Seeing and Doing

Historic Parks

Tubac Presidio State Historic Park

Once a small Pima Indian village, Tubac became a mission farm and ranch when Jesuit priest Eusebio Francisco Kino established the mission at Tumacacori in 1691, just a few miles to the south. A bloody battle in 1751 between the Pima Indians and the Spanish led to the construction of the Presidio San Ignacio de Tubac the following year. When the Tucson Presidio was established 45 miles to the north in 1775, the colonists and garrison were moved there. During the ensuing years the little settlement was plundered by Apaches, resettled, abandoned once again, then repopulated until in 1860 it was the largest town in Arizona. But the Civil War demanded that the troops protecting Tubac be deployed elsewhere, and once again it was abandoned.

In 1974 archaeological explorations unearthed portions of the presidio walls, foundation and plaza floor that now are open to the public as part of an underground display. The State Historic Park has a new visitor center where a nine-minute video gives a good history of what can be seen on the walking tour. The 1885 Tubac schoolhouse and artifacts from the town's history are part of the park as is the press used by Charles Poston to print the state's first newspaper, *The Weekly Arizonian.* On Sundays, October through March, from 1 to 4 P.M., volunteers in the park's living history program authentically portray Tubac life between 1752 and 1776. Open daily, 8 A.M.–5 P.M. Closed Christmas Day. Small admission. The visitor center is located where Tubac Road dead-ends into Burruel Street. **P.O. Box 1296, Tubac, 85646; (520) 398-2252, fax (520) 398-2685.**

Tumacacori National Historical Park

From Tubac, simply take the east frontage road 3 miles south to get to this lovely mission. It was the centerpiece of a thriving community terrified of Apache raids in the early 1700s, when a small adobe church was built. Construction on the existing larger church wasn't begun until the 1800s, with the final phase still in progress in 1823. The mission was abandoned in 1828 when a Mexican decree forced all Spanish priests to leave. The bell tower dome was never built. In 1908 it was declared a national monument, halting its rapid deterioration. The present visitor center was built in 1937, and in 1990 the mission received national historical park status and added protection. A self-guided walking tour takes you into the mission and around the grounds. It's easy to imagine what a pleasant community this must have been, with orchards and gardens flourishing along the banks of the Santa Cruz River. The mission's thick adobe walls keep its interior consistently cooler than the outdoors. Remnants of once-colorful paintings cover inside walls and a few of the original wood statues remain. Graves in the courtyard are marked with wood crosses. Adjacent to the visitor center is a lovely little patio garden where neatly tended mission period plants surround a trickling fountain. The small visitor center has books and videos about the mission. Open daily, 8 A.M.–5 P.M. Closed Thanksgiving and Christmas day. Small admission. Take Exit 29 off I-19. For information call **(520) 398-2341.**

The Mission at Tumacacori National Historical Park was established in 1691.

Old Tumacacori Bar

If you leave the mission after 2 P.M., head across the street to this wonderfully kitschy place, owned and run by Abe T. Trujillo for 47 years. The adobe building dates to the 1930s and Abe, who always seems to be there, says he holds the oldest liquor license in the same family in the state of Arizona. The barroom has a huge pool table surrounded by walls lined with gifts from customers, steins and figural bottles, his great-grandmother's coffee grinder and more. Bum checks hang alongside signed $1 bills that span four generations. At one time the place did a land office business, bolstered by the Tucson-Nogales bus that stopped at the bar to use the bathrooms. But the freeway passed Abe by, and he now stays solvent with local trade and the visitors that straggle over from the mission. Open daily, except Mon., 2 P.M.–1 A.M.

Santa Cruz Chili & Spice Company

The fragrance alone is enough to make you linger in this interesting shop and museum. Across the street and a few hundred yards south of the mission at Tumacacori, it's the place to stock up on spices at less than half of supermarket prices. Professional chefs make regular runs here to find the unique, gourmet seasonings not readily available in local markets. Most also are available by mail, including its famous chili paste. A small table is filled with bowls of chips and products to sample. Jean England Neubauer and her husband are the second generation to run the spice company, which began in 1943, along with the adjacent Rock Corral Ranch. The museum here is filled with artifacts from El Alamo, a stronghold on the Sonoran Desert that looked like a European castle. It eventually became a guest ranch. Open Mon.–Sat., 8 A.M.–5 P.M. **1868 E. Frontage Rd., Tumacacori, 85640; (520) 398-2591.**

Museums and Galleries

Titan Missile Museum

When you drive up to this desolate spot there is no indication that something as impressive as a Titan II missile lurks underground. A huge antenna looking like a denuded Christmas tree, a chain-link fence and a small building are the only structures. That's just the way the designers wanted it when this once-deadly projectile was installed here as part of the chain of 54 such defense mechanisms that guarded the nation during the Cold War. While it was active, few people in the surrounding area even knew the site was here. Missiles were kept at the ready in underground silos, complete with nuclear warheads, since removed. Within a minute of receiving the word, they could be launched by a specially trained team, on duty 24 hours a day. By 1987 the country was deemed safe and all Titan II missiles were dismantled except for this one, now available for public viewing. A one-hour guided tour takes you 35 feet underground to see the missile and the control center that fortunately never received the order to launch. Simulated countdowns and a walk through the 200-foot cableway to the silo are part of the tour. Take I-19 south from Tucson about 25 miles to Green Valley. Take Exit 69, Duval Mine road, and continue west just a few blocks to the museum entrance. Guided tours are offered at the Missile Complex Wed.–Sun., 9 A.M.–5 P.M., May 1 to Oct. 31; and daily, Nov. 1 to Apr. 30. Closed Christmas Day. Moderate admission charge. For information call **(520) 625-4759 or (520) 625-7736.**

Tubac Center of the Arts

At the corner of Calle Baca and Plaza Road, this tile-roofed center has changing fine art exhibits as well as music and cultural events scheduled from Sept. to June, Tue.–Sat., 10 A.M.–4:30 P.M.; and Sun., 1–4:30 P.M. Closed in July and Aug. In the Gallery Shop, the work of more than one hundred local craftspeople is for sale. For information on specific shows and events call **(520) 398-2371.**

Smithsonian Institution Whipple Observatory

Appearing as a white dot on top of Mt. Hopkins, to the east of I-19 near Amado and south of Tucson, the observatory interests mostly serious amateur astronomers, although everyone can enjoy the scenic ride into the mountains. Here, the Smithsonian uses one of the world's largest telescopes, the Multiple Mirror, to gain knowledge of the stars and planets. Six-hour public guided tours, conducted on Monday, Wednesday and Friday from March through November, begin at 9:30 A.M. with a half hour video presentation at the observatory visitor center in Amado. At 9:30 A.M., a bus takes you to the observatory, returning you by 3 P.M. Reservations are required. Open Mon.–Fri., 8:30 A.M.–4:30 P.M. **(520) 670-5707.**

Buenos Aires National Wildlife Refuge

Once a vibrant grasslands that supported pronghorn, falcons, Mexican wolves, bear and jaguar, the range was decimated in the mid-1800s by overgrazing and fire suppression. When a nonnative grass called Lehmann lovegrass was planted, it became a monoculture inhospitable to most species. In 1985 the U.S. Fish and Wildlife Service bought Buenos Aires ranch to preserve habitat for the masked bobwhite, whose breeding population is gaining a foothold in the refuge. Although it's a long process, restoring native plants is in progress. AZ 286 follows the refuge's western border, and is lined with giant sunflowers in early October. Paved Arivaca Road bisects the refuge about midway. You can explore more than 100 miles of back roads, taking care to stay directly on the roads, except to camp at any of a hundred-plus primitive campsites scattered in the backcountry. In the southeast portion of the refuge there are challenging mountain bike trails. In the refuge's far northwest corner, Brown Canyon provides an excellent birding spot, lined with sycamore and live oak. A guided hike (the only way at present to enter the canyon) leads to a 47-foot natural bridge. A good map showing back roads and campsites is available at the visitor centers. There are two entry points with information. Refuge Headquarters is open Mon.–Fri., 7 A.M.–4 P.M. Located at Milepost 7 on AZ 286. **P.O Box 109, Sasabe, 85633; (520) 823-4252.** The Arivaca Information Office is open Mon.–Fri., 9 A.M.–3 P.M., or as volunteers are available. It is located just off I-19 in the town of Arivaca.

Where to Stay

Because this area is widespread and sparsely populated, there aren't many places to stay. To find lots of luxury resorts you'll have to go back to Tucson. The ones that are here, however, are unusual and memorable.

Santa Rita Lodge Nature Resort—$$$

This quiet, secluded lodge is one of our favorite places for a weekend or a weeklong getaway. Situated above a stream in Madera Canyon at 4,800 feet elevation, units have tub and shower and color TV. Cabins accommodate two adults and two children or four friendly adults; efficiency units with fireplaces are perfect for two adults. Both have kitchens, so you can bring food in coolers, with outdoor barbecues at each unit and small decks overlooking the forest and creek. The nearest grocery store is about 13 miles away. Without ever leaving the cabin area, you can see noisy acorn woodpeckers and scrub jays, hummingbirds and nuthatches. One of the neatest things about this lodge is its natural history program. Hikes, classes and walks are conducted by local naturalists, recognized experts in their fields. Bird walks leave Monday, Wednesday and Friday at various times, Mar. 1–14 and June 1 to Aug. 31. They leave every weekday morning from Mar. 15 through May 31, and cost $12 per person. Additional nature programs are scheduled regularly and may include archaeology, geology, astronomy, birding and other topics for $15 per person; they last four to five hours, and include a light meal. Reservations are essential. Take Exit 63 off I-19 about 13 miles to the lodge. For lodge and nature program reservations, **HC 70, Box 5444, Sahuarita, 85629; (520) 625-8746, fax (520) 648-1186. Website: www.wm-online.com/lodging/madera/santarta.htm.**

At Rex Ranch, riding, hiking and being pampered at the spa are part of the total experience.

Rex Ranch—$$$$

Secluded in the Sonoran desert 30 miles south of Tucson, this lovely Territorial-Colonial ranch has gone from a beans-and-potatoes, dusty dude ranch to a rustic retreat with a spa. The attraction is the unspoiled outdoors. You can spend days hiking the fifty-plus acres of mesquite and chaparral, riding a spirited horse with no nose-to-tail mentality, or tracking feisty cactus wrens and Gila woodpeckers as they flit from saguaro to prickly pear. Then, return to the ranch for a massage. Cielo, the ranch spa, features a treatment called La Stone, in which the therapist moves smooth basalt river rocks heated quickly over the body. The stones are placed strategically under the body and on pressure points in a combination that results in ultimate relaxation. Accommodations are in adobe casitas, some with fireplaces and patios that offer desert views, some with kitchens. Three meals a day, with fitness-friendly choices, are prepared by a chef who truly understands how to combine European style with the flavors of the Southwest. Rather than the 10 o'clock news, evening entertainment can mean hot-tubbing under the stars that seem particularly bright in the clear desert air. Room-only and packages with meals are available. Because summers can be very hot, horses are at the ranch only from Oct. to May. Located about 12 miles south of Green Valley. From I-19 take Exit 48 (Arivaca/Amado) and go 3.5 miles south to the ranch. **P.O. Box 636, Amado, 85645; (888) REX RANCH or (520) 398-2914.**

Tubac Country Inn—$$$

Just off Tubac's main drag, this pleasant blue and white frame bed and breakfast truly looks like a country inn, even though it is just a block or two away from most of the interesting things in Tubac. Four suites open onto a friendly front porch. All have coffee makers and fresh coffee, two have full kitchens and two have wet bars, but no phones. Rates include an in-room continental breakfast. Corner of Plaza and Burruel. **(520) 398-3178.**

Burro Inn—$$$–$$$$

So-named because gentle resident burros, Louie and Andrew, are on hand to welcome guests. The inn, on a 12-acre plateau on top of Tubac Mountain, is surrounded by state forest land that is leased as open range to a working cattle ranch so drive carefully once you're off the main road. The inn has four two-room suites that sleep four, each with a wet bar, microwave, refrigerator (stocked with two carrots per day), phone and color TV. Remnants remain of the days when it was the site of Silo #7 in the 18-silo chain of Titan missiles that once crossed Southern Arizona. The missile was completely dismantled in 1982 to comply with the SALT Treaty, but its owners are slowly excavating the dirt-filled, 10-story silo. A small pond, created to extinguish the fire that would have been caused if a missile had been launched, now holds water hibiscus. One mile west of I-19 at Exit 40. **70 W. Burro Ln., P.O. Box 4188, Tubac, 85646-4188; (520) 398-2281.**

(For more accommodations, see **Rio Rico Resort** and **Tubac Golf Resort** listed under Golf.)

Where to Eat

See also Where to Stay, as many restaurants are part of resorts. A number of interesting cafes in Tubac offer fare a notch above the chain eateries in Green Valley.

Burro Inn Restaurant—$$

Open for lunch and dinner, this unpretentious place has huge, western-style, mesquite broiled steaks and equally huge Margaritas. If burro humor amuses you, take the time to read the captioned photos that line the walls. One mile west of I-19 at Exit 40. **70 W. Burro Ln., P.O. Box 4188, Tubac, 85646-4188; (520) 398-2281.**

Tumacacori Restaurant—$$$

It has been there almost a decade, drawing its loyal clientele from Green Valley, Tubac and Nogales, and attracting visitors that come to the mission just across the street. Small, homey and family-run, it serves reasonably priced Greek food as well as Sonoran Mexican, an odd combination that somehow seems to work. It offers full cocktail service. Located across the street from Tumacacori Mission. Open daily for lunch and dinner. **(520) 398-9038.**

Services

Green Valley Chamber of Commerce offers printed information on the area. Staffed with helpful volunteers, it is open daily, 9 A.M.–5 P.M.; open Sat. morning during summer months only. **270 W. Continental Rd., #100, Green Valley, 85614; (800) 858-5872, (520) 625-7575 or 7594, fax (520) 648-6154.**

Tubac Chamber of Commerce is a small, all-volunteer chamber so you'll probably get voice-mail when you call. Things slow considerably in the summer, but someone will always get back to you if you leave a message. Send a self-addressed, stamped, business-sized envelope and you'll receive information. **P.O. Box 1866, Tubac, 85646; (520) 398-2704.**

There are clean public rest rooms with composting toilets in Tubac, off Tubac Road across from The Country Shop.

Tarantulas

Those hairy, scary creatures you see scurrying across quiet desert back roads are tarantulas, long a part of Indian lore and desert tales. You'll see the greatest number with the onset of southern Arizona's summer rains, usually in late July or August when males start actively pursuing a mate.

They may be the largest and hairiest spider in the United States, but their bite is not lethal. Their venomous reputation, and their name, date back to the 15th century when people sometimes suffered from a form of hysteria thought to be caused by the bite of a large wolf spider named after the town of Taranto in Puglia, Italy. The only cure for the afflicted one was to dance himself into a frenzy to purge the effects of the spider's bite. Modern-day medical professionals have speculated that, once injected with the irritating venom of a tarantula, the gyrations of the dancer caused body sweat to dilute and wash away the toxin, thereby appearing to create a cure. The Italian folk dance called the tarantella is said to be named for this bizarre remedy.

The fuzzy arachnids don't spin webs to capture food. They seize their quarry by emerging cautiously from their burrows at night to pounce quickly on anything smaller than they are. The tarantula has a beaklike mouth from which it ejects a venom fatal to small creatures, along with enzymes that begin the digestive process. Thus disabled, hapless insects become a meal.

Tarantulas have been kept successfully as pets for many years. A female may live to be as old as 30, and a male has a life span of about ten years. If you held one in your hand you'd expect it to weigh more than the half-ounce it does, because the five-inch span of the hairy legs that extend from a two-inch body makes it appear larger than it really is.

A tarantula spends most of its life in its burrow, which may be an abandoned animal hole or a remote ledge. Males don't leave the sheltered hollow until they are sexually mature, at about eight years of age. That's when you're most likely to see them scampering about the desert, so please don't deter them and put a damper on their romantic quest. Their mating process is complication enough. Although they don't spin webs for food-catching, they do create one for mating purposes. The male creates a small network of web material in which he deposits his sperm. He picks up the little bundle and puts it into two sacs in the female's abdomen. Apparently this is not a gesture that she appreciates, because she can viciously turn on her new suitor at any time during this process, possibly killing him.

Being a single mom doesn't seem to phase a female tarantula. She stores the little bundles of sperm for a number of weeks, then spins a silk sheet on which she lays up to one thousand eggs. This may seem like a lot, but on average only two of the eggs will become mature spiders. Predation by small mammals like skunks, as well as birds, snakes, lizards and frogs takes its toll.

In six weeks tiny white spiders hatch, staying with mother tarantula for up to a week, when they leave home (but stay in the neighborhood) to build burrows of their own. Tarantulas don't generally stray far from their original burrow, so if you see one, chances are that others are close by.

As will most wildlife, a naturally timid tarantula tries to run away if threatened. If cornered, it will try to frighten away the interloper by rearing up on its back legs and displaying its fangs, which are located quite far back in its throat. If it does bite, its venom has about the same effect as a bee sting or mosquito bite on humans. If you walk an area at dusk and spot large half-dollar size holes in the ground, they probably belong to tarantulas. Hang around. They'll eventually come out to feed.

Nogales, Arizona, and Nogales, Sonora

The state's best-known border town, Nogales, is joined with Nogales, Sonora in Mexico to form a pair that consider themselves one community. Arizona's Nogales has just 25,000 people whereas the one in Mexico has a population of 250,000, but there is an active industrial and trade exchange between the two. With the signing of the Gadsden Purchase in 1854, the present-day boundary was established.

Early on, Native Americans used Nogales Pass to move between what now is Arizona and the Sea of Cortez, traffic verified by sea shells found in ancient Arizona ruins. The town itself was founded in 1880 as a center of customs control between the two countries. By 1910 it had become the most important city in the state of Sonora. During subsequent turbulent years it often was the target of forceful takeovers by various Mexican power factions. In 1976 then-President Gerald Ford visited to meet with Mexican President Luis Echeverria Alvarez to reaffirm an informal good neighbor policy. By then a stream of U.S. tourists heading over the border and a steady flow of Mexico-grown produce into the United States had created a strong economic bond. Sonora, an agricultural state, together with Sinaloa, another agricultural state on its southern border, make Nogales the largest port of entry for produce into the United States. During winter months Mexican farms fill U.S. produce departments with 80 percent of the cucumbers and zucchini and 66 percent of the tomatoes they sell. More than 65 *maquiladoras* employ close to 20,000 workers here. Working under a two-nation agreement, these plants assemble and manufacture computer parts, electronic components, medical products, typewriter ribbons, welders, battery chargers, sunglasses, auto parts and more.

Nogales (means walnut in Spanish), Sonora, has niched itself as a tourist destination, and is fun to explore for the better part of a day. Take I-19 south until it practically dead-ends into parking lots within blocks of the border. Park in one of them and walk across at Garita A, the place with the big double humps, which is the main 24-hour walking entrance. Just ahead is the Flag Island of the Americas, aflutter with banners from Mexican states. Note that street signs are at intersections on the corners of buildings. Turn right on Campillo Street and walk about three short blocks to Downtown Obregon Street, which is lined with shops. From there, just explore. Since a self-imposed spruce-up a few years ago, there are clean rest rooms located in most restaurants and at the border crossing. Opinions differ about where to change money, but it really doesn't matter unless you're changing thousands of dollars, because the rate of exchange will vary by just pennies from place to place. In fact it really isn't necessary to change money at all if you'll be across the border just for the day. U.S. dollars are accepted everywhere, as are credit cards. If you'd like a peso coin or note for a souvenir, just ask when you make a purchase.

If you're not a seasoned Mexico traveler it should be noted that a day's foray into Nogales, Sonora, is not "going to Mexico." This is a border town, with little of the charm of Mexico's marvelous beaches, spectacular canyons or sophisticated tourist resorts further south. But it has a low-key, naive appeal all its own that certainly has kept Arizona residents, and generations of tourists, coming back for decades.

To make a phone call to Nogales, Sonora, dial 011-52-631 and the five-digit telephone number. 011 is the international code, 52 is the country code and 631 is the city code.

Festivals and Events

Fiestas de Mayo

April–May

From the last few days in April until May 5, the traditional Battle of Puebla is remembered with a celebration that involves bullfights, *palenque* (cockfights), horse races, arts and crafts exhibits and industrial expositions. Whatever your feeling about bull and cockfights, keep them to yourself when you're across the border. Part of a tradition that residents are not ready to forfeit, their merits generally are not a favored topic of debate.

Seeing and Doing

Shopping

You're allowed to bring back $400 in duty-free merchandise monthly that can include a quart of liquor and a carton of cigarettes. Most shoppers generally consider Kahlua, the rich coffee-flavored liqueur made in Mexico, the most reliable buy. Heavy blue-rimmed Mexican glassware is a popular item, available at about half of what it sells for in trendy U.S. decorator shops. Wood and wrought iron furniture, ceramics, leather goods and colorful knickknacks of all sorts are plentiful and well priced. Floaty lightweight cotton dresses, often with intricate embroidery, are popular as nightgowns. On the Saturdays that correspond with big holidays such as Memorial Day, Fourth of July, Labor Day and Thanksgiving, merchants tend to take advantage of bigger crowds by reducing prices. **Little Mexico** on Campillo Street has a good selection of arts and crafts from all over the country. **El Cid Mall** on Obregon Street, the main shopping thoroughfare, is a collection of shops with higher quality leather goods, clothing and art. Haggling and bargaining become an art form here and are part of the fun of making purchases. Even in what appear to be fixed price shops, don't hesitate to try.

It is no secret that large numbers of U.S. citizens cross the border to buy prescriptions that, while available in the United States, are often a fraction of the cost in Mexico. Too, many drugs that doctors prescribe here are available without a prescription in Mexico. The danger is that there is no Food and Drug Administration that eagle-eyes these drugs. While many ill people, dependent on very expensive prescriptions, say they must use the Mexican versions or do without, others have had less pleasant experiences. A number of Mexican pharmacies are within blocks of the border. As with any unknown quantity, caveat emptor.

Museums

Pimeria Alta Historical Society

On the Arizona side of the border, this combination museum and archives traces the history of southern Arizona and northern Sonora, and gives a sense of how the two states relate. At varying times the 1914 building served as the firehouse, jail, courthouse, customs house and city hall. The old firehouse pole and a gleaming 1900s engine, a particularly grim jail cell and a rolltop customs house desk are remnants of the building's past lives. Open Fri., 10 A.M.–5 P.M.; Sat., 10 A.M.–4 P.M., Sun., 1–4 P.M. Closed Mon.–Thu. These odd hours have been established to serve the visitors that cross the border on weekends. Admission is free. It is at the corner of Grand and Crawford Streets. **136 N. Grand Ave., Nogales, AZ 85628; (520) 287-4621.**

Where to Stay

Many visitors prefer to stay in Tucson or nearby, then drive the 68 miles to Nogales for the day. But there are a number of reliable, if not luxurious, hotels on the U.S. side right at the border.

Nogales, Arizona

All of these middle-of-the-road places are in the $$ to $$$ range.

Americana Motor Hotel, 639 Grand Ave.; (520) 287-7211 or (800) 874-8079.
Best Western Siesta, 673 Grand Ave.; (520) 287-4671 or (800) 528-1234.
Best Western Time, 921 Grand Ave.; (520) 287-4627 or (800) 528-1234.
Super 8 Motel, 537 W. Mariposa Rd.; (520) 281-2242 or (800) 800-8000.
Mi Casa RV Travel Park is about 4.5 miles north of the border on Grand Avenue, and has full hookups. **2901 Grand Ave; (520) 281-1150.**

Nogales, Sonora

Fray Marcos de Niza Hotel—$$

This tall, pink building in the center of town has clean, comfortable air-conditioned rooms with phones and TV and is convenient to shopping. You'll find purified water and ice in the restaurant and bar. This is about as luxurious as it gets in Nogales, Sonora, but then, that's not why you come here. Anyplace you stay right in town will be noisy until the early morning hours, so it's a good idea to stay in an air-conditioned place so you can close the windows. **At the corner of Obregon and Campillo; phone 2-16-51.**

Where to Eat

If you are genuinely terrified of contracting Montezuma's Revenge, don't put a thing in your mouth while in Nogales, Sonora. However, big hotels and the major restaurants have purified water, even in ice cubes. By all means ask before you order. Most regular border-crossers report no problems with food in Nogales. Of course it isn't wise to lap up a colorful ice from a street vendor, or buy homemade tortillas from adorable, big-eyed children. On the U.S. side you'll find Arby's, Kentucky Fried Chicken, Pizza Hut and Shakey's Pizza conveniently positioned so that you could purchase a lunch before crossing the border, to eat later. Zula's Restaurant and Sweets 'N Subs bakery and deli, both on Grand Avenue, are convenient eateries. But don't be afraid to try the truly wonderful restaurant food available in Sonora. Stick to bottled beer and sodas if you really are concerned.

On the Arizona Side

Molina's Pete Kitchen Outpost—$$

On the historic Pete Kitchen Ranch established in 1854, in an old ranch building, you'll find the last remnant of a memorable pioneer. The thick-walled adobe building has a foundation laid of rock from a nearby canyon and door posts fashioned from oaks that grew on the property. Ranch artifacts and memorabilia decorate the dining room. The specialty is Mexican food with many flavorful fish dishes prepared in the Santa Cruz style. Open daily, 10 A.M.–10 P.M. Located 3 miles north of Nogales on **Frontage Rd. off I-19; (520) 281-9946.**

San Cayetano—$$$

Located at Rio Rico Resort and Country Club about 12 miles north of the border, the menu is typically upscale Southwest, with interesting salads and sauces as well as some Mexican dishes. Choose this resort if you're looking to linger over a well-prepared meal, share some wine, and perhaps snug into one of the resort's rooms from where you can peacefully memorize the mountains. **Off I-19 at Exit 17; (520) 281-1901.**

On the Sonora Side

El Cid—$$-$$$

This large, airy second-floor restaurant serves a continental menu as well as Mexican food. Truly delicious choices include Guaymas shrimp, cabrilla and other imaginatively prepared local fish. Run by a Greek gentleman who is much involved with Sonoran tourism, he will do his best to be sure you have a pleasant experience. **Av. Obregon #124 Altos; phone 2-15-00.**

Elvira's Restaurant—$$

Not far from El Cid, this lovely patio restaurant serves what U.S. residents think of as typical Mexican food. Chile rellenos, chimichangas, plus fish dishes redolent of garlic are no-fail choices. Margaritas are great. **Av. Obregon #1; phone 2-47-73.**

Services

Nogales-Santa Cruz Chamber of Commerce, Kino Park, Nogales, AZ 85621; (520)-287-3685, fax (520) 287-3688.

Delegation of Tourism, Edificio Puerta de Mexico; phone (direct dial from the United States) 011-52-631-2-64-46.

Because the states of Arizona and Sonora are partnering in a tourism endeavor, it's possible to get Nogales information from the **Arizona State Office of Tourism, 2702 N. 3rd St., Ste. 4015, Phoenix, 85004; (888) 520-3434.**

Patagonia

This unassuming little town is a good place to headquarter for exploring the Patagonia-Sonoita Creek Preserve, or as a jumping off point for visiting Nogales. Located about 18 miles north of the Mexican border at an elevation of 4,044 feet, it straddles AZ 82, in a pretty little valley with the Santa Rita Mountains to the north and the Patagonias to the south. It takes its name, as do the mountains, from the Patagonia Mine, later called the Mowry Mine, that produced substantial quantities of silver and lead ore. Surrounding grasslands have supported ranching for decades. A charming feature is a butterfly garden in the center of town, planted with desert senna, lantana and other blooming plants that attract pipevine swallowtails, queen butterflies, fritillaries and more. Picnic tables nearby provide shady sites for lunch alfresco. Along Naugle Avenue (AZ 82), shops include **Red Mountain Foods,** a natural foods place with fresh organic produce. The **Nature Center** has books, crafts and birding supplies. Garlic growing is part of the area economy, with dozens of organic varieties ready for purchase at **The Garlic Lady.**

Seeing and Doing

Patagonia Sonoita Creek Preserve

The Nature Conservancy's first preserve in Arizona, it recently acquired additional land that more than doubled its size from 355 to 770 acres. It includes an exceptionally rich cottonwood-willow riparian habitat with hundred-year-old trees that provide homes for more than 260 bird species. The greatest diversity of birds appears during April, May and June, before summer's heat sets in and chiggers become voracious. But because of the large number of migrants that pass through, any season will have good birding. The ever-running stream supports four native fish species that are critically endangered in the southwest. The Gila topminnow, among the most imperiled, recently has been found to contain cells that divide in ways to mimic cancer, making it an invaluable tool in the study of the disease. You can expect to see white-tail deer and perhaps a coatimundi, with plenty of fluffy-tailed Arizona gray squirrels to keep you entertained. A number of trails provide easy walking. A new visitor center has rest rooms, water and interpretive displays. Open Wed.–Sun., 7:30 A.M.–3:30 P.M. A guided walk is held Sat. at 9 A.M. The preserve is located about 60 miles southeast of Tucson. From Patagonia, turn west on 4th Ave., then south on Pennsylvania. Cross the creek and go about 1.5 miles to the entrance (this is a new entrance, opened in 1997, so if you think you've missed it, keep going.) **P.O. Box 815, Patagonia, 85624; (520) 394-2400 (phone and fax).**

Patagonia Lake State Park

More than 640 acres of rolling grassland make this a comfortable place to camp or picnic.

Hikers enjoy the trails at the Patagonia Sonoita Creek Preserve.

During many months it is underutilized, possibly because of its comparatively remote location. The 265-acre man-made lake regularly produces crappie, bass, bluegill and catfish. From October through February it is stocked every three weeks with trout. Expect to see white-tail deer, great blue herons, vermilion flycatchers and a number of hummingbird species. Try the easy Sonoita Creek Trail for a mellow stroll. Picnic areas have ramadas, tables and grills. The campground has 106 sites with showers, hookups, rest rooms and dump station. There are boat ramps and a marina and camper supply store. Small day use fee. **P.O. Box 274, Patagonia, 85624; (520) 287-6965, fax (520) 287-5618.**

Where to Stay

The Duquesne House—$$$

Built by the owner of the Duquesne Mine as housing for his workers when Patagonia was a copper and silver center, this turn-of-the-century adobe has been renovated so that each suite has its own bedroom, bath, sitting room and private entrance. Breakfast is served in the dining room or on a screened porch where guests also can gather to socialize. One efficiency with kitchenette and three suites are available. Located 60 miles south of Tucson and 20 miles east of Nogales. **357 Duquesne St., P.O. Box 772, Patagonia, 85624; (520) 394-2732.**

Stage Stop Inn—$$$

Located in downtown Patagonia, 43 rooms make this the largest hotel in the area. It has a heated pool and some kitchenettes. There is a restaurant and saloon next door. **303 W. McKeown (P.O. Box 777) Patagonia, 85624; (800) 923-2211 or (520) 394-2211.**

Patagonia RV Park is located on Harshaw Road and has full hookups with cable TV; **(520) 394-2491.**

Where to Eat

McGraw's Wagon Wheel Cantina—$$

"We don't have a town drunk. We take turns." The declaration on the wall pretty much characterizes this fun cowboy bar, where everyone looks up when you enter, then includes you in the conversation. There are a pool table, booths and hearty chow. An order of pork ribs, slaw and beans is a frequent special, along with chicken and burgers. **400 W. Naugle; (520) 394-2433.**

The Ovens of Patagonia—$$

This pretty, airy blue and white restaurant has good salads, tamales and quesadillas as well as vegetarian dishes and a bakery. Walls are lined with local art. Open daily, 10:30 A.M.–2:30 P.M.; Fri.–Sat., from 5 P.M. On AZ 82 on the town's north side. **(520) 394-2483.**

Wine Country

The word wine usually brings to mind California's hospitable Napa and Sonoma Valleys and the rich French countryside. But Arizona and wine have been compatible as far back as the days of the Spanish padres who gave wine-producing a fling. Since then it has been established by viticulturists that the soil and climate in parts of southern Arizona mirror those of Burgundy and Bordeaux so faithfully that producing fine wine is not only possible but happening regularly. Many vintners supply restaurants and beverage stores around the state with award-winning vintages. Vineyards in southern Arizona are clustered around Willcox, Vail, near Sonoita and in small areas east and west of Nogales, in a small wine belt that parallels the Mexican border. If you visit in August or early September you should be able to see grapes on the vines about to be harvested. Most wineries welcome visitors and offer tastings for a small charge, but because circumstances change seasonally, call ahead to verify hours.

La Capilla de Santa Maria Consoladora des Afligadoros

The name of this charming little shrine in the tiny village of Elgin means Chapel of St. Mary, consoler of the afflicted. Overseen by the Monks of the Vine, a group of area vintners, it is the site of the April Blessing of the Grapes ceremony and the August Harvest Festival. The little Santa Fe style chapel is nondenominational and welcomes all for quiet, contemplative moments.

Wineries and Vineyards

Sonoita Vineyards

Pack a picnic lunch and come for tasting at this recently expanded vineyard. The red, sandy loam soil here and a longer growing season than in France, produce award-winning cabernet sauvignons. Other favorites include a fume blanc and a sonora rossa, a spicy red chianti-style wine. The vineyards are owned and were developed by Dr. Gordon Dutt, professor emeritus of soil and water science at the University of Arizona, who is credited with having started Arizona's wine industry. Open daily, 10 A.M.–4 P.M. Located 12.5 miles southeast of Sonoita, south of Elgin. **HCR Box 33, Elgin, 85611; (520) 455-5893.**

Village of Elgin Winery

The only winery in Arizona to stomp its grapes, it uses new wood casks for aging. Winemaker/owners Gary and Kathy Reeves welcome visitors. Outstanding Pinot noir, Cabernet Sauvignon and Colombard. Next door to the chapel in downtown Elgin. Tastings daily 10–5 P.M. **HC1, Box 47, Elgin, 85611; (520) 455-5893; Website: www.concentric.net/~elgnwine.**

R. W. Webb Winery

This beautiful Spanish-style building at the base of the Rincon Mountains has a cool patio with a fountain and a graceful olive tree. Among its award winners are a cabernet

The Village of Elgin Winery relies on a bit of heavenly help for a good grape harvest.

sauvignon, Johannisberg Riesling and an Arizona gold sherry that is truly spectacular. Warm, sunny days, cool, dry nights and cold winters, plus the slightly acidic, sandy loam soils of the Sulphur Springs Valley produce the grapes necessary for these wines. It also is the site of the Dark Mountain Brewery, making it the only winery and brewery combo in the state. Located 20 miles south of Tucson in Vail. Informal guided tours and tastings of wine and beer are offered Mon.–Sat., 10 A.M.–5 P.M.; Sun., 12–5 P.M. **13605 E. Benson Highway (P.O. Box 130), Vail, 85641; (502) 762-5777.**

Santa Cruz Winery

The tasting room is located in downtown Patagonia, open Wed.–Mon., 11 A.M.–5 P.M.; Thur.–Sun. in summer. **(520) 394-2888.**

Arizona Vineyards

Further south, just above the Mexican border, this kitschy spot is as much showplace as winemaking establishment. They say they sell more wine than any other winery, due to their position on a well-traveled road to Nogales. It specializes in sweet wines and proudly offers an award-winning Rattlesnake Red. Their best-seller, a sweet, fruity mountain Rhine, combines French Columbard and muscat grapes grown in Chandler. A motion picture prop rental service also is centered here, hence the Roman chariot, oak icebox, crank phone, ancient license plates and other collectibles that line the walls. The owner, Tino Ocheltree, whose oil paintings are part of the decor, is a world traveler and seldom in residence, but the accommodating manager is more than happy to pour samples. On crowded winter weekends tasters are on their own to take a "wine barrel tour" with printed information directing them from bottle to bottle. Don't miss the rosemary garlic vinegar at $5 per bottle. Located 2 miles east of Nogales. Open daily, 10 A.M.–5 P.M. **1830 Patagonia Highway, Nogales, 85621; (520) 287-7972.**

Callaghan Vineyards

You can't go to the vineyards to taste the outstanding wines produced at this small operation, but they are available at restaurants including Karen's Wine Country Cafe in Sonoita (see Where to Eat), Janos in Tucson and AJs Markets in Phoenix and Tucson. It's worth seeking out their Callaghan, Cochise County Fume Blanc and their Callaghan, Sonoita, Buena Suerte Cuvee. For information call **(520) 455-5322.**

Kokopelli Winery

Located in Willcox, this is Arizona's largest producing winery. Its vintages reflect the expertise of the European heritage of the Italian grape grower, Don Minchella, and the fifth generation French wine maker, Herve Lescombes. Their award-winning brut champagne is outstanding. It is the only organically certified vineyard in Arizona. Take I-10 east to Exit 340 (Rex Allen Drive), to 1 mile south to Haskell, then 1.5 miles to the winery. Open weekends noon–5 P.M. **2060 N. Haskell Ave., Willcox, 85643; (520) 384-5205.**

San Dominique Winery

In Camp Verde in the Verde Valley, it is the state's first boutique winery producing only fine varietal and specialty wines. Located 11 miles south of Camp Verde. Take Exit 169 off I-17 and proceed southeast to winery. Open daily 10 A.M.–5 P.M. **(602) 945-4583.**

For more information on the Arizona wine industry and a map showing vineyard locations, call **Arizona Wine Commission (Dept. of Agriculture)** at **(602) 542-0877**, or **Vintage Voice** at **(520) 455-5285.**

Where to Stay

Crown C Ranch—$$$–$$$$

This ranch is truly unique because you are completely on your own. Chances are you'll never see the staff, except maybe on arrival. The rambling 60-year-old adobe ranch house has individual rooms with baths that can be connected in a number of configurations to accommodate groups or couples, and a separate guest house that's ideal for a family. There are two complete kitchens (no meals are served unless you arrange for them), barbecues, firewood for fireplaces, swimming pool and tennis court. Horses are available for riding from nearby **Arizona Trail Tours, (520) 394-2701.** You come here for total privacy, to enjoy the absolutely serene surroundings, watch the birds, read a book, appreciate that there is this much open land and peace and quiet left in the world. Take AZ 82, 2.7 miles west of Sonoita and look for the Crown C brand sign. Turn right and drive one mile to the ranch. **P.O. Box 984, Sonoita, 85637; (520) 455-5739.**

The Vineyards Bed & Breakfast—$$$

Set on a knoll overlooking tidy rows of vines, the Hacienda Los Encinos dates to 1916 when the original ranch was built. Today, Ron and Sue DeCosmo have completely refurbished the place to provide three guest rooms plus a separate casita with sitting room and bath. Set at 5,100 feet elevation, summers are warm enough so the pool gets lots of use, but there is snow in the winter. You'll be greeted by Nellie and Rosie, a pair of black labs, as well as Pepperoni, a classic Jerusalem burro with a crosslike marking on his back and withers. Ron cooks a full breakfast. From The Vineyard it's an easy drive to wineries and birding territory. **92 S. Los Encinos Rd., Sonoita, 85637; P.O. Box 1227, Sonoita, 85637 (mailing address); (520) 455-4749.**

Yee Haa Guest Ranch—$$$

Another good place to headquarter while exploring wine country, the ranch has three guest rooms decorated to reflect the Old West as well as the area's Mexican and Native American influence. Each room has a spa tub and shower, wood burning stove and feather beds, all with private entrances, TV and VCR. Full breakfast included. Located just south of Elgin, 8 miles southeast of the junction of AZ 82 and AZ 83. **P.O. Box 888, Sonoita, 85637; (520) 455-9285.**

Where to Eat

Karen's Wine Country Cafe—$$–$$$

Southern Arizona's flourishing wine industry has created enough cachet to support upscale fine-food restaurants. In Sonoita, this unexpected little gem, and Grasslands, below, are good examples. Karen's is a cheery mix of press-back chairs and blue mixed-print tablecloths. Many Arizona wines are stocked, so you can try them with a meal after you've been to the vineyards for tastings. The menu includes truly inventive salads (the soy ginger dressing is outstanding) served with Karen's fresh-baked bread, excellent steaks, always a grilled fish and desserts (like Mexican spice cake) to die for. Open Wed.–Sun. for lunch, 11 A.M.–4 P.M.; Thu.–Sat., 5–8 P.M. for dinner. **3266 Hwy. 82, Sonoita, 85673; (520) 455-5282, fax (520) 455-0075.**

The Grasslands Restaurant, Bakery, Bar—$$–$$$

Another fabulous place to eat in this out-of-the-way little town, Grasslands offers just-baked breads, muffins, Danish, breakfast breads, filled croissants, quiches and more. The family-owned place draws clientele from Tucson as well as surrounding ranches. The light wood decor, airy and bright, adds to its upbeat atmosphere. Local and organic wines, German beers and cocktails are available. Don't miss the feta and spinach–stuffed croissant, always freshly baked. On Saturdays there are authentic German entrees along with mellow guitar, mandolin or fiddle music. Open Wed., Thur., Fri. and Sun., 8 A.M.–4 P.M., Sat., 8 A.M.–8 P.M. **3119 S. Hwy. 83, Sonoita; (520) 455-4770.**

Sierra Vista

Once dependent on U. S. Army Fort Huachuca for its economic sustenance (the fort is located within the city limits) Sierra Vista has become a substantial city of its own, mainly through efforts by city directors to publicize its amiable climate and great diversity of area activities. Somewhat of a retirement mecca, cost of living is low and it has a small-town atmosphere, yet Tucson is just 70 miles to the northwest. Military retirees come here to use base privileges. Situated on the eastern slope of the Huachuca Mountains overlooking the San Pedro River Valley, Sierra Vista's name means Mountain View in Spanish. You can look in any direction and see the Mule, Dragoon, Whetstone or Huachuca Mountains. Its main claim to fame, besides reliably good weather averaging 75 degrees in summer and 50 degrees in winter, is its position at the hub of one of the country's finest birding areas. A variety of habitats attract more than one hundred species. These habitats include desert mesquite shrubland, grassland, brushland, riparian, oak woodland and pine forest with Douglas fir and aspen at higher elevations. In this part of the state, elevations range from 2,389 feet in Tucson to 9,324 feet at the top of Mt. Wrightson, with Sierra Vista at a comfortable 4,623 feet. The town itself, population 33,310, is low-key but lively, with 75 restaurants ranging from basic fast food to truly fine dining.

Festivals and Events

Southwest Wings Birding Festival

mid-August

One of the biggest birding festivals in the state, it includes field trips to the San Pedro Riparian Area, Ramsey Canyon, Coronado National Memorial and Patagonia/Sonoita, lectures by nationally recognized Audubon authorities, owl prowls, bat stalks and more. Thousands of local and international visitors come to this highly respected event. It is based at a Sierra Vista hotel where vendors and exhibitors set up tables and booths. Oftentimes live birds and animals are on display in connection with rehabilitative programs. Bird-banding classes, beginning birding workshops, identification skills, habitat recognition and choosing and using binoculars also appeal to outdoor lovers. If you're even thinking of going, book a hotel room early. If you're too late, try surrounding towns like Bisbee, one-half hour away. For information call **(800) 288-3861.**

Festival of Color Balloon Rally

mid-October

Calm desert air makes this countywide event an ever-increasing success as more and more balloonists participate. Although not as dramatic as the November balloon spectacular held in Phoenix, the assurance of clean, blue skies as a background for their colorful display makes this event a photographic delight.

Outdoor Activities

Birdwatching

Ramsey Canyon Nature Conservancy Preserve

The best-known of Arizona's Nature Conservancy Preserves, Ramsey Canyon is a shady, green 300-acre arroyo in the Huachuca Mountains that is practically a shrine to hummingbirds. From spring until early autumn this unique biological crossroads hosts more than 14 species, attracted by an all-season stream that also appeals to other wildlife. April and May are prime months (see Where to Stay). You'll see hummers hovering and darting, gorging themselves at feeders set up near the visitor center. Conveniently placed benches are best for quiet viewing. Among the 230 bird species that reportedly spend at least part of the year in the canyon, elegant trogons sometimes nest in the sycamores, and sulphur-bellied

flycatchers are easy to spot. Golden eagles nest high in the canyon and can sometimes be seen floating against an early morning sky.

The canyon's history includes a period in the 1880s when miners from Bisbee and soldiers from Ft. Huachuca flocked to the saloons and hotels that were built among the shady sycamores that line its walls. A few old cabins and foundations remain. You're likely to see a troop of coatimundis frolicking in the trees. The long-tailed critters, much like monkeys, are friendly and mischievous but can bite, so don't get close. White-tail deer, in groups of three and four, will watch placidly if you stroll by quietly. An irrigation pond has become a home for the Ramsey Canyon leopard frog, found only in the Huachuca Mountains, and one of only two frog species in the United States known to call under water. They depend on the preserve for their future.

Six creekside cabins are available for rent, and are booked as much as a year in advance for May and August, prime birding months. Just 13 parking spaces make whole and half-day parking reservations essential. Pets are not allowed in the preserve. About 6 miles south of Sierra Vista on AZ 92, take the Ramsey Canyon Road turnoff and follow it 4 miles to the preserve. **27 Ramsey Canyon Rd., Hereford, 85615; (520) 378-2785.**

Hiking

Ramsey Canyon

Hamburg Trail

Follow the main canyon's rough dirt road one-half mile from the Nature Conservancy visitor center. A sign on the left marks the Hamburg Trail, which heads uphill. You'll immediately realize the wisdom of the trail builders who placed benches to encourage hikers to rest. If you move steadily for about 45 minutes, you'll come to an overlook with a spectacular view of the forests, grasslands and the town of Sierra Vista. Watch for golden eagles floating on thermals.

From the canyon you can go directly into the surrounding national forest where there are more than 120 miles of trail. Violent thunderstorms often pelt the area in July and August, so be prepared. Ramsey Canyon is the first canyon south of Sierra Vista on AZ 92. Turn right at Ramsey Canyon Road and follow it approximately 4 miles to the Nature Conservancy Preserve.

Coronado National Memorial

A 1.5-mile, round-trip hike to Coronado Cave takes a leisurely two hours and requires a map and free permit from the visitor center, and two flashlights per person to explore the 600-foot cave. It was formed more than 250 million years ago when southern Arizona was a sea. Inside are stalagmites, helictites and flowstones, identified by numbers on the map. Occasionally bats inhabit the cave and should not be disturbed. Joe's Canyon Trail is tougher, climbing about 1,000 feet in the first mile, but levels out for the remainder of its 3-mile length.

Getting There

Sierra Vista is about 70 miles southeast of Tucson just off AZ 90, 30 miles south of I-10. Leaving Fort Huachuca, continue straight ahead from the main gate and you will be on Fry Boulevard, Sierra Vista's main drag. The municipal airport has daily flights to Phoenix and other area cities via Mesa Airlines.

Only the fittest of the fit should tackle the Crest Trail, which climbs for 2 miles, then follows the crest of the Huachuca Mountains to Miller Peak, the highest point in the mountains.

To join a group for a hike, the Huachuca Hiking Club has regular, local hikes that begin Tues. at 7:30 A.M. from Nov. through Apr. and 7:00 A.M., May through Oct. They usually begin at the east side of the grocery store parking lot, at the southeast corner of Fry Blvd. and 7th Street in Sierra Vista. Write to the club at **P.O. Box 3555, Sierra Vista, 85636-3555; (520) 459-8959. Website: www.primenet.-com/~tomheld/hhc.html.**

Biking

In 1997 *Bicycling* magazine rated Sierra Vista one of "America's 10 Best Bike Towns," lauding it for its "endless mountain biking and lightly trafficked, beautiful road loops." The town's moderate elevation and year-around climate that allows riding any month of the year also were mentioned as pluses. To qualify for this honor, a city must have both on- and off-road rides suitable for many abilities.

Mountain Biking

Brown Canyon

This ride, above the tree line, is a single track through the tall pines with a little bit of everything, incorporating almost every type of riding. The 5-mile loop crosses a creek, then comes back to Ramsey Canyon. It takes one-half to one hour, depending on strength and ability, and is do-able by riders at all levels. Six miles south of Sierra Vista, off AZ 92, turn right onto Ramsey Canyon Road and proceed 1.5 miles to Brown Canyon, which is marked, and turn right.

San Pedro River

This easy, flat, 14-mile, one-way ride extends from Sierra Vista to the Mexican border, following the river along a riparian area filled with large cottonwoods. Stop and dangle your feet in the river, bring a picnic and enjoy the cool shade. It starts on AZ 90, which you follow to Hereford Road, then to AZ 92, which goes to the Mexican border.

Road Biking

One of the reasons that Sierra Vista is so cycling-friendly is that roads have wide shoulders, motorists are generally courteous, and so are other riders. These on-road routes require caution, but generally are not heavily trafficked.

Charleston Road to Tombstone

Named for the ghost town it passes through along the San Pedro River, this easy-to-moderate ride starts in Sierra Vista at the corner of Charleston Road and AZ 90 (there's a Wal-Mart on that corner), follows Charleston, and ends on Allen Street in Tombstone.

Bisbee Loop

This challenging loop is part of the annual La Vuelta de Bisbee Stage Race, the oldest continuous road race in the United States. It follows AZ 90 east to AZ 80 up over Mule Mountain, through the tunnel, then descends into Bisbee. It returns to Sierra Vista via AZ 92.

West Gate Ride

On Fort Huachuca Army Post, this up-and-downer keeps you shifting gears for 17 miles. A dozen trails on the post (see page 260 for how to get on the post) include Stampede Trails, mainly a horse trail, that begins across from Wren Arena, and Arena Loop that begins at the post cemetery and loops around Wren Arena with some steep, rocky climbs.

For more information on cycling in the Sierra Vista area, stop in at **Sun 'N Spokes Inc.** Friendly folks will provide you with a detailed trail map of Cochise County that has virtually all the county's best cycling trails on one map. **164 E. Fry Blvd.; (520) 458-0685.** Visit the website of the **Dawn to Dust Mountain Bike Club** at **www.primenet.com/~tomheld/ddtraiils.html.**

Golf

Retirees lament that there are just two golf courses in the immediate Sierra Vista area. Fortunately they're both good ones. **Pueblo del Sol Golf Course,** part of Sierra Vista's Country Club community, has Kentucky bluegrass fairways and bentgrass greens that wind through lovely homes with mountains all around. It's been around for 25 years, so has the comfortable look and feel of a truly mature course. The 6,600-yard, par 72 layout is PGA rated and open to the public. Off AZ 92 in Country Club Estates. **2770 Saint Andrews Dr.; (520) 378-6444.**

Mountain View Golf Course, on Fort Huachuca property, is open to civilians. Come through the fort's main gate for directions. **(520) 533-7092.**

Seeing and Doing

The Amerind Foundation

Between Willcox and Benson, 64 miles east of Tucson in rugged, rocky Texas Canyon, the foundation has a museum, art gallery and museum store in a series of clean-lined Spanish colonial revival buildings. Founded by archaeologist William Fulton in 1937, its name is a combination of the words "American" and "Indian," which describes its diverse contents. It houses one of the most respected privately maintained archaeological and ethnological collections in the country, including artifacts found during excavations in the Southwest and Mexico. Included are examples of crafts, weapons and household items used by various Indian cultures. The art gallery has paintings and sculptures fashioned around western themes. This serene, tranquil place is an au-

Pueblo del Sol Golf Course in Sierra Vista is surrounded by mounatins and upscale homes.

thoritative source for information on Native American culture and history. Open daily, 10 A.M.–4 P.M., Sept. to May; open Wed.–Sun., 10 A.M.–4 P.M., June to Aug. Closed major holidays. Small fee. Located one mile off I-10 at the Dragoon exit (318). **P.O. Box 400, Dragoon, 85609; (520) 586-3666.**

Parks and Preserves

San Pedro River Nature Conservancy Preserve

Forming the eastern edge of the town of Sierra Vista, this lovely area along the San Pedro River is so environmentally important that it has been designated one of the "Last Great Places" by the conservancy, one of just a dozen such places in the Western Hemisphere. The river flows north from Mexico, joining the Gila River near Winkelman. The area shelters more than three dozen species of amphibians and reptiles including the Gila monster. Almost 400 bird species, two-thirds of all North American species, including grey and red-tailed hawks, green kingfishers, coots and grebes have been observed on the river. The slender, rust-capped green-tailed towhee breeds in northern Arizona, then comes to the San Pedro for the winter. The river flows all year long, providing a reliable water supply for 80 species of mammals. Walnut, ash and huge

Near Sierra Vista, hikers explore the river, lined with cottonwoods, in the San Pedro Riparian Area.

cottonwoods, among the most water-dependent trees, line the river, providing bird and insect habitat. You may spot a giant bullfrog hiding among the bulrushes, or you may just hear the splash as it plops into the water, scattering the tiny mosquito fish that dart in the shallows. Bullfrogs were introduced for food as froglegs that are delicious delicacies, but the downside is that they are voracious and will eat anything. At one time beavers were plentiful along the river, but were trapped out decades ago. At the point where a small bridge crosses the San Pedro, a town named Charleston once flourished, in the 1880s when mines were working overtime. But when the mines died, so did Charleston, and today adobe walls and sheets of tin are all that remain. The area is 7 miles east of Sierra Vista just off AZ 90. **(520) 378-2640.**

Arizona Folklore Preserve

In addition to its hummingbirds and coatimundis, another treasure lies in Ramsey Canyon. The Arizona Folklore Preserve, part of the University of Arizona Sierra Vista Campus, is open now, with additional facilities scheduled for a mid-1999 completion date. The project is spearheaded by Dolan Ellis, Arizona's Official State Balladeer for more than three decades. His goal is to provide a place that protects the songs, legends, myths and stories of Arizona. The not-for-profit preserve has a 44-seat theater to showcase presentations and performances highlighting Arizona legends. In an audiovisual recording facility, visiting folk artists produce tapes and compact disks, offered for sale in the preserve's bookstore. Ellis, an original member of the New Christy Minstrels in the 1960s, earned a number of gold records and a Grammy during those years. Longtime Arizona residents and visitors to Scottsdale in the 1960s will remember Ellis as the talented proprietor of Dolan's, a folk music nightspot on the corner of Camelback and Scottsdale Roads in Scottsdale. Take AZ 92 south from Sierra Vista about 6 miles. Turn west on Ramsey Canyon Road for about 3 miles to the preserve. For more information and reservations contact the preserve. **44 Ramsey Canyon Rd., Hereford; (520) 378-6165. Website: www.dolanellis.com.**

Coronado National Memorial

Here, at the southernmost end of the gently folded Huachuca Mountains, a paved road winds through colorful oaks to the visitor center. Almost 5,000 acres commemorate the first major exploration of the American Southwest by Europeans. The memorial follows the route traveled by Coronado and his men in the 1500s in search of riches. White-tail deer, coatimundi, gray fox and javelina are frequently seen residents. From the visitor center you can drive to Montezuma Pass over a mostly dirt and gravel road for a spectacular view.

The visitor center has displays tracing the explorations of Don Francisco Vasquez de Coronado and the Spanish conquistadors in 1540. Authentic 450-year-old armor including a chain-mail helmet, dagger and spurs are displayed under glass. You're invited to touch replicas of these to see how Spanish soldiers must have felt under their protective weight. A small gallery of nature photographs shows the area's wildlife. Adjacent to the visitor center a 50-yard nature trail introduces some of the area's plants. There is no camping. The memorial is staffed daily, 8 A.M.–5 P.M. Located 5 miles

The Arizona Trail

As Route 66 bisects Arizona horizontally, providing a historic path for motorized vehicles, the Arizona Trail reaches from north to south in a swath designed for nonmotorized use. With the famous Appalachian Trail and the Colorado Trail as successful models, it was funded by a coalition of state and U.S. agencies. About 500 miles of the total 780 miles opened at the beginning of 1998, with a grand opening set for January 1, 2000. Its planners declare that it ties Old West with New West. It begins at the Coronado National Memorial and ends on the Utah line just north of Jacob Lake. It links special places that include the Huachuca Mountains, Saguaro National Monument, Mount Lemmon, the Superstition Mountains, the Mogollon Rim, Mazatzal Wilderness, Four Peaks, Walnut Canyon, San Francisco Peaks and the Grand Canyon. It spans seven mountain ranges and crosses seven life zones, from Sonoran Desert to Canadian Alpine. It is designed to accommodate hikers, backpackers, cross-country skiers, mountain bikers (outside of wilderness or other specially managed areas) and equestrians, and is off-limits to motorized vehicles. Besides scenic wonders, the trail provides access to old stagecoach routes, ghost towns, Native American ruins and trails used by early explorers. It is divided into 44 sections called passages that go from trailhead to trailhead. Maps and information are available for completed passages. Some portions may be extremely hot in summer, others can be covered with snow in winter. It is not yet possible to do the entire trail. But on New Year's Eve in the year 2000, a group of horseback riders will cut the ribbon at the Mexican border and begin a two- to three-month inaugural trek to Utah, covering the entire trail and opening it for use. For access points and more information contact **Arizona Trail Association, P.O. Box 36736, Phoenix, 85067; (602) 252-4794, fax (602) 952-1447. E-mail: aztrail@primenet.com. Website: www.primenet.com/~aztrail.**

south of the town of Hereford and 21 miles south of Sierra Vista off AZ 92. The turnoff to the memorial is clearly posted. **(520) 366-5515.**

Fort Huachuca

Established in 1877 as a cavalry post to safeguard settlers, the fort was the center of operations for thwarting the marauding Geronimo. Deactivated at the end of World War II and reactivated during the Korean conflict, it became part of Sierra Vista in 1972. It now is headquarters for the U.S. Army Information Systems Command, the Intelligence Center and School, the Electronic Proving Ground, the Department of Defense Joint Test Element of the Joint Tactical Command, the 11th Signal Brigade and the U.S. Army Communications Security Logistic Activity. Currently about 11,700 military and civilian employees work there. An additional 11,200 military family members live in Sierra Vista.

Museums

Fort Huachuca Museum and U.S. Army Intelligence Museum

On the post, these thoughtfully planned museums are outstanding places to get a sense of U.S. Army history on the Southwestern frontier. The main building, complete with creaky wood floors, at various times served as Bachelor Officers' Quarters, a chapel, home to the base chaplain and finally a museum in 1960. The series of rooms has displays on the last Indian scout who retired in 1947, and on types of horse- and mule-drawn wagons used for freight, as ambulances and for personnel

At Fort Huachuca near Sierra Vista, the statue called "The Eyes of the Army" commemorates the Indian scouts who became trusted guides.

transportation. The base's earliest residents, the Hohokam Indians, are represented with pre-Columbian artifacts.

Don't miss the area dedicated to the Buffalo Soldiers. At one time the post was home to all four famous black regiments, the Army's 24th and 25th Infantry and the 9th and 10th Cavalry. These men, former slaves, were commanded by white officers to help control the Indians, an irony that received little attention at the time but has been remarked on recently in books and motion pictures. Buffalo Soldiers got their name from the Plains Indians who thought their hair had an appearance similar to the curly buffalo.

Enter the post through the main gate at the corner of Fry Blvd. and Buffalo Soldier Trail. You will be asked for drivers license, registration and proof of insurance, then issued a temporary base pass and a map directing you to the museum area. The museum is open 9 A.M.–4 P.M. on weekdays, 1–4 P.M. on weekends. Closed Thanksgiving, Christmas and New Year's Day. **Fort Huachuca Museum and Gift Shop, (520) 458-4716.**

Scenic Drive

Most travelers heading south to Sierra Vista leave I-10 at AZ 90 and head on into town. But there's another route on AZ 83 that exits I-10 and continues south 29 miles to Sonoita. If you are coming from the other direction, you can stop at the Sierra Vista Chamber of Commerce and pick up (for $10) a driving tape called "How the West Was Fun" narrated by Rex Allen. It points out landmarks and fills you in on historical notes. Part of the drive, marked by colorful Scenic Route signs, crosses the Coronado National Forest, which covers most of southern Arizona in a patchwork of preserved areas and was named for the famous Spanish explorer who came through here in 1540. Unless you're accustomed to the Arizona notion of forest, you may wonder where the trees are. In this state a forest may consist of cactuses, scrub, low vegetation and just about any living thing that covers the surface of the earth. To the west are the Santa Rita mountains, stretching almost to the Mexican border; on the right are the Empire Mountains, behind which are the Whetstones. The mountains catch the moist air that creates rainfall, essential to keep the desert flourishing. The road passes through primitive areas where hunting, fishing and bird-watching are popular pastimes. The town of Sonoita was a railhead for the cattle industry in the 1920s and 1930s, an understandable position when you consider the open grasslands and prairie that you've just passed through. It now lies on the edge of Arizona's emerging wine industry around Elgin. From Sonoita you can hook up with AZ 82 and proceed east. The tape narrates your trip to Sierra Vista, Tombstone and Bisbee.

Where to Stay

In Sierra Vista, accommodations range from basic motels to multiroom resorts, many with housekeeping units. Some have birders' packages if you plan to stay several nights. The ones we mention here offer something other than a traditional motel stay.

Bed & Breakfasts

Ramsey Canyon Inn, Bed & Breakfast—$$$–$$$$

Adjacent to the Ramsey Canyon Preserve and leased by the Nature Conservancy for visitors to the preserve, this delightful inn has six rooms with private baths in a main building, and two one-bedroom housekeeping units that accommodate four and overlook Ramsey Creek. Duplex units appropriate for four (breakfast not included) are equipped with cooking utensils and staples (flour, sugar, coffee, spices) so you need to bring only fresh foods. **31 Ramsey Canyon Rd., Hereford, 85615; (520) 378-3010.**

Casa de San Pedro Bed & Breakfast—$$$

This brand-new territorial-style inn with hand-carved furniture from Mexico, ten guest rooms around a central courtyard and fountain creates a gracious oasis. Rooms have private baths, king or two double beds. It's adjacent to the southern end of the San Pedro Riparian Area so birding and hiking are just out the door. It includes full breakfast and is located 20 miles southeast of Sierra Vista. Take AZ 92 south to Palominas, and go north (left) onto Palominos Road. Continue 2 miles, turn east (right) onto Waters Road and proceed one mile to Yell Lane. **8933 S. Yell Ln., Hereford, 85615; (520) 366-1300. Website: www.theriver.com/casadesanpedro/.**

Hotels

Windemere—$$$

What takes this large, comfortable hotel out of the ordinary category is that the double room rate includes a happy hour with table service and a good spread of hors d'oeuvres, and a complete buffet breakfast with all kinds of hot entrees. Rooms have coffee makers. For total comfort in the center of Sierra Vista, this place can't be beat. **2047 S. Hwy. 92, Sierra Vista, 85635; (800) 825-4656 or (520) 459-5900.**

Camping and RV Parks

Sierra Vista Mobile Home Village

It has 30 spaces and full hookups in a mountain setting. Coyotes call at night, and it's not unusual to see javelina and quail near the park. Fairly upscale, with an indoor pool, spa, minigolf, a weight room, lending library, barber and beauty salon. On AZ 90, 2 miles south of Sierra Vista. **733 S. Deer Creek Ln., Sierra Vista, 85635; (520) 459-1690.**

Lakeview Campground

Centered around Parker Canyon Lake, one of the few sizeable bodies of water in the area, there are rest rooms and drinking water, but no hookups at its 64 sites. The lake gets a fair amount of day use by anglers pursuing channel catfish, sunfish, rainbow trout and largemouth bass. Open all year, at an elevation of 5,422 feet it's a cool respite from summer's heat in other parts of the state. Take AZ 83 (good gravel road) south from Sonoita about 25 miles to the lake.

Where to Eat

As you come into town there are any number of fast food restaurants and coffee shops along Fry Blvd. that cater particularly to dashboard diners. This proliferation has led locals to dub the street "French Fry Boulevard." There also are steak houses, Vietnamese, Chinese and Mexican restaurants, informal cafes and buffets.

The Grille at Pueblo del Sol Country Club—$$$–$$$$

This is our favorite place to eat in Sierra Vista. It has the best menu in town and overlooks a lovely golf course in an upscale setting that doesn't require getting dressed up. Clean jeans and a shirt are perfectly appropriate. Try to get there at sunset and watch the sky change colors behind the mountains. Truly gourmet fare is presented in the evening, while breakfast and lunch feature inventive, well-priced choices. Even in the desert, count on at least one flown-in fresh fish selection each evening. Located in Country Club Estates. **2770 Saint Andrews Dr., Sierra Vista; (520) 378-2476.**

Mesquite Tree—$$$

Entertainment comes from a number of sources in this friendly place. A model train chugs overhead as it travels around the perimeter of the ceiling, and the patio is filled with vintage stoves. During most months, meals are served outdoors to take advantage of the view of the Huachuca Mountains. Count on good steaks and ribs in large portions. Hikers often pop in after a day in the canyons, so you're assured that the atmosphere is casual and comfortable, and you can come as you are. **Hwy. 92 at Carr Canyon Rd., (520) 378-2758.**

Outside Inn—$$–$$$

We like the casual, personal atmosphere of this smaller inn. You have to watch for it on your left as you drive south on AZ 92 as it is set back a bit from the highway. The floor is covered with saltillo tile, and furnishings are attractive natural wood. Try the outstanding veggie club sandwich, and if you happen in on a Friday, don't miss the clam chowder. During appropriate weather, meals are served on an umbrella-shaded patio that doubles as an herb garden, providing fresh mint to complement iced tea. Open Mon.–Fri., 11 A.M.–1:30 P.M. and 5–9 P.M.; Sat., 5–9 P.M. **4907 S. Hwy. 92, Sierra Vista, 85635; (520) 378-4645.**

Services

Take time to visit the gallery at the **Sierra Vista Chamber of Commerce,** which has well-respected work by local artists. There is also a gift shop. Knowledgeable volunteers, cheerfully enthusiastic about their community, will patiently take as much time as you wish to answer questions. **21 E. Wilcox Dr., Sierra Vista, 85635; (800) 288-3861 or (520) 458-6940. Website: www.arizonaguide.com/sierravista. E-mail: chamber@c2i2.com.**

Arizona Hummingbirds

Their movements are so swift and precise they look computerized. Their colors are as brilliant as precious gems, displaying jewel-like iridescence that seems to come and go. They'll attack a bird many times their size and can beat their wings at more than 870 flutters per minute. They can fly sideways and backwards, hover in place and execute amazing aerobatic displays that are the envy of pilots everywhere.

During Victorian times hundreds of thousands of the tiny birds were killed and stuffed to adorn women's hats. Fortunately fashion's whims changed and legislation protected future hummingbirds from such devastating indignities.

Hummers, so called because of the sound produced by their wings, have a special job in nature. They aid bees, moths and bats in the process of pollination. While drawing nectar from blossoms, their heads and long slender bills become dusted with pollen that they brush on the next blossom they visit.

Of the 14 species (the state as a whole claims 17 species) of hummers found in Ramsey Canyon, five are common, and are the ones you will most likely be able to identify.

Blue-throated—Its broad tail, with big white patches, and overall larger size make this hummer identifiable, rather than its light blue throat, which sometimes is difficult to see.

Magnificent—Almost as large as the blue-throated, it has a bright green throat. From a distance it looks all black, but has white streaks around the eye.

Black-chinned—It has a white collar under a black throat that is fairly easy to identify. It is difficult to distinguish this little guy from a Costa's or a ruby-throated, common in the east.

Anna's—At about four inches long, it's medium-sized by hummer standards, and the only U.S. hummingbird with a red crown. Its metallic green back is absolutely dazzling when it catches the sun.

Costa's—Smaller than Anna's and not as common in Ramsey Canyon, it has a brilliant purple or amethyst throat and long side feathers. Its high whistling song sounds like a zinging bullet. An identifying behavior is soaring between flower clusters rather than zeroing in on a straight line.

Even if you never identify a single hummer, you'll be mesmerized by their collective beauty.

Tombstone

This little town has done a good job of reinventing itself. Part history, part fun, it has all the elements for a wholesome good time. Considered high desert and surrounded by mountains at an elevation of 4,600 feet, it is probably the most glamorized mining town in America. So-named because prospector Ed Schieffelin, upon being told he would find only his tombstone in the Apache-infested San Pedro Valley, named his first silver claim Tombstone. The surrounding hills, rich in silver ore, created a booming economy in the 1880s. The town became notorious for saloons, gambling houses and the famous Earp-Clanton shoot-out at the OK Corral. More than 10,000 folks called Tombstone home. But by 1886, collapsing silver prices and a huge increase in groundwater in the mines contributed to the town's decline. Yet it survived, pulling through the Depression and the indignity of Bisbee taking over as the county seat, earning the title "The Town Too Tough To Die." It built on its reputation to recreate itself as a Registered Historical Landmark that rapidly became a tourist attraction. Today its population includes about 1,400 hardy souls, some of whom are employed in nearby Sierra Vista and Fort Huachuca.

Much of the fun of Tombstone is simply exploring. Start by picking up a map and list of sites and sights at the visitor center at Fourth and Allen Streets, plan your route and set out. Stagecoaches and buckboards drawn by mules, Clydesdales and other steeds clatter through the streets providing local color and offering narrated tours.

Festivals and Events

Vigilante Days
early August

Western reenactments, fashion shows and a chili cook-off are part of this three-day event. Tombstone Vigilantes, identified by their six-sided badges, belong to an organization that promotes a western atmosphere locally and statewide. Proceeds from this event go to the Vigilantes Charity Fund. The fashion show features originals and copies of clothes worn in Tombstone from the early 1880s through 1915. Other events are a 10K run, a 2K fun run and street entertainment that goes on throughout the event.

Rendezvous of Gunfighters
late August

If you're into shooting and the craft of guns, you'll love this event that draws gunfighter groups from across the country to participate in demonstrations and activities. An authentic costume parade features great gunfighter gear as worn by the men who blasted their way through the West.

Seeing and Doing

Boot Hill

On AZ 80 as you enter Tombstone from the north, the famous final resting place covers a sunny little hill reached via a gift and curio shop. Used from 1879 to 1884 when it was considered full, more than 250 graves trace a rough and tumble history. "Here lies Lester Moore, Four slugs from a 44, No Les, No More," and "John Heath, taken from County Jail & lynched by Bisbee Mob in Tombstone Feb. 22, 1884," are among the eloquent epitaphs. Open daily, 7:30 A.M.–6 P.M. **(520) 457-3421.**

Tombstone Courthouse State Historic Park

The brick courthouse, Cochise County's first, was built in 1882 at a cost of nearly $50,000, a princely sum for a public building in those days. To assure that justice was swift, a gallows was built in the adjacent courtyard. When the county seat was moved to Bisbee in 1931, the courthouse had no real use, so it stood vacant until 1955 when restoration began. It opened as a state park in 1959 and now contains photos and memorabilia from Tombstone's salad days. Small fee. Open daily, 8 A.M.–5 P.M. **Corner of Third and Toughnut; (520) 457-2311.**

Bird Cage Theatre

A registered national monument, the theatre was more famous for "private performances" than for stage productions. The 14 "bird cage" crib compartments that hang from the ceiling were really small rooms used by ladies of the evening to entertain their clients. Opened in 1881, turmoil and rowdiness dominated the saloon and dance hall's existence. It was the site of more than a dozen gunfights, remnants of which are obvious in the bullet holes that riddle the walls and floor. An 1889 showbill advertises the "Human Fly," a troop of lady gymnasts, and a rosy, rotund Fatima smiles down from a painting onto a bar pierced with a massive bullet hole. The Birdcage closed in 1889 and through fortuitous far-sighted thinking, the owner boarded it up completely intact so when it was reopened in 1934 its contents were close to their original state. Although its heydays lasted just 8 years, from 1881 to 1889, the distant *New York Times* referred to it as the "wildest, wickedest night spot between Basin Street and the Barbary Coast." Open daily, 8 A.M.–6 P.M., for self-guided tours. **6th and Allen Sts.; (520) 457-3421.**

OK Corral, Tombstone's Historama, *Tombstone Epitaph*

You can visit the site of the famous Earp-Clanton gunfight, then get a reprint of the edition of the *Tombstone Epitaph* that reported the shootout. The *Epitaph* was started in 1880 and is still going strong, with the original presses still in place, if not in use. Located on the corner of 5th and Fremont. The Historama, a half-hour audiovisual presentation narrated by Vincent Price, details Tombstone's history. It's also a comfortable spot for a rest during a tour de Tombstone. The OK Corral and Historama are next to each other on Allen Street near the city park.

The Rose Tree Inn Museum

This delightful museum owes its existence to a Lady Banksia rose bush shoot brought from Scotland in 1885 and lovingly tended. Millions of white blossoms appear each year, the sheer size of the bush earning it a place in the *Guinness Book of World Records.* Rooms at the inn are furnished with 1880s antiques brought by a young bride and her husband who hoped to prosper from the rich silver mines. Open daily, 9 A.M.–5 P.M. **Located at Fourth and Toughnut.**

Where to Stay

You'll find a number of bed and breakfasts and a few smaller motels right in town. You'll have to go about a mile north on AZ 80 to the **Best Western Lookout Lodge** to find a conventional

Getting There

From Tucson you can take scenic route 83 through Sonoita and the Coronado National Forest, where overlooks will lure you to pause. The speediest route from Tucson is via I-10 to AZ 80, then south to Tombstone. Tombstone Municipal Airport is accessible to private aircraft.

large chain motel. Rates may go up at all Tombstone accommodations on special event weekends.

Bed & Breakfast Inns

Boarding House—$$$

Two side-by-side 1880s adobe houses surrounded by a picket fence have seven guest rooms decorated with antiques and collectibles, each with a private bath. It's about as close to what overnight digs were like in 1880s Tombstone as you'll get. There is also a small miner's cabin that's romantic and private. A full breakfast is served in the country kitchen. **P.O. Box 906, 108 N. 4th St., Tombstone, 85638; (520) 457-3716, fax (520) 457-3038.**

Marie's Bed and Breakfast—$$

Four rooms are furnished to Tombstone's glory days in a 1906 adobe home with original floors, windows and woodwork that shows generations of good care. A player piano provides entertainment, as does sittin' and rockin' on the front porch. Includes continental breakfast, or a voucher for breakfast next door at Don Teodoro's, at Fourth and Safford. **P.O. Box 744, Tombstone, 85638; (520) 457-3831.**

In Tombstone, the brick courthouse built in 1882 is now a state historic park. The hanging yard is handily situated in the courtyard next door.

Victoria's Bed and Breakfast—$$

Next to the courthouse, this 1880 stucco-adobe home is cottagelike and comfortable. Rooms have queen beds, cable TV and private baths. Near Toughnut and Third. **P.O. Box 37, Tombstone, 85638.**

RV Parks

Wells Fargo RV Park

Located right in the middle of Tombstone a block from the Courthouse and half a block from the OK Corral on AZ 80. What it lacks in charm it makes up for in convenience. You can walk to everything. Full hookups with cable TV, showers and laundry facilities. **P.O. Box 1076, Tombstone, 85638; (800) 269-8266 or (520) 457-3966, fax (520) 457-2307. Website: si-systems.com/wellsfargorv. E-mail: wellsfargorv@si-systems.com.**

Where to Eat

There are lots of fun, old-style places like **Big Nose Kate's 1880 Saloon,** the **Longhorn** and **Nellie Cashman's Restaurant.** Since you don't come to Tombstone for an epicurean experience it's no surprise that none particularly stands out, but most serve good, basic steak-and-potatoes fare.

Services

Tombstone Chamber of Commerce & Visitor Center, Box 995, 4th & Fremont, Tombstone, 85638; (520) 457-9317 or 457-3925, fax (520) 457-3929.

Public rest rooms are located in the city park at Third and Allen, and on Allen across 6th Street from the Bird Cage Theatre.

Bisbee

Drive along Arizona 80, through the Mule Pass Tunnel, around a curve, and you're in the walls of Mule Canyon that shelter Bisbee. The surrounding Mule Mountains, which put Bisbee at a 5,300-foot elevation, are the cradle for some of the richest copper ore ever taken from the state. The town has become a popular weekend destination for antiques and collectibles shoppers, where browsers search for local arts and crafts, and travelers seek a fun and funky getaway. Its streets, a warren of slim alleys, nooks and crannies filled with shops, invite exploration. Old miners' cottages and larger edifices that once were brothels climb up steep hillsides. Some have been converted to cafes and bed and breakfasts. Shops are eclectic and interesting, including a number purveying fine Bisbee turquoise in handmade silver settings.

The resident philosophy is a mix of humor and an acceptance of reality. "The only way to make a small fortune in Bisbee is to come with a large one," jokes one cafe owner. Or, as another resident puts it, change your notion of what constitutes a fortune.

Before the turn of the century an emerging electrical industry, spurred by Thomas Edison's invention in 1879 of the first widely marketed incandescent lamp, created an increased demand for the copper wire that conducted this new energy source. By 1880 the Copper Queen Mine was flourishing, and Bisbee was on its way to becoming a sophisticated urban center. It once was the largest city between San Francisco and St. Louis. The elegant Copper Queen Hotel, built in 1902, welcomed noted guests including Black Jack Pershing and young Teddy Roosevelt. By 1910 Bisbee's streets were lined with aristocratic Victorian mansions, miners' cabins and ornate buildings of commerce. For decades the town flourished, at one time boasting a population of close to 20,000. Miners, saloon girls, bankers, restaurant and hotel operators and families coexisted happily (except for some labor disputes between workers and mine owners) on a number of economic levels.

But inevitably the rich ore that fed the open pit and underground mines ran out, and in 1974 the huge Lavender Pit Mine was closed, marking the end of an era. The area is left with more than 2,000 miles of underground tunnels that channel through the surrounding mountains. Today the town laps at the edge of the open pit, its boundaries shaped by the huge hole, its personality cast in the rubble that came from the mine. Bisbee, named for Judge DeWitt Bisbee, an early stockholder, has a present population of about 4,000.

Festivals and Events

Brewery Gulch Daze
Labor Day Weekend

Held the Saturday and Sunday of this long weekend for more than a decade, the celebration includes a sale of photographic reproductions from the Bisbee Mining & Historical Museum, and craft vendors in Brewery Gulch selling pottery, jewelry, prints and posters by local artists. Other fun, small-town events are a pet parade, cake walk, waiter-waitress tray-run and waterball tournament. A highlight on Sunday is the chili cook-off, the products of which are offered to interested spectators for tasting. For more information call **(520) 432-5421.**

Seeing and Doing

Historical Site

Lavender Open Pit Mine

The consequences of this type of mining (380 million tons of ore and the soil that surrounds it were taken from the chasm) are eerie and unsettling. You can park and look into the gaping hole through a chain-link fence with viewing ports. The mine was named not for the vivid colors that paint its walls, but for an early mining official. Located one mile south of downtown Bisbee off US 80.

Mine Tour

Queen Mine Tours

The Copper Queen Mine is such an icon that in 1997 it became part of the Smithsonian Institution's Hall of Geology, chosen for the large collection of gems and minerals as well as the copper it has given up. A crystallized cave has been authentically replicated in the Smithsonian, complete with dim lights dangling from cables and the sounds of dripping water. You can see the real things in Bisbee on an organized tour. After outfitting guests with hard hats, slickers and 5-pound light packs, former miners take guests underground into a once-active copper mine, closed since 1943. You'll learn how drilling and blasting dislodged the copper ore from the rock, to be loaded into carts and brought to the surface for smelting. The 75-minute tour, in open cars with guests straddling padded seats, goes 1,800 feet into the 10-level mine. The train runs on level eight. The 8 x 6-foot tunnel is just big enough for the train. Chilly 47-degree mine temperatures and claustrophobia might deter a few. The tour is moderately priced and leaves the Queen Mine Building daily at 9 A.M., 10:30 A.M., noon, 2 P.M. and 3 P.M. Reservations suggested. Take the Hwy. 80 interchange entering Old Bisbee. **(520) 432-2071.**

Bisbee Self-Guided Walking Tour

Pick up a free map from the visitor center on Main Street and set off on your own. You'll see the Copper Queen Library built in 1907 and still in service with the post office on the ground floor, the 1904 Pythian Castle whose gas-lighted tower served as the city timepiece, and the Bisbee Convention Center built in 1939 by Del Webb. It's easy to spend an entire day wandering, with stops for cappuccino, lunch and a frosty brew. Take a look at the architecture. It seems that very little is newly built in Bisbee, and that almost every building was once something else.

Museums and Galleries

Bisbee Mining & Historical Museum

In the old Phelps Dodge General Office Building that dates to 1897, it's an excellent place to begin a walking tour. An award-winning exhibit includes a mural-sized photo, taken in 1908, that shows throngs of residents celebrating the arrival of the trolley. The town's population, about 9,000 then, peaked out at about 15,000 in 1910 when the mine was in full swing. Between 1881 and 1975 more than 7.7 billion pounds of copper were removed from the Bisbee district. The museum's second floor houses an outstanding cowboy retrospective, with recollective quotes and grainy black and white photos paying tribute to the most important things in a ranch hand's life—horses, chuck wagon food, roping and women. A separate room, Shattuck Memorial Archival Library, is filled with reference tomes. Bisbee's daily newspaper, dating back to 1902, is available on microfilm. Small fee. Open daily, 10 A.M.–4 P.M. **At the corner of Brewery and**

Howell Aves. in Copper Queen Plaza; (520) 432-7071.

Nightlife

Once an infamous street that roared with gunplay, rowdy saloons, sporting houses and alluring ladies of the evening, **Brewery Gulch** remains a toned-down version in a number of establishments.

Stock Exchange Bar has the original stock board from Bisbee's heyday. Located in the Muheim Block in a 1905 building that housed offices, a restaurant and a stock exchange. **15 Brewery Gulch; (520) 432-9924.**

St. Elmo Bar, just down the street from the Stock Exchange, is said to be the oldest continuously operating bar in Arizona. Bartenders cheerfully point out bullet holes from contentious days gone by. Take time to check out the multitude of memorabilia that decorates the walls. On weekends, blues groups usually perform. **36 Brewery Gulch; (520) 432-5578.**

Where to Stay

Winter months are high season here, when accommodations fill up quickly. Reservations, especially on weekends, are recommended. Bed and breakfast inns, restored and refurbished to varying degrees of comfort, are particularly interesting for what they used to be.

Hotels & Inns

OK Street Jailhouse Inn—$$$$

Built in 1904, this former jail was in use until 1915 when it became too small, then sat empty until 1989 when it was renovated. Where big-time crooks once languished, upstairs there is a bedroom with shower and whirlpool tub. It also has a full kitchen, living room and half bath. More of an apartment than an inn, it is very unjaillike now. Two large metal doors are the only reminders of its first incarnation. Accommodates four. **9 OK St., Bisbee, 85603; (520) 432-7435.**

Getting There

Bisbee is about a 190-mile drive from Phoenix, a 90-mile drive from Tucson, and is about 11 miles north of Arizona's border with the Mexican state of Sonora. From Tucson take I-10 to Benson, turn south on AZ 80 to Bisbee.

Copper Queen Hotel—$$$

In 1902, a decade before Arizona became a state, when Bisbee was the largest mining town in the world, the Copper Queen Mining Company (later Phelps Dodge Corporation) built the elegant Copper Queen Hotel. The four-story hostelry hosted mining executives, traveling men, territorial governors and well-heeled cowboys in an atmosphere of grace and elegance. Those that were not so flush went around the corner to Brewery Gulch where Muheim's Brewery and an array of shady ladies guaranteed an exciting evening. When the ore played out the Copper Queen went into a temporary decline, but because she was built to last, her architectural integrity allowed her to undergo restoration that returned her to her former level of luxury. The Queen's 45 rooms, updated to today's comfort level, retain their historic ambiance with period draperies and wallpaper as well as genuine antiques. **11 Howell St., P.O. Drawer CQ, Bisbee, 85603; (800) 247-5829 or (520) 432-2216.**

Bed & Breakfast Inns

School House Inn—$$$

Bisbee children once attended classes in this 1918 structure, but kids now must be 14 and older to spend the night. Rooms have names like The Principal's Office, private baths and great town views. A full breakfast is included. **818 Tombstone Canyon; (800) 537-4333 or (520) 432-2996.**

Main Street Inn—$$–$$$

In the middle of the historic district, this 1888 hotel was formerly called The Mann, and then became a boardinghouse for miners. Present furnishings give a Southwestern flavor, which works unexpectedly well with its bay windows. There is one suite with private bath, plus seven rooms with shared baths. Continental breakfast is served. **26 Main St. (P.O. Box 433), Bisbee, 85603; (800) 467-5237 or(520) 432-1202.**

Mile High Bed and Breakfast—$$$

This quiet inn is set on three tranquil country acres of cottonwoods and rose gardens. Guest suites, located away from the main house where breakfast is served, have private baths and separate sitting rooms. Kitchenettes are available. Bird-watching here is a treat. You can simply plunk down on the lawn, sit quietly and nature will come out to greet you. Full breakfasts include huevos Mexicana as well as more traditional dishes. One mile from downtown historic Bisbee at the west end of Tombstone Canyon. **901 Tombstone Canyon, Bisbee, 85603; (520) 432-4636, fax (520) 432-3395. E-mail: kga@primenet.com.**

RV Parks and Camping

Shady Dell RV Park & Campground

Not to be missed for its collection of vintage trailers that you can rent for an overnight or a whole season, we think this is one of Bisbee's biggest draws. It is a living museum of travel's bygone days and the era of the tin-can tourist. Stay in a 1957 El Rey, a 1954 Crown, a 1949 Airstream or even a tiny 1947 Kit, complete with pink plastic flamingos on the lawn. Magazine racks hold decades-old issues of *Arizona Highways,* aluminum coffeepots have the characteristic curvy designs of the 1950s, Art Deco radios play swing music, beds are covered with chenille spreads and nostalgic cookie jars are filled with treats. White picket fences surround the hitches. Dot's Diner (see Where to Eat), a gleaming stainless steel monument to the 1950s, opened recently. Nightly stays in a vintage trailer are around $$ with central bathrooms and showers nearby. The park also has full hookups with cable TV and laundry facilities for present-day RVers. Located just off the traffic circle. **1 Douglas Rd., P.O. Box 1432, Bisbee, 85603; (520) 432-3567 or (520) 432-4858.**

Queen Mine RV Park

This is possibly the only park in the world that practically hangs on the edge of an open pit mine, and the only RV park in historic downtown Bisbee. On the upper terrace of the Queen Mine Tour, it has amazing views that some consider beautiful and others perceive as silent admonishments of the devastation that man can do to the earth. From here you can walk to the historic district. Full hookups, showers, laundry and cable TV. **P.O. Box 488, Bisbee, 85603; (520) 432-5006.**

Where to Eat

There are many restaurants here, at least half of them in Old Bisbee, ranging from basic home cooking to what borders on haute cuisine. A stroll through city streets will lead you past half a dozen, so you can read menus then choose your eatery.

Copper Queen Hotel Dining Room and Saloon—$$$$

A sophisticated menu and impeccable continental service at first seem out of place in this little mining town. But as you settle into the mood created by lace curtains, candlelight and fresh flowers, the seared rare ahi seems appropriate. The chef's European background is evident in the very thin, crispy-crust pizza, suggested as an appetizer, and in menu offerings that include pheasant confit with Belgian endive salad and grilled mallard duck breast. If you feel that someone is looking over your shoulder, it could be the ghosts of diners past, who included governors, gamblers and presidents. In the Copper Queen Hotel. **11 Howell St.; (520) 432-2216.**

Cafe Roka—$$$

This trendy place, a one-time department store in the 1907 Costello building, still has the huge metal doors through which stock was received. The original tin ceilings and maple flooring keep it connected to the past. Its two most-requested dishes are white corn and pine nut risotto cakes with jalapeno cream sauce, and roasted half duck with cranberry, honey and merlot sauce. It is often fully booked during winter months, so make reservations early. Listed in *100 Best Restaurants in Arizona,* it has built a reputation for its contemporary Italian food. Open for dinner Wed.–Sat.; Jan. to May it is also open Tue. **35 Main St.; (520) 432-5153.**

Dot's Diner—$

This place is a mandatory stop. At the Shady Dell Trailer Park (see Where to Stay), this classic 1957 Deco-style eatery has all the great memories of diner days, including the food. The diner includes ten swiveling stools with magenta metal-flake tops, shiny stainless steel interior, a green malt machine and hand-lettered signs with features and specials unchanged from Sputnik days. Silver and red with glowing neon, the diner was transported from the Los Angeles area. Dot (yes, there really is a Dot) says she loves the steam table, grill, deep fryer and malt mixer. "If you come in you gotta be prepared to wait a bit for the fried chicken," she cautions, "'cause it's all done from scratch. But most folks don't mind. They just chat and wait their turn, 'cause the food's that good," she laughs. Burgers, shakes and fries plus local favorites like red beans and rice with corn bread are served on green three-compartment plates. The daily $1.99 Workman's Special may be a huge pork chop with rice, green beans and corn bread; meatloaf; chicken-fried steak or a hot roast-beef sandwich with sides of mashed potatoes and peas. Sweet potato pie is her specialty. Open 6:30 A.M.–2 P.M. for breakfast and lunch five days a week, and for breakfast on Sat. **1 Douglas Rd.; (520) 432-3567.**

Dot's Diner in Bisbee, a throwback to the 1950s, serves home-cookin' at its best.

Services

The **Bisbee Chamber of Commerce and Visitor Center** has its home in what once was the Miners & Merchants Bank, built in 1902. High tin ceilings and dark wood are reminders of a time of green eyeshades and hand-scribed ledgers. Remodeling created the present neoclassical facade and replaced the original imposing Ionic columns, with a result that is nonetheless impressive. If they're not too busy helping others, senior citizen volunteers will answer historic questions and reminisce about Bisbee's past. Some of the stories are not the kind you'll find in any book. **7 Main St.; Bisbee, 85603; (520) 432-5421, fax (520) 432-2597.**

Douglas and Agua Prieta

Douglas, a typical small mining town 118 miles southeast of Tucson with a population of about 14,820, is unlikely to grow since the Phelps Dodge company closed its smelter there in January 1987. During peak production, more than 375,000 tons of ore per day were brought north from Mexican mines to be processed in Douglas, where in 1902 two large-capacity smelters, the Calumet and Arizona and the Copper Queen, were built. The companies merged in 1931 and the Copper Queen was closed. Today all that remains of the smelters is a black slag pile about 1 mile west of town. Named after Dr. James Douglas, a Phelps Dodge executive at that time, the town attracts retirees who like its slow pace and low living cost. It also ships 125,000 head of beef cattle each year.

Douglas and Agua Prieta, its sister city across the border in Sonora, Mexico, have become economically bonded in the last few years because of the *maquiladoras,* factories that draw on Mexico's cheaper labor pool to assemble products made in the United States. Two dozen such businesses exist in Agua Prieta, employing more than 10,000 workers. The factories, and the ancillary services they generate, have swelled Agua Prieta's population to more than 100,000, most of them family folks who venture across the border by the thousands to shop. The state's largest Safeway is in Douglas.

Outdoor Activities

Golf

Douglas Golf and Social Club

Recently expanded to 18 holes, this public course has inexpensive greens fees and offers year-round play. The swimming pool and playground are for member use only. There is also a small RV park at the club with 28 full hookups. On N. Leslie Canyon Road .75 mile north of the AZ 80 junction. **P.O. Box 1220, Douglas, 85608; (520) 364-3722.**

Seeing and Doing

Gadsden Hotel

One of Douglas' biggest attractions is also its premier hostelry. Built in 1907 and rebuilt in 1929 after a devastating fire, the Gadsen Hotel ($$–$$$) is named for James Gadsden who negotiated the 1853 purchase of $10 million worth of land that later became Arizona and New Mexico. Once the hub of Douglas' cattle and mining interests, it thrived for years as a grand social and economic center. But as so many hotels do, it became the victim of neglect. In 1988 it was reprieved, and today the 150-room Gadsden retains its original grand staircase, Italian marble columns, manually operated elevator and 42-foot span of Tiffany murals depicting Sonoran Desert scenes. More than 200 cattle brands decorate the bar. A chip in the marble of the grand staircase supposedly was gouged by Pancho Villa's horse in 1911 when he rode the animal into the lobby during a clash between his forces and Mexican *federales.* Display cases on the balcony hold photos from the hotel's past. If you're looking for a ghost encounter, ask for room 333. A number of guests, and hotel housekeepers, have reported spirit sightings. The hotel, listed in the National Register of Historic Places, is undergoing a refurbishment. **1046 G Ave., Douglas, 85607; (520) 364-4481.**

Walking Tour

Historic Douglas

Pick up a map at the chamber of commerce and set out to enjoy representations of Sonoran row houses, Queen Anne cottages and period revivals that include gothic, Spanish, colonial and mission architecture. The town has 335 buildings listed in the National Historic Register dating to the period between 1905 and 1920 when copper mining was at its peak. You also can see the El Paso and Southwestern Depot (it later served Southern Pacific Passengers) built in 1913 and impossible to miss as you enter town heading south on Pan American Avenue. As many as eight trains stopped here daily during the 1920s, releasing passengers under the impressive Beaux Arts porticos. Rail passenger service ended in 1961. The station was rehabilitated using asset sharing money, Douglas's portion of cash and property seized from arrested drug lords, and in the spirit of meting out just deserts, the building now houses the Douglas Police Department. A few blocks south on the right the distinctive mission revival building once was the YMCA, built in 1906 with a bowling alley, basketball court and indoor pool. It gave up athletic purposes in 1958 and is now a recreational center under the Douglas Parks Dept. The elaborate classic revival Grand Theater on G Avenue, built around 1917 by the Lyric Amusement Company for $175,000, hosted luminaries including Edgar Bergen and Charlie McCarthy. It closed in 1962. Four churches on four corners in the same block in Church Square make it unique in the world. It is bounded by D and E Avenues and 10th and 11th Streets.

Slaughter Ranch Museum

Adjacent to the San Bernardino Wildlife Refuge, this 19th century cattle ranch has been restored to show what rural life was like at the turn of the century. The old adobe ranch house, ice house, wash house, granary and commissary built by John Slaughter, Texas Ranger and sheriff of Cochise County, are on the tour that is offered Wed.-Sun., 10 A.M.–3 P.M. Take 15th Street east out of Douglas and follow it (the name changes to Geronimo Trail) 15 miles to a large white gate marked with a "Z" that is the Slaughter family cattle brand. **P.O. Box 438, Douglas, 85608; (520) 558-2474.**

Farms and Orchards

0-6 Ranch

In Elfrida, north of Douglas, the Overfield family grows organic produce including grapes, peaches, pears, apples and cherries. "U-pick" is available if you bring your own containers. They also raise two breeds of sheep, one of which they slaughter for lamb and mutton. You can choose your "standing lamb," which means the fuzzy creature is still alive and gamboling, and the Overfields will make arrangements to have it slaughtered and packaged to your specifications. The ranch is located on US 191 midway between Douglas and Sunsites, about 30 miles south of Sunsites. Watch for the 0-6 Ranch, Registered Navajo-Churro Sheep sign on the right, just north of Elfrida. **(520) 642-9309.**

Shopping

Across the Mexican Border to Agua Prieta

Brief visits do not require visas or documentation, but you should carry personal identification. You can lock your car and leave it in the city-owned vacant lot on the Douglas side and walk across into Mexico. Within 20 minutes you can do an overview. Head south on Pan American Avenue (Avenue 3) and in the third block you'll find a saddle shop, **La Azteca Curio Store,** and a second curio shop around the corner on Calle 3. Turn right at Calle 6, a one-way eastbound street, right again at Avenue 4, and you'll be headed back to the border. For a pleasant lunch, try the modern, clean **La Hacienda Hotel** at the corner of Calle 1 (First Street) and Avenue 6, one block south and three blocks east of the border. There are fewer than half a dozen curio shops, but their merchandise is a notch above that offered in other border towns. Prices are equitable and bargaining is not a part of the experience.

Where to Eat

The Grand Cafe—$$-$$$

Gourmet magazine reviewed this unexpected little place for its top notch Mexican food and unusual ambiance. One of the owners is a Marilyn Monroe fan, attested to by hundreds of photos of the blond goddess papering the walls. The other owner, a native of the state of Chihuahua, is the chef responsible for the cafe's good reputation. Located across the street and one block north of the Gadsden. **1119 G Ave.; (520) 364-2344.**

Services

Douglas Chamber of Commerce/Visitor Center, 1125 Pan American Ave., Douglas 85607; (520) 364-2477, fax (520) 364-6535.

Douglas Municipal Airport served as an army air field during border troubles with Mexico from 1911 to 1935. The country's first international airport, it hosted Amelia Earhart and the pilots who flew the first regularly scheduled coast-to-coast airmail service in 1930. In 1928 the city of Douglas took over its operation. Scheduled commercial air service was discontinued a number of years ago, but private air traffic is welcome.

The Magic Circle of Cochise

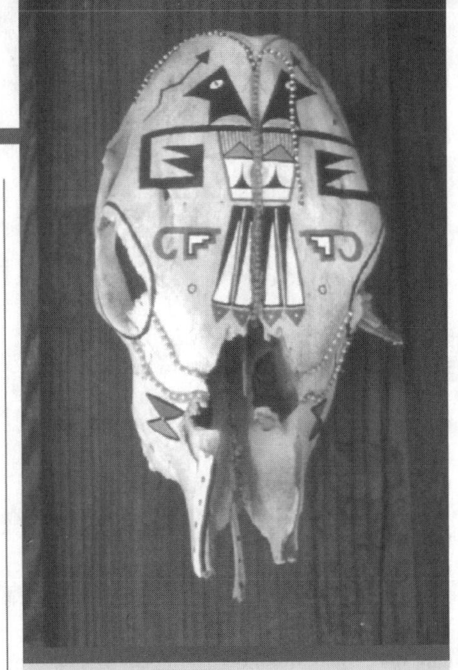

On a map it's easy to see this "magic circle," bounded by AZ 186 and 181 on the east and south, US 191 on the west, and Interstate 10 on the north, with the city of Willcox at its northernmost point. While the magic may be mostly in the mind of the beholder, its history contains a definite mystique. The Chiricahua Apaches supplemented their hunter-gatherer culture here as early as the 1500s with frequent raids against neighboring peoples. The county is named for their leader, Cochise, who besieged settlers and the military, but was widely respected for the commanding authority he held over his tribe. In 1872 Cochise made peace with the military for an exchange of land, a reservation where the Indian leader eventually died. As years went by, clashes often escalated because the government broke faith with the Indians and reappropriated reservation land. Geronimo took over where Cochise left off but to no avail. He surrendered in 1886 and the remaining Chiricahua were moved to forts in Oklahoma, Florida and Alabama. It closed another chapter on the existence of the American Indians in their longtime homeland.

Travelers usually begin the 100-mile route in Willcox, heading south 15 miles on AZ 186 to the ghost town of **Dos Cabezas.** From 1854 to 1859 it was the base for members of the commission that established the boundary between the United States and Mexico. Although all public buildings are closed, you can see remnants of the stage station built by the National Mail & Transportation Co. in 1884. You can still identify the old stage depot, one block off the main road, as well as the main street post office with its fading Dos Cabezas sign.

Seven miles farther on AZ 186 is the turn off to **Fort Bowie,** a National Historic Site in Apache Pass. Or, from the town of Bowie drive south 12 miles on the partly paved road that leads directly to Apache Pass. "Remember boys, nothing on God's earth must stop the United States mail," said John Butterfield to his drivers when he began his 24-day mail service from St. Louis to San Francisco in 1858. The stage used Apache Pass as a water stop, even though it took travelers and the mail through dangerous Indian territory. A brief halt to hostilities, which for two years had allowed stages to proceed unhindered, ended in 1861 with the Bascom Affair, in which an army officer wrongly accused Cochise of raiding stock from a local rancher. Cochise retaliated with more than two decades of attacks. Fort Bowie, established in 1862, consisted of tents surrounded by stone breastworks that were replaced six years later by adobe brick barracks, officers quarters, a hospital and other buildings. Despite the fort's growth to a total of 38 buildings, its isolation, crude quarters and constant threat of Indian attacks made it tough duty for early military men. Yet it played an essential role in the wars against the Chiricahua Apaches. It was abandoned in 1894. Today Apache Pass Road, a graded dirt thoroughfare that can be in various states of repair depending on the season, leads to the crumbling fort where a small National Park Service office is open daily, 8 A.M.–5 P.M., except Christmas. From there it is a moderate 3-mile round-trip hike into the ruins of the fort, a trek that can be beastly hot in summer. For more information call the **National Park Service** at **Fort Bowie** at **(520) 847-2500.**

Chiricahua National Monument

With a name that means Big Mountain to the Apaches, this area presents a wonderland of monumental spires, colossal columns and precariously balanced boulders that seem about to teeter at any moment. Geologists believe that 27 million years of violent volcanic activity created these mountains, which were then shaped and formed by the elements into the twisted formations that exist today. In 1924 President Coolidge established the area as a national monument, and footpaths were built in 1933.

The monument once was the stomping grounds of Cochise, Geronimo and his successor Massai, and the Chiricahua Apaches. They used its protective forest and rocks as a hideaway from which they launched attacks on encroaching settlers. Its position 50 miles north of Mexico, and the cool, damp forest, provide habitat for a number of unusual birds including elegant trogons and hepatic tanagers. Coatimundis, fox squirrels and peccaries live among the oaks, cypress, manzanita and juniper. Huge Ponderosa pine and Douglas fir are found at the high elevations.

For a super quick overview, take the scenic drive along Bonita Canyon Drive that winds 8 miles up to **Massai Point** and a sweeping view. Roadside pullouts allow access to exhibits and rock formations.

The best way to explore, however, is on foot, a pursuit made easy by the availability of detailed trail maps. Stop at the park visitor center first to see a well-produced video about the park and to pick up trail and topographical maps. All of the park, except the road, is designated as wilderness, so ask about regulations and be forewarned that nature can be unpredictable, weather may be harsh and altitudes that range from 5,400 at the visitor center to 7,010 feet near **Inspiration Point** can trigger unexpected physical reactions. Spring and fall are best times for amiable temperatures, although you can hike any time of year. It often snows in winter, but the white stuff melts quickly. Trails range from easy quarter-mile strolls to challenging treks of up to 9 miles. A park shuttle leaves the visitor center at 8:30 each morning and will drop you at trailheads at Sugar Loaf, Echo Canyon, Massai Point and "wherever you want to go that the shuttle can take you," say park rangers.

An easy hike of just over a mile from the visitor center leads to **Faraway Ranch** and the Stafford cabin. You also can take the entrance road, then walk in a quarter mile. Tour guides explain that this was a farm and cattle ranch in the early 1900s, and by the 1920s it had become a guest ranch where visitors came to ride horseback and explore the rocks. By moving slowly and quietly you are practically guaranteed great bird sightings. The raucous call and flash of blue may be a Mexican, or gray-breasted jay, one of the jays without a crest. The rufous-sided towhee, a robinlike bird with black back and rusty-red sides is also a common resident. The 7-mile **Heart of Rocks Trail** begins at Massai Point and appeals to the whimsical as it winds past formations called Punch and Judy, Duck on a Rock and others. A pleasant picnic area at Massai Point provides a posthike resting spot. **Echo Canyon Trail** is a photographer's dream, with massive rock columns, pillars and boulders along a 3.5-mile loop. To verify how the canyon got its name, just let out a whoop if you can bear to interrupt the stillness.

There are overnight campgrounds without hookups or showers in Bonita Canyon and a few RV parks scattered throughout the area. For campgrounds with amenities, head 36 miles north to Willcox. The monument is located 25 miles southwest of Fort Bowie and 70 miles north of Douglas at the junction of AZ 186 and 181. The park is open daily, 8 A.M.–5 P.M. daily. An extensive telephone menu answers many questions about the park. For more information call the **Chiricahua National Monument Visitor Center** at **(520) 824-3560.**

Cochise Stronghold

From the Chiricahua National Monument, continuing the circle south leads to the junction of AZ 181 and US 191 and heads back north again. To reach **Cochise Stronghold,** turn off US 191 onto Ironwood Road, a mile north of the small town of Sunsites, where there are restaurants and services. Don't let the paved road fool you. It turns to gravel in less than a mile, but is passable in a regular passenger car. As you head into the Dragoon Mountains the elevation gain is apparent as the vegetation changes from desert scrub to madrones, walnut and cypress. It's easy to see why Cochise chose this beautiful canyon, wooded with twisted oak and whispery cottonwood, for his hideaway. It is believed that his bones are still here. One account says his braves buried him in a deep crevasse along with his horse, dog and rifle. Another says that Cochise was buried on a verdant mesa, his grave site then ridden over by men on horseback so as to hide the burial site from desecration. It doesn't seem to matter which version is true, because many visitors say that among the boulders, manzanita and cottonwoods the spirit of Cochise is abundantly present.

On the temporal plane, keep an eye out for coatimundis, monkeylike creatures that forage for grubs, roots, lizards and fallen berries in the underbrush. You may also spot them in trees, swinging from branch to branch, usually in groups. Along the **Cochise Trail** is Cochise Spring, sometimes dry, but the area is green and pleasant. Just beyond is Half Moon Tank, built so local ranchers could water their cattle. In summer months it is usually alive with frogs among the cattails. At the Stronghold's apex is a boulder-strewn vantage point with spirits in every shadowy crevice and behind each looming pinnacle. It's easy to understand how the 40-mile view of the high desert floor below gave the resident Apaches an unsurpassed advantage over approaching enemies, whose dust clouds could be seen while they were still a day away. There is a Forest Service campground in the West Stronghold that has water during summer months. A number of dirt Forest Service roads in the Stronghold require four-wheel-drive vehicles. For information call the **National Forest Service** at **(520) 826-3593.**

Sunsites, Pearce, Courtland and Gleeson

Three little ghost towns in the Sulphur Springs Valley formed by the Dragoon Mountains can make an interesting side trip for serious aficionados of towns of the past. **Sunsites,** which was developed a number of years ago as a retirement destination 28 miles southwest of Willcox, is very much alive, with two golf courses and a community rec center. But half a mile south on US 191, a turnoff called Ghost Town Trail leads to **Pearce,** about 1 mile down the road. Miner and rancher James Pearce, whom it is believed to be named for, discovered gold near the town and inspired an influx of fortune hunters from nearby Tombstone. The Commonwealth Mine opened and findings were rich. But when water began to fill the shafts faster than was economically feasible to pump it out, the mine closed. Today the general store and church are closed. If you follow the sign that says "Pearce Cemetery" for half a mile, on your right you'll see the entrance and a large rock full of symmetrical holes, created by Commonwealth Mine workers testing their drills. Inside the cemetery are the graves of Abraham Lincoln's bodyguard and General Sherman's adjutant, as well as a number of Union and Confederate soldiers. For information contact **Pearce-Sunsites Chamber of Commerce, P.O. Box 308, 133 Frontage Rd., Pearce, 85625; (520) 826-3535.**

Courtland, named for miner Courtland Young and established in 1909, lies 10 miles south of Pearce on a graded dirt road. All that remains are a few concrete slabs with the exception of the sturdiest building, the jail. The leaching tanks of the Mame Mine are still standing. Follow the road south for another 10 miles and you'll come to **Gleeson,** named for an early rancher, where mines and buildings are posted as off-limits because their ramshackle condition makes them dangerous. But the crumbling adobe post office and the Gleeson Saloon remain picturesque in a quirky way. To make this little side trip coming from the south, turn left off US 191 a mile north of the town of Elfrida, at the sign that says Gleeson. The first 6 miles are paved, and Gleeson is 2 miles beyond the marked turnoff to Courtland. You'll have to backtrack those 2 miles to continue north to Courtland and Pearce.

Willcox Playa and Sandhill Cranes

From US 191 look toward the east to see a huge lake bed called **Willcox Playa** that's usually dry, but if it's been raining it may be filled with shallow water. The 60-square-mile, 37,000-acre lake bed was once the bottom of a Pleistocene sea. Visitors sometimes find unexploded shells and casings left over from World War II, when the Army used the surrounding area as a gunnery range. Despite its barren, desolate appearance, magnificent sandhill cranes have come here to winter for decades. Their numbers, once around 800, increased dramatically in the 1970s when agriculture took hold, providing bountiful grain and water for the wintering birds. Today an estimated 8,000 to 12,000 cranes come each year. In mid-July great thunderstorms drench the Playa, bringing to life the tiny crustaceans that have been dormant under the parched surface. The cranes feed on the little shrimps, which also attract avocets, sandpipers and killdeers. One of nature's largest birds, the greater sandhill crane can be as tall as 5 feet and weigh up to 12 pounds. Once widely hunted for their spectacular feathers, today they live protected in the Willcox area from mid-October until late February or early March. Their sheer numbers and sleek gray bodies with red-crowned heads provide one of nature's most dramatic spectacles.

Sky Islands

Rising above grassland and low scrub, high on the slopes of various mountains are what have become known as "sky islands." These ecosystems, where plant and animal life develop independently from the flora and fauna on lower slopes, are distinct mountaintop habitats. The arid distances between them, the "seas" that make them "islands," have allowed their biotic communities to evolve without outside influence. Darwin credited the same principle with creating the ecosystems on the isolated Galapagos Islands. There are sky islands in the Huachuca Mountains, the Chiricahuas and in the Santa Rita Mountains near Tucson. San Jose Peak, which pokes up from the Mexican desert, is a sky island. The greatest concentration of these lofty ecoregions lies in the area where Arizona, New Mexico and Mexico meet. To explore one of them, you ascend from the grasslands of the desert, pass through low oak woodlands and finally emerge among elegant pine and fir at the summit.

An easy-to-get-to sky island is accessible from the Chiricahua National Monument off AZ 186 and AZ 181 south of Willcox. It takes a high clearance vehicle and two or more hours. At the visitor center you can get a map (essential) that shows Pinery Canyon Road. By following it, and road signs, you will get to Onion Saddle and Rustler Park Campground, and eventually to the mountain village of Portal. From here you can head north to paved roads and I-10.

Willcox and Benson

Fast gaining favor with retirees for its inexpensive land and housing, mild high desert climate and rural lifestyle, Willcox, population 3,600, holds current as well as historic interest. First a base camp for construction workers building the railroad's southern route, it then became a central spot for local cattlemen to receive supplies and ship their steers. At one time it was known as the Cattle Capital of the nation. In the 1880s Army personnel stopped here on their way to Fort Grant and in fact it is named for General Orlando B. Willcox. The Southern Pacific Depot, the oldest original railroad station still standing on the line's southern route, was built in 1881. During the town's real boom years, from 1914 to 1920, ranchers ran cattle on huge spreads and nearby mines were rich. Today Willcox is a one-stoplight town, best known as an agricultural and ranching center. Where other areas have ecotourism, Willcox says it has agritourism because so many people come to do their own picking (see Seeing and Doing).

Benson, just down the road, now a quiet little town of about 4,000, was an 1880s railroad town on the Southern Pacific line, shipping supplies south to Bisbee and Douglas. Its position in the San Pedro Valley gave it an economic boost in the early 1900s as copper and silver were mined in the surrounding hills and shipped from Benson for smelting.

Festivals and Events

Wings over Willcox Sandhill Crane Celebration

mid-January

More than 1,200 visitors come from all over the world to witness the regal sandhill cranes overwintering in the Willcox Playa lake bed and surrounding fields. The three-day weekend event includes guided tours of best places to view, seminars on cranes and other wildlife, and an art auction and banquet. Birders stay overnight to get an early jump on the day, which means accommodations fill up quickly.

Rex Allen Days

first weekend in October

The famed cowboy star was born in Willcox in 1920 and stayed until lured to the West Coast by performing opportunities in music, movies and television. Over a 35-year span his Decca Records hit songs included "Crying in the Chapel" and "Streets of Laredo." Since 1951 Willcox has honored its famous son in an annual celebration that includes parades, rodeos, stage shows and dances. Allen presently lives on a ranch near Sonoita, 75 miles from Willcox, and is married to a member of a longtime area ranching family. He still actively performs.

Livestock Auctions

throughout the year

Every Thursday morning ranchers bring cattle to Willcox for auction. You'll see a gaggle of trucks and trailers just off I-10 half a mile north of Rex Allen Drive. You're welcome to watch while Herefords, Angus, Charolais and many other breeds go to the highest bidder. Don't raise your hand unless you want to go home with a heifer.

Seeing and Doing

Farms and Orchards

From the 4th of July through Halloween, peaking in early September, an amazing variety of produce comes from the fields around Willcox. Southeastern Arizona has the largest variety of direct-sales farms in the state, attracting more than 120,000 fruit and vegetable lovers who come to pick each season. Most of the farms, about 20 miles northwest and southwest of town, offer big plastic buckets, inform you of a few simple picking rules and you're on your own. When finished, you pay for your fruit and vegetables by weight. Available at varying times you'll find more than 40 varieties of squash, sweet corn, pears, apples, peaches, tomatoes, peas, green beans, hot chilies, bell peppers, okra, pumpkins, cucumbers and at least five varieties of apples. Wear old shoes that can get muddy, pick in cool morning hours, wear gloves and bring a cooler for toting your pickings home. The farms listed here all are off I-10 at Exit 340, left on Ft. Grant Road. Watch for signs for various farms. Because they're so close together, you can visit several in a day. It is essential that you call first to see what's available, because a late frost easily can wipe out all of a particular crop, and previous pickers may have depleted a field.

Jernigan Farm Produce & Orchards

Dozens of vegetable varieties are available including sweet corn, green and lima beans, melons, blackeye, crowder and other peas, yellow, green and red tomatoes, potatoes, onions, peppers, cucumbers, okra, squash and more. Open July to Oct., daylight to dark. **(520) 384-3123.**

Hunsdon Farms

Crops include sweet corn, summer squash, bell peppers and eggplant. A special watermelon festival is held Labor Day weekend and a pumpkin festival is held weekends in Oct. Open July to Oct. **(520) 384-4362 or (800) 351-6698.**

Briggs Orchard

Pears, peaches and apple varieties include Granny Smith, red and golden delicious, criterion, Jonathan, gala, fuji and winesap. Some are organically grown. Bring your own containers. **(520) 384-2539.**

Apple Annie's Orchard

The Holcomb family grows freestone peaches, Asian pears and many apple varieties. An onsite bakery has apple pies in dozens of varieties, dumplings, bread and other baked goods. **(520) 384-2084 or (800) 840-2084.**

Stout's Cider Mill

The fragrance of apples and spices is overwhelming as soon as you set foot into Stout's Cider Mill. Cider, of course, but also apple butter, apple nut cake and fabulous apple pie are their stock-in-trade. You can have a single warm slice to eat there, or take home a whole pie. In nearby orchards Stout's grows its own tart green Granny Smiths, as well as red delicious and other varieties for use in cider blends. Open daily, 8 A.M.–6 P.M. The tourist information center is next door. **1510 N. Circle 1 Rd., Willcox, 85643; (520) 384-3696, fax (520) 384-2007. Website: www.cidermill.com.**

Ostrich Farms

More than two dozen ranchers in the Willcox area have eschewed cattle to raise ostriches. Farmers of the long-legged birds say they're one of nature's most perfect creatures, as all parts can be used—feathers, hide and meat, which looks like beef and has a similar flavor, if a bit chewy. At Oak Tree Ostrich Ranch, owners Larry and Mary Beth Gately offer daily walking tours of their spread by appointment only. Visitors can take a look at their herd of about 400 adult birds, as well as 400 to 500 chicks in various stages of incubation and hatching. If you want to experience the life of an ostrich wrangler, the Gatelys invite you to bring your camper (they furnish water and power), then contribute 30 hours of your time per week. Arizona Ostrich Design has a small gift shop at the ranch, where you can purchase USDA ostrich meat (it's frozen, bring a cooler with ice), feathers, ostrich leather belts, wallets, ladies' shoes and handbags. To make an appointment for a tour, contact the ranch at **P.O. Box 727, Willcox, 85644-0727; (520) 384-0135, fax (520) 384-3788.**

Willcox Historic Walking Tour

Pick up a pamphlet at the chamber of commerce and start at the 1881 Schwertner House on Stewart Street. Merchants, cafes and saloons from days past line Railroad Avenue and Maley. The Railroad Dining Car/Sonora Express may or may not be operational as a restaurant, but it is interesting as an authentic Pullman car built for the Santa Fe Railroad.

Cochise Lake

A pond that holds overflow of treated effluent from the city sewage plant doesn't sound terribly attractive, but this small gray-water lake has become a magnet for birds. From November to February as many as 42 species have been identified in a single day. Located adjacent to the golf course off AZ 186 southeast of Willcox at the end of Rex Allen Jr. Drive.

Kartchner Caverns State Park

The newest of Arizona's state parks, this spectacular cave is destined to put the little city of Benson on the map. Steady progress is being made to construct trails and lighting systems in this delicate environment. The mandate to do the job right, without disrupting the natural process that created this spectacular cave, necessitated a $28.4 million total budget. A pair of spelunkers discovered the caverns in 1974. They kept it a secret until they were sure protective measures were in place. Arizona State Parks acquired it in 1988, naming it for the family on whose land the cave was discovered. It has two enormous 1,200- foot rooms connected by 2.75 miles of tunnel. Brilliant colors, the result of natural chemical reactions, plus stalactites, stalagmites and whimsical geologic formations have been created from hollowed-out limestone rock. The "live" cave will have more than a half mile of trails inside. Despite the surrounding desert heat the cave has a constant 68 degree temperature and a humidity of almost 100 percent. Services at the cave site include a 16,000-square-foot discovery center and a "cavatorium" that recreates the experience of going beneath the earth's surface. Hiking trails invite exploration of the surrounding area. Located off AZ 90, 8 miles south of Benson. Contact the Arizona State Parks at **(520) 586-4110** for more information.

San Pedro and Southwestern Railroad

This four-hour, 54-mile round-trip takes passengers on the Gray Hawk over tracks laid more than a hundred years ago. It departs from Benson and heads south into the Nature Conservancy's San Pedro River Preserve (see page 257) while experts on board provide narration. You'll learn about Wyatt Earp, Geronimo and the gunfight at the OK Corral, all of which figured prominently in area history. Sharp-eyed guests may glimpse white-tail and mule deer, javelinas and dozens of bird species. A lunch stop at the ghost town of Fairbank allows you time to purchase a barbeque lunch prepared by the nearby Ironhorse Guest Ranch. Bring your own lunch if you wish, but no alcohol. Snacks and drinks may be purchased on board. Fully enclosed cars are air conditioned and heated, but open-air cars can be chilly in winter. Trains depart Thu.-Sun. on a timetable that varies seasonally. **796 E. Country Club Dr., P.O. Box 1420, Benson, 85602; (520) 586-2266.**

Colossal Cave Mountain Park

The first thing you notice about this hollowed-out mountain is the cool 70-degree temperature, a welcome relief from summer surface highs that can top 100 degrees. This is a dry cave, which means there is no moving or dripping water inside to make the limestone formations "grow." It has a rich history of use dating to prehistoric times, but most recently has served as a hideout for gold-rustling outlaws. One of its areas is called Bandits Escape Route. In 1923, when the cave was first explored, visitors were roped to guides and to metal pins embedded in cavern walls. They wore miners' hats with built-in lights or carried lanterns. Since then lights and flagstone steps have been added, which makes exploration much easier, but still involves more than 350 steps, up and down, covering a height of six and a half stories. It's OK to take flash photos and videos inside. You can bring a picnic lunch to eat at tables in an adjacent wooded area. The cave is operated by the Pima County Parklands Foundation and is on the National Register of Historic Places. Moderate fee. Open mid-Mar. through mid-Sept., Mon.–Sat., 8 A.M.–6 P.M.; Sun. and holidays, 8 A.M.–7 P.M. Open from mid-Sept. to mid-Mar., Mon.–Sat., 9 A.M.–5 P.M.; Sun. and holidays, 9 A.M.–6 P.M. Located southeast of Tucson. From I-10 take Exit 279 and follow the signs for about 6 miles to the entrance and gift shop. **Vail, 85641 (mailing address); (520) 647-7275.**

Holy Trinity Monastery

St. David, a small town 7 miles south of Benson, is marked by a large white cross on the right as you're going south on AZ 80. This community of monks, sisters and laity follows the covenants of the Catholic Benedictine order. The 92-acre property has a 1.3 mile bird sanctuary trail bordering the San Pedro River that visitors (no pets) are welcome to stroll. Just remember it is a monastery, so no shorts or beachwear. A small RV park with some hookups offers sites on a first-come, first-served basis. The farm has goats, sheep, chickens and grazing cows. Beef from monastery cattle highlights the annual barbecue dinners held in spring and fall, drawing up to 12,000 people in a weekend. Browse the bookstore and gift shop, small art gallery and museum, with Civil War artifacts and an antique Bible collection. Benedict's Closet, their thrift shop, gives the word bargain real meaning. This tranquil place offers retreats of one day and longer. For more information contact the guest coordinator. **P.O. Box 298, Saint David, 85630; (520) 720-4016, fax (520) 720-4202.**

Getting There

Willcox is on I-10 about 200 miles southeast of Phoenix and 85 miles from Tucson. Use Exit #340 to get onto Rex Allen Drive and turn right onto Haskell, the town's main street. Benson is about 35 miles west of Willcox on I-10 (use exit 304) and 45 miles southeast of Tucson.

Museums

Rex Allen Arizona Cowboy Museum and Willcox Cowboy Hall of Fame

Early photos, elaborate costumes, and posters from some of the 19 movies he made for Republic Pictures between 1950 and 1954 trace this singing cowboy's career. The Cowboy Hall of Fame in the same building contrasts working cowboys with their celluloid counterparts. Across from the museum a larger-than-life Rex strums away in bronze permanence beside the grave of his horse, KoKo, whose epitaph says, "Belly high in the green grass of horse heaven." The museum occupies an 1890s adobe structure that was the Schley Saloon until 1919. Next door the 1935 art deco Willcox-Rex Theater shows weekend movies. Between the two structures a new little park has an open-air stage for concerts. Open daily, 10 A.M.–4 P.M. **155 N. Railroad Ave.; (520) 384-4583.**

Museum of the Southwest

The Willcox Chamber of Commerce and Agriculture's Visitor Center contains historically significant artifacts from Native Americans and cavalry, minerals and rocks of the area and maps tracing the route of the Butterfield Stage Line that once stopped nearby. A beautifully crafted bronze of Cochise is at the entrance. This is a good place to pick up free brochures about the area. Outdoors in Heritage Park there are a mine display and nature trail. Free admission. **1500 N. Circle 1 Rd.; (520) 384-2272.**

Where to Stay

Many basic chain motels cluster around the Willcox exit off I-10. By far the more interesting accommodations, the ranches some miles out of town, get you close to nature and give a sense of the area's history.

Heritage Manor Bed & Breakfast—$$$

Set in quiet countryside surrounded by green agricultural fields, it looks like a lovely transplant from the South or Midwest. The white frame inn with second-story dormers, shuttered windows and wide front porch is warm and welcoming. It has one room with private bath and two with shared bath. Call for availabilities and information. Located 10 miles from Willcox. From I-10 exit at Fort Grant Road and follow it past the Country General Store to the inn. **HCR 1, Box 93, Willcox, 85643; (520) 384-2953.**

Muleshoe Ranch/The Nature Conservancy—$$$

Owned and managed by The Nature Conservancy in conjunction with the U.S. Forest Service and the Bureau of Land Management, come here when you really want to get away from civilization. The quiet, secluded area encompasses 48,120 acres of rugged beauty on a Nature Conservancy preserve 30 miles northwest of Willcox in the foothills of the Galiuro Mountains. The preserve has hiking trails and excellent bird-watching. In January and February you're likely to see troops of coatimundis in the canyons, and in July and August whitetail deer are plentiful in the mesquite bosks. Hummingbirds practically storm the feeders set out at headquarters.

Within this vast back country area Pride Ranch lies about 6 miles from Conservancy headquarters and may be rented overnight. Jackson Cabin, about 14 miles away, can be used for basic shelter, but there are no furnishings, water or even much of a roof. Both are accessible with a four-wheel-drive vehicle. Camp overnight or stay in refurbished ranch buildings and casitas with bathrooms, kitchens or kitchenettes, some with fireplaces. One of the bonuses, available to overnight guests only, is use of the natural hot springs. Reservations are a must. From Willcox, follow Bisbee Avenue past the high school to Airport Road. Turn right and proceed 15 miles, bearing right at the fork just past mailboxes. Follow the road another 14 miles to the Muleshoe Ranch Headquarters at the end of the road. The headquarters is staffed Thu.–Mon., 9 A.M.–4 P.M. **RR#1, Box 1542, Willcox, 85643; (520) 586-7072.**

Grapevine Canyon Ranch—$$$$

About 35 miles southwest of Willcox, this popular ranch, niched in a secluded canyon, has an exceptional number of options for all riding abilities. Adventure rides take guests to abandoned mining camps, Apache lookout points, ghost towns and burial grounds. Special weeks each month are devoted to learning the techniques of cutting, how to be a cowboy and how to buy and enjoy a horse. During history week, guests ride to the Cochise Stronghold, along the Butterfield Stage Trail and to Apache hideouts. Rates include three meals a day, all horseback riding, and accommodations in casitas or large cabins. From I-10 near Willcox, take the Dragoon Road exit (318) that dead ends on US 191 south. Turn south to Sunsites and at the south end of Sunsites, take Treasure Road west and follow ranch signs. **P.O. Box 302, Pearce, 85625; (520) 826-3185 or (800) 245-9202, fax (520) 826-3636. Website: www.badude.com. E-mail: egrapevine@earthlink.net.**

Sunglow Guest Ranch—$$$–$$$$

Fifteen miles south of Chiricahua National Monument, with peace and quiet guaranteed by the surrounding national forest and wilderness, Sunglow provides an almost spiritual getaway. Owners Bob and Sue Paral say it's so quiet you can hear the stars twinkle. The ranch was once a town built to serve the sawmill teamsters. Although it has everything you'd expect in a ranch—trail rides, hayrides, bird-watching, hiking—there is a sense of remoteness. Spanish mission-style casitas have fireplaces, courtyards and kitchens so you can cook for yourself, or let the dining room know and they'll do the cooking. You also can stay in a rustic tepee on the shores of Sunglow Lake. Hiking, horse rentals and fishing are available on the property. They'll arrange a ranch-to-ranch ride that takes you to Price Canyon Ranch, a working cattle ranch a day's ride away. Take AZ 186 south out of Willcox to AZ 181, then to Turkey Creek Road. Call for availabilities. **HC 1, Box 385, Pearce, 85625; (520) 824-3334.**

Skywatcher's Inn, The Arizona Astronomy and Nature Retreat—$$$

One of the state's neatest, most interesting and unique bed and breakfast inns and part of Vega-Bray Observatory, the inn comes fully equipped with seven major telescopes, ranging from 6 to 20 inches. One is completely computerized. You can arrange an astronomy session with an amateur astronomer or professor and be almost guaranteed of seeing one major planet, and certainly the Milky Way. Because it is 47 miles from a major city, light pollution is negligible. There are two main bedrooms, each with private bath, and a smaller bedroom and bath in the adjacent observatory. A living room and kitchenette are communal. Even if heavenly bodies aren't your thing, the observatory's location, on top of a small hill overlooking the San Pedro River Valley, is filled with birds, wildlife and hiking trails. Located 47 miles from Tucson, 4 miles south of Benson. Take Pomerene (Exit 306) off I-10, and go east on Frontage Road to Airport Road. Turn south for 1.9 miles to Serenity Ranch, go past the lake on your right, to the Inn. **420 S. Essex Ln., Tucson, 85711; (520) 745-2390 (phone and fax).** From Benson call **(520) 586-7906.**

Cochise Hotel—$$

Opened in 1899, this wood-frame inn was built at the junction of the Southern Pacific and old Arizona Eastern Railways. Trains still rumble by, lending validity to the old Wells Fargo freight office still filled with antiques of the era. Rooms are small, sunny and pleasant with touches like patchwork quilts, oak dressers, brass headboards and lace curtains. All rooms have private updated baths. Located 5 miles south of I-10 on US 191. Watch for Cochise signs. **P.O. Box 27, Cochise, 85606; (520) 384-4314.**

RV Parks

Many of the RV parks near Willcox are not much more than parking lots. There is a better selection 35 miles west in Benson. Here are a couple of good ones, though.

Magic Circle RV Park

Full hookups, tent area, shower and laundry facilities, swimming pool, shade trees and picnic tables under redwood shelters. You can see it from the freeway. **I-10, Exit 340; (520) 384-3212 or (800) 333-4720.**

LifeStyle RV Resort

Full hookups plus fitness center, indoor pool and spa, laundry facilities. On-site restaurant and pizza parlor. In town. **622 N. Haskell Ave.; (520) 384-3303.**

Where to Eat

McDonald's, Burger King and Pizza Hut are here, plus a number of homestyle cafes and places with good Mexican food, but nothing's a particular standout.

Regal Cafe—$-$$

In this comfortable biscuits-and-gravy sort of place, retirees and ranchers congregate over coffee in a homey atmosphere. Everyone seems to know everyone else. Expect a minute of silence when you walk in as the regulars try to figure out who you are. **301 N. Haskell Ave.; (520) 384-4780.**

Solarium Dining Room—$$

At the Best Western, this pleasant restaurant is probably the closest thing to fine dining in Willcox. Each night the chef whips up something special, like stir-fry, in addition to standard seafood and steaks. **1100 W. Rex Allen Dr.; (520) 384-3556.**

Kokopelli Winery, the largest producer and seller of wines in the state, is well represented on the Solarium's wine list. Among the best are the Pinot Noir that recently received national recognition. The Muscat de Canelli is a wonderful partner for dessert or cheese. The winery has tastings on Saturday and Sunday from noon to 5 P.M. Take Exit 340 (Rex Allen Drive) off I-10 and proceed south less than a mile to Haskell. Turn left and follow Haskell 1.5 miles to the winery. For information call **(520) 384- 5205.**

Services

Willcox Chamber of Commerce has a good selection of pamphlets and books on the area and exceptionally friendly personell. The Museum of the Southwest is in the same building, and Stout's Cider Mill is just across the parking lot. **1500 N. Circle 1 Rd., Willcox, 85643; (520) 384-2272 or (800) 200-2272, fax (520) 384-0293.**

Benson Chamber of Commerce, 363 W. 4th St., P.O. Box 2255, Benson, 85602; (520) 586-2842.

A comfortable rest area sits among picturesque boulders in Texas Canyon on I-10 between Willcox and Benson, just past "The Thing" (you'll have to see it for yourself; admission 75 cents).

Safford

The largest city in Graham County and also the county seat, it was founded in 1874 by four farmers looking for arable land near a water source, which they found in the Gila River. It is named for Anson B. K. Safford, territorial governor at the time. Safford was influenced by Mormon settlement early on, as missionaries obeyed the edict of leader Joseph Smith to colonize the west. Agriculture is Safford's *raison d'etre* today, with 22,000 of its 35,000 irrigated acres planted in cotton. In the town of Pima just west of Thatcher (named for Mormon apostle Moses Thatcher), Glenbar Gin processes more than 20,000 bales annually. You have only to drive a few miles in any direction to see flourishing cotton fields and, depending on season, tomatoes, grain crops, apples and pecans. The Graham County Courthouse, an imposing brick building with white Greek columns at the end of Main Street, built in 1916 and still in use today, tells you that this is a town with history. Along roads and highways near Safford, signs warning not to pick up hitchhikers reflect the presence of three correctional facilities in the area. Arizona State Prison Complex currently houses about 715 minimum security inmates and 40 medium security inmates. Fort Grant, at varying times a cavalry post, army post and juvenile industrial school, now is a minimum security state prison. "Club Fed," the Federal Correctional Institution is the building with circular razor wire ringing it that you pass on your way up Mount Graham. It houses about 700 low security prisoners.

Outdoor Activities

Rockhounding

Near the south end of the scenic byway (see below) the Black Hills Rockhound Area regularly yields fire agates. Formed by volcanic activity, the agates are a variety of silica in which mineral impurities have created vibrant colors. You can bring a pick and shovel and dig, as most agates are found within two feet of the surface, but ardent rockhounders say you'll be just as successful scouring the surface near washes and other areas where the soil has been disturbed. Primitive camping is allowed. Located about 20 miles east of Safford. Proceed east for 10 miles on US 70, then follow US 191 toward Clifton to Milepost 141. Just beyond there is an entry sign on the left. Follow the dirt road for 2 miles to the rockhound area. For more information contact the **Bureau of Land Management, 711 14th Ave., Safford, 85546; (520) 348-4400.**

Seeing and Doing

Mount Graham International Observatory

Safford is a favored region for astronomy because big-city light pollution is far distant, air stability is unaffected by thermals from city

Discovery Park in Safford offers glimpses into other universes with its interactive galleries.

heat and skies are consistently clear. At the 10,720-foot summit of Mount Graham, considered a sky island (see page 278), you may arrange a tour to the Vatican Advanced Technology Telescope and the Heinrich Hertz Submillimeter Telescope during summer months. You are not allowed to go to the observatory on your own. You must book a tour and travel in the observatory van. Once there, you can see how the telescopes work and learn a bit about the projects under way, which currently include galactic and extragalactic research. Not much planetary work is being conducted. No one "looks through a telescope" anymore because video screens provide the viewing area. Everything is controlled by computer. Tours are conducted approximately Apr. 15 to Nov. 1, ceasing when winter ice and snow make the road unsafe for van travel. The last unpaved 9 miles to the observatory creates such tricky driving conditions in freezing weather that observatory workers who must travel it nicknamed it the "luge run." For information on observatory tours, arranged through **Discovery Park** (see below) call **(520) 428-6260.**

Discovery Park

This work in progress offers plenty to see and do even before its scheduled completion at the end of 1999. Interactive galleries let you measure radio emissions from the sun with the 0.5-meter radio telescope, and hear sounds from distant galaxies. An especially well-planned Origins Room displays varying cultural theories on how the world began. On clear nights you can look at the planets through a 20-inch reflecting telescope. Jupiter and its moons and ringed Saturn are reliably visible. The Shuttle Polaris, a full-motion flight simulator, blasts you at warp speed to the surface of the moon, then to planets beyond during a 13-minute journey. On the park's 200-plus acres, 65 of which are wildlife habitat, a small train chugs along a 2-mile track through a riparian area, past ponds and a marsh, and eventually will circle a planned 1860s ranch house. A self-guided nature walk helps you identify common desert plants including variations of prickly pear, night blooming cereus, yucca, ocotillo and desert lavender. The park is open Wed.–Sat., 3–9 P.M. From US 70 in Safford, turn south onto 20th Avenue and follow it to the park. Or, from US 191 just south of Safford, turn west onto Discovery Park Blvd. and follow it to 20th Ave. Turn south on 20th Ave. to the park. Signs clearly mark the way. **1651 Discovery Park Blvd., Safford, 85546; (520) 428-6260, fax (520) 428-8081. Website: www.discoverypark.com or discovery@discoverypark.com.**

Pinaleno Mountains/ Swift Trail

Take AZ 366, the road that goes up to the observatory area and the top of Mount Graham, for an experience in ecology. As you follow its switchbacks and twists you pass through five life zones in 30 miles. The scenery from so high up is nothing short of amazing. Though paved and well-maintained, the road is not recommended for overlong trailers and motorhomes. If there is any chance at all of snow, be sure to check the number below before setting out. The road was built in the 1930s along the route of a turn-of-the century logging road, and paved in the 1960s. A number of campgrounds including Hospital Flat, for tents only, are along the way, as are private cabins used mostly during summer months. The mountain to the right is Heliograph Peak, where in 1886 Col. William A. Glassford constructed a heliograph station for the US Army Signal Corps that was used for troop communication. One of a system of such mountaintop stations across southern Arizona and southwestern New Mexico, it functioned with a system of movable mirrors that reflected sunlight. Called the Swift Trail for T. T. Swift, the first supervisor of the Coronado National Forest, it is open the year around except when closed for snow removal. This road eventually leads to the other side of the mountain and Riggs Lake, a popular summer vacation site. Pick up a guide, which includes mileage for points of interest along the drive, from the Safford Ranger District Office on the third floor of the **Post Office Building** at **504 Fifth Ave., 3rd Floor, Safford, 85546; P.O. Box 709, Safford 85548-0709 (mailing address); (520) 428-4150.**

Roper Lake State Park

This attractive park surrounds 30-acre Roper Lake, which is large enough to attract a good variety of water and shore birds, and other avian species that depend on water. Within about one hundred feet of each other you may see a grebe on the lake diving for dinner, a spindly-legged killdeer searching the shore, and in the brush around the lake, a strutting roadrunner with a trophy lizard. Picnic tables are thoughtfully placed for privacy. Some are within feet of the water, so you can settle in for the day, get in some fishing (the lake is stocked with rainbow trout, bass, crappie and a few other varieties), and take short local hikes. The Hacienda Campground has 20 hookup sites with electric and water. At Cottonwood Campground there are 26 campsites with water and a ramada at each site. Lesser developed sites at Gila Campground are in a more natural setting. Hacienda and Cottonwood have showers, rest rooms and vending machines. Very few local lakes offer good swimming, but here you'll find a beach and large ramada in the Island area. About one mile away, the park's Dankworth Ponds section has a smaller lake with picnic ramadas. The park is located 6 miles south of Safford, one-half mile off US 191. **Rte. 2, Box 712, Safford, 85546; (520) 428-6760.**

Scenic Drive

As part of the Bureau of Land Management Backcountry Byway Program, the old Safford-Clifton road was graded a few years ago to make its bumpy 21 miles passable by many conventional cars, although high-clearance and four-wheel-drive vehicles will do it in more comfort. It also is popular with mountain bikers and hikers. Once a wagon trail through the canyons, it was built by prisoners incarcerated nearby. You can see the grave of one who tried to escape near the kiosk at the trail's south end. The rugged Black Hills, formed by volcanic uplifting more than 20 million years ago, today provide habitat for deer, javelina, eagles, red-tailed hawks, deer and other creatures. The road passes through five working ranches that lease 65,000 BLM acres for grazing and support close to 700 head of cattle. A number of scenic overlooks create sweeping views of the Gila River on its way to San Carlos Lake. At Milepost 7, the Black Hills Overlook, you can see Mount Graham in the distance, the Gila Mountains to the west, and to the north the enormous Phelps Dodge open-pit copper mine in Morenci. The picturesque old rock bridge, built by prisoners in 1918, spans the Gila River and is still structurally sound. This is a popular put-in point for rafters and kayakers, and for picnickers who seek the cool shade near the river. There are kiosks with maps and current road information at either end of the trail, but no services on the road so be sure to bring water. A cell phone works in most places. An audiocassette with cowboy narrative is available at the Graham County Chamber of Commerce in Safford. For more information contact the **BLM Safford Field Office** at **(520) 348-4400. Website: azwww.blm.gov.**

Gila Box Riparian Area

Named for a canyon, this specially designated area includes 15 miles of Bonita Creek and 23 miles of the Gila River, popular spots for birdwatching, hiking and picnicking. Hiking here is excellent from October to mid-December when fall colors are magnificent and the weather is comfortable. You can get to cliff dwellings and historic homesteads from graded dirt roads with a high clearance vehicle. Major access points are usually passable in a passenger car. From Safford take 8th Avenue north to the airport and continue 2 miles beyond the airport to Sanchez Road. Turn left (pavement ends) and follow Bonita Creek signs to the creek and river. You can also enter the area from the north, from US 191 at Milepost 160, 4 miles south of Clifton. The dirt road is marked with a large, colorful Black Hills Backcountry Byway sign. Follow it 4 miles to the Old Safford Bridge and you'll be in the Riparian Area. For information contact the **BLM, 711 14th Ave., Safford, 85546; (520) 348-4400.**

Eastern Arizona Museum and Historical Society

This interesting museum building, once the Bank of Pima, was constructed in 1916 and still has the original ornate tin ceiling. It houses collections of Southwest artifacts found locally, as well as memorabilia donated by local residents. A large barbed wire collection and a number of old quilts are among the highlights. The adjacent "pioneer rooms," housed in the old tufa stone Cliff Hall built in 1882, include a sitting room, bedroom, music room and kitchen of the past. Open Wed.–Fri., 2–4 P.M.; Sat., 1–4 P.M. Located on the northwest corner of Main and Center (US 70) in the town of Pima. **P.O. Box 274, Pima, 85543.**

Where to Stay

Olney House Bed & Breakfast—$$$

On the National Register of Historic Places, this 1890 mansion, built in the Western Colonial Revival style, once belonged to George A. Olney, the sheriff of Graham County. Today it offers rooms and cottages in a quiet residential area. There are three rooms with shared bath in the main house, behind which two cottages with kitchens and cable TV open onto a rose garden. **1104 Central Ave., Safford, 85546; (800) 814-5118 or (520) 428-5118, fax (520) 428-2299. Website: www.zekes.com/olney/. E-mail: olney@zekes.com.**

Services

The **Graham County Chamber of Commerce** offers a good assortment of literature, as well as displays that explain the county's agricultural personality. Dioramas with mammoths and condors show the area in ancient times. There are clean public rest rooms next door. **1111 Thatcher Blvd., Safford, 85546; (520) 428-2511, fax (520) 428-0744.**

Clifton and Morenci

Northeast of Safford, in Greenlee County, these are mining towns in every sense of the word. Depending on whom you believe, Clifton was named either for the cliffs surrounding the site where copper was discovered along Chase Creek, or for Henry Clifton, an early prospector. Morenci was named after a town about 75 miles from Detroit, Michigan, which had ties to the Detroit Copper Mining Company that later became one of the entities making up Phelps Dodge. Though proclaimed the official birthplace of Geronimo, accuracy is questionable.

Currently Clifton is restoring historic Chase Creek Street, a narrow byway that once was the town's rough and tumble main drag. Highlights include the Catholic Church built of local rocks in 1917, and the 1913 Eagle Hall that currently houses the Greenlee County Historical Society. You can pick up a walking tour brochure at the Greenlee County Chamber of Commerce located in the Clifton Passenger Railroad Station, built in 1913, where there are public rest rooms. The chamber is open Mon.–Fri., 9 A.M.–5 P.M. **P.O. Box 1237, Clifton, 85533; (520) 865-3313.**

Seeing and Doing

Morenci Mine

Owned by Phelps Dodge, this enormous amphitheaterlike open-pit relinquishes more copper than any other mine in North America. About 2 miles long and nearly as wide, it covers 32,000 acres and is about one-half mile deep. The town of Morenci quite literally sits inside the mine. US 191 winds through the mine and climbs to the Sitgreaves National Forest and the Colorado Trail, leading to Alpine. A 180-degree mine lookout reveals layers, terraces, water, tailings and equipment chewing away at the earth far below. Depending on your point of view, you are looking at either one of man's greatest examples of doing violence to the earth, or one of his greatest achievements.

In about 1865, while chasing Indians, Union cavalry discovered minerals in the area. The news immediately brought prospectors looking for gold. They found outcroppings of blue and green copper oxides, hardly worth much of a risk in this wild country rampant with Apaches. But claims were staked, and by 1881 Phelps Dodge bought half interest in what would become the Morenci Mine. A "baby gauge" railroad with tracks only 20 inches apart was built in 1879 with mules pulling cars down the mountain to the smelter in Clifton. An 1888 locomotive that replaced the mules stands spiffed and shiny at the Morenci Plaza. At first all mining was underground, and during the Depression copper was priced so low that mining ceased entirely. In 1937 Phelps Dodge reopened the Morenci Mine as an open pit, and when World War II broke out two years later, copper prices soared. Since then the operation has become a computerized behemoth that has removed more than 3 billion tons of material from the mine. Mine tours (no charge) leave from the Morenci Motel, across the street from Phelps Dodge Mercantile, the present-day version of the company store. Tours run Mon.–Fri. at 8 A.M. and 1 P.M. For information and reservations call **(520) 865-4521, ext. 1-6435.**

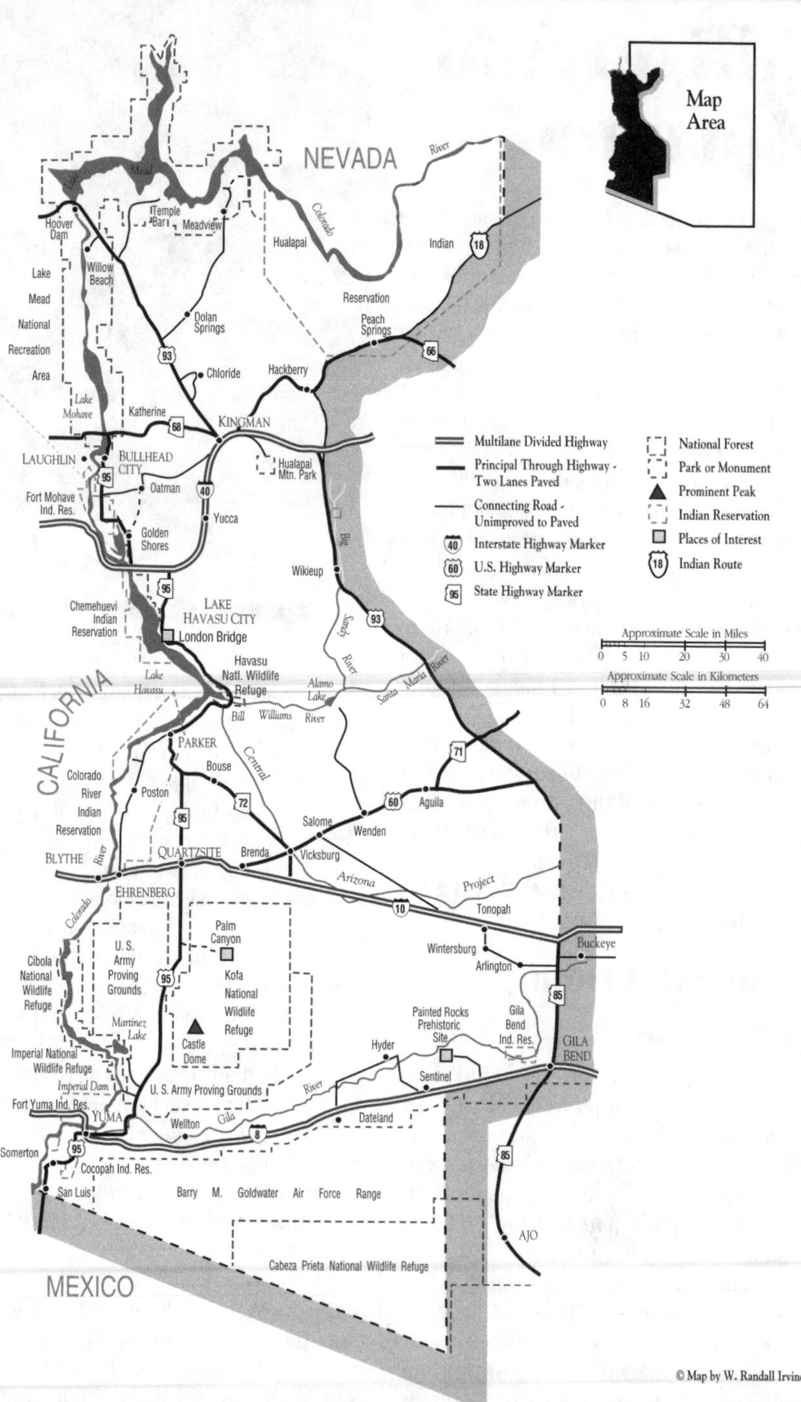

Arizona's West Coast

Arizona's West Coast

Lake Mead Recreation Area and Hoover Dam

This long, skinny area has become one of the most popular water sports and fishing destinations in the state. It includes more than 3,000 square miles of desert that borders on Lake Mead and Lake Mojave to the south. Both were created by damming the Colorado River, which flows almost 150 miles through the area beginning at Grand Canyon National Park. At Bullhead City, Davis Dam created Lake Mojave, while to the north Hoover Dam backs up Lake Mead. Both lakes generally follow the natural path of the Colorado, basically expanding it to overtake surrounding land. An amazing diversity of terrain ranges from a high of about 6,990 feet above sea level to 517 feet at the south end of Lake Mojave near Davis Dam. Lake Mead National Recreation Area was established by President Lyndon Johnson in 1964, and is administered by the National Park Service.

Hoover Dam has made Lake Mead one of the largest man-made lakes in the world. Its protracted length stretches 105 miles from Hoover Dam to Separation Canyon. With a maximum depth of 500 feet, its 550 miles of shoreline are broken by steep canyon walls, sheltered coves and beaches. Fishing is a big attraction, with anglers gathering for a number of major tournaments here each year. Striped bass, bluegill, crappie and catfish are among the game fish regularly caught. In Meadview, guide service is available for fishing the lake and the Grand Canyon. Call **South Cove Guide Service** at **(888) 564-2804.**

The massive structure of the Hoover Dam straddles the Arizona-Nevada state line, holding back two years' flow of Colorado River water in Lake Mead. It was completed in 1935 and named for Herbert Hoover, the 31st president of the United States. Sometimes called Boulder Dam, Congress made the name Hoover official in 1947. It took 16,400 men to build it, 96 of whom lost their lives to accidents and heat exhaustion.

The party line is that the dam was constructed to control the Colorado, which was running amok because melting snow frequently swelled it to the point where spring and early summer floods destroyed property, crops and lives. The production of hydroelectric power, so say the guides, was a secondary purpose. Yet 13 years before its completion, power had been parceled out to high bidders, with California getting 56 percent, Nevada 25 percent and Arizona 19 percent. The dam has been named one of America's Seven Modern Civil Engineering Wonders by the American Society of Civil Engineers for its arch gravity construction between the narrow walls of Black Canyon. It is 726.4 feet high and 45 feet wide at the top. When water is released, its temperature is a constant 52 degrees. Mammoth diversion channels, used to redirect the river during construction, are still part of dam tours. The dam has become such an attraction that a large parking structure had to be carved out of the canyon wall to accommodate cars, and a "snacketeria" has been built to provide sustenance. A 22-minute film shown at the visitor center, shot in the 1930s, presents an interesting background to the dam's construction.

Options for touring include a minimally priced 35-minute overview that takes you through the dam. It is offered daily, 8:30 A.M.–5:45 P.M. The Hard Hat Tour (which we highly recommend to anyone seriously interested in dams), lasts about 75 minutes and covers about 1.25 walking miles. For $25 (you get to keep the dusty blue hard hat), you may descend into the dam's interior. It is not for the claustrophobic. A dozen or so visitors at a time squeeze into an elevator for a 506-foot drop (yes, ears do pop) to the dam's powerhouse for a close-up of 8-story generators. Dials and gauges installed when the dam was built, their function now replaced by computers, remain as interesting relics. The tour gives a look at intricately designed terrazzo floors created by Italian designers who replicated patterns found on Southwest Native American pottery. Workers use the three-wheel bikes that you see leaning against walls and posts to quickly cover long distances within the dam. Both tours provide the humbling experience of being surrounded by billions of tons of cast concrete. For information on tours contact the **Lower Colorado Dams Facilities Office, P.O. Box 60400, Boulder City, NV 89006; (702) 294-3522.**

Straddling the Arizona/Nevada border, Hoover Dam creates Lake Mead, one of the world's largest man-made lakes.

Lake Mojave

This roughly cigar-shaped lake south of Lake Mead extends for 67 miles along the length of the Colorado River. It has 45 square miles of surface area and is 4 miles across at its widest point in the Cottonwood Basin. Coyote, kit fox, desert bighorn sheep and roadrunners are frequently sighted along the shores. Feral burros and horses as well as domestic livestock drink from the lake's clear waters. Enthusiastic anglers fish for naturally occurring game fish, regularly restocked. Species include cutthroat, rainbow and German brown trout as well as bass, catfish, crappie, bluegill and perch. Striper fishing is also excellent, say locals.

Davis Dam

This dam, which creates Lake Mojave, pales in size and drama by comparison with Hoover, but it gets a fair amount of traffic because it is one of the few places in the area to cross the Colorado other than at Hoover Dam, two hours north, or at Topock to the south where I-40 angles across. You can bring a picnic lunch to linger over at the ramadas along the river below the dam. There is no set tour, but Mon.–Fri. between the hours of 7:30 A.M.–3:30 P.M. visitors can walk to the spillway gates overlooking the river for a pretty view. For information call **(520) 754-3628.**

Bullhead City, Katherine and Laughlin, Nevada

These three cities lie on the northeast edge of the Mojave desert at the south end of the Lake Mead recreation area, with Bullhead City at the hub, just across from Laughlin, Nevada. Cleverly marketed as "Arizona's West Coast," what the area lacks in expansive stretches of water found on the nation's true West Coast in California, it makes up for in avid water enthusiasts who quite literally clog the river with boats and personal watercraft during the summer. That's about the only time the water temperature is warm enough to swim without a wetsuit. Although spring and fall air temperatures are decidedly more pleasant, the water is icy.

Bullhead City, with a population of about 30,000, is linked to Laughlin, Nevada, by a bridge donated by Don Laughlin, its founder, who paid $3.5 million in 1987 for its construction. Bullhead City is home to many of the workers from the casino across the river in Laughlin, where there is little permanent housing. Almost two dozen RV parks between the two cities verify the area as a popular winter escape, harboring as many as 15,000 snowbirds who migrate from colder climes for four to six months a year. A popular aquatic destination, it offers water skiing, jet skiing, parasailing and even sailboating. Chaparral Country Club offers a sporty 9 holes as does Riverview Golf Course. South of Bullhead City at Spirit Mountain Casino on the Fort Mojave Indian Reservation, slot machines satisfy the gaming instinct.

Getting There

Bullhead City is on AZ 68 (from Kingman) and AZ 95 (from the south) on the Arizona-Nevada border. The Laughlin-Bullhead City Airport was recently expanded to accommodate Boeing 737s, DC-10s and MD-80s. Three charter services and two commuter companies, America West Express and Eagle Canyon Airlines, fly into the airport on a scheduled basis.

Katherine Landing has a resort and marina with boat slips and rentals that include houseboats and personal watercraft. There are a launch ramp, swimmer-friendly beaches with barbecues and picnic areas. The campground has 165 full hookups with spaces big enough to accommodate your boat. The resort also offers a small motel, store, restaurant and lounge. On hot summer weekends the place is chockablock with boaters.

Laughlin, Nevada, barely 30 years old, has nine hotel casinos that offer low-stakes, low-key gambling, well-priced hotel rooms and buffets, and top notch entertainment without the Vegas price tag. There are more than 13,000 slots in Laughlin, ranging from nickel to sky's the limit. Fun, themed hotels and casinos include **Ramada Express** (Victorian railroad theme), **Colorado Belle** (river steamboat), **Pioneer Hotel** (Old West) and others.

Services

Bullhead Area Chamber of Commerce, 1251 Hwy. 95, Bullhead City, 86429; (520) 754-4121, fax (520) 754-551.

Laughlin Visitors Bureau, P.O. Box 502, Laughlin, NV 89029; (800) 452-8445 or (702) 298-3321. This helpful office provides information on entertainment and special events and will make room reservations.

Kingman

At an elevation of 3,336 feet, Kingman sits in a mining and cattle area in high desert surrounded by the Cerbat Mountains to the northwest, the Hualapais on the southeast, with the Black Mountains defining its southwest landscape. The quick way to get to Kingman from Williams and towns to the east is to stay on Interstate 40 all the way. For a taste of history, however, veer off at Seligman and take Old Route 66 through Hackberry and Peach Springs, named for the fruit trees planted there by early Mormon settlers. The road loops through the southernmost tip of the Hualapai Indian Reservation, the proposed site of a new gaming casino.

As do so many towns that developed during the late 1800s, Kingman owes its existence to the Atlantic and Pacific Railroad. When surveyor Lewis Kingman found a natural right-of-way, the line was built and the town of Kingman grew up around it. This history carries on today, as more than a hundred trains chug through in any 24-hour period. It isn't quite as disturbing as you might think, because 5 miles outside of Kingman the tracks split, permitting trains to pass, which means that two trains usually rumble through town within minutes of each other. If you listen, you can tell the difference between the musical toot-toot of Amtrak, which goes through twice a day, and the strident blat-blat of other trains. The express stops here to change personnel. A park in the middle of town, built around 1927 steam engine #3759, now a historical monument, commemorates Kingman's locomotive history.

The town niches itself as being "The Heart of Old Route 66" because it lies on the longest stretch of the Mother Road, 158 miles, still in existence. The portion that runs through the city and parallels Route 66 is called Andy Devine Avenue in honor of one of Kingman's native sons. The downtown area has more than 60 buildings listed on the National Register of Historic Places. Clark Gable and Carole Lombard were married at the old courthouse here.

If you come into Kingman on I-40, get off at Andy Devine Avenue where the interstate crosses Route 66 to find lots of budget motels and fast food places.

Festivals and Events

Route 66 Classic Car Rally & Show

mid-April

During this popular event, part of the whole weeklong Route 66 celebration, vehicles caravan along the old road. Events include a parade, bed races, a hot air balloon glow and music by a 1950s-style band. In recent years Martin Milner from the original Route 66 television series has put in an appearance at the Saturday night barbecue.

Andy Devine Days
early October

Until his demise in 1977, Andy Devine showed up for this three-day celebration that includes a PRCA rodeo, parade and other festivities.

Outdoor Activities

Golf

Cerbat Cliffs Golf Course

Named for the bluffs that edge its western side, this high desert year-round course is noted for its rocky challenges. If there's a breeze and you're at the Lava Loop, holes number 10, 11 and 12, you can be in a world of hurts because you can be blown into a bed of destructive rocks on either side of the fairway. Another hole, the short par 3 number 8, is completely surrounded by rock. The 18-hole course has bent grass greens and a 71.9 rating from the blue tees. The Sand Trap restaurant serves three meals a day, and has wine and beer. **1001 Gates Ave., Kingman, 86401; (520) 753-6593.**

Seeing and Doing

Hotel Beale

Although we currently consider this 1900 hotel an attraction, it may be just a matter of time until it is welcoming guests. The Beale is part of a restoration project that eventually will include the Andy Devine Celebrity Theatre and Old Town Meeting Hall. The plan is to renovate hotel rooms and provide a place to display memorabilia honoring Andy and his parents, Tom and Amy Devine, who acquired the Beale in 1906. Once a commercial center, here salesmen purveyed goods and services to Northern Arizona businessmen. Andrew Timothy Devine, later known as Andy "Jingles" Devine to a movie-going public, grew up here, watching the horses and wagons along Front Street give way to automobiles as the street became Route 66. The Beale changed ownership a number of times, and is presently in limbo. But it is on the National Register of Historic Places and if all you do is look at it from the outside, you'll get a sense of its history. **325 Andy Devine Ave., Kingman, 86401.**

Mojave Museum of History and Arts

Just behind the chamber of commerce building, this little museum displays a 1/3-size Santa Fe stagecoach outside and Andy Devine memorabilia inside. It details his 176-movie career with posters and photos, and explains that as a child his larynx was pierced in an accident, giving him his characteristic scratchy voice. The museum also traces the area's Hualapai Indian history and the construction of Hoover Dam. Open Mon.–Fri., 9 A.M.–5 P.M.; Sat. and Sun., 1–5 P.M., closed major holidays. Small admission. **400 W. Beale St., Kingman, 86401; (520) 753-3195.**

Bonelli House

Built in 1915, this family home is a good example of the Anglo-Territorial style of architecture popular in Arizona into the 1920s. Its thick tufa stone (a porous limestone that makes up the Cerbat Mountains) walls and wide porches were early heat-beating features. The home is furnished with original family possessions as well as antiques appropriate to the period. Listed on the National Register of Historic Places, it is open Thu.–Mon., 1–4 P.M. **430 E. King St, Kingman, 86401.**

Chloride

An old mining town (is there a town in this area that wasn't?) in the Cerbat Mountains founded in 1862 with the discovery of silver, it is named for the ore that contains the precious metal. It's presently reincarnated as an artsy-craftsy place, a nice side trip from Kingman. The old jail, Jim Fritz Museum and the Silverbelle Playhouse attest to a town not letting itself slip into oblivion. Once more than

2,000 residents worked 75 area mines. The current population of 300 is a dedicated lot, with many fine artisans purveying their wares alongside antiques and collectibles in assorted shops and studios. Because this is a casual sort of place, you'll find store hours a bit iffy, but on weekends you'll usually find things open. It's probably the artistic influence that induces residents to turn old junk into yard art. Or, depending on your point of view, the art could still be junk. But it does add to the charm of this rustic little place. Another example of its history, the Chloride Fire Department owns a custom-built 1939 Ford fire engine, along with a contemporary Mack fire truck. You might want to mail a card from the local post office. Established in 1862, it is said to be the oldest continuously operating mail facility in the state. Painted on sheer escarpments in the hills southeast of town are the Purcell Murals, remaining amazingly bright and colorful since they were created in 1966 and 1975. Although they remain open to interpretation, the artist-miner Roy Purcell called them "The Journey: Images from an Inward Search for Self." Take Tennessee Avenue out of town, then follow signs for about a mile and a half to the murals. In town there are a couple of cafes, two saloons, a grocery store, one bed and breakfast and an RV park. From Kingman take US 93 north 17 miles to the Chloride turnoff. Head right (east) about 4 miles into town. **Chloride Chamber of Commerce, P.O. Box 268, Chloride, 86431; (520) 565-2204.**

Grand Canyon Caverns

Along old Route 66 near Peach Springs you'll see huge signs for Grand Canyon Caverns. Don't bother if you're claustrophobic. But if you are a truly spunky spelunker, you'll enjoy a look at the largest registered dry caverns in the country. They have been documented at 345 million years old. With a guide, you'll take an elevator underground 21 stories, then walk along lighted trails with handrails through lovely limestone caves. Ancient fossilized fish and the replica of a giant ground sloth are evidence of one-time cave dwellers. A mummified bobcat suggests a more recent casualty. The underground labyrinth can't rival the caverns at Carlsbad, New Mexico, but they are interesting for their "cave snow," a murky coating that covers rocks with soft white stuff, and for the oddly lovely flowstone, stalactites, stalagmites and helictites that give the caverns their personality. There is a restaurant and little market at this stop, too. Located about 10 miles east of Peach Springs on old Route 66. Watch for the turnoff signs. Forty-five-minute, guided tours leave every half hour. Open daily, 8 A.M.–6 P.M., Memorial Day to Oct. 15. Hours vary at other times of the year. Moderate admission fee. **P.O. Box 180, Peach Springs, 86434; (520) 422-3223.**

Hualapai Mountain County Park

Summer temperatures of about 78 degrees make this a favorite hiking and picnicking retreat for those escaping the heat of the Mojave desert in California and the Lake Havasu area. Mixed forests of Ponderosa, piñon pine and scrub oak shelter a truly wonderful variety of bird life, not commonly seen in other parts of the state. If you've never watched the spectacular acorn woodpecker with his red cap, or the dramatic black and white downy woodpecker, this is the place to go. The park is about 14 miles southeast of Kingman. From I-40 take Exit 51 to Stockton Hill Road south, which changes names to become Hualapai Mountain Road.

Where to Stay

Accommodations

Hotel Brunswick—$–$$$

In addition to the proliferation of reliable chain motels along Route 66 and I-40, there is a new historic option. Next door to the Beale and also listed on the National Register of Historic Places, this restored hostelry was built in 1909 to provide luxury accommodations for well-heeled miners and ranchers. The three-story hotel, constructed of locally quarried tufa stone, was the tallest building in the area. But by 1980, after countless renovations, the hotel was vacant and in decay. In 1994 a local couple, Rennie and Priscilla Davis, took a look at the original architectural details such as the pressed tin ceilings, mahogany wainscoting and wood floors, hired an engineering team that pronounced it structurally sound, and set out on an ambitious renovation program. They reconstructed the balcony that runs the full length of the front, and decorated rooms with handmade quilts and antique furnishings. The Brunswick reopened in April 1997 as a bed and breakfast hotel, with an excellent full-service dining room open for lunch and dinner. The wide range of prices represents little $25 "cowboy" or "cowgirl" rooms that are comfortably furnished with a single bed and shared bathroom down the hall, as well as large double rooms with private baths. The quietest rooms are near the back, away from the road and railroad tracks, but many guests say that train sounds in the night are welcome reminders of days past. **315 E. Andy Devine Ave., Kingman 86401; (520) 718-1800; www.hotelbrunswick.com.**

Hualapai Mountain Lodge and RV Park—$$–$$$

These six motel units and an RV park with 12 full-hookup spaces lie in Hualapai Mountain Park in the midst of a gorgeous Ponderosa forest. In the lodge's award-winning restaurant, breakfast is cooked right at your table, sometimes with resident elk and mule deer watching through the picture windows. Reservations in summer are essential for both the dining room and lodge. Located about 13 miles southeast of Kingman off County Road 147. **Pine Lake, Star Route, Kingman, 86401; (520) 757-3545.**

Camping and RV Parks

Hualapai Mountain Park

Within this remote, quiet park there are hiking trails and good bird-watching. Refreshing summer temperatures keep the 11 full-hookup RV spaces (open May to Oct. only) occupied most of the time. There are 70 tent campsites, with no facilities, scattered among the tall Ponderosas. You can also park a small RV here. Rustic cabins ($–$$) have beds, cooktop stove and shower. Bring your own bedding, towels, cooking utensils and dishes. The steep road, although paved, can be tricky in winter because at the 6,000-foot-plus elevation there usually is snow. Located at the end of County Road 147 about 13 miles southeast of Kingman. **(520) 757-0915.**

Kingman KOA

Within the city limits of Kingman, yet quiet and off the highway, this well-kept park has 90 pull-through sites with hookups, and about a dozen tent spaces with tables and rest rooms nearby. There is a convenience store and souvenir shop. The solar-heated pool is open from mid-May until Oct. 15. From I-40, exit at Andy Devine Boulevard (at the McDonald's) and continue north on Andy Devine to Airway. Turn left onto Airway and continue about a mile to Roosevelt. Go right on Roosevelt to the campground. **3820 N. Roosevelt, Kingman, 86401-3298; (800) 232-4397 or (520) 757-4397.**

Where to Eat

There's no shortage of chains and fast food spots along Andy Devine Avenue, but in the older part of town there are a few standouts.

Mr. D'z Route 66 Diner—$–$$

The best place in town to watch traffic go by on Route 66, the pink and turquoise diner is straight out of the 1950s, with poodle-skirted waitresses, plastic booths and lots of neon and chrome. Burgers and sandwiches are menu staples, as well as meatloaf with mashed potatoes and gravy and chicken-fried steak. Corner of Route 66 and First Street. **105 E. Andy Devine Ave.; (520) 718-0066.**

El Palacio—$$

Good Mexican beer and cocktails are served in this large, friendly restaurant and cantina run by the Serrano family. Come with an appetite for the huge tostadas, tacos and chili rellenos, always on the menu. The historic, high-ceilinged building was once a drugstore that served townspeople and guests who came to the Brunswick and the Beale just one block away. Open daily, 11 A.M.–9 P.M. **401 E. Andy Devine Ave.; (520) 718-0018.**

Hotel Brunswick Dining Room—$$$

Certified Angus beef carved into porterhouse, filet and New York strip steaks is the draw at the newly restored crystal-and-tablecloth dining room in the Brunswick. It is one of the town's few fine dining restaurants, yet has a casual atmosphere that invites jeans-clad cowboys as well as weary travelers. The lounge has live entertainment, beer and wine and a player piano. At the Hotel Brunswick, **315 E. Andy Devine Ave.; (520) 718-1800.**

Services

Kingman Area Chamber of Commerce, 333 W. Andy Devine Ave., P.O. Box 1150, Kingman, 86402-1150; (520) 753-6106. Website: www.arizonaguide.com/visit-kingman.

Kingman Visitor Center, 120 W. Andy Devine, Kingman, 86402.

Historic Route 66 Association of Arizona, 201 Andy Devine Ave., P.O. Box 66, Kingman, 86402; (520) 753-5001.

Oatman

Located 25 miles southwest of Kingman via Route 66, a designated scenic byway at this point, you approach this little mountain town by climbing through the Black Mountains along a series of stomach-lurching switchbacks. The quartz spire that interrupts the horizon in the distance is called Elephant's Tooth. At Sitgreaves Pass, named for 19th century army topographic engineer Lt. Lorenzo Sitgreaves, who also gave his name to the National Forest, the 3,652-foot elevation creates great views into Arizona, California and Nevada. The scenery has lured film makers here to make *Foxfire, How the West Was Won* and other less memorable flicks as well as countless commercials. The stories of how Oatman, once called Vivian, got its name vary with the storyteller. One version says it was named for a family killed by Apaches in the 1850s. Another, possibly the most reliable, says that in 1851 a young girl named Olive Oatman was captured by Indians and held at Ollie Oatman Springs just north of town. She was rescued in 1857 near the current town site. Yet another story says it was named for the son of Olive Oatman, a Mojave Indian who became a successful miner. It doesn't much matter which you choose to believe because the town's appeal remains the same.

Clark Gable was a regular at the Oatman Hotel, built in 1902. It's still the only hotel in town.

Founded in 1906 as a mining center, you can still see tailings mounded near town, and an old mine shaft opening, marked "Unsafe," just a hundred yards off the main drag. Oatman, first a tent city, within a decade turned into a boomtown of more than 10,000 industrious souls producing exceptionally rich gold ore. Prosperity was short-lived, however, and in 1924 United Eastern Mines permanently halted operations. What minimal mining continued was dealt a final blow in 1942 when even the few remaining mines were closed. The town seemed doomed. But it was infused with new life when Route 66 made it a logical stop. It became the last oasis for migrants pushing westward before they headed out into the desolate Mojave Desert on their way to California. Bypassed in 1952 when Route 66 was rerouted through Yucca to alleviate traffic on the challenging mountain road, Oatman floundered a second time. But it hitched itself up by its bootstraps by developing into a historic destination, complete with plank sidewalks and tumbledown buildings. A dozen or more burros freely roam the main street, cadging handouts from willing tourists and posing for snapshots so long as they're being fed. These long-eared Eeyores, descendants of burros used by prospectors a century ago, now earn their living as crowd-pleasers. On weekends Oatman really gears up, with gunfighters and saloon floozies strolling the streets, "holding up" tour buses and perpetrating shotgun weddings.

Oatman received a second shot in the arm in February 1995 with the re-opening of the Gold Road Mine by Addwest Minerals, who acquired mining rights in 1992. The mine now has more than 500 employees, with reports putting its yield at 500 tons of ore a day, or 54,000 ounces of gold a year. Currently the mine has three operating levels accessed by a 12 percent grade, with a fourth being explored. Not open to the public, you will be rebuffed by armed guards if you approach the entrance. It's not that the mining people are unfriendly, they explain, they are just guaranteeing your safety.

When spending time in Oatman, the best thing to do is try to find a parking spot wherever you can, no mean task on a holiday weekend or the last weekend of April when the Historic Route 66 Fun Run hits town. There's a parking lot on the left as you enter town from the east, and several smaller areas off the main drag. There are only four restaurants and no gas stations. But there are plenty of funky little shops and a number of classier establishments purveying trinkets and trivia as well as fine Indian crafts, leather goods and stone jewelry.

The only place to stay is the **Oatman Hotel** ($$), a 1902 double-walled adobe building, one of the few two-story structures in town. Clark Gable and Carole Lombard spent their honeymoon here on March 8, 1939. Legend has it that Gable, an inveterate poker player, returned often to sit in on games with local miners. The modest second-floor rooms have the bathroom down the hall. Enter through the gift shop on the first floor. Reservations are essential during high-season winter months. Call **(520) 768-4408**. For information, contact the **Oatman Chamber of Commerce, P.O. Box 903, Oatman, 86433; (520) 768-7400.** (Note: There is no chamber office. This number rings in a small shop, and if the "chamber lady" is there, she'll help you. But don't hesitate to call. "Uncle Charley" is usually there, and he'll pass along messages.)

In the little town of Oatman, burros left over from mining days become everyone's pets. Carrots are for sale at local shops.

Lake Havasu City

In 1963 when chain saw magnate Robert P. McCulloch began constructing Lake Havasu City, the place was pretty dismal. A body of water, formed when Parker Dam impounded the Colorado River, was surrounded by dirt terraces bladed bare of trees and vegetation. A single spartan motel didn't do much to entice visitors. But McCulloch was a visionary. He promised a job with his company to anyone willing to relocate. Early guests were flown in on a four-motor Lockheed Constellation that landed on a rough, graded airstrip adjacent to the Nautical Inn. McCulloch hoped to entice them to purchase property, not a bad idea when lakeview lots sold for $5,000. But the new city languished. Phoenix newspaper articles joked about the "big mudhole," smugly pointing out that summer temperatures there topped even Phoenix's legendary heat. For almost two decades Havasu's progress remained unremarkable, until the mid-1980s when the groundwork for this now-flourishing city and recreation area paid off.

Today Lake Havasu City is a sun-sparkled oasis. The once-harsh landscape is green with golf courses and gardens. Imaginative resorts cluster at lakeside and good restaurants offer eclectic dining. Beyond city borders the Sonoran Desert melts into the foothills of the Mohave Mountains on one side and the Chemehuevi on the other. The population has doubled within the last five years and the number of annual visitors has tripled. Mr. McCulloch passed away in 1977, but a main thoroughfare named in his honor keeps his memory apparent in this "Blue Water Paradise," which is what Havasu means to the Mojaves.

Festivals and Events

Annual Western Nationals F-100 Pickups, Ltd. and Hava Salsa Challenge

April

Lake Havasu and its sister City, Cuidad Guzman in Mexico, get together in April for a multiday festival to share deep-pit barbecue, fry bread, tamales, tacos, arts and crafts and performances by folkloric dancers and singers. "People's Choice" salsa judging is a highlight. Concurrent with the festival, one of the largest groups of F-100 pickups, those little 1950s Ford classics that have become the darlings of vehicle buffs everywhere, congregate in Havasu. It's great fun to see the time-honored trucks spiffed to their original perfection.

Skat-trak Jet Ski World Finals and Lake Havasu Classic Outboard World Championships

October

These two aquatic events, held in separate weeks in October, draw thousands of aficionados of these fast-paced water sports. Book hotel rooms well in advance as these are the two premier sporting events of the year.

London Bridge Seaplane Classic

early November

This in-the-air event for model radio controlled floatplanes and seaplanes is held on the beach at the Nautical Inn Resort. You can watch earthbound "pilots" guide their planes to (hopefully) safe watery landings. Half the fun is looking at the beautifully handcrafted models. After putting so much work into each plane, it might seem that an owner would be reluctant to launch his baby into the air and onto the water. But nope. Crashes and splashes are all part of the sport.

Major Attractions

London Bridge

In 1971 the famed London Bridge came to Lake Havasu. A decade earlier, when the bridge was still British, it was discovered that the storied landmark was indeed, as the nursery rhyme declared, falling down, sinking into the Thames under the burden of increased traffic. For close to 2,000 years, since the Romans built a bridge across it in A.D. 43, a bridge had spanned the Thames. The bridge in Lake Havasu was built in 1831 of granite quarried on Dartmoor and designed with five magnificent arches still in place today. When the bridge began its slow slide into the Thames in 1962, its British life was over.

Entrepreneurial Londoners put it on the market, and developer Robert McCulloch submitted the winning $2,460,000 bid. The bridge was dismantled, transported to Long Beach, California, by boat, then trucked to Havasu at an additional $4 million cost to McCulloch. Workers formed sand mounds along a 1-mile channel to the profile of each arch, and reassembled 10,000-plus granite blocks around them. They removed the sand after construction, and diverted water from the lake, under the bridge, and back into the lake.

Each piece was numbered when the bridge was disassembled. As you pass under its arches, you can still see four-digit numbers painted on many of the blocks. The first indicates which span, the second number places it in its proper row, and the last two digits denote the block's position in the row.

The bridge seems appropriate here in a Disneyesque sort of way, especially since the city of Lake Havasu was laid out by C. V. Wood, the man who designed Disneyland. But far from just a quirky anachronism, it attractively spans the lake, providing access to a small splotch of land called The Island and sheltering the shops of English Village at its mainland end.

Havasu National Wildlife Refuge

This is a truly beautiful refuge, especially if you see it during winter months when the river isn't clogged with boats. It is one of the most important riparian areas along the lower Colorado River, with more than 14,000 of its 44,000-plus acres designated as wilderness. Extending for 24 miles between Lake Havasu City and Needles, California, the refuge has for thousands of years supplied essential winter food for migrating geese, sandhill cranes, ducks and other wildlife. The area's position on a major flyway makes it a prime viewing spot for the Western grebe, great blue heron and other migratory birds. Three hundred miles of

The London Bridge was moved from England, brick by brick, and rebuilt at Lake Havasu.

shoreline, created by the Colorado River and its arms, shelter wading and shore birds. The endangered Yuma clapper rail, southern bald eagle and peregrine falcon all depend on the refuge for shelter and sustenance. In the area called Topock Marsh there are large heron and egret rookeries. The marsh suffers the effects of high boat traffic, and during the busiest summer months wildlife may be difficult to spot. But be patient and try to visit during early morning hours and you'll likely be rewarded with impressive sightings.

Topock Gorge

Within the refuge the soaring cliffs of 16-mile-long Topock Gorge, softened by centuries of eroding river water, look like large fists and giant dimpled kneecaps. In their random shapes imaginative watchers can clearly see the eye of Stargazer Rock open and close as the boat passes by. Other discernable rock creatures include an alligator, fish, dolphin, hippo, gorilla and praying Indian. Keen-eyed observers may catch a glimpse of desert bighorn sheep as the animals prowl the rocky ridges, sometimes drawn to the water's edge if drought conditions are severe. Near the waterline in some areas, ancient Indian petroglyphs are clearly visible. The gorge is closed to water skiing, camping and open fires. Boaters are cautioned to pay close attention to two-way water traffic. For information contact **Refuge Manager, Havasu National Wildlife Refuge, 1406 Bailey Ave., Ste. B, P.O. Box 3009, Needles, CA 92363; (760) 326-3853.**

Nature lovers can catch a jet boat with windows along the sides and in the roof for a three-hour cruise upriver to the refuge. Boats leave from the base of the London Bridge, cruise past petroglyphs and possibly big horn sheep, and make a rest stop at Park Moabi. For information, contact **Bluewater Charters Jet Boat Tours, P.O. Box 2032, Lake Havasu City, 86405; (888) 855-7171 or (520) 855-7171.**

Outdoor Activities

Four-Wheel-Drive Trips

Because it sits at the juncture of the Sonoran and Mojave Deserts, the area around Lake Havasu City has an amazing diversity of plant and animal life. Among the plants surviving in these arid conditions are the puffy smoke trees that look just like their name, yellow-flowering creosote bushes, red-blooming barrel cactus and ocotillo. Chuckwallas, a type of desert lizard kept almost invisible by protective coloration, sometimes pose languidly on shaded ledges if visitors keep their distance and watch quietly. The phainopepla, a striking black cardinal-like bird, and the capricious roadrunner are commonly seen. It's not unusual to spot antelope jackrabbits and an occasional sidewinder rattlesnake working its way in S-shape squiggles across the road. If you're going out on your own, always observe posted signs, especially when you head off on old mining roads. Besides disturbing ancient Native American sites, you could be moving into roads that are unsafe. Be sure you're carrying plenty of water.

Outback Offroad Adventures

For an interpretive look at these fascinating aspects of the desert, you'll be picked up at your hotel in a Bronco 4x4 outfitted with roll bars and a shade top. Guide Dave Griffiths' knowledge of plants and animals makes it possible to see life where none seems to exist. The half-day adventure includes snacks and cold drinks. Call for reservations at **(520) 680-6151.**

Houseboating

Lake Havasu's placid waters and the coves and inlets along its irregular shoreline invite houseboaters, who find their floating condos a popular alternative to conventional hotel and resort accommodations. It's a leisurely way to explore in comfort. Most houseboats, at 46 to 52 feet about the size of a large motorhome, come with standard-sized beds, complete galleys, living rooms and barbecue areas on deck, plus a lesson in captaining. Rentable for just a few days or a week, they're equipped with utensils, dishes and linens, and can accommodate 10 to 12 guests. These apartments afloat adapt to your own leisurely ad-lib itinerary, allowing for frequent stops to explore nooks and crannies along the 45-mile lake. For information, contact **H20 Houseboat Vacations, P.O. Box 2100, Havasu Lake, CA 92363; (800) 242-2628 or (760) 858-1008. Website: www. H20houseboats. com.**

Fishing

Houseboats provide a base from which fishermen can pursue the wily trout, bass, bluegill, crappie and catfish. You can launch your own boat from any of a number of public ramps and fish the river from shore or a craft, day or night, in any area that isn't posted. Fishing licenses and regulations are available at most marinas.

Water Sports

Forty-five mile long Lake Havasu forms a man-made boundary between Arizona and California and creates an extensive aquatic playground. Its waters chill to the mid-50s during winter months, but stay in the pleasant 80s from about mid-April into early fall. A number of natural sand beaches are jumping-off points for windsurfing, jet skiing, sailing, canoeing, water skiing, fishing and swimming.

Getting There

From Phoenix drive west on I-10 for about two hours, then go north on AZ 95 to AZ 72 through Parker, to Lake Havasu City. The drive takes about four hours.

Picnicking

Picnics are fun at the lake because there is so much pretty shore line. A number of carry-out restaurants preclude you having to pack your own. Rotary Beach Community Park along the Colorado has shady picnic tables and beachside volleyball sites so many families come and spend the day. The beach here has a gentle, toddler-accessible slope.

Golf

While winter months are glorious for getting in a round of golf, hitting the links in Havasu's 100-plus summer temperatures may sound like a bid for heatstroke. But many courses open at daylight so you can get in 18 holes and be home by eleven, before temperatures reach their late-afternoon high. Most courses have lower fees after 2 P.M., and even lower rates closer to the end of the day.

London Bridge Golf Club

Two par 71, semiprivate, championship courses wind among lakes, palm trees and lovely upscale homes. Almost every tee has a view of the lake. The east course is about 500 yards shorter than the west course, but the two are equally challenging. **London Bridge Golf Club, 2400 Club House Dr., Lake Havasu City, 86403; (520) 855-2719.**

Nautical Inn Golf Course

This mainly flat 4,012-yard executive course is adjacent to the little motel originally constructed by McCulloch to house the guests he flew in as prospective buyers. You can walk over from the Inn, which is on McCulloch Blvd. on The Island. **(520) 855-5585.**

Seeing and Doing

Parker Dam

Built between 1934 and 1938, it is the barrier that forms Lake Havasu and is one of the dams built by the Bureau of Reclamation that helped bring the once-mighty Colorado River to its knees. AZ 95S crosses over it into California, where the power plant is located. About 17 miles northeast of the town of Parker, the dam's main purpose is to store water for the Colorado River Aqueduct, which supplies southern California, and the Central Arizona Project aqueduct, which keeps water flowing to central and southern Arizona. The deepest dam in the world, 73 percent of its overall 320 feet lies below the original riverbed. Public parking, mostly on the California side, is available so you can get out of your car and walk across the dam for a good view of the downstream canyon. The power plant is open daily, 8 A.M.–4 P.M., for free self-guided tours. **(760) 663-3712.**

Scenic Drive

Parker Dam Road Back Country Byway

The dam begins this scenic route, one of three such byways established in Arizona by the Bureau of Land Management. The 11-mile road parallels the Colorado River and is accessible to most vehicles. You can stop and swim, fish, hike and do some rock hounding. An information kiosk is located in the Parker Dam parking lot. The byway goes from Parker Dam south to Earp, California. For information contact the **BLM Lake Havasu Field Office; (520) 505-1200. Website: azwww.blm.gov.**

Casinos

You can challenge Lady Luck at Havasu Landing Resort and Casino on the Chemehuevi Indian Reservation on the California side of the Colorado. Even though in a different state, it is very much a part of the Havasu scene. Games of chance (electronic only) include blackjack, bingo, lotto and conventional slots. If you're not accustomed to the newest in slot machines, you may miss the sound of coins jingling out your reward when your winnings appear as a printed receipt. Take the slip of paper to the cashier and exchange it for the real thing. The Colorado River Express offers five daily, 20-minute shuttles between the English Village underneath the London Bridge and the resort, which also has beaches, a restaurant and cocktail lounge. For more information, contact **Havasu Landing Resort & Casino, P.O. Box 1707, Havasu Lake, CA 92363; (800) 307-3610.**

Aquatic Recreation Center

This popular center is a good respite when even water-lovers need a break from the summer's 105-degree sunshine. Colorful windsurfers hang from the ceiling, over "surf" in the wave pool that washes up on a cement "beach." It's all fringed with frankly fake palm trees sprouting plastic coconuts that periodically dump water on anyone underneath. A four-story water slide keeps kids busy, and a gently sloping shoreline-style entry accommodates the aquatic PVC wheelchair, available to anyone who needs it.

Where to Stay

Accommodations

Havasu Dunes Resort—$$

We particularly like this lovely site overlooking the lake because the one- and two-bedroom condos have complete kitchens, so we can settle in for a number of days, getting our groceries locally, without having to go out to eat for every meal. Each unit is set up with a well-furnished living room, TV, table and chairs for dining and plenty of closet space. It has a pretty pool that hardly anyone seems to use. Nightly and weekly rentals. **620 Lake Havasu Ave. S.; (520)-855-6626.**

The London Bridge Resort—$$$
More than a hundred acres of shops and restaurants keep guests busy at this castle-like place. With flags aflutter from crenelated turrets it's a medieval castle transposed to the banks of the Colorado. Kids especially love it for its fantasy look. In the lobby is a replica of the elaborately decorated Gold State Coach, part of British coronation ceremonies in the 1800s. From its beach it's an easy launch into any number of water sports. The resort, whose rooms have kitchens and living rooms with sofa sleepers, recently has become a timeshare. Reservations may be booked no more than 14 days out from time of arrival except for holiday weekends, when some units may be available earlier. **1477 Queen's Bay Rd.; (800) 624-7939 or (520) 855-0888.**

Nautical Inn—$$
Originally built by McCulloch when he was marketing Lake Havasu City, recently all 120 guest rooms have undergone a complete renovation. Located on The Island, across London Bridge, all rooms face the water. It has a small golf course, tennis courts and laundry facilities. Cross the bridge and follow the main road. **1000 McCulloch Blvd., Lake Havasu City, 86403; (800) 892-2141 or (520) 855-2141.**

Howard Johnson Lodge & Suites—$$
Located in town but with good lake and mountain views, this Hojos comes with refrigerator and microwave in all suites, which is why we list it here. If you're settling in for more than a night, it's always a bonus not to have to go somewhere to get morning coffee. Indoor spa and swimming pool. **335 London Bridge Rd.; (800) 446-4656 or (520) 453-4656.**

Holiday Inn—$$
This is a bit different from many Holiday Inns because some rooms have lake views and balconies that really put it in the resort category (ask when booking). The heated outdoor pool and spa overlook the lake. All rooms have refrigerators. Ask about special weekly and monthly rates. **245 London Bridge Rd.; (888) 428-2465 or (520) 855-4071.**

The London Bridge Resort recently became a time share, but usually has some rooms available.

RV Parks and Camping

Havasu Landing Resort Campground
On the California side of the Colorado River, you can pitch a tent in a campground shaded by saltcedar within a minute or two of the water. Full hookup sites with river views adjacent to the full-service marina may be reserved in advance. There is no vehicle crossing at Havasu Landing between the two states. When driving your RV from the Arizona side you'll have to go north on I-40 to the town of Needles to cross the river, then return south on California Highway 95 to Havasu Landing. Campers and pedestrians can take the ferry that runs five times a day. **P.O. Box 1707, Havasu Lake, CA 92363; (760) 858-4606.**

Lake Havasu State Park Campground
The park begins two miles north of the London Bridge and extends for more than 40 miles along the shore. If you don't like desert camping, this place may not appeal to you. However, you'll be very close to the lake. Spaces are thoughtfully planned so that you're not on top of your neighbor, and there are palo verde trees and a cactus garden on the grounds. It has picnic tables, a swim area and 43 first-come, first-served dry campsites, no hookups. From Lake Havasu City come north on London Bridge Road 2 miles to park entrance. **(520) 855-2784.**

Cattail Cove State Park Campground

There is not a lot of vegetation here, but you can camp literally feet from the water, a decided plus during hot summer months. More than 200 RV and tent sites are on a first-come, first-served basis, with a number of sites accessible only by boat. Located 15 miles south of Lake Havasu City, off AZ 95. **(520) 855-1223.**

Where to Eat

Eateries include the fun and funky as well as the truly elegant. The common denominator is that all are well-priced as are most attractions and facilities in Lake Havasu.

Chico's Tacos—$

Locals come here for lunch. Situated "in town" and up the hill from the lake, this Baja-style taqueria has freshly prepared tacos for you to embellish from the fresh salsa bar according to your personal tolerance. It's also the place for a great margarita. Phone ahead and they'll have a bag of tacos waiting for you to pick up, to consume at one of the waterfront parks. In the Basha's Center. **1641 McCulloch Blvd.; (520) 680-7010.**

London Bridge Brewery—$$

Appropriately located in the English Village under the bridge, this English pub serves breakfast, lunch and dinner and does a good job of replicating its U.K. counterparts. Service on the patio is offered during summer. **(520) 855-8782.**

Bridgewater Cafe—$$$

In the London Bridge Resort, this is a fairly classic place to eat because it overlooks the lake and all its activity. You can opt for dining alfresco on the terrace to get even closer to the action. It is open for three meals a day, plus an opulent Sunday champagne brunch, offered seasonally. You'll find a fairly decent selection of mid-priced California wines. In the **London Bridge Resort, 1477 Queen's Bay Rd.; (520) 855-0888.**

Services

Call the Lake Havasu Tourism Bureau, and they'll send a free vacation information packet. **314 London Bridge Rd., Lake Havasu City, 86403; (800) 242-8278 or (520) 453-3444, fax (520) 680-0010. Website: www.arizonaguide.com/lakehavasu. E-mail: lakehavasu@interworldnet.net.**

Parker Chamber of Commerce, (520) 669-2174.

Quartzsite

Not exactly located at the crossroads of the nation, there may seem to be little reason to come to this small town unless you're taking I-10 from Phoenix to the Palm Springs area. However, it annually hosts 11 of the country's most important gem and mineral shows, including the Quartzsite Pow Wow during the first part of February. Known internationally as one of the world's largest gem and mineral shows, it attracts dealers (and bargain hunters) from all over the world. Almost 2,000 vendors arrive in November and December, settling in from colder climes to sell almost every product imaginable. Booths, trailers, stands and cars along Business Loop 10 become seasonal shops.

Hi Jolly Daze, held in the fall, are named for Hadji Ali, a Syrian camel driver whose name was anglicized to fit local tongues. He arrived in the state in the 1850s with camels ordered by the U.S. Army, who wanted them as desert pack animals. When the humped beasts proved incompatible with Army mules, Hadji Ali ended up with a small herd that he used in his guiding and prospecting business. He died in 1902. You can visit his grave at the Quartzsite Cemetery where a monument explains his history.

There are a few low-key hostelries here, with a Best Western and Super 8 a half hour away in Blythe, California. Almost a dozen RV parks fill up with snowbirds during winter months. A few fast food places, a steak house, a yacht club (a bit of Quartzsite humor there) and a pizza place make up the dining scene.

The town is located at the junction of I-10 and AZ 95, 130 miles west of Phoenix and 23 miles east of Blythe, California. **Quartzsite Chamber of Commerce** is open 9 A.M.–4 P.M., Mon.–Fri.; closed for lunch. **1495 Main Event Ln., P.O. Box 85, Quartzite, 85346; (520) 927-5600.**

Yuma

On the banks of the Colorado River in Arizona's southwestern corner, Yuma often has the dubious distinction of being the hottest spot in the nation. But with November through May temperatures well under 100 degrees, the town has plenty of warm, sunny days that are wonderfully pleasant. They attract a huge snowbird population, with more than 20,000 RV spaces generally crammed full by the end of January, swelling Yuma's 60,000 population to more than 100,000.

Its riverside location makes it a prime agricultural center. Those tidy rows of green that stretch into the distance are lettuce. Iceberg, leaf and Romaine cover more than 41,000 acres of desert adjacent to the Colorado River, securing the state's niche as the nation's number two producer of lettuce, just behind California. Between mid-November and mid-April, about 95 percent of the lettuce consumed in the United States comes from Yuma and, on the other side of the Colorado, Imperial County, California. Planting begins in mid-August with harvesting in full swing by early November through March. Other crops you'll see include wheat, alfalfa, corn, peanuts, bell peppers and cotton. The Marine Corps Air Station and Yuma Proving Grounds also add to the city's economy, which helps support the second largest K-Mart in the country.

Native Americans have farmed along the Colorado River near Yuma for centuries, with the Spanish showing up in the 1500s. Yuma became a river-crossing point and an important steamship port, and in 1877 the railroad arrived, further establishing the town's commercial value. When Laguna Dam was built upstream in 1909, the Colorado's now-controlled flow made it possible for commercial agricultural crops to flourish, but it was the military that made the biggest contribution to the city's ability to take hold in those brutal, pre-air-conditioning days (see Yuma Crossing State Historic Park below). Soldiers were assigned here whether or not it was where they wanted to be, and ancillary services developed to support them. To get a feel of the city's past, pick up a self-guided walking tour map of historic downtown Yuma at the Convention & Visitors Bureau (see Services). It guides you to the Art Deco-style Yuma Theatre on Main Street, built in 1911, and the Arizona Historical Society Century House Museum, once the home of steamboat captain Andrew Mellon, as well as to antiques and crafts shops.

Major Attractions

Yuma Crossing State Historic Park

The newest addition to the state system, this 19-acre park celebrates 500 years of crossing the Colorado River between Arizona and California. At this point the river executes a particularly narrow bend that created an ideal place to ford, to ferry and later to build a bridge. The military used steamboats to transport wagons and mules, stagecoaches and carriages. The Southern Pacific Railroad built a bridge there, a version of which still stands, and a community grew up around the crossing. Native Americans, Spanish explorers, settlers and miners on their way to California's 1849 Gold Rush have all contributed to the site's historic significance. Also part of the park, a refurbished U.S. Army Quartermaster Depot issued supplies to frontier forts. The mule barn, once housing 900 of the sure-footed creatures as they transported munitions and food inland, has been restored, along with a storehouse for crates and barrels that traveled from the Gulf of California up the Colorado to Yuma. A 1910 Model T Ford, a 1931 Model A and a 1907 Baldwin oil-fired steam engine donated by Southern Pacific are remnants of early river-crossing days. You can pick up a pamphlet at the visitor center for a self-guided tour, or call ahead for the schedule of ranger-guided tours. Open daily, 10 A.M.–5 P.M., Nov. 1 to Apr. 30; Thur.–Mon., 10 A.M.–5 P.M., May 1 to Oct. 31. Closed Christmas and Thanksgiving. Small fee. **201 North 4th Ave., Yuma, 85364; (520) 329-0471.**

Yuma Territorial Prison State Historic Park

A mile east of Yuma Crossing lies the most-visited historical park in the state system, attracting more than 100,000 visitors a year. In 1876, when seven inmates moved into two cells they had built themselves, it was on the cutting edge of penology. It had a library, hospital, tailor and shoe shops, blacksmith and bakery. The first prison in the Arizona Territory, it was originally planned for Phoenix. But through early sleight-of-hand legislation it ended up in Yuma, expanding from two cells to hold a 30-bad-guy capacity to more than 400. Today the prison museum records transgressions of female as well as male prisoners. Unfaithful wives, robbers and murderers did the crime and served the time. Recaptured escapees were made to wear a ball and chain. Because of overcrowding, the prison was closed in 1909 and converted to a high school. It is definitely worth a stop for the picture it paints of early Arizona and the way justice was meted out. On Halloween, cells are rented to local businesses so costumed children can Trick or Treat. Rangers and volunteers in prison garb, locked in cells, portray former convicts. Located off I-8 and Giss Parkway. Open daily, 8 A.M.–5 P.M., except Christmas Day. Small fee. **Box 10792, Yuma, 85366; (520) 783-4771, fax (520) 783-7442.**

Seeing and Doing

Kofa National Wildlife Refuge

Some people say they're hard pressed to find the beauty in this 665,400-acre desert refuge, but others absolutely revel in spotting a desert bighorn sheep or a sharp-shinned hawk. The sheep have a stable population of close to a thousand within the refuge, enough so that it is a source for transplanting animals to other traditional sheep habitats that have lost their populations. Take binoculars for spotting them, as it's unlikely you'll get very close. Try early morning or evening around a water source, when the bighorns come down to drink or you may catch a glimpse of one against the skyline at the top of Palm Canyon. Bird species in residence the year-round are sharp-shinned and red-tailed hawks, Gambel's quail, Western screech owl, Gila woodpecker and his colorful look-alike, the gilded flicker.

With no services anywhere in the refuge, you can camp pretty much anywhere you wish for 14 days, but you must be more than one-quarter mile away from a water hole. Hiking is an excellent way to get to know the refuge, but watch for abandoned mine shafts and open pits. The refuge's name, Kofa, is a remnant from mining days and an acronym for King of Arizona Mine. The Palm Canyon Trail, a 1-mile round-trip hike, has interesting plants along the way. Going is slow because of large rocks and a few steep scrambles. You'll see the palms for which the canyon is named (Washingtonia filifera) near the end of a side canyon to the north. You can hike up to them if you really want a workout.

To get there, head northeast on US 95, and once you're in the refuge look for the Palm Canyon to the right. Ten miles of dirt road lead to the canyon entrance. The southern boundary of the refuge is about 40 miles from Yuma on US 95 north. Coming the other direction, from Quartzsite, you travel due south on US 95 about 11 miles to the refuge's northern boundary. There are four clearly marked main refuge entrances along the highway. Stop for maps and information at the refuge office in Yuma. Open Mon.–Fri., 8 A.M.–5 P.M. **356 W. First St., Yuma, 85366-6290; P.O. Box 6290, Yuma, 85366-6290 (mailing address); (520) 783-7861.**

Imperial National Wildlife Refuge

This long, narrow refuge hugs the Colorado River for about 30 miles along the California-Arizona border and encompasses a number of small lakes, providing rich riparian habitat for many species. Its 25,625 acres protect both desert and river ecosystems. During winter months (best time to visit because summers are excruciatingly hot) migrating waterfowl include marsh and shore birds using the lakes for winter stopovers. You can do a lot of things in the refuge, like hunting, hiking, bird-watching, fishing, boating and even waterskiing on two sections of the river. You can drive your car on graded gravel Red Cloud Mine Road (if it's been raining, check at the visitor center for road conditions) to four lookout points that provide great views of the river and the Chocolate Mountains. The furthest, Smoke Tree Point, is at 4.2 miles. Beyond that the road leaves the refuge and winds through the U.S. Army's Yuma Proving Grounds, where you must stay on the road. It dead-ends in a refuge wilderness area with no facilities.

The **Painted Desert Trail,** a popular, easy walk through the Sonoran Desert, passes ancient lava flows, runs through dry washes and provides views of beautifully colored rock formations. It takes about an hour to walk at a leisurely pace, with one fairly steep, but brief uphill. You can pick up a walking guide at the refuge office. The refuge is located about 40 miles northeast of Yuma, 3 miles north of the resort community of Martinez Lake. Take US 95 north from Yuma to Martinez Lake Road and follow signs to the visitor center, which has natural history exhibits and the information you'll need for hiking, hunting and boating. Overnight camping is not permitted. For information, write to **P.O. Box 72217, Martinez Lake, 85365; (520) 783-3371.**

Cibola National Wildlife Refuge

We absolutely love this refuge because of its 4-mile Canada Goose Loop. You drive your car slowly along the one-way gravel road, staying inside so as not to frighten the geese, but getting very close to the fields where thousands of the dark gray birds are feeding. The loop is always open, but the time to see the geese is from mid-November through February, with peak numbers there in December and January. You'll probably also spot beautiful white snow geese, as well as impressive four-foot sandhill cranes that follow the same migration routes. There are hunting, fishing and boating, but no camping. Cibola is located just north of the Imperial Refuge. From I-10 take the Neighbours Boulevard/78 exit just west of Blythe, California and head south about 18 miles. The road will cross over Cibola Bridge, bringing you back into Arizona and the visitor center, about 3.5 miles beyond the bridge on the right. **Rte. 2, Box 138, Cibola, 85328; (520) 857-3253.**

Saihati Camel Farm & Desert Wildlife Center

More than three dozen camels, usually including babies, comprise one of the largest herds of these ships of the desert in North America. Fifteen years ago the owners started the farm as a hobby that grew to include more than a dozen denizens of the Arabian desert and other dry parts of the world. Today water buffalo, Watusi cattle, pygmy goats, ostrich, ibex, oryx (remember those for Scrabble), three species of wild cats and tiny little fennec foxes make their home here. Narrated one-hour tours are offered Oct. 1 to May 31, Mon.–Sat., at 10 A.M. and 2 P.M., with a Spanish language tour offered Sat. at 3 P.M. From I-8, exit onto Ave. 3E and continue south 8 miles to County 16th. Proceed west 2 miles to Ave. 1E and go north 500 feet to the entrance. From Hwy. 95 (Ave. B) go south to County 15th, then east 2 miles to Ave. 1E. Proceed south 1 mile to the entrance. **15672 S. Ave. 1E, Yuma, 85366; (520) 627-2553.**

Ehrlich's Date Garden

You can see how dates grow at this tidy farm, where a stand of 300 graceful date palms produces eight different varieties. Harvesting is in full swing August through October. You can get fresh, dried, stuffed, candied and other types of dates at the store, open daily, 9 A.M.–5 P.M. **868 S. Ave. B; (520) 783-4778.**

Outdoor Activities

River Tours

Yuma River Tours

An interesting, comfortable way to see the Imperial Wildlife Refuge is via jet boat. You can join a 5-hour trip to see petroglyphs, old ranch sites and 1800s rock cabins. A stop at Lonesome Knolls reveals the spot where prospector Roy Morgan buried his dog Lonesome. A headstone exhorts visitors to place a rock on the grave, which has resulted in an impressive cairn. This lovely riverside area is generally a picnic stop for the tour. A great variety of birds may be spotted along the river, commonly including double-crested cormorants, sandpipers, kingbirds, Western grebes and several varieties of herons. Winter months, November through March, are best for seeing migratory birds. Tours depart year around from Fisher's Landing, 32 miles northeast of Yuma. Take US 95 northeast to Martinez Lake Road. Turn west and proceed 10 miles to Fisher's Landing. The boat is moored behind Olsen's store. Senior's and children's rates are offered, and there is a minimum number of passengers per trip. The Yuma office is located at **1920 Arizona Ave.; (520) 783-4400.**

Getting There

Yuma is less than a three-hour drive from Phoenix. Take I-10 east toward Tucson (you're really going south at this point), and transition to I-8, which goes directly into Yuma. Delta and Mesa Airlines serve Yuma from Phoenix and Los Angeles.

Colorado King I Paddle Boat

Leaving from the same point on the river as Yuma River Tours (see above), this replica stern-wheeler does relaxing, slow-moving cruises along the river. Seating on the upper deck is covered so you're protected from the sun. Reservations are a must because the schedule is pretty much determined by when there is a full boat. A recorded message tells you when the next available cruises will go. **(520) 782-2412.**

Golf

Many snowbirds come specifically to use the well-priced, well-maintained links in the area. The 18-hole course at **Cocopah Bend (520-343-1663)** and the 9-hole, par 36 **Fortuna de Ray (520-342-5051)** connect with RV parks. You just walk next door. **Desert Hills Municipal Golf Course (520-341-0644)** has a par 72, 6,800-yard (blue tees) 18-hole layout. The 6,767-yard, par 72 layout at **Mesa del Sol (520-342-1283)** has 18 championship holes designed by Arnold Palmer, on-course beverage service and an upscale lounge and restaurant.

Where to Stay

Motels

Chains include Comfort Inn, Days Inn, Holiday Inn Express, Motel 6, Super 8 and Travelodge. Of the three Best Westerns, we like the **Best Western Inn Suites ($$–$$$), 1450 Castle Dome Rd., (520) 783-8341,** because it has in-room coffee makers, refrigerators and microwaves, plus a continental breakfast.

RV Parks

There are no less than 84 RV and mobile home parks in Yuma, ranging from basic to luxury. Most are senior-friendly, catering to a mature crowd rather than families. Pick up a list from the Convention & Visitors Bureau (see Services).

Where to Eat

The city has more than two dozen fast food places, and a good selection of Mexican restaurants including El Pappagallo, Don Quijote and the family-owned Chretin's on South 15th Avenue. The one standout is Lute's, which is just a hoot.

Lute's Casino—$-$$

The oldest continuing pool hall and domino parlor in the state, it has an almost Fellini quality about it. You can't believe so much stuff has been crammed into one place without hampering the movements of the waitstaff. The 1901 building has housed an investment company, grocery store and hotel. Although once rough and rowdy, today it has a family clientele, serving up giant burgers, sandwiches, tacos, burritos and hot dogs to wash down with beer or wine. The famous (or infamous) Especial, a combination cheeseburger and hotdog covered with hot sauce has been known to singe the nose hair of even the hardiest eater. Best time to stop in is Saturday afternoon when the place is rockin'. You can tell the tourists. They're the ones walking around with beers, looking at all the stuff. Join in. Lute's loves it. Open Mon.–Sat., 9 A.M.–8 P.M.; Sun., 10 A.M.–6 P.M. **221 Main St., Yuma; (520) 782-2192.**

Services

Yuma Convention & Visitors Bureau, 377 Main St., Yuma, 85366; P.O. Box 11059, Yuma, 85366 (mailing address); (520) 783-0071.

Index

Notes

About the Author and Photographer

Judy Wade and Bill Baker are a husband/wife writer/photographer team living in Phoenix. Judy earned a journalism degree from the University of Minnesota, and when she felt secure enough to quit her day job, she became a full-time freelancer. Presently she contributes to *TravelAmerica, Cruise Travel, Walking, Arizona Highroads*, the *Los Angeles Times Syndicate, Physicians Travel & Meeting Guide* and other national magazines. In May 1997 she received the Arizona Press Women Sweepstakes Award, the highest creative honor the society bestows. She also received the Governor's Media Support Award "for providing extraordinary attention and/or support for Arizona's Tourism Industry through use of the media" for the state of Arizona. She is a contributor to *Travelers Tales: A Woman's World*, an anthology of women's travel experiences that won the 1996 Lowell Thomas Best Travel Book award. The Society of American Travel Writers Western Chapter awarded her a 1998 first place in its annual competition for a piece she wrote on hot air ballooning.

Bill, a communications major at Akron University, honed his photography skills in Akron, Ohio as a retail fashion and product photographer. In the last ten years he has concentrated on travel photography, contributing to *New Woman, Arizona Highroads, Cruise Travel, Get Up & Go, Travel 50 & Beyond, Valley Magazine, Where to Retire* and other national publications. He is a member of the American Society of Media Photographers.

The Arizona Guide is the couple's second book for Fulcrum Publishing. The critically acclaimed *Seasonal Guide to the Natural Year: Southern California and Baja* was published in 1997 and received a First Place award in the Travel Book category from the Arizona Press Women.